THE NEW YORK METS

ALSO BY Leonard Koppett

24 Seconds to Shoot

The New York Mets

REVISED EDITION

by Leonard Koppett

Collier Books
A Division of Macmillan Publishing Co., Inc.
New York

Collier Macmillan Publishers
London

To HENRY B. CHADWICK,
who created the profession
of baseball writer a century ago

and to Suzanne, Katherine and David,
who must put up with it now.

Macmillan Publishing Co., Inc.
866 Third Avenue, New York, N.Y. 10022
Collier-Macmillan Canada Ltd.

Library of Congress Catalog Card Number: 70-116781

First Collier Books Edition 1974

Printed in the United States of America

Contents

Act III: Hodges

Act IV: Berra

COMING ATTRACTIONS

PROLOGUE

1 The Hungry Metropolis

To anyone who grew up in New York City during the first half of the twentieth century, there were certain unquestioned verities, facts of ordinary life to be taken for granted so completely as to sink beneath conscious thought. A subway ride, like a phone call, cost a nickel. Trolley cars and buses (some of them double-decked) stopped to pick up and discharge passengers at every block along their routes. On any avenue it was possible to drive in either direction. When immigrants arrived, they passed through Ellis Island. When one started a major journey or returned, one passed through Grand Central Station or Penn Station or a Hudson River pier. School life began for some at five in kindergarten, for most at six in first grade, but never earlier. The streets, in prosperous neighborhoods no less than in slums, were the primary playgrounds for children, outside of public school yards.

The theater, if taken seriously, was always "Broadway," whatever its exact address (except for an enclave in Greenwich Village at certain times). "Stage show" meant vaudeville, on its own at the Palace or along with movies in the larger movie "palaces" downtown (the Roxy, the Paramount) or in good-sized "circuit houses" (R.K.O., Loew's) around the neighborhoods. Traffic lights were strictly red or green, unpunctuated by yellow; but on the subway lines underground and the elevated lines above, which had always existed and always would, the signals did include amber for "slow down."

Major shopping meant Macy's or Gimbel's. Important indoor gatherings—sports events, political conventions—meant Madison Square Garden. Choosing a newspaper to read meant never less than nine or ten alternatives. Music meant Carnegie Hall or the Metropolitan Opera House on 39th Street.

The sun, each morning, approached Manhattan from the East River side and departed, each afternoon, via New Jersey.

And the New York Giants played baseball at the Polo Grounds while the Dodgers played in Brooklyn.

For 50 years or so, two full generations and more, such things were anchors of stability for New Yorkers, whose awareness of change in the world was always acute. In countless ways the city's institutions and habits shifted rapidly. In physical appearance no district remained untouched for long. In the memory of a middle-aged man in 1940, automobiles and trucks had replaced horses, planes overhead had ceased to be a neck-craning novelty, motion pictures began to talk, revolutions swept the world, political scandals and drastic realignments had swept the city and the nation, prohibition had come and gone, styles of clothing had gone through several pendulum swings, ethnic groupings and attitudes about them had been altered drastically, and the radio had become indispensable to life. Consciousness of dynamism and even uncertainty was a frame of mind in which New Yorkers took pride.

But there were, at bottom, these automatically unchanging, subliminal certainties, as familiar as snow in winter or stifling apartments in summer.

Right after World War II, however, tremors were felt even in this bedrock. The subway (and the telephone) suddenly cost a dime. The elevated tracks disappeared, miraculously revealing three new broad avenues beneath them—and these avenues, before you knew it, were converted to one-way traffic as cavalierly as if they had been narrow little crosstown streets. The trolleys disappeared, and then their tracks, under endless repaving, and the now omnipresent buses stopped only at designated corners, sometimes several blocks apart. Traveling began to mean finding a way to get to and from La Guardia or Newark, and then Idlewild, whereas the famous huge rail terminals were left more and more to commuters and the waterfront to strikes.

The streets, their curbs walled solidly by parked cars, were no longer suitable for children who had choices, and three-year-olds in increasing numbers were entering society through nursery schools or day-care centers. Something called "off-Broadway" was acquiring an identity, and vaudeville was dead, and bars had television sets, and food was being bought in supermarkets, and newspapers that died were no longer being replaced, and there was talk of a fantastic cultural center around a slum district called Lincoln Square, and the air was getting noticeably less fit to breathe, and apartment house "developments" were becoming commonplace. There was less and less to count on, and the pace of change kept accelerating, and New Yorkers were all too aware of it.

But the sun did still come up over the East River and set beyond the Hudson. And the New York Giants did still play at the Polo Grounds and the Dodgers in Brooklyn.

There was also another baseball team in New York, the Yankees. While the Giants and Dodgers were both in the National League and played each other 22 times a season, the Yankees were off by themselves in the American League and could meet their fellow citizens only in an occasional exhibition game or in a World Series. Under this arrangement, New Yorkers (and equally important, tourists) took for granted the fact that some major league game was being played in the city every day during the baseball season, unless it rained or the rare luxury of an open date for the players came up. The Yankees and Giants had interlocking schedules: when one was home, the other traveled; and the Dodgers played at their home (Ebbets Field, near Prospect Park) in competition with one or the other. All thrived.

Older people (around 1950) could remember that the Yankees had once played in upper Manhattan around 168th Street and had later shared the Polo Grounds with the Giants. But in 1923, the Yankees had moved into their own stadium—the most magnificent ever built for professional sports—in the Bronx, directly across the Harlem River from the Polo Grounds. And from that time on, the Yankees came to represent the elite of athletics. With Babe Ruth as their main attraction, to be followed by Lou Gehrig and Joe DiMaggio and a surrounding cast of dozens of stars, they set all sorts of records for home runs, attendance, and victories. They took over the position of dominance John McGraw had attained for his Giants in the first quarter of the century, and just before World War II, when the Dodgers were made strong by Larry Mac-Phail, the Yankees emerged as a new archenemy for Brooklyn, since now their World Series confrontations came frequently.

By the year 1955, therefore, not only the existence of the New York Giants and Brooklyn Dodgers, but the relationships among their rooters, were looked upon as islands of unassailable permanence in a world whose changes kept accelerating dizzily. People now, and not only in New York, were being frightened by the H-bomb, by increasing automation which seemed to threaten jobs and increasing traffic which did threaten sanity, by civil rights awareness (and a Supreme Court desegregation decision) that brought into the open increasing social tensions, by the hint of economic downturn (with the

Depression still real in living memory), by the unprecedented experience of the Korean War, and by the continuing military draft. It was more comforting than ever to be able to turn one's thoughts to that good old security, the immutable orbits of the baseball teams, and to that delightful brand-new toy called television, which even brought the games into the home.

And the Giant-Dodger-Yankee tripod seemed never more firmly planted than in 1955. That year, for the first time, the Dodgers had beaten the Yankees in a World Series, and Brooklyn had the right to call itself "Woild Champeens," after decades of frustration. But the Yankees, with Mickey Mantle, and the Giants, with Willie Mays (and the World Championship of 1954 behind them), were also at peak popularity and confidence. Back in 1951, all three teams had finished first, with the Giants beating the Dodgers in a play-off for the pennant (on Bobby Thomson's ninth-inning, three-run homer off Ralph Branca, in a shamelessly pulp-fiction example of life imitating art). Then the Yankees beat the Giants in the World Series.

So everyone knew that Yankee fans, who had started out in the 1920s as young rebels against the McGraw Establishment, had long since become arrogant, insatiable for victory, single-minded, snobbish, and generally unbearable outside the Bronx, because their team was too perfect after 21 pennants in 35 years. They knew that Giant fans, wavering between nostalgia for the McGraw days that had established such deep identification for their team with the glamour of Broadway and Wall Street, and frustration at the frequently degrading but sporadically new-glory years of the present, were middle-class to the core. And they knew that Brooklynites, not alone as baseball fans, were a breed apart, rooting for and suffering with "Dem Bums" with a passionate patriotism characteristic of their peculiar and outspoken borough—perpetual underdogs in essence, no matter how much outward success they enjoyed.

And these composite identities, strangely enough, had survived bewildering cross-fertilization of their teams by the men actually involved.

The Dodgers of 1916 through 1930, who had won two pennants, come close to a couple of others, and were often laughable in between, lived under the leadership of Wilbert Robinson—"Uncle Robby"—who had been McGraw's close friend and coach in the early days until they had a mysterious falling out. The Dodgers of the early 1930s, in the hands of a bank, had a colorful manager named Casey Stengel, who had been a colorful outfielder for both Dodger and Giant pennant winners, and a worshipper of McGraw—but whose Dodger team knocked the Giants out of a pennant on the final weekend of the 1934 season, barely two years after McGraw's retirement. And the rebuilt Dodgers that followed the Stengel era were the creation of Mac-Phail, the man who introduced night baseball to the majors (in Cincinnati in

1935) and who brought Leo Durocher to Brooklyn as manager. Leo, who had started his major league career as a minor Yankee and had flourished among the Gas House Gang Cardinals, became the very personification of the Brooklyn Bum. After the Yankees met (and conquered) the Dodgers in a World Series for the first time in 1941, good-natured hatred knew no greater intensity than that of the Yankees for MacPhail and Durocher, and vice versa, and that of the Giants for the now unforgivably successful Dodgers.

And yet, before the 1940s ended, MacPhail had bought and sold the Yankees, installing lights on the roof of the sacred Stadium, inventing the profitable idea of a Stadium Club where season-ticket holders could keep themselves lubricated, and stirring excitement (instead of aloof tyranny) wherever he turned. And Durocher—the hated Durocher—was suddenly, in mid-season 1948, manager of the *Giants*; and within three years, the biggest of heroes to the Giant fans and the ultimate renegade to Brooklyn. And who, of all people, was in charge of the Magnificent Yankees? Casey Stengel, that clown, that life-long National Leaguer, that incomprehensible and irresistible language-mangler who was embarking on a streak of Yankee victories that would eclipse even those of Ruth and DiMaggio.

Countless other players shuffled back and forth, as indeed they always had, without disturbing the existing loyalties and with no difficulty adjusting their own. Dixie Walker, originally a Yankee sidetracked by injury, became the "People's Cherce" in Brooklyn. Babe Ruth wound up, in 1938, on exhibition in the first-base coaching box at Ebbets Field. Johnny Mize moved his smoothly stroked bat from the Polo Grounds to Yankee Stadium. To rebuild the Giants, Durocher promptly acquired Eddie Stanky, who had helped him win in Brooklyn, and so on in endless convolutions.

There had been another factor, of course, that helped set the individualities of the teams. It was the Dodgers, under Branch Rickey (MacPhail's successor), who broke the color line. They signed Jackie Robinson in 1946 and won the pennant in 1947 with him playing first base as the first-avowed Negro in major league baseball since the 1890s. In the context of New York, not to mention the country, this gave the Dodgers a dimension that had nothing to do with geography. The rise of the Dodgers competitively had been painted as the triumph of commoners at a time when "The Century of the Common Man" was an idea widely circulated—by Roosevelt, by the alignments of World War II, by the economic revolution. It was fitting in a way that this sociological advance (disgraceful as it was that there existed a position to advance from) take place in Brooklyn; it certainly fit the mood of the existing Dodger fans. Soon there were several outstanding Negro players (only the outstanding need apply, then) in the major leagues, but liberal loyalties were-

wedded to the Dodgers forever. The Giants followed suit as quickly as they could, and soon boasted Monte Irvin and Mays. But the Yankees, from their pinnacle of nobility, moved cautiously and reluctantly and—since they were winning—without urgency. They acquired, quickly, a patina of conservatism that actually helped them with some of their immediate customers but cut them off permanently from any universally warm acceptance by a city of New York's outlook.

Still, the larger pattern remained indestructible. The Atlantic Ocean was to the east, the mountains were somewhere west, Florida was south, Yonkers was north, and the Giants played at the Polo Grounds while the Dodgers played in Brooklyn. Oh, sure, the Yankees played in the Bronx, too, but that was for their diehards—and tourists. The Bronx Zoo was there too, but one hardly agonized over its ups and downs.

When rumblings started to be heard that it might not be this way forever— something about moving a team to California—the standard response was impatient incredulity. Rumormongers deserved to be sneered and shrugged at. How ridiculous can you get?

Nevertheless there were signs that something was up.

The Dodgers, in 1951, had passed into the full ownership of Walter Francis O'Malley, a lawyer who had acquired an interest in the club years before when the Brooklyn Trust Company (the real owner then) was effecting the shift from MacPhail to Rickey.

The Giants were owned by Horace C. Stoneham, whose father had owned them.

Both were acutely aware that their ball parks were obsolete, however successful their teams were.

As owners, O'Malley and Stoneham represented opposite ends of the baseball spectrum. O'Malley was a "self-made" man, who had worked his way through law school. He started to prosper under a system, common during the Depression years, that often paid legal fees in stock, especially to lawyers who worked for banks. Whatever his private feelings, he didn't pay too much attention to sports until his connection with the Dodgers, and then his interest grew clearly in direct proportion to his involvement. There was never any question that, to him, baseball was a business enterprise first, however emotional he might become about the outcome of games; eventually, it became his primary, full-time business.

Stoneham, on the other hand, came from an "old baseball family." His father Charles, whose main business had been investment, acquired the Giants in 1919. Horace had grown up in the middle of a boy's dream come true, intimately associated with all the great players and glamorous accomplishments of the McGraw era (or anyhow, the second half of it). He took over the club in 1936, four years after McGraw had handed the managership to Bill Terry and two years after McGraw had died. He spanned, therefore, in his own experience, all the changes that had come into baseball for a generation.

But where O'Malley was outgoing, politically minded, a tireless promoter with broad legal-business experience, conscious of public relations, and a joyful manipulator, Stoneham was shy, withdrawn, oriented entirely toward his own closed circle of family, friends, and private activities. O'Malley circulated among the people of Brooklyn; Stoneham watched games from his secluded office atop the centerfield clubhouse in the Polo Grounds. O'Malley's strong suit, and his pride, was shrewd decisionmaking; Stoneham's was loyalty—loyalty given and taken—to the past as well as to associates.

Different as they were, however, they faced essentially the same problems.

The composition of the population, and therefore of their customers, was changing. The middle class was moving to the suburbs. The slums that were starting to encircle both ball parks contained people too poor, and too disaffected, to be ticket-buyers. Rising costs dictated a higher proportion of night games. Those two factors alone demanded adequate parking space around any stadium that was to thrive in the long run. Competition from television (as a free, at-home entertainment medium) and other new forms of recreation made necessary more comfortable structures (with better sight lines, fewer posts, wider seats and aisles, better concessions facilities) than the antiquated Polo Grounds and Ebbets Field could provide. (Both had been built before World War I, and in the case of Ebbets Field, even the seating capacity was inadequate).

During the 1955 season then, both O'Malley and Stoneham were actively exploring alternatives to their existing homes—entirely behind the scenes, with utmost secrecy, but exploring. The explorations focused on the only two possibilities: a new ball park in New York or the shift of a franchise to another city.

The attractions of the second possibility had just been spelled out, unmistakably, for the whole world to see. Just before the 1953 season opened, the Boston Braves, who had shared Boston with the Red Sox for more than half a century, had moved to Milwaukee, into a fine new stadium built entirely by county funds, surrounded by parking space for 12,000 cars, rented to the club at a nominal figure. In their last season in Boston, the Braves had drawn 281,000; in their first in Milwaukee, 1,826,000; in the next, more than 2,000,000.

In 1954 the perennially hopeless St. Louis Browns, who had shared that city with the Cardinals for more than 50 years, were moved to Baltimore, where the city had enlarged and refurbished a municipal stadium. As weak as ever on the field, the reidentified Baltimore Orioles drew more than 1,000,000. And, before the 1955 season began, one of the most fabled of all baseball teams, the Philadelphia Athletics, left Philadelphia to the Phillies and became the Kansas City Athletics—pulling in 1,000,000 and more customers to an enlarged, refurbished municipal stadium.

The willingness of hitherto "minor-league cities" to spend their own money to acquire big-league representation was established, and the profitability to the moving club was demonstrated. If New York wanted their teams to remain, O'Malley and Stoneham decided independently, it would have to help them in some way to build new parks. In the meantime, moves elsewhere would have to be considered.

Actually, it was Stoneham who was closest to moving first. The chances of rebuilding the Polo Grounds were nil; talk of building a 110,000-seat stadium on stilts over the New York Central freight yard alongside the Hudson River between 59th and 65th Streets never got beyond the talking stage. The top Giant farm club was in Minneapolis, and Stoneham thought very seriously about moving there in the wake of Milwaukee's success. But his thoughts and plans remained private, and for the time being there was little public speculation that the words New York and Giants could ever be separated.

With O'Malley it was different, and quite public—although there was much misdirection in what was made public. O'Malley's stay-in-Brooklyn contingency was grandiose: he proposed that the city acquire and turn over to him the land around the Long Island Railroad station in downtown Brooklyn, an area which was Brooklyn's equivalent to Times Square. As part of a redevelopment of this entire neighborhood—which was deteriorating—O'Malley would build privately a $9,000,000 domed stadium seating 55,000.

And as his leave-Brooklyn contingency, O'Malley wanted only the best: Los Angeles, the target of several premature expansion plans for the past few years and obviously the largest, most important, untapped dollar-market in the United States.

So Walter went ahead busily on both fronts and opened a couple of diversionary ones. Soon after the 1955 World Series triumph over the Yankees, with Brooklyn's ecstasy at its height, O'Malley made a startling announcement. In 1956 the Dodgers would take seven of their home games (one against each opponent) out of Ebbets Field and play them in Jersey City, where a 30,000-capacity ball park built by public works programs during the Depression had been abandoned by the International League when the televising of Yankee, Giant, and Dodger games had driven minor league baseball out of Newark and Jersey City.

By this stunt, O'Malley hoped to prove that (1) he considered suburbs very important, (2) he would not hesitate to shrug off tradition, and (3) the ball club was his property and would play wherever he decided it should. He would also reap, in the meantime, extra publicity and a few extra bucks by creating seven special events out of seven ordinary dates.

To most people in 1956, it seemed like exactly that: a stunt. Only a handful of insiders realized that this was a major step in untying the bonds between Brooklyn and the Dodgers, and even some of these didn't really want to believe it. In their annual show the New York Baseball Writers referred to Walter's "Oldest Established Permanent Foating Franchise in New York"—with little awareness that they were being more prophetic than funny.

During the 1956 season while the Yankees and Dodgers happily marched toward another World Series confrontation, the possibility that one or the other, or both, National League teams might someday leave New York started to seem less ridiculous.

Minneapolis opened that season in a new, municipally built park easily convertible to major league standards. Rumors about the Giants, shrugged off in New York, were becoming common in Minneapolis.

More attention was being paid to the other part of O'Malley's Jersey City announcement, one that had been glossed over at first. After 1957, O'Malley had predicted the Dodgers wouldn't play in Ebbets Field at all because they would have a new park by then. In July 1956 the city appointed a three-man Brooklyn Sports Center Authority to evaluate O'Malley's plan as part of a $30,000,000 project for the Atlantic Avenue area. Meanwhile, O'Malley had sold the minor league park the Dodgers owned in Montreal, raising $1,500,000 for something or other.

Soon after the 1956 World Series (in which the Yankees got even by beating the Dodgers in seven games, and in which Don Larsen pitched his perfect game), an attempt to move the Washington Senators to Los Angeles was blocked by a Washington stockholder. At about the same time, O'Malley completed the sale of Ebbets Field to a real estate developer (named Marvin Kratter) and leased it back, but only through 1959.

What baseball fan, in those days, could pay attention to such dealings—especially when his team was winning pennants?

But by 1957 even some baseball fans began to listen, and wonder, and ponder, and worry.

In February 1957 O'Malley bought the minor league park in Los Angeles from the Chicago Cubs for $2,000,000. And Stoneham, in his low-key fashion, let it be known that Minneapolis, San Francisco, and a large Texas city (Houston or Dallas) were bidding for his Giants—and that he would go to the highest bidder, which he hoped would be New York. But only hoped.

A week later, a key Supreme Court ruling frightened baseball people. In denying certain antitrust exemptions to professional football even though baseball enjoyed them, the Court all but suggested that Congress act to weaken baseball's exemptions, too.

In March a delegation from Los Angeles visited the Dodgers at Vero Beach, their Florida training camp, and in early May O'Malley went to Los Angeles and informally agreed to move (a step he kept denying publicly as long as there were tickets to be sold at Ebbets Field).

The same month, Stoneham found acceptable an offer from San Francisco (to build him a new park there), and on May 28 the National League voted to give both clubs permission to move whenever they were ready.

On June 4 Mayor Wagner of New York met with both owners. Both the plans, in Brooklyn and on the West Side, were too expensive, he told them, but the city would build a 55,000-seat undomed, $12,000,000 stadium in Flushing, near LaGuardia Airport. Both said no thanks.

On June 17 congressional hearings on baseball's antitrust status began.

Exactly one month later, Stoneham testified that "New York can't support three teams" because "the baseball population is moving to the suburbs . . . our current location is such that it is impossible for us to operate profitably."

The stable structure was crumbling before the eyes of unbelieving New Yorkers, so most closed their eyes and continued to disbelieve.

On August 19 the board of directors of the Giants, with one dissenting vote, approved a move to San Francisco.

There was nothing left to disbelieve.

But O'Malley, whose deal with Los Angeles had been closed in May, insisted a better offer would still keep him in Brooklyn (and who knows: it might have). He withheld his formal announcement until October 8, in the middle of a World Series in which the Yankees were being beaten by the Milwaukee Braves.

And that was that.

Like legendary Atlantis, National League baseball in New York had suddenly sunk into the sea and disappeared. The continuous history of the New York Giants dated from 1883, of the Dodgers from 1888. Just like that, with the scribble of a pen and the wave of some California checkbooks, it was gone: poof.

And New Yorkers, who prided themselves on being able to take absolutely anything in stride, found themselves, for once, truly shocked.

The Yankees, of course, were still there—but so were the Statue of Liberty and the Empire State Building and the subways, and Wall Street. All were estimable institutions, and the Yankees were similarly reliable—and just about as exciting to those whose emotions had been nourished by the imperfect unpredictabilities of National League pennant races and the accessible characters of Giant and Dodger heroes.

But the empty feeling in people who had been rooting, heart and soul, for generations—literally from grandfather to father to son—for the Giants and Dodgers was unbearable. There were three principal reactions. Some had their interest in baseball killed, forever. Some, susceptible to a masochistic loyalty, kept an interest (necessarily curtailed but lively) in the transplanted teams. Some subsided into a sort of hibernation, or coma, or anesthetic trance as far as baseball was concerned, continuing to follow the events of the day but keeping them emotionally at arm's length.

Almost no one, however, transferred affection or even real curiosity to the Yankees.

A vacuum had been created.

And if nature abhors a vacuum, a politician who may be blamed for its creation abhors it even more.

October 8, 1957—the day the Dodger announcement made the abandonment of New York irrevocably public—was less than a month before a mayoralty election. Mayor Wagner, a Democrat running for his second term, was not exactly threatened in a city that never elected routine Republicans like Robert Christenberry. Nevertheless, the loss of two ball clubs was politically embarrassing. It hurt the economy of a city heavily involved with hotels, restaurants, transportation, and tourism; it hurt psychologically, too. The Mayor had to try to do something about this. He didn't have to succeed, but he had to try.

So Wagner tried. He set up a committee of "prominent citizens" to find a replacement. Another National League team must come to New York, and the park in Flushing offered to O'Malley and Stoneham could be the bait. The four-man committee had two well-known names (Jim Farley and Bernard Gimbel) and two obscure ones (Clint Blume and Bill Shea).

The one that counted was Shea.

As an energetic lawyer, active behind the scenes in Democratic politics, a sincere and enthusiastic sports fan and—ironically—once a stablemate of O'Malley's as a young lawyer for Brooklyn Trust, Shea went to work with remarkable effectiveness.

Before 1958 was over, he had approached the Pittsburgh, Cincinnati, and Philadelphia clubs about moving to New York. The first two expressed interest but finally backed off from accepting the stigma in their localities for the "kidnapping" accusation being hurled at O'Malley in New York. Philadelphia simply wasn't interested.

That convinced Shea that New York would never get a team within the framework of an eight-club league, which the National had been since 1900. Machinery to expand to 10 teams had been on the books of the league since 1947, but with the move into the gold fields of California now accomplished through the unforeseen abandonment of New York, there was a stone wall of opposition to any increase in size. No owner possessing one-eighth of a valuable monopoly wanted his share reduced to one-tenth.

Always quick to recognize and accept reality, and well-versed in where the leverage points of our society really lay, Shea promptly went to work in another direction.

If the existing leagues didn't want their monopoly diluted by new members, a new league could be formed to challenge the monopoly itself.

Ever since the move to Milwaukee in 1953, eager franchise-seekers had been trying to bring major league baseball to their cities. Most had failed. Now Shea got in touch with some of the more likely prospects, and the idea of a third major league took shape. Everyone knew that several times in baseball history, third leagues had been tried and had failed. But times were different now.

What Shea was counting on, of course, and what previous third-league attempts lacked, was congressional pressure. Baseball's special status as exempt from antitrust regulation, based on a 1922 Supreme Court decision reaffirmed with qualifications in 1953, had just been under highly publicized scrutiny in both the House and the Senate. Each new area, seeking the major league label, had Senators and Representatives whose interest (and interests) could be stimulated. The High Court had said, in effect, that Congress ought to write a law. The nature of that law—restrictive or permissive—could be greatly influenced by how Organized Baseball exercised its existing monopolistic powers when confronted by a legitimate new enterprise.

Like a third league.

And so the whole Continental League charade began. An eight-team league was formed on paper. Branch Rickey was made its president, but Shea was its workhorse. People with money were found to back clubs. Polite discussions (on the surface) explored how a third league could get started and gradually be absorbed into the established baseball structure. For the existing teams, this strategy was largely a holding action, a delaying tactic; the pushy newcomers would get discouraged and go away. For the Continental League people, the real goal was not an independent league but entry into the accepted, prestigious structure, a sort of oblique expansion.

An agreement was reached, with the existing majors spelling out the conditions a third league had to meet in order to be accepted. But Congress failed to pass any law (one bill was permissive and supported by baseball, another was restrictive), and suddenly there were charges of obstructionism and bad faith. Cities involved in the Continental League were suddenly being offered expansion spots in the majors.

By July 1960 it was clear that the Continental League would never become a reality, and the infighting between the American and National leagues for expansion plums was in full swing. The Yankees, technically, held a veto power over any new team in New York, but the American League was panting to share O'Malley's success in Los Angeles (where his anticipations had proved correct and where the Dodgers added to the excitement by winning the pennant and the World Series in 1959). The Yankees would demand, they announced, an American League team in Los Angeles if the National put a team back in New York.

The showdown came in August. The Continental agreed to dissolve for the promise that four of its groups would be accepted for expansion. The promise was half-kept. The two new National League teams, New York and Houston, were to be owned by people who had been in the Continental League setup; but when the American took in Los Angeles, moved the Washington Senators to Minnesota, and set up a new Senator team in Washington, it ignored the agreement and took in entirely new groups.

From Shea's point of view, however, he had been successful. There would be a New York team in the National League, to begin play in 1962, by which time, it was promised, the new stadium in Flushing would be built. The Baseball Establishment had succeeded in maintaining its unity; but Shea had succeeded in prodding, if not quite forcing, it to open its doors to newcomers.

The American League did not want to wait. Abruptly, in December 1960, it decided to field 10 teams in 1961. But the National stuck to its original plan: the new teams would organize during 1961 and be well prepared to begin competing in 1962.

Agreements were fine, but real life requires money.

When the Continental League's New York franchise was being organized, the principal financial backers, putting up roughly 30 percent each, were: Mrs. Dorothy J. Killiam of Canada, a rabid Dodger fan whose fortune was rooted in many industries but who was devoted, in part, to hiring a private railroad car to attend the World Series in Brooklyn; Dwight F. (Pete) Davis, Jr., whose family name was well known to all sports fans through the Davis Cup of tennis; and Mrs. Charles Shipman Payson, née Joan Whitney, whose brother owned, among a large number of other things, the New York *Herald Tribune*, and who herself was a familiar figure at race tracks as the owner of Greentree

Stable and countless fine thoroughbreds. Others, with smaller shares, were Herbert G. Walker and William Simpson. M. Donald Grant, a financier closely associated with Mrs. Payson, was active but not an actual shareholder at first.

Mrs. Payson had been a baseball fan and, in particular, a New York Giant fan for a long time. Once it was suggested to her that she buy a token interest in the Giants, and she did. So did Grant. When the Giants voted to move to San Francisco, it was Grant who cast that lone dissenting vote.

Mrs. Killiam, it turned out, wanted to be president of the club and not merely an honorary president. When this did not seem like a good idea to the others (nor to the National League people who would have to accept the franchise when it became obvious that the Continental League was done), she withdrew. Mrs. Payson took her share, motivated primarily (as she had been from the start) by the need to keep the enterprise going. (Eventually, Pete Davis, who was the most active in starting the project, sold out too, and Mrs. Payson wound up with about 80 percent of the stock.)

On October 17, 1960, at a National League meeting in Chicago, New York and Houston were formally awarded franchises.

It was three years since the Giants and the Dodgers had left. The Yankees had won two pennants and had just lost the seventh game of a wildly eventful World Series to Pittsburgh. The New York football Giants, who had moved from the Polo Grounds to Yankee Stadium in 1956, were the sports toast of the town. The traffic was worse than ever and the air less breatheable. Mayor Wagner was preparing to run for a third term, and the presidential campaign between John F. Kennedy and Richard Nixon was at fever pitch. One-way avenues were an accepted hazard by the pedestrians who tried to cross them. The Broadway Theater, for the 25th consecutive year or so, was dying, and off-Broadway and Greenwich Village beatniks were permanent tourist attractions. The airports were already overcrowded, rent-controlled apartments were to be treasured, more and more skyscrapers presented glass-and-shiny-metal faces instead of noble brick, and television had passed from novelty to wasteland.

The sun still moved from east to west, but it didn't shine as brightly or give any real warmth to baseball fans of National League persuasion.

But a glimmer of hope did lighten their horizons. A New York National League team did exist again. It had no players, no manager, no ball park, no minor league system, no equipment, and no history—but it did exist. At least there was something to look forward to.

It also had no name.

Would you believe Mets?

ACT I—STENGEL

2 *Birth of a Ball Club*

A carbon copy exists of the first official press release issued by the baseball team that was to become known as the Mets. It is dated October 17, 1960, and the typed copy begins:

"We haven't been officially notified of our acceptance into the National League, but if true, we are justifiably proud that the National League has entrusted our group, the Metropolitan Baseball Club of New York, Inc., with the franchise awarded New York City."

But, in pencil, "haven't" is crossed out and replaced by "have," and the phrase "but if true" is crossed out and replaced by "and."

That's how quickly things were moving. The Metropolitan Baseball Club of New York was all set to announce its existence on the basis of "reports."

The second paragraph, however, left no bases untouched.

"We accept this as an obligation to baseball followers the world over; to Organized Baseball; to the National League, and particularly to the people of the New York City metropolitan area whose needed support we are confident we will earn."

It went on to thank various people, including Shea, Rickey, and Mayor Wagner, and was signed by Grant, president; Davis, vice-president; Walker,

Simpson, and Mrs. Payson. Mentioned in the body of the release was Charles Hurth, who had been named general manager of the nonexistent club earlier in the year after serving as president of the Southern Association, one of baseball's oldest and best known minor leagues.

The owners, and Hurth, and Lou Niss (a former sports editor of the defunct *Brooklyn Eagle,* and subsequently a public relations man connected with Yonkers Raceway, who started handling publicity details for the new club in its Continental League phase) were more or less the entire organization at this point, except for office help.

So far, however, no major organizational effort had been required. The Mets (and within the group, they were already being thought of as "Mets") were still in a passive phase. The possibility of their existence had arisen from the actions of other people: the move west by the Giants and the Dodgers, and New York's search for a replacement. For the next few months, their development would continue to be merely a reaction to external events.

But this time, the external events would be those created by the Yankees.

Before Yankee business started to become Met business, however, the name "Mets" was taking root.

In mid-summer 1960, while it was still unclear whether there would be a new league or not, the ladies involved in the enterprise formed a committee to consider a name for the team. Mrs. Payson, Mrs. Grant, Mrs. Simpson, Mrs. Davis, and Mrs. Walker composed it. The announcement of its formation generated quite a few newspaper stories, and people were asked to send in suggestions. By mid-August, just about the time the Continental League idea died, about 1,500 letters had been received.

These letters contained suggestions for 468 different names.

The ladies decided to call in the press to help. A 12-man "advisory committee" was invited to a cocktail party at Mrs. Payson's home on Long Island. There were some husbands on hand, too. It was decided that the final selection would rest with the club itself, but that the writers would vote on the most frequently suggested names as a guide. The writers would narrow the list down to 10, and the public would be asked to vote (without having the final say, of course).

The top ten choices were: Continentals, Burros, Skyliners, Skyscrapers, Mets, Bees, Rebels, NYBs, Avengers, and Jets.

Two days later (September 2), the public was asked to vote on the ten names—but with no restriction about suggesting others. In a short time, about 1,000 letters were received, containing some 5,000 suggestions, about 500 of them different.

The top vote-getter was Mets—with 32 votes.

Skyliners got 31 votes.

However, there were several variations on the Met theme: Metropolitans, Metros, Metro-Giants, and so forth.

Here's how some of the suggestions were evaluated within the organization:

"*Burros*—originally considered in the spelling of BOROS, representative of the five boroughs but watered down to a hidden meaning with the small donkey as the emblem or insignia. Not truly representative of New York City in its present sense, and there is doubt that it will catch on.

Rebels—Might lend itself to humor, discussion, and argument for a while, but seems to be misplaced geographically.

Jets—Does not appear to have permanency. Has no true meaning. It describes the present age but could be outmoded in a few years.

Continentals—Weakness, if any, is in the shortening to Cons, but name may grow on fans and it has many things in its favor.

Avengers—Too long for headlines and cannot be shortened. Will mean nothing after the first year or so.

Skyliners—No apparent weakness. Question is, will it take hold with the fans?

Skyscrapers—Same goes for this one as Skyliners.

Mets—A shortened version of Metropolitans. Has a flat sound and does not lend itself to emblems or insignia."

But Mrs. Payson *liked* Mets. She liked Meadowlarks (for Flushing Meadow), too—but she did like Mets.

So they were the Mets.

Actually, it was a fine choice. It was a natural shortening of the corporate name; it was easy to handle in headlines; it was admirably broad in scope for identification with the entire New York area; and it had authentic historic overtones for those few who could hear them since the New York Metropolitans of the American Association had enjoyed an eventful career in the 1880s.

On October 17, however, the day of official entry into the National League, this tacit and gradual decision was months away from announcement—and it wasn't much of an issue. The news was being made by the Yankees.

Only four days before, on October 13, the Yankees had lost the seventh game of the World Series at Pittsburgh, on Bill Mazeroski's ninth-inning home-run off Ralph Terry. Now, one day after the Met announcement, the Yankees startled the world: they dropped Casey Stengel as manager.

Casey was 70 years old, and a complex situation had grown up around him. His Yankee teams had won 10 pennants in 12 years and had been completely rebuilt twice in the process. But in three of the last five World Series they had played, the Yankees had come in second. Players who had never known anything but victory were convinced it was they, not Stengel, who were entirely responsible. Dan Topping had taken over complete control of the Yankees while his partner, Del Webb, had become less active—and Stengel's original appointment to the Yankees had come through Webb, not Topping. Stengel, the word went out from confidential Yankee sources, was "too old."

Behind this lay a more realistic problem for Topping. Obviously, a 70-year-old manager might have to be replaced at any moment. (Stengel himself, at a birthday party in his honor in his native Kansas City, had told an attentive audience: "A lot of people my age are dead at the present time.") And Topping was absolutely sold on the identity of the successor: Ralph Houk, once a third-string catcher, later a manager of the Yankee farm club at Denver, and in the last couple of seasons a coach on Stengel's staff. Houk's baseball and leadership qualities were highly, and vocally, admired throughout baseball, and especially by Yankee players. Other clubs were offering him managerships. If Topping wanted to keep him for the Yankees, he couldn't afford to wait.

So Stengel was asked to "retire," in line with a newly discovered Yankee policy of retiring employees at 65, regardless of anything. But Stengel would have none of it. "My services are no longer required," he said bluntly and with unconcealed bitterness when it was his turn to speak. Houk was named manager, and the Yankees suddenly had a new image as well as a new regime.

But Stengel was only half the story. Within two weeks, George Weiss, the Yankee general manager, was gone too.

Weiss and Stengel had always worked closely together and had known each other for more than 35 years, going back to the days when Stengel was starting to manage in the minor leagues at Worcester, Massachusetts, and Weiss was running the New Haven ball club. In the 1930s, while Stengel was in Brooklyn, Weiss had taken charge of the Yankee minor league system and had helped build it into the unique talent-supplier it became. When MacPhail had divested himself of Yankee holdings after a fight with Topping and Webb right after the 1947 World Series, Weiss became the general manager, the professional man at the top of the Yankee pyramid. His regime was universally successful, in victories and dollars, but also aloof, cold, impersonal, and all the other unpleasant adjectives that people started to heap on the perpetual winners. When the Giants and Dodgers left, the atmosphere that Weiss's organization had projected (and that Topping had done nothing to dispel) helped prevent any mass switch of allegiance to the Yankees; but about Weiss's competence as a baseball executive, there had never been any question.

Now, on November 2, Weiss followed Stengel out of the Yankee picture—with a good deal less candor. He accepted the term "retirement" and would continue to be paid for five more years as an "advisor," while agreeing not to become general manager of any other team. He was 66 years old.

The passing of Stengel and Weiss from the New York baseball scene was accepted on all sides as final, and their professional obituaries filled the sports pages, blotting out speculation about the amorphous new team. It was just as well, in a way, because there were slight struggles going on in private.

Davis had decided by January 1961 that he did not want to be part of the new setup unless he could head it, and most of his stock was bought by Mrs. Payson, making her, to all intents and purposes, the sole real owner (since the other holdings now were minor fractions). Her position strengthened the hand of Grant, who was actually her representative. They intended to make Rickey the active head of the club, since the Continental League experience had brought them all into Rickey's orbit, and rarely did anyone exposed to Rickey fail to be impressed by the man's mental powers. But Rickey insisted on a completely free hand in operation and knew that this would take money; he wanted carte blanche to the extent of $5,000,000 or so—and that was a little too blanche a carte for Grant or Mrs. Payson to agree to. Meanwhile, Wid Matthews, a long-time Rickey protégé, had been hired as assistant to Hurth, but no agreement with Rickey himself could be reached.

So Grant had to look elsewhere for an experienced, prestigious, influential baseball executive to take charge of the day-to-day business of building and running a ball club. At any given moment, there are very few such men in America (or anywhere else), and fewer still at liberty.

But there was certainly one, right there in the New York area: George Weiss.

Even more than Stengel in his bank in Glendale, Weiss was chafing at inactivity in his home in Greenwich, Connecticut. When the Met opportunity arose, he grasped it eagerly.

Technically, of course, he could not accept a post as general manager; his agreement with the Yankees prohibited that. So Weiss became president of the Mets with Grant abandoning that title and becoming chairman of the board. But no one doubted for a moment that Weiss would be performing all the usual general manager's functions, even though Hurth's name would appear in releases for months afterward.

Weiss insisted that the difference in titles was real and that, anyhow, the $35,000 a year the Yankees were still paying him was "deferred payment for past services" rather than a continuing retainer. Topping, rather caustically, agreed that Weiss had the right to take any position that wasn't labeled "general manager."

"He is in the clear as far as the Yankees are concerned," Topping said. "Whether he is in the clear under the rules of baseball is for someone else to decide."

But the point was never pursued further, at least not publicly, and whatever matters of ethics or conscience were involved, they served only to heighten the emotional rivalry that began to grow between the two clubs.

This happened in mid-March, when the sports world's attention was focused on Florida. On Saturday, March 11, the first spring exhibition games had been played. On Monday, in Miami Beach, Floyd Patterson knocked out Ingemar Johansson in the sixth round, retaining the heavyweight championship, with most of the nation's most important sports columnists and television commentators on hand. The next day, in Miami, the Mets made their startling announcement: George Weiss, architect and symbol of the aristocratic Yankees, was taking over the still unnamed, undescribed but very definitely unaristocratic new National League team.

As a Yankee, Weiss had expressed strong opposition to all plans for a municipally built ball park—the key to attracting a new team which would, of course, compete with the Yankees. He had advanced many arguments why such a plan was (1) too expensive to be justified as a city expenditure; (2) unfair to a tax-paying, private business (the Yankees) that remained loyal to New York; and (3) a bad plan period, at a poor location (Flushing Meadow). On this Tuesday in Miami, however, Weiss suddenly saw the light. The new stadium was a fine idea, he said.

"I have a different picture now," he explained, not batting an eye. "With the additional information I have received, I think the new stadium is a good deal for both the city and the club."

The estimated cost, originally $9,000,000, was now $18,000,000, and back in New York there had been noisy opposition to it within the city government from January on.

That was on March 14.

On March 15 in Albany, the State Assembly voted down the Stadium bond authorization, 80–58.

Panicky phone calls went in all directions throughout New York's political machinery. No ball park, no ball club.

Within 24 hours, the State Assembly reversed itself and approved the issue. A week later, the State Senate did too. What remained to be done was to work out the details of a lease favorable enough for the club to make a profit, but also big enough to pay off the city's investment—and it would be Weiss's job to make the basic decisions for the club in this negotiation.

However, it was obvious by now that no new stadium would be ready for use by the opening of the 1962 season, just 12 months and a couple of weeks away. It was suggested that the new team share Yankee Stadium, but this was never a real possibility. Topping promptly threw cold water on the idea by announcing (on March 20) that the Yankees were opposed to it; but from the Met point of view, too, it would have been undesirable financially to be a tenant and perhaps fatal to establishing any individuality. The Polo Grounds still existed, and it was taken for granted it would be used.

Another popular speculation, voiced within minutes of the appointment of Weiss, was that Stengel would join him as field manager. Both Grant and Weiss insisted that it was too soon to talk of such things. "It will be a year before we need a manager, there are so many other things to do," said Grant; but they didn't deny it. The other possibility discussed most often was Leo Durocher, who hadn't managed anywhere since leaving the Giants after the 1955 season, but who was still a hero to old Giant fans—like Mrs. Payson.

But once the 1961 baseball season began, all kinds of speculation about the new team dropped to standby levels. It turned out to be an all-Yankee summer, surpassing Houk's and Topping's fondest hopes. Roger Maris and Mantle started hitting home runs early and just didn't stop. By June, the standard "10 games ahead of Babe Ruth's 1927 pace" comparisons were being made about both men, and the assault on the most glamorous of all baseball records—Ruth's 60 home runs—was getting national attention.

By July, the assault was being taken seriously, and no newscast failed to report on whether or not Maris and Mantle had hit another. By August, their progress was a national obsession. In September, the Yankees suddenly broke open the pennant race too, and although Mantle was injured and wound up with 54 homers, Maris went on to hit No. 61 in the last game of the season, off a Boston Red Sox rookie named Tracy Stallard—and arguments raged about the relative merits of Ruth's mark in a 154–game season and Maris's in the first 162-game season. As for the Yankees, who set a team homer record and brought Whitey Ford to new heights as he started every fourth day and won 25 games, their 11th pennant in 13 years apparently vindicated the youth movement that had swept out Weiss and Stengel.

During this Yankee summer then, few noticed how the Mets methodically went about creating an organization.

A baseball team needs, even before players, scouts. The great success of Weiss with the Yankees was based on his ability to hire talented scouts and administer efficiently their discoveries. By early May, Weiss and Hurth had signed up 23 scouts—including Rogers Hornsby, a Hall of Famer; Babe Herman, an outstanding hitter for the Brooklyn Dodgers of the 1920s and early 1930s, best known symbol of those zany days and hero of endless anecdotes (tripling into a double play, getting hit in the head by line drives, and so forth); Gil McDougald freshly retired as a Yankee player.

Listed as a scout at first, but actually brought in as a right-hand man for Weiss, was Johnny Murphy, a New Yorker to the hilt. He had played baseball at Fordham. As a Yankee pitcher during the 1930s, he became one of the first famous relief specialists in baseball history, especially when the man he relieved was Lefty Gomez. Murphy's brother was a well-known judge. Murphy himself, in his last year as a player right after World War II, was one of the leaders in the formation of the Players' Association, a rudimentary union. Through the late 1940s' and all the 1950s, he had worked for the Boston Red Sox, becoming their farm director. A self-effacing, infallibly pleasant, straightforward man with basically conservative views, Murphy had always enjoyed a friendly relationship with Weiss and was generally regarded as easy to work with (which Weiss was not). Technically he was "New England and New York Metropolitan Area Supervisor," but he would get more and more involved with building the farm system.

During this period, the Mets also acquired two other essentials: a man to take charge of selling tickets (and other fiscal matters), and a farm club. The ticket man was Bill Gibson, long associated with the Dodgers but one of those who stayed behind when most of the O'Malley employees moved west with the team. The farm club was in Raleigh, North Carolina, in the Class B Carolina League. This club was playing during the 1961 season, and players signed to Met contracts could play there.

But signing players, at that stage, meant signing free agents—players who were not under contract to any other professional team. In October, the Mets would get their chance to "draft" professionals from the rosters of the existing National League teams; so far, they could only get high school and college players and perhaps a semipro.

Somehow, somewhere, they found them, and a steady stream of announcements began in June. Ray Apple, Ohio State right-handed pitcher . . . Bill Haberman, Fordham outfielder . . . Sandor Tabor, St. John's third baseman . . . Tracey Rivers, Georgia Southern College pitching star ("the biggest prize," the release called him; "it took a five-figure bonus to get him.") . . . Bruce Grady . . . J. E. Rowe . . . Ted Gruber . . . Gene Huband . . . Dawes Hamilt . . . Hank McGraw . . . Bill Robinson . . . Doug Linehan . . . Eddie Wine . . . Dick Zeitler . . . Oscar Steadman . . . Alan Baade . . . Dubois McCullough . . . Paul Thomas Serra . . . Isaac Robinson . . . Ron Gasper . . . Ernest W. DeBruler . . . Grim Mason . . . Carmen Lemma.

Two of those names echo down the years. Hank McGraw was a catcher, "rated one of the finest high school athletes ever produced on the Pacific

Coast," who "cast his lot with the Mets despite offers from many other major league teams as well as 14 colleges" for a bonus of "better than $20,000" at the age of 18. His biggest asset, it turned out, was a kid brother named Frank and nicknamed Tug, a left-handed pitcher who followed him into the Met organization three years later and eventually helped lead the Mets to glory.

The other name is Ron Gasper, and its significance is strictly coincidental. He was an infielder who knocked around in the lower minors for several years before leaving baseball; but his name is almost the same as Rod Gaspar, a much younger, unrelated Californian who was a rookie on the Met championship team of 1969. The coincidence is this: just before the 1969 World Series, Frank Robinson, elder statesman of the Baltimore Orioles, tried to put down the Mets by asking "who is Ron Gaspar?"—purposely mixing up Ron Swoboda's first name with Gaspar's to prove that the Mets were nobodies. But Robinson was completely unaware that he was uttering the actual name of one of the first players signed by the Mets, even though the spelling was slightly different.

On May 8 the Mets announced that their name was the Mets.

On June 15 they announced that Red Ruffing, the dominant right-handed pitcher of the great Yankee teams of the 1930s and 1940s, had been signed as a pitching coach for the entire system.

On June 21 they announced that agreement had been reached with the city on terms of the lease for the new stadium in Flushing.

In July, with no announcement of any kind and quite a few evasions if not outright denials, Weiss spoke to Stengel at the All-Star Game in San Francisco. Stengel said he'd think about coming back to manage, but he didn't say yes. He had already turned down a couple of other offers.

Meanwhile, another important person had joined the team, this one with both Dodger and Yankee experience behind him: Jim Thomson, who had performed stadium-manager functions at Ebbets Field and then at Yankee Stadium, was now ready to handle the manifold and hard-to-define tasks of running the Polo Grounds and eventually (if it ever got built), Flushing Meadow Stadium.

By and large, though, it remained clearly the year of the Yankees, while Weiss worked quietly at lining up the internal affairs of a new organization.

Until late September.

As Maris and Mantle kept hitting homers, Commissioner Ford Frick had set off, not really intentionally, the great Asterisk Controversy. Once a ghost writer for Babe Ruth in his newspaper days, and revering the Babe perhaps a little beyond prudence, Frick declared that Ruth's "record" would not be "broken" unless Maris (or Mantle) hit homer No. 61 within 154 games, even though the American League schedule now called for 162 games. This not only cheapened the record Maris did set, but compromised the excitement possible in the closing days of the season. Game No. 154 (not counting an early-season tie) came up on September 20, when the Yankees were in Baltimore. Maris hit a home run off Milt Pappas—No. 59. Now, instead of shooting for an unadulterated record through the remaining 10 days of the season, Maris was in an ambiguous position.

What this meant was that there was more opportunity than there might have been for the Mets to get their share of the headlines.

A psychic sports fan might have suspected that something bizarre was in the air on September 22. At Madison Square Garden, the first six-day bike race held there in 22 years was supposed to start at 8 P.M., but it was discovered, when the riders took the track, that the boards had been put together the wrong way and were dangerous. Carpenters and riders then worked for hours, reassembling the track correctly, and the race finally began at 2:54 A.M. It ended on September 28 with Oscar Plattner and Armin Von Buren of Switzerland the winners.

What message could this convey to the psychic? Well, a six-day bike race is the closest sports event equivalent to an ordinary conversation with Charles Dillon Stengel, the Glendale banker.

On Monday, September 25, with the bike race not quite half over, Weiss was calling Glendale, pressing Casey for an answer.

On Wednesday, with the bike race winding toward a weary ending, the long-distance phone calls were mounting up.

On Thursday, when Nando Terrizzi and Leandro Faggin of Italy were finishing second, Weiss had Mrs. Payson call Stengel and ask him herself.

Casey gave in.

On Friday, September 29, the Mets announced the big news in New York, and Stengel began talking in California.

"It'll be great to be back in the Polar Grounds," he declared. "It's a great honor for me to be joining the Knickerbockers."

The sports world laughed and felt the glow of familiarity. That Casey! Calling the Mets Knicks! Did he think he was going to coach the basketball team?

The more penetrating Caseyologists, however, had a different explanation for the Master's slip. In Casey's mind, baseball history was a living force. He knew, subliminally at least, that the name "Mets" connoted the original Mets of the 1880s. He also knew that staple of baseball lore, the fact that the first organized baseball club and the first to write standardized rules was the Knickerbocker Club of New York, in 1846.

In his usual elliptical but circuitously relevant mode of thought, the Casey-ologists insisted, Casey was referring to the baseball Knickerbockers, not the basketball Knickerbockers. It was still a slip of the tongue but a more interesting one.

And Stengel's tongue, slipping or not, instantly became the largest asset the Mets had.

On Sunday, October 1, Maris hit his 61st homer at Yankee Stadium.

On Monday, Stengel and his wife Edna arrived in New York and put the impending World Series deep into second place, attention-wise.

On the same day, the Mets announced that Cookie Lavagetto and Solly Hemus, who had been fired as major league managers during the season just completed, would join Stengel's staff as coaches. Hemus had been guiding the St. Louis Cardinals, Lavagetto the Minnesota Twins (who were the transplanted original Washington Senators). Either was qualified to take charge if anything did happen to incapacitate Stengel, but both had a more important, more immediate function to perform. In a few days, the expansion draft would be taking place, and Hemus and Lavagetto were in a perfect position to offer up-to-date evaluations of the players who would be available.

And this, now, was the most important thing that had happened so far and the first activity with which fans could really identify. A complete framework of a ball club had been constructed during the past 12 months. At last the day of operational birth was arriving. As soon as the World Series was out of the way, the world would learn just who the first real Mets would be—and so would the Mets.

The plan devised by the National League for stocking its first new members since 1892 was simple enough: as simple as an entry fee (the kind view) or a holdup (the cynical view). Either way, no reasonably informed person doubted that the talent offered would be inadequate to compete with established teams, and startlingly overpriced. The Mets and Houston accepted this as a condition of going into business, but even they were startled and complained when they saw the actual proposals, although without real hope and without effect. When the American League had added two teams a year before, the decision to do so had been taken too late for the existing teams to get promising young players off the availability lists, and such prizes as Dean Chance and Jim Fregosi had been obtained; even so, the two new teams, Los Angeles and Washington, had finished no higher than 38½ games out of first place, with Los Angeles eighth and Washington tied with Kansas City for ninth. But National League teams had enjoyed a full year in which to manipulate their personnel so that desirable prospects were safely buried on unavailable minor league rosters.

This was the National League plan:

Each of the eight existing teams were to put 15 men into an expansion pool—seven from their active roster of 25 as of August 31, and eight from the rest of the players under their control.

From this pool, each new team was to draw 16 players at $75,000 apiece, taking exactly two from each old club. This was required. Then, if a new club wanted to, it could take one more player from each club for $50,000.

After these selections were made, each existing team put up one more player—a premium pick—with a $125,000 pricetag. Each new team would wind up with four such players, no more than one from any old team.

That meant each new team was committed to pay $1,700,000 for 20 players the other teams decided they didn't want and possibly $400,000 more for eight more men. In one sense, this wasn't as bad as it sounded. For tax purposes, it was in the interests of all concerned to have each player assigned a high dollar value, because players could be depreciated over a period of a few years. The really valuable item, the franchise, was assigned a nominal value. Everyone concerned understood that what it all amounted to was an admission fee of almost $2,000,000, which meant that about $4,000,000 was to be divided equally among the eight old teams. This made the slight dilution of the monopoly a little easier to bear.

The World Series ended in Cincinnati on Monday, October 9, with the Yankees winning in five games, and the expansion draft took place the next morning at the Netherland–Hilton Hotel there.

A coin was tossed to decide which team would choose first in the $75,000 phase of the draft. Houston won the toss—and in their first competitive action of any kind, the Mets were off and losing.

Houston chose Eddie Bressoud, the San Francisco Giant infielder, as its first pick.

The Mets then selected Hobie Landrith, a Giant catcher. (Later, Stengel was to explain the choice with one of his memorable aphorisms: "You gotta start with a catcher or you'll have all passed balls.")

Four hours later, the first all-pro Met roster was complete.

For $75,000 each, the Mets had obtained:

Pitchers: Roger Craig from Los Angeles, Al Jackson from Pittsburgh, Craig Anderson from St. Louis, and Ray Daviault from San Francisco.

Catchers: Landrith, Chris Cannizzaro from St. Louis, and Clarence (Choo-Choo) Coleman from Philadelphia.

First basemen: Gil Hodges from Los Angeles and Ed Bouchee from Chicago.

Other infielders: Elio Chacon from Cincinnati, Felix Mantilla from Milwaukee, and Sammy Drake from Chicago.

Outfielders: Gus Bell from Cincinnati, Joe Christopher from Pittsburgh,

Bobby Gene Smith from Philadelphia, and John Demerit from Milwaukee.

With these 16 in hand, the Mets went back and picked up two "bargains" for $50,000 each: Jim Hickman, an outfielder from St. Louis, and Sherman (Roadblock) Jones, a pitcher from Cincinnati.

And now came the real opportunity: four premium players at $125,000 apiece had to be selected. The Mets took Jay Hook, from Cincinnati, and Bob Miller, from St. Louis, two hard-throwing right-handed pitchers, universally regarded as fine prospects; Lee Walls, an outfielder from Philadelphia; and Don Zimmer, who had arrived at Ebbets Field as an understudy to Pee Wee Reese years ago, from Chicago.

The total cost of the 22 players was $1,800,000

Of the 22, only three could be classified as proven major league regulars: Hodges, who was 37 years old and suffering from a damaged knee; Bell, who would soon be 33 years old and whose productivity had dropped sharply in the last two seasons; and Craig, who was 30 years old and had suffered a broken shoulder in 1960.

Obviously, it was time for Weiss to start wheeling and dealing.

He began—with a definite pattern in mind. The Mets would be playing before sophisticated New York audiences, accustomed to watching Yankee teams win every year and, usually, Giant and Dodger teams too. They had to be given recognizable names, Weiss believed. It would take two or three years, Weiss and Stengel acknowledged, to build the team up to contending quality. In the meantime, the main thing they had to trade on was the nostalgia of the deprived National League fans who still remembered Giant and Dodger heroes and some of their former opponents. Besides, older players might have a better chance to keep the team "respectable," to win a few more games right away, and Weiss fervently believed that the only worthwhile entertainment in a ball park was a victory for the home team. Immediate help, immediate recognizability, and experienced hands—that's what the Mets needed at first. Young players could be brought along eventually in a farm system being built from the ground up. In Houston, perhaps, with its minor league history, they could afford to put youngsters on display from the start. But the Mets, in the most major of major league settings, had to have major league names whenever possible.

So Weiss started collecting them.

The day after the draft, he purchased Johnny Antonelli (and a lesser-known left-hander named Ken MacKenzie) from Milwaukee.

Two days later, he bought Jim Marshall, a first baseman, from the Giants, and three days after that, Billy Loes, also from the Giants. The same day, the Mets acquired Bob (Butterball) Botz and Neil Chrisley from Milwaukee—not "names" but presumably usable bodies.

Then Weiss signed Ted Lepcio, an infielder just released by Minnesota, known to New Yorkers from his Red Sox days.

Then he acquired Frank Thomas, a well-known slugger from Milwaukee, for the famous "player to be named later." This kind of deal was to cause Weiss considerable trouble when "later" came.

And on December 8, Weiss bought Richie Ashburn, once a league batting champion, from Chicago.

A week later, he traded Walls—one of the $125,000 picks—to the Dodgers for Charley Neal, their regular second baseman. And six days after that, he picked up Howie Nunn, a relief pitcher, from Cincinnati.

So by Christmas, the roster looked a little better. It contained 35 names, about half of them recognizable to ordinary fans, and in addition to those already mentioned, there were three pitchers whose names were not familiar: Aubrey Gatewood, Bob Moorhead, and Herb Moford.

The trouble was, of course, that too many of the names were just names. The same roster, with the clock turned back about four years for the veterans, would have done all right; but then, none of these veterans would have been made available if expansion had taken place four years earlier.

But it was a roster, and it was Christmastime, and there were no laws against hoping.

On other fronts, progress has been made. Stengel, upon his arrival in New York, had set forth his personal program with perfect clarity. Someone asked him if he was afraid that a weak Met team would tarnish the managerial record he had compiled as a Yankee.

"How big is baseball and how big is a record?" Stengel replied. "Well, I'll tell ya—baseball is far bigger than any record, including my own. I'm here to help baseball by helping Weiss rebuild this new club in a hurry."

It was a loyalty and obligation Stengel felt with deep sincerity—that he might be able, by his promotional flair and perhaps by his instruction on the field, to contribute something to the game-business-sport that had been his life and had made him wealthy. That he could indulge his ego while doing so was simply icing on the cake.

So on Thanksgiving Day, in cold weather, Casey was back in New York, far from the California sunshine, to take part in the celebrated Macy's Parade, promoting his Mets, which he had already dubbed "Amazing," sight unseen. ("I may be able to sell them some tickets with my face," he would confide, knowing his own value to the tireless and appreciative cameramen.)

And, by Thanksgiving, other kinds of milestones had been passed. Now that there were players to be transported from place to place, a road secretary was needed, and Niss took that job. (When the question of salary came up, Weiss pointed out to him, with a completely straight face, that road secretaries normally received a full share of World Series money.) Tom Meany, a former newspaperman and author who had worked with Weiss at Yankee Stadium, became the publicity man. Jules Adler was to handle special promotions.

On October 28, ground had been broken for the stadium at Flushing Meadow, and Weiss was telling people confidently that it would be ready for the 1963 season, if not earlier.

On November 13, a most important announcement was made: Liebmann Breweries, makers of Rheingold beer, had signed a five-year contract with the Mets, giving them $1,200,000 a year for radio-television rights. This assured financial stability regardless of fan response at the ticket windows.

A triple-A farm club was acquired, to be shared with the new Washington Senators (whose general manager, George Selkirk, knew Weiss from his own Yankee farm system days onward; baseball is a very inbred business). The team was Syracuse, in the International League.

Three broadcasters had been hired: Lindsey Nelson, nationally known for his work in college football and as Durocher's professional partner for the last five years on N.B.C. "Game of the Week" baseball telecasts; Bob Murphy, who had done major league baseball in Boston and Baltimore for the last nine years; and Ralph Kiner, home-run hitter extraordinary who had tried his hand as a general manager (in San Diego) after retiring as a player and was now entering a new career.

In short, as the year 1961 came to an end, all the complex elements of a major league baseball operation had been put together. With President Kennedy completing his first year in office, the aura of "New Frontier" was at peak intensity. But for baseball-minded New Yorkers, coughing more than ever as they spent more and more time traversing the same few blocks through traffic, the real new frontier was still on the horizon, impatiently awaited. National League baseball was coming back to a city that still pined for it, and all the backstage preparations were in motion, if not completed. All that remained was to put a team actually on a field.

Everyone knew, of course, that it couldn't be a good team, or a winner. Fortitude and loyalty would be required in rooting for it, and a certain amount of disaster could be anticipated. But at least it would be a real team, playing real National League opponents again, and perhaps in time some of the old, glorious excitement could be regenerated. And, just as it was not illegal for Met officials to hope, it was not illegal for those intending to be Met fans to dream.

Before long, though, all concerned—hopers and dreamers alike—were to relearn an old proverb: you can lead a man to dreamland, but you can't make sure he won't have nightmares.

3 The Original Mets

WITH Weiss and Stengel in command, and Gus Mauch installed as head trainer, and Murphy in the front office along with Thomson, the Mets headed into their first season with a heavy ex-Yankee flavor. It was heightened considerably by the fact that they also inherited the old Yankee training base in St. Petersburg, Florida.

The Yankees had always trained in St. Petersburg, it seemed. It wasn't quite always, but they had since the late 1920s, in the heyday of Babe Ruth. They had a practice field all their own, called Huggins Field in honor of their manager of the 1920s, and they used its clubhouse as their permanent headquarters. For exhibition games, they took taxis about 18 blocks farther downtown to Al Lang Field, the permanent training base of the St. Louis Cardinals. The Yankees and Cardinals shared playing dates there, and the baseball-mad citizens of St. Petersburg (whose average age seemed to be about 71) had a game to watch every day.

Once, in 1951, the Yankees had traded training camps with the Giants, going to Phoenix while the Giants used St. Pete. But in every other season, the Yankees were considered a natural part of Florida's west coast. All through the Yankee careers of Weiss and Stengel and Mauch (who had become trainer in 1944), they had been spending March in St. Pete, with that one exception.

But Dan Topping, now in sole command of the Yankees, lived in Fort Lauderdale, a little north of Miami, on the east coast. His decision to move the Yankees to Fort Lauderdale, where the city had built a beautiful small-scale, million-dollar stadium, really had nothing to do with the Mets. It was coincidental that the move was to take place at the start of the 1962 season—and a lucky break for the Mets, who would have been hard put to find a fully equipped training base elsewhere. The Houston Colts were using Apache Junction, Arizona and would shift in 1964 to Cocoa, Florida, not far from Cape Canaveral (which was not yet Cape Kennedy). Neither the weather nor the facilities nor the accessibility were terribly desirable, but Florida had more teams to play against.

Fort Lauderdale was a different world, best described by the old-fashioned word "swinging." It fit the Yankee top-hat image quite well, especially the spring after the Maris–Mantle home run explosion. St. Petersburg was the haven of the retired, especially mid-Westerners, proud possessor of a softball league in which the minimum age for players was 70.

These circumstances, naturally, worked all in favor of the Mets. From the very start, they had warm fan support in St. Pete. The old folks identified strongly with Stengel and Weiss, discarded by their former employees for being overage, and the Mets were a perfect antidote to whatever bitterness St. Petersburgers felt at being abandoned by the Yankees (for those young Gold Coast floozies, yet!). And a friendly atmosphere always helps—especially when you have as little talent as the Mets did then.

So the Mets moved into the Colonial Inn, a motel in St. Petersburg Beach that the Yankees had used in recent years, and there they found that the featured artist in the supper show was none other than Nelson Eddy.

And with them came a rather remarkable press corps.

Shea, in his work to bring a team to New York, had forged a strong alliance with the newspapers, who also wanted a team to replace the Giants and Dodgers because baseball interest sold papers daily. It happened that, through no particular plan, the older baseball writers in New York had been covering the Giants in the middle 1950s. When the teams left, most of them shifted to the Yankees, with attrition taking care of the surplus. The Dodger writers, on the other hand, were a younger and more aggressive group, and they included the single most influential (and, in the opinion of many, the most talented) baseball writer in America: Dick Young of the *Daily News,* the paper with the largest circulation in the country.

Young had a colorful writing style, a nose for news, tireless ability to dig up stories, a truly fantastic rapport with the mind and feelings of the average fan, and crusading zeal of the highest order. He needed no encouragement, or help, in launching a campaign for a National League team in New York. He and Shea could, and did, help each other immensely. And whatever the *News* paid attention to, the other papers had to follow too. Furthermore, Young had enormous personal influence among his colleagues, partly because of his status and information, and partly because of an irrepressible sense of humor that enlivened every press box and helped set a tone of joyful irreverence.

While Young occupied a key position in the creation of communication between the new enterprise and its potential followers, other writers were also very important. One was Jack Lang, of the *Long Island Press,* also a Dodger veteran, also quick to note items of humor and interest, and now the representative of the "home" paper, since the team was scheduled to move to Queens. No less involved, nor less attuned to the possibilities of the new situation, were Leonard Shecter of the *Post,* Barney Kremenko of the *Journal-American* (whose previous close associations had been with the Giants), Harold Rosenthal of the *Herald Tribune,* Jack Mann and Stan Isaacs of *Newsday* (the rapidly growing paper in Nassau County on Long Island), and half a dozen others. From the very first day of spring training, their stories focused on the bizarre, the offbeat, the human, the mock-historic, the endless *bon mots* of Stengel, the refreshing candor of players who knew they had nowhere to go but up or out. They expressed cheerful defiance of the perfectly clear reality that the future meant defeat. Their approach to the new team brought into being a new attitude that was quickly absorbed by many fans back north, a "let's have fun with this, no matter what it is" attitude. It is safe to say that no other club would have been launched in quite this light; it is a matter of record that no other club ever was.

And they certainly had plenty to work with.

Weiss (who took a dim view of the lighthearted and fundamentally frank reports Stengel and the writers were constructing) was wheeling and dealing with the throttle full-out. Before spring training began, he signed Joe Ginsberg, a catcher, and Clem Labine, once a famous Dodger relief pitcher, who had been simply dropped by other major league clubs. He also had to scratch from his list Antonelli and Loes, both of whom decided to retire without donning a Met uniform.

After a few exhibition games had been played, Chrisley and Botz were returned to the Braves and Nunn to Cincinnati. (These were, it turned out, "conditional" deals, in which the Mets were taking players on trial—but Weiss had neglected to make this feature of the trades clear when they were first announced. This left writers, who had written well-publicized stories about these Met acquisitions, feeling silly and unfairly used; and since Weiss had brought with him his Yankee reputation for being secretive, sensitive, inaccessible, and not always fully informative, all hope that this would be a "new Weiss" was undermined right at the start.)

However, as long as Stengel was around, spinning his yarns, dropping his marvelously confusing but often brilliantly insightful comments, no one worried too much about Weiss. Besides, there were all these new ball players with personalities to be explored and side issues to pursue. One young man turned up, uninvited, for a tryout as a pitcher—and was actually given one by Johnny Murphy. Hornsby, who was in camp to coach hitters, was apparently snubbed by Roger Maris, who was already being castigated by writers all over the country for being "unfriendly," and that incident became a three-day wonder. (Actually, Maris *was* unfriendly; but he was also insulted by Hornsby's comments before the snub took place, so it was more a retaliation than an affront, and no one had ever accused Hornsby—one of the greatest baseball players ever—of being gracious.) There were, along with the roster players, such conceivably exciting minor-league invitees as Evans Killeen, Marsh Hamilt, and Bill Robertson (pitchers), Bruce Fitzgerald (infielder), and Rod Kanehl (listed as an outfielder). A Yankee reject, "Hot Rod" Kanehl was to become a major symbol of the early Mets and a personal favorite of Stengel's.

By January, in fact, the Mets had 128 players under contract—35 on the Met roster, 19 assigned to Syracuse, 30 to Santa Barbara (Class C), 25 to Auburn (Class D), and 19 to Quincy (Class D). Since no one really knew what the Mets would look like when the season began, one could write about any of the kids as legitimately as one could about the familiar names.

And when it rained—as it did from time to time in St. Petersburg—one could always write a piece about the Polo Grounds itself, which was being painted and otherwise refurbished for its new temporary tenant.

So the Mets had begun to acquire an identity in the minds of New York readers before they had ever played a game. Baseball in New York had thrived on the perpetual argument between Dodger and Giant fans; now, to a lesser degree, Met fan could argue with Yankee fan, and everyone could argue about exactly how bad the Mets would be.

The high spots of the spring training season were, of course, predetermined: the two games against the Yankees. On March 22, at St. Pete, the teams met for the first time. For the Met official family, it was a holy war; for Met players, one more afternoon of struggle for survival, no different from any other; for the Yankees, something weird and funny that they didn't know quite what to make of.

The Mets won, 4–3, and Met readers and writers made the most of it. It is hard to name anything more completely meaningless than the outcome of a spring training exhibition game, but the emotional values of this one were real enough. Five days later in Fort Lauderdale, however, the Yankees beat the Mets, 3–2, so their face-to-face competition for a year at least ended even —unless, of course (big joke) they met in the World Series.

For that matter, the Mets held their own all through spring training, winding up 12 victories and 15 defeats. ("But I ain't fooled, they play different when the other side's trying too," Stengel observed.) In the process, they arrived at a starting lineup composed entirely of experienced players: Thomas, Ashburn, and Bell in the outfield; Hodges at first, Neal at second, Chacon at short, and Zimmer at third; Landrith catching and—for opening day at least—Craig pitching. On the day they left Florida, the Mets dropped Lepcio, so he too didn't last long enough to become an official Original Met. Those who survived the last cut and actually started the National League season were the nine starters and Anderson, Daviault, Hook, Jackson, MacKenzie, Moorhead, Jones, Labine, Moford, and Bob Miller, pitchers; Coleman, Cannizzaro, and Ginsberg, catchers; Smith, Christopher, Hickman, Kanehl, and Demerit, outfielders; and Mantilla and Neal, infielders. Lavagetto coached at first base, Hemus at third, Ruffing took charge of the pitchers, and Hornsby and Red Kress were also on Stengel's staff. The Mets may have lacked something in physical talent, but they had no shortage of baseball brains.

The first official Met game was scheduled for St. Louis on April 10.

It got rained out.

There should have been a victory celebration right then and there.

Instead, fate forced the Mets to actually play the next night. Craig started against Larry Jackson and lasted three innings. By that time St. Louis led, 5–2. Hodges and Neal hit home runs, but Moorhead, Moford, and Labine had to pitch, too. The final score was 11–4, and it was a fair sample of the rest of the season: the Mets would be able to score, but their pitching and defense would be totally inadequate.

Just as typical was the greeting the Mets got the next day when they finally reached New York. Mayor Wagner decreed a parade up lower Broadway to a City Hall reception, and the affair turned out to be appropriately festive— making the Yankees gnash their teeth some more. The Yankees were, after all, World Champions and record breakers; they had never left New York, had always paid taxes, had asked only for some extra parking space that was summarily refused; and they had opened the baseball season at home while the Mets were on the road. But the Mayor reserved his official recognition for the newcomers—and boasted of the new park the city was building for them. It didn't seem fair.

But the New York fans and the papers didn't seem primarily concerned with what was familiar stuff—Yankee victories—whether it was fair or not. All curiosity centered on the Mets.

The home opener was scheduled for—why not?—Friday the Thirteenth. The opposing team was Pittsburgh, the same team that had helped close the Polo Grounds "forever" in September 1957.

That day Pittsburgh had won.

This day Pittsburgh won too. The score was only 4–3, on a cold, rainy day that produced a few snow flurries. The attendance was 12,000, about 10,000 less than the Yankees had drawn on Tuesday.

The next day the Pirates won again.

The following day was Sunday, but that made no difference to the Pirates. They won again. The weather was still miserable, but the crowd was beginning to take on character. It cheered every pitch; it encouraged every move. (Yankee officials, coming back from the airport after being rained out in Detroit that Sunday, heard the Met game on the radio and couldn't believe that the crowd noise was real. "Imagine their nerve, using canned crowd noise to make the broadcast sound presentable," one of them said. But the few thousand on hand were really making the sort of sound experienced ears associated only with packed stadiums.)

The Mets had now lost four in a row, but they still disdained a victory celebration on Monday, a day off. The Cards and Pirates were, after all, established teams and probably in the midst of terrific hot streaks. But the next opponent would be someone their own size, the fellow-expansion Houston Colts. Things would be different on Tuesday.

They were. The Mets needed extra innings to lose.

Another pattern was being set. In this game, the Mets were losing to Houston, 2–1, with two out in the ninth when Bell hit a homer and tied it up. In the 10th Mantilla doubled with one out—but got caught in a rundown and was tagged out on Chacon's grounder to short. In the 11th, Don Buddin hit a three-run homer off Moford and Houston won, 5–2.

The Mets were discovering their trademark, the futile rally.

On Wednesday, the Mets played Houston again and guess what happened? That's right, they lost.

And they lost two more to the Cardinals before going on to Pittsburgh and losing another.

Their record now was no victories, nine defeats. The Pirates, meanwhile, had won 10 straight. The season was 12 days old and the Mets, having played only nine games, were already 9½ games out of first place.

The possibility of losing all 162 had to be given consideration, at least by the romantically inclined. Realistic baseball men knew, however, that you can't avoid winning some time.

And the realists were right, of course. On Monday night, April 23, in Pittsburgh, the Mets won one.

Hook pitched it, backed up by plenty of runs. The score was 9–1. Hook was the handsome, bright, graduate engineer whose Cincinnati career had been sidetracked only by arm trouble. He could throw as hard as anyone, and he was intelligent and eager, and he could even show with diagrams and equations why a ball curved. It was only a question of time, now, until the Jay Hooks and Elio Chacons and Jim Hickmans would become big stars.

This time, there was a victory celebration, with champagne and everything. Optimism ran rampant.

And things really did start to look up—relatively speaking. For the next three weeks and more, the Mets were to win more often than not. They won 12 out of 22, and people began to believe that they would be no worse than respectably bad.

Two series stimulated such fantasies and helped capture the imagination of more and more New Yorkers. One was against the Cubs in New York, the other at Milwaukee.

On May 15, a Tuesday night, the Cubs were at the Polo Grounds. The Mets, their record 7–18 now, could leave last place for the first time by beating the Cubs, who were 9–21. It was a particularly attractive battle of wits, too, because the Cubs did not have a manager; they had 10 coaches, who were supposed to take either turns or votes in running the club, but none was designated as manager. Pitting Stengel against 10 minds, or none, was a delightful matchup, any way you looked at it.

And Stengel had some new forces at his disposal. A new catcher, Harry Chiti, had been purchased from Cleveland (for a player to be designated and delivered later); Sammy Taylor, another catcher, was obtained from the Cubs for Bobby Gene Smith. (The desperate catcher hunt had followed the discovery that Landrith, who could catch, couldn't throw; Cannizzaro, who could throw, couldn't catch; and Coleman could catch low pitches but not much else.) Labine and Ginsberg had been released. Cliff Cook, an infielder, and another Bob Miller—this one left-handed and with the middle initial G instead of L—had been obtained from Cincinnati for Zimmer, who had gone hitless in 34 times at bat. (As the players put it, Zimmer was "oh-for-Met-career" although he actually had made four hits in 52 tries for an .077 average.) Wilmer (Vinegar Bend) Mizell, a distinguished left-handed pitcher who could no longer pitch, had come from Pittsburgh for Jim Marshall, the first baseman who had been booed lustily when he had to replace Hodges in the starting lineup of the first Polo Grounds game because Gil's knee had stiffened.

And, oh, yes; the Mets now had a first baseman named Marv Throneberry, who would have a chance to be a regular because it was obvious that Hodges had chronic knee trouble and would need an operation. ("You're 38 years old," Dr. Peter Lamotte, the club physician, told Hodges, "but that knee looks 76.") Throneberry was no stranger to Stengel and Weiss; he had been one of their prize slugging prospects at Denver in 1955 and 1956 under Houk, in an infield that included Tony Kubek and Bobby Richardson. As a Yankee, Throneberry had modeled every gesture on his idol, Mantle; but he had not played effectively and had been passed on to Kansas City and then to Baltimore. On May 9 with great fanfare, Weiss announced that Throneberry had been "purchased" from the Orioles (estimates were $40,000). He did not announce that another player would have to go to Baltimore subsequently.

So, on May 15, Stengel's lineup against the managerless Cubs had Hickman in center, Cook at third, Taylor catching, and Mizell pitching. Chicago's starter was Bob Buhl.

Going into the bottom of the ninth, things were normal enough. Chicago led, 4–3, and Stengel's maneuvering had helped make it a three-hour game. As Thomas came to bat to lead off the Met ninth, a fan in the upper stand behind home plate stood indecisively at the head of a ramp, and uttered the quintessence of the Met fan's life problem: "I hate to leave," he told his companion, "but I hate to stay."

He was so right.

Thomas hit a high foul. Cuno Barragan, the Cub catcher, dropped it. Thomas singled, and Stengel sent Kanehl in to run for him. Bouchee took a third strike, Kanehl stole second, Cook flied out, and Bell, after fouling off several pitches, pulled a ground single through the right side, scoring Kanehl with the tying run.

Extra innings.

With one out in the 10th, Billy Williams hit a home run off Craig Anderson, and Ernie Banks singled to left—only to be thrown out by Kanehl (who had gone to left field) when he tried to stretch it into a double, so no further damage was done. Hickman doubled with one out in the Met 10th. With two out, Neal bounced a single through the middle, and it was 5–5.

It was also nearing midnight. Two walks filled the bases for the Mets, but Cook flied out to deep center, missing a chance to end things.

Now Stengel wasn't taking any chances. He brought in his ace, Craig. With one out in the 12th, Williams singled. Craig picked him off first—just in time, as it turned out, because Hickman promptly dropped a fly by Banks for a two-base error. But Craig survived, and the game went into the 13th as the clock climbed toward 1 A.M. About half the crowd of 8,000 was still present.

Kanehl started the 13th with a single and Hodges, who had replaced Bouchee in the 11th, walked on four pitches. Cook struck out, Bell walked, and Chiti had his chance to be a hero. But all he could do was bounce to Ron Santo, whose throw home forced Kanehl.

Two out, at 12:59 A.M., and Landrith batting for Craig against a pitcher named Cal Koonce, who had just been brought in to retire Chiti.

Landrith was about 5 feet 4 inches tall. Koonce missed his strike zone with four straight pitches. The winning run was forced in, and the Mets were in ninth place. Time of game: 4 hours 54 minutes.

About 13 hours later, the teams were at it again. The Cubs seized a 4–0 lead in three innings, but the Mets chipped away and were even by the fifth. Cook's error gave the Cubs an unearned run in the eighth, but the Mets got it back in their half when Hodges, of all people, hit an inside-the-park homer to left center with two out.

So it was extra innings again, and again Stengel pulled no punches. He called in Hook—his big winner with two victories to his credit—to pitch the 10th, and in the 11th the Mets won again: Demerit, who had hit his only Met homer in the fifth inning, walked, and Hook singled. Hickman executed a rare play for the Mets—a sacrifice that worked—and after an intentional pass to Chacon, Mantilla bounced a hit through the left side for the ball game.

These two 6–5 extra-inning victories, within 24 hours, had a disproportionate effect on Met popularity. There were two types of baseball fan in New York at this time: those who had forgotten how much fun National League games used to be, and those who had not forgotten. The Mets were now reminding everyone, and educating those too young to remember.

But the weekend ahead was more exhilarating still.

Warren Spahn stopped the Mets Friday night in Milwaukee, 5–2, although Hodges and Thomas hit homers. That was all right; Spahn beat everybody. On Saturday, however, the Mets won, 6–5, with a four-run rally in the eighth inning. And on Sunday they equaled a major league record: they won two games in one day. They scored four runs in the ninth inning to pull out the opener, 7–6, in 3 hours 1 minute; and wrapped up the second, 9–5, with a six-run seventh which included home runs by Mantilla, Thomas, and Neal.

This was a high point indeed. The Mets virtually swaggered into a private dining room at a motel near the airport, to eat, drink, and be merry while waiting for a charter to take them to Houston, the next stop. Their record was 12–19; they were hitting the ball, which always cheers up ball players; Thomas had 11 home runs already; they had won five of their last six games with late-inning rallies; and now they would get another crack at those Colts, who had no right to be as good as the Mets. It was a high-spirited evening.

And it marked, unknown to anyone at that moment, the true birth of the real Met syndrome. The masochistic pattern—no basis for hope, the arousing of expectations, the ultimate failure, the hint of revival, the dashing of all hopes, and the institutionalizing of futility—was about to be stamped indelibly on the whole Met entourage.

The party went on and on, with no one paying much attention to the fact that the flight was being delayed. The itinerary called for a 9 P.M. departure, and arrival in Houston by 12, gaining an hour on the clock along the way. But now it was 10, 10:30, 11:30—and still no departure.

It was the usual charter hazard—equipment trouble or shortage or something. Finally, shortly after midnight, a plane appeared. It was a Viscount, with 44 seats, just big enough to carry the entire party if the hostess sat on someone's lap. The bats and equipment trunks were strapped into the open luggage compartment opposite the door.

A writer sitting next to Ashburn found that they were both eying the overloaded plane nervously.

"If we had any sense, we'd get off right now," the writer said to Ashburn.

"Or guts," said Richie. "It just shows we're more afraid of what people will think than of crashing."

The flight turned out to be safe enough. Safe, but not accurate. About 4 A.M. the plane landed in Dallas. Houston was fogged in, they said.

By 6 A.M., Houston was unfogged. Everyone climbed aboard again and the plane flew to Houston. By this time, Houston streets were in the grip of morning traffic and the Mets' motel, near the temporary ball park the Colts were using, was completely across town from the airport. The bus ride took more than an hour.

At about 8:30 A.M. Houston time—less than 10 hours before they were due to report for the next game—the Mets scattered to their motel rooms. The double-header victory in Milwaukee seemed like a week ago.

"If anybody wants me," Stengel told Niss, "tell 'em I'm being embalmed." And he disappeared into his room.

And that's how the famous 17–game losing streak began.

First of all, they found that Bell was no longer with them. He had been left behind in Milwaukee, as deferred payment for the acquisition of Thomas the previous November. It was a bad moment for this sort of thing, since it seemed that the club was doing better and certainly needed every capable hand it could get, and since the news that any payment at all was still due came as a surprise to Met followers.

That night, the Mets lost, 3–2. The next night, they lost again, 3–2, and flew all night on to Los Angeles. Before they knew it, it was Wednesday night and they were in O'Malley's brand new Taj Mahal at Chavez Ravine for the first time. Craig and Don Drysdale battled 1–1 until the eighth, when the Dodgers scored twice and won, 3–1. On Thursday night, the Mets led 2–1 into the seventh but were beaten again, 4–2.

On Friday night, the Mets scored eight runs—but the Dodgers got 17. It was a "getaway" game, with the Mets scheduled to play in San Francisco Saturday afternoon. This one lasted 3 hours 38 minutes, and it was about 3 A.M. when the Met bus pulled up to the Jack Tar Hotel in San Francisco. Stengel, sitting in his usual front seat, looked like a wax figure of a man 150 years old. Everyone was sleepy and depressed.

But as the bus pulled into the driveway, applause and cheering could be heard. Dozens of attractive ladies, of all ages, were in the lobby and on the sidewalk, waiting for a glimpse of Stengel. It seems that a convention of California Business Women was in session and when its members heard, at their dinner, that the Mets were due, they decided to stick around.

In a flash, Stengel pulled himself upright, shed about 100 years in appearance, shot adrenalin through his system and color into his cheeks, and was in midsentence before his foot touched the sidewalk.

"Now we haven't been doin' so great but let me tell ya why that is and what would you do if. . . ."

He was engulfed by admirers and autograph seekers.

At 7 A.M., looking perfectly fresh, he could be found in the coffee shop, having breakfast with new listeners, saying, "Now, if ya could only. . . ."

By noon, he was out at Candlestick Park, for more torture.

Hook pitched against Billy O'Dell. The Mets led, 5–4, going into the eighth. Willie Mays led off with a home run, and it was 5–5. In the 10th, Mantilla's homer put the Mets ahead, 6–5, but Mays was due to bat third in the Giants' half. Sure enough, Harvey Kuenn singled, Chuck Hiller failed to bunt him over—and Willie drove one over the left field fence for a 7–6 victory.

All the details, of course, were being devoured back in New York, since Nelson, Murphy, and Kiner were describing every step of every disaster by radio and occasionally by television. But the best was yet to come.

On Sunday, the Mets had a doubleheader, completing as exhausting and nerve-fraying a week as anyone could wish (on an enemy). In the first game, they were minding their own business, absorbing a defeat. In the seventh inning, with San Francisco leading 4–1, Mays was on second and Orlando Cepeda, having just been hit by one of Craig's pitches, was on first. Craig tried to pick Mays off second and Chacon, making the tag, tumbled over Willie and appeared to think he'd been attacked. All of a sudden there was a fight going—and Cepeda was going straight for Craig. When order was restored, the Mets promptly proved that they had lost neither their nerve nor their touch: Craig tried to pick Cepeda off first, Bouchee let the ball get away, and Felipe Alou singled in two more runs. It wound up 7–1.

The second game, mercifully, would be the end of the road trip that started apparently 25 years ago in Milwaukee. Hickman hit a three-run homer and the Mets took a 5–2 lead into the eighth, with Jackson pitching. Kuenn singled, and Craig Anderson came in, and got an out. But Mays singled, Cepeda doubled, Alou singled, and it was 5–5, with Bob (Righty) Miller coming in to face Jim Davenport.

Ready?

Wild pitch, Alou to second; on ball four to Davenport, Alou steals third. With Willie McCovey pinch-hitting, a passed ball lets Alou score. Giants win, 6–5.

The catcher in this exciting inning was Chiti, for whom the Mets still owed a player to Cleveland. The arrangement had been that within 30 days the Mets would send a player to Jacksonville, Cleveland's farm club in the International League. The 30 days were up. A few days later, they sent Chiti, in effect trading a player for himself.

No wonder people loved the Mets.

The losing streak now stood at eight, and the Mets were coming home to the first real test of New Yorker's loyalties: to play the Dodgers and Giants, returning to New York for the first time as enemies.

First the Dodgers, for a holiday doubleheader on May 30. Attendance— 55,704, largest crowd in the majors so far that year. It was a historic week on at least three counts.

One: the crowd, about half-and-half in its sympathies (since the Dodgers were involved in a pennant fight with the Giants), showed how profitable the rivalry with the defectors could be.

Two: the banners, which were to become the life blood of Metdom, became a public issue. There had been banner-carriers, and clever ones, at the previous home games, but the crowds were small. Now, for the first time they got full attention—and the first attention they got was from park police and ushers, who tried to stop them. Weiss considered them both undignified and an affront to other spectators whose view was being blocked. (He never did understand, as Stengel did instantly, that looking at the banners was often better than looking at what the Mets were doing on the field.) Banners were torn and trampled, banner-carriers were ejected. Full descriptions of the official reaction filled the papers, obviously sympathizing with the banners. Thus the Met management was intimidated into accepting what it soon adopted as a big selling point.

Three: the Mets showed, to their own fans in the flesh, that reports of their ineptitude had not been exaggerated. In the first game they made 13 hits and scored six runs off Sandy Koufax, no less—and lost, 13–6. In the second, they made a triple play (line drive to Chacon with men on first and second, relay to Neal, relay to Hodges)—and lost, 6–5, when Willie Davis, the man who hit into the triple play, hit a ninth-inning homer off Anderson. With their 10th straight loss, they had set a club record, barely six weeks after setting the original mark.

On Thursday night, the Mets got a terrible break: rain, which held up the start of the game for an hour, stopped. The Dodgers went on to beat them, 6–3.

On Friday night, the Giants arrived and 43,742 people paid their way into the Polo Grounds. McCovey hit two homers, Mays one, and the Giants won, 9–6. On Saturday, the teams played a doubleheader, drawing 41,001 and provoking the largest anti-banner pogrom. The Giants won 10–1 and 6–4. On Sunday, the Giants turned nasty and used Juan Marichal: score, 6–1.

This brought the losing streak to 15, the last 13 in a row against the Dodgers and Giants, living reminders of what had made the Mets necessary. The Mets went to Philadelphia and lost two more games, 2–0 and 2–1, before they finally won a game.

The three weeks that this losing streak encompassed forged the true Met image. All the ideas that caught on so widely during the next three years were circulated by the events of these superpublicized games with the Giants and Dodgers. The same picture might have emerged eventually anyhow; probably it would have. But this way, by accident of schedule, it was given an immediacy that proved indelible. The rest of the season was a repetition, a deepening, an elaboration, of the same themes.

There was no longer much question about where the Mets would finish. They would be last. But the Mets had shown they could give losing a new dimension. It wasn't the fact of defeat, but the variety of ways in which it came about that fascinated onlookers, amazed even Stengel, frustrated the faithful, and depressed the players. Anyone, after all, could simply lose; but the Mets perfected ways to do something that became a cliché: snatch defeat from the jaws of victory. There were two basic methods. They would take a lead into the late innings and then, inevitably, infallibly, lose it through some mistake of their own or through some spectacular play by an opponent. Or they would fall far behind, rally to close the gap and come within sight of a tie or victory—and fall short.

During that first season, as they moved toward a record total of 120 defeats, they managed to bring the potential tying run to bat in the last inning in 56 of them. Since they won 40 games, that meant the diehards had at least the hope of victory until the final pitch in 60 percent of the games played. That this simply reflected the nature of baseball didn't seem to detract from the suspense generated in those who kept hoping.

As June began, Hodges' leg gave way, and his playing career, to all intents and purposes, was over. That made Throneberry the first baseman, and many of the new legends crystallized around him.

Only part of it had anything to do with Throneberry himself, who was basically a quiet Tennesseean. He was, it was true, a poor fielder; and like any ordinary power hitter, he struck out more often than he hit a home run. But several factors conspired to focus attention on him.

First there was the nature of his acquisition. He had been built up as, potentially, a real help, once an examination of his injured knee (yes, he had one too) showed he could play. By the time he had been with the Mets a month, he had failed a few times in dramatic pinch-hitting situations, but he hadn't done anything terribly wrong, at least nothing more wrong than anyone else, and he hadn't made any unforgettable contributions to the 17–game losing streak.

But on June 6, between games of the doubleheader at Philadelphia in which the Mets were losing Nos. 16 and 17, it was announced that Landrith —the first player chosen by the Mets—was going to Baltimore to "complete the deal for Throneberry."

Since the press and the fans didn't know there was anything to complete, the loss of Landrith—who hadn't been doing anything terrific himself—made it seem that the Mets were paying an excessive price, and that therefore Throneberry was expected to be something special. Consequently, all his routine failures (and he made plenty that weren't routine) were put in a special spotlight, and he became the symbol of disappointment.

Disappointment among the Mets, however, was not simply that. Young had promptly labeled the enthusiastic new fans "The New Breed," and The New Breed transformed Throneberry into a favorite, precisely because he could be counted on to disappoint.

Then there was the fact that the locker next to his was occupied by Richie Ashburn. ·

Ashburn was a wit, aware, and a whale of a personality. Behind him lay a successful National League career. Outside of baseball, he had done well in the banking business and was that rarest of combinations—an ultraconservative Republican from Nebraska with a thoroughly hip attitude toward daily life and an enormous capacity for fun. He actually wore Tyrolean shorts and other bright outfits, many with a yachting motif.

The first few times Throneberry messed something up, and reporters clustered around seeking explanations, Marv was simply polite and open and helpful, but not that much different from any other ballplayer. It was Ashburn who started to guide him, who convinced him that he should go along with instead of resist the image being created, who set him up with straight lines and who often provided the punch lines. It was Ashburn who popularized, whether or not he invented, the appellation "Marvelous Marv." It was Ashburn who grasped, as quickly as any of the writers, where the real success of the Mets lay, and Throneberry was his great project.

Once Marv got to play regularly, his deficiencies (especially on ground balls hit toward him) started to show. But the performance that established his true flair took place in one inning at the Polo Grounds, just two weeks after he had become the regular first baseman. It was June 17, and the Mets were starting a doubleheader with the Cubs, who were now three games ahead of New York in the standings but not out of reach. In the top half of the inning, Marv got in the way of a runner who had been picked off first, and after the interference, the Cubs went on to score four runs with two out. In the bottom half, with the score 4–1, two men on base and one out, Throneberry "tripled" two runs across—but was declared out himself because he missed first base (and second base too). Neal followed with a homer, but the run Throneberry would have scored was lost forever, not to mention the extra out; and the Mets went on to lose, 8–7—with Throneberry striking out for the final out of the game after a two-out rally had produced two runs and put the potential tying run on first.

When Marv opened the second game by booting a grounder, and the Mets went on to lose 4–3 on a ninth-inning homer by Santo off Mizell, Marv's career as a lightning rod for all jokes about the Mets was on its way.

But it would be wrong to believe that, in the context of the time, Throneberry enjoyed the special status he acquired retroactively. There was too much else going on. In that same first inning, for instance, Lou Brock had hit a home run off Jackson. Brock was a left-handed hitter, not very big; yet he hit this home run into the centerfield bleachers at the Polo Grounds, about 460 feet from home plate, an area into which only one home run had ever been hit before (by the huge Joe Adcock of Milwaukee in 1953).

The very next day, off Hook, Hank Aaron hit one into the same bleachers (but to the left of the runway instead of to the right), and with the bases loaded for good measure. In two days, Met pitchers had served up prodigious home runs matched for distance and direction only once by all the great players of National League history.

And the day after that, with Craig pitching against the Braves, Ed Mathews hit a pop-fly homer into the right field stands, which were only 257 feet from home. In the next inning, with the score 4–4 and Mack Jones on first base, Mathews came up again—and Craig threw over to first base 14 times, less to keep Jones from stealing than to drive Mathews crazy. It worked, too. Mathews fouled out, and the Mets went on to win, 6–5.

By this time, the Mets had another prominent ex-Yankee in their group. On June 15, the trading deadline, they had purchased Gene Woodling from Washington. Woodling had made mighty contributions to Stengel's five straight World Championships in his first five years with the Yankees, 1949–53, and had been kicking around Baltimore and Cleveland since. Almost 40 years old, Woodling had little mobility left when he joined the Mets, whose outfield was already largely uncovered by Thomas and Ashburn, but he could still swing the bat effectively.

One way or another, then, the Mets gave people something to read about every day. For instance, on June 28, they announced the signing of Ed Kranepool (about whom more presently) in the afternoon in New York, and lost a 13-inning game in Los Angeles that night. On June 29, they scored one of their most notable victories as Hook defeated the Dodgers, 10–4— notable because the Mets got 16 walks in the game, seven of them in succession during a six-run first inning. It was an incomparable triumph for passive resistance.

And the very next night, Saturday, June 30, with the game televised back to New York even though it started at 11 P.M. New York time, the Mets went hitless against Sandy Koufax, who started the game by striking out Ashburn, Kanehl, and Mantilla on nine pitches. In pitching the first of his record four no-hitters, Koufax struck out 13 Mets and walked five, coasting to a 5–0 victory after the Dodgers scored four in the first.

So much for passive resistance. In their 73rd game, less than halfway into their first season, the Mets had achieved baseball's ultimate indignity. What else could happen?

Plenty.

4 The Met Mystique

THE 1962 season was the last in which baseball had two midsummer All-Star Games. The first one was in Washington, on July 10, and the Mets were represented automatically. The rules said that at least one player from every team had to be on the all-star squad, so Ashburn was chosen, as the currently active Met with the most distinguished past record. Since Richie was on his way to a .306 average for the season, he needed no apology for his presence, even in 1962; but he didn't get into action during the 3–1 victory the National Leaguers scored.

That didn't mean, however, that the Mets didn't usurp their usual lion's share of attention. Stengel was on hand, having been named a coach, and he was the hit of the pregame kaffeeklatsch that took place in front of the Presidential Box alongside the home dugout. President Kennedy, Vice-President Johnson, and every political leader who could arrange to bask in the periphery of their spotlight were on hand. The President seemed particularly delighted to see Stengel, who had been managing the Boston Braves most of the time Kennedy was at Harvard. He, and probably all the other politicians, undoubtedly envied Stengel's gift for filibustering double-talk. But Stengel, who became honestly embarrassed in situations where he felt he didn't really deserve to be the center of attention, cut the conversation short. "Mr. President, I'd love to stay but I gotta go 'cause I'm not working for myself today but for the other fella," he said, indicating Fred Hutchinson, the Cincinnati manager who was managing the All-Stars because his team had won the pennant the year before. Before the startled Hutchinson could say anything, Casey added, "I gotta get back to business," and was gone.

The incident is not without significance, because the Met Mystique that blossomed in the first two years cannot be separated from the Kennedy Era in which it was embedded.

It is easy to forget, since the Assassination, that for one brief period while Kennedy was in office the official cultural stance of the United States stressed youthfulness. Entirely apart from political considerations, and despite frightening international developments, the prevailing tone set by the White House was hopeful, forward-looking, sophisticated, humorous, and exciting to young people. Until 1960, the political leadership of the country had been in the hands of a succession of older generations, throughout the twentieth century. Kennedy had campaigned upon, and had won converts to, the idea of turning over a new leaf, of having the sources of power pass into the hands of younger-minded, as well as chronologically younger, men and women. However one judged his specific actions and policies, no one could deny that the image he projected—vigorous, intelligent, fun-loving, willing to break with the past, self-confident, dedicated to "let's get things moving again"—had tremendous appeal for young people. By identifying with such attitudes, and seeing them prevalent at the highest levels of the hierarchy, adolescents, and postadolescents in particular, suddenly felt that they counted, that "their kind" of people were less ignorable than they had been, and that an underdog had somehow triumphed. That the new President had set a style notably different from the Eisenhower years—and different from those which followed—was a major factor in the way the Met "thing" developed.

And it is just as pertinent to keep in mind what had not yet happened in 1962 and 1963. The civil rights movement was at the peak of its nonviolent phase. The urban riots had not yet exploded. Campus radicals were still unknown outside their immediate orbits, and the only college issue that got national attention was the semiludicrous free-speech turmoil at Berkeley. What hippies there were, were still originals and unpublicized; in fact, the general population still thought of them as "beatniks," as if there were no difference. Open advocacy of drug use, long hair, draft-card burnings, miniskirts and maxiskirts, and "safety in the streets" were not yet major issues. Discussions that castigated the young condemned their passivity and conformity, not their involvement and radicalism. And most of all, there was no antiwar movement because there was no war, and there was no universal awareness of "polarization" (a word not yet actively in use) until the Assassination, overnight, changed America's view of itself.

This was the time of the Peace Corps, of nightclub comedians making fortunes by mimicking the President and his family, of lip service at least (and much real attention) to intellectuality and culture, and of the first wide distribution of transistor radios and stereo, which shifted so much commercialism to the teenage markets. And it was the time when the space program was becoming visible. When the President of the United States promised that the moon was within reach, there was little reason to limit one's imagination in any other way.

And it was to the young that the Mets first appealed, to the surprise, not to mention consternation, of Weiss and Grant—and the Yankees.

The Mets had expected to tap the nostalgia of the fans who remembered, and yearned for, the Giants and Dodgers. They did. What they did not foresee was The New Breed.

It contained several strains.

First there were the teenagers, whose older brothers and fathers had been Dodger, Giant, or Yankee fans. Younger siblings rarely get as golden an opportunity as the Mets provided for getting in on the ground floor of something new. Here was a subject—the Mets—on which the teenagers did not have to put up with older people's reminiscences and judgments. The kids could know, for themselves, every detail of every experience in the entire history of the new club. It was something their very own to root for, like a stray puppy brought home. Let the pompous oldtimers dream of bygone victories, and make invidious comparisons to Met talent; what did it matter to us, today, how Jay Hook compared to Lefty Gomez? Who the heck was Lefty Gomez anyhow? This was now, and the Mets were now, and the very fact that the older generation tended to sneer or be distinterested made the Mets that much more satisfying to the high school and college kids who now found it possible to reach the Polo Grounds by subway and always be sure of getting in.

Then there were the intellectuals. It had been fashionable, for many years, for those who considered themselves the more enlightened, better educated, more serious segment of society to turn away from spectator sports. Rooting for a team, identifying with sports heroes was incompatible with maturity as they defined it. But, having grown up in America, many of them had formed strong emotional attachments to sports while they were children. It is hard, in later life, to recapture the soulsearing excitement a 12-year-old sports fan feels. But the craving for that peculiar type of satisfaction lies dormant in many an intellectual breast.

To this group, the Mets provided a beautiful escape. They would feel foolish really rooting for a team, hoping it would win; but they wouldn't feel silly rooting for the Mets as long as they could pass off the whole thing as camp, as parody of the less sophisticated, well-advertised (and therefore justifiable) escapism. The very fact that the Mets were sure to lose made it all right to root for them and to laugh at the frustration that arrived on schedule. And since support of any underdog was an acceptable stance for any intellectual, the Mets clearly qualified on that ground alone.

A third segment of the New Breed consisted of those who were, more realistically, underdogs. It had been made unmistakably plain that the Mets were playing with a stacked deck, that they lacked talent because the existing clubs had arranged it that way. For the black, the poor, the henpecked, and the underage, this was strong material for identification. For anyone who felt alienated for any reason, the Mets were, instinctively, partners in misery. Defeat didn't hurt so much because they lived with defeat anyhow, so even a rally that didn't make it offered at least a sensation of hope—and an occasional victory could be savored in a way the "haves" could never appreciate.

And all three segments found themselves united on several levels by the Kennedy climate. The New Frontier psychology made the young, the disadvantaged, and the intellectual feel that they were more effective, more noticed, more a part of things than they had been—and it made the central middle-class mass of society more receptive to the self-expression of off-center groups.

To boil it all down: a few years earlier, the New Breed might have felt too intimidated to come out of the woodwork; a few years later, it might have aroused only hostility. The Kennedy Years were not only the right period for the New Breed to take root but also the right time for its character to be met with acceptance and amusement at its kookiness.

The great instrument of the New Breed's exposure was the television camera. It was not coincidence or any mysterious psychic force that made these fans choose banners as their means of communication. A banner—simple or elaborate, on a piece of paper or painted on a bed sheet, to be held up or carried around the aisles—might be readable to a few spectators in the immediate vicinity; it might be spotted by a press box observer with field glasses; but it would certainly be seen, fully legible, by thousands or even millions of television viewers every time the camera focused on it.

And a clever sign, one that made a point or showed originality, perfectly served the interests of both parties. The fan got the exposure he (or she or they) wanted; the television director got a good, lively, talk-stimulating shot. Baseball, because of its leisurely pace and built-in delays, is ideally suited to camera-roving through the stands; and the Mets made an ideal subject for wandering attention, because no championships were at stake in their games and no one was terribly interested in their routine ineptitude. The banners, as Stengel had pointed out, were more fun to watch than the players.

So it was, that what the newspapermen had saved by their quick reaction to repression, the telecasts fostered. The signs, and the puckish mentalities they revealed, made converts and brought out more sign-makers. These early pop artists realized, of course, that a sign had to have something special to make TV. There was no point in simply inscribing flat, if worthy, sentiments, like "Hurray for the Mets." Even the new chant, "Let's Go Mets," which in its vocal form was part exhortation and part self-derision, lost its power when simply written out. (Circumstances alter cases, of course; when President Kennedy landed at Frankfurt, West Germany, and in the crowd at the airport someone held up a "Let's Go Mets" sign, it was effective indeed.)

A twist, then, was the essential feature of a worthwhile banner. "Eamus Metropoli"—Latin for "Let's Go Mets"—was more like it. The word "love," hitherto rare in sports banners, became commonplace, as in "Boro Park Loves the Mets," and the subliminal significance of bringing this word into the open was worth thinking about. It reflected a depth of attachment beneath the laughter and foreshadowed much hippieism. Eventually, such masterpieces of simplicity as "Pray" would be displayed. And Throneberry inspired a remarkable team effort: five young men in white T-shirts, each with a different character painted on the back—"M," "A," "R," "V," and "!." They could not only line up to spell "Marv!"; they could, and did, line up to spell "Vram!."

Right after the Washington All-Star Game, the Mets returned to the Polo Grounds to find the Dodgers waiting for them and the banner-carriers in full stride. Their record was 23–59, and their friend Koufax was facing them again.

One might think it would be hard, at that point, to steal headlines from a Yankee team that was heading for another pennant. But that would be underestimating the Mets.

They hit safely against Koufax this time—three hits in seven innings: two bunts and a double by Thomas—but that wasn't the big news. Sandy had to quit after seven innings because his forefinger was numb. It turned out to be a circulatory ailment that finished him for the season and finally cost the Dodgers the pennant. But he did get his 14th victory, 3–0.

That was Thursday. Friday was Don Drysdale's turn, and he won, 5–4. And Saturday was Oldtimers' Day.

Oldtimers' Day? Halfway through the very first season of a new club?

Well, why not? Weiss believed in Oldtimers' Days. He was extremely sentimental about former baseball people, and during his Yankee days the

Yankees had established such affairs as immense commercial and public-relations successes. All he had to do was invite back to the Polo Grounds a full complement of former Giant and Dodger stars, to give the Mets nostalgia-by-proxy. It worked, too. A crowd of 37,253 turned out, probably indifferent to the fact that July 14 was also Bastille Day. At any rate, there was no uprising of the downtrodden this time. After the ceremonies, the Dodgers beat the Mets 17–3.

On Sunday, though, Hook beat the Giants 5–3, in the first game of a doubleheader that brought out 35,000 more people and the Mets had their first victory at home over an ancestor. The Giants corrected that in the second game, taking a 9–2 lead into the eighth inning and finally using Marichal to choke off the Met rally just when it had produced six runs.

The Mets were reaching mid-season form. On Monday night they lost to the Giants, 3–2: Bob (Righty) Miller wild-pitched the deciding run across in the top of the ninth, making the score 3–1, and the Mets of course scored in their half before Kanehl flied out.

The season was starting to drag. Presently they were on the road and had lost 11 in a row. Stengel was playing Kanehl at second base now and Neal at short. The game that broke the losing streak was a 1–0 victory for Al Jackson over Bob Gibson at St. Louis on July 27, with the Mets scoring their run in the third on a bunt single, a sacrifice, and an error, while the infield backed up Jackson with three vital double plays. The Mets won another game in that five-game series and came up to the second All-Star Game (this one in Chicago) with a 26–76 record. In baseball parlance, they were 50 games below .500, and it wasn't even August yet.

This All-Star Game the American Leaguers won, 9–4, but with the game safely out of reach Ashburn was given a chance to pinch-hit. He singled, so the Mets could claim to be the only team in baseball with a lifetime average of 1.000 for all its hitters in all-star play.

Such a silly statistic was an example of another fad that was growing around the club: the negative statistic.

A negative statistic was just what its name implied: a figure that measured some uncomplimentary achievement. A losing streak was a negative statistic. Zimmer's 0-for-34 had been a negative statistic. The fact, just being unearthed, that the Mets had yet to win a game on a Thursday, was a negative statistic.

Weiss hated negative statistics with a passion. So did Meany, whose job it was to keep the press informed. Meany had been, in his days on the *World Telegram,* one of the wittiest sportswriters. As an after-dinner speaker in great demand, he was positively brilliant and a virtuoso wielder of the needle.

He was the author of many sports books, an outstanding magazine writer, and in general an extremely capable man, with excellent contacts among his generation of baseball people. But for acting as a publicity man, serving the daily newspapermen (and others, of course), he had one terrible handicap: he hated newspapermen. Oh, there were exceptions, naturally. He respected some and was friendly with others, but he felt great contempt for them en masse, for the younger writers in particular, and for what he felt was the deterioration of journalism generally. He took a cavalier attitude about disseminating any kind of information, so even positive statistics weren't easy to come by. The one thing Tom never failed to announce, moved by unbreakable habit, was the exact time of day the lights were turned on if it was cloudy or a game ran late.

The new Met writers, however, had no intention of depending on anyone for statistics. They had the unique opportunity to keep their own, covering the entire history of a club, and Lang quickly surfaced as their chief archivist. He, with plenty of help from his fellows, came up with negative statistics every bit as original as the banners. For reader interest, and argument material, negative statistics were the best kind, and they certainly added a factual base to the new Met Mystique. But Weiss cringed and never ceased complaining.

It must be made clear that in many respects Weiss was doing a fine job. He did organize the structure, and he did demand (and get) loyal hard work from everyone in the organization. He knew his business, and he paid attention to detail, and he never stinted his own effort. That he was squabbling with the press was really his hangup, not theirs. To them he was at most an inconvenience; to him, they were a perpetual pain, and he insisted on carrying around clippings of stories he didn't like.

On two major topics, he seemed to be wrong—although on one he quickly corrected himself, and on the other an argument can be made that he wasn't wrong. These were the promotion question and the name-player question.

Promotionally, Weiss had every intention of marketing the Mets straight. The one thing he wanted to plug was that they would be a winning team as soon as possible. He never did understand, emotionally, where their true appeal lay. But he did recognize, intellectually, that the New Breed was turning defeat and its own presence into assets, and within one year he completely changed direction and went with the tide. The Mets began to promote the banners and the fans, and to act less embarrassed about their excessive humanity ("To Error Is Human, to Forgive Is a Met Fan," one banner read). It is to his credit that he shifted.

On the other point, no one will ever know for sure. It's clear enough that opting for recognizable names over young talent held back the development of the Mets competitively; it is also a fact that they succeeded commercially. Most of the press believed they would have succeeded just as well by building faster, but the press had none of its own money invested. Whatever might have been, Weiss's way did pay off in dollars and cents.

At any rate, the meaning of the Mets was well established by August 1962. It was certainly established in the minds of the opposition. Hutchinson proved that on Saturday, August 4.

His Reds expected to win the pennant again, but they were running behind the Giants and Dodgers. They came to the Polo Grounds for a five-game series and sweated out an 8–6 victory Friday night. But in Saturday's doubleheader, Craig beat them, 9–1, in the opener, and the second game went 14 innings and 4 hours 20 minutes. The Reds had bases full, one out in the ninth, but were checked by McKenzie. They got the first man on base in the 10th, 12th, and 13th, but couldn't score. Then Thomas led off the Met 14th with a home run off Moe Drabowsky at 9:35 P.M., and the Mets had a 3–2 decision and a sweep of the eight-hour doubleheader. Hutchinson, who knew he had a terrible temper, didn't trust himself to go into his team's clubhouse, and remained in the dugout in the darkened park for 20 minutes before he went in to dress.

That's what it meant to a manager to lose a doubleheader to the Mets.

By September 1, the Met record was 34–102, and they were 54½ games out of first place—and they still had a 13-game losing streak ahead of them. The conveyor belt, meanwhile, was bringing players in and taking players away without a break. They had added Rick Herrscher, Joe Pignatano, Dave Hillman, Willard Hunter, Galen Cisco, Larry Foss. But the most interesting addition was a 17-year-old Bronx boy named Ed Kranepool, their first real bonus baby.

He came out of James Monroe High School in June, his slugging there being compared to Hank Greenberg's of 30 years before. He was big, running to baby fat, and hit left-handed. The Mets gave him an $85,000 bonus, took him on a western trip as a tourist, and shipped him off to Syracuse. It took 14 games there to make it plain he belonged down a step, in Knoxville. It took only seven games in Knoxville to convince the organization that he belonged down in Class D, at Auburn. That seemed to be right, because in 20 games at Auburn he hit .351 and knocked in 18 runs. At the end of the season, he came back to the Mets and got into three games. He hit one double in six times at bat.

The funny part was, there were Met fans who said, "This may be our first championship player."

On September 23, a Sunday, the season had one week to go, the Mets had a 38–116 record, and they were playing the Cubs again, at the Polo Grounds. The Cubs, in ninth place, were 19 games ahead of the 10th place Mets, with six to play, so that issue had been settled long ago. But there were three items of special interest about this game.

It was, once again, a final farewell to the historical Polo Grounds, since Weiss had assured everyone that the new Stadium would be ready by next season. (The suggestion that it be called Shea Stadium, put forth September 2 by Bernard Gimbel, was gaining support.)

It was, also, the last chance for the home fans to see the Mets close in on the modern major league record of 117 defeats in a season.

And it was Bob (Righty) Miller's next-to-last chance to win a game. His record was 0–12.

As things turned out, it wasn't a farewell, because the Mets had to use the Polo Grounds all of 1963. And they didn't get their 117th defeat, because they won the game. And Miller didn't get credit for the victory because the Mets didn't break a 1–1 tie until the ninth, after Craig had replaced Miller.

The Mets then proceeded to wind up their first season in a blaze of ignominy.

On Tuesday night, September 25, they were definitely small stuff even though they lost No. 117, 7–3, to Spahn in Milwaukee. That night, Sonny Liston knocked out Floyd Patterson in the first round at Chicago and became heavyweight champion; and the Yankees in New York clinched another pennant by beating Washington, 8–3. Furthermore, Mantle was making a run for the American League batting title, and the Dodgers were clinging to a two-game lead over the Giants out on the West Coast.

On Wednesday, Craig lost at Milwaukee, 6–3, and it was official. The Mets, with 118 defeats, had lost more games than any major league team since 1899. This was one negative statistic that could not be downgraded, the way Jay Hook's wild pitch—the 71st of the season for the team, a National League record—had been the night before.

On Thursday the Mets rested, on Friday they lost at Chicago, and on Saturday it was Miller's turn again. The negative-statistics students had established that 0–12 equaled the worst record ever compiled by a major league pitcher: no one had ever lost 13 games without winning at least one. Miller could enter the record book by losing, or escape it altogether by winning. "Imagine," said Kremenko, a dedicated gin rummy player, "still being on the schneid after 158 games."

Miller won. With the score 1–1 in the seventh, a magnificent rally produced the winning run: Thomas got a scratch single and took second on an infield out. Hickman lined a single to left, and Thomas, trying to stop after rounding third, fell down and was put out while scrambling back. (Here was thoroughgoing Metism—getting a safe hit that added up to plus one out and minus one base, since Hickman stopped at first.) But Throneberry sliced a two-base hit to left field and Hickman scored all the way from first, and Miller made the 2–1 lead stand up. Not only did he pitch his first victory of the season—two days before October—but he also posted his first complete game in two years.

There was one game to play, and any red-blooded American who can recall his feelings about the last day of school at the age of 10 can imagine how the Mets felt that Sunday in Chicago.

They lost, of course. The score was 5–1. They walked in the first run, wild-pitched the third across, and when they started the eighth inning with singles by Drake and Ashburn, Pignatano hit into a triple play—a looping fly to short right that, Drake and Ashburn both thought, Ken Hubbs would never catch.

They were wrong, which was par for the course. Hubbs caught the ball, threw to first, and a throw to second completed the inning. It was a failure of poetic justice that the Mets had to bat again in the ninth, but they did nothing to prolong the season.

At least they had completed it—80 games below .500. They had not succeeded in playing all 162 games scheduled; the last two with Houston had been rained out and forgotten, so those who had doubted, sarcastically, that the Mets would finish at all had a talking point. A better talking point was the strange but indisputable fact that the Mets kept losing ground even after the season was over. The Giants and Dodgers had finished in a tie for first place, and had to have a two-out-of-three playoff to decide the pennant—a replay for the West Coast (and on the West Coast) of the 1951 drama at Ebbets Field and the Polo Grounds. Playoff games were counted as part of regular season statistics, so when the Giants won two out of three, they gained another half-game on the Mets, three days after the Mets had scattered to their homes. New York's final resting place was 60½ games out of first—and 18 games out of ninth.

Talking points were their triumph however. They had established an identity, gained a following, won attention, and made history. Better to make history in reverse than never to historicize themselves at all. As a result, all their between-season activities received wide publicity.

First there was the tax tangle involving Ashburn and Throneberry. Both were now proud owners of boats. Throneberry got his $7,000 cruiser because his drives had hit the Howard Clothes sign on the Polo Grounds wall more often than any other player's. Ashburn received a $5,000 craft for being voted the Most Valuable Met. It then developed that Throneberry had to pay income tax on the value of his boat, because it was a prize in a contest involving skill; but Ashburn's award was tax free because it was simply an honor for which he was chosen. (Years later, while a Philadelphia broadcaster, Ashburn would confess that he never knew exactly how to take that honor. "Most Valuable Player on the worst team ever? Just how did they mean that?")

Then came the ball park sweepstakes. Flushing Meadow Stadium would not be ready, it appeared, for opening day, but it would be ready in May. Then, not May but June. Then July. Then August. Then 1964, maybe.

And the player shuffle. While the World Series was still on, the Mets bought Norm Sherry, a catcher, and Dick Smith, an outfielder, from the Dodgers. In December, they sent Bob (1–12) Miller to the Dodgers for Tim Harkness, a first baseman, and Larry Burright, a second baseman. They sent Mantilla to the Red Sox for Stallard (that's right, the fellow who had thrown up Maris's 61st homer), Pumpsie Green, and Al Moran, infielders.

As for Ashburn, he estimated correctly that the microphone held more future for him than the Mets, and retired to take the Philadelphia broadcasting job.

Not too much help could be counted on from the minors. Syracuse had finished last in the International League, losing 101 games. For 1963, the Mets would have a triple-A team all their own, at Buffalo in the International League, but it was more likely to be stocked with Met rejects than with future prospects.

In December, a strike of all the New York papers made the Mets, and many other things, virtually incommunicado. The strike lasted into March, and the ordinary spring training flow of information was blocked. No satisfactory explanation was received, therefore, when Woodling was abruptly released on March 8. There was some story about sticking up for Throneberry in an argument about who was allowed to eat the apples at the clubhouse lunch counter, but what really happened was never made clear. It's a safe bet it had something to do with money. By March 22, when the Mets bought Carl Willey from the Braves, one paper (the *Post*) was back in business, and it was better known that the Mets had acquired a professional pitcher.

By April 1 the strike was over, and all good Met fans could read all the implications of the latest deal. Duke Snider, one of the Ebbets Field greats, was bought from the Dodgers. Of course, Duke couldn't run much any more, but he might hit some homers, and he represented King Nostalgia. The Mets, at this point, had eight players who were recent Dodgers—Snider, Hodges, Neal, Craig, Sherry, Burright, Harkness, and Smith. (Pignatano was assigned to Buffalo.)

In the course of a wildly successful exhibition season (15 won, 12 lost), young Kranepool had won a job, and Stengel didn't see why he couldn't play the outfield as well as first base occasionally. Another native New Yorker who made the club was Larry Bearnarth, a right-handed pitcher from St. John's University, who had finished up the 1962 season in Syracuse. The scouts and coaches doubted that Bearnarth threw hard enough, but Stengel liked his ability to keep the ball low, his toughness, and his ability to try to do what Stengel asked.

The important newcomer, however, was a scrappy kid from St. Louis named Ron Hunt, an infielder.

Hemus had seen Hunt play in the lower reaches of the Milwaukee organization, and on his recommendation the Mets bought him. He had no "can't miss" tag (which baseball organizations evidently buy by the gross) and was supposed to be "unready." He was just 22 years old, not very big, and suffered from a bewildering variety of allergies. But he also managed to hit the ball consistently and to play second base well enough—to hold his ground fearlessly in making the double-play pivot. He couldn't run fast but he ran bases hard. He was exactly the kind of hard-driving, eager young man that Stengel loved most. He made the club, although not the starting lineup, during spring training and soon developed into the first "real player" the Mets had.

When the team came north to start the 1963 season, against the Cardinals at the Polo Grounds, Stengel had a regular lineup that contained only one holdover from the opener of a year ago: Thomas, in left field. The rest of it had Harkness at first, Burright at second, Neal at third, Moran at short, Snider in center, and (a surprise) Kranepool in right. Craig was the pitcher again, and people called it the Dodger B team, since it contained five ex-Dodgers.

There was a new set of coaches, too. Kress and Hornsby had died during the winter, and Ruffing was sent out to work with younger pitchers in the system (which had been his original assignment). Lavagetto and Hemus were still on the base lines, but Ernie White was now the pitching coach, working in the bull pen, and Clyde McCullough had been brought in to try to help the catchers.

Because of the good record in spring training, the lack of descriptive detail during the strike, and the soothing forgetfulness of an intervening winter, there was real optimism in the air. The Mets obviously had new faces, and since they couldn't be worse, they'd have to be better. The fact that Houston, the true measuring rod of progress, had finished eighth, 24 games ahead of the Mets, was a fluke; this year the Mets would catch them, at least, and begin to build a true winner.

It took about a week to dissipate all those happy thoughts. Once competition began in earnest, it became evident that 1963 would be just like 1962—only a little different.

The difference was that the 1962 team could hit but do little else. This team couldn't hit. Its pitching was considerably better, its fielding about the same, but scoring runs was simply beyond it. This was unfortunate, because if you have to lose, it's more fun to lose while getting a lot of hits.

The very first game, on a gray, chilling day in the Polo Grounds, conveyed the message. Curt Flood began the game by hitting a slow grounder to Neal, who threw it far past Harkness into right field. Three singles and a wild throw by Craig later, the Cards had two runs. On the Met side, Burright led off with a single, and he also led off the ninth with a double—and those were the only hits the Mets got off Ernie Broglio. The final score was 7–0.

The score of the second game was 4–0, although this time the Mets amassed four singles off Ray Washburn.

In the third game, the Mets scored—once, on a home run by Snider. This was in Milwaukee and Spahn beat them, 6–1.

In the fourth game, both Hickman and Snider hit home runs off Lou Burdette—who beat them, of course, 5–2.

In the fifth game, the Mets went back to zero. Craig also held the Braves scoreless for nine innings, but he walked the first man in the 10th and when Bob Hendley (the rival pitcher) bunted to Harkness, the throw to second was too late, and Ty Cline mercifully ended the game with a single.

In the sixth game, the Mets set a season high of three runs and took a 3–2 lead into the ninth. Stallard had replaced Jackson in the seventh and had retired six Braves in a row. He started the ninth by striking out Mathews and Joe Torre. But Mack Jones singled, Lee Maye hit a home run, and the Mets were back in the clubhouse, 0–6, with people trying to find a tactful way to mention Maris to Stallard.

The next stop was Cincinnati, a small park ideal for hitters. Sure enough, Snider hit a two-run homer. But Cincinnati won the game, 7–4.

The Mets had now been playing a full week, and had scored 10 runs—four on homers by Snider, one on a homer by Hickman, one on a double by Hickman, one on a pinch single by Throneberry, one on a pinch single by Cook, one on a throwing error, and one on a scoring fly that turned into a double play. It was not what you would call a well-balanced attack.

And it didn't improve in the eighth game. The Mets got shut out again, by Jim O'Toole, 5–0.

One more defeat would tie last year's start of 0–9. Was this to be the way they were to start *every* season? Fortunately, the answer was no. They had made their point, that they were fundamentally as helpless as ever. It was time for a revival, just as there had been early the previous year. The Mets came back to the Polo Grounds and defeated the Braves, 5–4. In fact, they swept a four–game series from them, using late-inning heroics of their own. On Friday they scored two in the ninth after Milwaukee took a 4–3 lead in the top half; on Saturday, it was 3–1; in the Sunday doubleheader, the Mets had a five-run eighth in each game, winning 8–5 and 9–2.

But the flurry, like all Met flurries of the Polo Grounds years, quickly died out, and the season settled down to a repetition of 1962, with which there were constant comparisons. They did bring their record up to 13–15, and to 14–17 in a glorious 13–12 victory over Cincinnati in the second half of a Sunday doubleheader on Mother's Day in the Polo Grounds. Right after that, though, they lost 11 out of 13. In July they lost 15 in a row, and a few days later started an 11-game losing streak. By August 1 they were 33–73; by August 17, they were mathematically eliminated from the pennant race; on August 24 they set a club record by posting their 41st victory; but by the end of the season they had 111 defeats and only 51 victories. It may have looked better in numbers, but it really wasn't.

Throneberry was gone, sent down to Buffalo in May. His place as an antihero was immediately taken by Craig, whose 24 defeats in 1962 had been pretty evenly spaced out. On his way to the same total in 1963, Roger put together an 18-game losing streak that stimulated curiosity nationally. When he pitched well, which was often, the Mets simply couldn't score; when he did get a lead, an error or a home run or something totally unforeseen would turn him into a loser again. Actually, Throneberry's fame grew greater in subsequent years, when he became such an easily identifiable object for nostalgic Met fans' memories. During the 1963 season, with such an infield as Harkness–Burright–Moran to watch every day, the spectators didn't miss Throneberry quite so much.

In 1962, every game seemed unique, historic, tradition-setting. In 1963, everything was more familiar, and what emerged was a discontinuous sequence of vignettes rather than a coherent chronology. A steady stream of new, familiar faces—new to the Mets, but well known from elsewhere—created isolated minichapters of Met lore.

There was Jimmy Piersall. A decade before, as a young Boston infielder, he had suffered, and recovered from, a nervous breakdown. His story was told in a widely read book and a popular movie, and he continued to make headlines by strange behavior as he developed into a first-rate player in the American League. Was he a little crazy, or was he a master put-on? Straight baseball people leaned toward the first view, while more and more evidence pointed to the second. In 1963, he was with Washington, his career nearing its end because his biggest asset, speed afoot, was fading. On May 22, the Senators hired Hodges as manager to succeed Mickey Vernon. The Mets, of course, had to release Hodges. The next day they announced that they had "purchased" Piersall in an entirely "unconnected" deal. It was, in effect, a trade, and Weiss's insistence that it wasn't did not help his press relations.

Piersall seemed to be a natural for the Mets: he was zany, outspoken, and (by now) a flawed player. He had also worn, for years, No. 37, the number Stengel wore; it was promptly suggested that Piersall be assigned 37½. On the other hand, Piersall had a long history of uncomplimentary remarks about Stengel through the years of losing to Yankee teams, so it wasn't as perfect a match as it seemed. Piersall did his best to be amusing. When he hit the 100th homer of his career (at the Polo Grounds on June 23), he carried out his vow to run backward around the bases (in the proper order, of course). But there was inherent friction in the juxtaposition of two comedians with conflicting egos.

What could not be evaded was the fact that Piersall hit .194, which was not enough to help a team hitting .219, so after 40 games he was gone, simply released. He signed on with the Los Angeles Angels and played there a few more years, winding up in their promotion department.

Before he left the Mets, Piersall participated in what was, by all odds, the high point of the season: the rout of the Yankees in their own Stadium.

It had been the custom to play mid-season exhibitions between the Yankees and Giants or Dodgers for the benefit of sandlot baseball in New York. After those teams went to California, each came back to Yankee Stadium to play such a game and drew immense, enthusiastic crowds. The creation of the Mets made this charity game an intramural affair again, but it had not been held in 1962. Now a rags-versus-riches confrontation would give the Met and Yankee fans a chance to enjoy it in person. The two Yankee-Met games in Florida had been split again, but the newspaper strike had minimized their impact. Anyhow, this was the real thing in mid-season.

On June 20, a Thursday night, 50,000 people came out to the Stadium, the House that Ruth Built, the Home of Champions, the focal point of American Sports Glamour, the hallowed ground of countless stars—and about 49,000 of them were Met fans, equipped with banners and bugles and firecrackers. The Yankees had already played (and won) a regular American League game there that afternoon; the Mets had returned from a western trip. To the Yankees, this was a nuisance-necessity for charity, and Manager Houk employed a makeshift lineup of substitutes (since the regulars had done their work that afternoon). To Stengel and the Mets, this was pure World Series, and he not only used his regulars (such as they were) but two first-line pitchers, Hook and Willey.

The Yankee gendarmes, naturally, tried to bar, confiscate, or tear down the banners. They weren't evil, they just had no exposure to this sort of thing and couldn't understand it. ("It blocks the view of the other spectators," was the perpetual explanation.) There was no serious trouble, but there was constant turmoil.

Piersall opened the game with a double off Stan Williams and soon scored on a wild pitch. The Yankees tied it in their half. In the third, Piersall led off with another hit, triggering a five-run rally which included two walks, a wild pitch, an error by Pedro Gonzalez, a hit by Kanehl, a two-run single by Harkness, and a scoring double by Moran. Hook held the Yankees through the fifth, Willey pitched the last four, and it ended 6–2.

To that moment, Met fans had seen their team lose 163 games in less than a season and a half, but this one victory made up for everything. The favorite argument of National Leaguers—that the Yankees always won in an inferior league—got an unexpected boost.

Within two weeks, the Mets had another ex-Yankee in uniform, Jesse Gonder, a catcher–outfielder, for whom they gave Cincinnati Neal and Sammy Taylor. Gonder just happened to be playing in the minors at the time.

Jesse was always a dangerous left-handed batter with power, but he was an even more dangerous catcher. He was to figure, in August, in the vignette that sums up the 1963 season as well as anything can.

It was, to be specific, Tuesday night, August 27, in Pittsburgh. The Mets scored an unearned run in the second inning off Bob Friend. Grover Powell, a cheerful young left-hander who was one of their recent discoveries, shut out the Pirates for five innings but was clipped by a line drive during the fifth. Cisco took over in the sixth and remained in complete command, getting the first out of the ninth inning by making Willie Stargell, pinch-hitting, ground out. The score was still 1–0.

Cisco then walked Ducky Schofield. He had just pitched to 12 batters, had struck out one, had made eight hit grounders, and two hit harmless flies. He made Manny Mota hit a grounder, too.

And lost the game on it.

Mota's bouncer went right back through the mound, just past Cisco's glove.

Moran, the shortstop, and Hunt, the second baseman, converged on it behind second base, but it got through them.

At the start of the inning, Stengel had put Joe Christopher in right field for Snider, and Kanehl in left field for Thomas, to strengthen the defense. But he had left the center fielder, Duke Carmel, alone.

Carmel charged the ball. It bounced over his glove.

But Christopher, the right fielder, was hustling. He backed up Carmel and retrieved the ball.

Schofield, running from first base, was rounding third and heading home with the tying run. Mota, having seen the ball bounce past Carmel, was on his way to second. Cisco, like any well-behaved pitcher, had gone over to back up third.

Christopher wasn't sure whether he should throw home to try for the tying run, or to third to keep the winning run from getting there.

So he threw it halfway between.

Cisco, trying to change direction as the ball sailed toward the stands, fell down.

Schofield scored.

Cisco got up and raced to retrieve the ball, which had caromed off the box fronts to a point behind home plate.

Mota, rounding second, went full speed into third.

The coach held up both hands, trying to stop him there.

Mota ran right through the stop sign and headed for home with the winning run.

Cisco, finally reaching the ball, had plenty of time to throw it to the plate before Mota arrived. He did so, perfectly.

Gonder was waiting for the ball, his back to the field of play, facing Cisco.

The ball arrived while Mota, several feet from home, was starting his slide.

Gonder caught the ball and, with the same motion, spun around to tag the runner—a picture play by a fearless, experienced catcher.

Only————

Where Gonder spun, there was no home plate.

He had wandered about five feet into foul territory urging Cisco to throw. So when he wheeled and lunged, there was no one to tag. And about five feet away, Mota was sliding across the plate, unmolested.

Pittsburgh 2, New York 1. Final score.

Stengel, for all his half century in baseball, couldn't believe what he had seen. A little grounder! For five minutes, he stood bareheaded and motionless on the dugout steps, before he could bring himself to walk across the field to the Pittsburgh dugout, through which one had to go to reach the clubhouse.

That's what it meant to be a Met, actual or vicarious, in 1962 and 1963.

Only Craig, whose losing streak had ended about three weeks before, expressed no surprise. "The minute Mota hit the ball," he said, "I got off the bench and started for the clubhouse."

But it also meant unquenchable spirit, as displayed on May 4 at the Polo Grounds, in what happened to be the first of Craig's 18 straight defeats. The Giants hit six home runs in the first six innings that Saturday afternoon before some 32,000 spectators, and the Mets committed their third, fourth, and fifth errors of the game in the ninth inning to give the Giants three more runs. The score was 17–4 in the last of the ninth, with two out and nobody on base, when Harkness pinch-hit. The count went to two strikes.

And the chant reverberated beneath Coogan's Bluff: "Let's Go Mets . . . Let's Go Mets . . . Let's Go Mets."

Thirteen runs behind, with nobody on base and one strike away from the final out.

Harkness struck out on the next pitch.

And the next day, for the doubleheader with the Giants, there were 53,880 customers in the stands, still chanting "Let's Go Mets."

That's how it was. Everyone had a favorite memory, a favorite incident, a favorite fan reaction, and they all added up to the same thing: an orgiastic mixture of defiance and futility. Two observations were being made frequently, both completely true. One was that the Met fans had found a way to cut from their consciousness anything that happened in the "other" half of an inning, so that they could be oblivious to the errors, the enemy runs, and the Met pitching, and so that any time the Mets scored it was sufficient reason to cheer, a triumph in itself. The other was that they were having far more fun than the Yankee fans, even though the Yankees had just won their fourth straight pennant and 13th in the last 15 seasons.

"It stands to reason," someone wrote. "If the Yankees win 100 games and lose 62, the Yankee fan has endured 62 disappointments. If the Mets win 50 and lose 112, the Met fan has had 50 thrills."

There, in a nutshell, was the Met Mystique as it blossomed in the doomed Polo Grounds. And it was about to change drastically, just as people were beginning to publish books about it.

EAMUS METROPOLI

Among the banners carried by that apparently endless stream of Metophiles at Shea Stadium last Sunday was one that read: "Et tu, Wes?" In another part of the procession was the Latin version of "Let's Go Mets," the "Eamus Metropoli" sign first seen at the Polo Grounds two years ago and now classic. And, of course, the grand prize winner was only one of several versions of a paraphrase of the same line from Pope: "To error is human, to forgive is a Met fan."

It was perfectly obvious, therefore, that Met fans were steeped in literary allusions, and this fact was not lost upon the group watching the proceedings on their three-dimensional, full-color, wall-size television screen in Elysium.

"Next year," said Willie Shakespeare, a former actor who possessed one of the liveliest imaginations of his set, "we ought to enter the Banner Day contest."

"I have my banner all ready," declared a bearded Russian named Dostoevsky. "Their Crimes Are My Punishment."

That Side of Paradise

"How about," suggested Voltaire, thinking of all the uncaught fly balls that had caused them so much agony in Heaven, "Let Us Cultivate Our Outer Gardens."

"I prefer the one you mentioned the other day," said Shakespeare, "the one that goes: 'I disagree with the way you play, but I will defend to the death your right to play that way.' "

"It's not quite certain I said that," demurred Voltaire.

"I am a Ron Swoboda fan," announced Coleridge belligerently, "so don't knock the outfielding. My Swoboda sign will read: 'Twice As Good As The Ancient Mariner—He Stoppeth Two of Three.' "

"Stop repeating that tired gag, Sam," broke in Andrew Marvell. "And stop harping on the future. I'm impatient. I'd like to see us win a few now. Or, to put it another way:

"Had we but world enough and time
"These last-place endings were no
  crime
"But from the Mets I always hear
"Some promise that we'll win next
  year
"Tenth has become our private place
"But I'd prefer a pennant race."

"If you think you'll get all that into one sign," said Shakespeare, who could never resist a pun, "you really will be a Marvell, Andy."

E Equals MC Squared

A kindly-looking man with unruly hair removed his pipe from under an equally undisciplined mustache and spoke softly.

"If I may point out," said Albert Einstein, "it is all a matter of relativity. The Mets are at one extreme end of the league standings—and relativity teaches us that it is impossible to describe motion or position in absolute terms. It is all relative to the observer. I would suggest, then, that the young man with the banner reading 'Turn the League Upside-Down' was on the right track, from a mathematico-physical view of the cosmos. A simple shift in viewpoint can change everything."

The literary men listened with respect, but with obvious mental discomfort, to the man of science.

"My famous formula," Einstein continued modestly, "applies even to the Mets. E stands for errors, M stands for Mets, C stands for customers. Substituting in the equation, we get: errors equal Mets multiplied by the square of the number of customers—which should not be confused with square customers, which Met fans are not."

"Bravo!" roared an energetic Frenchman with a triangular beard. "Science, geometry, philosophy, metaphysics—they will help overcome those errors of omission that cost us ball games. I think, therefore I exist; they exist—why can't they think?"

Signs of the Times

"That a little unkind seems," said Goethe, one of the most respected members of the community. "To me, their most interesting figure Casey Stengel remains. Always by the Faust legend I fascinated have been, and the way Herr Stengel has his youth retained makes me wonder if—well, if he some similar arrangements with you-know-who had made.

"Nevertheless, my banner will to his interim successor dedicated be: 'The Sorrows of Westrum.' "

Shakespeare summed up: "We have the makings of some pretty good banners. I know it's hard to keep track of earth-time but let's try to remember next year's Banner Day. Perhaps this thought will help: When winter comes, Cannizzaro be far behind? As for myself, I'm not yet sure whether I want them to improve or not . . . to win or not to win . . . you know, this above all, to thine own self be true. . . ."

"What gets me," said King Midas, "is how they reversed my touch by buying all those players. All the gold they touch turns to Mets."

5 The New Home

W HEN Weiss and Stengel had been with the Yankees, one of their most successful innovations was a "rookie camp," a preliminary training period before regular spring training began, at which they could concentrate on young players who weren't ready to compete with the regulars, but whose development (if they were top prospects) could be accelerated. They had done this in 1951, their one year in Arizona, and had been able to promote Mantle and McDougald to the varsity ahead of schedule.

In 1964, they felt the Met organization had accumulated enough kids to warrant such an early camp in St. Petersburg. It would be held during February, and serve the double purpose of preparing everyone for a three-game exhibition trip to Mexico during the first week in March, before the Florida exhibitions began. They were formulating these plans while the dismal 1963 season dragged to a conclusion.

But by February 1964, they—along with everyone else—found themselves living in a different world.

President Kennedy had been killed in November. A few months before that, the mass civil rights demonstration in Washington had taken place. In Vietnam, the situation was getting stickier every day. Barry Goldwater had announced his candidacy for president, making clear that sharp lines would be drawn between the political right and the political left. On all sides, on all levels, Americans were viewing life with more seriousness and apprehension. The carefree optimism of the three preceding years was shattered, perhaps permanently.

One result was that many people could no longer look at the Mets in the same light. The glorification of kookiness and ineptness just didn't sit so well in the suddenly darkened world. As escape and respite from serious things, such entertainment as sports (and specifically the Mets) could be more sought after than ever; but the same degree of whole-hearted involvement was harder to come by. Nor could people react with the same tolerant amusement to the sign-carrying actor-fans of the Mets when the process of polarization in the society was becoming so visible. Signs could say other things than "We Want Marv," and the "generation gap" was hardening into real conflict, and increasingly politicized young people were starting to find other outlets for sheer rebelliousness than rooting for the Mets.

Consequently, a series of subtle shifts, many not recognized for a while, started to take place. The original Met fans who remained loyal were getting tired of the joke and impatient for a little victory—and they were a couple of years older too. Those who continued to enjoy their own antics now provoked some hostility from the unconcerned mass, not only amusement. Those who had accepted Stengel as a symbol of the invincibility of the spirit, now started to blame him for lack of result. His age, an asset when it meant defying the Yankees, was again being cited as a handicap. And the subway-riding city-dwellers, who had found the Polo Grounds as accessible as the car-driving suburbanites found it impossible, were not at all sure they would get to the new stadium so easily.

For a major change had taken place here too. The new structure, now formally named Shea Stadium, had actually been built. It was right next to the World's Fair, which would open that spring and which itself was the target of much criticism. A subway line did stop there, and there would be Long Island Railroad special trains while the Fair was open. But what really mattered was that Shea Stadium was located in the middle of a huge network of superhighways, fed by all the roads leading in from Long Island, and by bridges across Long Island Sound and the East River, as well as by the city streets that went through Northern Queens. A huge parking area, surrounding the circular park, was part of its basic design. The right way to go to Shea Stadium would be by car.

Stengel, who used to urge everyone to join his "Metsies," now talked first about the new park and its marvels—the escalators "so you won't get heart attacks going to your seats," the luxurious and numerous rest rooms, the wonderful Diamond Club that would put the Yankee Stadium restaurant to shame, and other sensational facilities. Back in December, when there was still doubt that the new park could be made ready in time, there had been scare stories about Shea Stadium's "sinking"; it was built on land fill, and the water level was just below the surface of the field. (It turned out to be safe enough, but the playing field was repeatedly subject to sogginess from underneath as time went on.) That the new building would be a success, however, was not being seriously questioned in the spring of 1964, as construction workers hurried to prepare it for opening day.

The Polo Grounds, finally, officially, and for positively the last time with no encores, had been retired. The last game played there, on September 18, 1963, had gone according to form: the Mets lost it to Philadelphia, 5–1, equaling the "farewell game" record set by the Giants in 1957. The first year there, the Mets had drawn 922,530—half of it for Giant and Dodger games. The next, they had increased the total to 1,080,108—with only 41.5 percent of it accounted for by the former New York teams.

In the new park, things would be different. Weiss knew that and planned accordingly. Organizing and carrying through a detailed program was his strong point, and he went to work well ahead cultivating the Long Island suburbs that would produce future customers. His off-season ticket-selling and promotional plans were functioning well. A couple of million people lived just east of Shea Stadium, predominantly middle-class. It had been the shift of the middle class from central city to suburbs that had worried O'Malley and Stoneham; it was exactly that group that O'Malley hoped to tap with his grandiose plan for a stadium at the Long Island Railroad terminal in Brooklyn. (Years later, when a new Madison Square Garden was built above Penn Station, at the Manhattan terminus of the L.I.R.R., this thinking was vividly vindicated by the huge numbers of Long Islanders drawn to basketball and hockey games there.) Weiss, in his Yankee days, had worked at drawing suburbanites from Connecticut, Westchester, and northern New Jersey to Yankee Stadium. Now the future of the Mets lay in the hands of the Long Island equivalent of those areas.

With a new park, and millions of visitors streaming to the Fair next door, the Mets had every reason to expect more customers than they had drawn to the Polo Grounds, even though those totals were already considered phenomenal by traditional thinkers who related attendance to victories.

In recognition of a new situation, Weiss had even improved his press relations. Meany was made director of promotion, a post he enjoyed more and excelled at, and a new publicity director was brought in: Herb Heft, who had worked for the old Washington Senators and new Minnesota Twins, and was well known in the newspaper community.

Further startling changes had taken place in the opposition. The Yankees, while winning, had seen their attendance drop while the Mets' rose, and in terms of newspaper space they were taking a beating. In word-of-mouth baseball interest, there was simply no contest; New York was a National League town again. Maris had failed to become folk hero, and his homer production had returned to routine; Mantle was injured more often than not; the end of the road could be foreseen for Whitey Ford; and simply winning, again and again, without the added ingredient of exciting baseball personalities, would make the Yankees more and more a part of the scenery, always there but seldom exciting. To make matters worse, the whole American League was starving for star attractions, while the National not only had more spectacular individuals, but also the Giants and Dodgers. In the two years of Met existence, each had won the pennant, so when they came to town they weren't merely arousing sentimental curiosity; they were the top attractions in baseball. Willie Mays was still going strong. Koufax and Drysdale were the dominant pitchers in the game. It was getting harder and harder for the Yankees to keep their share of the limelight.

Since they were still winning, however, neither Topping nor his staff could believe for a second that they missed Weiss or Stengel or that their organization was showing cracks. In an overconfident frame of mind, they made a decision that showed abysmal ignorance of the real factors in their situation.

In 1961, alone in town and having the benefit of the Maris–Mantle home run spree and a tight pennant race which they won, the Yankees had drawn 1,747,736. The next year, the first of the Mets, they had drawn 1,493,574. In 1963, winning easily again, they had drawn only 1,308,920. A drop of more than 400,000 in two seasons meant that something had to be done. The something they decided upon was a beaut.

Roy Hamey, who had come to the Yankees as an assistant to Weiss and had been promoted to general manager when Weiss was forcibly retired, had been ill, and wanted to retire himself. Topping was reluctant to lose him. But Hamey had an idea. Why couldn't Houk, with whom Hamey worked so closely and who was so admired by Topping, step up to the general managership? And why couldn't Yogi Berra, whose hold on the sympathies of Yankee fans was so secure, be made field manager? Yogi had a reputation for malapropisms; Stengel had sold the Mets with malaprops. People said Yogi was "lovable" (although Yankee ball players did not say that); people thought Stengel was lovable (although neither Yankee nor Met ball players thought that). Yogi would be a good weapon in the publicity war, Hamey could retire, Houk could move up (the dream of every field manager), and the team would roll along as well as ever on the field because the material was so great that even an inexperienced manager could win with it. And Houk would always be there behind the scenes.

This was the Yankee plan. Houk went for it, because moving into the front office meant much more money and security. He didn't really want Yogi as a manager, but that was the price of advancement. Topping went for it because it was what Houk and Hamey wanted. Yogi went for it because every player yearns to manage, even though Yogi hadn't expected an opportunity like this.

Overlooked completely, of course, was the fact that Yogi, even in the realm of publicity, was nothing like Stengel. Both were subjects of humor, but Yogi had always been the butt, not the originator, of jokes, as Stengel was.

But it was a measure of Met growth that they had helped influence the Yankees to take such a step. The Berra-versus-Stengel idea was never as much a factor in the change as interpreters later made it, but it was a real, if minor, factor.

So when Weiss and Stengel headed for St. Petersburg in February 1964, they were moving into a totally new context of Met operation.

They had some new coaches. Hemus was gone, reportedly for some falling out with Stengel, and so was Lavagetto, who had suffered a frightening illness during 1963. He had recovered, but decided he wanted to be closer to his California home, so the Mets had arranged a sort of trade: Lavagetto went to work as a coach with the Giants, and Wes Westrum came to the Mets. There was a new pitching coach, Mel Harder; a new third-base coach, Don Heffner (a 1930s Yankee infielder and subsequently a successful minor-league manager); and Sheriff Robinson, who had worked within the organization on a minor-league level.

And they had lots of new players, not expected to make the varsity this year, but interesting enough.

There was a big kid from Baltimore, built like a football player, named Ron Swoboda. There was a skinny little kid whose name, Derrel McKinley Harrelson, was taller, if stood on end, than he was. There were some pitchers whose strong arms excited Stengel—Dick Selma, Jerry Hinsley, Rob Gardner, Ron Locke. There was a freckled infielder with the delectable name of Wilbur Huckle. There was a 21-year-old kid from Mobile, painfully shy, who had compiled a fine minor-league record in 1963 and had reached the Mets for a few games in September (two hits in 15 tries, for .133). His name was Cleon Jones.

There were also some new men the Mets had acquired who were not kids.

During the 1963 season the Mets had obtained Carmel from the Cardinals. A little later they had traded McKenzie to the Cards for Ed Bauta, an aging but knowledgeable Cuban who offered hope of effective relief pitching. In November, the two clubs did more business, the Mets sending Craig to St. Louis for George Altman, an outfielder who had spent most of his career with the Cubs, and Bill Wakefield, a young pitcher too tied up in his studies at Stanford to make spring training.

Meanwhile, in a special draft set up to help the Mets and Houston, right after the World Series, the Mets were allowed to buy Jack Fisher, a still-young but experienced right-handed pitcher, from the Giants and a minor-league first baseman named Bill Haas from the Dodgers, for $30,000 each. They also purchased, from the Braves in December, Bob (Hawk) Taylor, who had been a $100,000-bonus rookie five years before and had not made it as a catcher, outfielder, or hitter. And also from the Braves they got a young utility infielder named Amado Samuel.

The rookie camp, therefore, was as much a tryout camp for older players as an "instructural" (Casey's word) session for the youngsters.

Stengel's three favorites were "Saboda" (Swoboda, who could hit 450-foot flies), Selma (who was cocky, combative, and in a mental world of his own), and "that kid who can throw" (Harrelson). He had grave doubts about Haas (a left-handed hitter who infallibly hit the ball within five feet of the first base line, fair or foul—unless he struck out). And his plan for Burright, who had hit .220 right-handed in 1963, was to turn him into a switch hitter and a new Maury Wills.

The camp was productive—of fun, of instruction, of exposure to some major-league ideas for the kids, and of publicity back north. There wasn't much reason to think the 1964 team would be better, but at least there were tangible signs that a Met farm system did exist. Within six years, Jones, Swoboda, Harrelson, and Kranepool would be winning a World Series in Met uniforms.

Stengel was in his best form. "Take those fellows over to that other diamond," he told Heffner during an infield drill one day, "I want to see if they can play on the road." The base was now called Stengel–Huggins Field (or Huggins–Stengel Field, no one was quite sure), and all the pre-camp activity took place there. The Mets were in their best form, too. In one practice game, they made a play that is still unique in the scorebooks writers keep. Each position is assigned a number in baseball scoring shorthand, so that a ground out, second to first, is written 4–3, third to first 5–3, a fly to center 8 and so forth. A 3–4–5 out at first base sounds like an impossibility, but the Mets of the future managed it, proving their right to be associated with the Mets of the present: on a little pop fly between first and the mound, Huckle, the third baseman, came racing over while Haas, the first baseman, camped under it. Haas put his glove up and deflected the ball instead of catching it; Huckle ran right past him and continued to first base, where he took the throw from Burright, the second baseman, who had retrieved the ball.

And the Mets were about to take this act out of the country.

The visit to Mexico City was scheduled for a weekend, March 6–8. Thursday was devoted to travel, from Tampa Airport to Miami, to Merida in Yucatan Province to Mexico City. (In Merida, Stengel found his picture on page one of the local paper, but the customs man was not impressed.) In Mexico City, a huge crowd of baseball fans greeted the Met plane and almost trampled Stengel to death as he tried to reach the team bus.

On Friday night, with 25,000 people in the stands, the Mets played their first game of their third season, making their first international appearance. It goes without saying that they lost; for that matter, most teams coming to Mexico City for such exhibitions lost their first game, because of the unusual altitude. But the Mets found their own unusual aspect to their 6–4 defeat. The man who hit a three-run homer off Fisher in the first inning, and added three singles later, was Harry (Suitcase) Simpson, once a major disappointment on one of Stengel's Yankee teams and long remembered as one of Weiss's less successful trades.

At an International Press Club cocktail party the next day, a European journalist asked Stengel sympathetically, "Did the altitude bother your players?"

"The altitude bothers my players at the Polo Grounds, and that's below sea level," Stengel rasped.

This sort of remark, the essence of Stengel's public relations success, was also the essence of player dislike for Stengel. That it was true only made it worse in the eyes of the players. That it would have been still worse if interviewers concentrated daily on making the players explain their mistakes, instead of being beguiled by Stengel (who knew what he was doing), was something few players ever understood.

Having lost to the Mexico City Red Devils, the Mets turned around and walloped the Mexico City Tigers on Saturday night, 7–1. They won again on Sunday, against a combined team of Reds–Tigers, and proved that there was at least one country on earth where they could compile a winning record. Unfortunately, it was the wrong country.

On Monday morning, they awoke at 5 A.M. to make the trip back to Tampa, a trip made more harrowing by a two-hour delay in leaving Mexico

City. Edna Stengel, who had traveled all over the world without undue complication, had left her exit visa locked in her luggage this one time, and the party could not leave until it was dug out.

Back in St. Pete, with the first regular exhibition game only a few days off, Stengel had to forget about the kids and concentrate on devising a team that could play this year. Both he and Weiss believed it was essential to be more "respectable" in the new ball park, and once again they sacrificed systematic development of young players for major-league retreads who might win a few more games. In retrospect, it is fair to say that their decision wasn't as wrong as it seemed to many baseball people at the time, because the young talent they had was still insufficient. Nevertheless, it was a conscious policy that the new customers in the new stadium would have to be given as much immediate satisfaction as possible.

Snider was eager to be traded and didn't hesitate to say so to anyone who would listen. He had his eye on the Detroit Tigers, who could have used him and who had a home-run hitter's park. They also had, as manager, Charley Dressen, Snider's manager in the heyday of Ebbets Field success, and Stengel's old friend. All Casey wanted in return was an untried (but plainly not unevaluated) rookie outfielder named Willie Horton. Dressen laughed.

So on the day the regular season opened, April 14, the Mets sold Snider to the Giants. They were no longer attached to "names," even though they wanted experienced players.

They had a depressing spring training season, with a 10–17 record, although for the third straight year they split their two games with the Yankees. The matchups between Stengel and Berra got the expected publicity, but they were not really stimulating. What everyone was waiting for was the new park.

Yogi's debut as Yankee manager, on April 14, was rained out. That night in Philadelphia, the Mets began their third season with their usual defeat, 5–3, even though Stengel used 17 players. The next day the Yankees were rained out again, and the Mets took their second loss, 4–1, as Stallard was tagged for a three-run homer by Tony Gonzalez in the eighth inning, right after an error by Harkness. When the Yankees finally got to play on Thursday, they opened before a crowd of 12,000 at Yankee Stadium and dropped an 11–inning decision to the Red Sox.

Twenty-four hours later, five miles away at Shea Stadium, 50,000 turned out in perfectly fine weather to see the Mets. The predicted monumental traffic jam materialized, since no one was familiar yet with entrances and exits, but even this didn't dampen the enthusiasm of the crowd.

The team Stengel had for them this time still had Harkness at first, Samuel and Burright alternating at second, Moran still at short, and Hunt shifted to third. The outfield was Thomas in left, Altman in right, and Hickman alternating with a left-handed rookie named Larry Elliott in center. Gonder and Hawk Taylor were the lefty-righty catching platoon, with a rookie named John Stephenson (who was also a college basketball coach) in reserve. Jackson, Stallard, Fisher, and Hook were supposed to be the first-line starting pitchers since Willey had suffered a broken jaw when hit by a line drive in an exhibition game.

Fisher was stepping into Craig's shoes, figuratively and in pitching style. He would be the one, for the next couple of years, to log a great many good innings, win the respect of opponents, yet pile up the large total of losses, often on tough breaks or untimely homers. He drew the assignment of starting the first Shea Stadium game, against Bob Friend of Pittsburgh. He lasted into the seventh, when Bauta relieved him while the Pirates were tying the score at 3–3. In the ninth, Mazeroski drove in a run and Pittsburgh won, 4–3.

No one could really complain. The Mets had lived up to their image. They had made it close, and lost. The important thing, the remarkable thing, was the crowd. It was not only more than four times as large as the crowd the Yankees had drawn the day before, but it was noticeably different in character from the Polo Grounds variety. Even allowing for the fact that an opening day brings out a higher proportion of "important" or "respectable" people than an ordinary game, these people seemed better dressed, and somehow less passionate even though they were just as noisy. It was, in fact, the first capacity crowd the Mets had drawn that didn't have the Giants or Dodgers to yell at (or for), so perhaps that in itself made a difference.

On Saturday, 31,000 more came out for the second game at Shea Stadium, and saw the Pirates administer a 9–5 licking.

That made the Met record 0–4, and arguments raged among the amateur students of trends. The Mets had lost the first nine in 1962, and the first eight in 1963; were they due to lose the first seven in 1964, or go back to nine?

The next day, the question was answered. With 30,000 on hand again, Jackson pitched a six-hit shutout, and the Mets knocked out Bob Veale in the fourth inning. The final score was 6–0, and the trend-studiers could prove conclusively that the 1964 Mets were twice as good as the 1963 Mets, at least in the amount of time it took them to win one game.

But it was the other statistic that opened the eyes of more serious analysts: 110,000 paid admissions in the first three days, with a traditionally "weak draw" like Pittsburgh.

The new era of the Mets, officially under way, promised to be a bigger gold mine than the old Met era. One could expect the games themselves to be less bizarre, because Shea Stadium was a symmetrical and roomy park (although the ball did "jump" and carry well over a fence if hit squarely). At the Polo Grounds, with those short foul lines and ridiculously wide spaces in the outfield, a lucky (or unlucky) homer was always a possibility, no matter who was at bat, and the amount of ground to be covered by poor outfielders was awesome. In this, as in the crowd, an element of respectability had been introduced.

But in a showdown, Mets were Mets, and Stengel was certainly Stengel, and the negative statistics were taking on a life of their own, and Kiner, Murphy, and Nelson were telling the people all about it, and the newspapers were full of Mets, and Mrs. Payson's box near the dugout was just as identifiable here as it had been in Harlem, and all over America people who were planning to visit the World's Fair were making a mental note to be sure to look in on the "Amazin' Mets" and their "New Breed" of sign-carrying fans, and that funny-talking old man.

They would not be disappointed. The ones who would be disappointed would be the true Met fans, who had expected some sort of improvement by this time and weren't getting it. And still more disappointed were Stengel, Weiss, and their official family, who had expected the same. The start of the new era would mean financial prosperity, it was clear; but it also became, almost in direct proportion, a period of emotional poverty.

For the Met cosmos as well as the world at large, 1964 was to be a year of darkening mood.

6 *Treadmill*

Ron Hunt was one of the Met players who was not completely happy with the way Stengel ran things. In 1963, Hunt had become the best day-in day-out player on the team. He had just missed winning the rookie-of-the-year award in a close contest with a Cincinnati second baseman named Pete Rose, and all Met followers still felt this was terribly unjust. If ever a player had a right to feel he had won a job, Hunt believed, he was it. Yet Stengel now wanted him to play third base, to give up that important feeling of security, to try a strange position. Hunt wasn't happy.

And, for the first time, a large proportion of the fans were siding with Hunt.

Stengel's reasoning was clear enough. Third base had been a terrible problem from the beginning, ever since Zimmer's quick, spectacular failure. Nine different men had tried it the first year, including Thomas and Cook who were outfielders. In 1963 a total of 11 men played there, including Hickman, another outfielder, for 59 games and Hunt for 1. Hunt had proved he was a fine ball player, indispensable as a hitter, courageous as a pivot man. But he didn't cover much ground at second, and if someone else could play second better than someone else could play third, why wouldn't Hunt be the man to solve the problem at third? Burright and Samuel could, it seemed, get by at second defensively, but not at third. Hunt could. To Stengel, it was open and shut.

That Hunt didn't see it that way cooled some of Stengel's ardor for the young player whose competitive toughness he admired so much.

The experiment lasted just four games, those first four that the Mets lost. In the fifth game, Hunt was back at second, with Kanehl at third. Before another week had gone by, the Mets had bought a third baseman, Charlie Smith, from the Chicago White Sox.

That didn't solve the problem either, but at least Charlie hit some home runs.

About two weeks after that, in Milwaukee, Hunt slid home with what would have been the tying run in the ninth inning of a 2–1 game, and tried to knock the ball loose from Ed Bailey, a large and very experienced catcher. There was a free-for-all, and Stengel got into it, having his arms pinned from behind by Dennis Menke of the Braves. There were no serious consequences, but Stengel, at 73, undoubtedly set a record for being the oldest man in a baseball uniform ever to get into a fight on the field. It showed he was willing to stick up for Hunt, too.

Through all this, the defeats were piling up at a rate alarming even for the Mets. They had scored their first victory earlier than ever, in the fifth game, but their second victory came in Game No. 10 and their third in Game No. 14. Two days after the big fight, their record was 3–13, exactly what it had been the first year. The third-base problem was living on alongside the catching, pitching, shortstop, and outfield problems, not to mention first base. Something (again!) had to be done.

On May 8, something was, and it stabilized the team considerably. Roy McMillan, still an outstanding shortstop in his declining baseball years, was obtained from the Braves for Jay Hook and a minor-league player, and for the first time the Mets had someone who could not only play shortstop but who could unify the infield and help the younger players. McMillan was approaching his 34th birthday and had both leg and arm trouble, but he was a great improvement nevertheless.

It was already being taken for granted that the Mets would finish last again, and the charm was going out of just plain losing. What made 1964 memorable, finally, was a series of extraordinary games, and the crowds.

The crowds, which totaled over 1,700,000 for the season, combined some of the features of past and present. Although they were distinctly more orderly, and undoubtedly more prosperous, than the Polo Grounds people, they were just as diligent about cheering and making signs, and equally oriented toward Giant and Dodger visits as their special thing. The added factor was tourists: the visitors to the Fair came to Shea Stadium to see these crazy Met fans they had read about, as much as to see Stengel, or the new park, or the Mets.

The games themselves were something special too.

A hint of what was to come occurred on May 16, on the road. In San Francisco, the Mets went into the last of the ninth leading Marichal, 4–3, only to have Mays hit a home run off Bearnarth to tie it. The game dragged on through 15 innings, until Jim Davenport hit a two-run homer off Cisco and won it, 6–4. The next day they got shut out in both ends of a double-header. When they reached Chicago on May 25, they had scored a total of 16 runs in their most recent 10 games, and were rivaling the 1963 lineup for impotence. The 1963 Mets had been shut out 30 times, which was almost every fifth game played. This year's rate, seven in 49 games, wasn't quite as bad, but with four shutouts in the last 10 games, there was still hope for the negative statistics aficionados.

New York quivered with disbelief, therefore, on the afternoon of Tuesday, May 26. Kiner, Nelson, and Murphy had obviously cracked under the strain and lost their minds. According to what the radio was saying, the Mets were beating the Cubs in Chicago, 19–1. But it turned out to be true: 19 runs; 23 hits; three singles, a double, and a triple by Dick Smith; a home run by Charley Smith; four hits for Hunt, three hits for Hickman; two doubles for Cannizzaro; and four-hit pitching by Jack Fisher, the most privileged pitcher in Met history. It was a "laugher." Leading 13–1 in the ninth, the Mets scored six more runs. ("That's when I knew we had 'em," reported Stallard later.) And since baseball dugout jokes are as predictable and restricted as the courses of the planets, there were plenty of "save some for tomorrow" comments.

The Mets should have. Tomorrow, they scored one whole run and lost, 7–1. The next day, they didn't score at all and lost 2–0. They had managed to lose two out of three by concentrating their fire.

After which they came back to Shea Stadium for a series with the Giants. Friday, Stallard won, 4–2. Saturday, May 30, was Fisher's turn again, and he won, 6–2. At the same time, the Mets made some personnel changes. They purchased Frank Lary, the famous right-handed pitcher, from Detroit, and they called up Kranepool from Buffalo, so that both could help out during the big Sunday doubleheader coming up.

Both arrived in time to get a full dose.

The crowd was 57,037. Marichal won the opener, 5–3. The Giants took a 6–1 lead in the second game, but the Mets fought back and a three-run homer by Joe Christopher tied the score at 6–6 in the sixth.

It was still 6–6 after nine. And after 12. And after 14, as McMillan speared a line drive and turned it into the second triple play ever made by the Mets. And after 16, 18, 20, 22 innings, it was still 6–6.

Gaylord Perry of the Giants, and Cisco, who had been the decision pitchers in the 15-inning game at San Francisco, had now been pitching the equivalent of a full game. Perry had started the 13th as the fifth Giant pitcher. Cisco came on in the 15th as the sixth Met pitcher.

When the 23rd inning began, it was past 11 o'clock and only a few thousand spectators were still in Shea Stadium, but the television rating was something fantastic. People had come home from the beach, from the movies, from European vacations perhaps, and found the game still being played on Channel 9. In the park, some concession stands had run out of hot dogs, but home ice boxes were being depleted too by between-inning raids. At one stage, Willie Mays had actually played shortstop, before shifting back to the outfield. Giant manager Alvin Dark had been tossed out of the game. It was unbelievable, incredible, amazing, etc., etc. (The Yankees, having lost a game in Kansas City, were flying a charter to Minneapolis and picking up the broadcast on the pilot's radio.)

Davenport led off the 23rd with a triple into the right field corner. After an intentional pass, Del Crandall batted for Perry and broke the tie with a ground-rule double to right. An infield hit by Jay Alou brought in another run. Bob Hendley, pitching for the Giants in the bottom of the 23rd, fanned Cannizzaro and Stephenson and made Samuel fly out.

It was over, actually over! The time was 11:25. The doubleheader had lasted 10 hours, 17 minutes. Thirty-two innings had been played, a major league record for one day. Twenty-two dozen baseballs—that's 244 balls— had been used, most of them winding up as souvenirs in some fans' pockets.

As for Kranepool, he had played a doubleheader with Buffalo on Saturday, had traveled during the night to reach New York, and had played through all 32 innings Sunday. But neither he nor the other Mets could plan on a day off to catch up on their rest. On Monday night they were scheduled for an exhibition game with their farm club at Williamsport, Pennsylvania.

Mercifully, it rained at Williamsport, and the Mets were allowed to scatter after meeting at the airport.

The following weekend, the Dodgers came in, and Cisco greeted them with a four-hit shutout, 8–0, before a crowd of 55,000. Saturday's 9–2 Met defeat was attended by 34,000. Sunday's doubleheader (a 6–1 Dodger victory and a five-inning 1-1 rain-ended tie, in which Hickman's fifth-inning homer averted a five-inning 1–0 rain-ended defeat), drew 55,000 again.

Two successive weekends, with the Giants and Dodgers for company, had produced 294,000 paid admissions.

People were catching on to the new pattern. The routine games, in the third year of the Mets, were becoming more routine—but every once in a while something really noteworthy was likely to pop up, and you never knew when: 19 runs, 15 innings, 23 innings, triple plays, last-gasp homers. This more experienced club might not produce the unusual quite as often, but it seemed to have acquired the knack of producing the extremely unusual periodically.

Like on Father's Day.

A perfect game.

There hadn't been one in the National League since 1880.

And—need it be specified?—the Mets were the party of the second part.

Jim Bunning, a tall, business-minded pitcher who was then the father of seven children, started the first game of the June 21 doubleheader for Philadelphia. Bunning had spent most of his career in the American League, with Detroit, and had once pitched a no-hit game against Boston in 1958. A no-hit game, of course, is not that unusual: there are three or four pitched in the majors every season. A perfect game is something else: 27 men up, 27 men out, no walks or errors to interfere with the absolute minimum a baseball attack can be held to. In all baseball history, only seven men had pitched such a game, the most recent (Don Larsen of the Yankees in 1956) in a World Series.

There were 32,000 people at Shea Stadium. Two of them were Mrs. Bunning and 12-year-old Barbara, the oldest of Bunning's three daughters. The Met pitcher was Stallard, the pleasant Virginian, who was history-prone the way others were accident-prone (or maybe the same way). When history was being made, Stallard contributed as victim, not maker.

Bunning had a run to work with before he went to the mound. By the time he'd gone through the batting order once, he was telling his teammates that something special was in the works. The second time through, with one out in fifth, Gonder almost lined a hit to right, but Tony Taylor lunged, knocked it down, and threw him out. In the ninth, with the score 6–0, Charley Smith hit a foul to short left, where Cookie Rojas caught it. Altman batted for Samuel and struck out. That left it up to Stephenson, the rookie catcher who was also being tried out at third and in the outfield, to contest Bunning's low-breaking curves and high slider.

Bunning struck him out, for his 10th strikeout of the game.

In the second game, the Mets amassed three singles while losing 8–2. Their batting average for the day was .050, a negative statistic to be cherished even by those who were becoming jaded.

A couple of weeks later Shea Stadium customers saw another worthwhile show, although it didn't involve the Mets as such. The All-Star Game was played in the new park, and it turned out to be one of the best. The American

League was winning, 4–3, going into the last of the ninth, only to have Mays walk, steal second, race to third on a looping hit by Orlando Cepeda, and continue home when Joe Pepitone (a Yankee!) made a wild throw. With two out, Johnny Callison hit a three-run homer, and the home team won, 7–4.

That was July 7. Hunt had played in the game as the first authentically selected Met, and that added to the fitness of the occasion. But the Met record was 23–58, and by July 31—the day after Stengel's 74th birthday—it was 32–72. Exactly a year before it had been 33–73. If this was progress, it was indiscernible.

In this climate, the anti-Stengel cabal was getting a hearing. At the highest levels of the Met hierarchy—Mrs. Payson, Grant, Walker—there was talk of choosing a successor. None of them felt anything but gratitude for what Stengel had done, but he just couldn't go on forever. The familiar reasons were trotted out: being old, Stengel couldn't "communicate" with the younger players; where they needed encouragement and gentle handling, he gave them endless, incomprehensible lectures and was too tough in his language and in his platooning policies. The experienced players, whom Stengel could presumably manipulate, had brought the Mets absolutely nowhere. At last, full commitment to a youth program had to be faced. Was a 74-year-old man really the best one to handle it?

Stengel's promotional function had been carried out, brilliantly. The Mets had identity, they were established, their crowds were surpassing the wildest optimism expressed by Shea when he was plugging the Continental League. Besides, a man Stengel's age could fall ill, or even die, with little warning. Could the Mets afford, having achieved prominence, anything less than a worthy successor? Could they afford to wait for whoever might be available when Stengel did suddenly stop, or did they have to act fairly soon to tie up an appropriate personage?

Two names were being mentioned. One was, as always, Leo Durocher, still a Dodger coach, mentioned any time any managerial job was open. But there was no real possibility of Durocher coming to work for Weiss, who did not look upon Leo's type as the right working partner. Nor was the ownership group, having been close to the Giants at the time of Leo's falling out with Stoneham in 1954, unaware of the difficulties presented by Leo's personality.

The other name was Alvin Dark.

Dark was a special hero to the old Giant fans (which meant to Mrs. Payson, Grant, and particularly Walker) because of the leadership role he had played as shortstop on the Giant teams of 1951 and 1954. Taking over the San Francisco Giants after a period of turmoil, he had brought them through another playoff victory over the Dodgers to a pennant in 1962. That had been accomplished with an aging pitching staff, and when it collapsed and the Giants ran third in 1963, no one blamed Dark. Throughout the baseball community, Dark's "baseball brains" were universally admired, although some found his vocally moralistic attitudes hard to take on "holier than thou" grounds.

What happened next was complicated, far-flung, and hectic, much of it obscure at the time and full of hidden relationships and consequences understandable only later, by hindsight.

On August 1, while the Mets were deep in 10th place, the Yankees were leading the league again, by the slightest of margins over Baltimore and Chicago, despite a poor start. Nevertheless, Houk and Topping, in the privacy of their minds, had just about decided that Yogi would have to go. He, too, it seemed, "couldn't communicate," and the players who had adored Houk's handling of them were complaining to the general manager that the new manager, Yogi, just wasn't the same.

On August 3, the day before the Giants were to visit Shea Stadium, a smoldering story about Dark erupted on a national scale. Stan Isaacs, the *Newsday* columnist, and an old friend from Dark's playing days in New York, had dropped in on Alvin in San Francisco a couple of weeks before. They had a long talk, apparently informal, about "what's wrong with the Giants." Some time later, Isaacs decided to write two columns on the basis of that conversation. The gist of the columns, which quoted Dark directly and indirectly, was that the Black and Latin players, of whom the Giants had so many, weren't as bright or as dedicated to victory as might be.

The column itself didn't get abnormal attention at first. But July was also the month in which the Civil Rights Act had been signed into law; in which a Negro reserve Army officer who was also assistant superintendent of the Washington (D.C.) public schools was murdered in Georgia; in which a five-day racial riot had erupted in Harlem, and a three-day riot in Rochester; in which a month-long search for three missing civil rights workers in Mississippi was in the headlines daily; in which, in short, the shift from nonviolence to militancy was gaining momentum.

At such a moment, in such a context, the description of Dark's alleged attitudes was the most serious sort of indictment. Some of Isaacs' colleagues circulated reproductions of the column, and it became an issue for many days on a phone-in radio sports show conducted by Bill Mazer for WNBC—all without direct comment from Dark.

But now that Dark was coming to New York in person, a full exploration of the subject could not be avoided.

Everyone knew that Dark was Louisiana-bred (although Oklahoma-born), that he spoke with a Southern drawl, that he was a militant Christian (of

the Fellowship of Christian Athletes school). He certainly shared the funda-
mental racial prejudices of most of his generation, all of his home region,
and 98 percent of the whites in baseball—no more, no less. In behavior,
however, he had always been exemplary. Objective judgment of ball players'
abilities was his stock in trade, and he never let bias, conscious or otherwise,
interfere; in personal relationships, he had always been scrupulously fair, if
for no other reason than that he recognized the necessity for it as an element
in winning. At Louisiana State, he had been a football star, not a philosophy
major; pressed to put into words his views on racial differences, he certainly
expressed ideas unacceptable to liberal ears. But if progress meant acting
fairly in spite of childhood-imbued prejudices, and working conscientiously
to overcome their effects, Dark certainly represented progress.

On August 4, before that night's game, Dark held a press conference in
his office in the visitors' clubhouse at Shea Stadium. He denied holding, or
acting upon, racial-superiority views and generally defended himself well.
Many old friends and enemies, and most importantly Jackie Robinson, issued
statements clearing Dark of this charge.

But its mere existence was enough to knock Dark out of two jobs—
and to keep him, for a while, in his present one.

What no one knew at the time was that Stoneham had already decided
to drop Dark as manager of the Giants—over an entirely private matter
that had been building for some months, in no way related to Dark's so-
ciology, politics, or relations with ball players. When the racial issue came
up, Stoneham simply could not dismiss Dark without making the impression
indelible that this was the reason, and Stoneham, a decent man, would not
do that. So Dark remained.

But from the Met point of view, the mere accusation, and the impossibility of ever puting it to rest conclusively among those who would be
naturally suspicious (after all, Dark was a Southerner, and whatever he was
he certainly wasn't a liberal), was enough to knock him out of the box. When
the Mets would choose a successor to Stengel, they would still have a terrible team whose financial health would depend more on public relations
than on managerial brilliance. You simply didn't borrow trouble by raising
an issue that was now attached to Dark. As good a friend of Dark's as
Walker was, he had to agree that New York was no place to be selling
Alvin Dark.

And from the Yankee point of view, the same argument applied.

Yes, the Yankees were interested. Houk had always admired Dark, and
when he learned that there was some sort of coolness between Dark and
Stoneham, he had sounded Dark out.

Meanwhile, on August 5, Dark's second day in town, a rumor that he would replace Stengel made the national press association wires and drew denials from all directions.

On August 7, the Mets traded Thomas to Philadelphia for a hulking pitcher named Gerry Kroll and an infielder named Wayne Graham.

On August 8, they traded Lary to the Braves for a young pitcher named Dennis Ribant.

On August 13, in a truly astounding announcement, the Columbia Broadcasting System bought the New York Yankees from Topping and Webb.

On August 17, Bing Devine, general manager of the St. Louis Cardinals, resigned because he felt he had lost the confidence of the owner, Gussie Busch of the Anheuser–Busch beer empire.

The four events were strangely related. The first two represented a shift in policy by Weiss and Stengel, from using veterans to trying more young players. (They had acquired another one, infielder Bobby Klaus, in mid-July.) It may have been just that Weiss and Stengel changed their minds, or that Weiss changed his and Stengel lost some power, or—most likely— that they were both moved by some genteel needling from the Board of Directors. But it was a sign that things would not go on as before.

The acquisition of the Yankees by C.B.S. created a wholly new—and un-predictable—situation. Theoretically, C.B.S. resources could bury any opposition if fully employed. Practically, no one could tell who would wind up running the Yankees, along what lines, or how, or even when. Topping was supposed to remain in charge for at least five years, but those who knew a little about the Byzantine workings of television and corporate executives doubted it would be that simple. In any case, the Mets would eventually have to think differently about their neighbor-rivals.

The St. Louis story had still more wheels within wheels. Devine was a life-long Cardinal organization man, predating Busch's acquisition of the club in 1952. He had worked his way up the ladder to the general manager-ship, had promoted Johnny Keane to manager, and had put together a team that unexpectedly challenged the Dodgers for the 1963 pennant. But Busch had hired Rickey, now 82 years old, as a special consultant, and Rickey (about as opposite a personality from Weiss as one could find) wanted Durocher as manager. Devine went to bat for Keane, felt he didn't get the proper reception, and decided he had to step out. For a quiet, rather shy, salary-dependent career baseball man like Devine, this was quite a step. He was looked upon with sympathy and even greater respect by working base-ball men, who had always entertained a high opinion of him.

On the morning of August 18, therefore, the baseball fan found that Devine had stepped out with the Cardinals in fifth place, only a little above

.500, and a major disappointment. He found the Yankees in third place, slumping and struggling through costly losses to the Orioles and White Sox, the other contenders. He found the Mets buried in the cellar, 12½ games below ninth-place Houston, having been officially eliminated from the pennant race again three days earlier.

Evidently, being free of pennant pressure was what the Mets needed. They promptly won 9 of 11, and by September 11 had 49 victories, 93 defeats. The young players were getting more work, and at least it was a sure thing that the Mets would break their own record for victories for the second year in a row.

It was also a sure thing that the Phillies would win the pennant, since they had a six-game lead with 22 to play. The Cardinals had been doing better and were now third behind Cincinnati, but no one outside St. Louis was paying much attention to that.

The action, in fact, was in the American League for a change. Yogi's Yankees, after falling six games behind on August 22, had started winning and were putting on one of the great finishes in the illustrious history of Yankee clubs. They won 26 out of 33 and took a three-game lead into the final week of the season.

Although this served to eclipse the Mets a little bit, it didn't really turn people on about the Yankees. "They always win, don't they? This time, they just got started a little late." Trying to clinch the pennant at home after that marvelous stretch run, the Yankees drew only 15,000 for a night doubleheader with Detroit, 7,000 for a day doubleheader, 7,000 Friday night with Cleveland, and 14,000 Saturday afternoon, when they actually clinched. But the Mets, winding up their home season on the preceding Sunday against Cincinnati, had sold 26,589 tickets to people who watched them lose their 104th and 105th games.

The ones who were really commanding attention, though, were the Phillies. On September 21, they had a 6½-game lead with 12 games to play. They proceeded to lose 10 straight, the last three in St. Louis, and all of a sudden the Cardinals were in first place.

It was September 29. The Cards, those disappointments, were tied for first place with Cincinnati; the Phillies, those cinches, were third, with four games to play.

Could the Mets steal headlines on such a day? They could.

Casey Stengel would be back to manage the Mets in 1965, it was announced.

Bing Devine would join the Mets, as assistant to Weiss and heir apparent for general manager (which was still called "president"). With him would come Eddie Stanky, to supervise player development in the minors, a job he had done well for the Cardinals.

Murphy and Thomson, in routine promotions, were made vice-presidents.

So much for reorganization. There still remained the statistical matter (negative or positive, depending on how you loked at it) of setting the club record in victories. The Mets had needed four tries to win No. 50, and five tries to win No. 51, which tied the record. They then lost eight in a row, and on October 2, arrived in St. Louis with three games to play, still needing that victory.

The Cardinals needed victory even more. They led Cincinnati by half a game, Philadelphia by 2½, and Dark's Giants, who had been quietly sneaking back into contention, by 3.

Abruptly, Stengel and his Mets found themselves in the middle of a pennant race, just as surprised to be there, even as potential spoilers, as Keane and the Cardinals were.

The Cards had their ace ready: Bob Gibson. The Mets had their oldest reliable pitcher ready too: Al Jackson. Guess who won the 1–0 game? The Mets. Jackson pitched a five-hitter, and Kranepool knocked in the run with a single in the third. However, the Phillies beat Cincinnati, even though the Giants won. So the Cards still led by a half, with Philadelphia 1½ behind and the Giants 2. The Phillies and Reds were not scheduled Saturday and had only one game to play against each other Sunday. All the Cards had to do Saturday was beat the Mets to eliminate the Phils and Giants and guarantee no worse than a tie with Cincinnati.

The score was 15–5. In whose favor? Why, the Mets, of course. They got 17 hits, including five home runs, and polished off Ray Sadecki, the Cardinals' 20-game winner, in one inning.

It was their proudest moment.

The Giants lost on Saturday, so they were out of it, averting an embarrassing situation for Dark and Stoneham. The next day, Dark's dismissal was announced.

Back in Busch Stadium (the "little, old" Busch Stadium that used to be known as Sportsman's Park, not the huge, luxurious circle of concrete that now bears that name in downtown St. Louis), the Cardinals still needed one victory over the Mets. Cisco started against Curt Simmons. The Cards scored in the second, but the Mets tied it in the fourth. The Cards made it 2–1, but the Mets knocked out Simmons in the fifth and took a 3–2 lead— forcing Gibson into the game as a relief pitcher.

The Cards thereupon scored three runs off Cisco, Wakefield, and Fisher in the fifth inning, for a 5–3 lead, but the scoreboard showed that Philadelphia was beating Cincinnati decisively, so the pressure lessened a bit. The Cards finally won, 11–5, but not without using Barney Schultz to get the last two outs for Gibson's 19th victory. The Reds lost, 10–0, and the Cardinals were champions.

But that was only the beginning, as far as New Yorkers were concerned.

The World Series went seven games, and the Cardinals beat the Yankees as Gibson established his superstar status. The day after it ended, Keane astounded everyone by resigning instead of accepting an offered raise. He had decided, before the Series began, that Rickey and Busch didn't have the confidence in him Devine had had.

The same day, the Yankees fired Berra, offering him a $25,000 job as a roving scout.

Three days later, Busch dropped Rickey.

The day after that, the Yankees signed Keane as Berra's successor. "Knew him in the Minors and always liked him," explained Houk.

During the same week China exploded its first hydrogen bomb, and Khrushchev was deposed from power in Moscow, and Jean-Paul Sartre turned down the Nobel Prize.

Anyone who felt bewildered had a perfect right.

But the Mets still had a couple of surprises up their sleeve.

On November 17, they had a press conference and unveiled Berra, who had spurned the Yankee consolation prize and had accepted an offer to join the Mets as a coach. Rumormongers decided immediately he was being groomed as Casey's successor.

On November 23, the Mets got the media people together again and unveiled Warren Spahn. Having won more games than any other left-handed pitcher in history (356, all for the Braves in Boston and Milwaukee), Spahn, at 43, was going to join the Mets as a pitcher and pitching coach. Rumormongers decided immediately that Spahn was grooming himself as Casey's successor.

Thus ended a two-month period of spectacular developments rarely matched, for diversity and interaction, in baseball history. They could not mask, however, the condition true Met fans were beginning to recognize: stagnation. Hiring Berra and Spahn made good stories, but it could hardly alter the future field performance of the Mets, who had now lost 340 games in three years.

But the hiring of Devine and Stanky could.

In fact, it did.

But not right away.

7 Casey Exits

THE Mets who puttered through spring training in 1965, winning 11 games, losing 15, and struggling with bad weather, hardly looked like a team on the move. One of the regular starters was Spahn, who would be 44 years old in April. The next two were Jackson (the fixture) and Fisher. The fourth, it was hoped, would be Willey, trying to come back from his severe injury of the spring before. Then it might be a very tall young man named Tom Parsons or that bulkier fellow, Gary Kroll. Hickman was now being tried at first base, alternating with Kranepool. The catchers, all too familiar, were Cannizzaro, Taylor, and Gonder, and familiarity bred despondency. The shortstop was McMillan, the third baseman Charlie Smith, the second baseman Hunt, who was turning out to be injury-prone. Christopher was now a regular in left field.

There were two new faces in the outfield. Altman, having won many friends but precious few ball games, had been traded back to the Cubs for Billy Cowan, now installed as "the" answer to the center field question. And, on Devine's recommendation, the Mets had acquired Johnny Lewis, an "all the tools" left-hander hitter with a strong arm, from the Cardinals in a trade for Stallard. The Cards had been grooming Lewis as a possible successor to Stan Musial, and he had hit .280 in the minors in 1963, Musial's last year. But when Musial did retire in 1964, and the Cards won the pennant without him, Lewis spent two-thirds of the season in the minors and was probably one of the "disappointments" charged against Devine in St. Louis. But Bing had faith that the 25-year-old outfielder could still be brought around. As for Cowan, who had hit 19 home runs and struck out 128 times for the Cubs, he was a trifle more self-assured than might be fully justified.

And Yogi was catching every day, getting into shape just in case.

Even Frank Lary was back, repurchased from the Braves.

This group then could hardly be called young, or new, or capable. Some of the newest were the oldest, some of the most familiar were established mediocrities. The sociologists who were now posing the question, what would happen to Met "charm" if they rose from abject incompetence to run-of-the-mill ineffectiveness—the celebrated "will mediocrity ruin the Mets?" thesis— were not even being put to the test.

But things were happening beneath the surface.

Stanky had taken over as Director of Player Development, and he was good at it. The Mets had also found a gem buried within their own organization, a young fellow named Joe McDonald, who had acted as statistician for the broadcasters the first season and then moved into office work. He had grown into an indispensable, reliable, and efficient "living memory bank" as an administrative assistant in the minor league department, the kind of right-hand man without whom all sorts of brilliant leaders can go nowhere. And since Weiss took a dim view of grooming anyone at all to succeed him— and since Devine, fully qualified anyhow, needed no grooming—there was not much for Devine to do directly as "assistant to the president" but answer when asked. So Bing quite properly, and wholeheartedly, devoted his effort to building at the minor league level.

As the 1964 "instructural" camp had shown, there was something with which to build. Swoboda had done well at Williamsport, Jones at Buffalo, Harrelson at Salinas, Selma so-so at Buffalo. In training camp, Swoboda did so well that Stengel decided to keep him on the varsity for 1965, at least for the first month (when you were allowed to carry 28 men instead of 25), but the rest were "futures." There were also two more good-looking kid pitchers, Frank (Tug) McGraw, who was the kid brother of the Hank McGraw signed by the prenatal Mets, and Jim Bethke, only 18 years old. There was a bonus-baby infielder named Kevin Collins who impressed people. And buried in McDonald's file was the name "Jerry Koosman," representing someone who had not yet thrown a ball professionally. He was in the Army at Fort Bliss, Texas, and his catcher on the team he pitched for was the son of a Shea Stadium usher, John Luchese. "Send someone to look at him," the father begged the Mets at his son's urging. The Mets sent Red Murff, who signed the Minnesota-farmer-playing-soldier for future delivery, with no fanfare or great expectation.

More important, a new baseball regulation had come into being in December 1964, one opposed deeply by Weiss (and others brought up in the "have" tradition of Yankees, Dodgers, Braves) but supported strongly by Devine (while with the Cardinals): the free-agent draft, modeled on the pro football and pro basketball system of giving negotiation rights to players coming out of college in reverse order of the previous year's standings. This would do away with the fantastic bidding for untried high school and college hotshots, which had reached the $250,000 level in the case of Rick Reichardt (signed out of Wisconsin by the California Angels, who outbid the Yankees). It would shift the emphasis in scouting from the star scout who could persuade the top prospects to choose his client, to painstaking staff work in evaluating hundreds of players. A secondary purpose was to give the weakest teams—like the Mets—first crack at the best new talent.

And it would give the Mets, in an unpredictable and indirect way, their greatest jewel: Tom Seaver.

None of this, however, impinged on the awareness of the Met fans in the spring of 1965. To the outside world, always the victim of cultural lag, the Mets seemed as cute as ever, in the sense that they remained born losers. Interviewers swarmed over Spahn and Berra as well as Stengel, and appropriate hoopla surrounded the first clash (in Fort Lauderdale) between the Mets and Keane's Yankees. Spahn pitched six innings, knocked in the lead run with a scoring fly, then hit a home run and won, 3–2, with Bearnarth's help—and it was a day of celebration in New York for the habitually downtrodden, for Met loyalists, and for the geriatric set everywhere. When the Yankees came over to St. Pete a few days later and walloped the Mets 8–0, no one paid attention. Firmly entrenched as a stereotoype of themselves, the Mets were accepted by the general press and by the casual public as a fixture on the American scene.

But the true Metophiles—including their closest newspapermen like Young, Lang, and Kremenko—knew better. They knew what the real fans knew: the joke had gone far enough. A fourth year of indulgence with the treadmill just wasn't right. Their stories began to reflect less humor and more criticism (although no less love). It was time to start winning. The writers, however, differed from most fans (the inside, day-to-day-dying fans, not the mass of amused followers) in one important respect. The fans publicly, like the players privately, were blaming Stengel. The writers blamed the organization as a whole, the players, and occasionally Stengel in a mild way, but remained deeply loyal to the manager. They appreciated what he did do and recognized what no one at all could do (turn such a roster into a winning team), bound by their years of proximity to Casey's lack of pretense. "We're a fraud," and "the attendance got trimmed again" (meaning by "attendance" the word "customers") were epic truths seldom uttered to newspapermen by more popular, colorless leaders.

On the airwaves, one strident voice staunchly opposed the press and sided with the anti-Stengel faction. It belonged to Howard Cosell, of the American Broadcasting Company, a broadcaster of unique ability and tremendous I.Q. (Irritation Quotient). Cosell's vendetta with Stengel went back to Yankee days, and during the two years in the Polo Grounds when WABC Radio carried the Met games, Howard did a pregame show with "Ralph Big No. 13 Branca" that gave full vent to anti-Stengel viewpoints in a Stengel-worshipping era. As a nightly commentator with less direct contact with the Mets, Cosell maintained his stance, and by 1965 was amplifying a growing feeling.

With all this, Opening Day 1965 at Shea Stadium (Monday, April 12) was in no sense an upbeat occasion. Even with the Dodgers as visitors, the crowd was below par at 37,999 (which would have been great anywhere else, of course). The appointed defeat arrived on schedule, inflicted by Don Drysdale, 6–1. That Hunt was unavailable, and would be for a couple more weeks because he had damaged his hand somehow during the winter (playing handball?), didn't help morale or offense.

The second game was worse. It was against Houston on April 14, and Christopher tied it, 3–3, with a one-out homer in the ninth, saving Spahn from a defeat. But in the 11th, the Astros (who had just changed their name and had moved into their Astrodome) scored four runs off Larry Bearnarth in the following fashion: one out, error McMillan, two out; wild pitch, wild pitch, walk, walk; walk, forcing in the tie-breaking run; with Cisco now pitching, a bunt toward third for a hit, an error on it by Smith letting another run score; a steal of home.

And naturally, trailing 7–3, the Mets scored three in the bottom of the 11th before losing, 7–6. The first of those runs was a pinch homer by Swoboda on his second major league time at bat.

The next day the Mets struck early: in the second inning, they made their third triple play in four years. (Of course, since there must be at least two men on base with none out before a triple play can occur, the Mets were getting more chances at one than most teams did.) Walt Bond was on third and Aspromonte on first after a pair of singles when Wynn lined out to Lewis in right. One out. Bond tried to score. Throw to Cannizzaro, two out. Aspromonte tried for second. Throw to McMillan, three out.

Buoyed by that, Fisher took a 4–2 lead into the ninth and retired the first two men. But he walked Aspromonte on four pitches and Wynn hit a homer, and suddenly it was extra innings again. Happily, though, Willey and Bethke managed to stop Houston in the 10th and Bobby Klaus (Hunt's substitute) led off the 10th with a home run.

So the Mets won, 5–4, and in only their third game! How could anyone deny now that progress was being made? Nine straight, eight straight, four straight—and now only two straight losses before that first victory. One more, in fact, would mean the still untasted thrill of a .500 record.

Alas, the next visitor was Juan Marichal: Giants 4, Mets 0. In the opener of the Easter Sunday doubleheader the day after it was Giants 4, Mets 1, with 44,000 on hand. But the Mets did win a rain-shortened second game, 7–1, triggered by Swoboda's second homer, on his first time up in his first game as a starter.

With a 2–4 record, the Mets headed west quite unprepared for the emotional roller coaster of the next two weeks.

On April 20 at Dodger Stadium, the trip began with Spahn facing Claude Osteen in the Dodger home opener. Spahn was determined to prove he could pitch nine innings and win—and this was three days before his 44th birthday, his last start as a 43-year-old. His career with the Braves had ended in bitterness because the manager, Bobby Bragan, had wanted him to become a relief pitcher, and one reason Spahn had joined the Mets was that it was his opportunity to indulge his obsession to be a starter. In his first start, he had certainly pitched well enough to win, but the Mets had lost in extra innings. Now he was getting another chance.

The first three Mets filled the bases on two safe bunts and an error, but on Hickman's fly to right Jones was doubled up trying to score, and Smith struck out. Cowan led off the second with a pop-fly double to right—and the next 28 Met batters failed to hit the ball past the infield. That's how tough Osteen, 19 years younger than Spahn, was that night. But Spahn stayed even, scattering a few singles, and was finally given a 1–0 lead in the eighth on a walk, a sacrifice, an infield hit by Jones and a perfect squeeze bunt by McMillan.

Could Spahn hang on? He was weakening. With one out in the eighth, he blocked a line drive with his leg but threw the man out. The next batter (Al Ferrara hitting for Osteen) tripled, but a fly provided the third out, and suddenly the Mets made it 3–0 in the ninth. Their old friend, Bob (Righty) Miller, helped them fill the bases by making a wild throw on a grounder, and Lewis singled home two runs off Ron Perranoski. That should have wrapped it up.

Oh, no; not that easily. Not with the Mets. Wes Parker singled. Kranepool booted a routine grounder. Tommy Davis singled sharply, making it 3–1. John Roseboro singled sharply, making it 3–2.

Stengel was on his way out of the dugout before the ball Roseboro hit was back to the infield. Nobody out, tying run on third, winning run on first, a hot rookie named Jim Lefebvre coming up.

At the mound, Stengel was confronting not only his pitcher but his pitching coach, who was supposed to help decide about relievers.

"You got Ribant out there, you got McGraw," Casey rumbled. "Which one you want?"

Spahn didn't particularly want either, and Stengel, judging by his expression and next words, didn't either.

"How do you feel yourself?" Stengel asked.

Spahn needed no further opening.

"Let me pitch to this kid," he replied.

Stengel went back.

Spahn struck Lefebvre out.

Stengel stayed put.

Spahn made Ron Fairly tap weakly toward the mound and fielded the ball. Davis, caught between third and home, was run down and put out.

Then Spahn struck John Kennedy out and jumped three feet high with joy while Stengel led the congratulatory charge out of the dugout.

Spahnie (in an instant, he was now "Spahnie" to the Met fans as he had been for years to the Braves) had proved his point, and the baseball world talked of little else for the next two days. Among other things, the strikeout of Lefebvre had been the 2,500th of Spahn's career—a positive statistic that stood out nakedly among Met statistics. But the theme of vindication-despite-age was the captivating factor, an echo of Stengel's original entrance on the Met scene, and back in New York the Yankee home opener (and Keane's debut) was completely overshadowed by the middle-of-the-night melodrama on the other side of the continent.

The next two days, however, meant Drysdale and Koufax, so the Mets lost two more and arrived in San Francisco on April 23 (Spahn's birthday) with a 3–6 record. One more defeat, that night, would put them neatly in their ancestral niche, 10th place, which they had not yet occupied alone, and the universe certainly seemed orderly enough as the Mets were succumbing to Gaylord Perry, 8–2, in the eighth inning at Candlestick Park.

But.

With two out, Smith singled in two runs and it was 8–4. Swoboda led off the ninth with a pinch home run, and Gonder (who had pinch-hit earlier and stayed in) followed with another. Bob Shaw came in. There was a throwing error by Jim Hart, and a walk, and a single by Christopher, and a wild throw on a double-play attempt, and the Mets had tied it up. Bearnarth got through the Giant ninth, leaving two men on base. The Mets did nothing with three walks in the 10th, and Ribant got through the Giant half, making Mays hit into a double play. In the 11th, Christopher walked, stole, and continued to third on the catcher's throw past second, and came in on Smith's fly to Mays, just beating a fine throw. Ribant got through another inning, and the Mets had a 9–8 victory, their greatest "comeback" to date.

It was 12:10 A.M. in San Francisco—3:10 A.M. for the radio listeners back home.

About 15 hours later, they were losing again, 6–4, in the ninth inning, despite two homers by Kranepool. But Smith opened the ninth with a safe bunt, and with one out, Shaw (relieving again) missed Cannizzaro's checked-swing grounder.

Stengel had only one left-handed pinch hitter left: his pitching coach, Spahn (who had always been an outstanding hitter for a pitcher).

So Spahnie produced a grounder to Willie McCovey, who might have thrown to second for a force but didn't, settling for an out at first that moved the tying run into scoring position with Lewis coming up.

Herman Franks, the Giant manager, knew that you're not supposed to put the winning run on base intentionally. He also knew that the next hitter was McMillan and that the Mets had no more left-handed pinch hitters. So he put Lewis on.

But Stengel did have a pinch hitter up his sleeve, right-handed though he was. One of the rookies who had stuck through spring training was a stocky Negro who had hit .351 in his one professional season the year before (at Auburn, in the lower minors). His name was Daniel Napoleon, and he had been to bat exactly twice against major league pitching.

Shaw embarrassed him on the first two pitches, both strikes.

But Napoleon slammed the third one to right center, up into the wind, off the glove of Jay Alou as the outfielder hit the fence, for a three-run triple and a 7–6 lead.

And Ribant, asked again to preserve it, had to do so with Cowan playing second base, Smith short, and Napoleon (an outfielder) third. He did it.

"Vive La France!" Stengel screamed in the clubhouse, in honor of his latest hero.

Back in New York, they couldn't buy papers fast enough. In spite of the long, dismal spring, strange hopes were stirring in the breasts of the fans.

Twice within 24 hours, and against the Giants, no less, the typical futile-rally situations had turned into real rallies. Stengel's magic with pinch hitters and odd lineups, and his mysterious pitching changes (or nonchanges) were potent again. Rookies were doing things. Kranepool was hitting over .400 and leading the league. Spahn could pitch again. Could it be deliverance was at hand?

The next day, Sunday, the enthusiasm fed on itself. Marichal shut out the Mets in the first game, but that was to be expected. What mattered was that Spahn went nine innings again and won the second game, 4–3, with Swoboda knocking in three runs with a double and a homer. The homer was his fourth, in only 16 major league times at bat, and wasn't that other big fellow—Babe Ruth—from Baltimore too, just like Swoboda?

Houston was the next stop, and that Monday afternoon the Mets really saw themselves on the threshold of better days. Their record was 6–7, and the negative statistics purveyors had made sure that everyone understood that no Met team had ever reached the .500 mark, not even at 1–1. To do so now, and to touch fifth place for the first time, would be to cross a symbolic Great Divide. The players, not only the fans, really felt this at the time, and even Stengel did. Shaking off the losing image, so dear to sociologists but now so galling to the Mets and their followers, was a real objective, and even a little statistical accomplishment like this could help.

And what better time to accomplish it than this, the first indoor baseball game ever played by the Mets? For the first game in Houston this time would be their first exposure to that self-proclaimed Eighth Wonder of the World, Judge Roy Hofheinz's Astrodome. Up to now, the only place the Mets could claim a winning record was Mexico; but even domestically, they had never been tried under glass. Perhaps this was their true medium.

Their truest medium, of course, was headlines, and they produced a new one even without playing on Monday. Yogi Berra was going back on the active list, it was announced. He could pinch hit, and catch occasionally, even though he hadn't played in a major league game since 1963, when he was a player-coach with the Yankees. He was a lot younger than Spahn (Yogi wouldn't even be 40 until May 12, to be exact), and his remarkable reflexes might just be sharp enough to provide a little help. Now that the Mets were obviously a pennant contender—on the basis of the last weekend —every little bit could help.

So the strengthened Mets took the field Tuesday bubbling with confidence and ready for conquest.

By the middle of the evening, all these modest goals were right in the hollow of the collective Met hand. McMillan had knocked in two runs in the second inning. Fisher had pitched seven scoreless innings. A couple of singles and a couple of errors had given Houston a run in the eighth, but it was still 2–1 in New York's favor when Fisher retired the first batter in the ninth.

Swoboda had played center field in this game, but Cowan had been sent there in the ninth for defensive strength. It was disconcerting, therefore, to have Cowan fail to hold a drive by Aspromonte that went for a double with one out—disconcerting to Fisher, to Stengel, and to the fans who reflexively steeled themselves for disaster. Rusty Staub (the Kranepool of Houston) was to bat next, so Stengel brought in the left-handed Jackson, and when right-handed Mike White hit instead, Jackson got him on a fly to right. Two out.

Next was Ron Brand, right-handed—and it was obviously time to call in the latest expert game-closer, Mister Dennis Ribant.

Ribant went to a 3–2 count—and walked Brand. A certain amount of animated debate with Umpire Ed Sudol ensued, but the potential tying run was on first base, unable to be argued away.

And the pinch hitter coming up was Eddie Kasko, experienced but hardly likely to hit more than a single.

Ribant threw one pitch. Kasko hit it high to left, fairly deep but apparently a routine third out. The runners circled the bases mechanically, out of obligation. The Great Computer Up There In The Sky was starting to register ".500" for the Met Account. Relief and confidence flooded upward through Met souls.

But soft! Yon left fielder, Christopher, was acting strangely. He moved in hesitantly, then back, in some sort of indecision. Where, actually, was the ball? Could he see it against the milky background of the roof? Wasn't he going to catch it?

Nope.

It fell behind him, a few feet short of the fence, for a two-run double. Houston 3, New York 2.

Noisy joy among some 16,000 Texans in the theater-type seats.

Stunned numbness among the Mets.

Right there—in game No. 14—the fourth Met season turned downhill. A few isolated moments of irrelevant excitement still lay ahead, but authentic optimism would never again be felt during Stengel's regime.

That night the Mets bled from the most painful single defeat they had yet suffered, most painful because it was the first such loss in a situation where they had something positive to expect. They second-guessed themselves endlessly. Why had Ribant walked Bateman? Why didn't the umpire call it a strike? What sort of pitch did Ribant throw to Kasko? What had Cannizzaro called for? ("And why don't you ask me," muttered Stengel, alone in the hotel lobby after the team had scattered, "why I didn't take out the left fielder when I took out the center fielder?") In a perverse way, this was progress, since up to this time no loss could mean so much. In that sense, it was literally a growing pain. But it was one from which the Mets did not recover quickly.

They lost the next five games. The Wednesday game in Houston was being televised back to New York, with Lindsey Nelson working from the gondola at the top and center of the Astrodome, 200 feet above second base. It was a scary, uncomfortable, joke-provoking assignment—and it became interminable when the game lasted 3 hours 24 minutes. The Mets got off in front, were caught, battered their way to a 9–6 lead by scoring four runs in the sixth—and gave the four runs right back in the bottom of the sixth, eventually losing 12–9.

The next stop was Cincinnati. Spahn nursed a 1–0 lead for four innings, lost it to an unearned run in the fifth, and was bombed for three home runs in the sixth: final score, 6–1. The next day, Hunt finally returned to work, and Berra made his debut as a pinch hitter, but the result was 9–2 (Cincinnati's favor, of course). On Sunday the scores were 9–4 and 10–8.

With so little bread coming into the Met world, it was a good thing there were so many circuses, for at this point the second Met visit to Yankee Stadium intervened as a perfectly timed distraction. The 1964 Mayor's Trophy Game had been played at Shea Stadium, and the Yankees had won it. But now the Met fans had another chance to relive the triumph of 1963—and the fact that Yogi was now on their side didn't hurt the emotional flavor of the affair. The Yankees had started poorly under Keane, but they were still champions—for five years in a row now—and the common people had to teach them again what rooting was all about.

That's what the newspapermen thought. The fans thought something else. Only 22,000 bothered to come to the Stadium on Monday night, May 3. It was an unmistakable sign that symbolism wasn't what counted to them any more. What they wanted was some Met victories, and they weren't getting them.

Those who did bother to go to the Bronx, though, got one. Over the weekend, the Mets had used up 18 pitchers (counting repeat appearances) in four games. So Stengel decided to use nine pitchers one inning each in the exhibition game—not allowing for the one thing that was sure to happen: extra innings. But it paid off, and the Mets won, 2–1, in the 10th.

It didn't count, but it did make people feel a little better. So for the next night, the restive populace would have to be diverted again.

So, back in Shea Stadium on May 4, the home folks were offered Berra as a regular.

Yogi caught and batted sixth as Al Jackson started against the Phillies. When he came to bat the first time, the Mets already had a 1–0 lead, with two out. Kranepool on second and Christopher on first. Berra lined a single to center—and ended the inning, because Christopher was thrown out trying for third, even before Kranepool (all of 20 years old) could reach home plate from second. The run didn't count, Yogi didn't get a run batted in, and Kranepool stimulated the banner-makers who had one reading "Is Ed Kranepool Over The Hill?"

It was still 1–0 when Yogi led off the seventh with a looping single over first base, and hits by Swoboda and McMillan brought him around with what proved to be the winning run. Jackson survived an uprising in the ninth, and by a score of 2–1 the Met losing streak was over.

And that was the sum total of Berra's contribution in his comeback. He couldn't really hit any more and after a couple of weeks was deactivated permanently.

Little disasters were occurring daily now. On May 5, Spahn pitched a brilliant four-hitter against Philadelphia—and lost, 1–0, because Bunning hit a home run in the sixth and also pitched a four-hitter. Over the weekend, the Mets did take two out of three from the Braves, but on Monday, May 10, they went up to West Point for their annual exhibition game against the Cadets. Before the game, Stengel slipped on the concrete path outside the dressing room and fell, fracturing his wrist. The embarrassment pained Stengel far more than the physical injury. Already, there were plans for the celebration of his 75th birthday, which would fall on July 30. His critics, silenced for one San Francisco weekend, were baying at him again. Sensitive about his age, he bristled publicly but winced inwardly at the thought that this accident suggested incapacity.

A much more serious injury turned up the next day. Hunt, fielding a grounder, suffered a severe shoulder dislocation when Phil Gagliano of the Cardinals crashed into him on the basepath. Hunt would be out for many weeks, and the Mets had to buy Charley Hiller from the Giants to share second with Klaus.

The home stand ended on a bright note when the Mets swept a doubleheader from Cincinnati on May 16, 6–2 and 8–5 behind Fisher and Spahn, but that merciless, treacherous schedule took them on the road again and they lost six straight in Milwaukee and St. Louis. They won a couple in Philadelphia, came home and split a pair with the Cubs, then were brutalized by the Pirates in a four-game series: 6–1, 7–4, and 9–1 and 12–0 in a double-header. That series pushed them back into 10th place, and they never got out again.

Early in June, they had a 10-game losing streak which included seven straight losses at Shea to the Giants and Dodgers, during which they scored a total of nine runs—and drew 257,000 people. During the same week, the first free-agent draft ever held by baseball took place, and the Mets, having earned it, got first pick. They took a big, left-handed, English-born, Montana-bred pitcher named Les Rohr. He was 19 years old and considered a fine prospect, but he was to provide no help to the Mets in the ensuing five years.

In addition to losing their second baseman, their enthusiasm, a lot of games, the use of one manager's wrist, the playing services of Yogi Berra, and the warm indulgence of many fans, the Mets now lost their publicity man, too. Heft's brother, Arnie, had been a well-known basketball referee but had moved to higher echelons by becoming a member of the group that bought the Baltimore Bullets of the National Basketball Association. Herbie, who was very nearsighted and wore thick glasses, always had to listen to jokes about lending his spectacles to his brother the referee. But now Herbie left the Mets to join the Bullets with a vice-president's status, and the Mets had to listen to jokes about being raided for executive talent by basketball, of all sports.

Heft's successor was Harold Weissman, a man with rich newspaper background. For years he was the working sports editor of the *Mirror,* the Hearst tabloid that battled the *News* for circulation and that folded finally in the fall of 1963. Since then, he had worked for a pay-television project and for Madison Square Garden. Dedicated to detail, his capacity for work was exceeded only by his capacity for worry and his passion for golf. Under Weissman, Met publicity took on a systematized professionalism it had not achieved before, but in June of 1965 Weissman's main contributions lay far ahead. The growing gloom among the fans and testiness within the family were not to be checked by public relations techniques at this point.

Another *Mirror* alumnus was already working for the Mets. Arthur Richman had joined the organization as promotion director back on February 22—and had proved he was a Met at heart by slipping on the ice and breaking his elbow on his way to the office on his first day. He was the replacement for Meany, who had died in September 1964.

Weissman and Richman were already deep in preparations for Stengel's birthday party when the Mets, carrying their 10–game losing streak, started a western trip in Cincinnati and produced another of their unexpected, electrifying moments.

Jim Maloney pitched for the Reds at Crosley Field, against Lary, who was now a frequent starter for the Mets. Maloney, a fast-ball pitcher, really had it this time. He held the Mets hitless for nine innings, but the Reds couldn't score off Lary in eight nor off Bearnarth in the ninth. So Maloney went out and pitched a hitless 10th, too, bringing his strikeout total to 17. The only two base runners the Mets had managed were Kranepool, on a walk in the second inning, and Smith, on a missed third strike in the fourth. But Bearnarth blanked Cincinnati again in the 10th, so Maloney had to go out for the 11th.

He threw two balls and a strike to Lewis—and Johnny lined the next one over the centerfield fence. Swoboda became strikeout No. 18, tying a record; McMillan singled, Gonder hit into a double play, Bearnarth got through the bottom half, and the Mets had one of the most unlikely 1–0 victories imaginable.

Whereupon they lost the next five in a row. That made it 15 losses in 16 games, with the only victory coming in a game in which they were hitless for 10 innings.

On June 21, exactly a week after the Maloney game, the Mets scored another 1–0 decision, on a ninth-inning homer by Cowan off Osteen in Los Angeles. Again the Mets got only two hits, while Jackson pitched a three-hitter.

Then they lost the next five in a row, including four in Houston.

But it was Monday again, June 28, and the Mets had somehow been touched by a Monday madness. They had just lost 20 of their last 23 games—but back in Shea, they swept a doubleheader from Milwaukee, as 38,000 people came out to show the Mets they still cared.

That inspiration enabled the Mets to break even for about a week, but on July 7 they launched another 10–game losing streak that bracketed the All-Star Break. (Kranepool, whose .407 average of May 1 was down to .286 on July 1, represented the Mets in the All-Star Game at Minnesota but never got into action; Swoboda, who had 11 homers by mid-May and was among the leaders at that point, also found reality catching up with him during June.)

There was open grumbling now, Spahn was being racked up regularly, but he resisted Stengel's suggestions that he assign himself to relief pitching. Willey had not been able to come back and had been sent to the minors in May. Ribant, hero in April, was optioned to Buffalo on June 1. The proven mediocrities were proving it again. The young hopefuls, like Swoboda and Napoleon, had bogged down. Stengel was no longer succeeding in distracting the customers, and he himself was disappointed by the lack of progress. Weiss, who was always getting a bad press anyhow, was the target of dissatisfaction, and his impending retirement was awaited eagerly by one segment of fans and newspapermen.

On July 22, when the Mets came home for the weekend series that would include Stengel's birthday party on July 25 (since the club would be on the road on July 30, the actual birthday), they had a record of 30–63. They were three games ahead of their 1964 pace at that point—but two games behind their 1963 pace. As a ball club supposedly in a "developing" stage, they were as close to complete stasis as living creatures could get.

And yet, on Friday night, there were 38,000 people on hand to greet them as the series with the Phillies began. The last game of the trip, in Pittsburgh on Wednesday, had been a 1–0 victory in which Jackson held the Pirates hitless into the eighth inning before Stargell singled, and little Alvin completed a two-hitter. This time, Fisher pitched a 10-inning 3–2 victory before the big crowd.

On Saturday, with the former players gathering for the Oldtimers' ceremonies that would be part of Stengel's birthday party, the Mets drew 36,000 to an afternoon game and took a 5–1 licking.

That night, at Toots Shor's restaurant, the Oldtimers' Party took place, and it was splendid. Usually, these parties are held after an Oldtimers' Game, but with the festivities scheduled for Sunday, the private party had to be Saturday night. The talk, the booze, the camaraderie flowed on and on and on and on. At some point, in the early hours of Sunday, Stengel decided it was time to go. He also decided to accept an invitation to sleep at the home of Joe DeGregorio, the comptroller of the club, who lived near Shea Stadium, since it would be that much easier to get to the ball park the next day.

At the party, hardly anyone noted Stengel's departure. For that matter, at that stage of the party, hardly anyone noted anything at all.

The next morning, all was confusion.

Stengel wasn't at the park. And he wouldn't be.

He was in the hospital, with a broken hip.

No one seemed to know what had really happened. He had stepped heavily, or fallen, getting out of DeGregorio's car. No, he had been lying flat in bed and had suffered some kind of muscular spasm that could, in a man that age, break the hip. No, it was something far more sinister, or secret, or something. (The first version, ultimately, proved true.)

All that was clear was that Stengel wouldn't be able to make the birthday party or receive the huge cake. He sent his apologies to the crowd and appointed Westrum as his emergency replacement. For Westrum, the Mets knocked out Bo Belinsky and won the first game but lost the second. The next day, Westrum was named "interim manager" for the rest of the year, and the day after that Casey underwent surgery that placed a small steel ball in his hip socket.

In this unforeseen, ironic fashion, Stengel's active career ended. He spent three weeks in Roosevelt Hospital in New York, and on August 30 announced his formal retirement. "If I can't walk out there to take the pitcher out, I can't manage," he said simply. "I can't pull him with this here crooked cane." He offered great praise and encouragement for Westrum, and remained tied to the Mets as a vice-president "and West Coast representative," to do scouting and public relations chores as they arose.

Before heading home to Glendale, Stengel had to visit Shea Stadium one more time. There was to be a ceremony at which his uniform would be retired and put on display in a glass case in the Diamond Club lobby, and he had to make a farewell address to the troops. About three hours before game time, before empty stands, he tramped out to the mound before a crowd of cameras and reporters. After the pictures, he went into the clubhouse and gave his final pep talk.

"I've been fortunate in being able to watch some of you men on television, where you can see some things you can't see from the bench," he said. "And if you could see yourselves, you might be surprised at some of the improvement you're making in which was possibly some of your weaknesses.

"You've got a month to go, and I think you can still do something. Your manager and coaches have been doing splendid work, and you see now that a baseball season is a long time, and that some of those good clubs can't win in August and September, especially when they play each other. The season is too long for some of them.

"But you've made progress, and I mean the green men as well as the others, and if you keep on you can be here four or ten years. Now, that's it."

Cisco, who held the office of player representative, answered for them. "You got us off the ground and I think we can go on," he summed up, after showing his own ability to garble syntax.

Like most events featuring Casey, this one went on and on in its own bizarre fashion. After cleaning out his desk in the manager's office, Casey went upstairs for a luncheon in the press room and made another speech. Then he went on Kiner's pregame television show and spoke some more. (Among his observations were: "that Cisco from Ohio State University seems to have picked up some Stengelese somewhere along the way," and "I'd like to see them give that No. 37 to some young player so it can go on and do good for the Mets," and "I hope they don't put a mummy in that glass case.") Then it was back upstairs for another little party, this one in the private dining room of the Directors. Then, out to the club box in the mezzanine, above first base, to watch a few innings.

By the fifth inning, he was gone, that crooked black cane hanging from his jacket pocket (so that he could have his hands free). Edna explained that they had to stop in Kansas City for a few days to visit his older sister, who was 78—and had recently broken her hip, too.

Leaving when they did, the Stengels were spared a final look at the team itself. They watched four innings, and left with the score 1–1. In the ninth, trailing 4–1, the Mets scored two runs on Christopher's single with the bases full and had the tying and winning runs on base with nobody out. But Stephenson bunted carefully into a force at third; Kolb, carrying a hitless streak of 0-for-23, took a called third strike; and Hunt lined to center. Another futile rally, another 4–3 defeat. It encapsulated Stengel's regime.

But the Stengel regime was over. Suddenly, finally, that afternoon of September 2, Casey Stengel was really out of the Met picture. No one dared predict what it would look like without him. He had built, with his own gnarled hands, not much of a ball club, but one whopping doozy of an institution. Now it was on its own.

And he would live to share its triumph.

ACT II—WESTRUM

8 Out of the Cellar

WESLEY Noreen Westrum was a squat, simple, humble man whose dedication to baseball could not be exceeded. His physical toughness was matched by an alert baseball mind that one became aware of only by knowing him well. He was instinctively self-effacing and anything but garrulous. He did not feel sure of himself in front of a crowd and didn't speak easily even in informal surroundings; he preferred to listen and form his conclusions.

It is hard to describe what a sudden promotion to manager of a major league club means to a man like Westrum. It is the emotional equivalent of the pauper being made prince. In absolute sincerity, Westrum had devoted his professional life to playing and learning baseball and, finally, to trying to share that knowledge. One rarely meets a manager with as little ego as Westrum had. He looked upon his elevation as a stroke of good fortune almost not to be believed—and the fact that his salary was to be doubled really was a minor part of it. He was suddenly thrust into a position with status and responsibility he didn't expect, although he had always yearned for the chance as all intelligent (and not so intelligent) players do. It represented, to him, the highest step on the ladder he would ever reach, and having been placed there, he intended to do everything imaginable to stay. His gratitude

to Stengel was boundless; his discomfort at living in the limelight was something to be borne; his job was purely and simply to win more games. Amusing
the citizenry was no longer a function of the manager of the New York Mets.

A person more different from Stengel in style could not be found even
though, in rock-bottom approaches to baseball, they were similar in that they
were old-school products.

Blind fate, after all, had put him in this position. Wes came from northern
Minnesota, where the baseball-playing season is shortened at both ends by
snow. He had turned professional at 17 in 1940, and the three years he spent
in service during World War II came when he was on the Minneapolis roster.
He spent the 1948 season with the New York Giants, was sent down to
Jersey City in 1949 but was brought back in mid-season, and became their
first-string catcher the next year. His strong point was defense, since whatever natural ability he had as a hitter was soon undermined by a succession
of broken fingers—not all of which kept him out of action. He was tough,
single-minded, always hustling, "a good handler of pitchers," and probably
the most uncolorful personality on the Giant teams that had their glorious
moments under Durocher. Mays, Irvin, Dark, Stanky, Thomson, Lockman,
Maglie, Jansen, Hearn, Antonelli, Don Mueller—all overshadowed Westrum,
who was every bit as important to the total success as any. When the Giants
moved to California, his playing days were over but he went along as coach,
under Bill Rigney and then under Dark. Only Lavagetto's illness and the
odd trade of coaches had turned him into Stengel's lieutenant.

Westrum's assignment set tongues wagging on another subject. Why was
Yogi passed over? After all, only the previous season, Yogi had been managing
in the World Series. Wasn't he the natural successor to Stengel?

The trouble with this reasoning was that no one on the Mets had ever intended Yogi to be a manager—the Yankees had gone that route—and it had
been made clear when he joined the Mets that his job was not to be thought
of as a stepping-stone to Stengel's chair. Whatever Yogi may have felt privately about this, he accepted it completely and never, in subsequent years,
expressed dissatisfaction in any way.

But if the Mets didn't intend to make Berra manager in 1966, they could
hardly embarrass him by letting him finish 1965 as an interim manager.
Besides, their real problem was further upstairs.

Weiss, it had been widely assumed, would be retiring at the end of the
year, with Devine moving into his place. It turned out to be a false assumption.
Weiss decided to stay another year, according to an option in his contract,
and that left Devine in an ambiguous position as far as the public was concerned. No complaint of any sort emanated from Devine, but the Weiss-haters
were only too ready to make it on Bing's behalf. This embarrassed Devine,

annoyed Weiss, disturbed the lower levels of the organization a bit, and made plenty of reading material for those who had tired of negative statistics.

If Weiss had decided to retire, the choice of a new manager would have been primarily Devine's. As it was, it became almost entirely Weiss's (and Grant's, of course). And that decision had to be made in the light of how the season had ended.

When Westrum took over, the Met record was 31–64. During July, Lary had been traded to the White Sox for a reserve catcher, Jim Schaffer. Gonder had been sent to the Braves in a waiver deal for Gary Kolb, a left-handed hitter usable at several positions; and Spahn, unable to arrive at a modus vivendi when Stengel was unwilling to keep starting him, had been released (on July 22). He promptly signed with the Giants, who were in a pennant fight.

So the stage was being set for a shift-to-youth movement even before Stengel's unforeseen incapacity. Westrum took up that theme for the remainder of the season: let youth play.

Thereupon the Mets lost 17 of the first 20 games he managed.

Under Stengel that year, they had put together two 10-game losing streaks. For Westrum, they quickly managed an 11.

On August 16, the Mets lost No. 82 (they had 36 victories) and were again mathematically eliminated from the pennant race, right on schedule. The pressure off, they started to win for a couple of weeks, and that was the period Stengel had watched on television to note "improvement." But now came a stretch of 13 defeats in 15 games, and it began to seem doubtful that the Mets would even match the modest victory total of the previous year (53).

Even the attendance dropped during September, after the Giants and Dodgers had made their last visits in August.

September was a rough month for New Yorkers in many ways. There was another newspaper strike, although this one lasted only three weeks, not three months. The Yankees, unaccountably, had collapsed and were limping home in sixth place, out of the first division for the first time in 40 years. People felt sorry for Keane but accepted this for the most part as a one-year aberration, perhaps a punishment by the gods for being mean to Yogi. Besides, there was a real war now in Viet Nam, and a virulent three-way mayoralty campaign in progress (among John Lindsay, Abraham Beame, and William Buckley), and other real-life problems that were rather disturbing, among them a persistent water shortage in the greatest city in the world.

No, the internal affairs of the Mets did not seem so momentous.

The 1965 season ended, for the Mets, on a note of obscure futility. There was to be a night doubleheader at Shea on the final Saturday and a single game Sunday. The Mets got shut out, 6–0, in the first game Saturday, then

played an 18-inning scoreless tie that was finally halted by curfew at 1 A.M.—
which meant that two games would have to be played Sunday too. They lost
the first, 3–1, and then went 13 innings before losing the second by the same
score. In their final series, then, they had brought forth two runs in 49
innings. And there were no papers in town to spread the story.

However, during the 1965 season the Mets had signed two kids in Texas,
a pitcher named Nolan Ryan and an infielder named Ken Boswell. In Iowa
they signed a pitcher named Jim McAndrew and in Kansas City one named
Steve Renko. They had brought to the coaching staff Sheriff Robinson, who
had been managing Buffalo until Spahn's departure and Westrum's promotion
stripped the daily advisory board, and Sheriff had been handling Cleon Jones,
Bud Harrelson, Bearnarth, Ribant, Selma, Napoleon, and the other hopefuls
down there.

So even though the Mets had finished 10th for the fourth straight year,
winning only 50 games and losing 112, it was possible, within the confines of
the Met offices at 680 Fifth Avenue, to hope that there was daylight ahead.

It was time to make decisions.

Weiss would stay one more year, definitely his last. The decision that went
with this was: we will get out of 10th place at any cost. On a personal level,
Weiss was determined to leave on the upswing; and, in all objectivity, what
the Met customers were really demanding was a move upward on the field
now, not more promises about a rosy future.

Westrum would stay as manager, although they took their time—six weeks
—before they told him. He was not, in the minds of Weiss and the Directors,
the perfect ideal they would have created had they been Pygmalions, but he
was competent, loyal, and familiar with the organization. Perhaps the contrast
to Stengel would be an advantage; since no one could live up to Casey's
standard as an attention-getter, perhaps it would be just as well to have a
man from whom no one would expect it.

Devine would remain too, despite rumors to the contrary, and perhaps
take a more active part in the decision-making process.

New coaches would be needed, although Berra would stay too. So would
Robinson. But Heffner was gone, appointed manager of the Cincinnati Reds,
and no pitching coach had been named after Spahn's departure. The two
choices were: Whitey Herzog, a Yankee-system outfielder of modest talents
who had become a scout and then a coach for the Kansas City Athletics; and
Harvey Haddix, the well-known little left-handed pitcher who had just finished
a 14-year major league career, highlighted by his 12 perfect innings in a
losing game at Milwaukee one night in 1959.

Those were the planned moves. Then there was one big unplanned move.

Stanky, who had spoken so often of being happy just "working with kids," accepted an offer by the White Sox to return to managing. That was on December 14. Two weeks later, the Mets hired Bob Scheffing, who had once managed the Tigers in a close race with the Yankees and who had outstanding credentials, as the new Director of Player Development. And when Kerby Farrell went to join Stanky as a coach, the triple-A managing job (which was now in Jacksonville instead of Buffalo as the Mets switched cities) went to Hemus.

These backstage events were more important, in the long run, than the various trades that excited the fans, but there was plenty of action there too.

Right after the World Series, the Mets sent Jackson and Charley Smith to St. Louis for Ken Boyer, a top-draw star—but one who would be 35 years old in May.

The day before that, the Mets had purchased a young catcher, Jerry Grote, from Houston's farm club at Oklahoma City. Grote had played for Houston all of 1964 but had been sent out after hitting .181. At Oklahoma City he had hit .265. Eventually, they sent Parsons to Houston as final payment for Grote.

At the winter meetings in Florida, the Mets traded Christopher to the Boston Red Sox for Ed Bressoud, an experienced infielder who had actually broken in with the Giants when they were still at the Polo Grounds. Bressoud would be 34 in May, but he could hit.

The Mets also purchased, from Cleveland, a left-handed hitting outfielder named Al Luplow. A concerted attack was being made on the .221 batting average the 1965 Mets had posted.

And in February, they acquired from the Phillies one of the big bats of recent years, Dick Stuart, the first baseman. They had to give Klaus, Schaffer, and Wayne Graham, none of them regulars.

The only pitcher acquired between seasons was Jack Hamilton, an experienced right-hander, who liked admitting that he threw spitballs, from Detroit.

So the blueprint was clear: the 1966 Mets would have more punch but would depend on young pitchers. It was a sensible enough formula that other teams had used for quick dividends.

But it had a flaw.

The flaw was that they weren't the right young pitchers.

Westrum devoted spring training to "reversing" the losing psychology. The shelter of Stengel's humor no longer existed, but that humor had also had a corroding element in it as far as players' confidence was concerned. Westrum, in his direct fashion, would be a positive thinker. Little signs and maxims appeared everywhere, all with the theme "you can if you think you can." Also, platooning would be minimized, which was good for the morale of regulars but didn't do much for the rest. At any rate, there would be no digressions into reminiscence, argument, or zaniness: plain baseball, as good as the Mets could make it, would be the product.

Could avowed mediocrity be sold? The Mets would soon find out.

Westrum's opening day lineup included Jones, finally promoted to the varsity for good, in right field. Hunt was at second, Boyer at third, Stuart at first, Hickman in center, Swoboda in left, Grote catching, and McMillan at short. The pitcher was Fisher, who had lost 24 games the year before.

Westrum had the team ready for a great opportunity. The Mets were to share the annual Monday opener in Cincinnati, a day ahead of everyone else in the league. If they could win that one game, they'd have first place all to themselves. It would be a small symbolic triumph but in keeping with the spirit Westrum wanted to instill. The Mets were sure they could do it, especially after storming through the exhibition season with a 14–10 record.

Unfortunately, it rained Monday.

It rained Tuesday, too. And Wednesday night.

The Mets didn't get to play at all until Friday, back in New York, against the Braves. By then, Philadelphia and Pittsburgh were tied for first place with 2–0 records. The Mets could still perform their feat if both lost, but the idea was tarnished.

Anyhow, they didn't win the first game. A crowd of 52,000 came out to see The New Mets, and came away with a feeling of *déja vu,* that vague sense of having had the experience before. Fisher took a 2–1 lead into the ninth. Joe Torre doubled off the centerfield fence. Lee Thomas lined a single to right, and when Cleon threw the ball into the Braves' dugout beyond third, it was 2–2, and Thomas was on third. Dennis Menke promptly dropped a squeeze bunt toward the mound, and Thomas scored while Fisher desperately threw the ball past Grote. That was it. The game ended 3–2.

But, wonder of wonders, the Mets won the next day, 3–1, on a five-hitter by Hamilton, and the next, 5–4, coming from behind with two in the eighth and one in the ninth. With two victories in their first three games, they were on the right side of the .500 mark for the first time and in the first division, even if it was fifth place and even if the season was only five days old. Maybe Westrum had the right answers after all.

But no. Not with a starting rotation that included Selma, Gardner, and McGraw, and a bull pen that relied heavily on Darrell Sutherland, Bearnarth, and Gordon Richardson.

The Mets lost five in a row and never got back to .500. They didn't fall far below it, but they sank steadily. Boyer was knocking in some runs. McMillan was wearing out but Bressoud was helping. Jones was coming along, Kranepool was doing better, Grote was doing all right. But the pitching staff simply wasn't ready. The youngsters would log many fine innings, but they would also make too many fatal mistakes.

Then there were two extraneous factors that entered into Met thinking in May.

The Yankees had troubles. They started so badly, losing 16 of their first 20 games and being obviously at odds internally, that they had to fire Keane. Houk resumed managing on May 7, and the team revived, so it seemed all the more important for the Mets to make some upward showing now— either to take advantage of a real Yankee decline or to protect against a spectacular Yankee resurgence.

And the Cubs had troubles. After years of using the committee-of-coaches system, they had made Durocher manager. Leo was boss, no mistake about that, and his first plan was to tear apart the team that had been floundering for years and rebuild it into the form he wanted. This had been his pattern of success elsewhere, and he embarked on it now with a vengeance. One consequence was that the Cubs lost 16 of *their* first 20 games, and Leo made it noisily clear that he didn't care how far down that year's Cubs finished, he was going to rebuild the way he wanted. To the Mets, who won nine of their first 20 games, this meant opportunity: a chance to get out of the cellar by staying ahead of the Cubs.

The thing to do, then, was to go for immediate improvement. The experienced daily lineup was producing. Put some experienced pitchers on the mound, and the team might do all right. Not make a run for the pennant or anything like that, but at least it might stay off the bottom.

So Operation Age Movement, as distinct from Youth Movement, began.

The first new pitcher wasn't particularly old: Gerry Arrigo, a left-hander purchased from Cincinnati. But he wasn't particularly good either, and soon he was on the disabled list anyhow.

The next new one was exciting. He was a right-hander from Notre Dame, named Dick Rusteck, who was called up from Jacksonville on June 9. The next night he pitched a four-hit shutout and beat the Braves, 5–0. But three games later he hurt his shoulder, went on the disabled list, then back to Jacksonville, and was rarely heard of again.

By this time, McGraw had also injured his shoulder and had been shipped down. Sutherland had preceded him, and Richardson had been sent down to make room for Rusteck.

On June 10, the Mets picked up Bob Friend, who had just been released by the Yankees. Friend had spent most of his 15-year career with Pittsburgh, where he was unable to win half his games but had always been a principal tormentor of the Mets. The Yankees had acquired him after the 1965 season, used him briefly, and dropped him. It took him a few weeks to hit his stride, but he became an effective pitcher again with the Mets.

On June 15, the Mets were able to buy, from San Francisco, an established big-league pitcher: Bob Shaw. A native Long Islander, Shaw had pitched successfully for several clubs but was an outspoken sort with very strong opinions on life, his place in it, and everything else in the universe. Every couple of years, the management of whatever club he was with and he would decide it was better to part. But he could pitch, there was little question of that, and he immediately became a regular starter for the Mets.

The rotation became Fisher, Hamilton, Shaw, Friend. Around mid-season, Ribant became part of it too. In July, Sutherland was back, and Selma was down in Jacksonville.

With the staff rearranged this way and a slightly better offense, the Mets were able to stay on an even keel for two months. On June 21, they had a record of 24–37. On the morning of August 24, they stood at 56–70, having won 32 games and lost only 33 during that long period. During that stretch, Shaw won six games, Friend four, Arrigo two, and Hamilton two—14 victories from "pick-ups." During July, by winning 18 and losing 14, the Mets set a club record: their first winning month.

Better still, the Mets were in eighth place at this point, half a game ahead of Houston and (what really mattered) 12½ ahead of Leo's last-place Cubs. They had already set a new high for Met victories, posting No. 54 on August 21, with 39 games still to play.

Hunt and Jones, two of their young regulars, were hitting around .290. Kranepool had 14 homers and 51 runs batted (and Stuart had been dropped back in June, having spent most of his Met career on the injured list). Swoboda was a disappointment, on the basis of his 19 homers as a rookie the year before, but he was driving in about as many runs as Boyer and Jones. McMillan, recently injured, was probably finished, but Harrelson, that little kid just called up from Jacksonville, looked like a pretty slick fielder, even though he'd never hit.

In short, the Mets were pleasing their customers, Weiss's critics to the contrary. The turnstiles were spinning faster than ever—even though the World's Fair was closed, and Stengel was gone. In a certain sense, Westrum's homely personality struck the same kind of chord the original Mets had struck: he was clearly the Met fans' own, not to be shared with the cold outside world or the celebrity chasers. They could identify with his aspirations and struggles; he was one of the family. The sociologists and the magazine writers might not like it, but what the real Met fans craved was that ultrasquare experience of a few victories. The present team was providing it, and they loved it more than ever.

A price was being paid, of course. To a great degree, the "development" program had been sidetracked in favor of immediate appeal. The Shaws and the Boyers and the Bressouds and the Friends and the Hamiltons would not, obviously, have any part in a winning future. A Swoboda belonged down in the minors, playing every day and improving, or up here playing every day regardless of mistakes; but he didn't belong in a situation where he was being yanked in and out of the lineup.

After September 1, young players were recalled and they played some more, and the Mets lost 25 of the last 35 games. The veterans were tired and not really motivated at that point; the youngsters weren't ready. They couldn't keep pace with Houston—but they had enough of a cushion over Chicago. When the season finally ended on October 2, with two losses to Houston at Shea Stadium, the final figures were rather pleasing:

Attendance—1,932,693, the best yet.

Victories—66, the most yet.

Defeats—95, the fewest so far, the first time under 100.

And this above all—ninth place. Someone, at last, had finished below the Mets. That the someone was Durocher only made it sweeter to old Giant fans who hated him from Dodger days, or old Dodger fans who hated him from Giant days, or anyone else who simply disliked Leo for his brash, present self.

Weiss could now retire with a certain measure of glory.

And Westrum, of course, would have to manage for another year.

All this was satisfying enough, but it was intensified by what had happened in the Bronx.

The Yankees had finished 10th.

That's right, the Mets finished higher than the Yankees. The team Houk had taken over, after spurting for about a month, had collapsed, completely and finally. It might have avoided the indignity of last place during the final week, but rain wiped out its last chance. And in the battle of attendance, the Yankees had fallen to 1,124,648—their lowest in 21 years, and more than 800,000 below the Met total.

While this meant satisfaction for the Mets, it also was food for reflection. The soundness of the Shea Stadium location had now been proven, beyond doubt. The "what if O'Malley or Stoneham had agreed to stay" speculation was reawakened. The wisdom of the Yankees (Topping's Yankees, not C.B.S.'s) in fighting the municipal stadium idea instead of moving in on it was certainly open to question.

But all in all, at the end of 1966, New York's sports scene was not exactly scintillating.

The two baseball teams had finished ninth and 10th.

The football Giants, once the elite, had finished last, winning only one of their 14 games.

The Jets, co-occupants of Shea Stadium, were generating excitement with their $400,000 quarterback, Joe Namath, but they hadn't won anything yet. They finished third in 1966, with a 6–6 record and two ties, and never in their history had they enjoyed a winning season.

The basketball Knicks had just finished last in their division for the seventh year in a row.

The hockey Rangers had just finished dead last, and it was eight years since they had won more games than they had lost.

So if you looked at it the right way, the Mets were now the class of the lot.

However, the way the Met fans looked at it, the future was all important. All the other teams (except the Jets) had seen better days. The Mets, for the first time, had moved up. All that counted now was moving up some more, continuing to improve. If the 1966 Mets could win 66 games, the 1967 Mets should certainly win 70 and close in on the magic number of 81, which would represent a break-even season.

As a goal, it was clear enough. As an accomplishment, Devine knew it might not be that easy.

Westrum had been rehired, formally, while the season was still on (September 6). On November 14, Weiss officially turned the reins over to Devine, who assumed the title of president and the function of general manager. All his baseball life, Devine had been an active trader. He understood, better than anyone, to what extent 1967 had been mortgaged by the composition of the 1966 team. He knew that it was his obligation to tear apart what had become popular, so that a reasonable chance would exist of moving ahead later. It was a thankless assignment at that moment, but Devine had no choice; what he did have (and always had had) was the courage of his convictions.

First he had to review the minor league events of 1966, to determine which players had to be protected from the draft. (Actually, this had to be done in October, but by then it was clear that the responsibility would be Devine's.)

Back in the spring, with no public awareness, a stroke of good fortune had occurred. The Mets had drawn Tom Seaver's name out of a hat.

Among the regulations that had been worked out when baseball adopted the free-agent draft was a provision to help college coaches and the professional game live together. A college player in his junior or senior year could not be signed once his college team's season had started. Seaver, a junior-college transfer to University of Southern California, had been drafted by Atlanta. His father (once a Walker Cup golfer—the Walker Cup that was put up by the family of Herb Walker, one of the Met owners) and Tom negotiated a $50,000 bonus with the Braves. But by the time they signed a contract, the U.S.C. season had begun. Seaver hadn't played in any college game and was assumed to be in the clear, but technically he wasn't.

The case went to Commissioner William D. Eckert, whose short career was not marked by shining successes, but he made an eminently correct decision this time. He had to uphold the rule. But he could not penalize Seaver for what seemed to be an innocent infraction in an agreement made in good faith. (One reason he couldn't penalize Tom was that Mr. Seaver made plain, in the politest possible way, that he knew where to find the telephone number of a good lawyer.) So Eckert ruled that any club except the Braves could offer Seaver the same bonus, and that if more than one club was interested, the choice would be made by lot. Only the Mets, Cleveland, and Philadelphia decided to take part. Eckert drew out the slip with the Mets' name on it. They paid Seaver his bonus and sent him to Jacksonville.

In this instance, the Mets were doubly lucky. The draw-by-lot was obviously pure chance, although they did deserve credit for being one of three clubs interested enough to try (on the firm persistent recommendation of scout Nelson Burbrink). But they were also lucky the draft existed in the first place. Seaver's ability was not hard to spot at an early age, and he was well known in California. It's entirely possible that, in an open-market situation, the Dodgers or Giants might have pursued and landed him, without any technicalities to intervene.

Well, Seaver had posted a 12–12 record at Jacksonville but had impressed the ears off everyone who had seen him pitch. He'd have to be promoted.

Then there was this fellow Koosman, the one recommended by the usher's son. He had pitched at Auburn and struck out 174 men in 170 innings. He had better not be left on the Jacksonville roster.

Then there was that young second baseman at Jacksonville, Boswell. His average was only .255 but everyone agreed he should be a good hitter. Promote him.

Down in Williamsport there was Rohr, the original draft choice, and a left-hander named Don Shaw. They looked good enough to keep.

O.K. So much for the system itself. Now to market.

From Kansas City, the Mets bought Larry Stahl, a left-handed hitting outfielder whose claim to fame was one 500-foot-plus home run.

In the draft (the minor league draft, in which major league teams buy unprotected players at a set price), the Mets picked up Tommy Reynolds, a young outfielder.

From the Dodgers, Devine got Tommy Davis—a native Brooklynite and twice National League batting champion before suffering a badly broken ankle—and an infielder named Derrell Griffith in exchange for Hunt and Hickman.

Now there was a real trade to set fans talking.

A week later Devine had another one: he sent Ribant to Pittsburgh for Don Cardwell, an experienced pitcher, and Don Bosch, an outfielder who had played 859 minor league games and three with the Pirates in seven years.

"Bosch is the man who can solve our problem in center field," Devine explained. "Pitchers must have the help of a good centerfielder. Everyone who has seen Bosch agrees he has outstanding defensive ability. Nobody knows how much he can hit, but when a man is a great fielder in the minors, there's no reason why he shouldn't be just as good in the majors."

That meant the Met outfield would contain Davis, Bosch, and Jones. Swoboda, it was decided, could become a right-handed half of a first-base platoon with Kranepool.

McMillan was gone, so Harrelson would be expected to be the regular shortstop. By trading Hunt, Devine risked the displeasure of the more dedicated Met fans (including Mrs. Payson), who had fallen into the habit of considering him their "best player." In reality, Hunt had become less effective since his injury. Going into spring training, it was obvious a second baseman would be needed, since Hiller didn't seem capable of handling it all by himself. Boyer would be back at third, and Grote was the regular catcher.

The starting pitchers would be Fisher, Shaw, Cardwell, and Seaver.

And some of the most promising talent—McGraw, Ryan, Boswell, Rohr—were on the military list, fulfilling tours of duty in various reserve programs.

That was the shape of the team Devine turned over to Westrum in St. Petersburg. There was one coaching change, too: Herzog was moved up into the minor league system as a special scout, and the third-base coach became Salty Parker, a friend of Westrum's and fellow-coach from the Giants.

This move, strangely enough, stirred a minor tempest. Some of the writers took exception to Herzog's departure. Whitey was a gregarious, talkative, extremely energetic third-base coach, who jumped up and down and sometimes stretched out in a prone position. He had an aggressive, cheerful philosophy, all the more noticeable by contrast with his predecessor, Heffner. They interpreted his replacement by Parker as some sort of victory for conservatism or perhaps buddyism. As it turned out, Herzog would have far more to offer in his new position.

But the real tempest swirled around Bosch.

All winter long, stories had built up his great fielding skill. When he showed up in camp, he turned out to be a small, chunky fellow, visibly nervous and clearly suffering from a crisis of confidence. In practice and exhibition games, he was under constant scrutiny for any sign that he was really Joe DiMaggio and Willie Mays rolled into one.

No such sign appeared.

In fact, he messed up even ordinary plays.

Privately, Westrum, Devine, and the rest of the Met family were puzzled, then appalled. Publicly, they deplored the intolerance of the press and insisted it was too soon to judge. Bosch agreed with this view: the press was just making him more nervous, he declared.

Before the season ever began, therefore, Bosch was suspected of being a total failure. The suspicion proved true.

But Devine was still busy, undeterred by the possibility of a bad trade and never, never apologizing or alibiing. He traded Griffith to Houston for Sandy Alomar, who could play second base. He traded Bressoud to St. Louis for Jerry Buchek, who was a better hitter than fielder but also capable of playing second or short. He signed Ralph Terry, the former Yankee star who had finished 1966 with the Mets, as a free agent after a spring training tryout. He picked up Ron Taylor, a relief pitcher he had brought to St. Louis, from Houston, and brought him up from Jacksonville just as the season began. He brought up Chuck Estrada, who had been a bright rookie for Baltimore years before, and was not recovering from a bad arm. And, two weeks into the season, when Taylor was injured, he bought Jack Lamabe from the White Sox.

It was becoming, very quickly, Devine's team.

But it had, lying in its path, a terrible trap: Durocher had straightened out his Cubs.

And it had, surrounding it, a distinctly different mood among the faithful. The success of 1966, modest as it was, had created a demand for more success, and this was something quite new in the cozy confines of Metsomania. It would require a difficult adjustment.

DEBATE IN HEAVEN

Readers of this column may recall that a year ago, a distinguished group of New York Met fans made plans to take part in this year's Banner Day. These rabid rooters, watching Met activities from their unique vantage point in heaven, included William Shakespeare, Feodor Dostoevsky, Voltaire, Samuel Taylor Coleridge, Andrew Marvell, Albert Einstein, Rene Descartes and Johann Wolfgang von Goethe.

Yet, last Sunday's Banner Day at Shea Stadium came and went, and no representative of this illustrious company appeared. Some explanation seemed in order.

An explanation has been unearthed (or perhaps, more precisely, un-celestialed). The following material, presented here exclusively, is highly classified; the Mets had hoped to suppress it, and the man primarily involved, an Unidentified Met Official, is ready to deny everything to his dying day. But the public has a right to know.

This Unidentified Met Official entered his office at Shea Stadium early Sunday morning. The television set in the corner was off.

Sudenly, to the U.M.O.'s amazement, the screen came alive, although no dial had been touched. The picture was in color, which was even more amazing, since it wasn't a color set.

The figure coming into focus was easily identifiable. He was a tall thin man with bushy eyebrows and a square-cut beard, wearing knickers and a belted jacket made of the same checked material. Over the breast pocket the monogram "G.B.S." was clearly visible.

The TV Medium

However, the U.M.O. was so startled that his brain refused to accept the obvious.

"Lindsey Nelson," he cried, "what are you doing in that get-up?"

The face on the screen, now seen in close-up, seemed confused at being addressed in this manner.

"My name," he declared dryly, "is George Bernard Shaw, and if you are some official of the New York Mets, I have a message for you. An apology."

And G.B.S. proceeded to explain.

The Met fans of Elysium had indeed planned to attend Banner Day, and had spent much time composing signs. Julius Caesar had come up with "We Came, We Saw, We Got Clobbered." Benjamin Franklin produced a cartoon of Poor Richard, saying, "A Run Not Saved Is a Run Unearned." Gertrude Stein had worked on a long strip, to be carried by half a dozen young men, reading: "A Rose Is a Rose Is a Rose, but We Still Prefer Ron Hunt on the Grass, Alas."

But complications arose.

Einstein, a cautious man, regarded a trip to earth as dangerous at this time, because so much hardware was floating around in orbit. A path through the various man-made satellites would have to be plotted carefully.

There were other objections and hesitations, but the crucial one was the news brought by Don Juan, who had just arrived in heaven after finally breaking off his interminable conversation with the devil in hell.

The Wrong Spirit

"Juan reported," Shaw told the U.M.O., "strong rumors that Lucifer was taking a hand, indirectly, in baseball. I needn't go into detail; simply consider the court decisions and Congressional inaction that satisfy neither Milwaukee nor baseball, the simultaneous infliction on Chicago of Leo Durocher and Eddie Stanky, and the plight of the American League, with the Baltimore Orioles getting too far ahead for a race and the Yankees falling so far behind as to be stripped of even residual glamor.

"It is the devil's influence, Juan told us, that has made so much in baseball today not noble, only aristocratic; not exciting, only turbulent; not eventful, only prolonged; not greater, only expanded; not famous, only publicized; not ambitious, only greedy; not dedicated, only committed; not enriching, only profitable; not—but you know how wordy Juan gets when he rambles on that way.

"The point is, the group became reluctant to associate itself too closely with what may yet be a controversial activity.

"Naturally," Shaw concluded, "I disapproved of such a craven attitude—so I was deputized to convey to you our apologies. Please understand it has nothing to do with the improvement of the Mets—we're all delighted with that. It's just that life in heaven carries certain obligations, and certain standards must be kept. Therefore—we're sorry we can't make it."

The screen winked out. For the time being, presumably, baseball is on its own.

9 A Changing Climate

SAME old Mets.

That was the universal reaction to Opening Day, 1967.

It was cold and windy at Shea Stadium, and the crowd of 31,000 was respectably large but less overwhelming than people had come to expect. Those who had faith in the abstract power of mathematics were sure the Mets would win. After all, they had been sneaking up on a quick first victory for five years. First they had lost the first nine games, then eight, then four, then two, and last year only the first one. Certainly, numerology indicated that the time had come. Certainly the law of averages was on the side of the Mets.

Perhaps, but there were subtler principles, and historical habits, at work also. In the first eight innings, with Cardwell pitching for the Mets against Pittsburgh's Bob Veale, the Mets made four errors. Still they had a 3–3 tie going into the ninth.

But Gene Alley opened the ninth with a double, and Gonder—who had beaten them so often when he was with them—lined a double off the right field wall and beat them again. Just to make sure, a passed ball, a squeeze bunt single by Alou, a stolen base and Grote's wild throw on the attempt, and a single by Maury Wills made the score 6–3. Pete Mikkelsen (the Yankee who had been sent to Pittsburgh for Bob Friend a year before) polished off the Mets, and the first game had been lost again. Mathematicians could now recognize the process: the Mets were approaching a first victory not by arithmetic or geometric progression, but asymptotically—ever closer without ever quite reaching it.

The Mets did win the second game, 3–2, on a two-run homer by Buchek and an eighth-inning pinch single by Hiller. This was Seaver's debut, although he didn't get credit for the victory because Estrada took over in the sixth. It also marked the first Met save for Taylor, who pitched a hitless ninth after Hiller had batted for Estrada.

But in Philadelphia, Fisher, Shaw, and Bill Denehy (a young right-hander) were beaten in succession. Cardwell won at Pittsburgh, Seaver posted his first victory (with Don Shaw's help) against the Cubs at Shea, and Fisher (with help from Don Shaw again) stopped Philadelphia and put the Mets back at .500. But they lost six of the next seven games and never saw .500 again.

They were the same old Mets, all right, but they weren't getting the same old laughs.

By the first week in May, the Met record was 7–13, and certain facts had to be faced. The offense was not carrying the load; the defense was not sound; Bosch wasn't going to make it; and Bob Shaw was having his usual second-year-with-the-club problems, leaving a big hole in a pitching staff not that secure to begin with.

So Devine went back to the market.

From Baltimore, he bought Bob Johnson to replace Hiller, who had just broken his hand.

From Kansas City, he bought Ed Charles, an aging third baseman considered "washed up" by various American League evaluators.

And, since it was time to cut the roster from 28 to 25, Terry was dropped, and Koosman and Stahl were sent to Jacksonville. A couple of weeks later, Lewis was brought back up and Alomar sent down.

Westrum did not, as Stengel used to, believe that platooning players was an art, but he was involved in as fast a shuffle system as Casey ever had. Devine was not the sort of man to sit still any time he saw even the slightest possibility of improving things, and he was not afraid of change or of risks.

Since the club didn't stabilize its record, the shuffle continued through June, which began with the Mets back in 10th place. Cardwell's elbow acted up, and Selma came back from Jacksonville. Bosch was sent down, and Hawk Taylor came back, for the umpteenth time. Hamilton was traded to the California Angels for Nick Willhite, and Bob Hendley, an experienced left-hander, was purchased from the Cubs.

Hiller returned to duty, and Estrada and Lewis were sent back to Jacksonville. Luplow was sold to Pittsburgh and Stahl brought back from Jacksonville. Dennis Bennett, a left-hander, was purchased from Boston and Willhite sent to Jacksonville. Then Denehy was sent down to make room for Hal Reniff, the pudgy relief pitcher taken on waivers from the Yankees.

None of it seemed to do much good, since July 1 dawned with the Mets in last place, their record 26–44—which happened to be exactly the same as their record at that stage in 1963.

But that wasn't the scary part. What hurt more was the way Leo had made good his threat to rebuild the Cubs. Chicago was challenging the Cardinals for the League lead, trailing by only half a game with the midpoint of the season drawing closer. The Mets, already 17 games back, could not depend on the Cubs to keep them off the bottom again. To avoid 10th, they would have to beat out Houston, something they had never yet done. And Chicago was a living example that rebuilding could be done quickly.

So Devine kept shopping.

Hiller was sent to Philadelphia in a waiver deal for Phil Linz, another former Yankee, called "Supersub" in his days as a utility infielder for championship Yankee teams. Lamabe was sold to St. Louis for a player to be delivered after the season (who turned out later to be our old friend Alvin Jackson, an original Met). Hawk Taylor went down to Jacksonville, and Greg Goossen came up. Cardwell came off the disabled list. Boyer, hitting only .235, was traded to the White Sox for another future delivery (who came after the season in the person of J. C. Martin, the catcher–first baseman). Two days later Bob Shaw was sold to the Cubs. A week after that, the Mets got Cal Koonce from the Cubs and sent Bennett to Jacksonville.

It's bewildering to read about these maneuvers, but it was still more bewildering to live through them. In the Stengel–Weiss partnership, arguments about personnel were common enough, but the manager carried a major share of the responsibility for the makeup of the squad. In the Devine–Westrum relationship, there was actually more harmony, but Devine's opinion carried far more weight than Westrum's. It was, really, a more traditional baseball relationship: the general manager supplied the players, and the field manager used them as best he could. Devine knew, from experience, that a revolving-door policy had harmful effects, but he was giving full priority to future development and was willing to take the consequences of immediate instability. He believed that, for the present, any move that might help was worth making, and even if it didn't work out it was worth the risk; but he also believed that a long-range program should not be disrupted in the process.

Strangely enough, the performance of this constantly shifting roster was remarkably consistent: not good enough. The April record was 6–11. May was 6–15, June 11–18, July 14–17, August 12–18. When September 1 arrived, the Mets were at 51–79. They were in last place, but Houston was only half a game ahead (and actually behind in the loss column), so the Mets still had reasonable hope of matching their 1966 showing.

Hope, however, was not enough to mask a deteriorating situation. For the first time, attendance was on the way down (although it was still amazingly high), and the patience of both fans and owners was being stretched.

It was hard to pinpoint the factors, but the mood was easy enough to read. There was affection for Westrum—but he wasn't very inspiring. The Board of Directors had nothing against him, but it hoped to do better. Between Devine and Westrum there were none of the deep ties that are so common in baseball—they hadn't come up together, they had no long off-field friendship, they weren't particularly alike in philosophy or background. They were two men who just happened to have the same employers; they worked together conscientiously, smoothly, with good will and loyalty—but in the long run, in baseball, a manager should be the general manager's personal choice (as Stengel had been Weiss's), and Westrum had not been Devine's.

On other levels, Westrum was having an uncomfortable time. He could read handwriting on walls as well as anyone. He had none of the security that some managers, who are independently wealthy, enjoy. He knew his livelihood, as well as his desirable status, rested strictly on Met victories. He knew that his power over his players was limited, because they realized his position was less secure than theirs. He knew that insufficient winning, and a drop in attendance, would orient Met management back to a "colorful" manager, and he knew he wasn't that.

Furthermore, he found the cumulative burdens of managing hard to take. A player or coach can go about his business with a reasonable amount of equanimity and clear conscience as long as he does his best and tries his hardest, which Westrum always did. But a manager takes upon his soul all the sins and omissions of 25 men, every day, in every game.

And with a team like the Mets, sins and omissions greatly outweighed the good things. Westrum's most characteristic expression, a mild-voiced but heart-felt "Oh my God, wasn't that awful!" tightened his nerves every time he was forced to utter it. The only cure for what was happening on the field was better players and Westrum didn't have better players.

In addition to everything else, Westrum found life in a manager's spotlight a strain. He got along well with his "regular writers" and was infallibly polite and cooperative with strangers, but the incessant need for public appearance did not sit comfortably on his basically shy, can-of-beer, simple-friends-and-virtues personality. At the same time, he lived with an irrelevant but ego-bruising situation that was no one's fault but a painful irritant even to so nonegotistical a man as Westrum: the presence of Berra. Everywhere the Mets went, in every hotel lobby, airport, and ball park, the autograph-seekers clustered around Yogi. With Stengel gone, and with no true playing star on the club, and with the old nostalgia-stimulators like Hodges and Snider no longer around, Yogi was by far the most identifiable "famous" Met in the group, as far as the casual public was concerned. Now, Westrum had played in New York, and won pennants, completely in the shadow of Berra the Yankee and Roy Campanella the Dodger. He was now the manager of the Mets, with Yogi one of his assistants—but almost no ordinary fan even recognized him whereas everyone knew Yogi. It was a humiliating, frustrating situation, all the harder to deal with because Yogi did nothing particular to provoke it, and because no one was expressing any antagonism toward Westrum. It was not an important thing in itself, but it added to the emotional pressure Westrum felt.

Meanwhile, there was no strong fan identification with Devine either. His roots were in St. Louis, and he had continued to commute to New York through most of his Met career. People who had close contact with him invariably developed admiration for his character and ability, and affection; but as a public figure, he had little personality. He was sensible, reasonable, low-key, frank, fair—and entirely without flair. It was ironic, in a way, because his thinking and decision making were often breathtakingly daring, by conventional baseball standards, but he never gave the impression of being controversial or exciting. Weiss could be hated by those who read about him, or admired by those who focused on his record, but in one way or another, despite his aloof inaccessibility, Weiss generated a reaction. Devine did not and did not want to. He believed attention belonged on the people in uniform (and so had Weiss, for that matter), and as president of the Mets, Devine's very virtues helped make him a bland figure.

Again, there was no built-in closeness between Devine and Grant, who was the active member of the Board of Directors. They worked together perfectly well, but there was no extra personal loyalty, as there had been in the relation between the owners and Weiss. It was Weiss, after all, who had set them up in business, and with such great profit. There was a bottom layer of gratitude that could never be dismantled. Devine, on the other hand, was a respected, well-liked, well-functioning employee—but an employee.

Nor did any of the internal lines contain ties to Devine. Murphy and

Thomson had been brought into the organization by Weiss, for whom they had worked earlier in their lives. They, too, got along perfectly well with Devine, but no more so than they would with anyone else. Devine's closest contact in the system, Stanky, was gone. None of this made problems, but it also meant a less cemented unity than baseball organizations often have.

On the field, fan identification with the Mets was weakening too.

Kranepool and Swoboda had been around long enough to be seen as disappointing, not the pure promises they had been. Hunt, the home-grown star, had been traded. None of the older players, like Boyer or Bob Shaw, had their earlier success identified particularly with New York. The younger men like Grote and Harrelson and Jones hadn't exactly set the league afire. And the constant shuffling of players made it hard to latch on to anyone emotionally.

The games themselves were less bizarre, and had less sense of history, than they used to. Part of this was due to simple improvement toward mediocrity. Another element had to do with the inevitable accumulation of events: even in negative statistics, it was inherently impossible to keep producing "firsts" as the number of Met games played inched toward 1,000. The old jokes had long since worn thin—and the promise of upward mobility in 1966 was being shattered in 1967.

All in all, the whole Shea Stadium situation was beginning to feel more and more like a huge treadmill.

The fans themselves had changed, too.

This was the fourth year in Shea Stadium. The Polo Grounds was a dim memory, mentioned chiefly when Marv Throneberry legends were being elaborated. The World's Fair was two years in the past, and the proportion of tourists in the crowd had decreased. Shea Stadium customers now were predominantly suburban, middle-class, running heavily to family groups. The teen-agers and young people who had flocked to the Polo Grounds in 1962 and 1963 had been good-natured rebels; the rebels of 1966 and 1967 had turned their attention to far more serious things than baseball, and the young people at Shea Stadium were very much Establishment: their banners, still clever, still enthusiastic, were now an expression of conformity—to Met tradition—instead of a spontaneous flowering of irrepressible expression. They were stoic about defeat and satisfied by what limited victories the Mets could provide—but it was an acceptance of short rations, not a masochistic glorification of the doomed-to-failure effort. They came more and more from Long Island and Queens and Brooklyn, and less from the inner city. They came more by car than by subway. They came in organized groups, whose presence was duly noted on the electric scoreboard as promised by the promotional department. They were every bit as loyal as the original Met fans—but if they were very young, they hadn't been in on the beginning, and if they had, they were no longer that young. The 14-year-old who had trekked to Harlem was now 21; the college boys of Polo Grounds days now had families; and the younger brothers who had welcomed their "own" team to root for, to escape the tyranny of fathers' and older brothers' reminiscences, were starting to have nephews and sons of their own on whom to inflict Marvelous Marv and Casey Stengel stories.

In fact, the whole subject of fan participation in the Met Mystique had long since become institutionalized.

Banner Day, which could bring out more than 2,000 sign-carriers in an hour-long procession, had become an official club promotion, with prizes for the winners. (A nonwinner, but a sign that went to the heart of American promotional attitudes, was a big bedsheet that read "Bedsheet Manufacturers of America Love the Mets.") There was Camera Day, when the fans could come down to the box fronts to take pictures; Fan Appreciation Day; giveaway days (bats, helmets, etc.); Players' Family Day; Senior Citizens Day; and so forth. Such things were sound, progressive business practice. They certainly served, in total terms, the interest of the fans. But they made official things that had been unplanned, spontaneous, fan-initiated, and that meant a different kind of atmosphere.

All of which was probably just as well, because New York City was different, too. The self-confident, blasé metropolis of the early 1960s no longer existed.

Racial tension, usually concealed in the past, was a daily concern in the press and on governmental levels. Air pollution, traffic, housing, welfare, the war in Viet Nam, crime in the streets were no longer topics for editorial-page readers but in the forefront of awareness for ordinary people. When Mayor Lindsay attended the Yankee–Met exhibition at Shea Stadium in 1966, a crowd of 55,000 booed him unmercifully and chanted "We Want Buckley," the Conservative Party candidate defeated the previous year. Many politicians, from Presidents down, have been booed in American ball parks; what was significant here was the partisanship of a Met crowd against liberalism—an attitude inconceivable in the Polo Grounds years.

Even within the confines of sports interest, New York was an altered, less carefree community. When the Yankees were perennial champions and the football Giants habitual winners, there was a certain charm and gallantry to the ineptness of the Mets. Fans could be amused by the contrast. But now, when there was no contrast, there was nothing to be amused about. One can root for an underdog in the presence of nobility, but one mangy cur in a pack of other mangy curs does not arouse the same kind of empathy. One can feel sorry for the whole pack, of course, but it is harder to keep focused on the plight of any one.

The combination of social unrest and sports losers accelerated another trend. New Yorkers didn't go out as much as they used to. The theater district was, more and more, an area for tourists and expense-account clients, less a cross-section of the city's permanent population. Restaurants (like Toots Shor's and Leone's) were no longer the late-night, after-event hangouts for the sports set: the sports set was hastening home to the suburbs. Television not only provided more "watching" entertainment at home than there used to be, but satiated the desire for "watching," so that when people did go out, it was more often to "do" something (golf, boating, skating, bowling) than to "watch" some more (theater, movies, or sports). The whole fabric of "in" night life had become unraveled for the sports community— and this, in turn, made the ball park experience itself a more isolated one than it used to be.

For the Mets in particular, these trends changed their crowd composition in another way as well. Thanks to Stengel, Shea Stadium, and the famous Mystique, they had become an attractive product for the business firms who bought season boxes. When the Yankees, traditional recipients of this celebrity-seeking business, lost their championship label, the switch to the Mets among these institutional customers became a stampede. Their clients, more and more, wanted to be entertained at Shea Stadium rather than Yankee Stadium. In this, the physical superiority of the new ball park and the superior accommodations in the Diamond Club and other Shea Stadium restaurants played a role, but the main thing was that to the business community—which always lagged behind the feelings of the true fans—the Mets had become most "in" just at the point when the fan behavior that made them "in" was changing to something else.

As the list of subscribers grew, the Charcoal Room on the fourth level at Shea became a nightspot in its own right. After a night game, it became the scene of an impromptu party. When Shea Stadium had first opened, the Mets had hired Jane Jarvis, who had worked at Milwaukee, to play the organ. Jane was, in every respect, a latter-day Gladys Gooding, the lady who had indoctrinated New Yorkers to organ music at sports events during the 1940s and 1950s at Ebbets Field and Madison Square Garden. But in addition to the stadium organ, there was one in the Charcoal Room, at the end of the long bar, and Jane would play that for a while after the game. The sing-alongs would echo far into the night sometimes, and why not? The car was safely parked in the lot outside, there was no other place to go to conveniently, and the trip home eventually would be away from the city, not toward it.

Such a setup helped form a close-knit, family feeling among the most regular Met customers and gave Met officials like Thomson (who made it his business to stick around) a chance to know them and their attitudes. But these were, basically, affluent, conservative, Establishment people—no less Met fans for all that, and no less loyal, but quite different from the kooks who had created the original Mystique.

The new Met population didn't take form just by accident, either, as the original group had. It was the product of hard, purposeful work. In off-season appearances at dinners and other affairs, in ticket-selling plans, in routine publicity and special promotions, the Mets worked tirelessly and effectively. Their players were encouraged to mingle, and many made Long Island their home. By and large, the players were highly cooperative in this respect, partly because of their own relatively humble positions and partly because the club had a high proportion of fine people among its players. It had long been Weiss's policy to scout "character" as well as ability. There were those who sneered that by "character" Weiss meant "conformity" and docility, and that it was presumptuous of Weiss to concern himself with such judgments about ball players; but that was one of the least legitimate criticisms of Weiss, and the policy did pay dividends. Devine, in his way, maintained it.

What all this amounted to, in 1967, was that the Mets had become a deeply rooted Long Island entity, less interesting nationally than they had been in the Stengel Era but more firmly planted in a consistently prosperous situation.

Provided, of course, that the fans stayed loyal.

And their loyalty was being tested by the accumulated negative statistics, once considered so cute. Fans did not, by and large, keep track of such things the way Jack Lang did in his notebooks, but they were aware—and not only subliminally—of the residue of the events that produced the statistics.

They knew the meaning, if not the smallest details, of the record of the first five years:

547 defeats.

2–17 against Koufax, with a 1.44 earned-run average.

3–19 against Drysdale, with a 2.12 earned-run average.

0–17 against Marichal, with a 1.17 earned-run average.

0–15 against Larry Jackson.

2–15 against Bob Gibson.

2–12 against Bunning.

They knew that they had lived through losing streaks of five games or more 35 times—and had enjoyed a grand total of two five-game winning streaks and the record-breaking seven-gamer in 1966.

They knew that 101 separate times, a Met winning streak had ended at one—and that a losing streak had been checked at one only 51 times.

They knew, finally, what the players had always known: losing is no fun. And there they were, late in 1967, losing as much as ever.

But as they groped for swatches of silver lining among the thickening clouds of the 1967 season, neither fans, management, nor players had the slightest inkling of what diverse, unrelated forces were already conspiring to lead them to glory.

10 Relapse

IN every respect, 1967 was the year in which the Mets got least attention.

On a national scale, they were no longer news. Having escaped the cellar, there was no longer anything special about them. The joke was used up.

Locally, the Mets suffered proportionately more than other teams from the disaster that cut New York City's daily papers to three. *The Herald Tribune, Journal-American,* and *World-Telegram and Sun* had tried to merge, setting off a prolonged labor dispute that closed all three papers without opening the new one. Finally, the *World Journal Tribune* came into existence —and in May 1967 died. The *Herald Tribune* had been the morning rival of the *Times,* more feature-oriented and therefore more involved with the Mets; the other two had been afternoon papers, the only two full-sized afternoon papers in the city, since the *Post* was a tabloid. They, too, had been major outlets for Met news. Now a city of 8,000,000 people had only the *Times,* the *News,* and the *Post,* which meant not only a cut by more than 50 percent of sports page space available, but an appalling decrease in diversity. Such nationally celebrated sports columnists as Red Smith and Jimmy Cannon suddenly had no New York outlet. The suburban papers on Long Island and in New Jersey, which had always done well by the Mets anyhow, did not enter the city proper in enough numbers to make a difference. The main nutrient of baseball interest, daily newspaper stories, was drastically curtailed.

Within the sports scene, the Mets were also being pushed into the background by comparison.

The Yankees, having touched bottom, still had a major newsmaker on hand: Mickey Mantle. They switched him to first base, which occupied the minds of baseball fans all spring, and Mickey was starting the season four home runs shy of a career total of 500, a marvelously glamorous round number. It was mid-May before Mantle hit it, and the event was milked thoroughly before and after. (In fact, he had a remarkably good year and hit 22 homers altogether, playing more games than he had in several seasons.)

This didn't help the Yankees finish any higher than ninth, but it did keep them in the forefront of conversation. There was also the final retirement of Whitey Ford, in May, and the trading of Elston Howard to Boston in early August, major events of tremendous emotional content to baseball fans; all served to distract writers and readers from Met affairs.

There was, too, a wildly exciting American League pennant race for a change—and a drop in interest in Met opponents. Sandy Koufax had retired, because of his arthritic elbow, and the Dodgers dropped deep into the second division, and for the first time there was no strong feeling attached to their visits to Shea Stadium. And Willie Mays, ill or injured more frequently now, was showing the inescapable scars of time.

The American League race, a four-team affair, included Stanky's White Sox, the Detroit Tigers, the Minnesota Twins and—what was pertinent to the Met psychology—the Boston Red Sox. In 1966, the Red Sox had finished ninth, just like the Mets. In the four years preceding that, they had been ninth, eighth, seventh, and eighth; they had been a tail-ender, although not to the same degree, just as long as the Mets. Although everyone acknowledged that the Red Sox had always possessed a lot of promising talent that somehow never clicked, the fact remained that they had made it from ninth place to pennant contention in one year. The song from *Man of La Mancha,* the rather ambiguous "Impossible Dream," became associated with the drive of the Red Sox.

Met fans could not refrain from asking: if them, why not us?

And, along with Mantle and the Red Sox, the limited newspaper space was being contested by a full-scale effort to sell professional soccer (through television); a certain amount of resurgence by the Knicks and Rangers; and the growing interest in the Jets.

Mike Burke, the mod C.B.S. executive, had taken full charge of the Yankees and automatically eclipsed Devine as a personality—and Grant and Mrs. Payson as an entry, for that matter. Among the town's managers and coaches—Houk, Allie Sherman, Weeb Ewbank, Emile Francis, even Dick McGuire—Westrum was the least glamorous.

All in all, the Mets had become a concern for Met fans only, with little outside attention paid to their activities.

Yet, for the insiders, there were high spots as well as disappointments during 1967.

The highest spot was Seaver. In personality, as well as in pitching ability, he had "winner" written all over him. He was articulate, enthusiastic, fun-loving but an instinctive leader. He liked to hit, run bases, and field as well as pitch. And no public relations genius could have manufactured as perfect a hero image for suburbia as this handsome, bright, white-middle-class youngster with the pretty, lively blonde wife named Nancy.

It was Seaver who made the first assault on negative statistics.

His first start had led to a Met victory, even though it wasn't his. His second start was also a winning game, although he needed help. His third start resulted in his first complete game victory, and it displayed some of his qualities.

It was April 25, a windy day at Wrigley Field in Chicago, with the field still soggy from the melted snow of only two days before. Seaver took a 1–0 lead into the ninth inning and walked a man. A sacrifice moved him up, but Seaver got the second out. Then he made Ron Santo bounce to Harrelson—and Harrelson let the ball kick off his glove, so that instead of having a victory Seaver was involved in a tie game. But he got the third out, led off the 10th with a single to right, moved around on a sacrifice and a wild pitch, and scored when Luplow lined a hit to right center with two out. Then he got the Cubs out again and walked off with a 2–1 decision.

The next time he started, on April 30 in Cincinnati, he suffered his first defeat. Gary Nolan outpitched him, 3–2, in the second game of a double-header. Then he beat Houston, 3–2; was knocked out early but not the loser in a game against the Cardinals; was beaten in Atlanta, 4–3, by Joe Torre's ninth-inning homer; polished off the Dodgers, 5–2; pitched six strong innings but didn't get the victory in a winning game against Atlanta; lost at Houston, to Mike Cuellar, whom he would face in far more dramatic circumstances at a later date; pitched the first six innings of a game the Mets won in 10 innings, 1–0, at Pittsburgh; beat Cincinnati 7–3; lost to Chicago, 4–3; and beat Atlanta, 9–1.

It was now close to all-star time. Seaver's record was 6–4, his earned-run average 2.60. A Met had to be picked for the All-Star team, and the managers around the league had seen him, and to see him was to be convinced. He was chosen for the National League squad for the game to be played in Anaheim, California, in the new stadium of the Angels. Since the team also contained Marichal, Gibson, Drysdale, Osteen, Ferguson Jenkins of the Cubs,

Chris Short of the Phillies, and Cuellar, Seaver didn't really expect to pitch, but it was nice to have the honor and to be able to enjoy it so close to home.

In early July, Seaver beat the Giants and Braves with complete games, so his record was 8–5 when the All-Star Game took place on July 11. It took an unexpected turn. For the sake of national television, it started at 4 P.M. California time, which would make it 7 P.M. and prime time back east. That meant twilight and terrible visibility for the hitters. Also, the plate umpire was Ed Runge, of the American League, a man notorious for calling a "large" strike zone. Under those conditions, the best batters in baseball played a 15-inning 2–1 game in which 30 batters struck out.

Tony Perez, of Cincinnati, hit the home run that gave the National League the lead in the 15th. Manager Walter Alston asked Seaver to protect it— the most responsible assignment ever given a Met. He made Tony Conigliaro fly out, walked Carl Yastrzemski, made Bill Freehan fly out, and struck out Ken Berry to end the game.

Whatever else was happening, it seemed the Met fans had a real one to root for at last.

Seaver started the second half of the season an instant celebrity, beyond the confines of Met activities—and promptly got whipped in Cincinnati, 6–1, getting knocked out in the fifth. He floundered for about a month, and his record became 10–8. But on August 9 he beat Atlanta, 6–1, and next he shut out Pittsburgh.

He now needed only one more victory to tie the Met record of 13, set by Jackson in 1963. Even with the ninth-place finish in 1966, no other Met pitcher had won more than 11. Seaver was about to become the best pitcher in the history of the club—while still a rookie.

The first time he tried for No. 13, he lasted only two innings against Pittsburgh. The next, he pitched nine innings but lost to Philadelphia's Rick Wise, 2–0. The next, he lost to Chicago, 3–1.

Maybe he was going to be an old-fashioned Met after all.

On August 31, he pitched nine innings, allowing six hits, at Chicago—but he left the game with the score 1–1, and Taylor lost it in the 11th.

("Oh my, that was awful," sighed Westrum.)

On September 4 in Cincinnati, Seaver gave up two runs in the first inning and went on to lose the game, 2–1. He had now made five tries, over a three-week period, for No. 13 and all that had happened was that his season record had come down to 12–12.

Finally, on September 8, he made it. The Mets got him four runs early, and he had to be rescued by Taylor in the eighth after a home run by Perez, but he did win it, 5–4.

On September 13, he fired a four-hitter at Atlanta, won 2–1, and was officially the winningest Met pitcher of all time.

On September 17, he polished off the Dodgers, 7–2, for No. 15.

On September 21 he had a new manager.

Salty Parker.

Westrum, as noted, could see what was coming and was reaching the breaking point in personal strain. Aside from Seaver, precious little was happening that was positive. Harrelson had proved to be a fine fielder at short; Swoboda had done well as the right fielder, hitting .281 and 13 homers; Tommy Davis, bad ankle and all, had performed as advertised, with a .302 average and 16 homers, the club high. But the team had only 57 victories with 11 games to play, and ninth-place Houston—coming in for a four-game series—was five and a half games ahead. Matching the 1966 record was still a mathematical possibility, but Westrum was realistic enough to shrug that aside. He knew the finish would be 10th place again, and that attendance would be a few hundred thousand off—and he knew what baseball's verdict was in such situations: fire the manager. He knew it without any particular bitterness, just as a wartime spy who gets caught behind the lines out of uniform knows he will be executed; it's just part of the game.

So Wes decided not to wait to be told. He walked into Shea Stadium on an off day, when the team was to hold a practice, and resigned. Just like that.

Devine and Grant, who could not be described as shocked, were decently saddened and appointed Parker to finish the season. They could now concentrate openly on finding a new manager for the Mets, someone who would be "right" for the Youth Program the way Stengel had been right for the original program. It would take some thought.

Meanwhile, under Parker, the Mets split the four games with Houston, one of which was a 1–0 victory for Seaver, his 16th. That finished the home season, with the attendance at 1,565,492—a drop of about 370,000, some small part of which could be attributed to abnormally bad weather.

Then Parker took "his" team to California for the last seven games, of which five were lost. He had with him a new "coach" in uniform—Johnny Murphy, who decided to suit up to get a firsthand look at some of the new talent.

When the final returns were in, some records had been set.

The most notable belonged to Devine. The Mets had used 54 players during the championship season, the most ever employed by a major league team. They had used 27 pitchers, setting a National League record and equalling the American League mark.

Seaver had set four club standards: 16 victories, 18 complete games, 170 strikeouts, a 2.76 earned-run average (which ranked 10th in the league). He was also named National League Rookie of the Year. Since the team's final record was 61–101, Seaver had accounted for more than one-fourth of the team's victories.

Tommy Davis had set Met records with his 174 hits and 32 doubles.

But the other accomplishments were few and far between.

A notable one occurred, appropriately, on July 4, Independence Day. The Mets finally won a game from Marichal. They knocked him out in the sixth, building an 8–3 lead, then managed to choke off a four-run rally by the Giants in the eighth, using three pitchers to bail out Fisher for an 8–7 decision.

On August 14, in Philadelphia, they caught up with Larry Jackson, too, and beat him for the first time, 8–3. Fisher won that one all by himself.

No longer was there a National League pitcher, active as long as the Mets, who had never been beaten by them. And it had taken only six years. Whew!

There was a happy interlude provided by Hal Reniff, the discarded Yankee. A relief specialist, he had contributed to Yankee pennants but was repeatedly in trouble for carrying a few extra pounds, saying a few extra words, getting in a few minutes too late, and walking a few batters too many in crucial situations. He had been one of Houk's pet projects in the early 1960s, and there had been a tendency to blame Yogi's handling for arm trouble Reniff had in 1964. At any rate, on June 29, Houk sold him to the Mets, after he had allowed 19 earned runs in 40 innings of relief pitching for the Yankees.

He came crosstown with considerable incentive. In his first Met appearance, July 1, he blanked the Cardinals on one hit for three innings and got credit for a 6–4 victory. The next day, as the seventh Met pitcher in the game, he went into a tie game in the ninth, with two out and Cardinals on first and second, to face Mike Shannon. He wild-pitched the runners to second and third—then got a called third strike past Shannon. When the Mets scored in their turn at bat (Harrelson singled, stole second, continued to third on John Romano's overthrow, and scored on a wild pitch), the cocky Reniff had two victories in two days.

In his next appearance, he saved the victory over Marichal in melodramatic fashion. He came in with a one-run lead, two on, nobody out, and Mays coming to bat—and got Willie to bounce into a double play. He made Jim Hart ground out too, ending the game.

On July 9, he picked up his third victory, pitching the last two innings against the Braves and getting the benefit of a two-out, two-run rally by the Mets in the ninth, in a game in which Westrum was simultaneously second-guessed and lionized.

Losing 4–3, Westrum let Grote, hitting .206, bat for himself. Grote struck out. Now Westrum had Jones bat for Reniff, and Cleon bounced out. Now down to the last out, Westrum removed Harrelson, who had made four hits in this game, in favor of Buchek—a right-handed batter with power (which Harrelson didn't have) to face the left-handed pitcher, Dick Kelley.

Whereupon Buchek hit the ball over the right field fence—the opposite field—to tie up the game. Kelley then walked Reynolds and was replaced by Claude Raymond, who was greeted by a looping single to right by Davis. This put Reynolds on third with the winning run, so Kranepool was purposely passed to get at Swoboda—who also walked, forcing in the winning run.

It was the sort of thing that used to happen to Stengel a lot but to Westrum all too rarely. In fact, Buchek's was the only pinch homer the Mets hit all year.

Reniff's hot streak lasted almost a month, but in the end he returned to ineffectiveness. He finished up 3–3, with an appalling 3.35 earned-run average for a relief pitcher. He was released as soon as the season ended.

With Reniff, Linz, and Terry in Met uniforms at various times, not to mention Berra, people were making jokes about this becoming an Old Yankees home. But the real significance was that the three ex-Yankees were each, in their way, entertaining characters, and that was the hallmark of the 1967 Mets—minor characters.

Reniff was the butt of endless jokes about his natural portliness. ("Hey Hal," Mantle had called to him once when a baby elephant paraded around Comiskey Park in a pregame promotion, "there's your kid brother.") Linz had earned enduring fame from his run-in with Yogi, during the 1964 Yankee pennant drive, about playing a harmonica on the team bus after a tough defeat. Terry, whose career had taken him to great heights and great depths, was as carefree a soul as the other two. His biggest moment had come in the seventh game of the 1962 World Series, when he was leading San Francisco 1–0 in the last of the ninth, with men on second and third and two out and Willie McCovey coming to bat. Orlando Cepeda would have been the next hitter.

"Whaddayathink," Houk had said to Terry at the mound conference, "you wanna walk him or pitch to him?"

"I'd just as soon get it over with now," Terry had replied. And everyone remembered how McCovey's blistering line drive went right at Bobby Richardson for the final out.

Terry was also an outstanding golfer and became a club pro when he left the Mets.

Linz, though, was the most interesting. He was a cheerful and sweet-natured bachelor, but, much more to the point, he was coproprietor of an East Side restaurant-bar called "Mr. Laff's," that was in the mainstream of the new type of young-folks hangout. It was usually jammed with what were called "young executives" and large numbers of airline hostesses and girls who looked like airline hostesses. Ball players liked to drop in there, especially between seasons, and Phil was a polished host. It was this generation's equivalent of having Toots Shor for a teammate, and Linz enjoyed a special respect.

Less flashy, but immensely popular with teammates and the many fans who got to know him, was Fisher. He and Kranepool, who was studying to be a stock broker, were the "labor experts" on the club, active in player-representative affairs.

Charles, when he joined the club, turned out to be an admirable gentleman who wrote poetry to express his philosophy of life. Younger players looked up to him.

Swoboda fascinated people. His muscular frame and lumbering stride gave him a muscleman image, but his mind, tastes, and comments ran to surprisingly intellectual interests. He had fluctuating moods, and he showed them all. At times, he looked like the next superstar; at other times, it seemed he would never make it as a major leaguer. Each winter, he would speak sincerely about how he had finally matured; each summer, he displayed the same old symptoms of immaturity.

Harrelson appealed to the imagination too. He was so small, so skinny—yet he could fire the ball across the diamond with remarkable speed. He committed 21 errors in the first month of the season—more than all but two other shortstops in the league made in the whole season. But he made only 11 after that, and in late August he was hitting .270. He tailed off and finished at .254, and that was attributed to "fatigue," but he had shown that he could be an effective offensive player as a switch hitter, even though his only home run was an inside-the-park drive in Pittsburgh.

Selma was a major character, not a minor one. He was uninhibited in speech, a creature of impulse, and capable of having an operation performed on his pitching shoulder without telling the club anything about it. He came from the same high school in Fresno that Seaver did and was his contemporary, but it was hard to imagine two more different personalities than the undisciplined, unintellectual Selma and the well-ordered, life-planning Seaver. It was Selma's cocky brashness (and fast ball) that so impressed Stengel in the rookie camp of 1964; but it was Selma's lack of self-control that kept him from improving as much as he might have.

Then there was McGraw, an amateur barber, a dog lover, another outspoken free spirit who was having trouble living up to his first promise. Both McGraw and Selma had dazzled the Mets late in 1965, shortly after Stengel left. On August 25 that year, McGraw had become the first Met pitcher to beat Sandy Koufax, 5–2 at Shea Stadium, and that made him a celebrity (and a favorite of Westrum's) even though seven of his other eight decisions were defeats that year. But in 1966 he had elbow trouble and a 2–9 record, and he spent most of 1967 at Jacksonville. As for Selma, he had made his major league debut just a week after McGraw's conquest of Koufax and had beaten the Cardinals, 6–3. In his second start and first Shea Stadium appearance, on September 12, he beat Milwaukee in 10 innings, 1–0, striking out 13 for a Met record that still stood. But he won only four games in 1966 and two in 1967, although he spent most of each season with the Mets.

There were, therefore, plenty of personalities for the Met fans to be interested in. And in September, when it was possible to call up the minor leaguers, some tantalizing new talents appeared. Koosman, having struck out 183 batters in 178 innings at Jacksonville, got into nine Met games—and was clipped for 15 earned runs in 22 innings as he walked 19 men. He was charged with two defeats. McGraw, having led the International League with a 1.99 earned-run average, came back as a "matured" pitcher—and made four starts, took three defeats and a no decision, and yielded 15 earned runs in 17 innings pitched. Boswell got into 11 games, and Amos Otis, a promising 20-year-old drafted out of the Red Sox organization, got into 19. They didn't hit for average, but they showed some ability. Bob Heise, an infielder brought up from Durham (two steps below the majors), hit .323 in 16 games and struck out only once in 62 at bats.

Bosch came back, and didn't look a bit different.

As September wore on, however, everyone's eyes turned more and more toward the American League race and in particular the drama of the Red Sox. They were hanging on to first place, right down to the wire, and much credit was being given to their rookie manager, Dick Williams—remembered by Brooklynites as a substitute on some of the outstanding Dodger teams of the 1950s and a widely traveled player after that.

The Red Sox won their pennant, beating Minnesota hand-to-hand on the last two days. The jump from ninth to first had been made, and a dynamic manager was obviously an important factor. In the National League, Durocher's Cubs had finished a strong third, having risen seven notches in the standings in one year. This seemed to teach the same lesson.

Choosing a new Met manager, the lesson seemed to say, might be the most important step taken yet—if the right manager could be found.

One .choice was such a natural that everyone talked about it openly: Gil Hodges.

Hodges had taken over the Senators in May 1963 when they were in their third season. They had finished tied for last and solo last in their first two seasons, and they finished 10th again in their first year under Gil. But in 1964 they had moved up to ninth, and the next two years they had been eighth, finishing ahead of both the Yankees and Red Sox in 1966. Now, in 1967, with a general level of talent considered to be no different from other expansion clubs, the Senators had finished tied for sixth—tied with, no less, the Baltimore Orioles, who had won the pennant and World Series the year before.

With a record like that, Hodges had proved that he had some sort of knack in handling and improving expansion-type teams, and that was exactly the problem to be solved in Shea Stadium.

Sentimentally, Hodges was just as perfect a choice for the Mets as he had been when taken as an original Met player. No Dodger had been more sincerely loved, and no Dodger had joined the Brooklyn community so thoroughly. Even as Washington's manager, Gil continued to live in Brooklyn, to operate businesses there (a bowling alley, an automobile agency), and to mingle quietly with neighbors and friends. His wife Joan, a native Brooklynite, had deep roots there and so did the four Hodges children. So a move to New York would be of great practical attractiveness to Hodges, too.

There was was only one difficulty.

Hodges belonged to the Senators.

Managers, like players, are supposed to be the property of the club that signs them, and Hodges had a long-term contract with the Senators, who appreciated him as fully as the Mets.

To even talk to Hodges—who would probably be very receptive to the opportunity to move back home—the Mets needed permission from the Senators. And the Senators were reluctant to give it for two good reasons: they knew how good Hodges was, and they were afraid of the reactions of their fans if they let him get away.

On the other hand, there was one reason for letting him go, and it was stronger than the reasons for keeping him: Hodges wanted to go. Not that he wouldn't stay and carry on in Washington as conscientiously as ever; he was a man of unshakable personal integrity, and everyone knew it. Yet, the meaning to him of being able to work in New York could not be ignored, and where his heart's desire lay was plain enough.

Devine was a man whose scruples were as famous, and as solid, as Gil's. To him, an approach to Hodges would be unthinkable unless the Senators okayed it first. In short, an indirect and informal approach to Washington officials had to be the first step.

Well, there was a perfect way to take it.

The general manager of the Washington Senators was George Selkirk.

The vice-president of the Mets was John Murphy.

Selkirk had been a regular Yankee outfielder on the great teams of the 1930s.

Murphy had been the relief pitcher extraordinary of the great Yankee teams of the 1930s.

In fact, for a time Selkirk and Murphy had been roommates.

They could talk.

They did.

Selkirk was troubled, but he couldn't really stand in Hodges's way. The World Series began in Boston and, as usual, constituted an annual convention of baseball people, a clearing house for job changes and trades, a true industry-wide convocation. There were plenty of chances for two old friends to go up to a hotel room and discuss things.

After the second game, the Series moved to St. Louis. There conversations reached the point that Devine and Grant could become involved.

On the day of the fifth game of the World Series, Shirley Povich, the *Washington Post* columnist, broke the story: Hodges was going to the Mets. He referred to the conversations with Selkirk as "asking a man permission to steal his wife."

Cynics promptly pointed out that in a surprising number of cases, such permission might be granted.

In this case, it was. On October 10, when everyone was back in Boston on the off-day preceding the sixth game, the details were settled. The Mets would "buy" Hodges from the Senators for a nice sum (reported as $50,000) and a player, the right-handed pitcher Denehy, whose 1967 record had been 1–7. Hodges would receive a three-year $60,000 contract.

The next morning, the announcement was made in a hotel room in Boston, with Hodges present.

He would bring with him his coaching staff from Washington: Rube Walker, his old Dodger teammate, as pitching coach; Eddie Yost, the New York University alumnus who had spent 15 of his 19 playing years with the original Washington Senators, as third-base coach; and Joe Pignatano, not only a former Dodger (8 games in Brooklyn before the move west) but a former Met (remember, he hit into the triple play at the end of the 1962 season? That was his last time up in the majors). Piggy would work in the bull pen and, as a native of Brooklyn, had long been a family friend of Gil's.

And Yogi would remain as first-base coach.

To Met fans, this new leadership was accepted immediately as a wonderful thing. Gil seemed like the right man in every respect.

To Devine, again, there were slight, but not imperceptible, reservations.

Hodges was, in Devine's opinion, a fine manager, and the right man for the right spot—but he was not a choice initiated by Devine. For a club president, such a situation is not totally comfortable. In this case, Grant, representing the directors, had taken the lead. Devine certainly had no objections, but it was one more instance of the less-than-perfect closeness that existed at the highest Met levels.

It may not have made any difference, but something else was brewing that made a great deal of difference. The St. Louis job was opening up again.

The Cardinals had gone through some strange experiences since Devine had been forced out in August 1964. The general manager who succeeded him was Bob Howsam, and when Keane quit, Red Schoendienst had been made manager. Howsam promptly tore apart the club Devine had put together, and not without reason, since the Cardinals who won the 1964 pennant and World Series had several aging key men—Boyer, Dick Groat, Bill White, Curt Simmons. In the long run, Howsam's rebuilding ideas proved sound enough, but in 1965 the Cards had finished seventh and in 1966 sixth. In January 1967, Howsam left to take a general manager's post with the Cincinnati Reds, and Gussie Busch, the owner of the Cardinals, appointed Stan Musial as general manager. Musial, since his retirement in 1963, had been serving the Cardinals in a loosely defined vice-presidential capacity and had been working for President Johnson in a national fitness program.

Musial's success as a general manager was as spectacular as his playing success. He persuaded Roger Maris, obtained in a trade with the Yankees (for our old friend, Charlie Smith), not to retire. His manager, Shoendienst, was his old roommate and closest friend, and never had there been more front-office harmony. The Cardinals took command in mid-June, fought off the Cubs in July, ran away in August, and won the pennant by 10½ games. In the World Series, they had to go seven games, but they did beat the inspired Red Sox. They were World Champions again and Musial, as executive, was one-for-one.

But Stan the Man wasn't really an office type, and during the summer he had lost an important friend. His partner in the restaurant they ran in St. Louis (Stan and Biggie's) died. Stan decided his other activities needed more time (he also owned a hotel in Miami Beach). He would quit a winner as general manager.

And the door was open wide for Devine.

All the same emotional forces that pulled Hodges to Brooklyn pulled Devine back to St. Louis. That was his town, his tempo, his people. The fact that the Mets would have new leadership, and that Grant had been so active in arranging it, made it easier for Devine to leave New York. On December 5, the official announcement was made.

Before that, though, Devine had been busy on behalf of the Mets. In addition to all the extensive, necessary juggling of players from minor league lists to the Mets and vice versa, Devine traded Bob Johnson, who had hit .348 as a utility infielder and pinch hitter, to Cincinnati for Art Shamsky, a young left-handed home-run slugger who had never been able to win a regular job with the Reds. And, although it was not completed until after he left for St. Louis, Devine set in motion a major trade with the Chicago White Sox (at the urging of Hodges, who knew the players involved so well). The Mets received Tommy Agee, rookie-of-the-year centerfielder in 1966 but a disappointment in 1967, and Al Weis, a utility infielder recovering from a knee operation (needed after a crash at second base with Frank Robinson of the Orioles, a crash which affected Robinson's vision for a year). They sent to the White Sox Tommy Davis, Fisher, and Billy Wynne, a right-handed pitcher.

It now remained to choose a successor to Devine, and the Board decided it had one right under its nose: Murphy. On December 27, the 59-year-old Murphy was made vice-president and general manager, and the title of president was handed, with great sentiment, to Mrs. Payson.

In this fashion, forces far removed from Flushing were shaping the destiny of the Mets. The Red Sox had provided an example the fans wouldn't forget. The front-office change was the result of decisions made in St. Louis, since Devine would not have been asked to leave. The availability of Hodges, which might have been resisted more, turned out to be related, however indirectly, to a determination by the Washington owners to sell the club.

And, really way out in left field, there was a storm brewing in the American League about Charley Finley's desire to move his Kansas City Athletics to Oakland, California. When he was given permission to do this on October 18, 1967—only a week after Hodges took the Met job—a chain of complex events was set in motion. It would lead, within two years, to another expansion of the majors and to the institution of six-team divisions in each league. It would be in that context that the Mets would eventually triumph, and it is very doubtful that they could have as soon as they did if that had not happened.

But few fans suspected, as they wallowed in the possibilities suggested by the Hodges announcement, that all baseball would be hardly recognizable within two years.

ACT III—HODGES

11 A New Outlook

THE first pitch thrown to the Mets in the first inning of the first exhibition game of spring training in 1968 was a fast ball by Bob Gibson.

It hit Tommy Agee smack on the head.

Agee was wearing a helmet, but he was stunned anyhow and suffered a slight concussion.

That pitch affected Met fortunes for two years.

Agee figured very prominently in Hodges' plans. He would be the center field answer that Bosch was supposed to be but wasn't. Agee could run, could cover all the necessary ground, catch the ball and throw. But he was also, unlike Bosch, expected to hit. In his first full major league season, he had hit 22 homers, knocked in 86 runs, batted .273 for the White Sox. The second year he had slumped badly, but Hodges had seen what he could do the first year and was willing to write off the second. After all, if the second had been like the first, Agee would never have been available.

There was another plus. Agee and Cleon Jones were lifelong friends and neighbors, high school teammates. Both were on the shy side and had their difficulties in adjusting to aspects of major league life that involved loneliness and loss of confidence. Together now, they should be able to help each other blossom. With Agee in center and Jones in left, the Mets could be set at two positions. And if Shamsky and Swoboda could be a lefty-righty platoon in right field, the Mets should have the best outfield they had ever been able to put on the field on a daily basis.

For the most part, of course, Hodges had to depend on the word of Murphy, Berra, Scheffing, and others who had watched the Mets daily for several years. He had no first-hand experience with most of their players, having spent five years in the American League. Most of spring training, and much of the early part of the season, would have to be devoted to forming his own judgments.

Harrelson, they assured him, was a fine regular shortstop. Kranepool, who often irritated people with his apparent indolence and sour viewpoints (but who was really simply the victim of having been around too long from too young an age), had established a certain consistency: for three seasons, he had hit between .253 and .269, had knocked in between 50 and 60 runs, and had hit 10 homers a year (and 16 in 1966). The first-base job was his to keep or lose.

Second and third were open positions, although Boswell had earned a look, and the catching seemed set on a platoon basis between Grote, who could catch and throw but whose lifetime average was an unacceptable .204, and Martin, a left-handed hitter whose bat had a little more to offer, and who could also play first base.

Mainly, though, the pitchers were exciting. There was Seaver, of course. Cardwell, Hendley, Koonce, and Taylor had shown useful qualities in 1967. And then there were the young ones to be straightened out: Koosman, Ryan, McGraw, Selma, Don Shaw, Renko, Rohr, Danny Frisella. It was hard to believe that with their arms, and various minor league performances, they wouldn't produce something among them. And there were also two older left-handers around: Jackson, the original Met (and still the leader in lifetime victories as a Met), back from the Cardinals in payment for Lamabe; and Billy Short, a promising Yankee almost a decade before, sidetracked by arm problems then and, after kicking around in major and minors, bought by the Mets from Columbus during the winter.

Hodges also had, to look at, three players who had been cut from the roster to make room for the young ones who had to be protected: Charles, Linz, and Reniff. They were invited to camp to win jobs if they could. Charles and Linz did; Reniff didn't.

The camp had a different atmosphere than previous Met camps. Stengel, as a visitor, had always outshone Westrum, even though Casey was scrupulous not to interfere; but he didn't outshine Hodges. Gil was among friends:

Young and Lang, in particular, had grown up with him in the Ebbets Field days, and there was now a definite "Old Dodger" axis that included Walker.

Furthermore, Hodges was working with his own coaching staff to a degree that no previous Met manager enjoyed. Even under Stengel, the coaches had been chosen by the front office, not by him, and no matter how much willingness there might have been, there was seldom full, automatic rapport. Now, all the coaches—and Yogi blended in beautifully—were of the same mind as the manager about how things should be done and about what instructions should be given, not merely as loyal employees but, through habit and experience, as men who thought for themselves on the same wavelength. They complemented Hodges more smoothly than the coaches of Stengel or Westrum ever had. This was part of Hodges's success in Washington, and it was a particularly effective way to run a young, limited-talent, building club.

Hodges himself was a different experience for the Met players who had been around, like Jones, Swoboda, and Kranepool. He was, they learned, an old-fashioned father figure with up-to-date mannerisms. His physical strength, and huge hands, always made an awesome impression. But he spoke very softly and not very often directly to players. He made very clear what the rules were—about behavior, attitude, performances expected, and individual responsibilities—and then demanded, ironlike but without fuss, that the rules be lived up to. He communicated by action much more than by words: if you didn't do it right, you didn't play, and it didn't matter what your name, record, or past affiliations were. When a reprimand had to be articulated, it was done quietly, without causing embarrassment—but with no possible misunderstanding of the manager's intent. When things were done right, attention was called to them by citing them as examples of things to be repeated.

In terms of instruction, Hodges hammered away at basics: learn how each play is supposed to be made, concentrate all the time, don't keep making the same mistake after it's been called to your attention, be ready to give your best effort every day.

Yet, with all this velvet-glove severity, Hodges was a pleasant man who appreciated the fact that life must be fun. His own sense of humor, surprisingly subtle in a man of his physique, ran to deadpan put-ons: his fencing with the press was a daily game. He could utter the most outrageous clichés, and slip in the wildest improbability, without changing expression, and many a newcomer was thrown off stride by this performance. But Hodges was also sensitive enough not to let it go too far, not to embarrass the visitor. His face would break up into the network of creases that formed his smile, and he would say seriously that he had nothing to say.

For he knew exactly what he wanted to reveal and exactly what he considered his own business, and without ever becoming impolite he was absolutely immovable about that boundary. Whatever he told you could be relied upon; if it contained a hidden meaning or an escape clause, it was up to you to find it. It was not his obligation to spell out every implication of everything he said, but he was dedicated to the literal truth of whatever he told you. In this, his behavior with interviewers reflected his behavior with players: he was not "affable," nor would he go out of his way to put into words anything and everything that might come to mind; but he was absolutely straightforward in his intentions and requirements: when he said it, he meant it.

Not all players respond automatically to a man like this, but more do than don't, and almost all, sooner or later, respond to the reciprocity of Gil's method: when they do things right, they are rewarded by displays of confidence that build their own confidence in turn. And nothing is more important to a baseball player's success than self-confidence.

To top it off, it was painfully clear that Hodges and top management were as one, that there was no higher court of opinion to appeal to above the manager. It had been that way at first with Stengel, but it didn't matter because the talent was either nonexistent or at career end. Later, Stengel's authority was undermined by the sheer weight of second-guessing and the rumors that he might retire, or be asked to, at any time. Westrum never escaped the lack of authority that goes with being, too obviously, not the first choice. But Hodges, everyone knew, had been the object of a very definite pursuit by the Met ownership, and no one could doubt how high he stood in management's esteem.

And Hodges was, in his quiet way, a positive thinker too. He didn't use the slogans and corny placards that Westrum had, but the substance of his message was the same: you have to think you can win, and sacrifice comfort and be single-minded about it, before you can. Under Stengel, defeat had been a way of life—against Stengel's will too, of course, but also, to a degree, acceptable. It may have been necessary promotionally; it may have been inescapable realistically; but it did not promote selfless, "winning" attitudes. Westrum had succeeded in making a beginning to turn toward a better attitude. It had not stood up, because the team he had in his second year was too disorganized, too heavily laden with the end-of-career psychologies (which had, it was true, helped the climb to ninth in 1966), too dependent on too few young players who weren't quite ready. But there had been seeds planted, and Hodges recognized them. It was his job to make them flower.

"I think," he said, when spring training ended with the worst record a Met team had ever compiled (it ended 9–18), "I think we'll win 70 games."

That was certainly positive thinking, since the Met record was 66 and since the previous year's total had been 61.

But the pitch that hit Agee in the head had left Tommy uncertain. He got off to a terrible start, bogged down, had a terrible year, and all sorts of other possibilities failed to materialize because of his failure.

The Mets were scheduled to open on the West Coast in 1968 and finished spring training with four games in Arizona and California. Hodges had arrived at some conclusions.

Among them were:

Seaver was his best pitcher and would open against the Giants in San Francisco.

Ryan was exciting. When he struck out a flock of Cardinals in an exhibition game, the champions universally pronounced him as fast as Koufax and (by reputation) Bob Feller.

Koosman should probably be sent down for more seasoning, but Walker liked him and was working with him, so he stayed.

Cardwell and Jackson would provide experience, but Hendley did not seem to be making it after an elbow operation the previous fall.

Selma could make it, but McGraw belonged back in Jacksonville.

Taylor and Short would be the short relievers, righty and lefty. Frisella, the left-hander who had divided his 1967 season among the Mets, Jacksonville, and the California National Guard, would also stay.

So would Koonce, another experienced right-handed reliever.

So would Rohr, whose potential impressed Hodges.

That made 11 pitchers, and that would be all, since the new rules required that the squad be cut to 25 men by opening day, not 30 days later as in the past.

Two catchers would be enough, Grote and Martin.

Kranepool would be the first baseman, Harrelson the shortstop, but second base would be shared by Boswell, Linz, and Buchek, third by Charles and Buchek, with Weis available at all three positions.

Jones, Agee, Swoboda, Shamsky, and Bosch were the outfielders.

And stashed away at Jacksonville, where they could play regularly to stay sharp but be recalled quickly when military commitments took people off the varsity for weekends and two-week tours of duty, were Don Shaw and Kevin Collins.

That was the team Hodges took to Candlestick Park for an opener that was embroiled in controversy before it came up.

Dr. Martin Luther King had been assassinated in Memphis the week before.

No universal baseball policy had been adopted for playing or not playing on Tuesday, April 9, the day scheduled for the opening of the baseball season but now also the day of the funeral. The Giants, and several other clubs, wanted to play the game. The Met players took a stand against it. The Giants changed their minds. The opener was set back to Wednesday and changed to a day game.

With Marichal pitching for the Giants, Hodges decided to use Shamsky in left instead of Jones, Swoboda in right, Boswell at second, and Martin to catch.

It was a splendid decision. Swoboda singled home Agee in the first inning after Agee had stolen second. The next time around, in the third inning, Boswell and Agee singled, and Swoboda smashed a home run. Seaver had a 4–0 lead.

By the ninth inning, Seaver still had the lead, 4–2, and Marichal was out of the game for an unsuccessful pinch hitter. Seaver needed three more outs to record that long-sought Opening Day victory and, incidentally, New York's second victory over Marichal. These were, indeed, the new Mets.

Er—not quite yet.

In the next few minutes, Hodges saw in the flesh what sadists had been eager to tell him about the Mets in the years he had been away.

Mays lined a single off the glove of Charles at third.

McCovey, who had hit a home run earlier, popped up.

But a passed ball moved Mays to second, a foul tip broke Martin's finger, and Hart's single through the left side scored Mays.

That made it 4–3, and Hodges brought in Frisella to pitch and Grote to catch. The batter was Nate Oliver, recently traded to the Giants by the Dodgers along with Hunt, the one-time Met hero who was now the Giants' second baseman.

Oliver also bounced a single through the third-short hole. The winning run was now at first base.

Jay Alou lined one into the left field corner. Jones, who had replaced Shamsky for defense, couldn't get near it. It was a legitimate double. Hart was coming around with the tying run. Jones retrieved the ball and got it to Harrelson. The shortstop wheeled and threw home—or rather, well past home. Oliver kept coming and scored. The game was over. The Giants had won, 5–4.

Opening Day was still unstained by a Met victory.

Hodges had learned two lessons. One: the Met Mystique was alive and virulent. Two: never be in a hurry to take Seaver out. But all he said was, "we'll win tomorrow."

He was right.

Tomorrow night came, in Los Angeles, and Koosman started against the Dodgers. He pitched a four-hit shutout and the Mets won, 4–0, with Swoboda knocking in another run and Shamsky two.

But when Cardwell pitched a strong game against the Dodgers after an off day, Drysdale beat him, 1–0, on Ron Fairly's homer.

The next stop was Houston, where Ryan and Frisella combined their efforts for a five-hit shutout. The Mets won by a 4–0 score again, with Shamsky driving in two runs and Jones one.

All in all, things hadn't gone too badly in the first four games. Agee had five hits and a .313 average. The outfield had driven in 10 of the 12 runs scored. All four starters, and three out of four relievers, had pitched well. Only the error by Harrelson, a forgivable type of error, had hurt. There was one more game to play in Houston, and then a home debut for Hodges, a return home after nearly two months on the road. It would be nice to come home 3–2, on the plus side.

But that last game in Houston wasn't so easily disposed of.

It started at 7:30 P.M., with Seaver facing Don Wilson, a fast-ball pitcher who had a no-hitter to his credit. It would be hard to score on either man.

In fact, it would be impossible. In nine innings, the Mets made five hits off Wilson, but no runs. In 10 innings, Seaver gave up only two hits, and no runs.

After 12 innings, it was still 0–0. The Mets had used four pitchers and the Astros three. The Mets had filled the bases in the 12th, but Agee had bounced out.

After 15, it was still 0–0. And after 18, and after 20, and after 22.

Well past midnight, the Mets caught and passed their club record by playing and completing the 23rd inning. It was still 0–0.

At about 1:30 A.M., Norm Miller led off the 24th for Houston with a single off Rohr, who had entered the game in the 22nd—some seven hours after he had thrown 20 minutes of batting practice.

As Jim Wynn squared around to bunt, Rohr took his stretch motion—and separated his hands, committing a balk. That moved Miller to second, and Wynn was purposely passed. Rusty Staub moved both runners up with a grounder to Boswell, so John Bateman was also walked intentionally, bringing up Bob Aspromonte.

What the Mets needed, to prolong the game, was a double play. What Rohr made Aspromonte hit was a perfect double-play grounder to the shortstop. What Al Weis did was let the ball go right through him for an error. Houston won, 1–0—the longest 1–0 game ever played.

Weis, making one of the longest speeches of his taciturn career, explained: "I just plain blew it."

And Hodges had one more example of what had been just plain happening to the Mets. His pitchers had just allowed two runs—one homer, one unearned—in the last 50 innings, and he had lost two games out of four.

With these adventures fresh in mind, the Mets appeared at Shea Stadium Wednesday afternoon to face the Giants. The crowd was 52,000 again, and the pitcher was Koosman.

Hunt, the first Giant batter, singled. Jim Davenport bounced to Weis, who booted the ball, his first chance since the last one in Houston. McCovey walked. Bases full, nobody out, Willie Mays up, and a rookie left-hander before a huge home crowd. One could say that the Mets were in a bit of trouble.

But Koosman struck out Mays on four pitches. He made Hart hit a high foul that Grote caught. And he struck out Jack Hiatt. Then he tacked on eight more scoreless innings. Jones hit a homer for him in the second, and the Mets went on to a 3–0 victory.

That gave the 52,000, and all the millions of readers and television viewers, something to buzz about.

It wouldn't have happened that way, they thought, with Jay Hook.

The next day, with Cardwell nursing a 3–2 lead in the seventh, Frisella relieved with the bases full—and Mays hit a three-run double which won the game, 5–3. He was still Willie Mays.

The next day, Ryan struck out 11 Dodgers in less than seven innings, but lost the game, 3–2, to Osteen.

The next day, Seaver beat the Dodgers, 3–2, although Bill Singer struck out 12 Mets.

The next day, the Mets lost a doubleheader to the Dodgers in front of 45,000 people.

The next day Koosman beat Houston, 3–1, allowing just four hits but finally giving up his first run of the season.

Then Seaver and Ryan lost at Cincinnati, 3–1 and 5–3, before Koosman salvaged the third game, 6–5, with help from Frisella, Short, and Taylor in the last two innings. With four straight victories, Koosman had already tied a Met record.

Back home, on April 30, Cardwell defeated Philadelphia, 1–0.

The pattern had been set. These Mets, for the first time, had amazing pitching. All around the league, people were talking about it. But they also had amazingly weak hitting. They had allowed only 41 runs in 16 games—but had scored only 45 themselves.

One reason was Agee. He had gone 0-for-10 in the 24-inning game, and he hadn't made a hit since. He was up to 0-for-33, one short of Zimmer's famous hitless streak of 1962, and the negative statistics purveyors had informed everyone of the fact. His batting average was down to .102. It wasn't his fault that the whole team was hitting .205, but he was certainly center stage.

On Wednesday, May 1, the Mets had their first home night game, against the Phillies. About 11,000 showed up. Seaver started against Larry Jackson. The first time up, Agee went out, equaling Zimmer's record and reducing his average to an even .100.

The next time up he singled—and the crowd gave him a standing ovation: a sincere one, not a derisive one. It was an important moment in Agee's career, in the history of the Mets, and in the context of the Met Mystique. The fans were displaying a kind of sensitivity and loyalty that most players don't receive, and it would lead to enormous dividends.

But not yet. The game went into the ninth with Seaver losing, 2–0. The Mets tied it, but the Phillies scored five in the 11th and won, 7–2.

Then Ryan and Taylor combined on a three-hit shutout, and Selma, in his first start, beat Chicago, 7–3. Koosman was beaten, 3–2, by Ferguson Jenkins and the Cubs, and Cardwell lost another 1–0 game to Chicago's Bill Hands. The Mets went to St. Louis, where Gibson beat Seaver, 2–1, in 11 innings. Ryan, who had made his impression on them in spring training, stopped the Cardinals, 4–1, but the Mets were shut out again the next day, 2–0, by Steve Carlton, wasting a fine effort by Jackson.

And so it went. Fine pitching, a steadying defense in the field, but no offense to take advantage of them. On May 17 against the Braves at Shea, another of Cardwell's good games went down the drain when the Mets finally lost, 3–1, in the 16th inning. Selma won the next day, but on Sunday the Mets lost a doublehcader to the Braves by scores of 3–2 and 2–0.

It was now May 19, and the Met record was 15–20, and they were on the brink of a familiar abyss.

For six years, their campaigns had followed a regular, sorry pattern: defeat at first, a revival during late April and early May to a position within sight of .500, and then a terrible plunge downward to the all-star break. Here were the figures:

Date	Record	Immediately afterward
May 20, 1962	12–19	4–26
May 10, 1963	13–15	12–28
May 15, 1964	9–19	11–31
May 16, 1965	13–17	10–32
May 15, 1966	11–12	6–17
May 15, 1967	10–15	7–20

But now, in May and June of 1968, for the first time the Met graph avoided the next dip. It was a barely perceptible change, but a real turning point in the history of the club. A baseball truism is that fine pitching, in quantity, prevents you from having sustained slumps, because sooner or later you get a shutout or a one-run performance, and you win even if your team is playing badly. Now, with the staff that Hodges and Walker were running, and that Murphy and Devine and their farm assistants had built, it was starting to be true.

For on May 20, against Pittsburgh at Shea, Koosman won again, 2–1, as Charles hit a home run in the fourth and another in the ninth off Bob Veale. The next afternoon, Seaver, Koonce, and Taylor battled through 17 innings to a 4–3 victory. They lost three of the next four but swept a Memorial Day doubleheader in Pittsburgh behind Koosman and Selma. They lost four straight to the Cardinals but bounced back at Chicago as Koosman, Seaver, and Selma won in succession and opened a visit to California with Ryan shutting out the Giants, 4–0, with Koonce's help. The next two games were lost, but in Los Angeles Seaver beat Sutton, 1–0, in 10 innings; Selma beat Osteen, 3–0; and Al Jackson defeated Drysdale, 2–1.

The whole baseball world was fascinated by the Met pitching now. The team's record was 27–29, and it was in eighth place, but the idea of laughing at the Mets was completely dispelled among professionals. The fans, still hoping with their fingers crossed, weren't quite ready to believe a permanent change had taken place; the more casual public clung to its conception of "hapless Mets," oblivious to even the possibility of change. Books and articles were still being ordered, and authored, on the worn-out theme of Met defeatism. But the players who had to face Met pitching, and their managers, and the scouts, and the more alert writers, all knew better. This kind of pitching was no accident, and the men doing it were, for the most part, alarmingly young, and it was the raw material from which baseball victories were built. Sure, a team still had to be built around that pitching, because you can't hope to break even or do better if your pitchers, no matter how good, must always work with a one-run margin; but it was clear that, at last, there was something to build upon. With the kind of pitching staffs the Mets had in their early years, even a daily lineup twice as good as the one they had would have brought them nowhere—out of the cellar, maybe, but not much higher. With this kind of pitching, though, even a modest improvement in the other eight positions might pay surprising dividends.

In one position, the Mets were already doing better. Jerry Grote was hitting .310.

Always a good catcher, with a strong arm that helped keep pitchers from worrying too much about the runner on first, Grote had been a typically stubborn failure as a hitter. He kept trying to pull the ball, to hit it hard enough to reach a fence, as did 90 percent of the players growing up in the home-run era. Finally, they had persuaded him to "go with the pitch"—to cut down on his swing, to hit the outside pitch to right field, to concentrate on making contact and to choose pitches better. He was doing it.

At third, Charles was a revelation. He was hitting .267 and already had nine home runs, having his best season in five years. But, of course, he had no future.

And elsewhere, there were disappointments aplenty. Jones, being platooned with Shamsky, was down at .243, and Shamsky wasn't much higher. Swoboda had nine home runs, but his average was .241. Agee was at an unbelievable .191. The outfield that was supposed to supply punch wasn't supplying it.

Kranepool, at .204, was at his low point as far as management, fans, and probably he himself were concerned. He was sharing first base with Greg Goossen, the third-string catcher, whose hitting was a disappointment in itself, and with Martin, and occasionally Shamsky. Boswell was hitting only .239. And Harrelson was showing Hodges none of the defensive skill Gil had been told about. There was a good reason for this: Harrelson had a bad knee, which destroyed his mobility and which would require an operation. In the meantime, though, it didn't help the situation, and if Weis played instead, the lineup had another bat with a .152 average.

But the pitching—ah, that pitching. Koosman was 9–2, Selma 6–0, Ryan 5–4. Seaver had only four victories, and five defeats, despite a 1.89 earned-run average, and one could be sure that things would start going his way. Cardwell, the other hard-luck starter, was 1–6 with a 2.70 earned-run average, a logic-defying combination of figures. Of the top 23 regular pitchers in the league, five were Mets.

When it came time to choose all-star players, three Mets were picked: Seaver, Koosman, and Grote, and for the first time tokenism was no factor in the selection of Mets.

On June 14, the Mets opened a home stand with Koosman beating the Giants, 7–3. It was his 10th victory, and put the Mets one victory away from the .500 mark. Although they were in eighth place, they were only six games out of first.

Now the negative statisticians had something to play with. It was well and good, as a joke, to fool around with the .500 mark in the first few days of a season. But this was mid-June, with the schedule more than a third complete. No Met team had ever been anywhere near .500 at this stage. If they could reach it now, the symbolic significance would be appreciable. This pursuit of the .500 mark became the dominating theme of the next two weeks.

The first obstacle was Marichal, and it could not be cleared even though the Mets made 16 hits off him. (The first hit was an incredible event: Don Bosch's second home run in two days, which was also the second home run of his entire major league career.) But Seaver was hammered out in the fifth, and Koonce became the loser in the sixth of a 9–5 game. The next day, Selma took his first defeat, 4–1 to Sadecki (as Mays hit a homer), and .500 was three games away.

The Mets won the second game of that doubleheader but then lost a double-header to Houston (although Ryan struck out 12 in a 3–2 loss). But Koosman and Seaver beat the Astros, and Selma stopped the Dodgers, 5–1, and .500 was one step away again.

This time the obstacle was Drysdale, and although he needed some help from Don Sutton, he scored a 5–1 victory.

The Mets won the next day, and moved on to Cincinnati. On Monday night, June 24, they went into the ninth inning losing, 5–2, but tied the score. But they lost in the 11th, 6–5, when Lee May tripled off Short.

Seaver's five-hitter meant a 4–0 decision on Tuesday, and the opportunity was there again on Wednesday. Selma was knocked out in the fifth, and the ninth began with the Mets losing, 7–3. But an error, four singles, and Swoboda's scoring fly made it 7–6, with two men on. However, Jones grounded out, and the opportunity was gone again.

Cardwell, with Taylor's help, opened the Houston series with a 3–1 victory, only his second of the season. But Ryan was beaten, 7–2, and Koosman lost a 2–0 decision to Wilson. Seaver beat Cuellar, 1–0, but then came three straight defeats in Pittsburgh, and the Mets never again got closer than three games below .500.

This little stretch underlined basic weaknesses. Boswell had suffered a broken finger in Cincinnati, leaving Linz as the regular second baseman. Phil had been hitting well on a platoon basis, but he couldn't play full time. During the Houston and Pittsburgh series, the Mets had scored seven runs in six games, and that was the problem in a nutshell.

So a split of four games in Philadelphia brought the Mets to all-star break with a 39–43 record.

It is important to get the feel of these day-by-day events of the first half of the 1968 season to understand fully what happened later. To the outside world, the success that came to the Mets in 1969 was completely sudden, unforeseen, inexplicable, and occult, but this is a degree of romanticizing that distorts what really happened. There was a gradual, if rapid, basic improvement in the Mets, rooted in authentic changes in personnel, group talent, and ways of playing. The Mets of 1968 were a far better baseball team than any previous Met team, mainly because of their large quantity of good pitching, but for other, lesser reasons, too. The Mets of 1969 were stronger still.

That they made a leap all the way to championship status was genuinely unexpected, a sports miracle, a stunning upset, a 100-to-1 shot and all the rest
of it—but it was not a sudden, magical transformation of a terrible team
into a great one. The terrible team had been left behind by the middle of
1968, a condition easily obscured by the fact that the 1968 Mets finished
ninth again. But it was a very different ninth from the 1966 ninth, and no
relation at all to the tenth-place finishes of other years. The one statistic
that indicated the truth was generally overlooked: although ninth, the 1968
Mets finished only 24 games behind the league champion; in 1967, they
had been 40½ games out; in 1966, although they were only 28½ out of first,
they were 18½ games out of the first division. This time, they finished only
eight games behind the fifth-place team. This was the valid measure of their
improvement.

But in baseball, such shifts in team ability are seldom visible from a distance or from the perusal of box scores. You have to see a team play every
day, to watch the accumulation of good fielding plays, to observe how one
pitcher after another works out of trouble, to note which hitters come through
when it matters. The first half of 1968 showed some notable improvements
in the Mets in these daily tasks. More and more, fielders did not mess up
the routine plays. The outfielders threw to the cutoff men instead of over their
heads—which had allowed runners to take an extra base. When plays needed
to be backed up, players were in position to do so. When pitchers had men
on base, they got the third out instead of giving up the damaging hit. The
Mets were still far from a "good" team, but they were just as far from the
"inept" team their predecessors had been.

And that was the main point of it all. Seaver, Ryan, Koosman, Grote,
Boswell, Charles, Shamsky, Agee, Martin, Cardwell—they had never been
part of the comedy years. Swoboda, Jones, and Kranepool, who had, were
young men who were the victims more than the causes of those early defeats,
men who were tossed into big league competition before they were ready but
not necessarily incapable of living up to their promise in the years still ahead.

Such things could be recognized by those who worked with the Mets every
day, the writers who traveled, the club officials, and most of all, the opponents. The Met veterans, "shell-shocked" (in Casey's phrase) from the defeats
of the past, hesitated to emphasize the new look, for fear of being accused of
senseless bravado. The fans, who could grasp the change only partially, were
inhibited by hoping against hope. But the changes were real. The methods
of Hodges—painstaking concentration, a calm atmosphere, low-key but no-
nonsense discipline, careful instruction, and patient faith in young men's
abilities—were paying off.

In the All-Star Game, at the Astrodome, some of the new Met qualities got wider recognition. It was another nightmare for hitters. (This was the Year of the Pitcher, and all through baseball people were wondering at the all-time low to which major league offense was sinking.) The National League got a run in the first inning, when Mays singled, took second on a wild pick-off attempt, third on a wild pitch (for ball four), and came in while a double play was being made. It turned out to be the only run of the game, but there was some excitement before it ended.

Grote caught the first five innings, having been elected a starter by fellow players, and went hitless in two trips. Seaver pitched the seventh and eighth. He made Rod Carew bounce out, fanned Yastrzemski again, was tagged for a double by Tony Oliva but struck out Joe Azcue. Then he struck out Boog Powell and Mantle, gave up an opposite field double to Don Wert, and fanned Rick Monday, for five strikeouts in two innings.

In the ninth, with two out and nobody on base, Yastrzemski came up representing the tying run. Manager Red Schoendienst brought in Koosman to replace the right-handed Ron Reed—and Koosman struck Yastrzemski out.

In two years, now, Met pitchers had faced 12 American League All-Stars and struck out seven of them. People couldn't fail to notice.

When the regular schedule was resumed, the first Met game was a 1–0 victory by Selma over the Cubs, but the second game of the doubleheader was a 2–0 loss. Then Koosman beat Chicago, 4–0. It was the 14th Met shutout in the team's 85th game. But then an 11-inning 2–1 loss to the Cubs started a six-game losing streak, the longest of the season.

Now Seaver was starting to win, and Selma was starting to lose, but no one was starting to hit.

As important as what was happening were some of the things that were not happening. Very few personnel changes were being made. Goossen was shuttling back and forth to the minors, but he was about the only one. Boswell was still on the disabled list. Rohr had been sent down early, Shaw was showing up for weekends, and Kevin Collins had been called up in late May, when Harrelson went into service for a couple of weeks. Mainly, though, it was the same group, and they were learning how to live together and play together.

But on July 19, a few changes were necessary. Ryan was going on weekend duty, and Frisella hadn't done well. Two pitchers were brought up from Jacksonville, a right-hander named Jim McAndrew who wasn't supposed to be too overpowering and a relief pitcher named Billy Connors, who had been in the Cubs organization. Also, Larry Stahl was called up to try to add a little punch while Goossen went down again.

McAndrew was 24, with a college degree in psychology, and a proud citizen of Lost Nation, Iowa. He'd been in the Met system for three years, and his 8–3 record at Jacksonville was considered a little surprising. The hot pitcher down there was Gary Gentry, a 21-year-old Arizona State product, but he was considered too good to disturb. The Mets, after all, weren't going for a pennant; building still took precedence.

McAndrew's first assignment, on Sunday, July 21, was to face Bob Gibson and the champion Cardinals in the opener of a doubleheader in the new Busch Stadium, where the temperature was about 100 degrees. He was being thrown to the wolves, so that Koosman could pitch the second game against Nelson Briles. And Gibson, in the midst of one of the most fantastic hot streaks any pitcher had ever enjoyed, was in top form. He struck out 13, scattered seven weak singles, and didn't let the Mets score.

But McAndrew seemed to have a little more stuff than had been reported. He kept pace with Gibson for five innings. Bobby Tolan tagged him for a homer in the sixth, and doubled in another run off Connors in the eighth, so Gibson won, 2–0; but McAndrew had made an impression.

Then Koosman went out and pitched a 1–0 four-hitter striking out 12.

McAndrew had to go back to Jacksonville as Ryan returned, but he had earned another look. But what really got the Cardinals, and other baseball people, thinking, was this: last year the Mets had come up with Seaver; now Koosman looked even tougher; the next hotshot on the way up, according to grapevine gossip, was Gentry; yet here was this McAndrew, considered secondary, looking good too. Was there no end to the young pitching the Mets had coming?

It was a more pertinent question than the Cardinals realized in July 1968—although Devine certainly must have had a better idea than most.

Koosman won his 14th game against Cincinnati on July 26, by 2–0. He now seemed certain to break Seaver's club record of 16 victories, and he had six shutouts, approaching a National League record for rookies. The Mets were running seventh in a league so bunched that the gap between fourth place and 10th was only six and a half games. But the batting weakness was too big a burden for the pitchers to carry daily. The Mets were about to lose 19 of their next 28 games, scoring three runs or less in 20 of them.

McAndrew was brought back on July 30. He pitched in Los Angeles on August 4 and lost, 2–0. He pitched in San Francisco on August 10 and lost 1–0. On August 17 he faced Houston at Shea and lost, 1–0. He now had a 0–4 record despite a 1.44 earned-run average and had not seen the Mets score a run while he was pitching. The major leagues were tough, all right.

On August 21, he started against Marichal in New York and was losing, 1–0, when the Mets scored two runs in the third. This seemed to put McAndrew into shock, although it took an inning for it to take effect. In the fifth, the Giants knocked him out, scored six runs, and won the game 13–3. But five days later, in St. Louis again—where people were saying: watch what the Cardinals do to him now that they get a second look at his stuff—he pitched a five-hitter and posted his first victory. The score? Why, 1–0; what else? And he didn't get the run until the eighth inning, when Agee's single, a steal, a sacrifice, and Cleon's fly produced it.

There were other hard-luck stories in this period. On August 16, Seaver, having brought his record to 10–9, had a 1–0 lead over Houston in the ninth but couldn't hold it. The Astros then beat Taylor in the 12th, 3–1. Three days later, with the Giants at Shea, Koosman pitched 12 scoreless innings in pursuit of his 17th victory and got nowhere. In the 17th, when everyone was making reference to the 24–inning game in Houston, the Giants finally scored off Taylor on a hit by Hunt and won 1–0. But the next day Seaver shut the Giants out, 8–0.

The next time Koosman tried for the Met record, he was hit hard in Cincinnati and beaten 10–7. He faced them again in New York a few days later and was knocked out in the fourth, for an 8–3 defeat. And on Labor Day, he pitched well but lost to Atlanta, 3–1.

On September 6, the Mets started a series in Pittsburgh with their record 64–79. Hodges and the coaches weren't admitting it, but they were getting impatient about beating the club record of 66 victories, and reaching Gil's predicted total of 70. It didn't really matter, but—it mattered.

McAndrew opened the series in the way to which he had become accustomed: he lost, 2–1.

Then Koosman, staked to a 4–1 lead early, lasted six innings and got his long-awaited 17th with help from Koonce and Taylor. The victory total now stood at 65, with Seaver ready.

But Seaver lost, 3–0, the 20th shutout suffered by the Mets. And at Chicago, two days later, they were routed, 8–1.

But on Wednesday, September 11, in Chicago, McAndrew won a game the only way he knew how—1–0, on a fourth-inning hit by Grote, whose average was still a healthy .280.

And on Friday, back in New York, Koosman held Pittsburgh to three hits and won, 2–0, with the aid of Shamsky's 12th home run. It was official. This was the greatest Met team of all time—even though it was tied with Houston for last place.

They celebrated by not scoring any runs at all for Seaver and Cardwell in the next two games.

Now there were two objectives left. Koosman had a crack at 20 victories—

an inconceivable distinction for a Met pitcher—and the team still had to win three games to reach Hodges's 70.

McAndrew brought the second goal closer with a 3–2 victory over the Cubs, luxuriating in the most explosive batting support he had ever received: Three whole runs! But Koosman stymied both by weakening in the eighth and being beaten, 7–2. However, in a Friday night doubleheader at Philadelphia, Seaver posted No. 69, 3–2, and the hitters overcame a four-run first inning to win the second game, 5–4.

Now there was nothing left to do but nail down ninth place and try for seventh, which was only two games above, and then relax and enjoy contemplation of the real progress that had been made. Next year, the sights could be set higher; even though the world had chosen to ignore the Mets, the insiders knew that things were on the upgrade. The fans semed to know it, too, because attendance had climbed back to 1,700,000, and with a final weekend scheduled at home, it would be the second highest in club history.

There was nothing to do, in short, but prepare for celebration.

But it didn't turn out that way at all.

12 A Familiar Story

FROM Philadelphia, the Mets went to Atlanta on September 23, 1968. They had two more road games to play there, then three at home against the Phillies, and their first year under Hodges would be complete. Since they were only two games behind the Phillies, who also had five games to play, they would get the chance to finish eighth in the final series. And the seventh-place Dodgers were only a game further up. On the other hand, Houston was only one game behind the Mets, and the possibility of finishing last again was very real.

Harrelson was not with the club. He had been left behind in New York to have an operation on his knee which had bothered him so much all year. Bob Heise, who had been up at this time the previous year, was playing short-stop. Koosman and Seaver would start the two games in Atlanta and two of the games with the Phillies.

These were the considerations the Mets had in mind as they went to Atlanta Stadium on Tuesday evening, September 24. Hodges, who had been unable to shake a heavy cold for some time, pitched some batting practice, as he often did, but he looked drawn and didn't feel well. Soon after the game began, he felt so unwell that he told Walker to take charge of the club and went back into the dressing room. He complained to Mauch that he had chest pains. Mauch called a doctor, who decided Hodges belonged in the hospital. Long before the game ended with Atlanta winning, 7–4, Hodges was lying very still in a hospital bed.

He had suffered a heart attack.

The exact nature of his illness wasn't made public immediately, and there were a few hours of confusion. But by morning, everyone knew what had happened. The medical reports classified the attack as "mild," and Hodges seemed in no danger. But the mere words, "heart attack," were serious enough. Joan Hodges promptly flew down from New York, and all the good will Hodges had accumulated over the years was quickly concentrated on wishing him recovery.

And it was taken for granted, of course, that his managing career was over.

By most people, that is.

The doctors, as soon as possible, assured Hodges and Met officials that "there was no reason why he couldn't make a full recovery and return to work." A basic principle of heart patient rehabilitation, it turned out, was to get a person back to his normal occupation and way of life. If the attack itself was diagnosed promptly, and if no excessive damage had been done, with proper care and rest a person could go back to almost any routine he was used to. The tension of considering oneself an invalid might prove more of a strain than any normal activity.

But the baseball world thought it knew better.

How could a man with heart trouble manage a ball club? Aside from the tensions and frustrations naturally associated with the games themselves, there was the ridiculous traveling, the irregular hours, improper meals, plane and bus rides, 3 A.M. arrivals, and so forth. It was a tough grind for a fully healthy person. It was ridiculous to think of a man who had had a heart attack carrying this burden.

Baseball people in fact wrote Hodges off. They, and especially the newspapermen, could see everything clearly except the possibility that they didn't know what they were talking about.

For Met officials, the situation was much more delicate. First of all, they were close to Hodges on a personal level and concerned about his well-being. But then, they also had a ball club to run. No one could guarantee that Hodges would be able to come back. What if he could not? Vital and basic decisions about playing personnel, and the procurement of another manager, had to be made during October and November. One couldn't operate on the assumption that Hodges would not be back, and one couldn't assume the opposite, either. It was a difficult time to stay cool, patient, and unruffled, to wait for firmer medical opinion and evidence, and to encourage Hodges.

In this atmosphere of uncertainty, the Mets played out the season. Seaver won the last game at Atlanta, 3–0, matching his 1968 total of 16 victories. But when the Mets lost an 11-inning, 3–2 decision to the Phillies at Shea Stadium on Friday night, they were mathematically eliminated from finishing higher than ninth. And their margin over Houston was still only one game, with two to play.

On Saturday, Koosman, who had been knocked out in the first game at Atlanta (the night Hodges became sick), posted his 19th victory, beating the Phillies 3–1 with a three-hitter. He had completed his rookie season with three Met records to his credit—the 19 victories, a 2.08 earned-run average, and seven shutouts. He had actually surpassed Seaver's first-year achievements, and his seven shutouts equaled a National League rookie record shared by the legendary Grover Cleveland Alexander. In the balloting for Rookie-of-the-Year, he would just lose out to Cincinnati's Johnny Bench.

If encouragement was needed to hasten Hodges' recovery, Koosman had provided it in its most graphic form.

However, Houston had also won on Saturday, and although the Mets had now clinched at least a tie for ninth, they weren't assured of not having a share of the cellar. On Sunday in the final game, Seaver weakened badly in the late innings, and the Mets were beaten, 10–3, as Richie Allen slammed three home runs. But the Astros, playing in St. Louis, lost too, 11–1, and the Mets had ninth to themselves.

That was certainly an encouraging item for Hodges, who now had so much time to think. His stated objectives—70 victories, a move up in the standings, improved play and attitude on the field—had all been achieved.

There were other satisfactions, too. Agee, as terrible a year as he'd had, had never stopped hustling in the field and had hit well during September, bringing his average "up" to .217. And Jones, who had suffered through a bad first two months, had done so well from June on that his final average of .297 was good enough to rank sixth in the league. Grote, another major improvement project, had finished at .282. And then there were those pitchers—ah, those (sigh!) delicious pitchers. They had thrown 25 shutouts, eight of them the work of more than one man, and their combined earned-run average of 2.72 was surpassed only by that of the champion Cardinals.

So there was plenty to look forward to, Hodges thought, when I can get back on my feet.

For the fans, the illness of Hodges and the uncertainty it cast over the future made it hard to exult in the season's achievements. The fact of ninth place—one game out of 10th—was hard to shake off, and to the more casual observers it meant "almost same old Mets."

It was a time for purely Met considerations to take a quiet back seat, and there were plenty of other things happening to make it harder than ever to look ahead.

Back in April, the National League had voted to expand to 12 teams in 1969—voted unwillingly, but forced to go along because the American League was going to 12 teams as a result of allowing Kansas City to move to Oakland. Fear of Congress—the same fear that had brought the Mets themselves into being—dictated a new A.L. team in Kansas City; that made 11, so there had to be a 12th, and Seattle was chosen. The National Leaguers coveted the Seattle territory themselves, but for the distant future. Relations between the two leagues were strained.

In May the American League decided to split into two six-team divisions, the only sensible pattern for a 12-team league—but the National petulantly refused, after identifying San Diego and Montreal as the two new members. Grant was one of those opposed to the two-division plan, on elemental grounds: in an East and West plan, teams would play fewer games with opponents in the other division, and the Mets "couldn't afford" to give up a few lucrative Giant and Dodger dates.

However, there would be two new expansion teams, and any chance that the Mets would fall back to last place was gone.

By July, at the All-Star game in Houston, the National League club owners had come to their senses. They adopted two divisions, modifying geography so that Chicago and St. Louis would be in the East with the Mets, whereas Atlanta and Cincinnati were put in the West with the three California teams and Houston. It was an illogical, shortsighted, strictly expedient compromise—which produced undreamed-of benefits.

Thus, by a show of hands in a closed meeting in the Shamrock Hotel in Houston, the Mets were instantly assured of the highest standing in their history. They could not be lower than sixth by definition; and, since one of the expansion teams (Montreal) would be in their division, they could not in practice be lower than fifth. Any expansion team was virtually certain to be weaker than any existing team since the plan to stock new teams with players was designed with that in view. The two new teams would pay $10 million each to get in (ostensibly for 30 players from the existing teams), which meant the Met share would be $2 million—a complete return of their original investment.

But finishing first in a division would not make one a pennant winner, of course. There would have to be a playoff between the two division leaders. (A three-of-five series was decided upon.)

So all aspects of baseball in 1969 were hard to foresee. The two-division set up was unprecedented in major league baseball. Fans had trouble learning which teams were in which division. The necessity for a playoff disturbed the simplicity of "most victories make the champion." The unbalanced schedule—18 games against the teams in your own division but only 12 against the others—made things harder to figure.

Three other important between-seasons stories, apparently unrelated to the Mets specifically, were to have profound effects on the Mets of 1969 in ways no one could anticipate. These were the concern of baseball officials with decreased scoring, the sudden dismissal of General Eckert as commissioner and the subsequent installation of Bowie Kuhn, and the spring training boycott by the Players' Association in its negotiation for a new pension contract.

There was no escaping the fact that 1969 was the Year of the Pitcher. Marvelous as the Met staff's pitching statistics were, the ascendancy of pitchers was universal. When much publicity was given to the fact that the level of scoring and batting had fallen to the lowest point in modern baseball history, lower even than in the "dead ball" days of the early 1900s, baseball authorities were provoked to react. That the whole American League could produce only one .300 hitter (Carl Yastrzemski of Boston, who won the batting championship with .301) could not be shrugged aside. When analysis showed that the alarming drop in offense coincided with an enlarged strike zone adopted by rule revisions in 1963, the pressure to "do something" mounted. Baseball officials, unaccustomed as they were to public admission that anything about the game was less than perfect, decided to bring the strike zone back to its 1962 (and earlier) definition and to lower the pitching mound from 15 to 10 inches. These two steps, it was hoped, would help hitters. At the same time, half a dozen clubs decided independently to bring their outfield fences in somewhat.

What did this mean to the Mets? It helped them two ways. Their pitchers were, really and truly, good pitchers—and young pitchers, with good stuff. If the new rules would have an effect, the Mets would suffer relatively less than the teams which depended on older or less talented pitchers. All pitching might suffer, but the Mets would suffer less. At the same time, Met hitting needed all the help it could get, and if there was a tipping of the balance in favor of hitters, the Mets might get a few extra runs off mediocre opposing pitchers while their own top-drawer pitchers remained effective. Whatever these changes, they would be undramatic, showing up in "averages" and in "percentage situations"—but these small advantages could be translated into at least a few extra victories.

The near-strike of the players came about when pension negotiations dragged on past the first of the year. The Association (in which Fisher, the

ex-Met, was a prominent leader and in which Kranepool was the Met representative, elected by his teammates) urged its players to refuse, individually,
to sign 1969 contracts until the pension dispute was settled. Most teams
began spring training in mid-February, although the player contract didn't
require anyone to report until March 1. If the players didn't sign, and stuck
together, and boycotted spring training, the owners might become more mal-
leable about negotiating the pension agreement.

The burden of this strategy fell on pitchers, who always begin spring
training at least a week before the other players so that they can work into
shape to pitch to hitters by the time the hitters arrive, and so that they can
pitch in rotation often enough to get ready for the season. The key date was
March 1, and the dispute was settled on February 25 (with the players getting most of what they asked for). Solidarity among established players had
been remarkably good; but, by February 25, daily players had not missed any
important work; the pitchers had.

As a result, many teams got off to a poor start because their pitchers
weren't really ready by April 7 when the season began.

The Mets, however, were in a special situation. The success of the boycott
depended on the togetherness of the mass of big-league regulars, sure of their
positions and essential to their teams. Everyone recognized that rookies and
other youngsters were not really in a position to defy their managements and
that older players of borderline ability couldn't either. As it happened, the
Met pitching staff was loaded with youngsters and borderline oldsters.

None actually broke the boycott, because it never came to that: Murphy
(one of the first player representatives himself two decades before) handled
the situation delicately and correctly. There were no formal spring practice
sessions called and no threat of reprisals for those who weren't signing. On
many teams, not-so-subtle persuasion, with a slight hint of economic black-
mail, was widespread; public statements by club officials were quite insult-
ing to some players and vice versa. But Murphy kept the Met situation polite
and cool at all times—and by fair dealing in the past, the Met management
had created a stockpile of good will among its employees.

So Seaver took it upon himself to organize an informal "conditioning"
camp, which many Mets attended, and the Met pitchers, through their own
initiative, lost no working time.

No one can measure how much of a factor this became later, but the fact
remains the Mets didn't have some of the problems other clubs developed.
And as a by-product of this situation, the "team spirit" aspect of the Mets
was enhanced and displayed.

The Commissioner mess, in the strangest way, had the most direct effect.

Eckert was fired, unexpectedly, on the last day of the winter meetings in

San Francisco (December 6). No successor could be agreed upon. On December 20, in a historic meeting that lasted all night, a deadlock developed between the two leading candidates, Chub Feeney of San Francisco (backed by the National League) and Mike Burke, president of the Yankees (backed by the American). It had to be adjourned without decision in a highly embarrassing fashion. On February 4, when the owners met again at Miami Beach, the deadlock was intact, and a surprise compromise candidate was found: Bowie Kuhn, 42-year-old Wall Street lawyer from the firm that had been representing the National League for 30 years.

Kuhn was unknown to the public but intimately informed on all internal baseball matters and an insider of 10-years' standing. He took office with immense leverage because he was a unanimous choice, impressed by the need to upgrade the image of a "decisive" commissioner. The player pension struggle was at its height, with bitterness growing on both sides—and Kuhn had been, up to this moment, part of the negotiation on the side of the owners.

Eventually he played a helpful role behind the scenes in bringing both sides to agreement, but that wasn't what mattered to the Mets. What mattered was a decision he took in another case, a decision colored by his need to make crystal clear that he could make decisions while protecting the interests of individual players. The cases that brought out this issue involved a retired player.

Donn Clendenon, a right-handed hitter with power, had been picked by Montreal in the expansion draft from Pittsburgh, where he had played his entire major league career. Clendenon, 33 years old and coming off a relatively poor year, was an executive with the Scripto Pen company and had other extensive business interests in Atlanta, where he lived. Montreal then traded him and Jay Alou to Houston for Rusty Staub, and Clendenon announced his retirement. He had no intention of playing for Houston.

This, naturally, killed the whole deal, according to baseball law at the time. If anyone involved in a trade refused to report, the trade was off.

But it wasn't that simple.

Clendenon didn't "retire" as soon as the trade was made. He waited several weeks. In the meantime Staub, who had been unhappy at Houston, had become involved promotionally and emotionally with Montreal. He, too, had no intention of going back to Houston.

Kuhn approached this problem by refusing to recognize Clendenon's retirement and negotiating privately for a settlement. Perhaps another trade could be arranged, involving Atlanta, so that Clendenon could play there. Perhaps Clendenon would reconsider about Houston. Perhaps Houston would accept other players in payment for Staub.

Nothing worked, and the case dragged into spring training, with Staub vocally impatient about being in limbo and Houston vocally demanding his return. The problem was that it would be very awkward for Kuhn to make a ruling which obviously went against one player's very strong desires and underlined the chattel-status of everyone under baseball's right to trade players—a right that doesn't exist in ordinary life.

So Kuhn finally ruled, in early March, that Staub could stay in Montreal and that Houston had to accept another player as compensation.

Then Montreal persuaded Clendenon to come out of retirement (for more money), and he was free to play with the Expos too.

And what that meant to the Mets we'll soon see.

But the point was, Kuhn's ruling was against the book and against tradition. It was, from the standpoint of the players, a fair decision at a time when passions were highly inflammable. But it is hard to imagine Eckert, who did everything by the book, taking an action so clearly at variance with the written rules and with accepted practice. Therefore, the whole tangle that made Kuhn commissioner led to Clendenon's being placed where, in June, he would become a Met.

All these disparate happenings, therefore, were combining to make possible the Met miracle no one yet anticipated—Charley Finley's move to Oakland, which forced the American League to expand, which forced the National League to expand, which forced divisional play; the dissatisfaction with Eckert, and the internal political struggle that followed, which brought Kuhn to the commissioner's chair to make his Clendenon decision; the various steps to help hitting, which made Met pitching relatively more valuable than ever; the player boycott, which had the incidental effect of cementing Met unity; and the adoption, back in 1964, of the free-agent draft through which, by luck, Seaver had come to the Mets, since it is doubtful they would have landed him in an open market.

Finally, there was a trade the Mets didn't make.

Joe Torre, the slugging catcher–first baseman of the Braves, was available. Atlanta wanted young players in return, particularly Ryan and Otis. The Mets balked at, of all people, Otis, who had hit .286 at Jacksonville, Thereupon the Braves traded Torre to the St. Louis Cardinals for Orlando Cepeda, making the overwhelmingly favored Cardinals stronger than ever.

Young, in his column, was particularly critical of this nonmove. "With Torre, the Mets would be a pennant contender," he wrote. Colleagues snickered at Young's overestimation of Met potential but in general agreed that it seemed foolish not to get Torre (who was also a native Brooklynite) if he were available. On the other hand, the Mets were doing what the majority of the writers had always advocated, passing up short-run illusion for long-range building, so it was hard to knock it. Otis was not yet 22, Ryan just 22, and Torre almost 29. And everyone knew no immediate pennants were at stake, not for the Mets.

Meanwhile, Hodges was recovering on schedule, and routine business went on.

After four weeks in the hospital in Atlanta, Hodges was released. Naturally, he took no part in between-season promotional activity, but he was able to be in on all necessary decisions and discussions about the club itself. He spent some time in St. Petersburg, where he was able to look at some of the kids playing in the instructional league during November. He came back to Brooklyn and returned to Florida in February, taking long walks as therapy, thinking baseball, and no longer smoking.

During October, the standard roster shifts had to be made. Linz, Short, Connors, and Buchek were dropped to make room for McGraw, Otis, Gentry, Hendley, Frisella, Renko, Duffy Dyer (a catcher), Jim Bibby (a pitcher), and Rod Gaspar (an outfielder) on the parent roster.

For the expansion draft, the Mets had to list 15 players as untouchable; then, after they lost one, they could protect three more; when they lost another, they could protect three more; and so on, until they had lost six men altogether, three to each expansion team. The decisions about this were cumulative, and pretty well decided before Hodges became ill. But he was still in the hospital in Atlanta when the expansion draft took place on October 14, and the Met losses were not disturbing at all. Selma was chosen quickly by San Diego, and Stahl, and an infielder named Jerry Morales, a 19-year-old kid; Montreal took Don Shaw, Ernest McAnally (a 22-year-old pitcher from the low minors), and John Glass, a 21-year-old pitcher of promise. In this draft, unlike the one the Mets had drawn from in 1961, the new teams could choose not only from the major league roster but from anywhere in the system unless a man was on the protected list, and they went for prospects, figuring they would buy the major league rejects later. To the Mets, whose best prospects were close enough to major league level to be protected, this meant they lost only Selma and Shaw from the probable 1969 club, and since pitching was their strength, they could afford it. Many other teams were hurt more seriously by the draft, although none terribly.

Sure enough, a couple of days later Montreal bought Bosch from the Mets. In the draft, he would have cost the Expos $200,000. This way they got him for perhaps $25,000.

During the winter meetings (on December 2 in San Francisco), the Mets chose one player in the regular draft of minor leaguers. For the set price of $25,000, they took a red-headed, 21-year-old kid named Wayne Garrett from the Braves' system. He had played at Shreveport in the Texas League and had hit .239, but he was considered a useful utility infielder defensively. His chief claim to fame was that an older brother, Adrian, had been with the Mets briefly in 1964 on a conditional deal, and that both Adrian and Jim, another older brother, were still playing in the Atlanta organization.

And that was the only real personnel change the Mets made between seasons. They made no trades.

In training camp, there were several developments.

Koosman had a sore elbow—a frightening thought.

Shamsky developed a bad back, was unable to work, and was persuaded to transfer to the Jacksonville roster so he could work into shape while the team went north.

Gaspar, a 23-year-old Californian who had hit .309 at Memphis, was scheduled for Jacksonville. But he sprayed hits so well and looked like such a good fielder, with a good arm, that he simply played his way onto the squad.

Garrett was far less impressive, but he hit a couple of home runs and did well enough. Infielders were needed because it remained to be seen how quickly, and how thoroughly, Harrelson would come back after his knee operation.

Harrelson said he felt fine—and bigger. He had worked with weights, gorged himself on ice cream, and was heavier than he had ever been.

Weis came to camp with new muscles and extra pounds, too. He was now one year beyond his knee operation, and more optimistic.

Hendley didn't make it. In weeding out the pitchers, Hodges and Walker decided that McGraw could be made into a relief pitcher, because he had such good stuff and competitive cockiness in tight situations. For the last three years, he had been strictly a starter. With McGraw and Al Jackson in the bull pen, the Mets had enough left-handers there, but with only Koosman as a left-handed starter, they could have used Hendley. But Hendley's arm had not recovered and he simply didn't throw well enough to stay.

The ten pitchers chosen, then, were Seaver, Koosman, Ryan, Gentry (who looked as good as advertised), and Cardwell as starters; McGraw, Taylor, Koonce, and Jackson as relievers; and McAndrew, who was having some arm trouble.

Hodges also tried using Cleon Jones at first base, to platoon with Kranepool. "Cleon can make the All-Star team at either position, if he wants to," Hodges declared. Kranepool responded to this threat to his security by going on a hitting spree for a week.

Gil also tried Otis at third base, where he did poorly. It was a Met tradition going back to Hickman and Thomas to try outfielders at third base. The main thing was, though, that Otis didn't hit much.

As opening day approached, it became more and more obvious that an important transformation had taken place in the Mets, tradition or no tradition. The team that would play in 1969 would contain fundamentally the same players as the 1968 team, and this had never happened before. At long last, the Mets had achieved a degree of stability. The outside world could question whether it was a good thing that a team, barely finishing ninth the year before, was going into a campaign with the same lineup. But Hodges and the other Mets knew better: it was a young team, and another year meant more experience and natural improvement.

Picking a number, Hodges predicted 85 victories. Some laughed. That meant a 12-game improvement on last year's 73. But the manager meant it. He also made it plain he intended to use the platoon system, and basically along lefty-righty lines. Jones or Swoboda could spell Kranepool at first; Weis could share second with Boswell and short with Harrelson, and Charles and Garrett could share third. Agee and Jones seemed set, but Swoboda could be platooned with Gaspar and, eventually, Shamsky. Grote and Martin could share the catching, with Dyer in reserve.

Did Hodges believe platooning was a good system? Maury Allen, of the *Post,* asked.

"It is for this club," replied Gil. He meant, of course, that he had available many players of roughly equal ability and few so good that they had to be used every day regardless of circumstances. Platooning is generally detested by players, each of whom wants to play every day, but it has several hidden benefits. Among these are protection against fatigue and the fact that substitutes, having seen action fairly often, are always ready to play when emergencies (and injuries) disrupt the normal planning. It also protects against a prolonged and costly slump by any one player, since he is being frequently replaced anyhow.

All these things would work out just right for Hodges, whose own playing days had been spent on Dodger teams so set at every position that platooning was a rarity. Stengel had been the apostle of platooning and had achieved unprecedented success with it as a Yankee—but had achieved only variety in failure as a Met, because the players he was platooning weren't good enough, period. Now Hodges, who saw nothing inherently desirable in it but who knew all the angles in how to use it properly, would soon press all the right buttons like a Yankee-era Stengel.

No one, however, was thinking such grandiose thoughts as the Mets went from Florida to New York by way of New Orleans. Objective No. 1 was the still unattained feat of winning an opening game. As for the full season, well—everyone knew that the Cardinals would run away and hide from the rest of the Eastern Division. Their only conceivable challenge would come from Durocher's Cubs. Montreal, of course, would be last. So the Mets had to fight it out with Pittsburgh and Philadelphia for third place. They should certainly beat Philadelphia, since the Mets looked stronger and Philadelphia weaker than in 1968, when the margin between them was only three games. And Pittsburgh, which had finished only seven games ahead of the Mets, had injury, age, and other problems. Fourth place, therefore, could be called the legitimate expectation and third place a reasonable aspiration for the Mets. Fifth would be a bitter disappointment and sixth a disaster.

And when Young picked the Mets to finish second—far behind the Cardinals but able to overtake the Cubs—he was chided again for being carried away by loyalty to the Mets.

And out in Las Vegas, the official price on the Mets was exactly the same as in 1968: 100 to 1—and no takers.

But Objective No. 1 was in its most attainable form. The game would be at home. The opponent would be Montreal, managed by Gene Mauch (fired by the Phillies in the middle of the previous season). Tom Seaver would be the pitcher (against Mudcat Grant). An Opening Day victory could not possibly elude the Mets this time, and 44,000 people were there to bear witness.

It couldn't, eh?

An error by Boswell, followed by a walk and Bob Bailey's double with two out, put Montreal ahead, 2–0, before the Mets came to bat. But in the second inning, a three-run double by Agee, also with two out, gave the Mets a 3–2 lead and brought in Dan McGinn, recently of Notre Dame, as Montreal's relief pitcher. Seaver yielded the tying run in the third, and McGinn hit a home run in the fourth, but the Mets scored twice in their half, on Boswell's single and a double by Jones, so that they led, 5–4, when Koonce replaced Seaver at the start of the sixth.

Koonce promptly gave up two runs and another in the seventh. In the eighth, Staub hit a home run off Jackson and Coco Laboy a three-run homer off Taylor. Going into the ninth, Montreal led 10–5.

Remember the futile rally of early Met days? Here it came again. Jones singled, Charles walked, and with two out Grote singled in a run. Dyer pinch-hit a home run, and it was 10–9. Otis singled. Agee walked, pushing the tying run to second.

But Gaspar struck out.

The Mets couldn't make it on Opening Day even against a team playing the first game of its career.

And in the course of the three-and-a-half hour struggle, Boswell had made three errors, Seaver had done poorly and the bull pen worse, and nine runs—a week's supply for the Mets—had been wasted.

Some way to treat a heart patient.

Hodges, though, remained his imperturbable self. The next day, McAndrew started, was handed a 4–0 lead, but got knocked out in the second inning, giving up three runs. But McGraw took over and pitched five scoreless innings before tiring with an 8–3 lead, and Ryan had to finish for him. It ended 9–5. And on Thursday, Gentry stopped the Expos, 4–2, although Koonce had to come in and get the final out for him. In this game, Agee, who was now the lead-off man, hit two home runs, one of them an unbelievable smash into the fifth (and top) deck in the left field corner, an unmeasurable shot of something more than 500 feet. Maybe, the alert analysts wondered right away, the lively ball that had been tried in spring training had found its way into a real game.

Anyhow, after three games, the Mets had a 2–1 record, equaling their high point of 1966. Koosman, whose arm had felt better during the last week in Florida, would test it now against St. Louis.

He lasted seven innings, went out trailing 4–2, and the Mets lost, 6–5. On Saturday, Dave Giusti beat Cardwell, 1–0—that dear familiar score. On Sunday, Gibson beat Seaver, 3–1. And on Monday, McAndrew lost in Philadelphia, 5–1.

Same old Mets. Having lost four of the first six, they were tied for last with Philadelphia, and even Montreal was a game ahead of them.

Gentry, aided by Koonce again, stopped Philadelphia 6–3, but a two-game visit to Pittsburgh resulted in losses by 11–3 (with Koosman hammered to cover within three innings) and 4–0.

The Cubs, having won nine of their first 10 games, were already six games ahead of the Mets, whose record was 3–7. But the Cards were struggling too, unable to win a home game. When the Mets moved into St. Louis, the trend continued. Seaver beat Gibson, 2–1, and Ryan, relieving McAndrew in the fourth inning, was the beneficiary of an 11–3 victory.

But things didn't get much better, although Koosman pitched a 2–0 shutout against Pittsburgh. The Cubs came to New York and won the first three games of a four-game series, losing the second game of the Sunday doubleheader only when a three-run homer by Jones with one out in the ninth broke up a scoreless game. At 7–11, the Mets shared last place with Montreal and St. Louis, while the Cubs remained six games ahead with 14–6.

Now the Mets made their first visit to Montreal. The good news was that Kranepool's two homers produced a 2–0 victory; the bad news was that Koosman's shoulder "popped" and Ryan had to relieve him in the fifth. Seaver won the next day, 2–1, but the Mets lost the final game of the series, 3–2, when Mack Jones hit a home run off Cardwell in the ninth inning with the score tied. Two losses in Chicago followed.

It was now Sunday, May 4. The Mets, at 9–14, were ahead only of Montreal, by one game, and eight games behind the Cubs. A doubleheader would complete the first "intra-division" cycle of the new schedule. For the next six weeks, the Mets would play only Western Division teams.

Turning Point No. 1 had arrived.

The Mets had just lost 13 of their last 20 games. Their vaunted pitching was proving quite ordinary. They weren't playing well in other respects, either. Agee had bogged down again, and Hodges had benched him. Jones was hitting .422, but Grote was back to .207. Two more defeats at the hands of the hot Cubs, and they would be deep in just the sort of hole their predecessors had always dug for themselves.

Instead, Seaver and McGraw pitched and won two tough 3–2 games before a capacity crowd of 40,000, amid much hostility.

Durocher's teams had always been known for their willingness to use "beanballs"—pitches thrown at a batter's head—as a means of intimidation. His Dodger and Giant teams had been involved in numerous "beanball wars" that sometimes spilled into mass fist fights. Here at Wrigley Field, when Westrum was managing the Mets and Durocher the Cubs, there had been such an incident. Hodges, like Westrum, had played under Durocher and was sensitive to any hint of such tactics. In baseball, the accepted and manly response was retaliation. It wasn't always easy to tell "who started it," because sometimes the first close pitch could be an honest mistake, misinterpreted as malevolent; but past reputation played a large role in the climate that made beanball wars.

At any rate, provoked or not, Seaver made Ron Santo, Chicago's clean-up hitter, fall flat under a close pitch in the second inning. Later in the same inning, a hit by Randy Hundley and a triple by Al Spangler gave Chicago a run.

Seaver came to bat in the third, and Bill Hands, the Cub pitcher, hit him between the shoulder blades. When Hands came up in the bottom of the third, Seaver hit him in the stomach. There was a moment of potential riot, but it passed, and the double retaliation seemed to satisfy everyone. Kranepool hit a home run in the fourth, Boswell and Swoboda drove in runs in the fifth, and Seaver hung on for his 3–2 victory. Once he struck out Santo with the bases full, and twice he retired Ernie Banks with the bases full.

McGraw was given his first start in the second game because both Koosman and McAndrew were out of commission, and Ryan (whose 1968 season had been punctuated by finger blisters) had one of a series of leg injuries that plagued him most of 1969. Since McGraw had been converted to bullpen duty, there was a question about his stamina. Further drama lay in the fact that the opposing pitcher was Selma, obtained by the Cubs from San Diego. Each team scored twice in the first inning, but McGraw permitted nothing after that, and a seventh-inning run gave him the game.

That double victory, which merely seemed a good day's work at the time, was important as a brake on two sets of momentum. It checked the possibility of a sustained losing spell for the Mets, and it turned the pendulum in New York's favor in hand-to-hand combat with the Cubs.

Back home to play the western clubs for the first time, the Mets split a two-game set with Cincinnati and another with Houston. Ryan reinjured his leg and was placed on the disabled list for 21 days, so a left-hander with years of minor league experience but no major league exposure was brought up from Jacksonville: Jack DiLauro, purchased by the Mets from the Detroit organization over the winter.

After splitting the first two games of a series with Atlanta, the Mets lost the third—their last home game on this stand—in discouraging fashion. Trailing 6–5 in the ninth, they had the bases full with two out when Jones lined an apparent game-winning hit toward right—only to have Felix Millan, the second baseman, end the game with a leaping, backhanded catch. The Mets had been playing careless baseball in several respects, and in an exceptional clubhouse meeting after this game, Hodges spelled out to the whole squad what he considered unacceptable. The steel inside the glove made itself felt.

In Cincinnati, they won two slugfests, 10–9 and 11–3, and escaped defeat on Sunday when the game was rained out in the fourth inning while they were still hitless and while Cincinnati already had three runs off Seaver.

That was a mere hint of the favors fortune was storing up for the Mets, and few noted it.

On Tuesday, May 20, the Mets had to stop off in Memphis for an exhibition game, en route to Atlanta. It proved to be a big occasion. Koosman, trying his arm for the first time in three weeks, worked five innings, struck out 10, and declared he "felt great." It was a big boost to club morale to have him ready, and the next night there was a bigger boost to the morale of experienced Mets: Seaver's three-hit 3–0 victory in Atlanta brought the team's record to 18–18.

There it was: the .500 mark, 36 games into the season.

The object of so much struggle in 1968, and of such dim dreams before that, had been reached almost without warning.

And the reactions were revealing.

The writers were excited, and wrote exultant stories about the historic achievement. Met officials beamed. Fans sighed, laughed, cried.

But the players couldn't care less. In fact, they were sort of insulted at the idea of being fussed over. "What's .500?" said Seaver. "Let us reach first place. That'll mean something. We're looking far beyond .500."

The one exception was Kranepool, the only one who had been there almost from the beginning. He understood the significance of it the way the writers did.

"After all those losing years, it's a good feeling," he admitted. "Now that we're at .500, we can start proving we're a good ball club. I don't think the Cubs can win it; I'm more worried about the Cardinals."

It was a prophecy he never got credit for later. But the indifference with which the other players (and Hodges) met this milestone indicated how really unconnected most of these men were with the Met past. They wore the same uniform, but they were different men with different experiences—and they did have a winning attitude, a belief in their own abilities. To them, the old Mets were strange legends, evidently funny to the public but simply irrelevant to the players of today.

However: the next night, the Mets got bombed by the Braves, 15–3. They went on to Houston and lost three more, 7–0 (with 13 strikeouts for Tom Griffin, a Houston rookie), 5–1 (as Koosman started and pitched seven innings) and 6–3 (with Seaver lasting only four innings).

They were four games below .500. They might never see it again. "Now do you admit it was significant?" Young asked Seaver, good-naturedly. Seaver smiled sheepishly. "I'm beginning to see what you mean."

On Tuesday, May 27, they opened a home stand by facing San Diego, the other expansion team, for the first time. McAndrew was the starter, presumably recovered. He pitched well. But the Mets left 11 men on base against Al Santorini. They lost, 3–2.

That put them five under, at 18–23, virtually tied for fifth place, nine games behind the Cubs. They had been 18–23 the year before; they hadn't been very much worse off in 1966 or 1965—or even 1963—after the same number of games. That old treadmill feeling was getting started. Would it be the same old Mets after all?

Turning Point No. 2 was coming up.

13 *Excitement*

B Y the morning of Wednesday, May 28, 1969, the New York Mets had played 1,177 National League games. They had lost 760 and tied five, had used 168 different players for at least one inning, and had played before more than 17.5 million ticket buyers. Yet, that morning, the intensity of the world's concern with their activities was probably at low ebb. Among the large minority of Americans who were dedicated sports fans, the small minority who were dedicated Met fans continued to follow their fortunes. But Met Mystique had become a cliché suffering from overexposure, and baseball games themselves were being taken less seriously than ever. During the last 15 months, there had been the two shocking assassinations, Dr. King's and Robert Kennedy's; the forced retirement of a President of the United States, Lyndon Johnson; a presidential campaign of exceptional bitterness, marked by the violence at the Democratic Convention in Chicago and the strident third-party voice of George Wallace; widespread eruption of campus conflict, the headlong pace of polarization on the issues of race and war, a completely uninhibited antagonism between generations, an accelerating inflation, a new and increasing awareness of the scope of drug use. It was, indeed, a far more sombre and frightening world than it had been even two years before.

And for those who found their taste for sports news undiminished, the trite story of Met travail had been pushed far into the background, not only by their own repetitiveness but by new heroes. The New York Jets had humbled the National Football League in the Superbowl, and Joe Namath was king; the basketball Knicks had set New York on its ear with a whirlwind finish during the spring of 1969, a winning team at last with a great future; even the Yankees, who had startled everyone by their strong finish to claim fifth place in 1968, had just completed an eight-game winning streak and had a better record than the Mets.

In short, only those directly concerned were paying any attention at all when Koosman went to the mound that evening to face San Diego, before a crowd of only 11,000 at Shea Stadium. And no one, concerned or not, recognized that Turning Point No. 2 was taking place.

Koosman had his good stuff. San Diego, a weak team, was overmatched. In nine innings, he allowed three hits, no runs, and struck out 14, equaling a Met record held by Ryan.

Trouble was, the Mets didn't score either. Not that they didn't have chances. They put six men on base with nobody out in the first five innings.

In the tenth, Koosman gave up another scratch hit, posted his 15th strikeout, and retired. Walker and Hodges were great believers in watching carefully that no pitcher worked longer than he should or more often than he should. Koosman had shown he was in top form, and that was good news, and there would be no risks taken.

The Mets failed to score again, after a leadoff walk, because Boswell's line drive was turned into a double play. McGraw then walked the first San Diego batter on four pitches in the 11th, but Grote bailed him out by pouncing on a bunt and turning it into a double play. McGraw walked the next man, too, but struck out Nate Colbert and became the winning pitcher when the Mets finally scored on Harrelson's single with one out and the bases full.

It was an 11-inning, three-hour, 1–0 victory, enough to check the losing streak, but it was hardly reason to celebrate.

The reasons would soon appear, however. In the next two weeks, the Mets would reclaim a piece of the spotlight.

On Memorial Day, the Giants came in for a three-game series—the first of only two visits they would be making to New York under the new schedule —and the faithful turned out 52,000 strong. Trailing 3–0 after six innings, the Mets scored in the seventh and rallied for three in the eighth, giving Seaver a 4–3 victory. On Saturday, the Mets won again, 4–2.

On Sunday, 41,000 came out, and judging by the sound they were wholeheartedly in favor of a Met sweep. Nostalgia belonged to the past. It was a seesaw game and reached the ninth inning with the score 4–4. Joe Gibbon, an aging left-hander, was the Giant pitcher, having held the Mets scoreless since the fifth. Now he walked Harrelson. Agee bunted him over, Garrett bounced out, and Jones (still the league's leading hitter at .369) was purposely passed. Otis, who had replaced Kranepool in the seventh, now fouled off several pitches and worked a walk on a full count, filling the bases. And Swoboda also walked, forcing in the winning run.

The Met entourage was delighted. A sweep of the Giants, and in such a manner! Why, that's the way the Mets used to hand games to the Giants, not the other way around. This was fun.

Next came the Dodgers. Boswell was gone now, for a two-week tour of Army duty, and Weis and Garrett were being platooned at second. Since Claude Osteen, a left-hander, was pitching against Koosman, Weis played. In the third, Weis doubled to right center with two out, driving in the second run of the inning. Koosman made it stand up and won, 2–1. The next night, Seaver pitched a three-hitter and won, 5–2, as Kranepool hit two homers.

All of a sudden, the Mets had a six-game winning streak going and had passed the .500 mark for the first time—with little attention being given this negative-statistic-turned-positive. There was a much more exciting accomplishment in the wind: one more victory would give Mets back-to-back sweeps of the Giants and Dodgers. It was still a parochial concern of Met fans, but up to this point they could imagine nothing sweeter.

One of the things Hodges and Walker were dedicated to, in their pitching plans, was a five-day rotation for young pitchers. Baseball tradition calls for starters to work every fourth day. Hodges and Walker believed there was danger to young arms on such a schedule, and that Seaver and Koosman must be given proper rest, regardless of temptation. To stick to his schedule, Hodges now had to use DiLauro as a starter in this game, the last of the home stand, on Wednesday night, June 4.

DiLauro rose to the occasion. He shut the Dodgers out, allowing only two hits—only to find, as so many Met pitchers had found before him, that this wasn't good enough. The Mets hadn't scored either. And as both sides mounted threats in extra innings, the scoreless tie remained intact through 14 innings.

In the top of the 15th, the Dodgers put men on first and third with one out, and Willie Davis hit a one-hop liner off the pitcher's glove, with the infield playing in. Weis, racing to his right, made a completely unbelievable stab and throw home—and nailed the runner. Taylor promptly got the third out, and the Mets opened their half with Harrelson's walk. Agee failed to bunt, and forced him, but Garrett lined a single to center—where Willie

Davis, racing in, let the ball skip under his glove and out toward the fence, letting Agee race around with the winning run.

A 15-inning 1–0 game full of spectacular plays would be a conversation piece any time, any place. This one, though, also represented the longed-for double sweep of the Giants and Dodgers and tied a Met record by stretching the victory streak to seven. In New York, the Amazin' Mets were on people's tongues again, even as the team headed for California to play the same three teams on their grounds. At the unprecedented altitude of two games above .500, they were recapturing their audience.

Only for a few hours, though. As they arrived in San Diego, the story that Namath would quit football rather than sell his interest in his Lexington Avenue bar blanketed sports pages—and front pages—across the nation. It remained a hot story for weeks, until Namath finally gave in, in time to start his season on schedule.

So the Mets, what with the time difference and the Namath news, went about their San Diego weekend without too much fanfare. With Taylor supplying the last two outs, Gentry won the first game, 5–3, and set a new high for Met winning streaks. Koosman, striking out 11, took the second game, 4–1, losing his shutout only with two out in the ninth. And Seaver, striking out 14, took the third, 3–2, with Garrett driving in the winning run in the eighth.

San Francisco, full of lovely restaurants and other attractive places, is always a favorite stop for ball clubs. It's better still with a 10-game winning streak going and a day off. By Tuesday night, the Mets were feeling better than ever, and they took it out on the Giants: 9–4, two homers for Agee, one for Jones, a victory for Cardwell, a save for Taylor.

Eleven straight! It was not to be believed. Why, they might never lose another. The Mets now had a clear grip on second place, although still seven games behind the Cubs. Not that it was time to think of pennants, even though the Mets were six games over the .500 mark, a dizzying height. But with the Phillies and Pirates struggling as predicted, and the Cardinals still unaccountably under .500, the chances of finishing third were excellent. The Cards would wake up, sooner or later, and probably overhaul the Cubs. But even third place—in the money—would be progress indeed.

On Wednesday afternoon, the streak ended at 11. Gaylord Perry pitched a four-hitter, and Gentry was polished off early, 7–2. But the accomplishment remained. The winning streak brought to the attention of baseball fans what the opposition had realized some time back: the Mets really were a pretty good team, getting better, with pitching no one wanted to face. It still didn't mean much to the general public, beyond the oddity that the words

"Mets" and "winning streak" wound up in the same sentence, but the real fans recognized a new situation. Their hopes—for third place or even second this year, and a pennant in the near future—had a legitimacy they never had before. Most of all, it increased immensely the self-confidence of the players.

In Los Angeles, Koosman lost a 1–0 game to Alan Foster, giving up an unearned run on two singles in the second inning because Shamsky, in right field, bobbled the first one and gave up an extra base. But Shamsky hit a homer and a single the next night, helping Seaver to a 3–1 victory which made Seaver's record 10–3. Meanwhile, the last original Met slipped away. Room on the roster had to be made for Boswell, returning from military duty, so Al Jackson was sold to Cincinnati. He left with 43 Met victories to his credit—a club record which would last until Seaver could win a couple more.

And on Sunday, the last day of the trip, the Mets lost the game but won the pennant.

It was June 15, the last day on which real trades are permitted. Johnny Murphy, who had made the whole trip with the team, had an announcement before game time: the Mets had acquired Clendenon from Montreal, for four young players, none of whom figured in immediate Met plans. One was Collins, the infielder, who had been sent down to Jacksonville in May; another was Renko, one of the promising pitchers; the other two were pitchers in the lower levels of the organization, Dave Colon and Jay Carden.

The trade greatly overshadowed the 3–2 defeat that day in Los Angeles. Any trade, any time, stirs up baseball fans. But the meaning of this one stimulated more than ordinary interest.

Clendenon was a tall, strong, right-handed hitter, noted for power more than for average, and a good first baseman. He could play the outfield if necessary.

The Mets had just proved how strong their pitching was, and pitching was by far the most important factor in the game. The 11-game winning streak had focused attention on it, but it had really been consistent now for a season and a half and could not be regarded as a fluke. Koosman's return to health and Seaver's obvious excellence would make any staff a strong one, just by their presence; but the Mets also had half a dozen others who could be relied upon.

The winning streak had also made people recognize other improvements. The fielding was sound, no matter how the lineup was juggled, and the Mets were making plays correctly in key situations—exactly the thing the old Mets had never done. The play Weis made in the 15th inning was a constantly cited example.

Yet, although all these could make a club respectable, and bring it to .500 or even a little higher, they could not overcome a persistent batting weakness. Pitchers, no matter how talented, must have a reasonable number of runs. They need an easy inning, and an easy game, once in a while. Even with Cleon hitting .343 and Agee .278, the Mets were offense-starved. They were better than they used to be but too vulnerable too often. Opposing pitchers could "pitch around" Jones, by walking him or not giving him a good pitch to hit, when the game was on the bases. They could pitch around Agee, or Shamsky, or Swoboda, when one of them happened to be the feared batter, and the rest of the Met lineup was not that frightening.

But if you added Clendenon, the picture changed in more than one slot in the batting order. If Clendenon was a home-run threat, the men ahead of him in the batting order could not be "pitched around" so blithely. With a man on second and two out, for instance, a left-handed pitcher might well risk walking Jones if Kranepool were up next—but if it were Clendenon, it might cost three runs, so better to take one's chances with Jones. Thereupon, Cleon might drive in the run.

And Clendenon was not ineffective against right-handed pitching either. Anyhow, he made the first-base slot in the batting order a strong one if he shared it with Kranepool; he could take over full time if Kranepool slumped; and he provided Hodges with an extra pinch hitter, a believably strong pinch hitter. If Clendenon were playing, Kranepool (or whomever else Clendenon replaced) would be on the bench, available to bat if the need arose or if the other team changed pitchers. If Clendenon were not in the starting lineup, he was the dangerous pinch hitter himself. Too often, Hodges used to find himself in situations where the bench contained no substitute batter the other manager had to fear if he brought in a left-hander or a right-hander, according to circumstances; now Hodges had a card in his hand that might force the opposing manager to think differently.

It was exactly this chain reaction that Young, and others, had in mind when they were so disappointed at the failure to get Torre. A right-handed power hitter like that, Young had insisted, could make the Mets a pennant contender. Hodges and Murphy weren't so sure it would have that great an effect so quickly and didn't want to mortgage the future, but they certainly agreed in principle.

Well, Clendenon wasn't exactly Torre, but he represented the same factors —and he hadn't cost anything at all that the Mets had to use.

The Mets who left Los Angeles on the morning of June 16, therefore, were fundamentally different from the Mets of before. If Clendenon came through as one could expect, the team was strong enough to hold the position it had gained: four games above .500 and second place in the east. And no one minimized what an achievement it would be for a Met team to finish second.

A doubleheader in Philadelphia was the next assignment, and after Gentry posted a 1–0 victory, Clendenon made his debut in the second game, which the Mets lost, 7–3. Koosman followed with a 2–0 shutout, and in the final game the Mets scored two in the ninth to win 6–5, although Seaver didn't get credit for the victory.

The Mets had completed the long trip with an 8–4 record—unheard of for a Met trip. They were only five and a half games behind the Cubs now, and people were beginning to say, in an offhand, semiembarrassed, obviously joking way, "you think they can catch the Cubs?"

Heh heh.

But wasn't it wonderful that one could even think this way? Suddenly, the schedule was worth looking at. Let's see: the Cubs will be coming to New York on July 8—less than three weeks away. And the next week, the Mets will be in Chicago. If we can stay this close. . .

A whole new set of emotions was gestating in the hearts of Met fans.

And the players were beginning to believe.

To welcome home the conquering heroes (Conquering heroes? Mets?!) the largest crowd of the season filled Shea Stadium—54,000. It included Vladimir Horowitz, the world-famous pianist, whose true interest was the visiting team, the Cardinals. He had become a baseball fan by watching them play in three of the last five World Series on television and was as excited as any teenager when he was allowed to go into the dugout to meet them. He also autographed a toy piano for Hodges, who reported that one of his three daughters was taking piano lessons, and shook hands with Seaver and Swoboda.

The Cardinals were in fourth place, one game under .500, three and a half games behind the Mets, with more than half a season to go. There was no reason to doubt that they would get straightened out and take charge of the pursuit of the Cubs at any moment—perhaps right now. Both the Cardinals and the Mets could be put in their proper places in this series, especially since it was starting with Gibson pitching against Ryan.

But a perfectly executed relay, Jones to Harrelson to Grote, nailed Pinson for the third out as he tried to score on Torre's double in the first inning, and the Mets promptly tore into Gibson for three runs. They added another in the second, on Agee's single and Boswell's triple, and then hung on. Ryan gave up two runs in the fifth on a couple of infield hits and Garrett's wild throw, and Gibson greeted McAndrew with a home run leading off the seventh, cutting the margin to 4–3. But McAndrew retired the next nine men, striking out the side in the ninth, and Horowitz went home disappointed.

The Cards won on Saturday, and 55,000—a new season high for the league—came out for Sunday's doubleheader. The Mets won the opener, 5–3, and Koosman, surviving several crises, took the second 1–0, not getting his run until there were two out in the seventh, when Harrelson tripled and Agee doubled.

The Met share of the spotlight was getting bigger.

Those who looked at the league standings with sophistication noted that there was only a three-game gap "on the loss side" between the Mets and the Cubs. That is, the Mets had lost 28 games and the Cubs 25. The Cubs had played more games, and had 42 victories to 36 for the Mets, so that their actual margin was four and a half games. But baseball people liked to say that only the loss column mattered: you could still win the extra games you had to play; you could never erase a defeat from the record. From this point of view, the Mets were actually closer to first place than the "games behind the leader" figure indicated. And this situation would persist through most of what followed.

On Tuesday, June 24, the Mets had a doubleheader with the Phillies at Shea Stadium. The Phillies had several men injured, and were kept out of last place only by the 20-game losing streak Montreal had just gone through. Nevertheless, 40,000 faithful turned out. To make things a little easier, Richie Allen, the awesome home-run hitter who always hit best at Shea Stadium, simply didn't show up. He had done that before, but this time it set off a struggle that kept him idle for a month, led to Manager Bob Skinner's dismissal, and got Allen traded to St. Louis after the season was over. That, however, was not Met business; Met business was winning the two games, 2–1 behind Seaver and 5–0 as McAndrew allowed two hits in eight innings and Taylor pitched a perfect ninth.

This made 20 victories in the last 25 games and put the Mets 10 games over .500.

Harrelson was leaving now, for two weeks of Army duty, and Weis would play shortstop. Bobby Pfeil, a right-handed hitter, was called up from Jacksonville for utility infield work. The Mets were a national topic of conversation again.

Even Hodges confessed he was surprised.

"I expected us to really come on strong the second half of the season," he said, "but I didn't think we'd have a streak like this so early. But," he added, with that slow smile, "I'll take it."

All streaks end, however. The Mets were due for a sag, and it arrived in the middle of the next game. They were leading the crippled Phillies, 5–0 after five innings, with Ryan pitching. But the Phillies scored three in the sixth and one in the seventh. Their one able-bodied substitute was a man named Dave Watkins, a reserve catcher who was now pressed into service at third base. He had hit two singles all year.

So Watkins hit a home run in the eighth to tie the score, and a triple in the 10th. John Briggs singled him home with two out and the Mets lost, 6–5.

They got shut out, 2–0, the next night by Grant Jackson and were beaten 3–1 by Steve Blass of Pittsburgh the night after that. This was the eve of Oldtimers' Night, which would be celebrated June 28, and Stengel was on hand, along with some 30 Hall-of-Famers. It was a gala party, and Stengel rambled on about how good a job Hodges was doing and what it meant to have Grote keep the pitchers from worrying about the runner on first, and how the Amazin's were really amazin' at last, but what they saw was a 2–2 game that fell apart in the eighth when the Pirates scored five runs after Kranepool had messed up a bunt. It ended 7–4, and the Mets had their fourth straight defeat. The gap in the loss column was six games, and the Pirates in third place were only two games behind New York. There was still plenty of time for the Mets to turn into pumpkins again.

However, these Mets had Tom Seaver. He stopped Pittsburgh, 7–3, on Sunday, bringing his own record to 12–3. This was what baseball men meant by a "stopper": a first-line pitcher so reliable that he usually supplied a victory any time a real losing streak threatened to get started. The getaway victory was all the more significant because the Mets were going to St. Louis for five games, where the growth possibilities of a losing streak were excellent.

Instead, they hit the Cardinals (who had just lost a doubleheader in Chicago) in a winning frame of mind. They exploded for six runs in the first inning and won, 10–2. The Cards reasserted themselves the next night by sweeping a doubleheader, but then came one of those pivotal ball games that belie the common remark that "all victories count the same." It wasn't quite a turning point, in the sense that they can be singled out as changing the direction of a season, but it was still a game whose consequences had more effect on the participants than just one more addition to the win column.

Koosman took a 4–0 lead into the eighth inning, but when he tired and filled the bases with two out, with the right-handed Julian Javier coming up, Hodges brought in Taylor, because Javier could hit a home run in such a situation. But Red Schoendienst, the Cardinal manager, switched to Vic Davalillo, a little left-handed pinch hitter who rarely hit homers—and Davalillo hit a grand slam, tying the game.

In the ninth, McGraw took over, and the tie remained until the 14th inning. In every inning, the Cardinals had men on base, and in every inning McGraw managed to work out of the jam. Finally, in the 14th, Agee singled, stole second, and scored on Boswell's hit, and a bases-loaded walk to Garrett (who had driven in three runs earlier) made the final score 6–4. McGraw, working six innings, was the winner.

"That game," Johnny Murphy said months later, "was the one that matured McGraw as a relief pitcher. After that, I think, he never lacked confidence that he could get through any situation."

(McGraw's confidence never did lack expression. Once he found himself in trouble because of a bad-hop grounder and two errors by the infielders. Walker went out to the mound and offered the standard advice when a double play was needed.

"Make him hit it on the ground," said Walker.

"For God's sake, haven't you been watching the game?" bleated McGraw.)

Then the Mets wound up the visit to St. Louis with an 8–1 victory behind Gentry. Whatever resurgence the Cardinals had in mind was postponed again. And when the Mets pounded out two victories in Pittsburgh on July 4 (in a doubleheader that started at 10:30 A.M.), by scores of 11–6 and 9–2, they were 10 games over .500 again. They were rained out Saturday but won again on Sunday even though they fell behind, 6–1, in the first two innings. A three-run homer by Clendenon capped a four-run sixth inning and produced an 8–7 victory—exactly the sort that would have been so unlikely before Clendenon was acquired. The same day, the Cardinals obligingly beat Chicago twice.

In the past, this date (July 6) would have brought the Mets to the All-Star break. In 1969, because of the change to two divisions, the All-Star Game had been scheduled for July 22, well past the midpoint of the season. The pertinent comparison, therefore, was to all-star breaks in former years. With a 45–34 record, only five games out of first place, they were incredibly better off than they had ever been at any point of a season, let alone the midpoint. The big series with Chicago was coming up, they really did think of themselves as pennant contenders now, and they were the hottest sports story in America.

The sports editor of *The New York Times,* James Roach, asked Weissman what the Met policy would be on purchasing World Series tickets. Weissman, as fatalistically superstitious as he was worry-prone, tried to laugh and ignore him. His more immediate problem was handling the flood of requests for working accommodations from press, radio, television, and newsreels for the Cub series.

Book publishers were lining up authors in half a dozen directions, in unprecedented fashion for baseball. Almost every regularly assigned Met writer was being offered some kind of book deal. But these were for after the season, many of them contingent. The real indication of Met importance was their adoption by Dick Schaap.

Schaap was the latest, and most successful, entrepreneur of best-selling sports books that would go beyond the strictly sports-fan market. He had produced a best-seller with Jerry Kramer, the Green Bay Packer lineman, and was deeply involved with Namath for a book and television show. A former newspaper columnist, Schaap now ranked as a latter-day Dumas in operating a literary factory, a sort of Sol Hurok of sports literature, and he turned his forces full blast on the Mets. There would be no waiting to see what happened: it was clear enough that the Mets would not be last, wherever they finished. So Schaap, with the assistance of much of the regular press corps, embarked on an in-depth study of the two weeks coming up—the two series with the Cubs. (The book, called *The Year the Mets Lost Last Place,* came out even before the Mets won the World Series.)

Because Schaap was a gregarious, generally popular, and certainly well-known person in the writing community, his activity brought home to everyone what a new dimension of public interest the Mets had attained.

And they were, now, a national story equal in power to what they had been in Stengel's day. There were two main topics of barroom, tearoom, livingroom, and street-corner conversation in America at this time: man's impending landing on the moon, scheduled for July 20—and the Mets. Jokes were already being formulated about which event was more amazing, and harder to achieve.

Mrs. Payson, vacationing in Maine, had special arrangements made for a local radio station to bring her the games. In ticket brokers' offices in Manhattan, the Met games were the "hot ticket." In radio-television-land, where for so long baseball broadcasts had been considered a mixed blessing (because of the unpredictable time factor, the drop in glamor of the New York teams, and the greater profitability of movies and disc jockeys), Met ratings were going through the roof, and executives were congratulating themselves on their good fortune. At Rheingold, the beer whose 10-minute head had stayed staunchly on the Mets for eight years, they were pinching themselves.

Among Met insiders, there was not yet any real feeling that a pennant would be won. It was too satisfying merely to be in a contending position, an accomplishment that had seemed so far away only six weeks before. Sufficient unto the day, and so forth.

And, of course, underneath it all, gnawed the conditioned expectation that in a few days the whole bubble would burst. The Cubs, who looked so strong regardless of what the Cardinals did or did not do, would now polish off the Mets, who could then concentrate on saving second or third place.

As it happened, because schedule-makers are not soothsayers, the Tuesday and Thursday games of the series were day games, with only the Wednesday game scheduled for night. Also, all sorts of promotional plans had involved giving away free tickets for the day games, when they had loomed as ordinary dates. So although the paid attendance on Tuesday was only 37,000, and on Thursday 36,000, the park was filled to its 50,000-plus capacity for every game.

Turning Point No. 3 had arrived.

Koosman started the series against Ferguson Jenkins. Kranepool hit a home run in the fifth for the game's first run, but the Cubs tied it in the sixth (a homer by Banks), went ahead in the seventh (walk, sacrifice, single by Glen Beckert), and made it 3–1 in the eighth (Hickman's homer). "The first crucial game in Met history" was about to go against them, as if preordained.

Boswell led off the ninth, batting for Koosman, and hit a weak fly to short center. Don Young, the centerfielder, was confused by the sun, the background of the crowded stands, and by whatever else bothered him—and didn't break in on the ball. It fell for a double. Agee fouled out, and Pfeil was due up, but Hodges sent up Clendenon—that extra pinch hitter not available a month ago. Clendenon hit a high drive to left center, not far enough to reach the wall, and Young, racing into the gap, caught it—but couldn't hold it as he crashed into the fence. Boswell, who had to wait, moved to third, and Clendenon reached second, where he represented the tying run in scoring position.

Jones promptly doubled into the left field corner, and it was 3–3, with the winning run on second. Shamsky was purposely passed, to make a double play possible, and Jenkins did make Garrett hit a grounder. But it was hit too softly for anything but a play at first, and the runners moved up. Durocher now had to choose: he could have Jenkins pitch to Kranepool with first base open, or walk Kranepool and pitch to Martin, also a left-handed hitter. If he did the latter, a walk could force in the winning run, and Jenkins would have a little less freedom in trying to make the batter hit a bad pitch. Besides, there had been little wrong with the way Jenkins had pitched, only with the way the outfield had played. He would take his chances with Kranepool, trying to make him bite at a pitch off the plate.

Kranepool knew that too. He picked one out and lined it into left for a game-winning single.

Same old Mets? Not on your life. But the world hadn't seen anything yet.

Seaver started the second game against Ken Holtzman. He never looked faster, striking out two of the first three batters. Then Agee tripled into the right field corner on Holtzman's first pitch. Pfeil doubled to left. On three pitches, the Mets had a 1–0 lead and the crowd—59,000, the largest ever at a Met game—was boiling over with ecstasy.

Seaver struck out the side in the second, and with one out in the Met half, Santo and Don Kessinger made errors on successive ground balls. Seaver lined a single to right center, Agee doubled, and it was 3–0. All Seaver had to do now was hold the lead.

He did better. He got the side in order in the third, fourth, fifth, sixth, seventh. He was pitching a perfect game. Jones hit a homer in the seventh, raising the margin to 4–0. Now victory was taken for granted and the audience—in the park and out—was absorbed with a much greater stake. A perfect game is a once-in-a-lifetime experience not only for the man who pitches it but for the spectators. There had been fewer than 10 in all baseball history, and fans are aware of that. There is no counterpart in other sports for this particular tension-building possibility.

And Seaver moved toward it by posting his 10th and 11th strikeouts in the eighth.

Hundley led off the ninth by trying to bunt his way on but tapped it right back to Seaver, who threw him out.

Two outs to go.

Jimmy Qualls, 22 years old, left-handed batter, playing the 18th game of his major league career, was next. He was the centerfielder, in the lineup not because Young's difficulties the day before had annoyed Durocher (which they had) but because Seaver was right-handed.

And Qualls lined a clean single to left center.

In a haze of disappointment, glory, excitement, noise, triumph, exhaustion, unreality, Seaver got the next two outs. His near-miss was no less a story than the perfect game would have been.

And the standings showed the Mets only three games out of the league lead, only one behind in that "all-important" loss column.

Almost before one could realize it, the teams were back on the field the next afternoon, Gentry vs. Hands. Agee led off with a homer, and the Mets were in front again. Each team scored in the fourth, but the Cubs scored five in the fifth, and there were no more Met heroics that day. The Cubs won, 6–2, and left town four games ahead.

"Wait until we get them back in our park," Santo promised.

Regardless of what would happen there, Turning Point No. 3 had been passed through. The Mets had made their contender rating believable once and for all, not only by winning two of the three games but by the manner of their victories. Within the baseball world, they would not be taken lightly again—although no one really expected them to come out on top at the end.

Outside the baseball world, their renewed fame produced tangents. To the general public, it was as if the original Mets had really been transformed, magically, into princes. Having stopped paying attention while Stengel was still manager, the casual followers came back, four years later, with their mental stereotypes intact, oblivious to the gradual processes that had intervened. The name of Throneberry was being invoked over and over again; and the mental state of the Shea Stadium customers was being completely misconstrued by all the deep thinkers from other disciplines. Such topics as "Will success spoil the Mets," and masochism, and identification with defeat, and the aspirations of the deprived, were revived widely. That these things had nothing whatever to do with the rather square, mainstream suburban, honestly victory-hungry "nice people" who now patronized the Mets was blithely ignored. Kookiness had been the Met image and kookiness it would remain, unable to cross the abyss between the real world the Mets now lived in and the mythology of the past.

When the Cubs left New York, the Mets had a reaction to the emotional drain of that series and took an 11–4 licking from Montreal. Then, in one of those countless minor lucky breaks, it rained, giving them a day to relax. They returned to work Sunday and swept a doubleheader, 4–3 behind Koosman and 9–7 with Agee hitting two homers, and moved on to Chicago trailing by four and a half games, to confront Turning Point No. 4.

As uplifting as the series in New York had been, the Mets had to do as well in enemy country to keep from losing ground and to keep themselves believable in their own and Chicago's eyes. These would be all day games (since there were no lights at Wrigley Field), and all televised back to New York, by hasty arrangement. They had, therefore, a World Series type of impact on New Yorkers, since midweek working days were disrupted in countless offices as people tried to sneak a look at some television set. Ordinarily, that occurred only in October.

Seaver and Hands formed the matchup for the first game, and Seaver lost, by the classic Met score of 1–0. In the sixth inning, Kessinger bunted safely, moved up on a hit-and-run ground out, and scored on a single by Williams. The Mets made six hits but never two in one inning, and that was it.

That made the second game of the series a turning point. To avoid losing ground for sure, the Mets had to win now.

It was Selma against them again, facing Gentry. In the fourth, with the score 1–1 and two out and two men on base, Weis hit a home run—his first of the season, his second as a Met, his fifth as a major league player. The Mets were stunned and delighted; the Cubs, and their 40,000 fans, just stunned. An inning later, Boswell hit a homer, and that turned out to be the winning run, because Williams and Santo hit successive homers in the eighth off Gentry. Taylor came in, got the last four outs, and the Mets were in, 5–4.

Now for the rubber game. The teams would not meet again, after this, until mid-September. Cardwell, the hard-luck veteran (and once a Cub; he pitched a no-hitter for them nine years before), was the Met pitcher, against Jenkins. Every gambler knew that the Cubs were favored in a match-up like that.

But—Agee doubled, Boswell singled, Jones singled, Shamsky struck out, Garrett was walked intentionally, Kranepool singled, Martin singled—and Cardwell had a 4–0 lead before he went to the mound. In the second, Agee's homer and a couple of singles made it 6–0. Cardwell, however, didn't have it. The Cubs got four runs back in the second and scored off McAndrew in the third before Koonce got out with minimum lead intact, 6–5. What he needed now was working room, and in the fifth he got it from the most unlikely source: another home run by Weis, this time off Rich Nye.

Amazing.

At 7–5, the game was still in danger. With two out in the eighth, Santo's error was followed by Shamsky's home run, and at 9–5, it was safe. Taylor mopped up the last two innings. The confrontation, and Schaap's Operation Instant History, were over.

The Mets had done it again. They had steamed through Turning Point No. 4 in fine style; they had shoved Chicago's sneering challenge down Chicago's throat. They had asserted their baseball manhood beyond dispute. They had climbed to within one game of the lead in the loss column (3½ games altogether). They were 15 games over .500, and they had just won 34 of their last 47 games. Could it go on this way?

Why not?

July 17 was an off-day in Montreal, and the day of the launching of the moon shot. A new sort of suspense had been created. The moon landing was scheduled for very late Sunday night. By that time, the Mets would have played four games in Montreal and the Cubs four in Philadelphia. It was a mathematical possibility, therefore, that the Mets might set foot in first place before mankind set foot on the moon. The two staggering thoughts sort of knocked each other over.

It didn't turn out that way, however. The Mets had a terrible time winning two out of four in Montreal. Jones had a fist fight with Ron Brand after sliding home in the Friday night game, which Koosman won 5–2. But Seaver reported a sore shoulder and lasted only two innings on Saturday; that the Mets lost, 5–4, was much less frightening than the idea that Seaver wasn't right. On Sunday, Gentry lost the opener, 3–2, when he gave up three home runs in the fourth inning; and there was a scare in the second game when Agee ran into a fence and seemed to be seriously injured. Still, the Mets managed to win that one in the 10th, when Swoboda doubled with two out and came around on Pfeil's bunt, which was allowed to roll down the foul line until it hit third base.

Thus the Mets came to the All-Star break, firmly in second place. The Cubs, who had won three out of four from the Phillies, were 4½ games ahead of them; the Cardinals (only one game over .500) were 6½ games behind them. As all baseball's elite gathered for the special celebration in Washington to commemorate professional baseball's 100th year, the moon walk and the Met ascent got equal billing in over-cocktails discussions. Seaver, Koosman, and Jones were present as members of the All-Star team, and the front office people, naturally, were part of the elite. It was a festive three days. In the game itself (postponed by a violent rainstorm Tuesday night and played Wednesday), Jones got two hits, Koosman pitched an inning and two-thirds, and Seaver nursed his shoulder. The point was, no one any longer paid attention to what Mets did or didn't do in the All-Star Game, because it no longer mattered symbolically. It had become as routine an occasion for Mets as for any "regular club."

The two-month period that had started so unobtrusively with the 11-inning, 1–0 victory over San Diego on May 27 had been so intense that the pace simply could not be maintained. The break in routine represented by the All-Star game served to cool things off psychologically, to alter momentum, to put things back into perspective. The Cardinals, floundering so mysteriously for so long with no evident cause, still had plenty of time to make their run; the Mets certainly didn't figure to go the additional distance above .500 it would take to win themselves—especially with Seaver in questionable condition. The Cubs might be all right, or they might fall back—but if they fell back, what it would amount to was that the Mets had held them back for the benefit of the Cardinals.

That was the sound thinking among the hardheaded experts when play resumed on July 24, and for the next three weeks this logical approach seemed eminently justified. Boswell went into service; Harrelson returned but needed time to get his timing back; Seaver was not incapacitated but struggling; McAndrew was just coming around; none of the hitters were staying as hot as Jones had been earlier. In general, there was a sag in efficiency. The Mets were still playing far better than any previous Mets, but the expectations aroused by June and July were excessive, it had to be admitted.

A five-team race was developing in the Western Division, and for the next six weeks the Mets would be playing only Western Division teams, starting with Cincinnati. A slow decline set in, and the Mets faded a bit from the headlines as the football season's exhibition games (which would include a Giants-Jets clash at the Yale Bowl) approached.

The Mets finished July on a low note. After splitting four games with the Reds, they were humiliated by Houston at Shea Stadium. In a doubleheader, the Astros scored 11 runs in the ninth inning of the first game, which ended 16–3, and 10 runs in the third inning of the second game, which ended 11–5. It was during that 10-run inning that Hodges walked all the way out to left field to ask Jones if anything was wrong after Jones had given only perfunctory chase to an extra-base hit. Hodges took him back to the dugout and later announced that Jones was suffering from a muscle pull, but the disciplinary lesson was lost on no one, least of all the other players: you played all out for Hodges, or you didn't play, although you were afforded the protection of the benefit of the doubt: perhaps it was an injury that prevented you from doing your best, and in that case you shouldn't be playing. That Cleon Jones was an All-Star and a contender for the league batting title made no difference—and that was a large part of the lesson.

The next day, Jones sat, and Houston's Griffin shut the Mets out on four hits, 2–0.

The Mets perked up by sweeping Atlanta, 5–4, 1–0 (in an encouraging performance by McAndrew and McGraw, who was back from service) and 6–5 in 11 innings. But they lost three out of four in Cincinnati (with Koosman dropping the opener, 1–0) before getting another crack at the Braves. In Atlanta, they lost a frustrating 10-inning, 1–0 decision to Ron Reed but won three other games. From there they went to the Astrodome for three games with Houston. That would end their season's business with the three clubs they had just been playing, unless, of course, one of them finished first and the Mets did too—which did not seem likely on either side. In Houston, it was complete collapse: Griffin shut them out again, 3–0; Koosman, unable to hold a 5–1 lead, was beaten 8–7; and Gentry was polished off quickly, 8–2.

The universe was getting more orderly again. Since the all-star break, the Mets had won nine games and lost 12, proving (the experts said sagely) that the force of gravity had not been repealed when the moon had been trod upon.

And the Cardinals, as predicted, had been coming on, winning 16 out of 20. The Cubs were holding their own, but the Cards had a good crack at them, and the Pirates, their injured players functioning again, were not that far behind the Mets, whom they would play nine times in September.

And so, on August 15, the Mets sat in third place, 9½ games behind the Cubs (and eight on the loss side), one behind the Cardinals (who had actually lost one more) and only 3½ ahead of Pittsburgh. With 49 games to play, after all their Herculean accomplishments, the Mets still had a real task ahead of them to save third place.

They were at Turning Point No. 5.

THE HIGHEST JOY

Amid jubilation, exultation and rejoicing, the myriad members of the Celestial Chapter of the New York Mets Fan Club held this week's meeting on Cloud Nine. After the 15-inning, 1-0 victory that completed successive sweeps of the Giants and Dodgers and the rise to second place, so much enthusiasm had been whipped up that some Immortals seemed to be about to blow their minds.

"Next Year has come!" cried Percy Shelley, who always tended to get carried away by emotion.

"It's great to be immortal and a Met," roared Rabelais zestfully, more gargantuan than ever.

"Today Sol Three, tomorrow the whole Milky Way Galaxy," shouted Jules Verne, who tried faithfully to keep abreast of current terminology in science fiction.

"Fella, fellas, please, let's settle down," called out Will Shakespeare, informal leader of the gathering. "We have an important matter to deal with, and we want to get started, even though we do have all the time in the universe."

The Ultimate Thrill

The noise subsided, but the ether remained electric with excitement.

"After seven lean years as Met fans," Shakespeare began, "there are signs that seven years of plenty are beginning. We've all seen the tricky bounces and friendly gusts of wind that indicate Providence is starting to smile on the legitimately splendid efforts of our improved players. It is quite possible, in short, that the Mets will win the pennant, or come close.

"Our full enjoyment of this millennium, however, cannot be left to the inadequacies of the communications media. Radio and television reception is abominable because of interference from all that silly moonshot gadgetry, and newspapers and magazines insist on devoting much of their space, unaccountably, to countless other demonstrations of what fools these mortals be.

"We, therefore, will send our own correspondents to travel with the Mets and report directly the daily details of their developing epic. Obviously, our reporter must have the literary talent, the breadth of human understanding, and the intellectual dimensions needed to do justice to this new chapter of Met history. Our job now is to choose that man."

The nominations began.

"You used the word epic quite properly," Aristotle declared. "I propose we send my good friend Homer."

"With all due respect, I object," said Cicero. "Homer, being blind, will be instinctively too sympathetic to umpires. Vergil would be more objective."

"I must decline," Vergil demurred. "I am still at work on my epic about how Stan Musial vanquished a thousand pitchers: 'Of arms and The Man I sing, and . . . .'"

The pace quickened.

"Milton could give us a 'Paradise—At Last'—but no, he's as blind as Homer."

"Cervantes? Too quixotic."

"Balzac? He'd never fit in three-abreast seating on the plane trips."

"Chaucer's great on road trips. We'd get The Shortstop's Tale, The Manager's Tale, The Yogi's Tale . . . ."

The Supreme Satisfaction

"You know Omar Khayyam, over at Elysium East? He's got the good attitude—a hot dog, a can of beer . . . . . ."

"I love Jane Austen's style—but she couldn't do dressing rooms, could she?"

But finally it was Shakespeare himself who came up with the answer.

"We have one man uniquely qualified," he pointed out, "because his acuity of observation is unsurpassed and he has been through Hell as well as through Purgatory and Paradise: Dante Alighieri."

The motion carried. As he donned a rumpled suit and spotted tie to disguise himself as any ordinary baseball writer, Dante was thrilled, but vaguely apprehensive. His Inferno, after all, had always been far more widely read than his Paradiso, contrary to his intentions. Would the pattern be repeated? Could any author ever make fulfillment as fascinating as the agonies of Hell?

He—and the Mets—would soon see.

14 *First Place*

IN retrospect, everything falls into neat patterns. Living through anything
is different. When the eventual result is unknown, the flavor of the event is
less clearly defined. More important, memory is selective and telescopes the
time scale between significant moments; in real life, everything moves at the
same pace, each day has 24 hours, each week seven days. A baseball season
lasts six months, and it is easy to forget how long six months is. To a child
it is almost the whole school year. To a drafted soldier, it is one-quarter of
his military career. To a prospective mother, it is two-thirds of her preg-
nancy. And to anyone involved in a pennant race, it can seem like lifetime
torture, with ecstatic overtones.

If, by some edict, baseball had been abolished on August 15, 1969, the
Mets would have remained an interesting footnote, a warmhearted oddity in
the annals of dramatic entertainment. Their only real achievements had been
two: the Met Mystique of their early years and the spark of interest they had
imparted to an otherwise dull 1969 baseball season in June and July.

Even if, with no such drastic fantasy stipulated, they had simply puttered
along for the rest of the season at a win-one, lose-one pace, they would not
have made any real impact on their business. Their own coterie would have

basked in unprecedented success and the satisfaction of a real advance. But it wouldn't have mattered to anyone else. As perishable as all the commodities sold by the mass media, the Mets-Cubs excitement had run its course and was already half-forgotten.

Not everywhere, of course; not by everyone. Mr. Roach still wanted Mr. Weissman to tell him about World Series tickets, and now Mr. Weissman, underestimating Mr. Roach's blind faith, suspected he was being needled. The Met fans continued to hope, marking on their schedules the next visit of the Cubs to Shea Stadium on September 8–9, and noting that the schedule-makers had arranged the last two Met-Cub games of the season for Wrigley Field on October 1–2, the last two days of the regular season. And the Met players, as realistic as most athletes, didn't doubt they could and should do better than they had the last few weeks but recognized that any return to the excitement of July would depend on Chicago's failure, not their own success.

By and large, publishers and magazine editors were having second thoughts about their plans for Met stories, and Schaap's hasty production appeared to be cream-skimming of a high order. For a little while, the demands on Weissman, and on his assistant (Matt Winick, who had succeeded McDonald as statistician back in the dark ages and had worked his way up), seemed to ease.

Looking back, it is easy to identify the weekend of August 16–17 as a turning point. One should remember, though, that the day-by-day accumulation of game events is the truer picture. By noting how often, and how repetitively, certain names appear in daily triumphs, one can grasp more thoroughly how things really build up: Seaver, Koosman, Agee, Jones, Garrett, Kranepool, Weis—sometimes the names were the expected ones, but sometimes they were not. Those who were there every day could see how the fabric formed itself, what reality Hodges referred to when he spoke of "team effort," what the players meant by the endlessly quoted remarks about "someone always picks us up." The daily observers could also appreciate the little breaks, the lucky (and unlucky) bounces, the single plays that changed the color of a week's worth of games. These were, inevitably, interrelated; if not for Weis's fabulous play in the 15th, no 11-game winning streak; without Garrett's several hardly noticed key hits, no climb far above .500; and so forth.

But on August 15, back from the depressing series in the Astrodome, the Mets had no reason to consider themselves anything special, not being blessed with the gift of foreknowledge.

Turning Point No. 5, therefore, came about in the most unspectacular fashion imaginable. There was to be a four-game series with San Diego, the expansion club now deeply buried in the Western Division cellar. Because it rained Friday, there had to be two doubleheaders, on Saturday and Sunday. Then the Giants and Dodgers would come to Shea for the last time, perhaps for the last really large crowds the Mets could expect, despite the advance sale for the Chicago games in September.

This turning point consisted, then, of about 30 hours' work. The Mets swept San Diego by scores of 2–0, 2–1, 3–2, and 3–2.

Just think: any or all of the four games could have been lost. The Mets just squeaked by against the weakest possible opponent, showing not much offense of their own, cashing in on their deep pitching. It was, in a way, a lucky break of schedule placement. Any of the stronger teams might have beaten the same pitching, with the weak support Met hitters offered. But it was San Diego, at the right moment. In two days, the Mets had a four-game winning streak going and were looking up again. Besides, some highly encouraging items had appeared in those games.

First, Seaver. He pitched eight scoreless innings, allowing four hits in the first game and felt sound. It was an immense relief to him, to his wife Nancy, to Walker, to Hodges, to Murphy, to Grant, and to several million Met fans, and it brightened the future right there.

Then there was McAndrew, who also seemed sound in winning the 2–1 game (with McGraw locking up the last two innings).

Then there were Koosman and Cardwell, who won on Sunday. It was good to see Cardwell win for a change, and Koosman was looking more and more like the pitcher of a year ago.

And then there was Duffy Dyer, who was getting to catch a few games and doing a good job. It was his three-run homer that won Koosman's game.

The Giants and Dodgers were both in the thick of a Western Division race that now had five teams within two games of first place. The Cardinals, by losing one of their three games in Atlanta over the weekend, had nudged the Mets back into second place, but that didn't matter as much as the fact that they were driving on the Cubs at last. They were eight games behind the Cubs with 42 to play and would get seven cracks at them in September; many a Cardinal team had won a pennant from a worse position. Baseball was generating some interest in the pennant race at last, but it didn't involve the Mets.

Until a week later.

On Tuesday night, August 19, with 49,000 customers in Shea Stadium, the Mets and Giants put on another of their extra-inning specials. Gentry started against Marichal, and Marichal (as Seaver was to comment later) was the supreme artist that night. Gentry went through the classic Met-pitcher experience: he pitched a four-hit shutout for 10 innings and got nowhere, leaving the game with the score 0–0.

In the 13th inning, there came a portent, a sign that convinced at least some observers that Fate had made its choice and that somehow or other the Mets were destined for glory. It happened when Willie McCovey came to bat.

McCovey was now the most feared Willie on the Giants, having his greatest year. He led the league in home runs and runs batted in, and was on his way to the Most Valuable Player Award. The Mets, more than any other team, had suffered from his home runs over the years.

So, with nobody on base, Hodges went into his four-man outfield shift. He had done it before, against Richie Allen, and other teams had used something of the sort against McCovey. By spreading four outfielders evenly from foul line to foul line, the defense could be virtually certain of preventing an extra-base hit. The hole that was made on the left side of the infield could be used to punch a single through, but if McCovey chose to do that, he would give up all chance of hitting a home run, and the Mets would gladly take their chances if he settled for a single. If McCovey did swing for distance (as he had to, from his team's point of view), he might hit it over the fence; but anything short of that could be caught or held to a single. At the same time, the psychological effect of four outfielders, clogging the "power alleys," might just induce an extra effort to hit the ball farther—and that usually worked against the hitter, who might overswing. But that was a bonus. The main consideration was to prevent a double or triple at any cost; a home run couldn't be prevented anyhow, if the hitter could hit one that far.

Well, McCovey took his big swing at one of McGraw's pitches and drove the ball far and deep toward the fence in left center field. That's where Jones was playing (since Pfeil, who acted as the fourth outfielder, played the left-field corner). Cleon raced back and made a leaping, backhanded catch right at the wall. People still argue whether or not Jones prevented the ball from going over the fence, but there is no argument that he prevented at least a double or triple only because he had been placed where he could reach the ball. From a three-outfielder alignment, his catch would have been impossible.

An inning later, in the 14th, Marichal made his one and only mistake: with one out, he got a pitch to Agee "up"—higher in the strike zone than he wanted it to be—and Agee hit a home run, winning the game 1–0.

Nationally, this spectacular game didn't get the attention it might have, because that afternoon Holtzman had pitched a no-hitter for the Cubs, and because the Met game itself lasted until midnight, which meant missing many editions of newspapers on the eastern seaboard. To the Mets, however, it suggested that they were back in their June pattern. And to believers in faith, well, when you started using four-man outfields and the play worked. . . .

The next night, McAndrew fired a two-hit shutout and beat the Giants, 6–0. The next afternoon, with Seaver pitching poorly, the Mets made up a 6–2 deficit in the last three innings but lost in the 11th, 7–6. Then they swept a three-game series from the Dodgers again, drawing 138,000 increasingly enthusiastic fans, completing a home stand in which they won nine out of 10.

Suddenly, they were in the pennant race again. Both the Cubs and the Cards had gone through a losing week, and the Mets were only five behind now—three in the loss column—whereas the Cards were actually a percentage point behind Pittsburgh, 8½ games from the top. The thrilling possibilities dormant since mid-July were not only revived but more vivid: at this point, there were 39 games to play, and it became possible to see the finish line.

A certain amount of tension started to build within the Met office. Preparations of some sort for a championship playoff (and World Series) had to be considered. Mr. Weissman had to give Mr. Roach some sort of answer.

In the manager's office, Hodges and Walker plotted their pitching assignments far ahead, making sure Seaver and Koosman would come up for those two Cub games, ready now to move them into a four-day rotation if a real run for the pennant developed. The care in resting them properly could pay off now. The regular fourth-day pitchers on other clubs could not avoid a certain degree of fatigue in September; they always felt it. The Met pitchers might be a little fresher, able to handle an accelerated schedule; and, thank goodness, both aces seemed totally recovered from their ailments.

On the field, the Met players started watching the scoreboard with a new degree of interest. Ball players always watch scoreboards; they care about what other teams are doing, because it's their business. In a tight pennant race, "watching the scoreboard" is a term of derision, used to indicate "fear" of the opposing team and a certain "lack of concentration" about your own game. The Mets, new to this situation, and Hodges, so free of pretense, had no time for such traditional nonsense. Of course they watched the scoreboard to see how the Cubs were doing—with no loss of concentration and with no excessive emotional reaction to what the scoreboard showed. In all respects, the Mets were showing remarkable poise as they entered the "pressure" stage of a pennant race. Of course, it was easy for them in a way: no one had expected them to win it, so no stigma would be attached to losing; they had everything to gain and nothing to lose. Still, it took considerable sangfroid, confidence (in self and in each other) to withstand the ceaseless suggestions that the goblins of nervousness must strike soon.

And what about Hodges? After all, here was a man only 11 months removed from a heart attack. How could he take the mounting tension? Didn't he feel it? Weren't the physical demands of the season taking their toll?

Actually, Hodges was enjoying himself, and his iron self-control enabled him to keep in proportion both his emotions and his activities. Always a deeply religious man, in a completely nonpompous and non-self-righteous way, he had come to terms with all sorts of priorities during the early stages of his illness. He'd been through "nervous" pennant races before; he wasn't yet (as the team headed for California on August 26) that far into this one. But he carefully followed his prescribed diet, he didn't backslide into smoking, he got his rest, he did his work, and he succeeded in being involved in every moment without becoming submerged in it.

And close by, watching like a bodyguard to shoo people away if some situation became too tense for too long, was Pignatano, the family friend and loyal lieutenant, whose Chico Marx face often misled strangers about the warm common sense behind it.

The trip began in San Diego with a doubleheader. Seaver, strong again, gave up two homers but only two other hits and won, 8–4. McAndrew produced another shutout and won, 3–0. Koosman followed with a two-hitter, and won, 4–1. Through all this, the friendly scoreboard showed the Cubs losing twice at home, to Cincinnati.

So the Mets flew up to San Francisco even with the Cubs in the loss column, 2½ games behind because the Cubs had played and won five more games. The Giants were clinging to a half-game lead over Cincinnati and Atlanta. It should be quite a series.

It was pretty good, all right. Marichal, brilliant again, took the first game, 5–0, with a four-hitter, saved from any drawn-out frustration by a three-run homer in the first inning by Bobby Bonds. On Saturday, the Mets survived incredibly complicated Giant threats in the eighth and ninth innings with the score 2–2 and won in the 10th, 3–2. On Sunday, Seaver struck out 11 men in an 8–0 first game, showing his best stuff in weeks, but the Giants pulled out the second game in 11 innings, 3–2.

That brought the season, and the calendar, to Labor Day, Monday, September 1, the formal beginning of baseball's home stretch.

Since the Cubs had swept a three-game series in Atlanta, the margin was four games. And the Dodgers (the next opponent for the Mets), were only half a game out of first place in their race. The real excitement was in the Western Division.

The Mets entered the home stretch by taking a 10–6 licking; Koosman could get only one man out before he was shelled to cover in a five-run first inning, even though he had been given a 2–0 lead. The Mets made four errors. Koonce, who pitched through the sixth, had been hit hard. (He was having arm trouble.) It was, all in all, a miserable game.

And it provoked a remarkable reaction. The Mets entourage was grumpy, critical, almost outraged at the last two defeats. Not frustrated, or half-humorously appalled, as in the past; but sarcastically, almost bitterly, displeased. It was another Met first, a response to a defeat as if it really meant something because there was something meaningful to be won.

Weissman couldn't help but marvel at it. "Imagine," he said, "just yesterday it was going to be the end of the world if we reached .500. Now they're going to say we 'blew' the pennant."

It was true. From expecting nothing, the Met fans had shifted effortlessly to expecting everything.

Hodges, as always, retained a sense of proportion.

"I really didn't think we'd come so far so fast," he said, "but now we're here, and there's no reason to stop. I just hope I don't spoil things for the future by getting so far ahead of schedule. I remember what happened to Bill Rigney when he finished third with the Angels in their second year: after that, everything was bad by comparison. My master plan really was to move up a couple of notches this year, and a little more next year, and so forth. Maybe I've let it run away from me—so maybe we'd better win the whole thing right away."

And his deadpan face made it hard to tell exactly where the sincerity shaded into needling.

For the next two nights, Willie Davis upstaged the Mets. He had the season's longest hitting streak going, and when it reached 30 games it became a Dodger record, wiping out one that had stood since 1916. (It belonged to Zach Wheat, whose buddy, Casey Stengel, was sitting in a box seat next to Edna and Niss, rooting for the Mets. "We didn't know nothin' about streaks then," Stengel said, "we were busy winnin' our first pennant.") On Tuesday night, Gentry took a 5–1 lead into the ninth. But the Dodgers scored three runs off him and Taylor and had men on first and third with two out when McGraw came in to face Davis (who had gotten his hit in the sixth). McGraw struck him out and saved a 5–4 victory. But on Wednesday, after the Mets had scored four in the eighth to create a 4–4 tie, Davis came up in the ninth with one out, a man on second, and his hitting streak on the line after four failures. He could have been walked purposely, but Hodges had DiLauro pitch to him—and Davis lined a double to left, winning the game, 5–4.

The Mets were disgruntled again, but there was a more important indication of their new involvement in serious pennant contention. Koosman, who had been knocked out so quickly on Monday, had been used to start this game on Wednesday. It had to do with the schedule ahead. The way Hodges and Walker had planned it, Koosman would pitch Monday in Los Angeles, Friday at home against Philadelphia, and Tuesday in the second game of the Cub series, with Seaver skipping Philadelphia. Here was an opportunity to have Koosman pitch tonight and then on Monday, while Seaver could face Philadelphia Friday and the Cubs Tuesday. It was a chance to get an extra start out of the two big men, and it was seized. This was pennant-race thinking.

Heading back to New York on September 4, the Mets were five games behind the Cubs, who had shown no serious sign of faltering. The margin on the loss side was three games. Competition with the western clubs was over now, for both of them: from now on, everything would be settled within the Eastern Division. The Cardinals had slipped again, and the Pirates were the hottest team in the league, but both were more than 10 games out and not really in the race at this point. The Met-Cub series in New York would be a showdown after all.

First, the Mets had to play the Phillies four times at Shea, while the Cubs took on the Pirates at Wrigley Field.

On Friday, as the Mets were starting their night doubleheader at Shea, the scoreboard carried the happy news that the Cubs had been beaten by Pittsburgh, 9–2. Seaver increased the excitement by pitching a 5–1 five-hitter, but McAndrew lost the second game to Rick Wise, 4–2. It was Seaver's 20th victory, a minor millennium finally reached by a Met—but statistics were strictly incidental now.

On Saturday, while Cardwell and McGraw combined on a six-hit shutout, 3–0, the scoreboard fairly screamed the news that Pittsburgh had crushed the Cubs, 13–4.

And on Sunday, the game on the scoreboard was far more exciting than the game in the ball park. The Met game was close enough for six innings, but the Mets broke it open with two in the seventh and four in the eighth and won 9–3. Meanwhile, the Cubs fell behind 4–2, pulled closer, and apparently had a victory when Hickman's homer put them ahead, 5–4, in the eighth. ("That Hickman," old Met fans moaned, "after all the games he beat us out of when he was with us, he's beating us again.") But Willie Stargell's homer tied it for Pittsburgh in the ninth, and the Pirates won in the 11th, long after the Met game had ended.

Shea Stadium was bulging with news media representatives now, to a far greater extent even than in July. In New York City, one could hardly talk of anything but the Mets. The three mayoralty candidates were setting Olympic records for bandwagon jumping. The ratings of Channel 9 were not to be believed. The football season was not to be thought of, even though the Jets had opened their regular season that Sunday, and if the Mets kept winning, the Jets would be kept out of Shea Stadium until mid-October. National magazines and book publishers were going full steam ahead with Met material.

It was pennant fever of a virulence New Yorkers had not felt since the days of the Giants and Dodgers, more than a decade ago. The Yankees had been in pennant races since then, but they had been too machine-like. (Today, the Yankees were a fifth-place club, totally ignored except for problems with Joe Pepitone.) This was what Shea and Young—and Mrs. Payson—and millions of others had dreamed about when they wanted "National League baseball back in New York."

Here it was.

The Cubs came in leading by two and a half games, one up on the loss side. They could not be dislodged from first place even if they lost both games, because that would leave them still in front by two percentage points—but they could certainly be shaken. If they could win both, they would probably finish the Mets. A split would keep the pot boiling but represent a small net gain for Chicago—and aim more pressure at those last two games to be played in Wrigley Field.

Statisticians (all positivists now) were quick to point out that the Mets had won 18 of their last 24 games, while the Cubs had lost 10 of their last 18. Cub pitching, dependent on three outstanding starters (Jenkins, Holtzman, Hands) had been faltering badly, because the bull pen was weak and the first three were showing signs of wear. Met pitching seemed in peak health, peak form, and deep. Harrelson and Boswell both had completed their major military commitments now, and since late August, Hodges had settled upon two set platoons: Kranepool, Boswell, and Garrett were the infielders against right-handers; Clendenon, Weis, and Charles played against lefties. Shamsky and Swoboda shared right field, Grote and Martin the catching. Agee, Jones, and Harrelson played against all comers.

But Jones, leading the league with a .348 average, had pulled a leg muscle in Los Angeles. He had rested through the Philadelphia series, hoping to be ready for the Cubs. Now it was time to play, but he wasn't, so Shamsky played left and Swoboda right.

It was Hands vs. Koosman. The "crooshul" series was on.

Koosman made Kessinger fly out and struck out the next two men.

Hands threw his first pitch close to Agee's head, sending him sprawling. Then Agee bounced out, Garrett flied out, and Clendenon fanned.

Every sophisticated baseball fan knew what to expect next. Ron Santo,

Cub captain and most outspoken commentator on how the Mets would fold under pressure, and their most feared clutch-hitter, was first up in the second.

Koosman's first pitch cracked him painfully on the elbow.

No dugouts emptied. Santo went to first without a word. Koosman said nothing.

But the message had been delivered. Met pitchers protect their hitters if Cub pitchers throw at them. There was no beanball war the rest of the series, and the initiative seemed to pass to the Mets. Any nervousness they may have felt had been dissipated by anger.

Koosman then struck out three in a row, and in the third inning he received a 2–0 lead. Harrelson was on first after an infield hit when Koosman made the second out by popping up a bunt attempt—whereupon Agee hit a home run.

("Remember yesterday?" they said in the press box, "when Billy Champion knocked Agee down with the first pitch of the game and Agee hit the next pitch over the fence? I wonder if the Cubs knew that?").

The Cubs made their move in the sixth. Kessinger, Beckert, and Williams singled in succession. Santo flied deep enough to deliver the tying run. But Koosman got out of the inning on a couple of fly balls, and the Mets didn't let the tie last long. Agee ripped a double down the line past Santo at third. Garrett—the unknown, unnoticed, minor league draft pickup—pulled a single through the right side, and the Mets led, 3–2.

And that's how the game ended. The last crisis came when the Cubs opened the eighth with two singles, but Koosman made Santo hit into a double play and fanned Banks. He struck out three more in the ninth, for a total of 13.

New York was a summer festival.

Twenty-two hours later, Seaver went to the mound against Jenkins. One, two, three, the Cubs went out. Mets turn.

Agee walked. Garrett's line drive was caught by Kessinger. Jones (still hobbling), walked. Shamsky's roller to the mound moved the runners up while it made the second out. Poing!! A clean double to right center by Boswell— and Seaver had a 2–0 lead.

He swept through the first nine Cub batters, and Jones led off the Met third with a single. Shamsky forced him, and Hundley had Shamsky out by a mile when an attempted hit-and-run play misfired—so far out, that Shamsky backtracked and got caught in a rundown. But Beckert dropped the ball. Shamsky was safe, back at first and—Bong! Clendenon drove a home run over the right-field fence. It was 4–0, and who was folding under pressure now?

Seaver gave up three hits and a run in the fourth. There would be no more approach to a perfect game this time. But he also doubled and scored a run in the Met half of the inning. Shamsky hit a homer in the fifth. Seaver coasted through a five-hitter. It ended 7–1.

"Goodbye Leo," one of the signs told Durocher.

The Cubs were speechless. The Mets were chortling and jumping around and having fun. They actually had a one-game advantage in that famous loss column, even though the standings still showed them second. "Do you believe us now?" one Met after another would grin at visitors, most of whom were more involved in Met lore than these players had ever been. These players were quite relaxed, quite confident, eager for the next game.

And America had found its favorite new symbol.

Underdogism. The triumph of the lowly. The Impossible Dream. The frog turned into a prince by magic. The force of destiny, God loves the Mets, youth will be served, miracles still happen—the mangled images tumbled one over another. In one of the darker moments of America's national life, the gleam of this new chapter of the Met myth could not be resisted. Just as the original Mets had harmonized with the atmosphere of the Kennedy years, the possibility of Mets triumphant struck the exact chord needed now. Not for a century had national disunity been so much in the forefront of people's thought—disunity about race, war, schools, the control of crime, economics, politics, sexual mores—about anything you could name. And here, suddenly, the ages-old legend of redemption was coming to life in the corniest of American settings, a major league pennant race. The "nothings" could suddenly win it all or at least rise to the top. There was hope in a world where such a thing could happen—and if not hope, at least distraction.

It became unbearably important, at that moment, to have the Mets at least touch first place. It would be, then, an indelible fact for all eternity that they had gone from the bottom to the top. Whether or not they could stay there would matter less.

That the new Met myth was largely irrelevant to reality disturbed no one. These were not, after all, in any remote way the Mets who had suffered. They were young, more talented than they were being given credit for, eager, lucky, dedicated and cheerful—but totally different individuals than the ones who had formed the Mystique. That's precisely why they were winning, because Seaver and Koosman and Agee and Clendenon and Gentry and Boswell and Garrett and Shamsky and Taylor were unconnected to the defeatist days.

But who would dare, in a time of troubles, to be so un-American as to spoil a good story with facts?

There were exceptions. Kranepool really had lived through it all. Swoboda, Jones, McGraw, Harrelson, (and Berra) had caught the end of the Stengel era, but they had been its hopes for the future, not its constructors.

Essentially, though, these were young men, seizing the opportunity to make the careers all normal ball players yearn for—victory, earning power, fame, respect. They were no different from the dozens of other young clubs that had suddenly found themselves, all through baseball history, in some dramatic season. The comic origins of the name on their shirts did not really relate to them.

However, what was untrue for the players was true for the hard core of old Met fans. For them, as for Kranepool, it really was fulfillment after seven years in the desert. In their memories and emotions, there was an unbroken line back to 1962—and the glory now within reach was anything but sudden. They, it was true, were the lowly raised high—but only after several agonizing eternities.

It was only for the larger public that the Cinderella-like myth took form. It seemed a sudden rise to the outside world simply because the outside world never paid attention until the rise was complete. But the power of the myth was so great that it blanketed all national (and worldwide?) reaction: the Mets were the symbol of the impossible attained—not, as was so widely understood about the trip to the moon, as the impossible attained by purposeful hard work but as some sort of supernatural, mystical, logic-defying gift. It was probably the desire to have a mystical idea confirmed by events that made so many people begin rooting for the Mets at this point.

In this light, the night of Wednesday, September 10, took on a ritualistic aspect.

Montreal was coming to Shea for a doubleheader. If the Mets could win both games, they would take over first place no matter what the Cubs did in Philadelphia. If the Cubs lost their game, the Mets could still move ahead with a split. That Montreal was the second generation of expansion was somehow fitting. That the evening could be disappointing was realized by all who remembered the let-down loss the Mets had suffered at Montreal hands right after the big series with the Cubs in July. That there still lurked, in oldest Met breasts, a trace of fear that "if not tonight, maybe never," could not be denied.

In a sense, therefore, Turning Point No. 6 was this first attempt to actually move into first place. The series with the Cubs, in itself, did not deserve that designation because the margin had become so small, and the Met momentum so great, that it would have been a turning point only for the Cubs if the Cubs had won. There were still enough games to play to nullify almost anything that happened in those two. But the symbolic importance of touching the top had taken on value for the Met players as well as for the spectators: they felt the magic of it, the need for it; whether or not they would be able to grasp the opportunity now that it had finally arrived might determine the direction of their graph the rest of the way. In contrast to the first five turning points, this one's timing and meaning could be reasonably anticipated.

And it came in segments.

For the first few innings, the Mets displayed every symptom of inevitable letdown. Ty Cline started the game with a triple off McAndrew, and Harrelson's error let the run in. Mack Jones led off the second with a triple and continued home when Clendenon threw the relay wild. The Mets had scored a run themselves in the first, but they remained behind, 2–1, until the fifth. Then, with two out, Agee was safe on an error, Garrett singled him to third, Jones walked—and a balk by Mike Wegener, the Montreal pitcher, brought in the tying run.

That break seemed to wake the Mets up. When the Expos filled the bases with one out in the sixth, Harrelson started a crisp double play that ended the inning. After 11 innings, the score was still 2–2, even though Wegener had fanned 15 Mets. McAndrew, in nine innings of pitching after the second, had allowed just one hit. By now, the scoreboard showed the game in Philadelphia well in progress, and close.

Taylor, pitching the 12th, gave up two hits with two out but caught Angel Hermoso trying to steal home. Bill Stoneman, relieving Wegener, got two quick outs, but Jones singled. As the crowd began a nonstop roar, Gaspar walked on four straight pitches, and Boswell singled through the box into center, to end the game 3–2.

The Mets were in first place.

People danced in the aisles, literally.

But this was only the first segment of occupancy of the top. Technically, the Mets weren't in first yet because the Cub game was still on, and it is sort of purposeless to revise the standings while a team involved is still playing. If the Cubs won, the Mets would still be second, pending their second game.

Ryan started that one, while the scoreboard showed the Cubs tied, 2–2, after six. The scoreboard in Philadelphia, of course, showed that the Mets had won.

Ryan started that one, while the scoreboard showed the Cubs tied, 2–2, the first two in the second inning and Harrelson made an error, and Montreal had a 1–0 lead.

Then Grote opened the Met third with a double—and the scoreboard showed the Cubs losing, 3–2. Harrelson singled, and when Ryan bounced to third, Grote was run down. But Agee was hit by a pitch, and a wild pitch brought in the tying run.

Now Garrett, Jones, Shamsky, and Boswell singled in succession, and the

Expos made a couple of errors. The Mets had a 6–1 lead. The stands were in a frenzy. And the scoreboard was posting three more runs for Philadelphia in the eighth.

For all practical purposes, it was official. The Mets would sleep in first place that night. But it wasn't really official, because strictly speaking a league standing doesn't exist until all the games scheduled for that day have been completed.

At 10:13 P.M., it became officially official. The Cubs had lost, 6–2. Even if the Mets lost the second game, they would still be first. Millennium, we are here.

But the Mets were no longer in a mood to lose anything. Ryan, with a no-hitter for five innings, completed an 11-strikeout three-hitter. The final score was 7–1. A little past 11:30 P.M., the Mets were back in their clubhouse—their first-place clubhouse.

Imagine.

Even so, life went on. They had to be back at work the next afternoon, to close out the home stand before a trip to Pittsburgh, St. Louis, and Montreal. There were, after all, 21 games still to be played.

So Mr. McAndrew, the young psychologist from Lost Nation, Iowa, who had made his major-league debut amid some skepticism only 14 months before, went out and pitched a six-hit shutout, and won, 4–0.

Now let the Cubs, who had to play in Philadelphia that night, do the worrying.

And just incidentally, McAndrew's victory happened to be No. 85 of the season for the Mets. That was the number Hodges had set as a goal, back in April.

He beamed when reminded of it.

"I said, at *least* 85," he pointed out. Now 85 wasn't enough.

And the Cubs, with the scoreboard glaring at them in Philadelphia, took a 2–1 lead into the eighth inning that night with Selma, the ex-Met, pitching a fine game. But the Phils rallied, and with a man on third Selma committed one of his typical, impulsive acts: he tried to pick the man off third, and picked Santo off too. The ball sailed into left field, and when people stopped running the Phils had a three-run inning. They won the game, 4–3. It was Chicago's eighth straight defeat.

The Mets were ahead by two games—three in that all-important loss column. The Cubs were headed for a series in St. Louis, and neither the Cards nor the Pirates, encouraged by the Cub collapse, considered themselves hopelessly out of the race. The Pirates had nine games to play—half their season's work—with the Mets; the Cards had seven with the Cubs, and five with the

Mets. If the Cubs were really sinking, there was a chance for anybody, because everyone could see the Mets might blow up too at any moment. Just wait until the realization hit them that they were now the leaders.

To the Mets, Pittsburgh represented a truly dangerous obstacle. The Pirates were hitting like mad, and their pitching had steadied. In two months, they had won 31 games and lost 16. The Mets had to play them twice on Friday, once on Saturday, and once on Sunday. Then there would be two games in St. Louis, two in Montreal, and five more with the Pirates in three days at Shea.

If the Met bubble were going to burst, this was the likely time and place. Such a stretch required six starting pitchers, and the bull pen could be chewed up quickly if Pirate bats got rolling.

They had reached, as a matter of fact, Turning Point No. 7 in the doubleheader of Friday night, September 12. A bad start to this Pirate series could lead to disastrous consequences, and there were several additional handicaps:

Jones couldn't play again because of his persistent injuries.

Shamsky couldn't play that night: it was Rosh Hashanah, the Jewish New Year, a religious holiday to be observed.

Boswell couldn't play because he had a weekend military commitment.

That stripped the batting order of power just when it was needed most.

And, sure enough, the regular Met hitters could not produce a run in either game.

But Koosman, the weakest of weak-hitting pitchers, did drive in a run with a single in the fifth game.

And Cardwell, an acknowledged good-hitting pitcher, drove in a run in the second inning of the second game.

And those were the only runs scored at Forbes Field, Pittsburgh, on September 12, 1969.

Two 1–0 victories over the hottest hitting team in baseball, in their park.

To hard-core baseball people—like the Cubs and Cardinals—this was the most amazing accomplishment yet. Koosman had pitched a three-hitter, and Cardwell had given four hits in eight innings before McGraw pitched the ninth.

These scores, on the board in St. Louis long before the Cubs completed a 5–1 victory, provoked uncontrollable head-shaking. Two 1–0 games—with both runs driven in by the pitchers! Not only did it mean that the Mets had two victories in the bank, and that they could not have a losing weekend; it meant that the depth of the pitching staff was untapped for the games ahead. Imagine!

On Saturday, Seaver trailed, 1–0, until the seventh, when Weis knocked in the tying run. In the eighth, Swoboda unloaded a grand slam home run. The Mets won, 5–2—and that one was on the board in St. Louis before the Cubs and Cards went to work.

The loss on Friday night made the Cards feel they had blown their last chance. The Cubs, starting the game with a three-game deficit to the Mets, were still nervous. They had lost eight straight games before the previous night's victory, and they were bewildered; but at least they had won one, and if they could get started now—well, wait until they got the Mets in Chicago those last two days of the season.

They fell behind 2–0, battled back, and took a 4–3 lead into the eighth with Jenkins, their ace, pitching. But Jenkins got into trouble, and Durocher called in Ken Johnson, a veteran picked up during the season after being discarded by the Yankees—and Johnson walked in the tying run. Torre followed with a two-run single that should have been fielded, behind second, by Beckert. Tim McCarver singled too. The Cards had four runs and the game, 7–4.

The Cubs were dead.

They wouldn't admit it, but they knew it. Perhaps without even realizing it, they talked of the season in the past tense.

Unless, of course, the Mets started to feel the pressure and began losing. That would revive the Cubs right quick.

On Sunday the Cubs had their chance. The Mets lost finally, 5–3, ending a 10-game winning streak. Their result was on the board while Gibson and Holtzman, in a torrid pitching duel, battled into extra innings, 1–1. With one out in the 10th, Brock hit a home run, and the Cubs were beaten again, 2–1.

Leo was polite, philosophical, magnanimous—sure signs he knew he was beaten.

Into St. Louis rolled the Amazing Mets, an object of frank admiration to their spring training cotenants. Someone reminded Schoendienst that Red had cited the Mets, back in St. Petersburg, as a team that worried him, as a pennant contender. "That's right, and nobody would believe me," said Schoendienst. "But you could see they were stronger and getting better and had that pitching. I'm sorry I was right."

All across the country, stories about the predestination of Met victory were gaining currency. The game of Monday night, September 15, stimulated such stories.

Steve Carlton, the Cardinal left-hander, was speed-of-light fast that night. He struck out 19 Mets, breaking a major league record shared by Bob Feller and Sandy Koufax. Good, eh? But: leading 1–0 with a man on base in the fourth, he challenged Swoboda with his fast ball—and Ron hit a two-run homer. Leading 3–2 in the eighth, Carlton challenged Swoboda again—and Ron hit another two-run homer.

So Carlton lost, 4–3, and the Cubs got creamed in Montreal, 8–2, and the Mets led by 4½ games with 15 to play, and the "magic number" was 11. Any combination of Met victories and Chicago defeats adding up to 11 would clinch first place for the Mets.

Nothing, it seemed, could go against them now. It rained on Tuesday, so the game had to be transferred to New York, where the Cards would play next week—an extra home game for the Mets. In Montreal, Koosman and Seaver shut out all Canada, 5–0 and 2–0—and the Cubs, losing a game to Philadelphia, fell five games behind, six on the loss side. The magic number was eight. The pace was ever quickening, the rush to destiny becoming headlong.

A crowd of 51,000 greeted the Mets at Shea Stadium Friday night, giving them a club record of 1,969,000 for the season. This time, the anticipated ambush by the Pirates did take place: a double defeat, 8–2 and 8–0, with eight different Met pitchers in action. But it was too late to really hurt. The Cubs split a doubleheader, missing a chance to really gain, and the Mets had plenty of extra bodies now, because the farm club at Tidewater had finished its season (winning the International League pennant, but getting knocked out quickly in the play-offs). Even while losing two games, the Mets had come closer to clinching.

On Saturday, the Mets suffered the not unprecedented indignity of being held hitless. Bob Moose was the fourth man to do it in eight years. However, this had never happened in all major league history to a pennant-winning team involved in a stretch run.

But that didn't hurt either. The Cubs lost that day.

The magic number was six.

On Sunday, in Chicago, the Cubs beat the Cardinals. But in Shea Stadium, the Mets won two tough games from the Pirates, 5–3 and 6–1, with Koosman and Cardwell each going nine innings. The magic number was four.

On Monday night, the makeup of that rainout in St. Louis: Seaver, a four-hitter, 3–1, his 24th victory. The magic number was three.

On Tuesday, the Mets had to face Gibson, seeking his 19th victory and eyeing his 20th beyond that. Lots of threats, on both sides, in almost every inning—but the Mets tied in the eighth and won in the 11th, 3–2. The Cubs? They'd lost that afternoon.

The magic number was one.

If the Cubs could lose to Montreal Wednesday afternoon, the Mets would be divisional champions before they took the field against the Cardinals for their last home game of the season—not counting playoffs, of course. (Not counting playoffs! Remember when that was the ultimate sarcasm?)

But it would be more fun if they could do it themselves.

("Don't be silly," said Hodges, "we'll take it any way it comes.")

The Cubs didn't lose.

Gentry, the rookie, started against Carlton, the new strikeout record-holder. Gentry needed a victory to reach the .500 mark personally, at 12–12. He got the side in order in the first.

Now the Mets.

In the stands, 56,000 people, radiating their craving to be in on the kill. ("We'd like to do it in front of our fans," all the Mets remarked.)

Harrelson (that little, unappreciated pip-squeak) singled. Agee walked. Jones struck out.

Clendenon hit a home run.

Clendenon, who had retired, who had been persuaded to play by none other than the Commissioner himself, who had been worth four "futures" in a trade, who was to provide that one missing piece in the puzzle of insufficient power—Clendenon had just made it 3–0.

Swoboda—Carlton remembered him, all right—walked.

Ed Charles, 36 years old, committed to retirement when the season ended, 10 years in the minors before being given a chance (almost too late) by the Athletics, traded to the Mets as washed-up goods, cut even by the Mets so that he had to win a job in spring training—Ed Charles, poet and elder statesman, hit a home run, and the Mets led 5–0.

The roaring from the stands drowned out the low-flying jets wheeling into La Guardia Airport. All that lay ahead now was a two-hour working-up period to the damnedest celebration anyone wanted to imagine.

Ice the champagne, boys; we're ready.

Gentry never faltered. He allowed only two singles through eight innings. Clendenon had made it 6–0 with another homer in the fifth, off Dave Giusti. When Gentry needed only three more outs, most of the 56,000 were on their feet, yelling, leaning forward, pressing against field gates at the end of each aisle.

Brock scratched a single over the mound. Davalillo singled through the middle. Still three outs to get.

Gentry struck Pinson out—Vada Pinson, who hit .316 in the National League before Gentry was 12 years old.

Now Torre—the man who "might have made a pennant contender out of the Mets." If they had been willing to trade young talent, of course.

Torre rapped the ball sharply to Harrelson—to Weis—to Clendenon. Double play.

Game over.

Race over.

Miracle accomplished. Myth certified. America fulfilled.

The magic number was zero.

At 9:17 P.M., Eastern Summer Time, September 24, 1969.

Just 2,724 days after Stengel exposed his "Metsies" to the Cardinals in their first National League game.

The seven-year famine had ended.

15 *Pennant*

THEY poured out of the stands like deranged lemmings, like the mob attacking the Bastille, like barbarians scaling the walls of ancient Rome, like maddened initiates in some Dionysian rite—driven, however, by pure joy, by ecstasies beyond hope of control. Their destructiveness was spontaneous, unreasoned, free of malice. They wanted—they had to have—something tangible to freeze the moment into perpetual bliss. Chunks of sod, handfuls of dirt, a base, home plate, a slat from a chair, a piece of fence, anything—so long as you could touch it, feel it, take it home, keep it. To call it vandalism was to slander the motivation; to call it souvenir hunting was to demean the age-old power of relic worship; to call it attention-seeking was to pronounce a petty, mean, insensitive judgment. The sack of Shea Stadium that night was an instinctive act, possible only that one time in unpremeditated purity.

It would be repeated soon as cheap imitation, with full awareness of the television camera as an instrument of any fan's self-aggrandizement. It would become, indeed, the coarsest kind of souvenir pursuit and misguided destructiveness, an attempt to be "in" by the most slavish followers of instant fashion.

That night, though, the rush to the field was an act of honest originality.

Football fans, for decades, had torn down goal posts, and some basketball-crazed rooters would occasionally cut down netting, but baseball celebrants traditionally attacked only the players themselves as they raced for the dugouts. Caps, gloves, a torn piece of sleeve—these were the accepted baseball trophies. It took these Metsomaniacs, in one inspired instant, to change the target to the unresisting field itself.

Fifteen minutes after the Mets had clinched their championship, their followers had torn up the Shea Stadium surface. In their personal ascent to the moon, they turned the field into a moonscape.

And, being true Mets with their roots in 1962, they missed first base.

Somehow, the first-base bag had been overlooked while the mob appropriated everything that wasn't nailed down and quite a few objects that were.

The most remarkable feature of this milling, yelling celebration, which went on for about half an hour, was something that was not repeated in the similar scenes after the play-off and World Series. This night, even while some fans were gouging out huge chunks of turf on the field, dozens and perhaps hundreds of others climbed on the outfield fence—and just sat there, like so many perched birds, their feet dangling down, not cheering, not waving arms, not taking anything, not harming the fence: just sitting blissfully and watching others strip the stadium.

Inside the Met clubhouse, the expected hysterics could be found—and televised. The players used champagne as a weapon and as a medium to move through. Its function as a beverage was not really recognized until a couple of hours later, when a party in the Diamond Club for the players, their wives, and Met officials hit full stride. Mythology calls for wild celebration by sports winners: in this case, the Mets carried out in real life the mandates of mythology to the fullest.

And for once, another cherished legend proved true: this triumph meant even more to the fans than to the players, as involved as the players were. This time—this one time—the true Met fans had really made a greater, longer emotional investment than the actual Mets.

So overwhelming were the feelings all around that it took almost 24 hours to focus on the fact that the Mets hadn't won anything yet.

Under the new divisional setup, finishing first didn't make you a pennant winner. Baseball's rulers, in their decidedly finite wisdom, had made no provision to recognize a divisional leader as anything but a qualifier for the play-off. There would be no trophy, no flag, no official designation of any sort for the "Champion of the Eastern Division," so far as anyone could determine. All one could win in 162 games was the right to play a three-out-of-five series to become the champion—or the runner-up.

In one sense, it didn't really matter. The myth had been fulfilled by the words (and reality) "first place." But myths can be tarnished and their lives shortened by asteriskization, as Maris's home-run record had been. To make it stick, the Mets would have to win the play-off.

Play-off with whom? Well, on the morning of September 25, there were three possibilities: Atlanta, the Western Division leader; San Francisco, a game and a half behind; and Cincinnati, three games back. While the Mets spent their off-day making a mass recording of terrible singing, signing up to appear in Las Vegas with Phil Foster, and making other private commercial arrangements, a bit of America's attention allowed itself to shift to the problem of an opponent for the Mets. Emotionally, poetically, gastronomically, San Francisco would be best; Marichal and McCovey, not so good.

It turned out to be Atlanta, a team that got hot, like the Mets, when it counted. On August 19—the day the Mets beat Marichal in the 14th inning —the Braves had been fifth in the West but only three games from first. Since then, they had won 23 out of 33. On the weekend of September 26–28, they swept three games from San Diego, eliminating Cincinnati and reducing San Francisco's chances to hopes for a tie. On Tuesday night, in Atlanta, they polished off the Reds, 3–2, and clinched first place.

This was fine with the Mets, who had developed the winning habit so thoroughly now that they couldn't lose even when it didn't count. Over the weekend in Philadelphia, they had shut out the Phillies three straight times— Koosman on Friday for his 17th victory, 3–0; Seaver on Saturday for his 25th, 1–0; and Gentry, Ryan, and Taylor, all working just to stay sharp, on Sunday, 2–0. In the three games, the Phillies got 11 hits. Up in the broadcasting booth, Richie Ashburn just shook his head.

On Monday, the Mets had to come home and play the Yankees for the Mayor's Trophy, because the charity game had been rained out in June. For experimental purposes, a lively ball was used without the players being informed ahead of time. The Mets hardly noticed as they won 7–6.

On Tuesday, they moved on to Chicago for those last two games, so delectably meaningless now. The Wednesday afternoon game dragged through 12 innings, as Hodges used 21 players—and the Mets won 6–5. That made it 10 straight victories since Moose's no-hitter (a rather pointed answer to that embarrassing moment) and 100 victories for the season. How positive could statistics get?

Hodges, conservative that he was, had underestimated by 15 games.

On Thursday, the Mets finally lost, 5–3, and it was just as well. No sense tempting those friendly fates with too long a winning streak carrying over into the play-offs. They had won 38 and lost 11 since the day they left

Houston, 9½ games out, and had finished eight games ahead of the Cubs—
a gain of 17½ games in less than seven weeks. When people thumbed through
record books in the 21st Century, and saw that eight-game margin, they
would consider the Met victory an easy one, no doubt. That's how much
record books know.

And on Friday, the eyes of the world focused on the New York Mets in
Atlanta, Georgia.

The series would start with Saturday and Sunday games there, starting at
4 P.M. for the sake of national television exposure. (The Baltimore Orioles
and Minnesota Twins, the American League's divisional winners, would play
at Baltimore at 1 P.M., giving the home audience a doubleheader). Then the
next three games, or as many as needed, would be played at Shea Stadium,
at normal starting times. The World Series would start the following Saturday, October 11.

The myth slipped smoothly into a new setting. Met pitchers were great,
all right, but the Braves had power, and the power bats were hot: Hank
Aaron, Rico Carty, Clete Boyer, Orlando Cepeda—why, Felipe Alou wasn't
even playing. The Braves had some good starters, good enough to handle
the weak Met batting order, at any rate. Logic said power and experience
should prevail. On a greatly intensified, condensed level of competition, the
American public automatically looked upon the Mets as nobodies again.
Hey, remember that Marv Throneberry?

"We've made some believers," Hodges said with his slow smile. "Now
we'll have to make some more."

Actually, the Mets had won eight out of 12 from Atlanta during the
regular season. Seaver, the top Met pitcher, was 3–0 against the Braves.
Phil Niekro, the knuckle-baller who had won 23 games for Atlanta, was
0–3 against New York. And they were the match-up in the first game. But
those were mere baseball facts; America cared only for the metaphysical and
psychic aspects of the confrontation. "Lowly Mets" they had to be to make
the dream worth dreaming, so lowly Mets they were.

For the Met family, the occasion was socially festive in a new way. Many
of the players had brought their wives to Atlanta. Nancy Seaver was "covering" the games for the *New York Post*—and Casey Stengel was "writing"
for the *Daily News,* their ghosts following them around. Seaver himself had
moved into the Schaap orbit. Mrs. Payson, entering the park at a point in
the right-field corner, was transported to her box seat near the third-base
dugout by one of those golf carts used to haul pitchers in from the bull pen.
Gaiety outweighed tension.

Seaver, in the most important game of his young life, did not look so good.

His pitches kept coming "up." His stuff wasn't too bad, but his control was off. But Niekro, older but just as new to post-season competition, didn't look like a world-beater either. He gave the Mets two runs in the second inning, the second on a third strike that slithered past Bob Didier, his 20-year-old catcher—a type of mishap all knuckle-ball pitchers have to live with. But Seaver was shaky in his own way, and was tagged for four doubles and a single in the first three innings, and fell behind, 3–2. The Mets then put him ahead again, 4–3, with two out in the fourth, when Kranepool singled, Grote walked, and Harrelson bounced one down the first-base line, just out of Cepeda's reach, for a two-run triple.

Neither team was approaching perfection.

In the fifth, Tony Gonzalez greeted Seaver with a home run, and it was 4–4. In the seventh, with one out, Aaron drove one over the left-field fence. Noc-a-homa, the high school boy dressed as a Brave who sits in front of his tepee behind the left-field fence, came out and did his jubilant dance. The Braves were ahead, 5–4, and Niekro needed just six more outs, and the great Met pitching had failed them.

Here it was, Turning Point No. 8.

One could easily imagine the Mets losing this game, with Seaver, and losing the next two. The magic had run out. It had been a wonderful year, but mystique can take you just so far. In real life, gallant tries don't reach ultimate rewards.

But—as Dick Young's fellow journalist, Casey Stengel, liked to say—"Wait a minute, Doctor."

Wayne Garrett, the little red-headed kid the Mets had drafted out of the Braves organization, bounced a double past Clete Boyer at third—past the Boyer who never let anything like that bounce by, at least not once in a hundred times. It was a legitimate enough hit, but Boyer was Superglove and usually swallowed legitimate hits.

Not this time, though.

Now Jones had a chance with a runner in scoring position, and he looped a soft liner to left for a single, sending in Garrett and tying the score. New ball game.

Shamsky, who already had two singles, poked a third, Jones stopping at second. That called for a bunt from Boswell—and Didier picked Jones off second, only to have Cleon go on to third instead of back to second. Then Boswell hit away and tapped to the mound. Niekro, making sure Jones held third, got the force at second but not a double play.

Kranepool also hit a slow bouncer, toward Cepeda. With one out, Jones had to try to score. Cepeda raced in, and his 50-foot throw home would have Jones by yards—but Cepeda's throw was wild, bouncing past Didier, and the Mets were ahead, 6–5.

Believe it yet?

Grote hit the ball to Boyer, whose only play was to first base. With two out, men on second and third, Harrelson had to be purposely passed because Seaver was due up next. Either he would be Atlanta's best bet for the third out, or he would be out of the game for a pinch hitter, a plus for the Braves either way.

Hodges chose the pinch hitter, J. C. Martin.

Martin lined the first pitch to center for a clean single, and the ball bounced past Gonzalez besides. Three runs scored. Martin was out trying to reach third base, so the inning was over, but the Mets had a 9–5 lead. They had scored five runs on four grounders, two loopers, an intentional walk, a clean hit, and an outfield error.

Believe?

Ron Taylor was the relief pitcher. He gave up a couple of hits in the ninth but wasn't really threatened. The first divisional play-off game in 94 years of National League history was over, and it belonged to the New York Mets.

The second one was even more amazing.

Agee led off with a single, Ron Reed walked a couple, struck out a couple, and fell one run behind when Kranepool's bouncer could not be handled by Felix Millan, the second baseman.

In the second inning, Koosman got a walk with one out, and Agee hit a homer. Jones doubled, Shamsky singled, and it was 4–0.

In the third inning, Cepeda dropped an ordinary throw to first, and Harrelson promptly turned it into a run with a double past third. Agee was passed purposely to get to Garrett, and Garrett singled home Harrelson.

It was 6–0, and Koosman was pitching a no-hitter.

Shamsky singled, and Boswell homered in the fourth. 8–0.

Believe?

Koosman gave up a run in the fourth, but Garrett doubled, and Jones singled in the fifth, and it was 9–1.

If only the Mets had a little hitting to go along with that pitching, eh?

Suddenly, with two out in the fifth, Koosman was in trouble. An infield hit, a walk, a three-run homer by Aaron. A walk, a double by Cepeda, a two-run single through the box by Boyer, and it was 9–6, with half a game still to play. All at once, they needed a little pitching to go along with that hitting.

Taylor, throwing a few pitches hurriedly in the bull pen, wasn't really ready, but in he came. Didier hit a line drive, but right at Boswell. At least that inning was over.

Back to the bull pen went Taylor, to do more throwing, alongside McGraw. The Mets got two on with one out and Harrelson up, and Hodges got ready to use a pinch hitter for Taylor. But Harrelson took a third strike, and Kranepool was doubled up trying for third, on some kind of messed-up hit-and-run play, and Taylor was still in the game. He pitched a strong inning, and Martin hit for him in the seventh.

Martin flied out, but Agee walked and stole second. Garrett's long fly sent him to third. With Jones at bat, Agee decided to steal home—just as Jones decided to swing. The line drive, just foul, just missed decapitating Agee. Cleon had almost killed his best friend.

Both were shaken by the experience. Both decided to take no more chances: Agee held fast at third, and Jones hit the ball over the left-field fence. That was a nice safe way to make the score 11–6, and McGraw had no trouble keeping it that way.

The Mets, negative-positive statisticians noted, had never lost a play-off game in their lives.

Now they had to win one out of three at home to be pennant winners for real.

New York City, in the midst of a bitter mayoralty campaign that split loyalties along various lines—race, class, Manhattan vs. the outer boroughs—put hostilities aside that Monday, October 6. The lucky 53,000 who could get into Shea Stadium thought of nothing else; the millions of others would make sure they had access to a television set by 1 P.M.

Gentry, who had pitched a major league game for the first time only six months before, and who had been pitching for Arizona State in a college world series only two years before that, was the Met starter. He got only one man out before Aaron's titanic two-run homer put him behind. He got through the second inning, but the third began with another single by Gonzalez and a double by Aaron. With the count 1–1, Carty hit a long drive into the left-field stands—just foul, for strike two.

Hodges waited no longer. He brought in Ryan, mid-batter.

Ryan threw one blazing fast ball, and Carty was out on strikes.

He put Cepeda on base purposely and struck out Boyer. Didier hit a soft fly, and the Mets had teetered away from the brink.

"God," someone observed in the press box, "was a little confused by those 4 o'clock starting times in Atlanta. Today he came on duty late."

Agee cut the margin to 2–1 in the third. Shamsky singled, and Boswell hit a homer in the fourth, and the Mets led 3–2. But Ryan walked Carty on a 3–2 pitch with two out in the fifth, and Cepeda blasted a home run. Atlanta led, 4–3.

But only until the Mets could bat. Ryan himself led off with a single, and with one out, Garrett—Wayne Garrett, with one home run to his credit in his one-year major league career—lined a homer into the right-field bullpen.

Believe? Believe yet?

A 5–4 lead wasn't big enough. Jones followed Garrett's drive with a double to right. Shamsky went out, but Boswell singled, and it was 6–4.

One could say that the crowd, at that moment, numbered 106,000, because it seemed that each of the 53,000 was beside himself with joy. A bad joke? It was a time for jokes, bad or otherwise.

And now, as on the night the Mets clinched first place, there was nothing left but a crescendo of anticipation to the official ending. The Mets scratched across another run in the sixth and had a 7–4 margin. Ryan was making no more mistakes. A couple of men got on in the eighth, but when Alou pinch-hit and hit a line drive, it went right to Harrelson.

It ended 7–4.

The myth was complete. The New York Mets had won the National League pennant.

Today, league champions.

Tomorrow, the world—World Series, of course.

16 *World Series*

CAN a World Series be an anticlimax?

Sure. And it often has been. Who remembers that the Giants lost the World Series to the Yankees after Bobby Thomson's home run had given them the pennant? Who cares that the Dodgers, after inflaming Brooklyn's chauvinism to unprecedented heights by winning their first pennant in 21 years under Leo Durocher in 1941, went on to lose the World Series in five games? Who in New England, wallowing in memories of the 1967 Red Sox and their last-day victory, dwells on the World Series then lost to the Cardinals? And even when the end result is a victory in the Series, what Yankee fan recalling the glorious finish of 1949 (Stengel's first year), in which the Red Sox were beaten on the final two days, goes on to gloat about another routine five-game Series with the Dodgers?

But a World Series can also be the most exciting, most memorable feature of an entire season. In Pittsburgh, they talk about Mazeroski's home run in the seventh game against the Yankees in 1960, not about the long stretch drive to that pennant; in Los Angeles, they still thrill to the way Koufax and Drysdale stifled the mighty Yankees in a four-game sweep in 1963, ignoring the race that preceded that; and only the year before this one, in 1968, a dramatic seven-game Series in which the Tigers beat the Cardinals redeemed two runaway pennant races.

It took the Mets, however, to produce a World Series that was anticlimactic and the supreme thrill, both at the same time.

There were two senses in which the 1969 World Series was an anticlimax for the Mets. One was peculiar to them: so much had already happened that one's reactivity was numbed; the overwhelming significance of their rise from the bottom to the top could not be obliterated by any World Series event: it had been achieved by the winning of the pennant, and nothing could ever change that. The other sense was one that most teams share: both in terms of money and in professional pride, the big thing about the World Series is reaching it. It takes a full season to win a pennant (and now it took a play-off besides); but "anything can happen in a short series," and players know this better than anyone. When you win a pennant you prove yourself the best team, by definition, because good luck and bad luck are supposed to cancel out over 162 games; but a seven-game series is too subject to the fortunes of a particular bounce to prove anything. Financially, the big jump is between getting in and not getting in. The loser's share in the Series is still substantial money; the winner gets a few thousand more, but the loser has still had a good year. But the difference between finishing second (in the past) or losing the play-off (now) and even the loser's share in the Series is more meaningful.

So the Mets approached the Series with at least some feeling that nothing mattered that much any more, now that the pennant had been won. They were entertained privately at Governor Rockefeller's Fifth Avenue apartment, beseiged by agents and offers of money, publicly adored to the highest degree. They had made it.

On the other hand, there was the artistic side: if the Mets lost the Series, the future memories in themselves and their followers would of necessity revert to the season itself—but there would be a flaw. Having come so far, the compulsion to go to the summit was very great. In the long run, their pennant achievement could not be dimmed; but at the moment, defeat and disappointment could be felt deeply. In a perverse way, winning the World Series became all-important, to cap what could now be a perfect year.

In a way, and on a much more rarefied level, this was a repetition of the rooting situation Met fans had developed for themselves in the early years, the one-way-vision sort of rooting. It was impossible to be really hurt by defeat—then, because defeat was inevitable anyhow; now, because so much had been won already; but it was distinctly possible to be whipped into ecstasy by victory—then, because it was so rare; now, because it would be the ultimate one. That old observation about the Polo Grounds' faithful—"They get their money's worth anytime the Mets score, and it's as if the other team's turn at bat simply didn't exist"—applied now on a broader scale.

In short, the Series could be shrugged off as an anticlimax if they lost, yet hailed as the greatest triumph in baseball history if they won. One couldn't ask for a more enviable position.

The events of September had educated the entire country in the mystical quality of Met victories. All the key incidents of their march to the pennant—winning a game in which 19 Mets struck out, sweeping two 1–0 games in Pittsburgh, the Marichal game with the four-man outfield, the lucky bounces, the timely hits by .213 hitters, the way the hitters overcame the pitchers' semi-collapse in the play-off with Atlanta—were cited as proof that gremlins, or God, or Destiny, or something was seeing to it that the Mets won. The Orioles, who had left their own league far behind and had whipped Minnesota in three straight games in their play-off, were subjected to a full dose of such half-joking comment. Baltimore was a big favorite to win the Series, and legitimately so: its regular lineup was being hailed as one of the "strongest ever," and its pitching had been dominant beyond the individual reputation of its starters. Yet, at every turn, someone came to Manager Earl Weaver, or a player, with another story about how some unlikely circumstance had produced a Met victory. No more imaginative than most baseball people, and no less self-centered, the Orioles took such talk to be threatening rather than amusing. To them, it had a sacrilegious tinge, an implication that fate was supposed to be against Baltimore; and it carried a vague suggestion that their skills, of which they were so proud, were being demeaned by the idea that some supernatural force would be the deciding factor, not those skills.

So when the Orioles had won the third game in Minnesota, and wrapped up their pennant, Frank Robinson's remark summed up their attitude:

"Bring on Ron Gaspar."

"Not Ron—Rod, stupid!"

"O.K., bring on Rod Stupid."

Robinson, a prospective big-league manager himself, who had managed a team in Puerto Rico over the winter, knew perfectly well who Rod Gaspar was, as he knew all his opponents. The point he was making was simply that the Orioles were great, famous, and intimidating, whereas the Mets were young nobodies who might have won a National League pennant but hadn't proved anything yet to the American League.

And much of the country felt the same way. If black magic was an element in Met success, surely it lost its potency when the National League race ended.

The Oriole lineup would certainly test Met starters, who hadn't seemed so overpowering against Atlanta. Don Buford, Paul Blair, Frank Robinson, Boog Powell, and Brooks Robinson, the first five batters, were undoubtedly the most effective run-making unit in baseball. Dave Johnson, the second baseman, could hold his own. When Elrod Hendricks caught (against righties), another dangerous hitter was in the lineup; Andy Etchebarren, the catcher against lefties, was less feared. Mark Belanger, the superb shortstop, had always been considered a weak hitter, to be carried only because of his defense—until, in 1969, he had suddenly produced a .289 batting average and had batted in 50 runs.

And Baltimore pitching, the Orioles felt, could match anyone's, no matter what they said about Seaver and Koosman. Cuellar, obtained from Houston over the winter, had won 23 games (and would eventually be chosen the American League's outstanding pitcher); Dave McNally, who had pitched a shutout in the final game of the 1966 World Series and pitched an 11-inning 1–0 victory in the second playoff game against the Twins, had won his first 15 games during the season. Both were left-handed, which meant they would face the potentially less-dangerous, right-handed platoon of the Mets; all the slugging against Atlanta had been done by the lefty platoon, which included Shamsky, Kranepool, and Boswell (although Grote caught no matter who pitched). And for a third starter, the Orioles had Jim Palmer, restored to health, a fireballer who had shut out Sandy Koufax in the 1966 World Series and who had pitched a no-hitter less than two months ago. Behind them the Baltimore bull pen was well stocked. In fact, the earned-run average of the Baltimore staff, 2.87, was actually better than the 2.99 the Mets had.

Finally, the relatively long layoff fed the idea that natural forces would reassert themselves in the World Series. Because both play-offs had lasted only three games, they had ended on Monday; the Series would not start until Saturday, October 11. At this stage of a competition, four days was a long time to go without a real game.

On Wednesday, the Mets were supposed to work out at Shea Stadium, but it rained. So they worked out Thursday and went straight to the airport, where Mayor Lindsay was present for a send-off ceremony which included a piece of doggerel he read proudly. The charter flight took off an hour late, and the hotel in Baltimore turned out to be totally unequipped (in terms of telephone switchboard and room service) for a World Series crowd. Well, that was the rule rather than the exception at every "Fall Classic." In undergoing their particular inconveniences Friday night, the Mets were having their first true World Series experience.

On Friday, when both teams worked out at Memorial Stadium (and the Orioles, in uniform, were paraded in open cars through downtown Baltimore), a political story broke. It was reported that Seaver had announced he would take an ad in *The New York Times* if the Mets won the Series, saying "If the Mets can win the World Series, the United States can get out of Viet Nam." This was five days before the anti-war Moratorium, originally planned for college campuses but now a national issue, and Seaver's position as the supremely successful young American was of interest to all sides. Just what the logic of such a message might be he wasn't quite clear, but its anti-Viet Nam flavor was plain enough, and it stirred a storm within the fundamentally conservative, jingoistic baseball community. A day later Seaver put the matter in a different perspective: yes, he had been approached by someone connected with the Kennedys about giving his support to such an ad, and he was considering it; and yes, he had strong feelings about the war; but he considered these his private business and did not want to be "used" as a baseball celebrity for any external purpose. The thing that concerned him today was trying to win the World Series first. If that happened and if it encouraged people to think "if this is possible, anything is possible," well and good. But it hadn't happened yet.

And the next day, a glorious October Saturday with warm sunshine, it didn't seem that it would happen.

The first pitch Seaver threw was hit by Don Buford over the right-field fence, over an imperfectly timed leap by Swoboda whose back hit the canvas barrier.

Cuellar held the Mets to two hits for the first four innings, and with two out in the Baltimore fourth, Hendricks singled through the right side, and Seaver was suddenly in trouble. He couldn't seem to get the ball where he wanted it and walked Johnson. Belanger lined a single through the right side, and it was 2–0. Cuellar looped a single to center, and it was 3–0. Buford hit a line drive double on one bounce against the right-field wall, and it was 4–0.

And that was plenty. Cuellar did give up a run on a couple of singles, a walk, and Weis's fly in the seventh, and with two on and two out, the Mets "brought on" Rod Gaspar. He tapped weakly toward third, and Brooks Robinson, racing in and making a bare-handed scoop, threw him out on a magnificent play.

In the ninth, with two on and two out, the Mets got the tying run to bat in the person of Shamsky. If the fates, or whatever, were still at work, this was the spot for a homer. But Shamsky bounced to Johnson, and Baltimore had won the first game, 4–1.

Orthodoxy heaved a sigh of relief.

Koosman and McNally, on another beautiful day, were backed up by spectacular fielding plays (Belanger, Harrelson, Brooks Robinson) in the early innings Sunday. Then Clendenon led off the fourth with a curving drive sliced over the right-field fence, just about where Buford had hit his homer the day before. It was the first post-season run off McNally in 24 innings—and the only run in the game as Koosman went into the seventh inning with a no-hitter going.

But Blair spoiled that with a clean hit through the left side opening the inning, and with two out he stole second. Brooks Robinson promptly singled through the box, and it was 1–1.

When McNally got the first two Mets out in the ninth, he was pitching a three-hitter. But Charles succeeded in bouncing a single past Brooks Robinson and made it to third on a hit-and-run play as Grote grounded a single past Belanger. Weis promptly lined a single to left on the next pitch, and Koosman had a 2–1 lead, with the head of the Baltimore batting order up in the ninth.

He made Buford pop up and Blair ground out, and Hodges ordered his four-man outfield again, to keep Frank Robinson from getting an extra base hit. Robinson didn't but in an unexpected way: he walked on a full count—and so did Powell. So Hodges brought in Taylor, who fell behind to Brooks Robinson, three balls and one strike. However, Brooks fouled off the next pitch and then bounced to Charles, who started to tag third, saw the runner had him beaten, and threw to first, where Clendenon dug the ball out of the dirt.

The Mets had won, 2–1—on a hit by Weis. Maybe the gremlins weren't dead yet.

There was no game Monday, the "travel" day of every World Series between the second and third game, and it was cloudy but mild Tuesday when play resumed at Shea Stadium. The Mets were still underdogs, using their rookie, Gentry, against the reinvigorated Palmer, which meant New York's lefty platoon could go to work, its first game in eight days.

Agee, the double-platoon man, greeted Palmer with a home run.

With two out in the second, Palmer walked Grote, and Harrelson singled. Whereupon Gentry lined one between the fielders in right center (really over Blair's head) for a two-run double, and the Mets had a 3–0 lead.

And Gentry didn't even give up a hit until Frank Robinson singled with one out in the fourth. Powell's single sent him to third, Brooks struck out—and Hendricks belted a curving drive, high and deep to left center, sure to produce two runs.

Agee, throwing his gloved hand across his body, reached up and caught the ball, running at a fast but controlled speed, just as he hit the fence. The white of the ball was plainly visible in the top of the webbing of his glove—but he held it.

Believe?

Grote's double made it 4–0 in the sixth, and in the seventh, after two long flies to Agee, Gentry walked three men in a row, bringing up Blair as the tying run. Hodges brought in Ryan, who had relieved Gentry so spectacularly in the third play-off game, and it worked again—but not on a strikeout. Blair hit a long, curving drive to right center; Agee ran as far as he could, lunged as he reached the running track, slid on one knee, and got his glove under the ball inches off the ground.

("The second one was easier for me," he actually said later, "because it was on my glove side.")

Even the Mets found that one hard to believe.

In the eighth, Kranepool hit a home run—a home run unsurpassed for personal satisfaction and symbolic vindication. With a 5–0 lead, Ryan let the bases get filled in the ninth on two walks and a scratch hit, but he threw a called third strike past Blair.

The Mets were leading in the World Series, two games to one.

Wednesday was Moratorium Day, and Seaver's turn to pitch, and there were people giving out mimeographed handouts all around the ball park, but nothing really impinged on the sports drama now: a six-month saga was entering its last couple of hardly credible pages.

Seaver pitched eight scoreless innings, aided by two great stops by Clendenon (one that killed a potential Baltimore rally in the third, when with two on and none out and the Mets playing in for a bunt, Buford swung and hit a one-hop liner that Clendenon speared like a hockey goalie). And he nursed a 1–0 lead from the second inning on, thanks to Clendenon's homer off Cuellar.

With one out in the ninth, Frank Robinson singled to left, Powell singled to right, and the tying run was on third.

Brooks Robinson lined a sure hit to right center.

Swoboda thundered into the gap. He dove, full length, gloved hand outstretched—and caught the ball, just as his face smacked the ground hard.

Frank Robinson tagged up and scored, but it was only tied, and when Swoboda caught Hendricks' fly after almost overrunning it, it remained a tie.

Believe? Believe?

The Mets got two on in the ninth, but Shamsky, pinch-hitting, couldn't end the game. An error by Garrett helped Baltimore put two on in the 10th, but Seaver ended the threat by striking out Blair.

By now, Coach Billy Hunter was running the Orioles, because Weaver had been chased by Umpire Shag Crawford in the third inning for protesting a pitch. It was Hunter who had to make the decisions in what followed.

Grote led off the 10th with an ordinary high fly to medium short left.

Buford, blinded by the sun, or gremlins, or something, never broke in.

Belanger raced out. Blair came from center. Buford, finally, started to race in. None reached it. Grote reached second, with a double.

And the Mets had reached the threshold of ultimate victory: from this point on, it was all in their hands to achieve.

This little fly ball was Turning Point No. 9. The Mets could still lose, but only if they beat themselves, if they failed to carry out the normal things now expected of them. If Blair had caught it, Seaver was probably through pitching anyhow; even if he stayed in, he would be less and less effective as extra innings mounted. But now the Mets had a chance to win this game, right here, and that would give them a 3–1 grip on the series with Koosman ready to pitch and Seaver available for a seventh game if it came to that.

And wherefore were these 1969 Mets different from all other Mets? In that they cashed in on their opportunities and did not beat themselves.

Gaspar ran for Grote. Harrelson was purposely passed. Martin batted for Seaver. Pete Richert, a left-hander, came in to pitch: all standard moves. And Martin would have to bunt, also a standard move.

He did. Hendricks was a little slow starting after the ball. Richert reached it first. He fired toward first—too close to the runner. The ball hit Martin's left wrist and ricocheted into short right field. Gaspar, who had stopped safely at third, ran home and jumped on the plate. The Mets spilled out of the dugout and pounded him, and Martin (whose wrist hurt), and Seaver (who had led the charge). The stands were in turmoil. The Orioles were bewildered.

The threshold of Paradise had been reached. Believe?

(Richert for one, had doubts. Without making an issue of it, he wondered if Martin had run outside the foul line, as he was supposed to, so that he wouldn't interfere with a throw to first. Photographs that evening showed that Martin had, indeed, run well in fair territory when hit by the ball; he should have been declared out, and there was an 18-hour cause célèbre requiring a public statement by Crawford, the umpire, the next morning. In his judgment, Crawford said, Martin had touched the foul line with his right foot, and that was good enough for him; it was a judgment play; and, of course, it was—but a good thing for the Mets that Crawford's judgment ran that way.)

Anyone with the slightest faith in inevitability had to doubt that the Series would ever return to Baltimore.

Game No. 5, on Thursday, October 16, was played on a cold, cloudy day. If the Orioles won it, the next game would be in Baltimore Saturday. If the

Mets won it, the perfect ending would take place in the presence of the Met fans (or at least that small portion that could crack the World Series ticket barrier), poetic justice of the highest order—and the fans could repeat their field-destroying act, invented so spontaneously on September 24 and repeated so callously after the Atlanta series.

The day started badly for New York. McNally walked two Mets in the first inning, but Swoboda left them on base, striking out. Belanger singled, and McNally, instead of bunting, hit a home run off Koosman in the second. Two outs later, Frank Robinson hit one out of sight ("over a building," as Stengel liked to say), and the Orioles had a 3–0 lead.

And, if you thought about it rationally, what would be so unlikely about the Orioles winning two games at home if they won this one?

In the sixth inning, one of Koosman's pitches hit Frank Robinson on the thigh. (It did; pictures proved that, later.) But Umpire Lou DiMuro ruled it hit his bat first. There was a long argument, Robinson disappeared for repairs, came back, took a third strike. Powell singled, Brooks Robinson flied out. The umpire's mistake had prevented a threatening inning from getting started.

The first Met batter in the sixth was Jones. A pitch by McNally hit him on the foot. Again, DiMuro didn't believe it—but now Hodges produced the ball, which had bounced into the dugout, with a smudge of shoe polish on it. DiMuro was convinced ("the ball never left my sight so I knew it was the same one," he said afterwards). Jones was allowed to take first base.

Opportunity, right?

Right. Clendenon hit a home run, his third of the series, and the Mets were in business, trailing only 3–2.

The first Met batter in the seventh was Al Weis.

He hit a home run.

Honest.

It didn't clear the left-field fence by much, but it did clear it. Score tied, 3–3.

Al Weis, whose only two previous homers that season had burned the Cubs so badly in July, had saved his last shot for the best time. Al Weis, who had come to spring training with extra muscles. The glove man, the utility man, the silent one, the one who had made that incredible play in the 15th inning in June, the one who had wrecked his knee while wrecking Frank Robinson's vision, the "useful" player that Hodges had liked from his American League days. The man who "could help you in a lot of little ways."

But with a World Series homer?

Now do you believe?

Koosman believed. Brought even, he would give up his life easier than another run. He would hang on somehow until the Mets scored again.

They needed only one inning. Ed Watt, a right-hander, was the pitcher now. Jones led off the eighth with a blast that just missed clearing the fence at the 395-foot mark in left center. It bounced back in for a double.

Clendenon bounced softly to Robinson at third, and Jones took third.

Swoboda ("He may be the first true Met hero," they said back in 1965) ripped a sharp line drive, right down the left-field line. Buford raced over. He didn't dive; he backhanded the ball on a short hop. Swoboda had a double.

And the Mets had a 4–3 lead.

And the rumbling crescendo was beginning in the stands, in the streets, in offices, in homes, wherever a television set or a radio could be tuned in.

The Orioles messed up a bouncer wide of first, and Swoboda scored. It was 5–3. Koosman even had an extra run to work with. Three outs to go.

Frank Robinson walks, and Koosman is mad at himself for committing a pitching sin. Now a home run can tie it, and Powell certainly is the man who can hit one. But Koosman makes him hit on the ground, to Weis, who forces Robinson at second. No chance for a double play. One out.

Brooks Robinson hits a fly to right field. Swoboda is under it. (This used to be considered a Met adventure: Swoboda under a fly ball.) He catches it. Two out.

Johnson up. A fly ball to left, fairly deep. Cleon is under it. He waits. He catches it and holds it there, motionless for a second or two, almost down on one knee.

Then he races, faster than he ever did on a football field, with his friend Agee, for the bullpen gate, to escape the onrushing crowd.

And so, at 3:14 P.M., Eastern Daylight Time, October 16, 1969 A.D., at 40 degrees 45 minutes North Latitude, 73 degrees 50 minutes West Longitude, on the third planet of a solar system in the spiral arm of one of uncounted billions of galaxies, the New York Mets became baseball champions of the whole expanding universe.

At least, so far as we can tell.

The clubhouse celebration was properly hysterical. The fans tore up the field. A cascade of torn paper hit downtown Manhattan like a tidal wave. Someone's joy erupted in every corner of the country and in some places overseas.

Mrs. Payson cried. Casey Stengel hugged Gil Hodges. Joan Hodges and Joe Pignatano worried as they tried to keep the crowd around Gil within bounds, and as they tried to get him home before it went on too long. George

Weiss, a trifle embarrassed but thrilled to his marrow, wandered around the clubhouse with Grant and the other Directors. Murphy, as always, showed on the outside only a small fraction of what he felt inside. Dick Young and Jack Lang, whatever they felt, hustled harder than ever, with so much to be written. The "young writers," who had always taken the Met Mystique and the Met players to their hearts, moved as if they belonged in the general congratulatory haze. Kiner, Nelson, and Murphy, who had seen every bit of it, were as talked out as the fan with the multiple signs, who had held up the one that read: "There Are No Words."

And, of course, there weren't. When you come right down to it, myths aren't told, they are felt. In the intricate mythology that America had created around baseball, fashioning it so lovingly for more than a century, the Mets had produced a submyth of transcendent power. A cascade of interpretation inundated their victory: they represented the power of faith, love, the common man, the underdog uplifted, democracy in action; they had unified the soul of a city rent by dissension, had justified America, glorified sport, ennobled youth, deified the team spirit, enriched the quality of life, redeemed mankind—whatever the particular editorialist decided to extol was attributed freely to the Mets. Perhaps the one great contribution a mass-amusement athletic team can make to a culture is to turn itself into such a lightning rod for the ambient idealism adrift in the system.

What the Mets had really done, of course, was merely win a flock of ball games, within a period of exactly two months. They won because they had real, prosaic assets—two pitchers like Seaver and Koosman, a manager like Hodges who could instill and maintain a winning attitude, talented players like Jones and Agee, an essential pick-up like Clendenon and a fine mix of gifted young players and less-gifted experienced men—and because, like many teams before them, they "got hot." Their organization had built its club, painstakingly, with this in mind—but it was as astonished as anyone that it all came to fruition between August 17 and October 16, 1969.

Stengel, as always, put it concisely and inimitably:

"They came slow, but fast."

The celebrations went on. A ticker-tape parade (like those for Lindbergh, the astronauts, military heroes) was held on Monday; a reception at Mayor Lindsay's residence (Gracie Mansion) that evening; a party here, a personal appearance there; a trip to Las Vegas for seven of them, to do an act with Phil Foster; a tour of Viet Nam hospitals for Ed Charles and Ron Swoboda, at some sacrifice of personal earning power; a good rest for Hodges; a spate of books, articles, interviews, television shows, recording sessions, business offers, family conferences.

It would take a while to unwind. Each Met player, each Met official, each Met fan had his personal future to think of, brightened by what had happened. The general public, its mythological feast over, was already thinking of other things. The unitary, 60-day super-event of the New York Mets was over, and the historical Met Mystique was twisted into a new shape, to be seen from new perspectives.

Only one thing seemed quite certain: a baseball team wearing New York Met uniforms would have to play in 1970.

HEAVENLY FINALE

In Heaven, the victory party went on for aeons; being immortal, the ecstatic elect who were the members of the Celestial Chapter of the New York Met Fan Club had plenty of time.

They celebrated on a cosmic scale. The nectar, flowing like cheap champagne, was sloshed, spilled, squirted, and splattered more than guzzled. They were all as excited as children. They tore out huge chunks of firmament, with no purpose in view, and tacked two signs to every cloud within reach—one reading "No. 9," and the other, much larger, declaring "We're No. 1." They danced, sang, laughed, exulted, embraced, shouted, pounded one another on the back. The Heavenly Decorum was shattered cheerfully.

"I'm sure they haven't had anything so noisy here since the Revolt of Lucifer," said John Milton, a blind poet, beaming. "It's enough to wake the dead."

"Now that's one of your typically fatuous observations, John," said George Bernard Shaw, also beaming, "but this time, even I will forgive you. No one

can deny that we are the dead and the Mets have awakened us."

"They have shown the mortals, and us too, that miracles are still possible," cried the usually shy Bernadette of Lourdes, grinning broadly.

"It just didn't figure, I never would have postulated it," muttered Euclid through his beard, "but you have to give them credit, they earned everything they got. There is no royal road to the World Championship."

The largest single center of attraction was Dante, who had actually been there, sent down in June as the special correspondent of the immortals. He was pelted with endless questions: "What's Swoboda really like? Isn't Harrelson underrated? How about that Weis? Is Seaver really that good? Hodges is a genius, isn't he? When did they first think they could win it? Why was Shamsky platooned so much? Did you get Yogi's autograph?"

And all Dante could say, over and over, was "Amazing . . . amazing . . . amazing."

Already, bids were being made for

the right to accompany the Mets to spring training. An especially sincere Russian named Leo Tolstoy would make his pitch to anyone he could corner.

"Always I believed," he would say, tears streaming down his cheeks, "that all happy families were alike. That's why I became a Met fan: they were, naturally, unhappy in their own way. But now they have taught me a new vision: they are a happy family, and yet they are like nothing else in Creation. I must go with them, humbly, like a pilgrim, to rethink again all my philosophy, to reject again all my previous work, to spread the new gospel . . . and just think, to see again St. Petersburg. . . ."

And no one would have the heart to explain to him that it was St. Petersburg, Florida.

Over by the harp sector, glorious music poured forth from a chorus of thousands, directed by George Frederick Handel:

"Donnnn—Clen–den–on . . . Hallelulia . . . Hallelulia . . . Jehhh–ry Koos–man . . . Hallelulia . . . Hallelulia!"

"A toast, a toast!" shouted Epicurus. "Let us eat, drink and make merry, for tomorrow the Mets may have to play again. A toast to the Mets!"

"To Boswell," roared Dr. Sam Johnson, lifting a glass.

"To Charles the Great—the new Charlemagne," shrilled Joan of Arc.

"Hail to thee, blithe Agee," sang Percy Bysshe Shelley, "bird thou never wert—but you sure could go and get 'em."

"To Taylor," called out Thomas Edison, always partial to electrical engineers.

"To Gaspar—de la nuit and du jour, too," said an obscure but prosperous musician named Maurice Ravel.

"To all the K's" squeaked Immanuel Kant, "who made Met victory a Kategorical Imperative: Kranepool, Koosman, Koonce, Kardwell, Kleon-Chones, Klendenon, Muh–Kandrew and Duffy Dyer."

"If you're toasting K's," broke in Hegel, always prone to argue, "why Duffy Dyer?"

"Why not?" demanded Kant.

And the assemblage obviously sided with that sentiment.

The great scientist-philosophers, as usual, were off in a corner talking to themselves.

"It was as I tried to tell you," Einstein explained, "a simple matter of relativity. Turn the standings upside down, and the last-place Mets become first."

"But the standings weren't turned upside down," demurred Aristotle, a stickler for detail. "They were merely split into two divisions. Do you mean that helped?"

"Didn't hurt," answered Einstein.

"They certainly made a bum out of my laws of gravitation," sighed Newton. "All summer I kept waiting for what went up to come down. They never did."

"Everyone insisted they couldn't reach the top," said Galileo defiantly. "Nevertheless—they moved."

"To me," said Madame Curie, her eyes shining, "they were simply radiant."

"It came as no surprise to this writer," boasted Nostradamus.

Elsewhere, some saints were feeling more benign than ever. Many of those who had been, in earthly lives, members of religious orders had naturally become baseball fans then, so they felt in fullest measure the magnitude of the Met triumph.

"For the very first time," admitted Saint Francis of Assisi, referring to the World Series, "I found myself rooting against the Birds."

"I made no attempt to understand it," said Saint Thomas Aquinas, "I just sat back and enjoyed it."

"For a while," chuckled Saint Nicholas, "it seemed like every day was Christmas."

"I must confess one thing distressed me," said the gentle Saint Theresa. "When the fans tore up the field that way, I couldn't help thinking, pigeons on the grass, alas."

They were joined by Molière and a more recent arrival from Russia.

"Did you hear the gossip?" Molière announced. "Shakespeare and Mozart have decided to collaborate on a musical about the Mets."

"An ambitious undertaking," remarked his companion, Konstantin Stanislavski, in his methodical manner. "The only really successful musical ever done about a baseball team was *Damn Yankees.*"

"They're calling theirs *Blessed Mets,*" replied Molière.

The revel might have gone on for eternity had not The All-Pervasive Voice interrupted.

"Bless you, my children, and the capacity for joy that you express. The selflessness of your pleasure in a triumph, which can have only spiritual meaning to you, is a reflection of the worthy aspect of your imperfect race— which has always claimed a special place in My scheme. But even you, the most exalted of the humans, must be reminded not to lose perspective. In a few millennia—a mere blink of cosmic time—it will all be forgotten.

"Some have been so carried away by enthusiasm as to suggest that My influence was brought directly to bear on these remarkable but trivial events. That this is presumptuous does not matter; that it demeans the true accomplishment of your darlings should be clear; that it shows again such deep ignorance of My true scope is no longer surprising. But, having enjoyed yourselves, try to regain that most precious and rare attribute of sentient life, a sense of proportion.

"So celebrate a little longer, toast your Mets—and then return to your true function: contemplation. There is a time for all things, as you have been told before; a time to live, a time to love, a time for the Mets, a time for others. Even now, another baseball season is playing itself out on that little planet of yours; even now, new events, new melodramas, new heroes and new hopes are being manufactured —all equally absorbing for the moment, all equally transitory. It is, after all, only a game, that even children can play.

"But—" and now The Voice acquired an indescribable warmth, an infinitely compassionate chuckle, an indulgent smile—"even My Omniscient Omnipotence must confess, it was fun while it lasted. Let it be said, one more time: 'Let's Go Mets.' "

And all was serene in a cosmos that had produced, at least once, the Mets.

ACT IV—BERRA

17 Back to Earth

NOTHING could ever be the same. Nothing. But some of the differences would be more obvious than others.

The rewards of victory, pouring in through the rest of 1970, were clearly a new experience, for Met rooters no less than for the Mets themselves. Seaver won the Cy Young Award, as the National League's best pitcher, and was runner-up by a narrow margin to Willie McCovey for the Most Valuable Player Award. Hodges, naturally, was Manager of the Year. Murphy received the coveted Major League Executive of the Year Award from *Sporting News*, the trade paper whose recognition means so much to lifelong baseball people. For his three World Series homers, Clendenon won the sports car given by *Sport Magazine.*

And when Seaver added the posh Sportsman of the Year Award to his collection, Murphy made a memorable remark. This trophy, a replica of a fifth century B.C. amphora (a Grecian urn with handles that had Olympic athletes painted on its sides), is given by *Sports Illustrated*. At the presentation, Murphy declared: "Tom, if you and Nancy ever come up for adoption, Mrs. Murphy and I will be only too glad to take you."

Money, too, was a new experience, or at least a new level of an old experience. Each winning share of the World Series came to $18,332—the highest yet, and more than 10 times the annual salary of the highest paid members of the first professional team, the Cincinnati Red Stockings of 1869, whose 100th anniversary was celebrated with such pomp throughout the triumphal year of the Mets. Thirty-five Mets, including Hodges and the coaches, got full shares. And a full share, supplied by the club in accordance with baseball custom, went to Lou Niss, obliterating a nine-year joke.

Back in 1961, when Weiss told Niss that he would henceforth be the road secretary instead of the publicity man, he pointed out to the astonished Niss one advantage the new position would bring. "The road secretary, of course," Weiss said in all seriousness, "gets a full World Series share." In all his Yankee years, Weiss had never been associated with a club that failed to finish in the money, so it was, perhaps, a natural observation. But during seven seasons of finishing ninth or tenth, Niss had been the subject of much teasing on this point.

Now he had the last laugh.

And the players were making money in other ways, too. The seven who did a show in Las Vegas, under the direction of Phil Foster, the comedian long associated with Brooklyn, got $10,000 apiece for their two-week stint. They and others made personal appearances, endorsed products, cut records, joined businesses (and acquired agents), all for substantial cash. And there were fat raises, sometimes 100 percent, in their 1970 Met contracts.

A less obvious change, but clear enough, was one of status. Having won, the Mets would be expected to win again—and would expect it of themselves. They didn't know yet, although older heads tried to tell them, that winning again was a much harder thing to do than winning once. By winning, the Mets had forfeited the right to be tolerated fondly when they lost; but, perhaps more significantly, they also would not be looked upon as precocious miracle-workers when they won. In a perverse way, their achievement had turned them—from then on—into something less special.

It was this last factor, applied to the entire Met Mystique and its followers, that was the most subtle and most pervasive change. Again, it was obvious enough that the super-thrill of that first, unexpected, once-in-a-lifetime ascent from nothing to championship could never be re-experienced: anyone could understand that there can be only one first love. But the day-by-day consequences of this lost innocence were harder to grasp, and would be felt only gradually. Among the things now lost forever to Metdom were the qualities that had made each Met game so special for eight years—the uniqueness. Negative statistics, as camp, lost meaning. Minor accomplishments, like winning on a Thursday, could no longer be magnified, with humerous affection, into an event. The victory that was represented by merely existing could never again be enough. And each inning, now, each game and series and road trip and time at bat could never again be really considered in isolation, a happening to be savored for its own sake, because it had no greater significance. From now on, everything had to be put into the perspective of a serious baseball goal: it mattered toward the winning of a pennant, or it didn't. To the professionals, that's what baseball life had always been. But to the Met fans, and more casual onlookers, this assertion of reality was simultaneously welcome—since it did mean respectability—and sad. In a way that had never constrained them before, the Met followers were now prisoners of results, as other fans always had been. For better or worse, winning and losing would be the primary value from then on.

And, finally, there was another price to be paid for success: He who reaches the top becomes a target for those who see no point in attacking anything less than the top; and the new champion, inevitably, acquires a bit of arrogance that reacts to such attacks by becoming more arrogant and a little bitter. It's a universal process and the Mets would not escape it.

What would have been a private disagreement a year before suddenly became a well-publicized case of strained relations. Ed Charles was not going to be asked back for spring training, and he was ready enough to give up playing at 35. But it had been his understanding that the Mets would give him a promotional job at a salary on a par with his playing salary, or make up the difference with some sort of bonus arrangement. The Mets did, indeed, want to use Charles—but they had no such salary in mind. There were bitter remarks from Charles, widely quoted because he was so respected and liked, and embarrassed explanations from Murphy, who felt it was all a misunderstanding. The point, really, was not who was right or wrong in the specific instance: the point was that a surprising number of people, even while the afterglow of the Met victory lingered, were so eager to seize upon whatever meager facts they had to condemn the Met management. It was the beginning of an antagonism toward Mets as winners that they had never been subjeced to as losers. And it would persist.

And then, suddenly, shockingly, Murphy was dead.

At the winter meeting in Miami Beach, during the first week in December, Murphy had enjoyed all the recognition and congratulation a man could imagine, and far more than so essentially modest a man could absorb comfortably. He also had concluded what was widely held to be a promising trade, geting Joe Foy from Kansas City. But on Dec. 30, back home in Bronxville, New York, he suffered severe pain in his back and neck, and went to the hospital. It was, they discovered, a heart attack, and he went immediately into intensive care.

The memory of Hodges' attack, and his successful recovery, tended to calm people's first reactions. Murphy would be away from work for many months, but there was not, at first, real concern for his life.

But Hodges had been 44 years old; Murphy was 61. He never did leave intensive care. On Wednesday evening, January 14, he suffered another massive attack and died.

To the public, except for that portion that remembered him as a Yankee pitcher, Murphy had always been a dim background figure, quiet and self-effacing. To those who knew him personally, the loss was felt more deeply for its unexpectedness. But baseball life has to go on, somewhat less flexibly even than other segments of life, and already it was only a month until spring training would start. Grieving would have to be private; decisions would have to be made and actions taken.

As it happened, there was a well-qualified successor right at hand. Bob Scheffing, director of playing personnel, easily could be promoted, and he was made vice-president and general manager on January 19. He had been a catcher in the majors, a minor-league manager at the age of 24, a successful major-league manager with the Chicago Cubs and Detroit Tigers, a broadcaster and a scout. He had been brought in by Devine in December, 1966, when Stanky went back to managing (with the Chicago White Sox), and after Devine's departure had become Murphy's right-hand man in all player evaluation and development matters.

A better baseball man than Scheffing would be hard to find anywhere, anytime; on the business side, he was less equipped than Weiss had been, or even Murphy. But this fit neatly into a new pattern that was emerging. For day-to-day business operations, more and more was in the province of Jim Thomson. For traditional "club president" functions—top policy decisions, attending league meetings, and so forth—Grant had been moving ever more prominently into the foreground. This triumvirate, then, was to guide the Mets through the early 1970s.

And there was plenty of guiding to be done. Even without the tragic loss of Murphy, the euphoria of 1969 would have been dissipated quickly as soon as one contemplated 1970. The new season would start from scratch. Last year's victories wouldn't count or help. Scheffing understood perfectly the team assets, and the dimensions of its problems.

Jones had hit .340, third in the league behind Pete Rose and Roberto Clemente—but even with that, the 1969 Mets had hit .242, the lowest batting average ever posted by a pennant-winning team. Their success had been built on another statistic: in 28 regular-season games, they had kept the opposition from scoring at all, and in 24 others they permitted only one run. In the last four games of the World Series, the Mets had held Baltimore—that powerhouse—to just five runs.

With such pitching, a terrific attack had not been necessary.

And with such an attack, such pitching *had* been necessary.

In a new year, there was no guarantee that such a level of pitching could be maintained. The only sensible thing was to try to beef up the attack.

That was the rationale behind Murphy's acquisition of Foy. Without minimizing the contribution of Charles, there just didn't seem much future in filling third base with a Garrett-Charles platoon. Harrelson, so great defensively, couldn't be touched at short; Boswell had won the second-base job; Clendenon, Jones, Shamsky and Agee could supply the power, and a better catcher than Grote wasn't going to be found; so if a good-hitting regular was to be found it would have to be at third base.

The Mets had tried to solve that problem with Otis, one of their hot prospects, back in the spring, but it had had a bad effect on the young outfielder without helping the team. So Murphy had been willing to give up Otis for Foy, who had displayed both right-handed power and base-stealing ability in the American League.

It was, it turned out, a mistake. Otis became a star centerfielder for Kansas City, and if he had been given that position by the Mets he might have solved a continuing problem. Foy, who proved an unstable character, never got untracked at all: he wound up hitting .236, with only six homers and 37 runs batted in, and did poorly in the field. And while he stole 22 bases, he also got thrown out 13 times, an unsatisfactory proportion.

So Foy wasn't the answer, but he wasn't the problem, either. The attack in general became more ineffective, for no single reason. Jones dropped from .340 to .277, and no one else made any appreciable gain. The offense, by and large, compiled statistics roughly similar to 1969, but the hits weren't as timely.

Yet, there was enough run-making there to cash in on a pitching staff that could repeat its 1969 performance.

It couldn't.

Seaver and Koosman, the leaders in the miracle run, were less than they had been. Neither Gentry nor Ryan advanced as expected. McGraw and Taylor weren't as effective in relief. McAndrew seemed less effective as he became more familiar.

None of these, it must be noted, had a "bad" year; the way they pitched would have been good enough to win a pennant for a better offensive team. And there were newcomers who helped: a reliever named Danny Frisella (brought up in mid-season from Tidewater), and the experienced Ray Sadecki, a left-handed starter. (Sadecki and Dave Marshall, a left-handed-hitting outfielder, were obtained from San Francisco for Jim Gosger and Bob Heise— a deal as one-sided in favor of the Mets, in its way, as the Foy-Otis trade wasn't). But they just didn't produce, as a staff, the exceptional work needed by a Met-type offense.

There were reasons. The detractors—and the Mets now had the rank to attract detractors—would call them alibis. The dedicated followers would call them tough breaks. The professionals knew they were the typical vicissitudes of competitive life, the inevitable obstacles that arise for everyone sooner or later, sometimes greater, sometimes less; a part of the to-be-expected fabric that makes winning so difficult.

Koosman's reason was arm trouble. He'd had some early in 1969, but this was worse and lasted longer, and he didn't really find himself until the second half of the season.

Seaver's reason was simply fatigue, mental as well as physical. He had pitched 251 innings in 1967, 278 in 1968, and 273 (plus 22 post-season) in 1969. And he worked 291 innings in 1970. That much pitching by a man who was primarily a power pitcher simply takes its toll. He won only 2 of his last 12 starts in 1970.

Ryan's problem was that he simply hadn't matured yet, and his small-town personality and preferences made it hard to adjust to New York, among other things.

McGraw's problem was the typical one of outstanding relief pitchers: they are seldom at a peak two years in a row. Taylor, in terms of his career record, had enjoyed an exceptional year in 1969, and in 1970, quite simply, he didn't.

And so it was that the 1970 season, from the beginning, was a struggle—in the new vein. Now, from the very start, every possible defeat had pennant implications. It wasn't a matter of kooky records or let's have some fun, at least; it was the real business of serious baseball.

The new champions did win their first game (*that* tradition had been laid to rest, anyhow), in extra innings at Pittsburgh. But Koosman lost the second, 2–1, and the pattern was set. Well into June the Mets struggled to stay above .500, never far below but never much above.

But since no one else in the division was doing much better, the Mets were in the thick of a three-team fight for first place, and when they started to put a few victories together in late June and early July, they moved into the lead. Measuring the Mets against first place every day was a new experience for everyone, since the 1969 dash had happened too quickly for such worries.

In the course of this, the staff's capacity for brilliance displayed itself in some awesome flashes. On April 22, against San Diego at Shea Stadium, Seaver set a major-league record by striking out the last 10 men in a row, in a 2–1 victory. His 19 strikeouts in that game tied the mark set the year before by Carlton. On April 18 at Shea Stadium, Ryan pitched a one-hitter against the Phillies (but without suspense, since the single by Dennis Doyle came in the first inning). Seaver pitched a two-hitter during the same home stand. Three days later, at Los Angeles, Ryan lost a two-hitter, 1–0. On May 13, in Chicago, Gentry hurled a one-hitter (with plenty of suspense until Ernie Banks singled in the eighth), and two days later, in Philadelphia, Seaver produced another one-hitter, spoiled by Mike Compton's single in the third. And on May 24, Ryan chipped in with a two-hitter against the Cubs at New York.

Three different pitchers turning in three one-hitters and three two-hitters in the first six weeks of a season—there was no doubt this staff had extraordinary ability. What it couldn't supply was consistency at such a level.

Between June 12 and July 9, the Mets won 20 of 27 games. This put them in first place by a game and a half—and it was to be the high point. Five straight losses followed, three at the hands of Montreal and two in Los Angeles, and the momentum was shot. But the win-one, lose-one pattern that followed was being matched by Chicago and Pittsburgh, and on August 5 the Mets started a long road trip in St. Louis, trailing Pittsburgh by only one game.

It was an eventful trip, on several counts. After a split of two games in St. Louis, the Mets got their first exposure to Three Rivers Stadium, the new ball park in Pittsburgh, opened only three weeks before. They split four games there, winning a wild 12–9 Saturday afternoon game that was nationally televised and lasted 3 hours 44 minutes. From there they went directly to another new park, Cincinnati's Riverfront Stadium, which, like Three Rivers, had a carpet instead of grass to play on. The Reds were asserting their power over the Western Division, and had by far the best record in the League, so the Mets couldn't feel too bad about losing two of the three. They reached Atlanta on Friday, August 14, two games behind Pittsburgh, seven games over .500, very much in the pennant race and very aware that just about a year ago at this time the miracle had begun to happen.

They split a double-header on that brutally hot night, but the big item was a highly encouraging six innings by Koosman in a 4–2 victory in the second game. On Saturday night, they had Seaver—whose record was 17–6, better than at the same point in 1969—going against Phil Niekro, who was 10–14, and the chance to start something rolling, with a home stand just ahead, seemed good.

And up came one of those turning-point games, the kind that sticks in memories and in emotions and has more consequences than even the participants will admit until much later.

The Mets just couldn't touch Niekro's knucklers, and got one hit in five innings. Seaver, tagged for three singles and a run with nobody out in the second, pitched out of a couple of jams. In the sixth, with two out and Seaver on base, Clendenon bashed his 17th homer, and the Mets had a 2–1 lead. In the bottom half of the inning, with one out, Clete Boyer doubled and Seaver fanned Bob Tillman with a fast ball for the second out before getting Gil Garrido on a fly. Tillman, a free-swinging, seldom-connecting right-handed catcher, was a natural enough strikeout victim for a Seaver stalking victory. It didn't seem noteworthy at the time.

But that's one of the fascinations of baseball. Details become related in fantastic ways. The Met offense was through for the night, and Seaver got through the eighth with the aid of a diving catch by Tommie Agee, before Tony Gonzalez opened the ninth with a bouncing single that squirmed through the left side of the infield.

Orlando Cepeda, Rico Carty and Boyer were the next three hitters—each a major home-run threat in the Atlanta ball park, so favorable to homers. Cepeda flied out, but Carty topped a ball towards third and Garrett couldn't handle it in time to prevent a hit. The winning run was now on first.

But the next hitter wasn't Boyer after all: it was Hank Aaron, pinch-hitting.

And the hitter after that was Tillman, with no fearsome pinch hitters left on the Atlanta bench.

Seaver's stuff was still good. So was his thinking. He would not give in to Aaron. He made four straight pitches, with lots on them, just outside the strike zone. Aaron wouldn't give in either. He walked.

Now the bases were full, and Seaver's task was completely defined: he had to strike Tillman out, or make him pop up, or hit a grounder that could be turned into a force at home. By far the safest thing to do was strike him out. Then any kind of out on Garrido could end the game.

Seaver did strike him out.

And lost.

The 1–2 pitch was a blazing fast ball, so fast that Tillman looked completely helpless as he swung and missed.

But Grote missed, too. The ball flew past him, to the distant backstop in this wide-oval stadium.

For a moment, everyone seemed stunned and motionless. There was a moment of hesitation before Gonzalez ran in from third with the tying run. Seaver came down to cover home, but to no well-defined spot. Grote, after another momentary hesitation, threw the ball in his general direction, but it flew off into the middle of the infield.

And Carty, who had moved from second to third, trotted home for a 3–2 Atlanta victory.

The Mets couldn't believe it. This was exactly what had happened to opposing teams in 1969, not to them.

And it was exactly the way the old Mets used to lose. (Look back in Chapter 4 and refer to the game of August 27, 1963, in Pittsburgh.)

But then it was funny, and cute.

Now it meant a pennant was slipping away.

Some believe that Seaver never recovered from that game; whether or not that's so, he posted only one more victory, in six weeks. On his next start (he was trying a four-day rotation now, and that cost him something, too) he was hit hard early by Houston in New York and beaten. Next time out, against the Reds in New York, he was nursing a 5–4 lead in the seventh when he gave up a three-run pinch homer to Jimmy Stewart—Stewart's first of the season, on August 23.

There were also recriminations. Grote, always easy to anger, resented being questioned about the play. There were indications that Seaver had crossed him up—that Grote had called for, and expected, a curve, but that Seaver threw a high inside fast ball to which Grote had no time to react. Seaver half admitted that, saying he was concentrating so hard on throwing a fast ball to Tillman—remembering Tillman's previous time at bat—that he might not have even noted, consciously, that Grote had called for something else.

But the point was that such explanations, demanded of Choo Choo Coleman or Jesse Gonder or Marv Throneberry—or even of Grote a year earlier—meant only clarification of a weird play. Now, after 1969, they meant the sharpest of value judgments: whose fault is it that we're blowing the pennant?

Stengel would have ranted about someone being a dummy (making sure that no one could really tell which one he meant), added an anecdote about someone in 1916, and kept double-talking until most of the players had dressed and left. Westrum would have looked pained and said, "Oh my God, wasn't that awful?" Hodges would, and did, say there was nothing much to say.

And yet—nothing was settled, not by a long shot. McAndrew ended the road trip, not 16 hours after Seaver's mishap, with a gallant 2–1 victory, and the tight race continued. The Mets were now losing more often than winning, but so were the Cubs and Pirates, and Aug. 31 found New York only three games over .500, but only two games off the pace, in third place.

They were still World Champions, until proven otherwise, and the time to make a drive was now.

And they made one. They won nine of the next 12 games. On September 10, the anniversary of their first touch of first place, Cleon Jones hit a triple in the 14th inning for a 3–2 victory over Philadelphia, and the Mets were tied for first place again, with Pittsburgh.

All the decisions still lay ahead, with 19 games to go.

Only now did the real pressure start, a kind of grinding out-by-out pennant pressure they had not felt in 1969, when everything was surrounded by that happy haze of destiny, buoyed by that mysterious momentum.

The Cards came in, and Gibson beat Seaver, but McAndrew answered with a 3–0 five-hitter, his fourth straight victory. But the rubber game went to the Cardinals on Joe Torre's 13th-inning homer off Ron Herbel. (Here was another newcomer; the Mets had acquired Herbel from San Diego only two weeks before, and he hadn't given up a run in his first seven appearances for New York.)

At Montreal, after a 10-inning victory September 14, another of those nightmare losses in 10 innings occurred. Marshall had tied the game for the Mets with a two-out pinch homer in the ninth, and Agee had provided a 4–3 lead with a homer in the top of the 10th. But, with Koosman pitching, there came a single, a walk, a sacrifice—and a wild pitch with the count two strikes, no balls on Gary Sutherland, when a strikeout would have meant one routine out needed for the victory. Instead, an intentional walk to Rusty Staub, another one (after Staub took second unmolested) to Ron Fairly, and—Herbel having relieved—a single by John Bateman.

Trailing Pittsburgh by a game and a half, and the Cubs by a percentage point, the Mets got four cracks at the Pirates at Shea Stadium starting September 18, and plenty of time to do it. But Steve Blass beat McAndrew, 3–2, and Gentry lost, 2–1, as four relief pitchers stopped the Mets. Koosman won with a two-hitter in the opener of the Sunday double-header, but Pittsburgh won the second game (after knocking out Seaver in the sixth) with a four-run 10th inning triggered by Willie Stargell's homer off McGraw.

Three and a half behind now, with nine to play; life draining away, as through a mortal wound. But with three to play in Pittsburgh, it was not yet hopeless. Two one-run decisions over Philadelphia set the stage.

The series began on Friday, September 25 with the standings this way:

	W	L	GB
Pittsburgh	84	72	—
New York	81	74	2½
Chicago	81	74	2½

A sweep would put the Mets into first, and then their four remaining games would be against the Cubs in New York. Two out of three wouldn't really be enough, but it would keep hopes alive. The first game had to be the key. And at this moment the Mets still officially owned their title.

Koosman started, lasted four innings, went out trailing 2–0. In the first eight innings, the Mets managed to put 16 men on base, but only two of them scored. It was 4–2, Pittsburgh, going into the ninth. The proverbial wall was pressing against the collective Met back.

Swoboda led off the ninth with a walk, and scored on Agee's double. It was 4–3, tying run on second, nobody out. A chance.

Garrett walked. Jones and Shamsky were the next two hitters. A good chance.

Jones hit the ball hard and deep to right field, but not out of reach of Clemente, who caught it for the first out. Agee could have tagged up and made third after the catch—but he didn't. So it was still men on first and second, and it would take a hit, rather than another long fly, to bring in the tying run.

But Agee, having failed to do it the easy way, tried the hard way: he tried to steal third. He didn't make it.

And Shamsky struck out.

And the game was over.

And the season?

Almost.

Again, recriminations. Agee was finishing up a season in which he hit .286, made 24 homers, and batted in 75 runs while playing 153 games with a knee that wasn't really sound. In the old days—a year ago—he would have been only loved and admired, with sympathy expressed for whatever mistake he might have made. Now he was being castigated for not tagging up, and for trying to steal.

That was the difference between being a Met B.C.—before championship —and now. Only the result counted now.

However, there wasn't too much time for brooding. By the next afternoon, the teams were on the field again, nationally televised, with the Mets mathematically alive and Seaver on the mound.

He lasted only into the fifth—his shortest appearance of the entire season —and gave way to Herbel; but in the seventh it was still a 3-3 game. With one out, Bob Robertson singled to center and Agee came dashing in to try for a shoestring catch. He didn't get it. The ball went through and Robertson wound up on third. John Jeter ran for him.

Herbel made Manny Sanguillen hit a grounder to Clendenon—who dropped the ball. Sanguillen was safe on the fourth Met error of the game, but Jeter was still on third. Then the managers went to work, and their maneuvers resulted in McGraw facing Jose Pagan. A fly to center, Jeter scoring after the catch, and, a few minutes later, a 4-3 Pirate victory.

Pittsburgh was now assured of nothing worse than a tie for first.

"It's been a long, long, long season," said Hodges, barely clinging to the necessary fiction that one couldn't give up as long as there was a mathematical chance. Had he tried to inspire his team in the clubhouse? "No, I don't make speeches like Knute Rockne. I'm not the type," he said.

Sunday, a crowd of 50,469, a Pittsburgh record, filled Three Rivers Stadium. Officially, the Mets were defending champions (of the Eastern Division, the National League, the World Series) until formally eliminated.

It became official at 4:08 P.M., with the final out of a 2-1 Pittsburgh victory, that they were champions no more, and that was the end of the First Met Dynasty. As World Champions, they had lasted 348 days; as National League champions, 358; as the first holders of the Eastern Division title, 369. It had taken them 2,724 days to reach the top, and less than one-seventh of that to lose it.

"We didn't lose it this weekend," declared Agee, with profound accuracy. "We lost it in April and May and June."

"We gave away too much," said Hodges, thinking of the men left on base, the errors, the late-inning homers off relief pitchers.

Agee had set a club record with 182 hits, Clendenon a club mark of 97 runs batted in (he had 22 homers), Boswell a major league record by playing 85 straight games (between April 29 and September 27) without an error. These would have been glorious achievements once; now they were dross. The only thing that counted, winning again, hadn't happened, and the harsh lesson had been driven home once and for all: miracles are not forever.

And 1971 proceeded to reinforce every lesson taught by 1970.

Of course, 1970 hadn't ended in Pittsburgh. There were still those four games to be played with the Cubs in New York. The series began with the Cubs one game ahead. At stake was a few hundred dollars a man, the difference between placing second and third. And the games proved surprisingly spirited. The Mets won the first, on a three-run 10th-inning homer by Garrett, and the second, 3-1, behind Koosman. But Bill Hands and Ferguson Jenkins won the last two, 2-0 and 4-1, and the Mets finished third.

There, in a nutshell, was the frame that gave perspective to the last two years: a Met team had finished third in a close race—and was considered a failure. That was true success.

While others tried to sort out their emotional reactions, Hodges and Scheffing—who had been through this kind of disappointment before, and worse—set to work on the only thing they had spent their lives learning: how to try again.

18 Creeping Maturity

EVERYTHING considered, 1971 was probably the least satisfying year the Mets had ever experienced.

Not only were the mini-rewards of pre-championship days no longer possible, but also the status of champion was officially gone. All through 1970, it had been possible for dedicated Met fans (and the casually curious everywhere) to wonder if perpetual futility had actually been transformed into perpetual success. Until the finality of the end of the 1970 season was felt, the miracle aura of 1969 lingered. But going into 1971, the Mets moved into complete ordinariness. They certainly had the kind of roster that, given some good luck, could finish first—just like half the other teams in the league; and they had no built-in excuses if the team did badly—just like half the other teams in the league.

Furthermore, all sorts of outside forces were combining to change public attitudes towards the Mets, and in some ways Met attitudes towards themselves.

Of the most immediate effect was the overall sports picture in New York. The Met Miracle of September–October 1969 was an extended version of the football Superbowl victory scored by the Jets nine months before, vastly magnified by the fact that the football miracle lasted three hours while the baseball miracle took two months. But in May, 1970, the New York Knicks won the National Basketball Association championship, for the first time in 24 years of trying, and basketball, after all, was New York's native sport. The New York Rangers, a hockey power more than a generation ago but woefully weak for two decades, posted their best record in 31 years in the 1970 season, finished second, and just missed making the final round of the Stanley Cup playoffs. And even the football Giants, in eclipse since the early 1960s, came up with an unexpectedly successful 1970 season, in which they were in the running for a playoff berth until the final game, in mid-December.

Then there were the Yankees. At the end of the 1969 season, the balance of power between the Mets and Yankees reached the opposite end of the pendulum's original position. The last time the Yankees had won a pennant, 1964, was the first year the Mets had occupied Shea Stadium. As Met audiences grew and became more respectable in the new ball park, Yankee field power faded (to last place in 1966), attendance dwindled (it was less than half of what the Mets drew in both 1969 and 1970), and attention paid to them all but disappeared.

But during 1970, while the Met title defense died a slow death, the Yankees made real progress in a rebuilding program. They won 93 games, 10 more than the Mets; they didn't really threaten Baltimore, the powerhouse of the American League, but they did run a strong second and, in all respects, had their most successful season since their glory days. On September 23, two days before the Mets went to Pittsburgh for their final, painful elimination, the Yankees had a champagne clubhouse celebration at Yankee Stadium upon clinching second.

So, in two short years, New York's sports public faced entirely different prospects. On January 1, 1969, there was the long-established hunger for some sort of vicarious victory, a willingness to settle for crumbs, and a sort of logic-defying hope for better things. On January 1, 1971, there was the fresh memory of three emotional binges supplied by the Jets, Mets and Knicks, along with the conviction that the Rangers and Yankees were about to duplicate those feats and the belief that the Giants might. Nor was there much doubt that the Knicks and Jets, if their key players could avoid injury, could maintain their positions.

Therefore, in a perverse way, the Mets entered the 1971 season as once again the most questioned of the New York teams: it was their 1969 situation, in a way, raised to a much higher level. After 1970, 1969 could be seen as a fluke, and older habits of believing in other teams were easily restored. What was different, of course, was the demand. New Yorkers who,

24 months before, would have been happy to have anybody win anything, were now demanding nothing less than a championship from everyone.

Beyond the sports picture, things were different, too. The ecstasy of pennant celebrations, which had spawned so many editorials about bolstering civic "morale," had passed and left its bleak residue: life in the city had not improved. The streets were daily more frightening; night life was expiring restaurant by restaurant, theater by theater, club by club; transportation, by car, subway, or taxi, continued to become less comfortable; strikes and ethnic fragmentation continued to increase; the middle class continued to flee; the central city seemed to make little progress. When the realization sank in that the moment of unity and joy provided by a championship team really didn't produce any lasting after-effect, the mood of disillusionment was even stronger than it had been before the "miracles" occurred. And this disillusionment put sports back into perspective, underlining their limited importance. One might dream, beforehand, than when the Mets or Knicks or Jets "finally made it" (or that when man finally walked in the moon), some "new era" might dawn. But they had, and it hadn't, and the net effect was to make ball games only ball games again, with less capacity to move deep emotions in millions of people. The dedicated fans, and the involved players, were as immersed as ever, of course; but the much larger surrounding fringe, touched by the magic of those "first" triumphs of the Jets, Mets and Knicks, could not be touched the same way again.

And a change in the political climate affected the Met picture, as it did everything else, but with some special characteristics.

By 1971, the campus rebellion was waning and protest, in any form, was meeting with more and more hostility from the "silent majority." Being far out, which had been cute in the early years of the Mets, was now a facet of the universal polarization: you had to love it or hate it. Those who had been originally attracted to the Mets as a maverick phenomenon were either no longer amused by such things, or so hardened into anti-establishment attitudes that the no-longer-helpless Mets seemed much too square for them. Those who had become Met fans after the move to Shea, the new suburban majority, were merely annoyed by the presence of the remaining maverick-lovers, and were more likely to accept the increasingly prevalent view (so often espoused by President Nixon) that "only winning counts." Meanwhile, the war in Asia was dragging on, stimulating bitterness in exactly that segment of the young population that was most affected by military service and had been most susceptible to Met interest in more carefree days. Inflation was becoming a daily issue. "Crime in the streets" was a major feature of the Congressional campaign in the fall of 1970.

Another aspect of the political climate had an unexpected, often unrecognized, but measurable effect on the Met aura. There was open conflict between the administration (usually represented by Vice-President Spiro Agnew) and "the press." Whatever the merits of the dispute—and there were strong feelings on both sides—there was a noticeable increase in public distrust of the news media. And however this did or did not affect political questions, it did spill over into the sports world.

The news media, after all, were the daily point of contact for the vast majority of fans with their teams. The Mets, originally, were the product of bright reporting, in a time when readers and listeners didn't particularly question the purposes or essential accuracy of the reporters. When newspapers in general became vaguely more suspect, even their sports pages acquired some of that undefined but uncomfortable flavor. If this had happened during the Casey Stengel era, when all the Mets were good for was a joke, it might not have mattered; but once the Mets passed into mainstream pennant contention, there was blame to be assessed for defeat, and praise to be assigned for victory—and it became significant how reporters wrote and commentators commented. The net result, largely subliminal, was the loss of a few more degrees of pleasant amusement in following the Mets.

So when the Mets gathered in St. Petersburg at the start of spring training in 1971, they were further from the center of people's thoughts than they had been for some time, and a less cheerful object than they used to be for those who kept their thoughts on them.

To Hodges and Scheffing, such philosophic considerations hardly existed. Theirs was the straight baseball view: beef up the roster a bit, get a decent break, and try to win. They believed wholeheartedly that pitching was the name of the game, and they had every reason to believe that their staff represented a depth of talent no other club could match. With such a start, the end result of 1969 (although not the pattern) could well be repeated.

Their optimism was basically justified. They knew that Seaver, Koosman, Ryan, and Gentry were four first-line starters of unquestioned physical ability, that McGraw and Frisella could form an excellent lefty-righty bullpen, and that Sadecki and McAndrew provided an experienced reserve.

Anyone could see that much, but few knew as much as they did about the farm system, which had been producing so handsomely. It still had goodies to offer, because the high draft choices earned by years of finishing ninth and tenth were beginning to pay off. All fans read of future phenomena year after year, but couldn't really distinguish between standard hopefulness and actual promise; and the names constantly being dropped by farm directors and scouts seldom got sorted out and retained until the player in question made it as a major leaguer. But the Met organization knew who it had, and who could be used either for replacement or trading.

The policy going into 1971 was to go with replacement. There was a lot to choose from.

High draft choices in 1966 had provided Gentry and Duffy Dyer, rookies in the championship year. Both figured to improve and Dyer might be ready to share some of the catching burden with Grote. There were also Mike Jorgensen, Ken Singleton, Tim Foli and Jon Matlack. Jorgy was a 4th-round pick in 1966, Singleton a No. 1 in January, 1967, Matlack a No. 1 in June, 1967, and Foli a No. 1 in June, 1968.

During the 1970 season, Jorgensen and Singleton had spent a lot of time with the parent club. Jorgensen, a left-handed hitter, was a first baseman, but able to fill in as an outfielder. He stayed all year as Agee's back-up man and got into 76 games, although he rarely batted. Singleton, a large, switch-hitting outfielder, was tearing up the International League (.388, with 17 homers in 64 games) when he was called up in late June. He did well enough (.263) to make one believe that if he hadn't been unavailable most of September with a leg injury, the 1970 story might have ended more happily.

When Singleton had been brought up, Kranepool had been sent down, even though he was (at 25!) the oldest Met in terms of service. By his own testimony later, Kranepool benefitted from a two-month exile: he returned to the Mets thinner, more eager, more mature, more determined to prove his major-league skills. So, in a way, Singleton's arrival added two useful players to the roster.

Foli was a fiery young infielder, who spent all of 1970 at Tidewater, but clearly seemed destined for regular duty somewhere. Matlack, a tall, young left-hander who had been tabbed "another Koosman" after striking out 188 batters in 173 innings in his first pro season in 1968, had compiled an off-year record in 1970 in his second season at Tidewater, but his quality was not in question.

So the stock-taking went this way: Agee (despite a questionable knee) and Jones were set at two outfield positions. The third would belong to Singleton unless he lost it. Shamsky, platooned against right-handed pitching and moved between first base and the outfield, had chronic back problems, but Jorgensen could help there if need be. Dave Marshall fit the same category. The expendable one was Swoboda, albeit he was a folk hero. Hodges had never liked Swoboda's attitudes, which seemed frivolous and undisciplined to the quiet manager, and Swoboda's day-in, day-out performance didn't encourage making exceptions. (In the last three seasons, Swoboda had hit .242, .235 and .233).

Harrelson and Boswell seemed set as the middle of the infield, but Clendenon would have to be replaced soon—presumably by Jorgensen—and third base was still the blank. Foy was simply dropped.

Grote was certainly a first-rate big-league catcher.

All in all, then, few moves were needed, except for third.

In December, 1970, the Mets thought they scored a coup: they got Bob Aspromonte (a 32-year-old veteran of more than 1,200 National League games) from Atlanta for nothing more than Ron Herbel. Aspro was known as a good hitter and solid fielder, and his .213 batting average in Atlanta was simply shrugged off. He was too young to be washed up—and besides, Hodges knew him from pretty far back: at this point, Aspromonte was the last Brooklyn Dodger still actively playing, since he had appeared in one game (one at bat) as an 18-year-old in 1956 before being farmed out for several years. (Such items still loomed large in the affections of serious Met followers: they knew that Harrelson had been born on D-Day, and that Jorgensen had been born on August 16, 1948—the day Babe Ruth died.)

And on March 31, only a few days before the 1971 season was to start, they traded Swoboda to Montreal for Don Hahn, whose defensive capabilities as a center fielder would provide full protection for the Agee situation. In terms of fame (and salary), Swoboda was being given away for "nothing," and many Met fans took it that way. In hard baseball terms, it proved an eminently sound move (although those who remembered Don Bosch shuddered).

So that was the shape of the team Hodges honestly felt could win again, if all went well.

It didn't.

It started well enough. Pittsburgh, clearly, was the team to beat (although Pirate pitching was suspect), and on May 15, after winning the first two games of a series in Pittsburgh, the Mets were 21–10 and leading the division by 2½ games. Ryan was 4–0, Seaver 5–2, Koosman 3–1, and the offense was averaging 4.3 runs a game, which wasn't bad for early in the season.

But a five-game losing streak took the steam out of the fast break, although there was no immediate cause for alarm. Early in June, Agee injured his other knee, but the team seemed to survive. On June 30, when Ryan shut out the Pirates 4–0 at Shea Stadium, the Mets found themselves trailing Pittsburgh by two games and boasting a 45–29 record.

It was certainly a fine contending position for mid-season. It was, in fact, the best record any Met team had ever enjoyed at that stage of the season.

And there was no hint at all that the team would lose 11 of its next 12 games.

You couldn't fairly pinpoint any one factor, or one person. It started on a long home stand, with a loss to Pittsburgh and three more to Atlanta. The real shocker was losing three of the next four to Montreal. They left home, on July 9, for a four-game weekend in Cincinnati just before the All-Star break—and lost all four. Suddenly they were 10 games off the pace.

The brief vacation did no good. The trip resumed with two losses in three games at Houston, a split in St. Louis, and two losses before a final victory in Chicago.

It was July 23 when they got back home: in fourth place, only four games above .500, 12½ games behind Pittsburgh.

And that was just about how they finished: 83–79, tied for third place, 14 games behind the Pirates, who went on to win the World Series.

After it was all over, the reasons were plain enough.

A sore arm and a mysterious pain in his left side kept Koosman out of action for a total of more than two months, and he wound up with a 6–11 record. Seaver, although he had another imposing year (he led the majors with a 1.76 earned-run average and set a league record for right-handers by striking out 289), wasn't able to provide victories in proportion. He did get to 20 victories by winning twice in the final five days, but between June 30 and September 26 he was able to win only eight of the 85 games the Mets played. Ryan, after an 8–4 start, won only two more games in the last three months. Gentry, 13–12 as a rookie and 9–9 as a sophomore, was 12–11 this time, making little progress towards the consistency hoped for: he remained enormously impressive one time, unaccountably off the beam the next.

So the pitching, still the best in the league statistically, wasn't overwhelming enough to make up for other deficiencies. There was nothing to blame it for, but it just wasn't up to miracle standards.

And it would have had to be, when one considered the offense.

Clendenon was done. He played maybe half the time, hit 11 homers, struck out 78 times and walked only 21 times. The extra power ingredient he represented was gone.

Shamsky, bothered increasingly by his bad back, played hardly at all and hit .185 when he did. So that aspect of the power, or even a threat of power, was missing.

Agee, hobbled much of the time, did well enough in other respects (.285 and 28 stolen bases) but dropped sharply in power, with only 14 homers and 50 runs batted in.

Aspromonte did nothing to solve the problem at third. He hit .225 and in the last couple of months, when Garrett returned from a six-month tour of military service, turned over the position to the younger player (who hit 11 homers in 56 games).

Singleton never really got untracked, and hit .245, with 13 homers.

Harrelson, Boswell, Kranepool, and Grote hit as well as they were expected to, but they were singles hitters essentially, so much of their value was nullified by the power failure in the rest of the line-up.

And although Jones had a good year, at .319, he wasn't really a power producer either, and could be pitched around when necessary.

So here was a team that hit only 98 homers altogether; that struck out almost twice as often as it walked; whose R.B.I. leader (Jones) had only 69; and that hit into double plays more often than it made them.

In short, weak offense and good pitching, with adequate but unspectacular fielding, added up to exactly what the team was: a .500 club, give or take a few decisions.

Two years before, with the same personnel doing the same things, it would have been considered a banner year. Now it was a cause for grumbling.

Gentry articulated what some of the other pitchers didn't want to say out loud: Seaver, as good as he was, constituted a problem for the rest of the staff because his starting schedule was often maintained at their expense.

The other players, platooned so profusely, complained now about what they had accepted so blissfully during 1969.

And the honeymoon was over for Hodges.

Both the press and a sizable segment of the public began finding fault with a manager who had committed the sin of failing, two years in a row, to reproduce the victory no one had expected in the first place.

As a champion, Hodges had been seen as marvellously calm; now it was "lack of communication with the players." He had been wonderfully, paternally, a disciplined leader; now he was harsh and cold. His handling of the pitching staff (through Rube Walker) and platooning had been sheer genius; now every move was second-guessed.

In none of these respects, of course, was Hodges any different from what he had been in his first two years with the Mets—or in his years in Washington—or as a player. He was always an intensely private individual, outwardly calm but extremely strong-willed, somewhat rigid in his standards but extremely alert, aware, and flexible in his tactical thinking. He never had been particularly "quotable" and never tried to be, a characteristic that surprised the younger reporters, who had always heard of him as a "good guy" and took that to mean (by the standards of the new time) "easy to get answers from and write about."

Now the terrific unity and loyalty that existed in the coaching staff (which had come with him from Washington, and which gradually accepted the non-assertive Berra) was being described as "cliquishness."

All these things, as any experienced observer could see, were absolutely typical of any ball club that had won and was now not winning.

And here was one more sign that the Mets had become a "typical" ball club: by the end of 1971, all their specialness was gone, for better or worse. They had entered the mainstream, and had completed the transition into being routine. No longer were they a challenge to any Establishment: they *were* the Establishment. In 1970, in the wake of their triumph, they had sold more than 2,600,000 tickets, the third highest figure in baseball history. In 1971, their attendance was 2,266,000, making a three-year total of more than 7,000,000. These were not young kooks carrying home-made banners, or various representatives of the disenfranchised—not in such numbers. Whatever original Met fans were still around were swallowed up in the middle-class masses who poured into Shea Stadium from Long Island and other suburbs, who bought their tickets well ahead for specific dates, and who wanted only what sports fans everywhere seemed to want: victory, and no questions asked.

Nor did the Met management seem to mind this status. It was pretty establishment-minded itself.

Grant had now emerged as a major baseball figure. While Weiss had been in charge, everyone else had stayed in the background (except Stengel, of course). But since then, the nature of the problems facing baseball club owners had changed. There was an anti-trust suit pursued by Curt Flood, supported by the Players Association. There were franchise moves and expansion, on an unprecedented scale. There had been that terrible fight over the commissionership, and Kuhn, in moving from "pro tem" to permanent commissioner in 1969, had not really healed any wounds.

By the end of 1971, Grant's identity and his image as the man who really made decisions about the Mets were clearly established in the minds of all Met followers. And it was, by and large, an unfavorable image for fairly traditional reasons.

To begin with, Grant's first major public exposure, back in 1966 and 1967, had put him in an unfortunate light. The American and National Football Leagues had merged, and now the Giants and Jets would be able to play each other—the Jets with Joe Namath, the Giants still not that far removed from their most glamorous years. In New York, no single sport event could match the anticipatory excitement generated by this meeting, and a natural place to have it seemed to be Shea Stadium.

But the Mets were prime tenants at Shea and the Jets had to accept dates as the Mets directed (about which the Jets had always complained). As representative of the top of the Met pyramid, Grant was the man who had to deal with this question of stadium availability. There was one flimsy but realistic reason for keeping the football team out until the baseball season was over: football games do chop up a baseball field, especially one as

naturally soggy as Shea. But there was a much stronger, psychological reason. This was a time, it must be remembered, when football's status as the
"new" national sport was receiving maximum publicity. Whatever the facts,
the public relations offensive on behalf of football was going full blast, and
had most baseball people in a defensive, resentful frame of mind. Grant's
position, shared by many baseball executives, could be summed up as: "Why
should we help football upstage us in our own ball park in the middle of
our season?"

Of course, it wasn't exactly the Mets' "own" ball park; on the other hand,
the lease terms had been agreed to by the city with presumably open eyes.
(And it was perfectly true, as Grant pointed out again and again in subsequent years, that without the baseball Mets as a prime tenant, Shea Stadium
would never have been built and the Jets would have had no home at all.)

What hurt Grant with the public, however, was his avowal of the "I'm for
baseball and I don't want football to interfere" attitude. *The Daily News*,
with its circulation of about 3,000,000, was strongly in favor of a Giants-
Jets game at Shea in August, possibly with a charity tie-in, and in its pages
Grant emerged as the villain of the piece. The Mets never did back down on
the exhibition-game question, and the famous football game was played at
the Yale Bowl in New Haven. The Jets never did get to play even early-
season regular games at Shea until the Mets were through with it every
October. So Grant, in this case, was labelled an Establishment Power Sel-
fishly Opposing the Desire of the Majority.

Such an image was easily reinforced by his bearing and background. A
tall, distinguished-looking man, he was easy to caricature in top-hat and tails.
A Canadian by birth and education, he spoke English in accents not cozy
to native New York ears, and such speech was easy to associate with "snooti-
ness" (as "My Fair Lady" taught to those who missed the original lesson in
"Pygmalion"). Always being identified as a "Wall Street" figure, involved
with "investments," and a "financial advisor" to Mrs. Payson only increased
the distance between Grant and the ordinary, original Met fan.

However unjust much of the instinctive hostility towards Grant might
have been, it was aggravated by a trait he either acquired from Weiss or
naturally shared: he had the memory of an elephant for unkind remarks in
print, combined with a bland acceptance of favorable publicity, as if that
were only to be taken for granted. Over the years, many a minor friction
that might have been quickly forgotten deepened into a feud between the
Met management and some writer because of this one-way vision. Grant, in
this respect, was certainly no different from most club owners or other high

executives in all sports (and outside of sports); but in few situations was the gap between common-people fan-dom and upper-crust ownership made so strikingly apparent. Like most things about the Mets, these were mythical conceptions, but no less powerful for that.

And in a few months, in the spring of 1972, Grant's personality would be projected to center stage in ways no one could have foreseen.

Scheffing, less bustling than Devine, less a long-standing insider than Murphy, less superboss than Weiss, went about his business in a low-key way that emphasized the impression that the general manager was now a technician (and Scheffing, baseball man to the core and still fond of his Arizona home, had no objection whatever to a self-effacing role). He worked well with Hodges and was generally popular with the players, and gave a lot of time to the farm system.

However, the key opinion on all strictly baseball questions remained Hodges's. That's how the outside world saw it, and that's how it was. There wasn't the slightest weakening of the faith management had in him and in his methods, whatever criticism (still subdued and sometimes shamefaced) might be expressed.

Approaching the 1972 season, few basic changes seemed necessary. The pitching, after all, had led the league and there was only one big "if": Koosman. If he were all right physically (and he had shown encouraging signs late in 1971), that department was fine.

In the infield, it was time to turn towards youth: Clendenon and Aspromonte were simply released. Kranepool (who had hit .280 after his Tidewater experience) or Jorgensen could certainly be the lefty half of a first-base platoon. Garrett had shown that he might hold down third, and Foli might make it, too.

In the outfield, it was still hoped Singleton could be the third man, backed up by Marshall. And Grote was fine.

Still—when you added it all up, it still spelled "not enough power."

So a basic decision was made. In 1971, the fine farm system had been seen as a source of replacements. Now it would be used—as good farm systems have been used traditionally—for trading purposes. The last three seasons had proved, conclusively, that the basic Met roster was strong enough to contend for a pennant: in that time, the Mets had won 266 games, Pittsburgh 274, Chicago 259, St. Louis 253. The foundation was there. Now it was a matter of finding those one or two extra, experienced, special players who might make the relatively little difference that makes all the difference.

Such players, if they could be found, would have to fulfill the primary need, batting power. As the roster shaped up, the lack of right-handed power (now that Clendenon, Aspromonte and Swoboda were gone) seemed most acute.

So the first trade was really a "bench" trade. Shamsky and three young pitchers (Jim Bibby, Rich Folkers and Charlie Hudson) went to St. Louis for Jim Beauchamp, a right-handed utility man who could pinch hit with some power, and Chuck Taylor and Harry Parker, two right-handed relievers. The Mets also got a young infielder named Tom Coulter. Essentially, they had traded a lefty pinch-hitter for a righty pinch-hitter.

The next one, in December, was bigger, and a stunner.

The Mets gave up on Nolan Ryan.

His retrogression during the second half of 1971 seemed to convince management that he just wasn't going to make it all that big. Whatever the reasons (and there were plenty of theories), he wasn't progressing. He wasn't acquiring control, of the ball into the strike zone, or of himself into consistent performance. Few Mets were more personally popular than this pleasant Texan, but as a pitcher he was frustrating everyone, including himself. The Met management position became: "How long can you wait?"

He was traded, therefore, with three minor league players to the California Angels for one veteran infielder who was supposed to be a pretty good hitter and the latest answer to the third-base gap: Jim Fregosi. Four for one.

It was a questionable move even as a first guess, long before it became one of the most second-guessed of all Met moves.

Ryan was not yet 25, and his arm still had the velocity to make him a super-pitcher. Fregosi was 30, and not really a third baseman. He had been an all-star shortstop, but was coming off two years of arm and leg injuries and had hit only .233 in 1971. Even so, he was looked upon as an answer to the righty power problem, and if he got back his 1970 form (22 homers, .278) he might serve the purpose.

That the Mets also had to throw in Lee Stanton (an outfielder), Don Rose (a pitcher), and Francisco Estrada (a catcher) only underlined how much faith they put in Fregosi.

Of course, the decision to yield Ryan wasn't illogical. The fact was that the Mets were pitching-rich, and only so many starters can be used, anyhow. They had Seaver; they were sure that Gentry was more likely to blossom immediately than Ryan; they thought Koosman would come back; they knew Matlack was on the way; and they felt they had another promising right-hander in Charley Williams, still another fire-baller who had spent the second half of the 1971 season with the Mets after making the jump from Memphis.

And there was a talent flow at other positions, too: John Milner, a lefty first baseman-outfielder, had moved up with two strong years at Memphis and Tidewater. Teddy Martinez seemed able to play anywhere effectively. The others given up with Ryan wouldn't be missed. And if one strong right-handed hitter could help bring a pennant (as Clendenon had in 1969), Ryan wouldn't be missed either.

And yet, even with Fregosi (who promptly broke his thumb before his first exhibition game), real punch was a border-line commodity. Hodges and Scheffing kept yearning for one more really big bat—the game-busting type—and preferably left-handed, since Agee, Jones, and Fregosi were right-handed.

There was such a bat on the market. It belonged to Daniel Joseph (Rusty) Staub, who had captivated Montreal as "Le Grand Orange" during the last three years after several impressive but power-stymied years in the anti-homer Astrodome. Rusty was only 28, but an eight-year major leaguer. In 1969, when Commissioner Kuhn had involved himself in the Clendenon affair, he had also made it possible for Staub to stay in Montreal when Houston wanted to reneg on the trade. And now the Expos, entering the fourth year of their expansion existence, were willing to give up such a prize for a suitable package of young players who might lift the general level of their team. Montreal needed now what the Mets had needed in the 1960s, and a Staub was their best instrument for getting new talent from the highest bidder.

The Mets, Scheffing and Hodges decided as the 1972 spring training season neared its end, would bid high. Negotiations began.

On Easter Sunday, April 2, the Mets would play the Expos at West Palm Beach, in their last Florida game before a final pair of exhibitions with the Yankees on the way north. Perhaps the deal could be finalized then.

But two shocks intervened.

On April 1, the baseball players went on strike.

On April 2, Hodges was dead.

19 *Restlessness*

A HAZE of shock and bewilderment hung over the first week of April, 1972, for anyone connected with baseball or interested in the Mets.

All through March, a confrontation had been building between the players and club owners, ostensibly over a trivial pension question, but really over negotiating strength. On March 31, a Friday, in Dallas, player representatives of every club voted to strike. The regular season was scheduled to start the next Wednesday.

The same day, the Mets broke camp at St. Petersburg and moved to the Ramada Inn at West Palm Beach. They were to play the Yankees in nearby Fort Lauderdale on Saturday and the Expos at West Palm on Sunday. Then they would share a charter with the Yankees to Kinston, N.C., and Norfolk, Va., for the final two exhibitions between the clubs. The Mets would then go on to Pittsburgh to open the season on Thursday while the Yankees opened at home.

But by late Friday night, word of the strike had reached all players. Seaver and Ray Sadecki were the Met representatives at Dallas, and they promptly called their teammates with the news. By Saturday morning, instead of taking a bus to Fort Lauderdale, Met players were scattering, en route either to their homes, to New York, or to some Florida location to wait for the next development. There was not yet any widespread belief, that Saturday, that the strike would last, although it was clear that all the remaining exhibition games were off.

Grant was up to his neck in the player negotiations, as a member of a key committee of owners. Scheffing and Jim Fanning, Montreal's general manager, had just about agreed on the details of a deal for Staub, but this was no time to conclude it: each was buried in dealing with the adjustments forced by the strike situation.

The manager and his coaches, however, suddenly had nothing to do. On Sunday, which was Easter, Yogi and his wife Carmen went to Miami to attend a friend's funeral. Hodges, Walker, Pignatano, and Yost went to play golf.

About five o'clock Sunday afternoon, the golfers returned to the Ramada Inn. Before going to their separate rooms, they took a moment to set a time to meet for dinner.

As he turned away from the group, Hodges suddenly collapsed.

He didn't crumble. He fell heavily backwards, his head hitting the stone walk. He was unconscious instantly, and, if not already dead, beyond revival. The heart attack was that sudden.

He would have been 48 years old on Tuesday.

First reports were confused, not immediately confirming that Hodges had died, but by midnight it was known everywhere.

All the disruption of the strike situation added to the disorientation and the pain of the next few days. To people connected with the Mets, feelings towards Hodges were just this side of worship. While there were players who found him cold and distant, most players did not, and the rest of the organization felt unreserved love, from Mrs. Payson and Grant down.

Beyond that, few men in baseball history had struck so deep a chord of affection—in the minds of Met fans everywhere, and Brooklynites especially, since Brooklyn was the spiritual home of the club. Sympathy for his family, Joan and Gil Jr. and the three daughters, went far beyond routine compassion.

And yet—there was absolutely no way to make time stop.

Hodges died on Sunday. The same night, Scheffing and Grant reached Yogi and told him he was their choice to take over the club.

On Monday morning, the charter plane that had been ordered to fly both clubs to exhibition games was used to fly Yankee and Met officials, and newspapermen, to New York. The body of Hodges was carried north on the same plane.

On Tuesday night, in Chicago, the clubowners had a long, stormy, showdown meeting, which Grant had to attend. Decisions were taken that extended the strike, and now it was clear that the baseball season would be delayed.

But even if it had not been, the Met opener in Pittsburgh would have been cancelled. Because the funeral was on Thursday.

And immediately after the funeral, Grant and Scheffing called a press conference at Shea Stadium.

They had two announcements: Yogi Berra was the new manager of the Mets; and Rusty Staub had been acquired from Montreal for Ken Singleton, Mike Jorgensen and Tim Foli.

There was much criticism of the "haste" with which the news was given out, the "insensitivity" of announcing it the same day as the funeral. But many of those who uttered this criticism had spent the preceding three days speculating about the manager and the trade.

So there just wasn't any "graceful" way that would satisfy everyone to handle a tragic circumstance, and the emotional pressure of the strike only added to the difficulty.

But there, in a space of five days, the nature of the Mets had fundamentally changed.

It had been, for four years, Gil's team, indelibly stamped. Even those who had begun to second-guess Hodges as a manager assumed he would move up to the general managership, this year or next, and continue to be the dominant brain on baseball matters. And many who also thought that Walker would be his successor in the dugout.

But Grant and Mrs. Payson and Scheffing had immediately chosen Berra —the same man they had passed over when Stengel had to be replaced nearly seven years before.

A great deal had happened since then, however, to put Yogi in a different light. In a way, he was made manager of the Mets for exactly the opposite seasons that he had been made manager of the Yankees. The Yankees had thought, in 1964, that they would be getting someone to combat Stengel in attention-getting. The Mets recognized that Yogi's appeal lay in his self-effacing quality. People liked him—fans liked him—because he was down-to-earth simple and obviously sincere, not because of the quips he might or might not make. And what the Mets wanted, in the unexpected necessity of replacing Hodges, was a "comfortable" feeling above all else.

When he took over the Yankees, he was dealing with teammates of great personal reputation, arrogant in their winning habits, resentful (or contemptuous) of the difference between Yogi and Houk, their glamorous ideal as a manager.

Taking over the Mets, Yogi was moving into command of much younger men, whose only contact with him had been as a lieutenant of the strong-willed Hodges. He knew them all, they knew him, but not as former buddies (or non-buddies). He was both familiar and unabrasive.

In his seven years as a Met, Yogi had displayed some qualities best appreciated by insiders. For even-keel loyalty he could not be surpassed and, for so famous a figure, he was remarkably self-effacing. His baseball judgment, of course, was respected.

In all those years, he had never once publicly, and very rarely privately, expressed any bitterness about his Yankee dismissal. He had never gloated about their misfortunes. And he had never given the slightest hint that his status as a one-time pennant-winning manager elevated him above the coaching chores he had settled into.

Furthermore, Yogi had absorbed, very visibly, the Hodges system. It was remarkable in itself that this man, himself so famous, could blend so smoothly into a group that came from a totally different baseball background. After all, Hodges had brought Walker, Piggy, and Yost with him from Washington: they were already a close-knit management team. Yogi, the only holdover from previous regimes (and a product of the Stengelism that neither Hodges nor the others had ever found particularly congenial), could have stuck out like a sore thumb. Instead, gradually, he had become one of the comfortable fingers of a well-fitting glove. He pitched batting practice, coached at first base, gave batting advice when sought but didn't offer any hard sell, signed autographs, minded his own business, rooted hard for everyone, and contributed his rather sharp baseball judgments in private to the managing group. By 1972, he had grown into the intimacy of that group to a considerable degree.

Every player could see that as an individual Yogi would be quite a different manager from Hodges; but each could not miss the fact that a continuity in overall methods and evaluations was being maintained.

To higher management, Yogi seemed attractive in another way. He represented all of New York's best baseball traditions, combining past Yankee success and recent Met success in his persona. He had proved how cooperative and loyal a person he could be, and his public relations value was recognized much more accurately than it had been by the Yankees.

In general, Yogi's image had been enhanced by the decline of the Yankees. The Yankee attitude had been, until then, that "we're so good anybody can manage us to a pennant." The rap against Yogi had been that he wasn't "bright" or "communicative." But Yogi had managed them to a pennant—and no one else had since, not even the re-installed Houk; so how dumb could Yogi be? He had been dealt with shabbily by the Yankees—and had never complained subsequently. Wasn't it time he got another chance?

So Yogi's greatest asset—an ability to soothe, rather than an ability to inspire uphill charges—was very much what the Mets needed at the moment.

And here, mercifully, the strike helped the transition. It lasted another week, and all baseball attention was on the fight between the players and owners. There were no daily games to hash over, no decisions to be made that would glaringly contrast with the fresh memory of "what Gil would have done." Only a week, but a long week, long enough to let both Yogi and his players get their thoughts in order.

Positive thoughts.

Staub, without question, changed things. He could be exactly what Clendenon had been in 1969, only more so—younger, more versatile, left-handed. At Houston he had been a premature star-in-the-making at first, compared to Kranepool or Swoboda in the Met situation of the mid-1960s; but by 1967 he was a .333 hitter, and in his three years at Montreal had hit 78 home runs. With him, a Met offense was credible.

Nor would the men given up be missed immediately. An outfield of Staub (in right), Jones, and Agee shouldn't need too much backing up, and certainly didn't need platooning at bat. With Hahn available to spell Agee defensively, and Dave Marshall to pinch hit and play occasionally, and with John Milner a hot prospect (.290 with 19 homers at Tidewater in 1971), that department was the strongest in the history of the club.

With Harrelson at peak respect as a shortstop, Fregosi taking over at third, and Boswell and Garrett available for second, the infield was pretty good. Foli would have been a utility man, but there was another good young one in Teddy Martinez. Kranepool (who hit .318 in spring training on the heels of his strong 1971 performance) was reliable enough at first base. And Grote seemed better than ever behind the plate.

That certainly was a solid enough club to put on the field behind all that pitching—none of which had to be disturbed to add Staub.

The Mets saw no reason at all why they shouldn't win the whole thing.

Two days after Yogi became manager, the outstanding issue of the strike, the pension dispute, was settled. Now a wearing argument began about how the missed games would be made up. It dragged on for several days before it was conclusively decided to simply forget the unplayed games.

Which meant, for the Mets, four games with Pittsburgh and two with St. Louis would never be played.

An advantage? A disadvantage? The fact that such a point was debated indicated how truly the Mets considered themselves a pennant contender.

Within a month, everyone did.

When play finally began, at Shea Stadium on Saturday, April 15, Seaver shut out the Pirates, 4–0. The Mets lost to Steve Blass, 2–0, the next day, and to Renko, 7–2, in Montreal. But they won the next seven in a row, sweeping three from the Cubs at home, three in San Diego from the Padres, and starting a visit to Los Angeles with a 6–1 victory behind Matlack. They lost the next two, started May with a three-game sweep in San Francisco, and later in the month ran off an 11-game winning streak.

On May 21, they were 25–7, leading the division by six games. Seaver was already 7–1, Matlack 5–0. Staub was everything the Mets hoped, hitting over .300, hitting eight homers the first month. The team looked great.

And a spectacular development had taken place.

The Mets got Willie Mays.

THE Willie Mays. The one who owned New York's heart when the Giants were still in town, and whose periodic reappearances with San Francisco were the reason that the Giants were the biggest draw the Mets had. The one whom people had called "the greatest ball player." The one who (every story reminded us) used to play stickball with the kids in Harlem streets. Willie Mays himself.

This Willie Mays, of course, had just turned 41, on May 6. It had been seven years since he had hit .300 in a season. He had sore knees, couldn't throw any more, and had other natural middle-age ailments. In recent years with the Giants, he had needed more and more time off.

He had made a comeback of sorts in 1971, stealing 23 bases and helping the Giants win a Western Division title. But his average had slipped to .271 (lowest of his career) and his homer production had dropped to 18.

Yet, he was Willie Mays, and it was unthinkable that the Giants would ever let him go. In the early years of the Mets, Mrs. Payson had offered Stoneham $1 million, cold cash, for Willie's contract, and it hadn't even been considered. But Stoneham and his Giants had economic problems: since the Athletics had moved into Oakland to share the territory, attendance had dropped by half. In other respects, Stoneham wasn't as financially secure as he had been after the club first moved West.

Stoneham was, furthermore, the most sentimental of club owners, authentically so, placing loyalty above all things. He had always promised Willie, "Don't worry about the future," as some high salaries slipped through Willie's hands (as they had through Mantle's and so many other suddenly rich young men's). Now it was time to set Willie up (he was getting about $150,000 a year), and Horace didn't see how he could do it.

Mrs. Payson did. The Mets had all the money anyone could possibly use— and she had bought the Mets in the first place partly out of desire to see

Willie play in New York again, even as a visitor. She and Grant and Stoneham, with Willie's consent, were able to work out a deal. With the Mets, Mays would not only collect his high salary as long as he could play, but would be given a 10-year contract that would spread out considerable earnings when he stopped playing. And from a strictly business standpoint, his presence in Shea Stadium would quickly pay for itself as the New York fans resumed their love affair with him.

So on May 11, in one of the big stories of any year, Mays came to the Mets. Stoneham received some money he badly needed, and Charlie Williams, the right-handed pitcher.

To most of the fans, this was a glorious homecoming—and pennant insurance.

The Mets in uniform weren't quite so sure, but this was no time to talk about it.

That Willie was a mixed blessing was obvious to experienced baseball men. As the deified elder statesman, he would have to be deferred to: he would play when he felt he should, where he felt he should. This would undermine the authority of any manager (it had in San Francisco), affect some other players, raise issues of favoritism. Most of all, though, in the merciless judgment of men on the field, the burden of age was visible: by up-to-the-minute standards, Willie could not run, throw and hit as well as many quite ordinary young men. His bat could not get around on the fast ball. His legs could not reach every catchable drive.

This was the classic case of the aging star: it had happened with Mantle, and Musial, and several others—living legends who could still play well enough to excite the public, well enough to tell themselves they're not finished, but not well enough to avoid being a problem to the team as a whole.

What made this case peculiar, however, was that Willie wasn't an aging star the Mets had already lived with: he was being brought in at that stage. One could foresee the problem: if he didn't play much, the fans (and the Met front office) would demand that he did; if he played a lot, he might hurt a club that had a pennant in its grasp; and if the club lost some games when he didn't play, the manager would be second-guessed for that. The other possibility—that he might play frequently and well, and help the club win— just wasn't in the cards if one looked at Mays with cold realism instead of glowing nostalgia.

But who in the world wants to deprive himself of glowing nostalgia?

Certainly not Met fans, of all people.

Nor was it wise to underestimate the ability of Willie Mays to rise to a dramatic occasion.

His first game as a Met was on May 14, a Sunday—at Shea, against the Giants. In the fifth inning, with the score 4–4, he hit a home run that turned out to be the winning run in a 5–4 victory.

How could anyone knock that?

That game was No. 3 of the 11-game winning streak. Things were rolling. Milner played left field sometimes, with Jones switching to first, and Milner was great. Martinez filled in at second, and Martinez was great. Koosman had trouble with his shoulder, and had to be taken out of the rotation to work his way back through the bull pen, but McAndrew was doing surprisingly well, so why worry?

The issue of Yogi's brilliance or non-brilliance as a manager was dead. He had the horses. He obviously knew how to handle them. It was already June. Get ready for the World Series.

On June 1, a 4–1 victory by McAndrew over Philadelphia made the Met record 30–11, a .732 pace. With the season more than one-fourth over, the Mets had a five-game lead.

The club was solid, right?

No, not solid. Flesh and blood. And bone. And joints. And muscles.

All vulnerable.

On June 3, at Shea, Staub was hit on the right hand by a pitch thrown by George Stone, a left-hander from Atlanta.

He kept playing, but stopped hitting. Two weeks later, taking a swing in Cincinnati, he dropped the bat in pain. It took extensive examination to reveal that he had fractured a small bone in his hand, near the wrist, and although he tried from time to time, his season was over right there.

On June 9, in Chicago, Fregosi injured his shoulder. He hadn't been doing particularly well, but he was capable of taking up the slack, if sound. He wasn't. Later he hurt his leg. His whole season became a total loss.

On June 16, Jones, playing first base in Cincinnati, damaged his elbow when he collided with Joe Morgan. The after-effects dragged on for weeks.

And so it went, with no let-up. Agee injured his ribs. Harrelson's back went bad. Gentry had shoulder trouble. Grote turned up with bone chips in his elbow (which finally required surgery in September).

It was an epidemic.

Milner and Martinez, now forced to carry the lead on a daily basis, suddenly looked much less brilliant. Mays, with his legs, could help only sporadically. The pitching remained essentially sound, but the supporting cast had disappeared, re-creating the situation of 1971.

In the game in which Staub got hurt (a Met victory), the Mets made their record 31–12. By June 30 it was 41–26 and they had no lead at all. By July

23, at the All-Star Game break, they were 49–38 and 5½ games behind. By September 1 they were 63–59 and in third place, 14 games out.

That's how they finished: in third place, 13½ out, with an 83-73 record thanks to four straight victories at the end, in Montreal.

It was all a miserable letdown, but who could be blamed? The injuries had been simply brutal, insurmountable. Staub (who got back briefly in September) wound up playing only 66 games, able to contribute only nine home runs, all before his injury. Jones, in and out of 106 games, hit .245. Agee, shunted aside for the convenience of Mays but forced to play at other times with his own ailments, fell to .227. Fregosi, the latest savior, was .232; Harrelson, .215; Boswell, .211; Grote, .210. What else was there to say?

Wait 'til next year, that's what.

Staub would be all right. Fregosi would come around. Grote should bounce back, and Harrelson seemed capable of recovering.

About Agee and Boswell the Mets weren't so sure.

Agee had been in and out of the Met doghouse for several seasons now. The rap was that he didn't play up to his "potential," and since this was the same as the rap against Jones, their close friendship was looked upon as some sort of aggravation. Such reasoning may be hard to follow if you haven't spent your life around professional sports, but it's prevalent there. Since Jones was the more talented of the two, the decision was made to dispose of Agee—especially since he was the one for whom Mays was the complication, and Mays intended to play in 1973.

So Agee was traded to Houston for a centerfielder named Rich Chiles and a pitcher named Buddy Harris. Nothing was seriously expected of either, and nothing materialized. It was strictly an unloading of Agee.

But the other trade was something else again.

Assuming that Fregosi could play, and that Milner, Jones, Kranepool, and sometimes Mays would take care of first, the main gap was at second base.

Boswell had never been considered a first-class fielder, and now that he had hitting problems (and some physical ones), there was a lack offensively as well as defensively. Assuming the now available power did come through, people had to get on base in front of it.

A high-class, experienced, thoroughly professional second baseman who can field and bat is not easy to find, but there was one who happened to be available. Felix Millan, 29 years old, was a three-time member of the All-Star team, a .281 lifetime hitter. He played for Atlanta, and one thing Atlanta needed was pitching. The Mets had pitching, especially since Matlack, with a 15-10 record, had turned out to be Rookie of the Year.

How about Gentry? Well, something more, said Atlanta. Two pitchers, said the Mets, but we have to have another pitcher in exchange. So that's how the deal wound up: Gentry and Frisella for Millan and Stone, the left-hander who had started Staub's difficulties.

Adding Millan (who was an excellent partner for Harrelson defensively, and who would bat second in the lineup) immediately strengthened the Mets, but few realized how much. Rarely has a trade paid off so well, since Stone also turned out to be an outstanding addition, winning as many games as Gentry and Frisella had together, and losing 15 fewer.

The most discussed issues in the spring of 1973 were: would Mays play or retire? Would Staub be 100 percent physically? Would Fregosi get straightened out? Would Yogi, immunized from criticism last year, first because of the nature of his ascension and then because of all the injuries, run things effectively?

Mays came late, tried, decided he could play. Staub seemed better some days, not others. Fregosi didn't look much improved. And Yogi? He was just Yogi, telling everyone the club would be fine if all the players could play, and if they got hurt, what could anybody do about it?

The Yankees had been sold again, to a Cleveland-based group led by George Steinbrenner. The plan to refurbish Yankee Stadium, now owned by the city, was going through, and arrangements were made to have the Yankees play in Shea Stadium in 1974 and 1975. There was a new indoor arena on Long Island, the Nassau Coliseum, housing the basketball Nets and hockey Islanders, while the Rangers and Knicks seriously pursued their championships again. There was another fuss with the players and owners, but this one stopped short of a strike. All in all, the Mets were pretty well lost in the pack in the sports news of the spring of 1973. The Yankees had made a run, unsuccessfully, for the 1972 pennant, while the Mets had been fading, so there were more people in town who considered the Yankees a 1973 contender.

And the underdog pendulum had finally swung, too. It was the Yankees for whom one heard sympathy, the "I hope they finally win something" syndrome, and it was the Mets who found themselves increasingly criticized for arrogant management, "stagnation," and the whole potful of accusations usually thrown at top dogs.

By July, all these tendencies had intensified.

The Yankees were leading the American League East. The Mets were under .500. The injuries were coming just as fast as in 1972—Staub (the other hand), Jones, Harrelson, Grote, Milner, Matlack (his skull fractured by a line drive, but able to pitch again within two weeks), and of course Mays. The team fell to last place.

During this period, the "what's wrong with the Mets?" type of story pro-
liferated. (Again, the price of progress and maturity was being paid. Can you
imagine anyone asking that about the pre-1969 Mets? There was no need to
ask; one *knew*.) In a city steeped in that tradition—what's wrong with the
Knicks, what's wrong with the Rangers, what's wrong with the Yankees,
Giants, Jets—this was predictable enough, and the usual answer was predictable, too: we need a new manager.

At this point, Grant made two remarks, one in private, one in public, and
the public one was unfortunate. To the players, he made a clubhouse oration
on the necessity of believing in themselves and not giving up—sound sentiments, and if some players snickered at his pomposity, there was certainly
nothing wrong with his intention.

The most charitable view to take of the public statement, however, is to
assume Grant didn't realize its implications, and that would be an uncharitable
view of his astuteness.

What about the manager, he was asked; would Yogi be replaced? The
chorus was loud, because some never thought he was the right man in the
first place, and because losing always generates demand for a scapegoat. The
Met players, like Yankee players a decade before, found the not very articulate Yogi a perfect excuse for whatever was going wrong (the "uncom-
municative" bit again). In particular, it was easy for any player who thought
a teammate wasn't doing right to blame Yogi for not being severe enough
with the offender. (One never came across a player who thought Yogi wasn't
being severe enough with *him*.) And those fans who took their second-guessing
seriously had a field day with Yogi, because his moves were invariably conservative and orthodox, and any variation seldom got a good explanation in
print.

So, they asked Grant, what about Yogi?

Grant's answer was one of the strangest votes of confidence on record.
The Mets had no intention of dropping Yogi—who couldn't be blamed for
injuries—"unless the public demands it."

This invitation to the wolves was taken up in an unexpected way. *The New
York Post* promptly started a poll: who should be fired—Yogi, Scheffing,
or Grant?

After three days of balloting, some 4,000 replies were received. The tally:
Scheffing, 1,448; Grant, 1,207; Yogi 611.

That only adds up to 3,266, you say? Well, this was still the world of
the Mets.

The Post, of course, was just having some good clean fun. But the point
was made that no upswell of "public demand" could be blamed for dropping

Yogi. The management would have to take responsibility for that on its own.

Still, it was generally assumed that Yogi would be through at the end of the year. On July 15 they were 10 games out of first. A week later, at the All-Star break, they were only 7½ out, but still last. They couldn't help noticing that strange things were happening in the division above them, but this was whistling in the dark. The Pirates, three-time champions, couldn't get untracked. The Cubs, who had started fast, had begun a sensational collapse in June. The Cardinals, who started so badly, were now hot.

The standings that Yogi looked at when play was resumed in St. Louis on July 26 said:

	W	L	Pct.	GB
St. Louis	51	45	.531	—
Chicago	51	46	.526	½
Pittsburgh	46	48	.489	4
Philadelphia	46	51	.474	5½
Montreal	44	51	.463	6½
New York	42	51	.452	7½

"We're not out of it," he said. "Look at that: only six down on the loss side. If we can get everybody back playing, we still got plenty of time."

Well, sure; what would you expect any manager to say?

Whereupon the Mets stepped out on the artificial turf of Busch Stadium and lost a double-header, 13–1 and 2–1.

But Seaver outpitched Rick Wise, 2–1, the next night and the Mets went home for a 10-day stand at Shea with some hope of making a run for it. Staub seemed to be improving, and Jones and Harrelson were playing again. Koosman had pitched well a couple of times and Matlack, despite a losing record, was winning new praise each time he worked. A hot home stand could make things interesting, since the others had been kind enough not to pull away.

It wasn't to be, however. They lost seven of the 13 games at home, and lost Harrelson again (with a cracked bone in his chest). Staub's hand hurt again; he couldn't swing naturally and had to be benched against left-handers.

On August 8, the Mets started their final California trip of the season, still last, 10 games below .500, still amazed that they weren't further behind. The Cardinals, winning for the last two months, were starting to falter, too, and neither Pittsburgh nor Chicago was really picking up the slack.

The trip began with a 1–0 two-hitter by Matlack in Los Angeles. The same night, the Cards and Cubs lost (but Pittsburgh won). The next night, Koosman lost a 1–0 decision (on an eighth-inning triple misplayed by Hahn in center), while St. Louis lost, too. The next night, in San Francisco, Seaver won, 6–1, backed up by a three-run homer by Garrett. The Cubs, Pirates, and Cards all lost.

"Nine games under .500," mused one of the writers in a rather happy Met clubhouse. "You know, maybe this year nine under is a helluva pace."

That was truer than he knew—but it turned out to be too stiff a pace for the Mets to maintain.

They blew a 13-inning game the next day, with horrible things happening mechanically and tactically. (Martinez had hurt himself, and shortstop was being shared by Garrett and a young man named Brian Ostrosser, brought up from Tidewater as an emergency measure; Grote had to play third for a few innings.)

They lost the next game, and then the next two in San Diego, of all places, looking worse than ever. Behind Matlack, poor fielding in the ninth inning turned a 2–1 victory into a 3–2 defeat, and then Koosman got racked up, 9–0.

It was now August 15—the witching hour of four years ago—with one more game to be played in San Diego before returning home. Not even the four-game losing streak had cost them ground, because the teams above them kept losing also. But on this particular night, there wasn't anyone around the Mets who still clung to the idea that they could still be a contender—not because of the standings, but because of how badly they played.

Yogi, as always, wouldn't give in. He wouldn't blow his top at the ineffective (if not lackadaisical) play, although he did go around in private and have a talk with Jones, among some others.

"We're only 7½ out," he said. "There's lots of time yet. You can't give up, can you?"

But who would expect any manager to say anything else under the circumstances? In Yogi's case, he believed it; but even if he didn't, he'd have had to say it.

Nobody else believed it. Not that night.

That night, most Met thoughts were on next year. Who would be back? Who would be traded? Who would be the manager? What kind of future was there, altogether?

On the night of August 15, in San Diego, Seaver pitched in top Seaver form: two infield hits, one he deflected himself, stood between him and a no-hitter. A grand slam homer by Grote in the fourth inning made the 7–0 victory easy early.

And the scoreboard already showed that the Pirates had lost, 1–0; the Cubs had lost, 15–1; the Cardinals had lost, 3–0—and Philadelphia and Montreal had lost, too.

This was ridiculous, but it couldn't go on much longer. The Mets were going home now to play Cincinnati and the three California teams, and after that the last month of the season would have all the Eastern teams playing one another. Then they couldn't all keep losing.

Dreams are fine, miracles do happen—didn't the Mets know that better than anyone?—but there's a limit. Flying eastward through the night of August 15–16, twelve games below .500 with 44 to play, the Mets felt no contact whatever with destiny.

Which only shows how much *they* knew.

20 Triumph

TUG McGRAW was the quintessential Met. Kranepool had been with the team longer, but had never become as prominent. Nor did Kranepool have the same pixieish quality in his personality. Even though he had passed up college to be the first Met bonus baby, Kranepool had a serious turn of mind. He studied to be a stockbroker, and then went into the restaurant business (with Swoboda as a partner). He didn't appreciate being the butt of all those jokes in the early days, felt that he had often been treated unfairly by press and public, and thought he hadn't been given as many opportunities to play regularly as he had earned. He didn't hold grudges, and he appreciated his responsibilities in a public relations sense, but he was not what one would call a warm personality.

Tug was, and more: he had just that strain of kookiness, the quick humor and roller-coaster emotions that fit perfectly with the Met image—both the original image and the later miraculous one. No one enjoyed good times any more thoroughly than Tug, and few people displayed honest feelings about bad times more openly. In the last few years, he had become a star, with appropriate pay (about $75,000), but he retained a boyishness that seemed as fresh as when he had first come around, nine years before.

Then there was Jones, who had played in a few Met games in 1963, but hadn't really become part of the club until 1966. He was a much more reserved person than either of the other two, moody by nature and often defensive through long periods of being criticized. Cleon's image simply wasn't vivid.

Those three were the only players around who had played under every Met manager: Stengel, Westrum, Hodges, and Yogi. Not even the coaches were as steeped in Met tradition. Walker and Yost had come to the Mets for the first time with Hodges in 1968. Piggy had played one year for Stengel, but had been away until he returned with Hodges. Roy McMillan, who had joined the coaching staff this year, had played for Stengel and Westrum, but spent the Hodges years managing Met minor-league teams or serving as a coach with the Milwaukee Brewers. (But Yogi himself, of course, qualified as having been part of all four regimes.)

So, everything considered, McGraw came closest to incorporating the whole Met story in one human symbol: he had been youthful, hopeful, hapless but eager; then professional and successful and super-successful; and then still capable of having troubles on a spectacular scale.

Because it was Tug's trouble, on a spectacular scale, that had the Mets where they were on August 16, 1973.

For all the injuries, and all the other factors, one circumstance was enough to keep the Mets in last place through the summer: Tug McGraw was having a granddaddy of a slump.

"I got the best relief pitcher in baseball," Yogi had beamed when the season began, and McGraw's record made the claim plausible. He had posted a 1.70 earned-run average for two straight years, during which he had won 19 games and saved 37. He was 28 years old and free of arm trouble. He had a great screwball, a fine fast ball, a fine curve, and good control, and that special ice-blooded insouciance that makes relief pitchers thrive on pressure.

But all of a sudden, a couple of weeks into the 1973 season, McGraw forgot how to pitch.

Gradually, all his skill came apart, experience or not. It reached a point where he could say: "I've been standing on mounds since I was seven years old, but all of a sudden it was if I had never pitched a game of ball. I just didn't know what I was doing."

And all through June and July, as the Mets kept losing, Yogi would call on Tug in the usual game-saving situation—and Tug would come in and blow the game.

There was no physical reason for it. Others were hurt; he wasn't. And there was no conceivable way to avoid using him. But there it was: no rhythm, no real control, nothing.

By August 16, however, there had been some encouraging signs. Two starting assignments had been tried to help him out, and the second one (in July) seemed to. Some long sessions with Piggy and Walker helped. And then, just as suddenly as it had disappeared, it came back. In mid-July, McGraw stepped out there one day and saved a game. (Ironically, at just about the same time, Sparky Lyle, the left-handed relief pitcher on whom the Yankees counted, started to go sour, and the Yankees began to sink.)

By August 16, as the Mets arrived back in New York, the Yankee bubble had burst, and they had all but dropped out of their race, so the coast was clear for taking another look at what the Mets might do.

And by August 16—with the season three-quarters over—Tug McGraw had an 0–5 won-lost record with a 5.11 earned-run average.

The fact was, however, that McGraw had been pitching well for a couple of weeks, and the rest of the staff had settled into remarkable efficiency. Poor defense and lack of hitting were still costing every other game, but the general level of the pitching staff was turning out to be the best in the league.

It remained only to get the rest of the team functioning, and there were encouraging signs here, too. Fregosi had been dropped in late July, waived on by everyone, and traded to the Texas Rangers for a player to be named later (and he still hadn't been named when the season ended). Garrett was going to be the third baseman, as soon as Harrelson came back and let him escape short. (This was really looking ahead to 1974, and why shouldn't a last-place team look ahead?) Milner had been stationed at first base, permanently (also a look-ahead move). Grote was starting to hit, Staub was feeling a little better, Millan was worth his weight in gold.

Now, if the team could win some games, it should certainly get out of the cellar and finish at least fourth, perhaps third. That would be a good springboard for next season, and provide some confidence to carry over the long winter.

As for the dreamers, they couldn't be entirely turned off: there remained the amazing fact that first place was only 7½ games away, and that the leader—St. Louis—was only three games above .500.

Many fans hadn't realized it yet, but the two-division system altered some of the traditional mathematical principles of pennant races. When the whole league had a single standing, it was enough to lose one more than half your games to be eliminated; no team could finish first without being at least one game above .500.

This was no longer true. It was theoretically possible for all the Eastern teams, for instance, to lose all their games to all the Western teams; that would leave each with an 0–72 record in those games. Then, if all 90 intra-division games were essentially split, one team could win 46 of them and finish first—with a 46–116 record. While this extreme arithmetical example was ridiculous, the situation it described was not. The Eastern teams *had* lost more games than they had won against Western teams, and it was quite possible to win the Eastern division title without reaching .500 for all 162 games.

Now' wouldn't that be the ultimate Met feat? To finish first while losing more than half your games?

Those who had spent 11 years becoming sensitive to weird portents began to suspect that destiny did have something in store.

Even along such lines, though, it was all the more important that the Mets get hot on the home stand starting now, because this was the last chance to make hay while the others were playing Western teams. Once August 30 was reached, half the Eastern Division games would have to be won by Eastern teams the rest of the way.

That made the first game even more of a letdown than it would have been otherwise. Stone took a two-hitter and a 1–0 lead into the ninth inning against Cincinnati, which was fighting to overtake the Dodgers in the Western race.

Better still, that one Met run had been supplied by a home run by Mays, his sixth of the year, No. 660 of his career (and, as it turned out, the last he would ever hit).

But with two out, three straight singles tied the score. In the 10th, Hal King hit a pinch homer off Harry Parker, and the Reds won 2–1.

But the Cardinals lost that night, too, at home, to San Diego.

On Saturday, Milner hit a grand slam and got three other hits, Matlack pitched powerfully, and the Mets romped, 12–1.

On Sunday, Harrelson returned to action. He doubled and scored one run, then doubled to drive in a run in the eighth, breaking a 1–1 tie, and Koosman had a 2–1 victory.

But Monday night there was another great deflation: after 15 innings, it was still 3–3—and the Reds scored five in the 16th, winning 8–3.

It had been a treadmill weekend, but at least the team had played well against the hottest team in the league. Maybe things would be better next year.

On Tuesday, Sadecki pitched a four-hitter against the Dodgers, and Milner won it, 2–1, with a ninth-inning single after the Mets had pulled even in the eighth.

On Wednesday, there was an even better ninth-inning victory: trailing 3–2, the Mets got a pinch single from Jones, then consecutive singles by Millan, Staub, and Milner to win the game.

Winning pitcher: McGraw—his first victory of the season, in his 42nd appearance, on August 22.

Could they really be starting something?

Err—not quite.

Three of the next four games were lost—all one-run decisions. The Dodgers beat them, 5–4. Koosman beat Juan Marichal, 1–0 in 10 innings, but Tom Bradley of the Giants beat them, 1–0, the next day—on a first-inning run knocked in after a fan had prevented Grote from catching a foul at the box fronts. And the Giants took the rubber game of the series, 5–4, for Ron Bryant's 20th victory, despite a two-run Met ninth that narrowed the margin.

So August 27 dawned with the Mets still 12 under .500, taking precious little solace from the fact that the Cardinals and Pirates had also lost last night.

There were only 33 games to play. Time was running out.

And right then—just as it had four years before—a sweep of the Padres ignited enthusiasm. Staub's grand slam and McGraw's 14th save of the season (for Stone) produced a 6–5 decision. Tug saved an 8–6 game the next day, and Koosman, with a little help from Buzz Capra, closed out the home stand with a 3–0 shutout.

The same day, the Cards, Pirates, and Cubs lost.

Now the Mets headed into the final, intramural phase of the schedule, with St. Louis the first stop, only 5½ games behind—and, for the first time in weeks, no longer last. These were the standings:

	W	L	GB
St. Louis	67	65	—
Pittsburgh	63	65	2
Chicago	64	67	2½
Montreal	62	69	4½
New York	61	70	5½
Philadelphia	61	71	6

"It's beginning to feel like 1969," said Koosman.

"If we keep getting this kind of pitching—" said Grote.

"I been tellin' you, in this division anything can happen," said Yogi. "We're the only team that hasn't had a hot streak yet. Maybe we're gonna have one now."

"We may be the first team ever to be last in August and win the pennant," said McGraw. "You gotta bee-lieve."

A few weeks before, McGraw had met two nuns, who had used the "you gotta believe" phrase. He had picked it up, and it had become a clubhouse motto. There was a slight element of mocking Grant's inspirational speech in its use, at first; but as time went on, it became the true rallying cry, with emphasis on the first syllable: you gotta bee-lieve.

Poised, at last, for a serious effort, after all those abortive starts and sand-bagging disappointments, the Mets took the field in St. Louis on August 30 brimming with determination and hope. On top of everything else, they had Seaver going for them, and Seaver was absolutely in the top form of his career.

Sure enough, Seaver pitched nine scoreless innings.

And it wasn't enough to win.

The Cards won, 1–0, in the 10th.

The third extra-inning loss in two weeks.

The fifth loss by a one-run margin in that time (and the other loss had been the 16-inning game).

Some pennant drive.

Oh, yes: back in last place, too, because the Phillies beat Montreal that night.

In the immortal word of Charley Brown: rats!

Still, the glory of baseball is that every today is followed by tomorrow, at least until the end of September. The Mets won the next two games, 6–4 in 10 innings and 4–1, before losing the final game of the series, 7–4, and it was back to Shea Stadium for Labor Day. Thanks to Montreal's three victories over Philadelphia, the Mets were out of last place for good, as of August 31.

The Labor Day double-header was split. Koosman blanked the Phillies, 5–0, but the second game had to be entrusted to a rookie starter, Craig Swan, and the Mets lost 6–3. The Pirates split with the Cardinals, so the Mets lost no ground.

They were 5½ out now, with 23 to play, and it was time for a decision.

"From now on," Yogi announced, "starters go on a four-day rotation. Seaver, Matlack, Koosman, and Stone will start all the remaining games except the one Sadecki has to work Wednesday. We got a shot now and we've got to take it."

Seaver won, 7–1, with a five-hitter. Sadecki, with McGraw's help, beat the Phillies 4–0. The Mets were now 66–73, in fourth place, ahead of the Cubs.

The Cardinals had just turned around and beaten Pittsburgh three in a row, after the Pirates had climbed to within a game, and that provoked an explosion in Pittsburgh: Bill Virdon was fired as manager, an unheard-of change at that stage of a pennant race, and Danny Murtaugh was brought back for his fourth tour of duty in that post.

Which made the Pirates most likely to survive the staggering non-race that had developed. They were, after all, the champions, and the later it got, the more even a brief assertion of power would mean.

Meanwhile, the Mets were up in Montreal, where pennant fever, with a French accent, was being experienced for the first time. The Expos were riding a six-game winning streak and were in second place, only two games behind the Cardinals.

Things were tightening up.

The Montreal series began with a double-header. Garrett led off with a homer, Matlack made it stand up (while the Mets left 13 other runners on base), and McGraw got the last out in a 1–0 victory. The second game went 15 innings, with McGraw pitching most of the last six and Sadecki getting the final out, and the Mets won 4–2. The scoreboard showed that the Cards had lost to Chicago and Pittsburgh had beaten Philadelphia.

Seaver was beaten the next day, 3–1, as Singleton and Ron Fairly tagged him for homers, but Stone and McGraw produced a 3–0 shutout in the final game.

A day off made an easy trip to Philadelphia, and no one could deny that the Mets were right in the thick of it now.

The Mets? Wasn't everybody?

September 10, quite unnoticed, was the fourth anniversary of the day the Mets had first taken the division lead in 1969. On the morning of September 11, 1973, the standings were:

	W	L	GB
St. Louis	72	71	—
Pittsburgh	70	70	½
Montreal	69	73	2½
New York	69	74	3
Chicago	68	74	3½

The Pirates were clearly the team to beat, since the Cardinals had been fading so consistently—and the Mets had five straight games with them coming up starting next week, two in Pittsburgh followed by three in New York. It was important not to stumble before then.

On September 11 in Philadelphia, Koosman stumbled. Having pitched 31 consecutive scoreless innings (tying a club record held by Seaver), he got blasted even though two homers by Staub gave him a 4–0 lead in the third inning. He gave up four homers and was beaten, 6–4.

But Pittsburgh lost to Chicago, and the Cards lost, to Montreal. Incredible.

Now Matlack, backed up by McGraw, won 3–2, as Milner and Garrett hit homers. The Pirates won and took over first place as the Cards lost again. Now Seaver pitched 11 strong innings and the Mets finally won in the 12th, 4–2, with McGraw locking it up. Back at Shea, after a Friday night rainout, McGraw saved a 5–1 decision for Stone before the Mets dropped the second game, 7–0. He saved a 4–3 victory for Koosman on Sunday. The Pirates, having won seven of their first nine games under Murtaugh, lost to the Cardinals on Sunday.

So the confrontation came up right on schedule. Going into Pittsburgh for the Monday night game, the Mets found:

	W	L	GB
Pittsburgh	74	72	—
Montreal	74	73	½
St. Louis	73	75	2
New York	73	76	2½
Chicago	70	78	5

The task was clear: the Mets absolutely had to win three of the five Pirate games. That would leave them 1½ behind with eight to play, and breathing. If they lost three of the five, they would be 3½ out and dead, since Montreal and St. Louis would probably still be above them.

That made the opener the key game. They had Seaver going, and Seaver had been extraordinarily successful against the Pirates, in past years and this year. They needed the split in the two games at Pittsburgh, so that they could hope for two out of three at home—where they'd have Seaver again in the fifth game.

From the Pittsburgh point of view, beating Seaver in the first game meant a clear path for the remainder of the pennant run.

And Seaver got slaughtered. He was knocked out in three innings. The Pirates won, 10–3.

Nice try, Mets.

Miracles don't happen a second time, but at least the Mets had projected themselves into a wild scramble, and the humiliations of June and July had been somewhat erased. In view of all that had happened, a second-place finish was worth going after, because now that the Pirates had straightened themselves out, it was only a matter of cream coming to the surface, anyhow.

That's how it looked during the day on September 18, and even more so late in the evening when the ninth inning came up with Pittsburgh leading, 4–1. Three more outs and the Mets would be 4½ games behind.

But there was a rally. Ron Hodges (Ron who?) singled in the tying run as a pinch-hitter. Don Hahn singled home two more. The Mets were ahead, 6–4.

(Ron Hodges was a catcher, a rugged young man out of the farm system, drafted only in 1972, brought up in mid-season when various injuries had decimated all the replacements for Grote while Grote was out with a broken wrist. He had caught quite a few games impressively and hit well enough—he batted lefty—but had been pretty much forgotten since Grote got back into action.)

Now they had to get three outs to win the game. McGraw had already been used, but Yogi's choice to protect the two-run lead was an eye-popper: Bob

Apodaca, one of the rookies brought up when the roster limit went to 40 men after September 1.

Apodaca faced two men and walked both. The second-guessers went absolutely crazy.

Buzz Capra, who also seldom inspired tidal waves of confidence among the second-guessers, came to the rescue—and he got out of it, although he did walk two more men and make the final score 6–5.

But that was as good as 106–5. It was a reprieve.

The scene shifts to Shea Stadium.

Wednesday night, September 19. The Pirates are still shaking their heads. The populace is excited. The Mets have that same high feeling they had once before, and are mulling over Koosman's words: "It's beginning to feel like 1969."

"You gotta bee-lieve," echoes McGraw, and when you can build a five-run ninth on Ron Hodges and Don Hahn, why not bee-lieve?

Stone is the pitcher. Jones hits a homer—his first in Shea Stadium since Opening Day, can you believe that?—and then another. McGraw does his fireman act out of the bull pen. The Mets win, 7–3. The Cards and Expos lose.

Thursday afternoon, September 20. Willie Mays announces his retirement. "I want to end speculation about next year," he says. He hasn't been playing because of cracked ribs. "These kids are going for a pennant now and the best thing I can do for them is to step aside," he says. "But if they get in the World Series, I'll be there to help." He says a lot of other eloquent things, about his "love affair" with baseball for 22 years. Grant says: "Both Mrs. Payson and I love Willie, and we feel we got quid pro quo—one thing in return for another. We feel our fans and the public of New York deserved Willie in his final days." His future duties are not defined, but he says he doesn't want to coach or manage. Whatever he does, he'll get at least $50,000 a year for the next 10 years from the Mets.

New York is bathed in honest sentiment. And more excited than ever.

Thursday night, September 20. Koosman the starter. Pirates lead, 2–1 in the eighth; Mets tie. Pirates go ahead, 3–2 in the ninth; Mets tie. It's 3–3 in the top of the 13th. Richie Zisk is on first base for Pittsburgh. Dave Augustine, one of the Pirate rookies, belts one of Sadecki's pitches deep and high left —apparently a two-run homer.

Jones, the left fielder, is racing back, but he won't be able to reach the ball. If it doesn't go over the wall, it will certainly hit it, and an extra-base hit will be enough to score Zisk, running from first.

The ball hits the wall, all right—right on the top of the fence. It bounces up. If it falls beyond the fence, it's a home run. If it falls back within the field of play, it's in play.

It does neither.

It comes right back into the glove of the astonished Jones.

He wastes no time, instinctively whirls and throws. Garrett is in the right relay position. He fires it on to the plate. Hodges tags Zisk. Out.

You gotta bee-lieve—especially the unbee-lievable.

No one has ever seen a bounce quite like it. New Yorkers, bred on stoop-ball, recognize a "pointer," when a rubber ball comes off the point of a step. But in a major league game, such a bounce is as clear a sign of divine will as professional ball players ever want to see.

The Mets score in their half—of course—and win, 4–3.

And portent readers are convinced; the Mets are going to take the whole thing.

Mets with memories remember the four-man outfield that robbed McCovey of a possible homer at a vital time in the 1969 miracle.

It was Cleon who had caught that one, too.

But that was just being in the right place, with some intention. This bounce was more metaphysical.

The result had been earned, however: without the quick throw and perfect relay, it wouldn't have mattered. "Luck is the residue of design," that famous Branch Rickey observation again. Still—ball players are no less superstitious than most other people, and the odd carom made an indelible impression on the Mets—and on the Pirates.

Not that it determined what followed; but it certainly averted something different that might have followed.

The 13-inning game, televised (like most Met games) in New York, ignited 1969-intensity interest at last. It put the Mets in second place, half a game behind the Pirates, with Seaver coming up. One more Met victory would put them on the top—from last to first in 22 days.

Some 53,000 turned out Friday night to see if that would happen—the first time all year the Mets had drawn 50,000 or more (they used to do it 10 times a year in 1969 and 1970). And it wasn't just the size of the crowd: it was the same electric atmosphere, the perpetual-noise hysteria, that had been absent since the end of the 1970 season. Now it *really* felt like 1969 again.

And it proved glorious. The Mets scored four runs in the first inning. Milner, Garrett, and Staub hit homers. Seaver pitched a five-hitter. They won 10–2.

They were on top.

After everything, in spite of everything, along with everything, they were in first place.

And healthy.

And in command of their own fate. To be beaten now, they would have to be overtaken.

And the standings showed:

	W	L	GB
New York	77	77	—
Pittsburgh	75	76	½
St. Louis	76	78	1
Montreal	75	78	1½
Chicago	74	79	2½

With just nine days to go in a six-month baseball season, the Mets had taken over the lead by reaching .500—and everyone else under it. The jokes had become an actuality.

The Reds, having overtaken the Dodgers, were wrapping up the Western Division title with a victory total in the 90s. The pro football season had started. The Knicks and Rangers were deep into training camp, and there was all sorts of fussing about Wilt Chamberlain switching leagues, Congress lifting the home blackout of football telecasts, the move of the San Diego Padres to Washington (or maybe not), and so on.

But there was no question what the No. 1 sports story in America was: the Mets. Again.

Their Saturday afternoon game against St. Louis, from Shea, was the national television game. Matlack was overwhelming. Garrett hit a two-run homer in the third. The Cards got only four hits. New York won, 2–0. Since the Pirates were rained out in Montreal, the Met lead soared to a full game— and they were over .500.

On Sunday, Stone pitched the first two innings, Parker the next four, McGraw the last three and the Cards were beaten again, 5–2—before a crowd of 51,926. Now they were two games over .500, so high they might get dizzy, but because the Pirates won both ends of the double-header in Montreal, the lead was back down to half a game.

With one week left.

Only now did people begin to recognize what could happen in that week.

A five-way tie for first was entirely possible.

All sorts of alternatives had to be considered.

For one thing, the Pirates had an unplayed game. The Padres had been rained out in Pittsburgh on their last visit there, and such games are not made up unless they have a bearing on determining first place.

Now the league office had to reschedule it, just in case. The season would end on Sunday, September 30. The Padres would play in Pittsburgh on Monday, if necessary.

Then there was the question of resolving ties. If two teams tied, one play-off game would suffice. If three, one would get a bye while the other two played, and the winnner would play the one that got the bye. If four, it was simple: two games, with the winners meeting in another game.

And if five? As fantastic as it seemed, it was still quite possible. That would require a more complicated system.

Chub Feeney, President of the National League, fervently hoped it wouldn't come up. For a league president to say, as ritual, that he expected the race to end up with everybody tied for first was acceptable rhetoric; the reality, even involving five teams, was too horrible to contemplate.

The final week began.

The Mets, Cards, and Cubs were off on Monday, but the Pirates had a double-header to play at Montreal.

This had special meaning for the Mets. As things stood, if the Pirates won all their remaining games, the Mets would be beaten, even if they won all theirs, because the Pirates had one less defeat. It was unlikely, but possible— and who, at this stage, would shrug aside anything at all as unlikely?

So when the Pirates lost the first game, the Mets heaved a sigh of relief, and weren't too upset that Pittsburgh won the second game. The margin was still only half a game, but now it was even-up on the losing side and all the Mets had to worry about were their own games—including a playoff, of course, if one developed.

Tuesday was Willie Mays Night.

It had been planned some time back. When Willie had announced his retirement, it added steam to the occasion. The turnout was 53,603—the third time in five days the Mets had packed in more than 50,000. It was old times, all right.

The ceremonies were elaborate, and moving. He couldn't hold back his tears. And his keynote was: "I see those kids over there"—pointing to the Mets in the dugout—"and I see how hard they're fighting for a pennant, and to me it says one thing: Willie, say goodbye to America."

He said goodbye, and the kids fought: Koosman, with McGraw's help, turned back the Expos, 2–1.

And the Pirates lost, and the Cardinals lost. The Mets had gained a full game on the three closest pursuers. Breathing space.

And none too soon. Seaver got knocked out in the first inning by Montreal the next day, and the Mets went on to lose, 8–5. The Pirates and Cards won.

So it was back to half a game, with four to play.

The four remaining games were in Chicago—Friday, Saturday, two on Sunday. At Wrigley Field there was old-fashioned grass and there were no lights. Weather and darkness would be a factor.

Yet the Mets were in a strangely relaxed mood. In a sense, the act of reaching the top, from where they had been in August, had already established their self-respect. They wanted to win a pennant as much as anyone, but there was something less than desperation in their feeling. Perhaps the main motivation was to avoid the nagging regrets that would follow them all winter if they didn't make it now. But there was neither the unreal exhilaration that marked 1969, nor the painful tension that marked the late stages of 1970.

As for portent readers, they had no doubts.

On Thursday, the Pirates lost a 13-inning game to the Phillies. Now the Mets didn't even have to worry about finishing in a tie. All they had to do was beat Chicago four times and it was theirs.

Not on Friday, though. It rained. The ground was soaked. There would be two games Saturday and two games Sunday, with early starts.

Friday night, the Pirates lost again, 3–2 to Montreal. The Cards shut out the Phillies, 3–0.

The season had 48 hours to go, and five teams were still in it.

On Saturday it was still raining. The teams came to the park, waited; the umpires agonized. But you just couldn't do it. Two games tomorrow—and two on Monday, if needed.

Pittsburgh—would you believe it?—lost again to Montreal on Saturday. The Cardinals whipped Philadelphia, 7–1, and took second place.

All five still alive. The morning of Sunday, September 30—the last scheduled day—the standings read:

	W	L	GB	To play
New York	80	78	—	4
St. Louis	80	81	1½	1
Montreal	80	81	1½	1
Pittsburgh	79	81	2	2
Chicago	76	82	4	4

All the talk was of "ifs."

If the Cubs could win all four from the Mets, they'd be tied, 80–82. If Pittsburgh beat Montreal, and then lost to San Diego, the Pirates and Expos would also be 80–82. And so would the Cardinals if they lost their last game to Philadelphia.

Crazy. Just plain crazy.

The rain-soaked weekend also gave the Mets, and their growing band of historians, plenty of time to analyze what had been happening. Scheffing had said it all, two months before, in a conversation with Lee MacPhail of the Yankees, when the Yankees were riding high: "If McGraw was pitching for us the way Lyle is for you, we'd be first; and if Lyle was as mixed up as McGraw has been, you'd be last."

Neither had expected, then, that Lyle would suddenly lose his stuff, and that the Yankees would drop out of the race during August. But Scheffing had seen no reason why McGraw shouldn't get straightened out.

McGraw did, with a vengeance. It was just five weeks since he had scored his first victory, thanks to that two-run ninth against the Dodgers. In that time, he had earned five victories and 11 saves—a hand in 16 of the 23 games the Mets had won. At one point, 10 straight appearances had been victories or saves. He had regained, just in the nick of time, the skills the Mets counted on so heavily.

Then there was Harrelson. He had to be seen every day to be appreciated. He was both brilliant and steady in the field, and his defensive value was something of which the good Met pitching could make maximum use. And offensively he did his share, no matter how little he looked.

And Jones: making sensational catches and hitting in the clutch. And Staub, hitting over .300 since mid-August. And Garrett, a September terror at bat and suddenly a major home-run producer. And Grote, catching magnificently and hitting .280 since mid-August.

When it was all over, statistics would show that these four, who batted in 138 runs in the first three-quarters of the season, knocked in 76 in the last quarter—more than doubling their pace. But it was not all over yet. The games with Chicago would have to be played, even if it took until mid-winter.

It was still rainy on Sunday morning, but playable. One Met victory would eliminate the Cubs and whoever lost the Pittsburgh-Montreal game, but not the other two contenders. Two Met victories would clinch first place and make Monday's games unnecessary.

Matlack and Koosman would pitch, against Rick Reuschel and Ferguson Jenkins.

The opener was 0–0 until the eighth. Then a two-out single by Ron Santo produced a Chicago run. It ended 1–0. The race was still on.

In Pittsburgh, the Pirates were slaughtering Montreal, 10–2.

But the possibility of a five-way tie evaporated as soon as the Cardinals finished beating Philadelphia, 3–1. They had finished their schedule 81–81, and Montreal and Chicago were now eliminated.

Meanwhile, the Mets were off to a good start in the second game. Two errors helped them to a three-run first inning, and Koosman didn't let anything happen to the lead. They won 9–2.

They had clinched a tie—but you can lose a tie, eventually.

What did Yogi think now?

"I'll take my chances," he grinned. "I like where we're at."

Then he was told that Houk had just resigned as manager of the Yankees. He was sincerely surprised. But if he had any impulse to gloat at this confession of Yankee failure at the threshold of Met triumph, he gave no indication of it whatever.

Besides, he had his own problems to think about. The four-day rotation had taken its toll. Seaver wasn't quite the 100 percent Seaver. He had already pitched 284 innings, and almost 2,000 innings in his seven-year career. His arm was tired, and his shoulder ached. It was unthinkable to face a deciding game with anybody but Seaver on the mound, if he was available; but how available was he? There were two games scheduled for Monday. Winning either one would do the trick. If Seaver couldn't do it in the first game, everything would hinge on Stone in the second. Wouldn't it take some pressure off Stone to let him pitch the first, knowing that Seaver was there for the second if necessary?

Maybe—but Yogi didn't think in such fancy terms. He had Seaver. That was enough. Seaver it would be.

"If you gotta get beat," he said, uttering one of the oldest maxims of sport, "get beat with your best."

Monday was also a rainy but playable day. All of 1,913 people paid their way into Wrigley Field that morning for a game that meant nothing to anyone in Chicago except the Mets.

Seaver wasn't overpowering, but he kept the Cubs scoreless for four innings, aided by a couple of double plays, and great outfield catches. The Met hitters pecked away. They got Seaver a run in the second. He protected it. They added two more in the fourth and another pair in the fifth, for a 5–0 lead. Seaver began weakening, and yielded two of them. It went to 6–2 in the seventh—and Rick Monday's two-run homer cut it to 6–4 with nobody out in the Cub seventh.

Nine outs still needed. Any questions about what to do?

Right.

Call Tug McGraw.

The cocky left-hander, as confident now as ever in his life, marched in and did it. He did give up one hit in those last three innings, but that was all. Seaver's 19th victory was McGraw's 25th save—and the clincher.

Joyous Mets raced up the stairs to the antiquated visitors' clubhouse under Wrigley Field's first-base stands. They couldn't really celebrate properly, because another game had to be played, even though it didn't count.

Within five minutes, however, the umpires sent word that the field was too wet, and that there would be no second game. Rarely have umpires made a wiser decision.

So the celebration picked up steam: champagne and buckets of ice spilled all over the place. Mays, a non-drinker, gulped some bubbly and promptly got sick. Grote amused himself by dumping ice buckets on newspapermen he disliked, particularly Young and Lang. Kranepool beamed. McGraw and Seaver hollered. Jones, low-key as ever, talked more than usual.

Harrelson summed it up:

"Nothing can ever be like 1969 was. You can't repeat a first time. But in a lot of ways this is better. We're mature now. Then we didn't quite know what was happening to us, it was all a sort of haze. Now we knew we had a good club, and we knew what it took to win, and why we weren't winning. To keep fighting back through all those disappointments and injuries—that's what we're proud of. To win when you're expected to win, as we were when the year started—that's the greatest satisfaction of all. We showed everyone, finally, what we knew we were: a good, grown-up ball club."

Seaver?

"1969? My God, we were so young then, we didn't understand. This is nothing like that. This is professionalism. We knew what we had to do and went out and did it. This is a much better club."

McGraw?

"Yuh gotta bee-lieve. . . . Yuh gotta bee-lieve. . . . Yuh gotta bee-lieve!"

Yogi?

"I tol' ya, ya never could tell. I'm proud of all of them. Like I said, you can never give up."

And so on.

But, for all the joy and release, the Mets hadn't really won anything yet. Finishing first had certainly justified the last two years, restored respect, clarified the future—but the National League championship, and entry to the World Series, still had to be decided, hand to hand, with a Cincinnati team that had beaten the Mets eight times in 12 tries during the season.

"Yeah," grinned Yogi, "but we weren't always healthy then. When we had all our fellas, we did all right with them."

They had all their fellas now.

COMING ATTRACTIONS

21 *Questions*

LUCK—or at least unforeseen logical chains—always did play a part in deciding championships, any championships. In October, 1973, the Mets were lucky that the baseball schedule had been changed.

Ever since the last expansion of 1969, the final day of the regular season had been in mid-week, Wednesday or Thursday, with the championship playoff starting on Saturday (for television purposes, naturally). But in 1973 the closing day had been moved back to Sunday, leaving five fat days off before the playoffs. As it happened, the bizzare Eastern Division race had forced it to go to Monday, but there was still a four-day gap.

It was needed.

Seaver's shoulder soreness couldn't be hidden any longer. It was an open topic—the chief topic—of conversation even while the clubhouse celebration was going on. The Reds, having clinched their division title a week before, were rested and ready no matter when the playoff began. But there was a real question about when Seaver could pitch.

"We'll have to see," said Yogi, that Monday.

With the old pattern, of course, the Mets would have been stuck no matter what. If the season had gone the same way, but with a Wednesday-Thursday ending and a Saturday playoff start, Stone would have had to open against the Reds. This way, even if Seaver couldn't, Koosman and Matlack, who had pitched Sunday, would be ready, and whoever pitched the first game would be expected to pitch the fifth, if there was one.

On Wednesday, the Mets worked out at Shea Stadium. Seaver did some throwing, hard. Walker and Yogi were convinced he was all right. He would start.

The first two games, Saturday and Sunday, were to be played in Cincinnati —at four P.M. local time, to accommodate the TV network, which would carry the American League playoff at an earlier hour and, on Sunday, a football game. Four o'clock is a bad time to start any baseball game, because you quickly get into twilight, when visibility is poor; the artificial lights don't help much because it isn't dark enough, the bright sunlight is gone, and there are unfamiliar shadows by five or six o'clock.

Well, the Mets clearly had the pitching, and the Reds clearly had the hitting. Conditions worked against hitting. Would that mean a net loss to the Mets, whose weaker hitters needed every edge, or a net loss to the Reds, who were facing tough pitchers under tougher conditions?

It probably helped the Mets.

Seaver started against Jack Billingham, also a 19-game winner. The Mets filled the bases with one out in the first inning, but Jones hit into a double play. In the second, Harrelson walked with two out, and Seaver lined a double to left center, scoring him. That's why they called him Tom Terrific.

Now it was up to Tom Terrific to make that 1–0 lead stand up. The Mets never did get another hit, off Billingham or two relief pitchers who worked the ninth; and Seaver struck out 12 men in the first seven innings.

But with one out in the eighth, Pete Rose tied it up with a home run.

And with one out in the ninth, Johnny Bench won it with a home run, 2–1.

Once again the Mets had opened a crucial series by losing.

And once again, it didn't stop them. On Sunday, Matlack proved untouchable. He got his 1–0 lead in the fourth, when Staub smashed a home run, and he never did weaken. In the ninth, the Mets broke loose for four more runs, making the last inning tension-free for Matlack as he closed out the 5–0 victory. He had allowed just two singles, both by Andy Kosco.

That reduced the competition to a two-of-three series with all the games in New York. Yogi was able to say again: "I like where we're at."

There had been crowds of 53,000 and 54,000 in Cincinnati, and the people had been partisan, but they were just people. The 53,000 in Shea Stadium Monday were Metomaniacs of the first water. They started screaming before the game began, and from fever pitch started to work their way up towards a 32nd-degree frenzy. By the third inning, Koosman had a 6–2 lead, aided by two homers by Staub, and by the fifth it was 9–2.

At that point, Rose, trying to break up a double play, spilled Harrelson, and a moment later they were scuffling, with Rose on top. Both dugouts emptied and the usual baseball fight consumed the next five minutes or so. No serious damage was done, and neither ball player was thrown out of the game.

But while it may have been an ordinary enough baseball fight on the field, it wasn't accepted that way in the stands.

Some of the fans—obviously not all—were enraged at this attack upon the smallest and perhaps most important of the Mets, in a game already one-sided, with ultimate victory only another day away.

When Rose went to his position in left field for the bottom of the fifth, he he was bombarded with garbage, bottles, and anything else the fans could find to throw.

He didn't have to stand there and take that—and Sparky Anderson, the Cincinnati manager, pulled his whole team off the field.

Still the mad bombers in the stands wouldn't quit. There was a real danger of forfeit.

Twenty-nine years before, in the 1934 World Series, Joe Medwick had been subjected to the same sort of barrage in Detroit, and finally Commissioner Kenesaw Mountain Landis had told him to get out of the game. Medwick's Cardinal's were leading, 11–0, in the seventh game at the time.

Now Chub Feeney, the league president who represented the ultimate authority in a championship playoff, tried another tack. He asked Yogi and Willie, two of the most popular baseball figures New York has ever known, to walk out there and appeal to the fans for order.

Staub, Seaver, and Jones decided to go with them.

Now, how about that for a vignette in the Met album? The manager and four players pleading with their fans to be allowed to complete a victory the team was winning on the field.

In Stengel's day, the score probably would have been 9–2 the other way and Stengel would have asked them to keep throwing things.

The peace delegation accomplished its mission (which is more than many peace delegations can say), and the game ended uneventfully, a 9–2 eight-hitter for Koosman.

The rowdyism in the stands soured somewhat what followed. On Tuesday, Stone—who hadn't lost a game since July—made a magnificent effort in the most important game he had ever pitched. His 1–0 lead was provided in the third inning by Millan's single. But Tony Perez tagged him for a tying homer in the seventh, and McGraw came in. In the 11th, it was still 1–1, and McGraw had to come out for a pinch-hitter, who did no more than the rest of the Mets.

And in the 12th, Rose hit one over the fence off Harry Parker. The Reds had a 2–1 victory, Rose had his revenge, the fans in left field had gnashed teeth, and the National League had a one-game series coming up to decide its championship.

It was Seaver against Billingham again, this time in better light.

And Yogi didn't have all his fellas again.

In the 11th inning on Tuesday, Staub had crashed into the right-field fence while making a game-saving catch (temporarily game-saving, that is). Now his right shoulder was too sore to swing a bat.

Yogi's solution was to switch Cleon to right field and put Kranepool in left, where he had played only a few times in the course of his 11 years with the Mets.

Who knocked in two runs with a first-inning single?

Ed Kranepool.

Seaver, however, clearly didn't have the kind of stuff he'd had in Cincinnati. Once again, he was working on the fifth day, and it showed. Great pitchers are great because they can win anyhow, when their stuff isn't at its best, and that's the quality Seaver was showing now. It was much like the last game in Chicago.

Still the Reds nicked him for a run in the third and tied it, 2–2, in the fifth.

The season was down to half a game. Something had to break soon.

Something did—New York's way.

Garrett opened the Met fifth with a double. Millan bunted. Billingham, pouncing on the ball, threw to third in time to get Garrett.

But Dan Driessen, the rookie third baseman, drew a mental blank. He acted as if it were a force play, tagging the base but not bothering to tag Garrett.

Of course, it wasn't a force play. It was an historic boo-boo. The Mets had men on first and third with nobody out.

Jones doubled, for a 3–2 lead. Milner walked. Kranepool was up again and left-handed Don Gullett, who had come in to face Milner, was on the mound.

Yogi sent up a right-handed pinch-hitter.

Willie Mays.

Some 50,000 spectators, rowdies included, blew their minds.

Anderson countered with Clay Carroll, a right-hander.

Willie swung hard and chopped a high bouncer to the left side. Carroll couldn't do anything until the ball came down. When it did, he threw it home, not nearly in time. Willie was across first with a single—his last National League hit.

And the Mets led 4–2.

An infield out made it 5–2. A single by Harrelson, 6–2.

Tom Seaver, with a four-run lead, 12 outs to get for the pennant, and Tug McGraw in the bullpen.

How's that for liking where you're at?

Sure thing?

Yep.

Cleon knocked in another run in the sixth, making it 7–2. Seaver kept getting people out. By the ninth inning, the hysterical portion of the crowd was out of control. It had poured down the aisles, and with one out in the ninth, out onto the field. Once more, certain victory had to be delayed while order was restored, and the delay seemed to bother even Seaver. He couldn't get another out.

In came McGraw, and got the last two.

And the frenzy exploded.

Unlike the wild scenes of 1969, this one had an undercurrent of vicious-ness and random destructiveness. The Reds thought Rose might be attacked, and formed a protective cordon. Some players' wives, along with uncounted innocents, were all but trampled in the stands and seriously frightened.

Disgraceful, both sides agreed.

"Those people don't care anything about baseball, or that we won," said Seaver bluntly. "It's just an excuse to them to go tear something up."

"I never thought I'd see anything like this in America," said Anderson, as bitter at the tarnishing of the scene as at his own defeat. "But then, who says New York is America?"

So times had changed in this way, too. The occasion of the Miracle of 1969 had put a glow of comradeship on a beleaguered metropolis. At a moment when Watergate and a new Mideast war and the impending resignation of the Vice-President of the United States were what really concerned the country, the Miracle of 1973 was only an occasion for more bad publicity about the jungle New York had become.

Nevertheless, on the limited scale of the baseball world, miracle it was. The Mets had won their division by winning one more than half their sched-uled games. They had won the league championship by winning one more than they lost, three of five. They didn't doubt they could win the World Series the same way, four of seven. All you had to do to be successful, it seemed, was to win the last game.

And never, but never, give up.

*   *   *   *   *

Can a World Series be an anti-climax? Yes, it often had been in baseball history, and in a real sense it was exactly that for the Mets in 1973.

They lost it, in seven games, to the Oakland Athletics; but it would have been an anti-climax even if they had won.

Their story really ended with the 1973 pennant; it was the true completion of the cycle.

Born deprived, loved for their futility, the Mets had become, in 1969, the first expansion team ever to win anything. The symbolic significance of 1969 could never be matched, and it was important—in retrospect—that the symbolism be carried to a perfect conclusion then. Anything less than the World Championship would have diluted the miracle.

But in a longer time-frame, 1969 was only the beginning. The hope, the intention, the prayer of all those who rooted for expansion teams was not merely to be struck by lightning once, and forgotten; it was to have their team be built into a true year-in, year-out contender, capable of generating belief season after season that this year we might win.

Through 1970, and 1971, the victories of 1969 remained fresh, and served as a reminder of the possible. By the middle of 1973, there were doubts. If another pennant could not be won this year, would it ever be won? Was the team of 1969, many of whose players were still the backbone of this one, just a freak? Had the roster really been built to contending status? In mid-August, it seemed that the program, not merely this season, was a failure.

The comeback, and the winning of the league championship, settled that, once and for all. Any team that can be in pennant contention five years in a row, and win in two of those years, has attained true competitive respectability. It is not an "expansion" team any longer in any sense. It is a contestant among equals.

Within baseball, although not outside it, the measure of everything is the full season. Players and managers know, better than anyone, how much luck decides any short series. A World Series is an honor, an excitement, a spotlight, an achievement—but not a true test of baseball worth. The full season is. That's why, on the private scales of baseball people, finishing first in your division is the truest accomplishment: it takes six months to do it. The pennant playoff, to them, is an unwelcome innovation, but it's there and can't be shrugged off—and, when all is said and done, it is a face-to-face test for the championship with a team in your own league, a circumstance that might have arisen naturally in the schedule of a non-division league on the final weekend of the season.

And the Mets had won that. In the showdown, under pressure, they pitched better, hit more, made better fielding plays and committed fewer blunders than their opposition.

They had established, not a dynasty, but a solid sovereign state on the baseball globe. The Mets, as an organization and continuing competitive enterprise, had proved they belong. As always, hindsight was the key: anyone could shrug off 1969 as a Happening; anyone could point to the following three seasons as self-deception and lingering decline; but the 1973 performance pulled the three preceding years back up into a truer perspective. The injuries had been proved a valid handicap, not an alibi. The choice of Yogi as manager had proved viable (in fact, it was the very even-temperedness for which he was criticized that enabled the team to come through its dark hours without pulling itself apart). The decisions of Scheffing and Grant had been proved more often right than wrong.

A franchise had been built—and the uniqueness that had been lost after 1969, that had been dribbling away ever since, was now finally laid to rest.

There *was* nothing more exceptional about the Mets, and there could never be. The second victory was the last step in becoming—in the most welcome sense—"just another ball club." As time went on, sometimes they would win, sometimes they would lose, players and managers—and even owners—would come and go, but the building phase of their history was complete.

Their tradition, and identity, was established forever. If 1969 marked the end of childhood, 1973 marked the end of adolescence.

The Mets were fully grown.

And nothing about the World Series, win or lose, could alter that in the perspective of history.

Besides, the As were owned by a man named Charles O. Finley, whose capacity for upstaging anybody was unlimited.

The 1973 World Series was essentially an Oakland story, with the Mets definitely the party of the second part. Even if the seventh game had come out a different way, it would have been remembered as an Oakland defeat rather than a Met victory, except among the most dedicated Metophiles.

Yogi (who would soon be signed for two more years) was now at the pinnacle of a rather successful life. He was already a member of the Baseball Hall of Fame as a player (inducted in 1972), and he now shared with only one other man the distinction of being a pennant-winning manager in each league. That other man, Joe McCarthy, had been the symbol of Yankee invincibility in the 1930s and early 1940s, the man Yogi expected to play for when he signed his first Yankee contract. That Yogi's methods and personality were not in line with what the bright young geniuses expected of a field general, suddenly seemed unimportant when stacked up against his irrefutable record. He must have done something right.

Stengel, attending the Series at the age of 83, put his finger on it as sharply as ever, one night in the Shea Stadium press room, spewing forth Stengelisms as easily as he had 20 years before.

"Lemme ask ya," he rasped, slowly turning the glass in his hand and managing to look like an outraged gnome and benign statesman all at once, "how many big games was he in? He played more World Series games than anybody, right? And all those pennant races? Well, lemme ask ya: if you been in that many big games, you ought to know what to do even if you're a dummy, and he's not."

Experience counts.

And that, finally, was what the Mets collectively had achieved, something the franchise would never again be without, however young its new individual employees might be: experience.

The Mets were now The Establishment.

* * * * *

The Series played itself out rather quickly, not really able to capture the full attention of Americans living through a painful year on much more important levels—scandal, inflation, a new war, gas shortages. Television ratings set records, but the unmeasurable item called "involvement" did not. Even in baseball, extraneous issues (the not yet completed San Diego move, and the fusses Finley would make) intervened.

The first two games were in Oakland, in fine weather.

Seaver could pitch. Staub couldn't play. Oakland's pitcher, Ken Holtzman, was left-handed—and New York's starting centerfielder was Willie Mays.

But it wouldn't be Seaver's turn to pitch until the teams got back to New York, since the fifth playoff game had been on Wednesday. Matlack and Koosman would work the Oakland games.

Matlack lost, 2–1, in an embarrassing way: he was tagged for a double by Holtzman, his rival pitcher, with two out in the third inning—and two runs followed. It would be bad enough to give up a hit to a pitcher in any case; but the American League had used a new Designated Hitter rule all year, so that the pitchers had never come to bat, supposedly to their great disadvantage in the World Series. Instead, Holtzman doubled sharply past third, and scored when Millan let a grounder by Bert Campaneris go right through him. Campy stole, Joe Rudi singled, and it was 2–0. It was enough, because Rollie Fingers and Darold Knowles took over when Holtzman tired.

By now, no one agonized at a Met loss in the opening game of a big series. They *always* did that, didn't they?

And, sure enough, they evened the score the next day. In one of the sloppiest, and absolutely the longest, World Series games ever played, the Mets won 10–7 in 12 innings. It took four hours and 13 minutes, and was finally nailed down by Stone after McGraw had worked through six harrowing innings. Mays, entering the game in the top of the ninth as a pinch-runner for Staub (who forced himself to play), took over in center with the Mets leading 6–4. He lost a drive in the sun, igniting a two-run rally that tied the score and forced extra innings—but he singled to drive in the tie-breaking run and launch what proved to be a four-run 12th for the Mets. Then he lost another drive in the sun in the bottom half, but no disaster followed. It was probably the most humiliating experience of his baseball life—and yet, he had delivered the key hit, with two out. That's why Willie Mays was Willie Mays.

After Willie's hit, there had been two errors by Mike Andrews, the last reserve player the As had, and after the game Finley persuaded Andrews to sign a statement saying he was injured, hoping to have another player activated. The furor that followed monopolized conversation for the next three days, led to the Commissioner's reinstating Andrews and fining Finley $7,000, and distracted everyone.

While the Oakland players were stewing about the Andrews case—on the side of the player—Manager Dick Williams called a clubhouse meeting before Game No. 3, in New York. This was Tuesday, Monday having been set aside for travel.

In deference to television ratings, the weekday World Series games were being played at night, and it was about six P.M. when Williams got his players· together. He told them he was resigning as soon as the Series was over, no matter how it came out, and promised to deny that if they told anybody.

The secret was faithfully kept for at least 47 seconds, the length of time it takes to walk briskly from the clubhouse door, under the stands, through the dugout, to a field full of reporters.

This was supposed to inspire the As to greater effort, and perhaps it did, but they won only the first of the three New York games. Seaver, rested again, struck out nine men in the first five innings, nursing a two-run lead he had been given by Garrett's lead-off homer, a single by Millan, a wild pitch, and a single by Staub. But, as had happened so often for Seaver, the Mets never scored again off Catfish Hunter, Knowles, Paul Lindblad, and Fingers, while Seaver couldn't quite hold off the later innings. Doubles by Sal Bando and Gene Tenace made a run in the sixth, and the Campy-Rudi axis—single, steal, single—tied it in the eighth. Sadecki and McGraw had to be used to get through the ninth and tenth and Harry Parker was pitching in the 11th when a walk, a passed ball, and a single by Campaneris produced the deciding run in a 3–2 game.

The next night, even colder than the first, was much brighter for the Mets.

Staub socked a three-run homer off Holtzman in the first inning, and Matlack was in command. Three more runs in the fourth made it 6–1, and Sadecki pitched the ninth after Matlack had allowed just three hits in eight innings.

It was all even again, and the competition reduced to a three-game set.

On Thursday night, Koosman and McGraw combined on a three-hit shutout, and the 2–0 decision moved the Mets to within one game of the championship. Everyone could see now what the Mets meant about their pitching, and that sort of pitching didn't require exceptional support. Off Vida Blue, Jones doubled and Milner singled for a run in the second. With two out in the sixth, Grote singled and Hahn—yes, Hahn—blasted a triple to deep left center. Two runs isn't a lot, but it can be plenty when you have McGraw: he came into the game in the seventh, with men on second and third and one out, and got out of it by making Deron Johnson pop up and striking out Campaneris.

By the time the teams took the field again on Saturday afternoon in Oakland, it was October 20 and everyone was pretty tired, emotionally as well as physically. Too much had been happening, for too long. To the As, the issue of winning a second straight World Series had special meaning in their private war with Finley. The Mets seemed more fatalistic. They needed one more game, but somehow the world wouldn't end if they didn't get it.

And, of course, they didn't.

It was Seaver and Hunter again, and Seaver didn't have his super velocity. Reggie Jackson tagged him for a run-scoring double in the first inning, and did the same in the third. Nobody else hurt him, but he was still losing, 2–0, when it was his turn to bat in the eighth, with one out.

Boswell pinch hit and singled (as Yogi's pinch-hitters did with remarkable frequency). Garrett singled. Millan singled through the right side. It was 2–1 with the tying run on third.

But Knowles, the left-hander who had relieved Hunter after Boswell's hit, fanned Staub, and Fingers took care of the next four outs. A run off McGraw in the eighth made it easier. The final score was 3–1.

And this, on October 21, was finally to be the last game, no matter what. The pro football season was in its sixth week. The world's troubles seemed greater than ever, and the dismissal of Archibald Cox, special Watergate prosecutor, by President Nixon had penetrated even the World Series scene.

One or the other would win this one, and the loser would be neither shamed nor in despair. The winners would collect $25,000 a man, a record; the losers would get $15,000. (The Reds, who had been in the Series last year, had to settle for $7,000 a man; the Pirates, who seemed so well set up in mid-September, got $295 each for finishing third in their division.)

It was, after all, only a ball game.

The dominant player now was Jackson, but the unappreciated one was Campaneris. Matlack and Holtzman were facing each other for the third time.

It broke apart in the third inning.

Again, Holtzman doubled off Matlack, this time with a line drive into the left field corner with one out.

Campaneris followed with a home run.

Rudi singled. Bando popped up. And Jackson hit another home run.

Oakland, 4; New York, o.

It ended 5–2.

In the ninth inning, trailing by four, the Mets got a run in and had two men on. They brought the tying run to bat, then expired.

There had been a time when a powerful statistic had been built on how many times the Mets got the tying run to bat in the ninth inning of a losing game. It seemed a million years ago when such things were considered amusing. But it wasn't a million: only 10. Ten years. That's how long it took for the Mets to pass from American folklore into mainstream baseball. Reasonable men may reasonably differ on the true value of that transition. But no rational mind could deny that it had taken place.

The Mets were mainstream now, and perhaps this was the best measure of it: they had been able to play in a World Series without every detail becoming automatically, immortally, memorable; and they had been able to lose without creating a tragic myth.

They had won—acceptance.

And the ultimate achievement of storming the gates of heaven had turned out to be—to be taken for granted.

* * * * *

In Elysium, Will Shakespeare turned to George Bernard Shaw and said: "Well, they did it again, or almost. Isn't it great to be a Met?"

"Met who?" said Shaw.

(NEW YORK DAILY NEWS PHOTO)

Before they played their first
home game, the Mets had a
City Hall reception on April 12,
1962. Stengel was already
proving that you don't have
to win to have a ticker-tape
parade.

(UNITED PRESS INTERNATIONAL)

The Original Mets, on the
City Hall steps with Mayor
Wagner, Weiss, and Stengel.

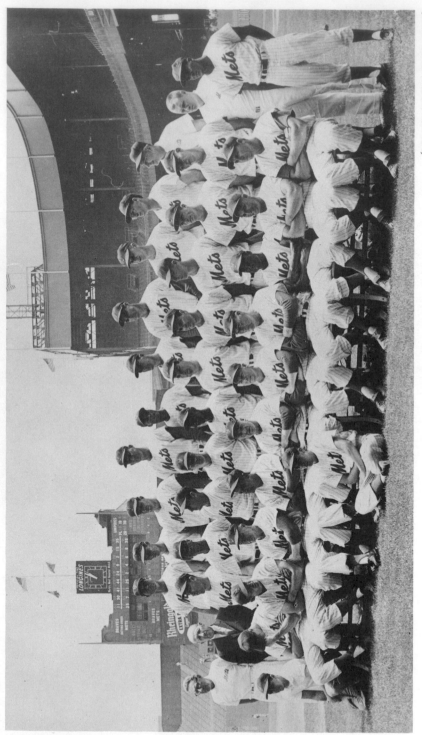

1962 Mets. Front row, left to right: Frank Prudenti (assistant equipment manager), Rod Kanehl, Frank Thomas, Red Kress (coach), Cookie Lavagetto (coach), Casey Stengel (manager), Solly Hemus (coach), Red Ruffing (coach), Joe Christopher, Gene Woodling, Gil Hodges. Seated on ground in front, Harvey Kamnitzer, (bat boy). Second row: Gus Mauch (trainer), Lou Niss (traveling secretary), Cliff Cook, Felix Mantilla, Chris Cannizzaro, Richie Ashburn, Al Jackson, Craig Anderson, Ray Daviault, Jim Hickman, Bob Moorhead, Bob Miller, Lynn Lischer (assistant trainer), Elio Chacon. Third row: Marv Throneberry, Sam Taylor, Bill Hunter, Roger Craig, Charlie Neal, Dave Hillman, Vinegar Bend Mizell, Jay Hook, Ken MacKenzie, Herb Norman (equipment manager).

(NEW YORK DAILY NEWS PHOTO)

(NEW YORK DAILY NEWS PHOTO)

Chacon, ss.

Mantilla, 3b.

(NEW YORK DAILY NEWS PHOTO)

1963 Mets. Front row, left to right on ground: Jimmy O'Connell, Harvey Kamnitzer (bat boys). First row: Al Jackson, Choo-Choo Coleman, Frank Thomas, Charlie Neal, Cookie Lavagetto (coach), Casey Stengel (manager), Solly Hemus (coach), Ernie White (coach), Duke Snider, Jim Piersall, Bob Taylor. Second row: Gus Mauch (trainer), Fred Cordetti (equipment manager), Al Moran, Jay Hook, Ed Kranepool, Jim Hickman, Roger Craig, Tracy Stallard, Larry Bearnarth, Tim Harkness, Lynn Lischer (assistant trainer), Lou Niss (traveling secretary). Third row: Galen Cisco, Chico Fernandez, Carl Willey, Ken MacKenzie, Rod Kanehl, Marty Kutyna, Don Rowe, Cliff Cook, Norm Sherry, Herb Norman.

Ed Kranepool and Mom,
the day he became a Met.

Seven and one-half years later, Kranepool's World Series Home run.

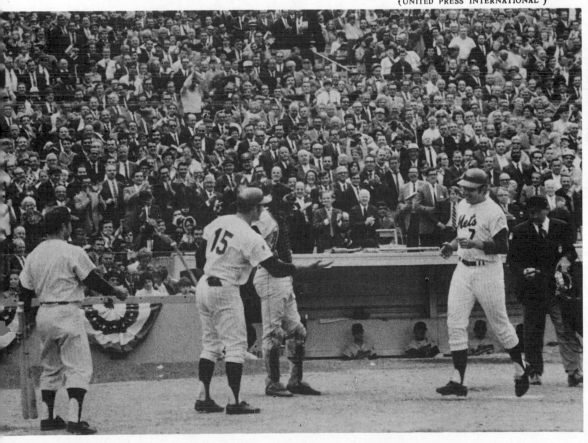

Shea
Stadium
under
construction.

Shea Stadium, opening day.

1964 Mets. Front row, left to right: Al Jackson, Charlie Smith, Wes Westrum (coach), Don Heffner (coach), Casey Stengel (manager), Mel Harder (coach), Sheriff Robinson (coach), Willard Hunter, Joe Christopher, Second row: Gus Mauch (trainer), Lou Niss (traveling secretary), Tracy Stallard, Jim Hickman, Gary Kroll, Ed Kranepool, Larry Bearnarth, Jack Fisher, George Altman, Rod Kanehl, Galen Cisco, Ron Hunt, Joe Deer (assistant trainer). Back row: Bobby Klaus, Dennis Ribant, Wayne Graham, Ron Locke, Roy McMillan, Jesse Gonder, Carl Willey, Chris Cannizzaro, Bob Taylor, Bill Wakefield, Herb Norman (equipment manager).

1965 Mets. Foreground: Dom Ardvino (bat boy). Seated: Chuck Hiller, Dan Napoleon, Chris Cannizzaro, Yogi Berra (coach), Don Heffner (coach), Casey Stengel (manager), Wes Westrum (coach), Warren Spahn (coach), Galen Cisco, Charlie Smith, Johnny Lewis. Second row: Gus Mauch (trainer), Al Jackson, Jack Fisher, Larry Bearnarth, Ed Kranepool, Dennis Musgreaves, Gary Kroll, Tom Parsons, Jim Hickman, Ron Hunt, Jesse Gonder, Joe Deer (assistant trainer), Lou Niss (traveling secretary). Back row: Ron Swoboda, Tug McGraw, Joe Christopher, John Stephenson, Larry Miller, Bobby Klaus, Roy McMillan, Billy Cowan, Frank Lary.

New
home,
same
act.

Bunning pitching
a perfect game.

Drysdale.

Marichal.

Stengel's farewell.

The retiring of No. 37
—Stengel, Weiss, and Westrum.

1966 Mets. Foreground, left to right: Sandy Reiss, Steve Barry, (bat boys). Seated: Al Luplow, Dick Selma, Bill Hepler, Harvey Haddix (coach), Yogi Berra (coach), Wes Westrum (manager), Sheriff Robinson (coach), Whitey Herzog (coach), Rob Gardner, Cleon Jones, Chuck Hiller. Second row: Gus Mauch (trainer), Lou Niss (traveling secretary), Bob Friend, Bill Murphy, Bob Taylor, Bob Shaw, Jerry Grote, Dick Rusteck, John Stephenson, Dennis Ribant, Jack Hamilton, Joe Deer (assistant trainer). Third row: Ron Hunt, Jim Hickman, Jerry Arrigo, Roy McMillan, Ed Kranepool, Larry Bearnearth, Ed Bressoud, Ken Boyer, Ron Swoboda, Jack Fisher, Johnny Lewis.

A new Met: Yogi Berra.

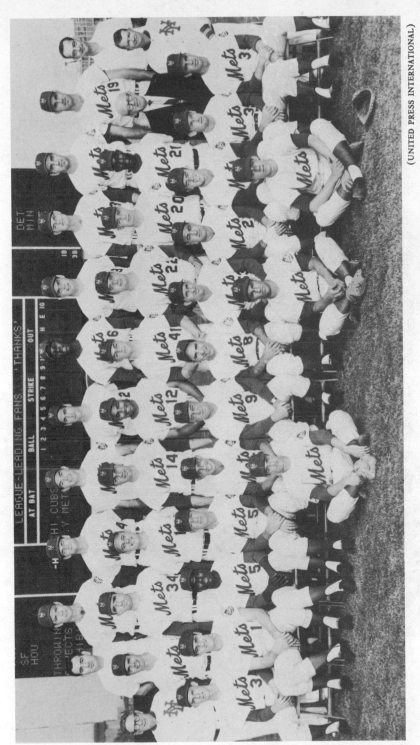

(UNITED PRESS INTERNATIONAL)

1967 Mets. Foreground: Joe Fitzgerald, George Forere, Bob Sanchez (bat boys). First row: Bud Harrelson, Jerry Buchek, Ed Charles, Salty Parker (coach), Harvey Haddix (coach), Wes Westrum (manager): Yogi Berra (coach), Sheriff Robinson (coach), Chuck Hiller, Jerry Grote, Dick Selma, Don Shaw, Second row: Gus Mauch (trainer), Bob Johnson, Jack Lamabe, Al Luplow, Ken Boyer, Tommy Davis, Tom Seaver, Jack Fisher, Johnny Sullivan, Cleon Jones, Lou Niss (traveling secretary), Joe Deer (assistant trainer). Third row: Nick Torman, Don Card-well, Bill Denehy, Ron Swoboda, Ron Taylor, Tommy Reynolds, Nick Willhite, Bob Hendley, Ed Kranepool, Bob Taylor, Jimmy Richards (clubhouse assistant).

Wes Westrum resigns.

(UNITED PRESS INTERNATIONAL)

1968 Mets. Front row, left to right: Gus Mauch (trainer), Joe Pignatano (coach), Eddie Yost (coach), Yogi Berra (coach), Rube Walker (coach), Wes Stock (minor league pitching coach), Joe Deer (assistant trainer). Second row: Bud Harrelson, Dick Kenworthy, Ed Charles, Jerry Buchek, Bob Heise, Gil Hodges (manager), Jerry Morales, Don Bosch, Bill Short, Dick Selma, Al Jackson. Third row: Al Weis, John Glass, Clyde Mashore, Don Shaw, Duffy Dyer, Tommie Agee, Cal Koonce, Tug McGraw, Phil Linz, Ken Boswell, Amos Otis, Danny Frisella. Fourth row: Nick Torman (equipment manager), Juan Rios, Ron Taylor, Joe Moock, Hal Reniff, Tom Seaver, Art Shamsky, Cleon Jones, Don Wilkinson, Greg Goossen, Lou Niss (traveling secretary), George Emirzas (clubhouse attendant). Back row: Bob Hendley, Steve Renko, Ed Kranepool, Les Rohr, Ron Swoboda, J. C. Martin, Kevin Collins, Ron Paul, Don Cardwell, Jerry Koosman, Al Schmelz, Nolan Ryan.

The clinching of first place.

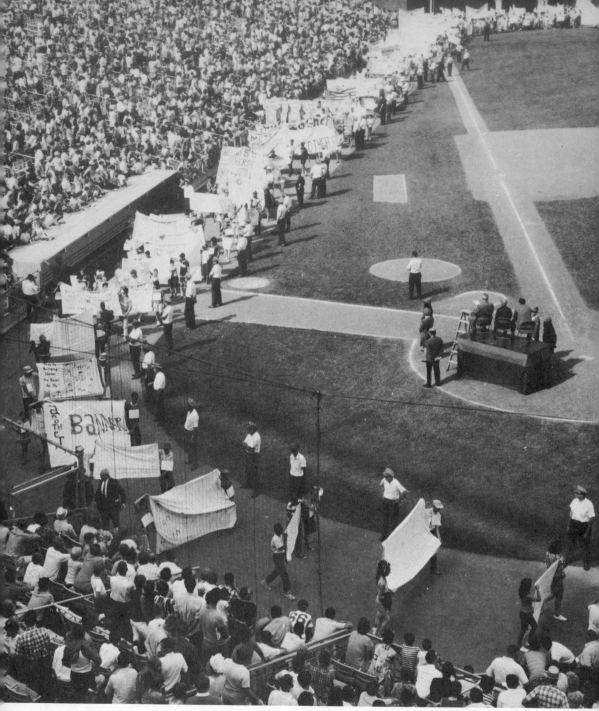

Banner Day at Shea.

Agee watches Jones climb the wall.

Bud Harrelson, brilliant shortshop.

World Series,
third game,
two on,
two out:
Agee robs
Baltimore's Hendricks
of a
two-run double.

(NEW YORK DAILY NEWS PHOTO)

City Hall, 7½ years after . . .

Victory parade.

1969 Mets. Front row, left to right: Gus Mauch (trainer), Joe Pignatano (coach), Rube Walker (coach), Yogi Berra (coach), Eddie Yost (coach), Joe Deer (assistant trainer). Second row: Tug McGraw, Gary Gentry, Al Weis, Cleon Jones, Gil Hodges (manager), Jerry Grote, Bud Harrelson, Ed Charles, Rod Gaspar, Duffy Dyer. Third row: Jim McAndrew, Tommie Agee, Cal Koonce, Ken Boswell, Tom Seaver, Jerry Koosman, Ron Swoboda, Wayne Garrett, Robert Pfiel, Lou Niss (traveling secretary). Top row: Nick Torman (equipment manager), J. C. Martin, Ron Taylor, Ed Kranepool, Don Cardwell, Donn Clendenon, Nolan Ryan, Art Shamsky, Jack DiLauro, Roy Neuer (clubhouse attendant).

371

1970 Mets. Front row, left to right: Tom McKenna (trainer), Bob Sacha (batboy), Yogi Berra (coach), Eddie Yost (coach), Rube Walker (coach), Bill Curtin (batboy), Joe Deer (trainer). Second row: Gary Gentry, Al Weis, Tug McGraw, Bud Harrelson, Gil Hodges (manager), Cleon Jones, Ray Sadecki, Duffy Dyer, Joe Foy, Jerry Grote. Third row: Tommie Agee, Jim McAndrew, Dave Marshall, Ken Boswell, Wayne Garrett, Mike Jorgensen, Danny Frisella, Ron Taylor, Rich Folkers, Lou Niss (traveling secretary). Top row: Nick Torman (equipment manager), Ken Singleton, Tom Seaver, Ron Swoboda, Jerry Koosman, Donn Clendenon, Art Shamsky, Nolan Ryan, Roy Neuer (clubhouse attendant).

Gil Hodges.

Art Shamsky.

(PHOTO BY L. KOMITO)

Gary Gentry.

Donn Clendenon.

1971 Mets. Front row, left to right: Tom McKenna (trainer), Bill Connors (coach), Joe Pignatano (coach), Rube Walker (coach), Yogi Berra (coach), Eddie Yost (coach), Joe Deer (trainer). Second row: Tug McGraw, Al Weis, Tom Seaver, Cleon Jones, Gil Hodges, Bud Harrelson, Jerry Grote, Ray Sadecki, Tommie Agee, Duffy Dyer. Third row: Lou Niss (traveling secretary), Danny Frisella, Mike Jorgensen, Tim Foli, Bob Aspromonte, Jim McAndrew, Jerry Koosman, Don Hahn, Gary Gentry, Ken Boswell. Top row: Nick Torman (equipment manager), Tommy Lagan (batboy), Donn Clendenon, Ron Taylor, Dave Marshall, Ed Kranepool, Ken Singleton, Art Shamsky, Charlie Williams, Nolan Ryan, George Palermo (batboy), Steve Torman (clubhouse attendant).

1972 Mets. Front row, left to right: Tom McKenna (trainer), Eddie Yost (coach), Sheriff Robinson (coach), Rube Walker (coach), Joe Pignatano (coach), Bill Connors (special instructor), Joe Deer (trainer). Second row: Buzz Capra, Cleon Jones, Tom Seaver, Duffy Dyer, Yogi Berra (manager), Tug McGraw, Teddy Martinez, Bud Harrelson, Gary Gentry, Jerry Grote, Ken Boswell (insert). Third row: Lou Niss (traveling secretary), John Milner, Wayne Garrett, Tommie Agee, Jim McAndrew, Jim Fregosi, Danny Frisella, Rusty Staub, Ray Sadecki, Jim Beauchamp, Willie Mays (insert). Top row: Nick Torman (equipment manager), Greg Cox (batboy), Jerry Koosman, Ed Kranepool, Jon Matlack, Dave Marshall, Chuck Taylor, Bill Sudakis, George Palermo (batboy), Steve Torman (clubhouse attendant).

Berra argues
with umps;
Boswell chips in.

Grote waiting
for a foul pop-up.

(PHOTO BY L. KOMITO)

Boswell and Kranepool.

(PHOTO BY L. KOMITO)

Garrett covers second base—Billy Williams is out.

Ted Martinez.

Millan covers the bag against Cincinnati's Boone.

Tom Seaver.

Seaver's winning form.

(PHOTO BY L. KOMITO)

(PHOTO BY L. KOMITO)

Jerry Koosman.

Jon Matlack.

Ray Sadecki.

Tug McGraw arrives.

(PHOTO BY L. KOMITO)

McGraw delivers.

Willie Mays and his fans. (PHOTO BY L. KOMITO)

The famous Mays swing.

Cleon Jones steals another base.

Jones at bat.

Rusty Staub.

(PHOTO BY L. KOMITO)

John Milner.

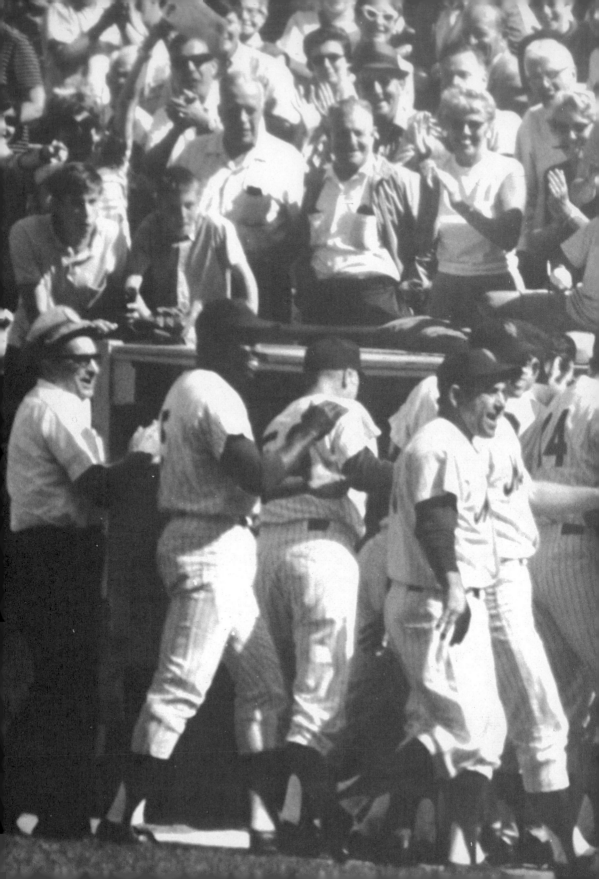

Another Met win and everybody is happy.

Met fans and the Sign Master.

More signs.

Bud Harrelson, accompanied by coach Roy McMillan, walks toward dugout after his fisticuffs with Pete Rose.

Trainer Tom "Doc" McKenna patches up Harrelson's eye.

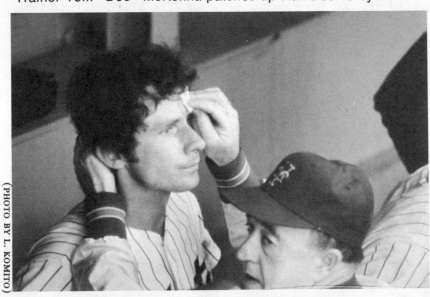

National League President Chub Feeney goes to Mets dugout to ask Willie Mays and teammates to talk to the fans to stop them from throwing objects onto the field.

Seaver, Mays, Staub, and Jones talk to the unruly left-field fans.

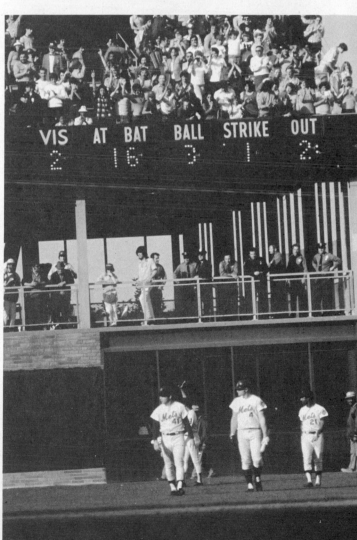

Wild crowd tears up the field after the Met victory over Cincinnati.
(PHOTO BY L. KOMITO)

1973 Mets. Front row, left to right: Tom McKenna (trainer), Roy McMillan (coach), Rube Walker (coach), Eddie Yost (coach), Joe Pignatano (coach), Joe Deer (trainer). Second row: Jerry Grote, Willie Mays, Wayne Garrett, Tug McGraw, Yogi Berra (manager), Felix Millan, Tom Seaver, John Milner, Duffy Dyer, Bud Harrelson. Third row: Herb Norman (equipment manager), Lou Niss (traveling secretary), Jerry May, Jim Gosger, Phil Hennigan, Jim Fregosi, Jim Beauchamp, Don Hahn, Ray Sadecki, Teddy Martinez, Ken Boswell, Bill Hampton (clubhouse attendant). Top row: Greg Cox (batboy), Harry Parker, Jerry Koosman, Ron Hodges, Cleon Jones, Ed Kranepool, George Stone, George Theodore, Jon Matlack, Rusty Staub, Jim McAndrew, Joe Fitzgerald (camera technician), George Palermo (batboy).

Mrs. Payson, owner of Mets, waves to the crowd.

APPENDIX

APPENDIX

THE METS AND THEIR PLAYERS
YEAR BY YEAR

This section is a chronological listing of every Mets season through 1973. All format information and abbreviations are explained in the following text.

Roster Information

POS	Fielding Position		R	Runs
B	Bats B(oth), L(eft),		RBI	Runs Batted In
	or R(ight)		BB	Bases on Balls
G	Games		SO	Strikeouts
AB	At Bats		SB	Stolen Bases
H	Hits			
2B	Doubles		*Pinch Hit*	
3B	Triples		AB	Pinch Hit At Bats
HR	Home Runs		H	Pinch Hits
HR%	Home Run Percentage		BA	Batting Average
	(the number of home		SA	Slugging Average
	runs per 100 times at			
	bat)			

A ★ (star) directly alongside the name of any player means he was *selected* to that year's All-Star team. If a PH appears under the Position Column, it indicates Pinch Hitter. A UT would indicate Utility Player, and if a player was a substitute at two positions, it would be indicated by the first letter or number of the position, i.e., S2 (Shortstop and Second Base); the position listed first is where the most games were played.

Individual League Leaders. (Applies to batting, fielding and pitching.) Statistics that appear in boldface print indicate the player led or tied for the league lead in the particular statistical category.

Traded League Leaders. (Applies to batting, fielding and pitching.) An asterisk (*) next to a particular figure indicates that the player led the league that year in the particular statistical category, but since he played for more than one team, the figure does not necessarily represent his league leading total or average.

Meaningless Averages. Indicated by use of a dash (-). In batting, the dash may appear in averages. This means that the player had no official at bats even though he played in at least one game. A batting average of .000 would mean he had at least one at bat with no hits. In pitching, the dash may appear in winning percentage. This means that the pitcher never had a decision even though he pitched in at least one game. A percentage of .000 would mean that he had at least one loss.

Anytime the symbol "infinity" (∞) is shown for a pitching average, it means that the pitcher allowed at least one earned run, hit, or base on balls without retiring a batter.

325

Individual Fielding Information

T	Throws L(eft) or R(ight)	E	Errors
G	Games	DP	Double Plays
PO	Put Outs	TC/G	Total Chances per Game
A	Assists	FA	Fielding Average

Each man's fielding record is shown for each position he played during the year. Those men who did not play at a position in at least 15 games are shown only with the number of games, in parentheses, that they played at the position. Fielding information for pitchers is not included.

Monthly Record

A "T" appearing next to a figure in the team's standing indicates the team was tied for the position when the month ended.

Team and League Information

W	Wins	*Fielding*	
L	Losses		
PCT	Winning Percentage	E	Errors
GB	Games Behind the	DP	Double Plays
	League Leader	FA	Fielding Average
R	Runs Scored		
OR	Opponents' Runs	*Pitching*	
	(Runs Scored Against)	CG	Complete Games
		BB	Bases on Balls
Batting		SO	Strikeouts
2B	Doubles	ShO	Shutouts
3B	Triples	SV	Saves
HR	Home Runs	ERA	Earned Run Average
BA	Batting Average		
SA	Slugging Average		
SB	Stolen Bases		

Team League Leaders. Statistics that appear in boldface print indicate the team led or tied for the league lead in the particular statistical category. When teams are tied for league lead, the figures for all teams who tied are shown in bold face.

Individual Pitching Information

T	Throws R(ight) or L(eft)	BB	Bases on Balls Allowed
W	Wins	SO	Strikeouts
L	Losses	R	Runs Allowed
PCT	Winning Percentage	ER	Earned Runs Allowed
ERA	Earned Run Average	ShO	Shutouts
SV	Saves	H/9	Hits Allowed Per 9
G	Games Pitched in		Innings Pitched
GS	Games Started	BB/9	Bases on Balls Allowed
CG	Complete Games		Per 9 Innings Pitched
IP	Innings Pitched	SO/9	Strikeouts Per 9
H	Hits Allowed		Innings Pitched

   The records for all the men who pitched for the Mets are shown in the table marked Total Pitching, and those who started and relieved are also shown in the Starting Pitching Table and the Relief Pitching Table. If a pitcher led the league and only started or relieved, his record would also be shown under the Starting or Relief Pitching Tables provided he did not lead the league in Games Saved, Games Started, or Complete Games.

POS	Player	B	G	AB	H	2B	3B	HR	HR %	R	RBI	BB	SO	SB	Pinch Hit AB	Pinch Hit H	BA	SA
REGULARS																		
1B	Marv Throneberry	L	116	357	87	11	3	16	4.5	29	49	34	83	1	21	5	.244	.426
2B	Charlie Neal	R	136	508	132	14	9	11	2.2	59	58	56	90	2	0	0	.260	.388
SS	Elio Chacon	R	118	368	87	10	3	2	0.5	49	27	76	64	12	3	0	.236	.296
3B	Felix Mantilla	R	141	466	128	17	4	11	2.4	54	59	37	51	3	17	3	.275	.399
RF	Richie Ashburn ★	L	135	389	119	7	3	7	1.8	60	28	81	39	12	31	13	.306	.393
CF	Jim Hickman	R	140	392	96	18	2	13	3.3	54	46	47	96	4	13	3	.245	.401
LF	Frank Thomas	R	156	571	152	23	3	34	6.0	69	94	48	95	2	11	4	.266	.496
C	Chris Cannizzaro	R	59	133	32	2	1	0	0.0	9	9	19	26	1	3	1	.241	.271
SUBSTITUTES																		
UT	Rod Kanehl	R	133	351	87	10	2	4	1.1	52	27	23	36	8	11	3	.248	.322
1B	Gil Hodges	R	54	127	32	1	0	9	7.1	15	17	15	27	0	9	2	.252	.472
3O	Cliff Cook	R	40	112	26	6	1	2	1.8	12	9	4	34	1	12	4	.232	.357
1B	Ed Bouchee	L	50	87	14	2	0	3	3.4	7	10	18	17	0	28	5	.161	.287
23	Sammy Drake	B	25	52	10	0	0	0	0.0	2	7	6	12	0	6	3	.192	.192
3B	Don Zimmer	R	14	52	4	1	0	0	0.0	3	1	3	10	0	0	0	.077	.096
UT	Rick Herrscher	R	35	50	11	3	0	1	2.0	5	6	5	11	0	8	2	.220	.340
1B	Jim Marshall	L	17	32	11	1	0	3	9.4	6	4	3	6	0	9	2	.344	.656
1B	Ed Kranepool	L	3	6	1	1	0	0	0.0	0	0	0	1	0	0	0	.167	.333
OF	Joe Christopher	R	119	271	66	10	2	6	2.2	36	32	35	42	11	18	3	.244	.362
OF	Gene Woodling	L	81	190	52	8	1	5	2.6	18	24	24	22	0	28	4	.274	.405
OF	Gus Bell	L	30	101	15	2	0	1	1.0	8	6	10	7	0	4	0	.149	.198
OF	Bobby Gene Smith	R	8	22	3	0	1	0	0.0	1	2	3	2	0	2	0	.136	.227
OF	John DeMerit	R	14	16	3	0	0	1	6.3	3	1	2	4	0	1	0	.188	.375
C	Sammy Taylor	L	68	158	35	4	2	3	1.9	12	20	23	17	0	16	3	.222	.329
C	Choo Choo Coleman	L	55	152	38	7	2	6	3.9	24	17	11	24	2	14	2	.250	.441
C	Joe Pignatano	R	27	56	13	2	0	0	0.0	2	2	2	11	0	3	0	.232	.268
C	Hobie Landrith	L	23	45	13	3	0	1	2.2	6	7	8	3	0	2	0	.289	.422
C	Harry Chiti	R	15	41	8	1	0	0	0.0	2	0	1	8	0	2	0	.195	.220
C	Joe Ginsberg	L	2	5	0	0	0	0	0.0	0	0	0	1	0	0	0	.000	.000
PITCHERS																		
P	Roger Craig	R	42	76	4	0	0	0	0.0	1	2	4	33	0	0	0	.053	.053
P	Al Jackson	L	44	73	5	2	0	0	0.0	5	2	2	27	0	0	0	.068	.096
P	Jay Hook	L	41	69	14	0	0	0	0.0	6	5	8	24	0	1	0	.203	.203
P	Bob Miller	R	40	41	5	0	1	0	0.0	2	0	1	17	0	0	0	.122	.171
P	Craig Anderson	R	50	32	3	0	0	0	0.0	2	0	1	12	0	0	0	.094	.094
P	Bob Moorhead	R	38	22	1	0	0	0	0.0	2	0	5	11	0	0	0	.045	.045
P	Ray Daviault	R	36	15	1	0	0	0	0.0	0	0	1	8	0	0	0	.067	.067
P	Willard Hunter	R	27	13	3	0	0	0	0.0	1	0	0	7	0	0	0	.231	.231
P	Ken MacKenzie	R	42	12	1	0	0	0	0.0	0	1	0	6	0	0	0	.083	.083
P	Vinegar Bend Mizell	R	17	8	2	0	0	0	0.0	1	0	0	2	0	0	0	.250	.250
P	Galen Cisco	R	4	7	0	0	0	0	0.0	0	0	0	1	0	0	0	.000	.000
P	Sherman Jones	L	8	7	3	0	0	0	0.0	0	1	0	2	0	0	0	.429	.429
P	Herb Moford	R	7	4	1	0	0	0	0.0	0	0	0	1	0	0	0	.250	.250
P	Larry Foss	R	5	1	0	0	0	0	0.0	0	0	0	0	0	0	0	.000	.000
P	Dave Hillman	R	13	1	0	0	0	0	0.0	0	0	0	1	0	0	0	.000	.000
P	Bob Miller	R	17	1	0	0	0	0	0.0	0	0	0	0	0	0	0	.000	.000
P	Clem Labine	R	3	0	0	0	0	0	–	0	0	0	0	0	0	0	–	–
	TEAM TOTAL			5492	1318	166	40	139	2.5	617	573	616	991	59	273	62	.240	.361

INDIVIDUAL FIELDING

POS	Player	T	G	PO	A	E	DP	TC/G	FA
1B	M. Throneberry	L	97	785	77	17	87	9.1	.981
	G. Hodges	R	47	315	32	5	23	7.5	.986
	E. Bouchee	L	19	137	23	4	16	8.6	.976
	F. Thomas (11G), R. Herrscher (10G), J. Marshall (5G), R. Kanehl (3G), E. Kranepool (3G)								
2B	C. Neal	R	85	187	240	13	54	5.2	.970
	R. Kanehl	R	62	183	187	22	53	6.3	.944
	F. Mantilla (14G), S. Drake (10G), R. Ashburn (2G), E. Chacon (2G)								
SS	E. Chacon	R	110	204	332	22	64	5.1	.961
	C. Neal	R	39	63	118	12	30	4.9	.938
	F. Mantilla	R	25	28	48	4	10	3.2	.950
	R. Herrscher (3G), R. Kanehl (2G)								
3B	F. Mantilla	R	95	76	179	14	22	2.8	.948
	R. Kanehl	R	30	15	40	8	4	2.1	.873
	C. Cook	R	16	14	21	5	2	2.5	.875
	D. Zimmer (14G), C. Neal (12G), F. Thomas (10G), S. Drake (6G), R. Herrscher (6G), E. Chacon (1G)								
OF	J. Hickman	R	124	265	7	8	0	2.3	.971
	F. Thomas	R	126	216	14	9	0	1.9	.962
	R. Ashburn ★	R	97	187	9	5	1	2.1	.975
	J. Christopher	R	94	133	5	4	4	1.5	.972
	G. Woodling	R	48	68	0	1	0	1.4	.986
	G. Bell	R	26	40	7	1	3	1.8	.979
	R. Kanehl	R	20	21	1	1	0	1.2	.957
	C. Cook (10G), J. DeMerit (9G), B. Smith (6G), R. Herrscher (4G), C. Cannizzaro (1G), J. Marshall (1G)								
C	C. Cannizzaro	R	56	218	34	7	3	4.6	.973
	S. Taylor	R	50	202	25	2	3	4.6	.991
	C. Coleman	R	44	187	22	1	2	4.8	.995
	J. Pignatano	R	25	100	10	1	2	4.4	.991
	H. Landrith	R	21	87	3	3	0	4.4	.968
	H. Chiti (14G), J. Ginsberg (2G)								

MONTHLY RECORD

	APR.	MAY	JUNE	JULY	AUG.	SEPT.	OCT.	FINAL
WINS	3	9	8	6	8	6	0	40
LOSSES	13	17	23	23	26	18	0	120
STANDING	10	10	10	10	10	10	10	10
GAMES BEHIND	10	19	28	43	54.5	60	60.5	60.5

MANAGER	W	L	PCT
Casey Stengel	40	120	.250

TEAM STATISTICS

	W	L	PCT	GB	R	OR	Batting 2B	3B	HR	BA	SA	SB	Fielding E	DP	FA	Pitching CG	BB	SO	ShO	SV	ERA
SF	103	62	.624		**878**	690	235	32	**204**	**.278**	**.441**	73	142	153	.977	**62**	503	886	10	39	3.79
LA	102	63	.618	1	842	697	192	**65**	140	.268	.400	**198**	193	144	.969	44	588	**1104**	8	**46**	3.62
CIN	98	64	.605	3.5	802	685	**252**	40	167	.270	.417	66	145	144	.976	51	567	964	13	35	3.75
PIT	93	68	.578	8	706	**626**	240	**65**	108	.268	.394	50	152	**177**	.975	40	466	897	13	41	**3.37**
MIL	86	76	.531	15.5	730	665	204	38	181	.252	.403	57	**124**	154	**.980**	59	**407**	802	10	24	3.68
STL	84	78	.519	17.5	774	664	221	31	137	.271	.394	86	132	170	.979	53	517	914	**17**	25	3.55
PHI	81	80	.503	20	705	759	199	39	142	.260	.390	79	138	167	.977	43	574	863	7	24	4.28
HOU	64	96	.400	36.5	592	717	170	47	105	.246	.351	42	173	149	.972	34	471	1047	9	19	4.54
CHI	59	103	.364	42.5	632	827	196	56	126	.253	.377	78	146	171	.977	29	601	783	4	26	4.54
NY	40	120	.250	60.5	617	948	166	40	139	.240	.361	59	210	167	.967	43	571	772	4	10	5.04
LEAGUE TOTAL					7278	7278	2075	453	1449	.261	.393	788	1555	1596	.975	458	5265	9032	95	289	3.94

TOTAL PITCHING

PITCHER	T	W	L	PCT	ERA	SV	G	GS	CG	IP	H	BB	SO	R	ER	ShO	H/9	BB/9	SO/9
Roger Craig	R	10	24	.294	4.51	3	42	33	13	233.1	261	70	118	133	117	0	10.07	2.70	4.55
Al Jackson	L	8	20	.286	4.40	0	36	33	12	231.1	244	78	118	132	113	4	9.49	3.03	4.59
Jay Hook	R	8	19	.296	4.84	0	37	34	13	213.2	230	71	113	**137**	115	0	9.69	2.99	4.76
Bob Miller	R	1	12	.077	4.89	1	33	21	1	143.2	146	62	91	98	78	0	9.15	3.88	5.70
Craig Anderson	R	3	17	.150	5.35	4	50	14	2	131.1	150	63	62	108	78	0	10.28	4.32	4.25
Bob Moorhead	R	0	2	.000	4.53	0	38	7	0	105.1	118	42	63	69	53	0	10.08	3.59	5.38
Ray Daviault	R	1	5	.167	6.22	0	36	3	0	81	92	48	51	64	56	0	10.22	5.33	5.67
Ken MacKenzie	L	5	4	.556	4.95	1	42	1	0	80	87	34	51	47	44	0	9.79	3.83	5.74
Willard Hunter	L	1	6	.143	5.57	0	27	6	1	63	67	34	40	41	39	0	9.57	4.86	5.71
Vinegar Bend Mizell	L	0	2	.000	7.34	0	17	2	0	38	48	25	15	35	31	0	11.37	5.92	3.55
Sherman Jones	R	0	4	.000	7.71	0	8	3	0	23.1	31	8	11	22	20	0	11.96	3.09	4.24
Bob Miller	L	2	2	.500	7.08	0	17	0	0	20.1	24	8	8	16	16	0	10.62	3.54	3.54
Galen Cisco	R	1	1	.500	3.26	0	4	2	1	19.1	15	11	13	7	7	0	6.98	5.12	6.05
Dave Hillman	R	0	0	–	6.32	1	13	1	0	15.2	21	8	8	12	11	0	12.06	4.60	4.60
Herb Moford	R	0	1	.000	7.20	0	7	0	0	15	21	1	5	15	12	0	12.60	0.60	3.00
Larry Foss	R	0	1	.000	4.63	0	5	1	0	11.2	17	7	3	6	6	0	13.11	5.40	2.31
Clem Labine	R	0	0	–	11.25	0	3	0	0	4	5	1	2	6	5	0	11.25	2.25	4.50
TEAM TOTAL		40	120	.250	5.04	10	415	161	43	1430	1577	571	772	948	801	4	9.93	3.59	4.86

STARTING PITCHING / RELIEF PITCHING

PITCHER	W	L	PCT	ERA	GS	CG	IP	H	BB	SO	W	L	PCT	ERA	SV	G	IP	H	BB	SO
R. Craig	6	**22**	.214	4.68	33	13	223	254	64	112	4	2	.667	0.87	3	9	10.1	7	6	6
A. Jackson	8	20	.285	4.45	33	12	228.2	240	77	116	0	0	–	0.00	0	3	2.2	4	1	2
J. Hook	7	19	.269	4.94	34	13	209.1	228	70	108	1	0	1.000	0.00	0	3	4.1	2	1	5
B. Miller	1	11	.083	5.03	21	1	118	122	51	75	0	1	.000	4.21	1	12	25.2	24	11	16
C. Anderson	0	11	.000	7.64	14	2	66	94	36	29	3	6	.333	3.03	4	36	65.1	56	27	33
B. Moorhead	0	1	.000	4.91	7	0	36.2	37	14	25	0	1	.000	4.33	0	31	68.2	81	28	38
R. Daviault	0	2	.000	8.49	3	0	11.2	18	7	7	1	3	.250	5.84	0	33	69.1	74	41	44
K. MacKenzie	0	1	.000	16.20	1	0	1.2	5	1	1	5	3	.625	4.71	1	41	78.1	82	33	50
W. Hunter	0	6	.000	8.06	6	1	25.2	29	20	15	1	0	1.000	3.86	0	21	37.1	38	14	25
V. Mizell	0	0	–	7.27	2	0	8.2	12	4	2	0	2	.000	7.36	0	15	29.1	36	21	13
S. Jones	0	3	.000	9.00	3	0	13	21	2	7	0	1	.000	6.10	0	5	10.1	10	6	4
G. Cisco	1	1	.500	2.40	2	1	15	9	10	10	0	0	–	6.23	0	2	4.1	6	1	3
D. Hillman	0	0	–	6.75	1	0	2.2	4	0	0	0	0	–	6.23	1	12	13	17	8	8
L. Foss	0	1	.000	10.80	1	0	5	10	3	1	0	0	–	0.00	0	4	6.2	7	4	2
TEAM TOTAL	23	98	.190	7.47	161	43	965	1083	359	508	17	22	.436	4.76	10	254	465	494	212	264

POS	Player	B	G	AB	H	2B	3B	HR	HR %	R	RBI	BB	SO	SB	Pinch Hit AB	Pinch Hit H	BA	SA
REGULARS																		
1B	Tim Harkness	L	123	375	79	12	3	10	2.7	35	41	36	79	4	16	1	.211	.339
2B	Ron Hunt	R	143	533	145	28	4	10	1.9	64	42	40	50	5	1	1	.272	.396
SS	Al Moran	R	119	331	64	5	2	1	0.3	26	23	36	60	3	1	0	.193	.230
3B	Charlie Neal	R	72	253	57	12	1	3	1.2	26	18	27	49	1	1	1	.225	.316
RF	Duke Snider ★	L	129	354	86	8	3	14	4.0	44	45	56	74	0	29	6	.243	.401
CF	Jim Hickman	R	146	494	113	21	6	17	3.4	53	51	44	120	0	11	1	.229	.399
LF	Frank Thomas	R	126	420	109	9	1	15	3.6	34	60	33	48	0	15	4	.260	.393
C	Choo Choo Coleman	L	106	247	44	0	0	3	1.2	22	9	24	49	5	11	2	.178	.215
SUBSTITUTES																		
SS	Chico Fernandez	R	58	145	29	6	0	1	0.7	12	9	9	30	3	14	1	.200	.262
S2	Larry Burright	R	41	100	22	2	1	0	0.0	9	3	8	25	1	2	0	.220	.260
3B	Pumpsie Green	B	17	54	15	1	2	1	1.9	8	5	12	13	0	0	0	.278	.426
UT	Ted Schreiber	R	39	50	8	0	0	0	0.0	1	2	4	14	0	10	0	.160	.160
1B	Gil Hodges	R	11	22	5	0	0	0	0.0	2	3	3	2	0	1	0	.227	.227
1B	Marv Throneberry	L	14	14	2	1	0	0	0.0	0	1	1	5	0	10	2	.143	.214
O1	Ed Kranepool	L	86	273	57	12	2	2	0.7	22	14	18	50	4	13	3	.209	.289
UT	Rod Kanehl	R	109	191	46	6	0	1	0.5	26	9	5	26	6	21	5	.241	.288
OF	Joe Hicks	L	56	159	36	6	1	5	3.1	16	22	7	31	0	16	3	.226	.371
O1	Duke Carmel	L	47	149	35	5	3	3	2.0	11	18	16	37	2	7	1	.235	.369
OF	Joe Christopher	R	64	149	33	5	1	1	0.7	19	8	13	21	1	21	3	.221	.289
OF	Jimmy Piersall	R	40	124	24	4	1	1	0.8	13	10	10	14	1	2	1	.194	.266
UT	Cliff Cook	R	50	106	15	2	1	2	1.9	9	8	12	37	0	19	4	.142	.236
OF	Dick Smith	R	20	42	10	0	1	0	0.0	4	3	5	10	3	5	1	.238	.286
OF	Cleon Jones	R	6	15	2	0	0	0	0.0	1	1	0	4	0	2	0	.133	.133
C	Norm Sherry	R	63	147	20	1	0	2	1.4	6	11	10	26	1	2	1	.136	.184
C	Jesse Gonder	L	42	126	38	4	0	3	2.4	12	15	6	25	1	11	2	.302	.405
C	Sammy Taylor	L	22	35	9	0	1	0	0.0	3	6	5	7	0	11	5	.257	.314
C	Chris Cannizzaro	R	16	33	8	1	0	0	0.0	4	4	1	8	0	1	1	.242	.273
PITCHERS																		
P	Al Jackson	L	49	79	16	2	0	0	0.0	8	4	1	23	0	0	0	.203	.228
P	Roger Craig	R	46	69	6	0	0	0	0.0	0	0	5	39	0	0	0	.087	.087
P	Carl Willey	R	30	54	6	0	0	1	1.9	3	5	2	32	0	0	0	.111	.167
P	Tracy Stallard	R	39	48	3	0	0	0	0.0	1	1	0	21	0	0	0	.063	.063
P	Galen Cisco	R	51	38	5	1	0	0	0.0	0	3	4	9	0	0	0	.132	.158
P	Jay Hook	L	41	38	9	1	0	0	0.0	4	1	2	13	0	0	0	.237	.263
P	Larry Bearnarth	R	58	30	6	1	1	0	0.0	2	3	0	12	0	0	0	.200	.300
P	Don Rowe	L	26	13	3	0	0	0	0.0	0	1	0	5	0	0	0	.231	.231
P	Ken MacKenzie	R	34	10	0	0	0	0	0.0	0	0	0	5	0	0	0	.000	.000
P	Grover Powell	L	20	10	2	0	0	0	0.0	1	0	2	3	0	0	0	.200	.200
P	Craig Anderson	R	3	3	1	0	0	0	0.0	0	0	0	0	0	0	0	.333	.333
P	Ed Bauta	R	9	3	0	0	0	0	0.0	0	0	0	2	0	0	0	.000	.000
P	Steve Dillon	L	1	0	0	0	0	0	—	0	0	0	0	0	0	0	—	—
	TEAM TOTAL			5336	1168	156	35	96	1.8	501	459	457	1078	41	253	49	.219	.315

INDIVIDUAL FIELDING

POS	Player	T	G	PO	A	E	DP	TC/G	FA
1B	T. Harkness	L	106	898	112	14	73	9.7	.986
	D. Carmel	L	18	185	10	4	13	11.1	.980
	E. Kranepool	L	20	150	13	0	16	8.2	1.000
	F. Thomas	R	15	146	9	1	9	10.4	.994
	G. Hodges (10G), C. Cook (5G), R. Kanehl (3G), M. Throneberry (3G), D. Smith (2G)								
2B	R. Hunt	R	142	350	416	26	85	5.6	.967
	L. Burright	R	15	29	44	3	11	5.1	.961
	R. Kanehl (12G), C. Fernandez (3G), T. Schreiber (3G)								
SS	A. Moran	R	116	189	332	27	57	4.7	.951
	C. Fernandez	R	45	57	79	8	16	3.2	.944
	L. Burright	R	19	40	66	6	10	5.9	.946
	T. Schreiber (9G), C. Neal (8G)								
3B	C. Neal	R	66	61	135	8	10	3.1	.961
	J. Hickman	R	59	45	103	14	14	2.7	.914
	P. Green	R	16	12	36	8	2	3.5	.857
	T. Schreiber	R	17	12	31	1	3	2.6	.977
	R. Kanehl (13G), C. Cook (9G), C. Fernandez (5G), L. Burright (1G), R. Hunt (1G), A. Moran (1G), F. Thomas (1G)								
OF	F. Thomas	R	96	158	8	2	1	1.8	.988
	J. Hickman	R	82	149	6	6	2	2.0	.963
	D. Snider ★	R	106	139	5	2	0	1.4	.986
	J. Hicks	R	41	83	1	3	0	2.1	.966
	E. Kranepool	L	55	78	5	4	1	1.6	.954
	R. Kanehl	R	58	69	5	2	2	1.3	.974
	J. Piersall	R	38	65	3	0	0	1.8	1.000
	J. Christopher	R	45	58	1	1	1	1.3	.983
	D. Carmel	L	21	47	1	1	0	2.3	.980
	C. Cook	R	21	26	2	0	0	1.3	1.000
	D. Smith (10G), C. Jones (5G), C. Coleman (1G)								
C	C. Coleman	R	91	418	54	15	9	5.4	.969
	N. Sherry	R	61	265	26	6	6	4.9	.980
	J. Gonder	R	31	120	16	3	3	4.5	.978
	C. Cannizzaro	R	15	49	6	0	0	3.7	1.000
	S. Taylor (13G)								

MONTHLY RECORD

	APR.	MAY	JUNE	JULY	AUG.	SEPT.	OCT.	FINAL
WINS	7	11	11	4	9	9	0	51
LOSSES	12	19	17	25	19	19	0	111
STANDING	9	10	9	10	10	10	10	10
GAMES BEHIND	6.5	12.5	16.5	31	38	48	48	48

MANAGER	W	L	PCT
Casey Stengel	51	111	.315

TEAM STATISTICS

	W	L	PCT	GB	R	OR	2B	3B	HR	BA	SA	SB	E	DP	FA	CG	BB	SO	ShO	SV	ERA
LA	99	63	.611		640	550	178	34	110	.251	.357	124	159	129	.974	51	402	1095	24	29	2.85
STL	93	69	.574	6	747	628	231	66	128	.271	.403	77	147	136	.976	49	463	978	17	32	3.32
SF	88	74	.543	11	725	641	206	35	197	.258	.414	55	156	113	.974	46	464	954	9	30	3.35
PHI	87	75	.537	12	642	578	228	54	126	.252	.381	56	142	147	.977	45	553	1052	12	31	3.09
CIN	86	76	.531	13	648	594	225	44	122	.246	.371	92	135	127	.977	55	425	1048	22	36	3.29
MIL	84	78	.519	15	677	603	204	39	139	.244	.370	75	129	161	.979	56	489	924	18	25	3.26
CHI	82	80	.506	17	570	578	205	44	127	.238	.363	68	155	172	.976	45	400	851	15	28	3.08
PIT	74	88	.457	25	567	595	181	49	108	.250	.359	57	182	195	.971	34	457	900	16	33	3.10
HOU	66	96	.407	33	464	640	170	39	62	.220	.301	39	162	100	.973	36	378	937	16	20	3.44
NY	51	111	.315	48	501	774	156	35	96	.219	.315	41	210	151	.967	42	529	806	5	12	4.12
LEAGUE TOTAL					6181	6181	1984	439	1215	.245	.364	684	1577	1431	.975	459	4560	9545	154	276	3.28

TOTAL PITCHING

PITCHER	T	W	L	PCT	ERA	SV	G	GS	CG	IP	H	BB	SO	R	ER	ShO	H/9	BB/9	SO/9
Roger Craig	R	5	22	.185	3.78	2	46	31	14	236	249	58	108	117	99	0	9.50	2.21	4.12
Al Jackson	L	13	17	.433	3.96	1	37	34	11	227	237	84	142	128	100	0	9.40	3.33	5.63
Carl Willey	R	9	14	.391	3.10	0	30	28	7	183	149	69	101	74	63	4	7.33	3.39	4.97
Galen Cisco	R	7	15	.318	4.34	0	51	17	1	155.2	165	64	81	88	75	0	9.54	3.70	4.68
Tracy Stallard	R	6	17	.261	4.71	1	39	23	5	154.2	156	77	110	89	81	0	9.08	4.48	6.40
Jay Hook	R	4	14	.222	5.48	1	41	20	3	152.2	168	53	89	104	93	0	9.90	3.12	5.25
Larry Bearnarth	R	3	8	.273	3.42	4	58	2	0	126.1	127	47	48	61	48	0	9.05	3.35	3.42
Ken MacKenzie	L	3	1	.750	4.99	3	34	0	0	57.2	63	12	41	35	32	0	9.83	1.87	6.40
Don Rowe	L	0	0	–	4.28	0	26	1	0	54.2	59	21	27	27	26	0	9.71	3.46	4.45
Grover Powell	L	1	1	.500	2.72	0	20	4	1	49.2	37	32	39	23	15	1	6.70	5.80	7.07
Ed Bauta	R	0	0	–	5.21	0	9	0	0	19	22	9	13	11	11	0	10.42	4.26	6.16
Craig Anderson	R	0	2	.000	8.68	0	3	2	0	9.1	17	3	6	15	9	0	16.39	2.89	5.79
Steve Dillon	L	0	0	–	10.80	0	1	0	0	1.2	3	0	1	2	2	0	16.20	0.00	5.40
TEAM TOTAL		51	111	.315	4.12	12	395	162	42	1427.1	1452	529	806	774	654	5	9.16	3.34	5.08

STARTING PITCHING | RELIEF PITCHING

PITCHER	W	L	PCT	ERA	GS	CG	IP	H	BB	SO	W	L	PCT	ERA	SV	G	IP	H	BB	SO
R. Craig	5	21	.192	3.63	31	14	216	225	52	102	0	1	.000	5.40	2	15	20	24	6	6
A. Jackson	13	17	.433	3.99	34	11	223.1	234	83	142	0	0	–	2.45	1	3	3.2	3	1	0
C. Willey	9	14	.391	3.15	28	7	180	148	67	99	0	0	–	0.00	0	2	3	1	2	2
G. Cisco	2	12	.142	5.13	17	1	94.2	110	44	53	5	3	.625	3.10	0	34	61	55	20	28
T. Stallard	6	14	.300	4.47	23	5	139	137	62	91	0	3	.000	6.89	1	16	15.2	19	15	19
J. Hook	3	14	.176	5.90	20	3	114.1	127	36	65	1	0	1.000	4.23	1	21	38.1	41	17	24
L. Bearnarth	0	1	.000	9.90	2	0	10	18	3	6	3	7	.300	2.86	4	56	116.1	109	44	42
D. Rowe	0	0	–	5.79	1	0	4.2	7	1	1	0	0	–	4.14	0	25	50	52	20	26
G. Powell	1	1	.500	0.86	4	1	21	13	13	10	0	0	–	4.08	0	16	28.2	24	19	29
C. Anderson	0	2	.000	5.19	2	0	8.2	13	2	6	0	0	–	54.00	0	1	.2	4	1	0
TEAM TOTAL	39	96	.289	5.82	162	42	1011.2	1032	363	575	12	15	.444	4.03	12	233	415.2	420	166	231

POS	Player	B	G	AB	H	2B	3B	HR	HR %	R	RBI	BB	SO	SB	Pinch Hit AB	Pinch Hit H	BA	SA
REGULARS																		
1B	Ed Kranepool	L	119	420	108	19	4	10	2.4	47	45	32	50	0	10	2	.257	.393
2B	Ron Hunt ★	R	127	475	144	19	6	6	1.3	59	42	29	30	6	6	2	.303	.406
SS	Roy McMillan	R	113	379	80	8	2	1	0.3	30	25	14	16	3	2	0	.211	.251
3B	Charley Smith	R	127	443	106	12	0	20	4.5	44	58	19	101	2	7	2	.239	.402
RF	Joe Christopher	R	154	543	163	26	8	16	2.9	78	76	48	92	6	9	3	.300	.466
CF	Jim Hickman	R	139	409	105	14	1	11	2.7	48	57	36	90	0	31	8	.257	.377
LF	George Altman	L	124	422	97	14	1	9	2.1	48	47	18	70	4	18	6	.230	.332
C	Jesse Gonder	L	131	341	92	11	1	7	2.1	28	35	29	65	0	43	8	.270	.370
SUBSTITUTES																		
UT	Rod Kanehl	R	98	254	59	7	1	1	0.4	25	11	7	18	3	15	3	.232	.280
32	Bobby Klaus	R	56	209	51	8	3	2	1.0	25	11	25	30	3	2	0	.244	.340
S3	Amado Samuel	R	53	142	33	7	0	0	0.0	7	5	4	24	0	2	1	.232	.282
1B	Tim Harkness	L	39	117	33	2	1	2	1.7	11	13	9	18	1	9	0	.282	.368
1O	Dick Smith	R	46	94	21	6	1	0	0.0	14	3	1	29	6	8	1	.223	.309
3O	Johnny Stephenson	L	37	57	9	0	0	1	1.8	2	2	4	18	0	21	2	.158	.211
3B	Wayne Graham	R	20	33	3	1	0	0	0.0	1	0	0	5	0	12	1	.091	.121
SS	Al Moran	R	16	22	5	0	0	0	0.0	2	4	2	2	0	0	0	.227	.227
2B	Larry Burright	R	3	7	0	0	0	0	0.0	0	0	0	0	0	0	0	.000	.000
OF	Larry Elliot	L	80	224	51	8	0	9	4.0	27	22	28	55	1	15	3	.228	.384
O1	Frank Thomas	R	60	197	50	6	1	3	1.5	19	19	10	29	1	11	3	.254	.340
CO	Hawk Taylor	R	92	225	54	4	0	4	1.8	20	23	8	33	0	34	8	.240	.329
C	Chris Cannizzaro	R	60	164	51	10	0	0	0.0	11	10	14	28	0	5	1	.311	.372
PITCHERS																		
P	Tracy Stallard	R	36	79	15	3	0	0	0.0	5	1	0	22	0	0	0	.190	.228
P	Jack Fisher	R	40	76	12	1	0	0	0.0	5	8	5	24	0	0	0	.158	.171
P	Al Jackson	L	50	72	11	3	1	1	1.4	6	4	2	26	0	0	0	.153	.264
P	Galen Cisco	R	36	54	6	1	0	0	0.0	2	4	4	19	0	0	0	.111	.130
P	Bill Wakefield	R	62	24	4	0	0	0	0.0	0	0	0	8	0	0	0	.167	.167
P	Dennis Ribant	R	17	20	2	1	0	0	0.0	2	1	1	2	0	0	0	.100	.150
P	Frank Lary	R	13	17	2	0	0	0	0.0	1	1	4	5	0	0	0	.118	.118
P	Larry Bearnarth	R	44	14	2	0	0	0	0.0	0	0	0	6	0	0	0	.143	.143
P	Tom Parsons	R	4	7	0	0	0	0	0.0	0	0	0	5	0	0	0	.000	.000
P	Ron Locke	R	25	5	0	0	0	0	0.0	1	0	0	3	0	0	0	.000	.000
P	Darrell Sutherland	R	10	5	1	0	0	0	0.0	0	0	0	4	0	0	0	.200	.200
P	Carl Willey	R	14	4	0	0	0	0	0.0	0	0	0	1	0	0	0	.000	.000
P	Craig Anderson	R	4	3	0	0	0	0	0.0	0	0	0	1	0	0	0	.000	.000
P	Jay Hook	L	3	3	0	0	0	0	0.0	0	0	0	1	0	0	0	.000	.000
P	Gary Kroll	R	8	3	1	0	0	0	0.0	0	0	0	1	0	0	0	.333	.333
P	Jerry Hinsley	R	9	1	0	0	0	0	0.0	0	0	0	1	0	0	0	.000	.000
P	Willard Hunter	R	41	1	1	0	0	0	0.0	0	0	0	0	0	0	0	1.000	1.000
P	Tom Sturdivant	L	16	1	0	0	0	0	0.0	0	0	0	0	0	0	0	.000	.000
P	Ed Bauta	R	8	0	0	0	0	0	–	0	0	0	0	0	0	0	–	–
P	Steve Dillon	L	2	0	0	0	0	0	–	0	0	0	0	0	0	0	–	–
	TEAM TOTAL			5566	1372	195	31	103	1.9	569	527	353	932	36	260	54	.246	.348

INDIVIDUAL FIELDING

POS	Player	T	G	PO	A	E	DP	TC/G	FA
1B	E. Kranepool	L	104	975	80	10	78	10.2	.991
	T. Harkness	L	32	251	28	2	32	8.8	.993
	F. Thomas	R	19	142	14	1	11	8.3	.994
	D. Smith	R	18	143	11	2	11	8.7	.987
	R. Kanehl (2G)								
2B	R. Hunt ★	R	109	244	317	12	73	5.3	.979
	R. Kanehl	R	34	78	84	2	15	4.8	.988
	B. Klaus	R	25	58	80	2	11	5.6	.986
	L. Burright (3G), A. Samuel (3G)								
SS	R. McMillan	R	111	217	353	14	64	5.3	.976
	C. Smith	R	36	50	55	7	17	3.1	.938
	A. Samuel	R	34	34	70	6	20	3.2	.945
	A. Moran	R	15	14	31	2	5	3.1	.957
	B. Klaus (5G)								
3B	C. Smith	R	85	89	166	23	9	3.3	.917
	B. Klaus	R	28	23	48	4	4	2.7	.947
	R. Kanehl	R	19	20	35	4	7	3.1	.932
	A. Samuel	R	17	8	40	5	3	3.1	.906
	J. Stephenson (14G), R. Hunt (12G), W. Graham (11G), F. Thomas (2G), J. Hickman (1G), A. Moran (1G)								

POS	Player	T	G	PO	A	E	DP	TC/G	FA
OF	J. Christopher	R	145	251	10	7	2	1.8	.974
	J. Hickman	R	113	237	8	6	1	2.2	.976
	G. Altman	R	109	202	12	7	3	2.0	.968
	L. Elliot	L	63	130	2	2	1	2.1	.985
	F. Thomas	R	31	58	2	0	1	1.9	1.000
	R. Kanehl	R	25	54	4	0	3	2.3	1.000
	H. Taylor	R	16	28	0	1	0	1.8	.966
	C. Smith (13G), D. Smith (13G), J. Stephenson (8G), E. Kranepool (6G)								
C	J. Gonder	R	97	397	70	10	7	4.9	.979
	C. Cannizzaro	R	53	225	28	3	6	4.8	.988
	H. Taylor	R	45	182	28	4	5	4.8	.981

MONTHLY RECORD

	APR.	MAY	JUNE	JULY	AUG.	SEPT.	OCT.	FINAL
WINS	2	12	8	10	12	7	2	53
LOSSES	10	22	22	18	14	21	2	109
STANDING	10	10	10	10	10	10	10	10
GAMES BEHIND	7.5	14	24.5	29	34.5	40.5	40	40

MANAGER	W	L	PCT
Casey Stengel	53	109	.327

TEAM STATISTICS

	W	L	PCT	GB	R	OR	2B	3B	HR	BA	SA	SB	E	DP	FA	CG	BB	SO	ShO	SV	ERA
							Batting						**Fielding**			**Pitching**					
STL	93	69	.574		715	652	240	53	109	**.272**	.392	73	172	147	.972	47	410	877	10	38	3.43
CIN	92	70	.568	1	660	**566**	220	38	130	.249	.372	90	**130**	137	**.978**	54	436	**1122**	14	35	3.07
PHI	92	70	.568	1	693	632	241	51	130	.258	.391	30	157	150	.974	37	440	1009	17	**41**	3.36
SF	90	72	.556	3	656	587	185	38	**165**	.246	.382	64	159	136	.974	48	480	1023	17	30	3.19
MIL	88	74	.543	5	**803**	744	**274**	32	159	**.272**	**.418**	53	143	139	.976	45	452	906	14	39	4.12
LA	80	82	.494	13	614	572	180	39	79	.250	.340	**141**	170	126	.973	47	458	1062	**19**	27	**2.95**
PIT	80	82	.494	13	663	636	225	**54**	121	.264	.389	39	177	**179**	.972	42	476	951	14	29	3.52
CHI	76	86	.469	17	649	724	239	50	145	.251	.390	70	162	147	.975	**58**	423	737	11	19	4.08
HOU	66	96	.407	27	495	628	162	41	70	.229	.315	40	149	124	.976	30	**353**	852	9	31	3.41
NY	53	109	.327	40	569	776	195	31	103	.246	.348	36	167	154	.973	40	466	717	10	15	4.25
LEAGUE TOTAL					6517	6517	2161	427	1211	.254	.374	636	1586	1439	.975	448	4394	9256	135	304	3.53

TOTAL PITCHING

PITCHER	T	W	L	PCT	ERA	SV	G	GS	CG	IP	H	BB	SO	R	ER	ShO	H/9	BB/9	SO/9
Jack Fisher	R	10	17	.370	4.23	0	40	34	8	227.2	256	56	115	124	107	1	10.12	2.21	4.55
Tracy Stallard	R	10	**20**	.333	3.79	0	36	34	11	225.2	213	73	118	111	95	2	8.49	2.91	4.71
Al Jackson	L	11	16	.407	4.26	1	40	31	11	213.1	229	60	112	115	101	3	9.66	2.53	4.73
Galen Cisco	R	6	19	.240	3.62	0	36	25	5	191.2	182	54	78	85	77	2	8.55	2.54	3.66
Bill Wakefield	R	3	5	.375	3.61	2	62	4	0	119.2	103	61	61	57	48	0	7.75	4.59	4.59
Larry Bearnarth	R	5	5	.500	4.15	3	44	1	0	78	79	38	31	38	36	0	9.12	4.38	3.58
Dennis Ribant	R	1	5	.167	5.15	1	14	7	1	57.2	65	9	35	35	33	1	10.14	1.40	5.46
Frank Lary	R	2	3	.400	4.55	1	13	8	3	57.1	62	14	27	33	29	1	9.73	2.20	4.24
Willard Hunter	L	3	3	.500	4.41	5	41	0	0	49	54	9	22	25	24	0	9.92	1.65	4.04
Ron Locke	L	1	2	.333	3.48	0	25	3	0	41.1	46	22	17	23	16	0	10.02	4.79	3.70
Carl Willey	R	0	2	.000	3.60	0	14	3	0	30	37	8	14	19	12	0	11.10	2.40	4.20
Tom Sturdivant	R	0	0	—	5.97	1	16	0	0	28.2	34	7	18	20	19	0	10.67	2.20	5.65
Darrell Sutherland	R	0	3	.000	7.76	0	10	4	0	26.2	32	12	9	26	23	0	10.80	4.05	3.04
Gary Kroll	R	0	1	.000	4.15	0	8	2	0	21.2	19	15	24	11	10	0	7.89	6.23	9.97
Tom Parsons	R	1	2	.333	4.19	0	4	2	1	19.1	20	6	10	9	9	0	9.31	2.79	4.66
Jerry Hinsley	R	0	2	.000	8.22	0	9	2	0	15.1	21	7	11	17	14	0	12.33	4.11	6.46
Craig Anderson	R	0	1	.000	5.54	0	4	1	0	13	21	3	5	9	8	0	14.54	2.08	3.46
Ed Bauta	R	0	2	.000	5.40	1	8	0	0	10	17	3	3	6	6	0	15.30	2.70	2.70
Jay Hook	R	0	1	.000	9.31	0	3	2	0	9.2	17	7	5	10	10	0	15.83	6.52	4.66
Steve Dillon	L	0	0	—	9.00	0	2	0	0	3	4	2	2	3	3	0	12.00	6.00	6.00
TEAM TOTAL		53	109	.327	4.25	15	429	163	40	1438.2	1511	466	717	776	680	10	9.45	2.92	4.49

STARTING PITCHING   RELIEF PITCHING

PITCHER	W	L	PCT	ERA	GS	CG	IP	H	BB	SO	W	L	PCT	ERA	SV	G	IP	H	BB	SO
J. Fisher	10	15	.400	4.18	34	8	221.2	248	55	111	0	2	.000	6.00	0	6	6	8	1	4
T. Stallard	10	19	.344	3.69	34	11	224.2	209	71	117	0	1	.000	27.00	0	2	1	4	2	1
A. Jackson	9	16	.360	4.35	31	11	196.2	211	52	104	2	0	1.000	3.24	1	9	16.2	18	8	8
G. Cisco	6	16	.272	3.96	25	5	161.1	159	48	70	0	3	.000	1.78	0	11	30.1	23	6	8
B. Wakefield	0	3	.000	9.82	4	0	14.2	20	10	4	3	2	.600	2.74	2	58	105	83	51	57
L. Bearnarth	0	1	.000	14.54	1	0	4.1	8	2	1	5	4	.556	3.54	3	43	73.2	71	36	30
D. Ribant	1	5	.166	5.55	7	1	47	53	4	32	0	0	—	3.38	1	7	10.2	12	5	3
F. Lary	2	3	.400	5.11	8	3	49.1	53	12	21	0	0	—	1.13	1	5	8	9	2	6
R. Locke	1	2	.333	4.86	3	0	16.2	15	9	5	0	0	—	2.55	0	22	24.2	31	13	12
C. Willey	0	2	.000	1.98	3	0	13.2	14	4	3	0	0	—	4.96	0	11	16.1	23	4	11
D. Sutherland	0	3	.000	9.22	4	0	13.2	20	10	6	0	0	—	6.23	0	6	13	12	2	3
G. Kroll	0	1	.000	7.88	2	0	8	10	9	9	0	0	—	1.98	0	6	13.2	9	6	15
T. Parsons	0	2	.000	6.00	2	1	12	14	4	6	1	0	1.000	1.23	0	2	7.1	6	2	4
J. Hinsley	0	1	.000	9.53	2	0	5.2	18	4	1	0	1	.000	7.45	0	7	9.2	13	6	6
C. Anderson	0	1	.000	3.86	1	0	7	11	2	4	0	0	—	7.50	0	3	6	10	1	1
J. Hook	0	1	.000	6.00	2	0	9	13	5	5	0	0	—	54.00	0	1	.2	4	2	0
TEAM TOTAL	39	91	.300	6.09	163	40	1005.1	1066	298	503	14	18	.438	3.80	15	266	433.1	445	168	214

POS	Player	B	G	AB	H	2B	3B	HR	HR %	R	RBI	BB	SO	SB	Pinch Hit AB	Pinch Hit H	BA	SA
REGULARS																		
1B	Ed Kranepool ★	L	153	525	133	24	4	10	1.9	44	53	39	71	1	11	4	.253	.371
2B	Chuck Hiller	L	100	286	68	11	1	5	1.7	24	21	14	24	1	27	6	.238	.336
SS	Roy McMillan	R	157	528	128	19	2	1	0.2	44	42	24	60	1	4	0	.242	.292
3B	Charley Smith	R	135	499	122	20	3	16	3.2	49	62	17	123	2	3	0	.244	.393
RF	Johnny Lewis	L	148	477	117	15	3	15	3.1	64	45	59	117	4	14	4	.245	.384
CF	Jim Hickman	R	141	369	87	18	0	15	4.1	32	40	27	76	3	29	5	.236	.407
LF	Ron Swoboda	R	135	399	91	15	3	19	4.8	52	50	33	102	2	26	7	.228	.424
C	Chris Cannizzaro	R	114	251	46	8	2	0	0.0	17	7	28	60	0	2	0	.183	.231
SUBSTITUTES																		
UT	Bobby Klaus	R	119	288	55	12	0	2	0.7	30	12	45	49	1	4	1	.191	.253
2B	Ron Hunt	R	57	196	47	12	1	1	0.5	21	10	14	19	2	4	0	.240	.327
SS	Bud Harrelson	R	19	37	4	1	1	0	0.0	3	0	2	11	0	0	0	.108	.189
3S	Kevin Collins	L	11	23	4	1	0	0	0.0	3	0	1	9	0	3	1	.174	.217
OF	Joe Christopher	R	148	437	109	18	3	5	1.1	38	40	35	82	4	34	10	.249	.339
OF	Billy Cowan	R	82	156	28	8	2	3	1.9	16	9	4	45	3	14	2	.179	.314
O3	Danny Napoleon	R	68	97	14	1	1	0	0.0	5	7	8	23	0	45	9	.144	.175
OF	Gary Kolb	L	40	90	15	2	0	1	1.1	8	7	3	28	3	12	2	.167	.222
OF	Cleon Jones	R	30	74	11	1	0	1	1.4	2	9	2	23	1	9	2	.149	.203
C	Johnny Stephenson	L	62	121	26	5	0	4	3.3	9	15	8	19	0	29	6	.215	.355
C	Jesse Gonder	L	53	105	25	4	0	4	3.8	6	9	11	20	0	35*	10	.238	.390
C	Hawk Taylor	R	25	46	7	0	0	4	8.7	5	10	1	8	0	13	0	.152	.413
C	Jimmie Schaffer	R	24	37	5	2	0	0	0.0	0	0	1	15	0	4	0	.135	.189
C	Greg Goossen	R	11	31	9	0	0	1	3.2	2	2	1	5	0	2	0	.290	.387
C	Yogi Berra	L	4	9	2	0	0	0	0.0	1	0	0	3	0	2	0	.222	.222
PITCHERS																		
P	Jack Fisher	R	43	78	12	2	0	0	0.0	2	2	2	22	0	0	0	.154	.179
P	Al Jackson	L	56	60	7	1	0	0	0.0	5	2	2	23	0	0	0	.117	.133
P	Warren Spahn	L	21	35	4	1	0	0	0.0	0	2	7	12	0	1	0	.114	.143
P	Galen Cisco	R	35	27	7	0	0	0	0.0	5	4	2	9	0	0	0	.259	.259
P	Gary Kroll	R	32	26	3	1	0	0	0.0	3	0	0	9	0	0	0	.115	.154
P	Tug McGraw	R	38	23	3	0	0	0	0.0	0	0	0	10	0	0	0	.130	.130
P	Frank Lary	R	14	19	4	0	0	0	0.0	3	0	0	4	0	0	0	.211	.211
P	Tom Parsons	R	35	18	1	0	0	0	0.0	0	0	1	14	0	0	0	.056	.056
P	Darrell Sutherland	R	18	13	2	0	1	0	0.0	0	0	0	4	0	0	0	.154	.308
P	Larry Miller	L	28	11	2	0	0	0	0.0	0	0	0	5	0	0	0	.182	.182
P	Larry Bearnarth	R	40	9	1	1	0	0	0.0	1	0	1	4	0	0	0	.111	.222
P	Dick Selma	R	7	9	2	0	0	0	0.0	1	0	0	4	0	0	0	.222	.222
P	Rob Gardner	R	5	7	0	0	0	0	0.0	0	0	0	4	0	0	0	.000	.000
P	Gordie Richardson	R	35	7	0	0	0	0	0.0	0	0	0	7	0	0	0	.000	.000
P	Dennis Ribant	R	19	6	0	0	0	0	0.0	0	0	0	1	0	0	0	.000	.000
P	Carl Willey	R	13	5	0	0	0	0	0.0	0	0	0	3	0	0	0	.000	.000
P	Jim Bethke	R	25	4	0	0	0	0	0.0	0	0	0	2	0	0	0	.000	.000
P	Dennis Musgraves	R	5	2	0	0	0	0	0.0	0	0	0	0	0	0	0	.000	.000
P	Dave Eilers	R	11	1	1	0	0	0	0.0	0	0	0	0	0	0	0	1.000	1.000
P	Bob Moorhead	R	9	0	0	0	0	0	–	0	0	0	0	0	0	0	–	–
TEAM TOTAL				5441	1202	203	27	107	2.0	495	460	392	1129	28	327	69	.221	.327

INDIVIDUAL FIELDING

POS	Player	T	G	PO	A	E	DP	TC/G	FA
1B	E. Kranepool ★	L	147	1375	93	12	116	10.1	.992
	J. Hickman	R	30	240	20	2	20	8.7	.992
	G. Kolb (1G), H. Taylor (1G)								
2B	B. Klaus	R	72	146	188	11	46	4.8	.968
	C. Hiller	R	80	145	182	14	39	4.3	.959
	R. Hunt	R	46	106	128	5	17	5.2	.979
	B. Cowan (2G), C. Smith (1G)								
SS	R. McMillan	R	153	248	477	27	80	4.9	.964
	B. Harrelson	R	18	28	36	3	6	3.7	.955
	B. Klaus	R	28	15	25	0	5	1.4	1.000
	C. Smith (6G), K. Collins (3G), B. Cowan (1G)								
3B	C. Smith	R	131	119	281	18	27	3.2	.957
	B. Klaus	R	25	18	41	0	3	2.4	1.000
	J. Hickman (14G), K. Collins (7G), D. Napoleon (7G), R. Hunt (6G), C. Hiller (2G), G. Kolb (1G)								

POS	Player	T	G	PO	A	E	DP	TC/G	FA
OF	J. Lewis	R	142	257	14	7	3	2.0	.975
	R. Swoboda	R	112	188	9	11	2	1.9	.947
	J. Christopher	R	112	180	3	2	0	1.7	.989
	J. Hickman	R	91	136	3	5	0	1.6	.965
	B. Cowan	R	61	80	2	0	2	1.3	1.000
	G. Kolb	R	29	37	4	1	0	1.4	.976
	C. Jones	L	23	36	2	0	0	1.7	1.000
	D. Napoleon	R	15	32	0	2	0	2.3	.941
	C. Hiller (4G), J. Stephenson (2G)								
C	C. Cannizzaro	R	112	435	69	12	8	4.6	.977
	J. Stephenson	R	47	146	13	3	1	3.4	.981
	J. Gonder	R	31	103	20	1	5	4.0	.992
	J. Schaffer	R	21	60	1	2	0	3.0	.968
	H. Taylor	R	15	46	5	2	0	3.5	.962
	G. Goossen (8G), Y. Berra (2G)								

MONTHLY RECORD

	APR.	MAY	JUNE	JULY	AUG.	SEPT.	OCT.	FINAL
WINS	6	11	9	8	9	7	0	50
LOSSES	10	19	21	20	20	19	3	112
STANDING	10	10	10	10	10	10	10	10
GAMES BEHIND	4.5	12	19.5	26.5	32.5	45	47	47

MANAGER	W	L	PCT
Casey Stengel	31	64	.326
Wes Westrum	19	48	.284

TEAM STATISTICS

	W	L	PCT	GB	R	OR	Batting 2B	3B	HR	BA	SA	SB	Fielding E	DP	FA	Pitching CG	BB	SO	ShO	SV	ERA
LA	97	65	.599		608	521	193	32	78	.245	.335	172	134	135	.978	58	425	1079	23	34	2.81
SF	95	67	.586	2	682	593	169	43	159	.252	.385	47	148	124	.976	42	408	1060	17	42	3.20
PIT	90	72	.556	7	675	580	217	57	111	.265	.382	51	152	189	.976	49	469	882	17	27	3.01
CIN	89	73	.549	8	825	704	268	61	183	.273	.439	82	117	142	.980	43	587	1113	9	34	3.88
MIL	86	76	.531	11	708	633	243	28	196	.256	.416	64	140	145	.977	43	541	966	4	38	3.52
PHI	85	76	.528	11.5	654	667	205	53	144	.250	.384	46	157	153	.975	50	466	1071	18	21	3.53
STL	80	81	.497	16.5	707	674	234	46	109	.254	.371	100	130	152	.979	40	467	916	11	35	3.77
CHI	72	90	.444	25	635	723	202	33	134	.238	.358	65	171	166	.974	33	481	855	9	35	3.78
HOU	65	97	.401	32	569	711	188	42	97	.237	.340	90	166	130	.973	29	388	931	7	26	3.84
NY	50	112	.309	47	495	752	203	27	107	.221	.327	28	171	153	.973	29	498	776	11	14	4.06
LEAGUE TOTAL					6558	6558	2122	422	1318	.249	.374	745	1486	1489	.977	416	4730	9649	126	306	3.53

TOTAL PITCHING

PITCHER	T	W	L	PCT	ERA	SV	G	GS	CG	IP	H	BB	SO	R	ER	ShO	H/9	BB/9	SO/9
Jack Fisher	R	8	24	.250	3.94	1	43	36	10	253.2	252	68	116	121	111	0	8.94	2.41	4.12
Al Jackson	L	8	20	.286	4.34	1	37	31	7	205.1	217	61	120	111	99	3	9.51	2.67	5.26
Warren Spahn	L	4	12	.250	4.36	0	20	19	5	126	140	35	56	70	61	0	10.00	2.50	4.00
Galen Cisco	R	4	8	.333	4.49	0	35	17	1	112.1	119	51	58	63	56	1	9.53	4.09	4.65
Tug McGraw	L	2	7	.222	3.32	1	37	9	2	97.2	88	48	57	47	36	0	8.11	4.42	5.25
Tom Parsons	R	1	10	.091	4.67	1	35	11	1	90.2	108	17	58	53	47	1	10.72	1.69	5.76
Gary Kroll	R	6	6	.500	4.45	1	32	11	1	87	83	41	62	48	43	0	8.59	4.24	6.41
Larry Bearnarth	R	3	5	.375	4.60	1	40	3	0	60.2	75	28	16	43	31	0	11.13	4.15	2.37
Frank Lary	R	1	3	.250	2.98	1	14	7	0	57.1	48	16	23	24	19	0	7.53	2.51	3.61
Larry Miller	L	1	4	.200	5.02	0	28	5	0	57.1	66	25	36	32	32	0	10.36	3.92	5.65
Gordie Richardson	L	2	2	.500	3.78	2	35	0	0	52.1	41	16	43	27	22	0	7.05	2.75	7.39
Darrell Sutherland	R	3	1	.750	2.81	0	18	2	0	48	33	17	16	16	15	0	6.19	3.19	3.00
Jim Bethke	R	2	0	1.000	4.28	0	25	0	0	40	41	22	19	24	19	0	9.23	4.95	4.28
Dennis Ribant	R	1	3	.250	3.82	3	19	1	0	35.1	29	6	13	16	15	0	7.39	1.53	3.31
Rob Gardner	L	0	2	.000	3.21	0	5	4	0	28	23	7	19	13	10	0	7.39	2.25	6.11
Carl Willey	R	1	2	.333	4.18	0	13	3	1	28	30	15	13	13	13	0	9.64	4.82	4.18
Dick Selma	R	2	1	.667	3.71	0	4	4	1	26.2	22	9	26	11	11	1	7.43	3.04	8.78
Dave Eilers	R	1	1	.500	4.00	2	11	0	0	18	20	4	9	11	8	0	10.00	2.00	4.50
Dennis Musgraves	R	0	0	–	0.56	0	5	1	0	16	11	7	11	2	1	0	6.19	3.94	6.19
Bob Moorhead	R	0	0	1.000	4.40	0	9	0	0	14.1	16	5	5	7	7	0	10.05	3.14	3.14
TEAM TOTAL		50	112	.309	4.06	14	465	164	29	1454.2	1462	498	776	752	656	6	9.05	3.08	4.80

STARTING PITCHING / RELIEF PITCHING

PITCHER	W	L	PCT	ERA	GS	CG	IP	H	BB	SO	W	L	PCT	ERA	SV	G	IP	H	BB	SO
J. Fisher	8	22	.266	4.00	36	10	243	242	63	110	0	2	.000	2.53	1	7	10.2	10	5	6
A. Jackson	8	20	.285	4.45	31	7	194.1	207	59	112	0	0	–	2.45	1	6	11	10	2	8
W. Spahn	4	12	.250	4.32	19	5	125	139	35	56	0	0	–	9.00	0	1	1	1	0	0
G. Cisco	4	8	.333	3.76	17	1	83.2	80	38	36	0	0	–	6.59	0	18	28.2	39	13	22
T. McGraw	2	6	.250	3.54	9	2	56	47	23	28	0	1	.000	3.02	1	28	41.2	41	25	29
T. Parsons	1	7	.125	4.34	11	1	58	66	11	30	0	3	.000	5.23	1	24	32.2	42	6	28
G. Kroll	2	5	.285	6.22	11	1	46.1	56	27	25	4	1	.800	2.43	1	21	40.2	27	14	37
L. Bearnarth	0	2	.000	4.50	3	0	14	18	6	3	3	3	.500	4.63	1	37	46.2	57	22	13
F. Lary	1	3	.250	3.65	7	0	44.1	42	15	19	0	0	–	0.69	1	7	13	6	1	4
L. Miller	0	4	.000	6.87	5	0	18.1	26	10	12	1	0	1.000	4.15	0	23	39	40	15	24
D. Sutherland	0	1	.000	4.15	2	0	13	11	4	5	3	0	1.000	2.31	0	16	35	22	13	11
D. Ribant	0	0	–	0.00	1	0	11	6	1	6	1	3	.250	5.55	3	18	24.1	23	5	7
R. Gardner	0	2	.000	3.33	4	0	27	22	5	19	0	0	–	0.00	0	1	1	1	2	0
C. Willey	1	2	.333	4.60	3	1	15.2	17	11	8	0	0	–	3.65	0	10	12.1	13	4	5
D. Musgraves	0	0	–	1.29	1	0	7	7	1	3	0	0	–	0.00	0	4	9	4	6	8
TEAM TOTAL	33	95	.258	6.00	164	29	983.1	1008	318	498	17	17	.500	3.82	14	301	471.1	454	180	278

POS	Player	B	G	AB	H	2B	3B	HR	HR %	R	RBI	BB	SO	SB	Pinch Hit AB	Pinch Hit H	BA	SA
REGULARS																		
1B	Ed Kranepool	L	146	464	118	15	2	16	3.4	51	57	41	66	1	7	1	.254	.399
2B	Ron Hunt ★	R	132	479	138	19	2	3	0.6	63	33	41	34	8	8	2	.288	.355
SS	Ed Bressoud	R	133	405	91	15	5	10	2.5	48	49	47	107	2	12	2	.225	.360
3B	Ken Boyer	R	136	496	132	28	2	14	2.8	62	61	30	64	4	7	3	.266	.415
RF	Al Luplow	L	111	334	84	9	1	7	2.1	31	31	38	46	2	19	5	.251	.347
CF	Cleon Jones	R	139	495	136	16	4	8	1.6	74	57	30	62	16	11	0	.275	.372
LF	Ron Swoboda	R	112	342	76	9	4	8	2.3	34	50	31	76	4	19	8	.222	.342
C	Jerry Grote	R	120	317	75	12	2	3	0.9	26	31	40	81	4	5	1	.237	.315
SUBSTITUTES																		
UT	Chuck Hiller	L	108	254	71	8	2	2	0.8	25	14	15	22	0	45	15	.280	.350
SS	Roy McMillan	R	76	220	47	9	1	1	0.5	24	12	20	25	1	5	2	.214	.277
SS	Bud Harrelson	B	33	99	22	2	4	0	0.0	20	4	13	23	7	2	1	.222	.323
1B	Dick Stuart	R	31	87	19	0	0	4	4.6	7	13	9	26	0	5	0	.218	.356
OF	Larry Elliot	L	65	199	49	14	2	5	2.5	24	32	17	46	0	10	2	.246	.412
OF	Johnny Lewis	L	65	166	32	6	1	5	3.0	21	20	21	43	2	16	2	.193	.331
O1	Jim Hickman	R	58	160	38	7	0	4	2.5	15	16	13	34	2	11	1	.238	.356
OF	Billy Murphy	R	84	135	31	4	1	3	2.2	15	13	7	34	1	25	5	.230	.341
OF	Danny Napoleon	R	12	33	7	2	0	0	0.0	2	0	1	10	0	1	0	.212	.273
OF	Shaun Fitzmaurice	R	9	13	2	0	0	0	0.0	2	0	2	6	1	1	0	.154	.154
C	Johnny Stephenson	L	63	143	28	1	1	1	0.7	17	11	8	28	0	25	4	.196	.238
C1	Hawk Taylor	R	53	109	19	2	0	3	2.8	5	12	3	19	0	28	4	.174	.275
C	Greg Goossen	R	13	32	6	0	0	1	3.1	1	5	1	11	0	2	0	.188	.344
C	Choo Choo Coleman	L	6	16	3	0	0	0	0.0	2	0	0	4	0	0	0	.188	.188
PH	Lou Klimchock	L	5	5	0	0	0	0	0.0	0	0	0	3	0	5	0	.000	.000
PITCHERS																		
P	Jack Fisher	R	38	67	6	2	0	0	0.0	2	0	7	26	0	0	0	.090	.119
P	Dennis Ribant	R	40	61	12	1	0	0	0.0	3	5	1	11	0	0	0	.197	.213
P	Bob Shaw	R	26	50	13	0	0	0	0.0	1	2	4	15	0	0	0	.260	.260
P	Rob Gardner	R	43	41	7	1	0	0	0.0	1	0	0	12	0	0	0	.171	.195
P	Jack Hamilton	R	57	38	5	0	0	0	0.0	2	0	1	13	0	0	0	.132	.132
P	Bob Friend	R	22	29	1	0	0	0	0.0	1	1	0	17	0	0	0	.034	.034
P	Tug McGraw	R	15	17	4	0	0	0	0.0	3	0	1	1	0	0	0	.235	.235
P	Bill Hepler	L	37	14	3	0	0	0	0.0	0	0	0	7	0	0	0	.214	.214
P	Dick Selma	B	31	14	1	0	0	0	0.0	1	1	2	7	0	0	0	.071	.214
P	Jerry Arrigo	L	17	10	5	2	0	0	0.0	2	3	2	1	0	0	0	.500	.700
P	Larry Bearnarth	R	29	9	1	1	0	0	0.0	1	0	0	3	0	0	0	.111	.222
P	Ralph Terry	R	11	6	1	0	0	0	0.0	1	0	0	3	0	0	0	.167	.167
P	Dick Rusteck	R	8	5	0	0	0	0	0.0	0	0	0	3	0	0	0	.000	.000
P	Darrell Sutherland	R	31	3	2	0	0	0	0.0	1	0	0	1	0	0	0	.667	.667
P	Larry Miller	L	4	2	1	0	0	0	0.0	0	0	0	1	0	0	0	.500	.500
P	Gordie Richardson	R	15	1	0	0	0	0	0.0	0	0	0	1	0	0	0	.000	.000
P	Dave Eilers	R	23	1	0	0	0	0	0.0	0	0	0	0	0	0	0	.000	.000
P	Dallas Green	L	4	0	0	0	0	0	–	0	0	0	0	0	0	0	–	–
P	Nolan Ryan	R	2	0	0	0	0	0	–	0	0	0	0	0	0	0	–	–
	TEAM TOTAL			5371	1286	187	35	98	1.8	587	534	446	992	55	269	58	.239	.342

INDIVIDUAL FIELDING

POS	Player	T	G	PO	A	E	DP	TC/G	FA
1B	E. Kranepool	L	132	1161	85	10	100	9.5	.992
	D. Stuart	R	23	216	13	6	20	10.2	.974
	J. Hickman	R	17	120	12	1	14	7.8	.992
	H. Taylor (13G), E. Bressoud (9G), K. Boyer (2G)								
2B	R. Hunt ★	R	123	295	384	21	81	5.7	.970
	C. Hiller	R	45	85	123	4	31	4.7	.981
	E. Bressoud (7G)								
SS	E. Bressoud	R	94	135	252	16	52	4.3	.960
	R. McMillan	R	71	112	203	8	35	4.5	.975
	B. Harrelson	R	29	52	91	1	26	5.0	.993
	R. Hunt (1G)								
3B	K. Boyer	R	130	113	292	21	33	3.3	.951
	E. Bressoud	R	32	20	68	5	9	2.9	.946
	C. Hiller (14G), J. Grote (2G), R. Hunt (1G)								
OF	C. Jones	L	129	275	10	6	2	2.3	.979
	R. Swoboda	R	97	145	7	2	0	1.6	.987
	A. Luplow	R	101	147	4	2	1	1.5	.987
	L. Elliot	L	54	73	10	8	0	1.7	.912
	J. Lewis	R	49	77	2	1	1	1.6	.988
	J. Hickman	R	45	63	5	1	2	1.5	.986
	B. Murphy	R	57	57	6	3	1	1.2	.955
	E. Kranepool (11G), D. Napoleon (10G), C. Hiller (9G), S. Fitzmaurice (5G), J. Stephenson (1G)								
C	J. Grote	R	115	516	55	11	7	5.1	.981
	J. Stephenson	R	52	187	30	6	4	4.3	.973
	H. Taylor	R	29	80	13	0	3	3.2	1.000
	G. Goossen (11G), C. Coleman (5G)								

MONTHLY RECORD

	APR.	MAY	JUNE	JULY	AUG.	SEPT.	OCT.	FINAL
WINS	5	10	14	18	11	8	0	66
LOSSES	6	16	19	14	21	17	2	95
STANDING	7	9	9	9	9	9	9	9
GAMES BEHIND	3	10.5	16	12.5	20.5	27.5	28.5	28.5

MANAGER	W	L	PCT
Wes Westrum	66	95	.410

TEAM STATISTICS

	W	L	PCT	GB	R	OR	2B	3B	HR	BA	SA	SB	E	DP	FA	CG	BB	SO	ShO	SV	ERA
LA	95	67	.586		606	490	201	27	108	.256	.362	94	133	128	.978	52	356	1084	20	35	2.62
SF	93	68	.578	1.5	675	626	195	31	181	.248	.392	29	168	131	.973	52	359	973	14	27	3.24
PIT	92	70	.568	3	759	641	238	66	158	.279	.428	64	141	215	.978	35	463	898	12	43	3.52
PHI	87	75	.537	8	696	640	224	49	117	.258	.378	56	113	147	.982	52	412	928	15	23	3.57
ATL	85	77	.525	10	782	683	220	32	207	.263	.424	59	154	139	.975	37	485	884	10	36	3.68
STL	83	79	.512	12	571	577	196	61	108	.251	.368	144	145	166	.977	47	448	892	19	32	3.11
CIN	76	84	.475	18	692	702	232	33	149	.260	.395	70	122	133	.979	28	490	1043	10	35	4.08
HOU	72	90	.444	23	612	695	203	35	112	.255	.365	90	174	126	.971	34	391	929	13	26	3.76
NY	66	95	.410	28.5	587	761	187	35	98	.239	.342	55	159	171	.975	37	521	773	9	22	4.17
CHI	59	103	.364	36	644	809	203	43	140	.254	.380	76	166	132	.974	28	479	908	6	24	4.33
LEAGUE TOTAL					6624	6624	2099	412	1378	.256	.384	737	1475	1488	.977	402	4404	9312	128	303	3.60

TOTAL PITCHING

PITCHER	T	W	L	PCT	ERA	SV	G	GS	CG	IP	H	BB	SO	R	ER	ShO	H/9	BB/9	SO/9
Jack Fisher	R	11	14	.440	3.68	0	38	33	10	230	229	54	127	108	94	2	8.96	2.11	4.97
Dennis Ribant	R	11	9	.550	3.20	3	39	26	10	188.1	184	40	84	78	67	1	8.79	1.91	4.01
Bob Shaw	R	11	10	.524	3.92	0	26	25	7	167.2	171	42	104	85	73	2	9.18	2.25	5.58
Jack Hamilton	R	6	13	.316	3.93	13	57	13	3	148.2	138	88	93	89	65	1	8.35	5.33	5.63
Rob Gardner	L	4	8	.333	5.12	1	41	17	3	133.2	147	64	74	82	76	0	9.90	4.31	4.98
Bob Friend	R	5	8	.385	4.40	1	22	12	2	86	101	16	30	52	42	1	10.57	1.67	3.14
Dick Selma	R	4	6	.400	4.24	1	30	7	0	80.2	84	39	58	47	38	0	9.37	4.35	6.47
Bill Hepler	L	3	3	.500	3.52	0	37	3	0	69	71	51	25	30	27	0	9.26	6.65	3.26
Tug McGraw	L	2	9	.182	5.34	0	15	12	1	62.1	72	25	34	38	37	0	10.40	3.61	4.91
Larry Bearnarth	R	2	3	.400	4.45	0	29	1	0	54.2	59	20	27	31	27	0	9.71	3.29	4.45
Darrell Sutherland	R	2	0	1.000	4.87	1	31	0	0	44.1	60	25	23	25	24	0	12.18	5.08	4.67
Jerry Arrigo	L	3	3	.500	3.74	0	17	5	0	43.1	47	16	28	20	18	0	9.76	3.32	5.82
Dave Eilers	R	1	1	.500	4.67	0	23	0	0	34.2	39	7	14	18	18	0	10.13	1.82	3.63
Ralph Terry	R	0	1	.000	4.74	1	11	1	0	24.2	27	11	14	14	13	0	9.85	4.01	5.11
Dick Rusteck	L	1	2	.333	3.00	0	8	3	1	24	24	8	9	10	8	1	9.00	3.00	3.38
Gordie Richardson	L	0	2	.000	9.16	0	15	1	0	18.2	24	6	15	19	19	0	11.57	2.89	7.23
Larry Miller	L	0	2	.000	7.56	0	4	1	0	8.1	9	4	7	7	7	0	9.72	4.32	7.56
Dallas Green	R	0	0	–	5.40	0	4	0	0	5	6	2	1	3	3	0	10.80	3.60	1.80
Nolan Ryan	R	0	1	.000	15.00	0	2	1	0	3	5	3	6	5	5	0	15.00	9.00	18.00
TEAM TOTAL		66	95	.410	4.17	22	449	161	37	1427	1497	521	773	761	661	8	9.44	3.29	4.88

STARTING PITCHING / RELIEF PITCHING

PITCHER	W	L	PCT	ERA	GS	CG	IP	H	BB	SO	W	L	PCT	ERA	SV	G	IP	H	BB	SO
J. Fisher	10	14	.416	3.83	33	10	218.1	218	50	118	1	0	1.000	0.77	0	5	11.2	11	4	9
D. Ribant	11	9	.550	3.50	26	10	164.2	168	34	71	0	0	–	1.14	3	13	23.2	16	6	13
B. Shaw	11	9	.550	3.76	25	7	167.1	165	42	104	0	1	.000	81.00	0	1	.1	6	0	0
J. Hamilton	4	7	.363	3.86	13	3	74.2	60	37	41	2	6	.250	4.01	13	44	74	78	51	52
R. Gardner	3	7	.300	4.97	17	3	99.2	109	41	54	1	1	.500	5.56	1	24	34	38	23	20
B. Friend	4	4	.500	4.46	12	2	66.2	82	8	25	1	4	.200	4.19	1	10	19.1	19	8	5
D. Selma	0	4	.000	4.55	7	0	31.2	36	15	16	4	2	.667	4.04	1	23	49	48	24	42
B. Hepler	0	2	.000	3.63	3	0	17.1	14	15	5	3	1	.750	3.48	0	34	51.2	57	36	20
T. McGraw	2	9	.181	5.52	12	1	60.1	70	24	31	0	0	–	0.00	0	3	2	2	1	3
L. Bearnarth	0	1	.000	15.43	1	0	2.1	5	2	1	2	2	.500	3.96	0	28	52.1	54	18	26
J. Arrigo	1	3	.250	3.25	5	0	27.2	32	7	17	2	0	1.000	4.60	0	12	15.2	15	9	11
R. Terry	0	0	–	6.75	1	0	5.1	6	2	3	0	1	.000	4.19	1	10	19.1	21	9	11
D. Rusteck	1	2	.333	3.86	3	1	14	16	3	4	0	0	–	1.80	0	5	10	8	5	5
G. Richardson	0	1	.000	20.25	1	0	1.1	3	1	0	0	1	.000	8.31	1	14	17.1	21	5	15
L. Miller	0	1	.000	7.20	1	0	5	5	3	4	0	1	.000	8.10	0	3	3.1	4	1	3
N. Ryan	0	1	.000	36.00	1	0	1	4	2	3	0	0	–	4.50	0	1	2	1	1	3
TEAM TOTAL	47	74	.388	6.21	161	37	957.1	993	286	497	19	21	.475	4.20	22	288	469.2	504	235	276

POS	Player	B	G	AB	H	2B	3B	HR	HR %	R	RBI	BB	SO	SB	Pinch Hit AB	Pinch Hit H	BA	SA
REGULARS																		
1B	Ed Kranepool	L	141	469	126	17	1	10	2.1	37	54	37	51	0	9	1	.269	.373
2B	Jerry Buchek	R	124	411	97	11	2	14	3.4	35	41	26	101	3	9	2	.236	.375
SS	Bud Harrelson	B	151	540	137	16	4	1	0.2	59	28	48	64	12	0	0	.254	.304
3B	Ed Charles	R	101	323	77	13	2	3	0.9	32	31	24	58	4	10	1	.238	.319
RF	Ron Swoboda	R	134	449	126	17	3	13	2.9	47	53	41	96	3	9	2	.281	.419
CF	Cleon Jones	R	129	411	101	10	5	5	1.2	46	30	19	57	12	13	2	.246	.331
LF	Tommy Davis	R	154	577	174	32	0	16	2.8	72	73	31	71	9	4	0	.302	.440
C	Jerry Grote	R	120	344	67	8	0	4	1.2	25	23	14	65	2	2	0	.195	.253
SUBSTITUTES																		
UT	Bob Johnson	R	90	230	80	8	3	5	2.2	26	27	12	29	1	31	12	.348	.474
3B	Ken Boyer	R	56	166	39	7	2	3	1.8	17	13	26	22	2	7	1	.235	.355
UT	Bob Heise	R	16	62	20	4	0	0	0.0	7	3	3	1	0	0	0	.323	.387
2S	Phil Linz	R	24	58	12	2	0	0	0.0	8	1	4	10	0	5	0	.207	.241
2B	Chuck Hiller	L	25	54	5	3	0	0	0.0	0	3	2	11	0	12	2	.093	.148
23	Ken Boswell	L	11	40	9	3	0	1	2.5	2	4	1	5	0	1	0	.225	.375
3B	Joe Moock	L	13	40	9	2	0	0	0.0	2	5	0	7	0	1	0	.225	.275
UT	Sandy Alomar	B	15	22	0	0	0	0	0.0	1	0	0	6	0	0	0	.000	.000
2B	Bart Shirley	R	6	12	0	0	0	0	0.0	1	0	0	5	0	2	0	.000	.000
2B	Kevin Collins	L	4	10	1	0	0	0	0.0	0	0	0	3	1	2	0	.100	.100
OF	Larry Stahl	L	71	155	37	5	0	1	0.6	9	18	8	25	2	30	5	.239	.290
OF	Tommie Reynolds	B	101	136	28	1	0	2	1.5	16	9	11	26	1	22	5	.206	.257
OF	Al Luplow	L	41	112	23	1	0	3	2.7	11	9	8	19	0	14	1	.205	.295
OF	Don Bosch	B	44	93	13	0	1	0	0.0	7	2	5	24	3	3	0	.140	.161
OF	Amos Otis	R	19	59	13	2	0	0	0.0	6	1	5	13	0	0	0	.220	.254
OF	Johnny Lewis	L	13	34	4	1	0	0	0.0	2	2	2	11	0	4	0	.118	.147
C	John Sullivan	L	65	147	32	5	0	0	0.0	4	6	6	26	0	26	4	.218	.252
C	Greg Goossen	R	37	69	11	1	0	0	0.0	2	3	4	26	0	20	4	.159	.174
C	Hawk Taylor	R	13	37	9	3	0	0	0.0	3	4	2	8	0	2	0	.243	.324
PITCHERS																		
P	Tom Seaver ★	R	36	77	11	0	0	0	0.0	5	5	8	24	0	0	0	.143	.169
P	Jack Fisher	R	39	70	7	1	0	0	0.0	3	3	3	23	0	0	0	.100	.114
P	Don Cardwell	R	27	38	6	1	0	1	2.6	1	3	3	15	0	1	0	.158	.263
P	Bob Shaw	R	23	25	1	0	0	0	0.0	0	0	0	10	0	0	0	.040	.040
P	Danny Frisella	L	14	23	2	1	0	0	0.0	1	1	1	8	1	0	0	.087	.130
P	Dick Selma	R	43	22	2	0	0	0	0.0	2	0	0	10	0	0	0	.091	.091
P	Bob Hendley	R	15	18	2	0	0	0	0.0	1	1	2	15	0	0	0	.111	.111
P	Cal Koonce	R	13	13	2	0	0	0	0.0	1	0	0	4	0	0	0	.154	.154
P	Bill Denehy	R	15	9	0	0	0	0	0.0	1	0	1	5	0	0	0	.000	.000
P	Dennis Bennett	L	8	8	2	0	0	0	0.0	0	0	0	3	0	1	0	.250	.250
P	Bill Graham	R	5	8	1	0	0	0	0.0	0	1	0	2	0	0	0	.125	.125
P	Ron Taylor	R	50	7	0	0	0	0	0.0	0	0	0	5	0	0	0	.000	.000
P	Les Rohr	L	3	6	0	0	0	0	0.0	0	0	0	3	0	0	0	.000	.000
P	Chuck Estrada	R	9	5	0	0	0	0	0.0	0	0	0	3	0	0	0	.000	.000
P	Jack Hamilton	R	17	5	1	0	0	1	20.0	2	4	0	1	0	0	0	.200	.800
P	Jack Lamabe	R	16	5	0	0	0	0	0.0	0	0	1	3	0	0	0	.000	.000
P	Tug McGraw	R	4	4	1	1	0	0	0.0	1	0	0	1	0	0	0	.250	.500
P	Hal Reniff	R	29	4	0	0	0	0	0.0	0	0	0	4	0	0	0	.000	.000
P	Don Shaw	L	40	3	0	0	0	0	0.0	1	0	2	1	0	0	0	.000	.000
P	Nick Willhite	L	4	2	0	0	0	0	0.0	0	0	0	0	0	0	0	.000	.000
P	Jerry Koosman	R	9	2	0	0	0	0	0.0	0	0	1	1	0	0	0	.000	.000
P	Bill Connors	R	6	1	0	0	0	0	0.0	0	0	0	0	0	0	0	.000	.000
P	Joe Grzenda	R	11	1	0	0	0	0	0.0	0	0	0	0	0	0	0	.000	.000
P	Billy Wynne	B	6	1	0	0	0	0	0.0	0	0	0	0	0	0	0	.000	.000
P	Jerry Hinsley	R	2	0	0	0	0	0	–	0	0	0	0	0	0	0	–	–
P	Ralph Terry	R	2	0	0	0	0	0	–	0	0	0	0	0	0	0	–	–
P	Al Schmelz	R	2	0	0	0	0	0	–	0	0	0	0	0	0	0	–	–
TEAM TOTAL				5417	1288	178	23	83	1.5	498	461	362	981	58	240	42	.238	.325

INDIVIDUAL FIELDING

POS	Player	T	G	PO	A	E	DP	TC/G	FA
1B	E. Kranepool	L	139	1137	87	10	103	8.9	.992
	R. Swoboda	R	20	143	17	4	7	8.2	.976
	B. Johnson	R	23	129	9	4	14	6.2	.972
	K. Boyer (8G), T. Davis (1G)								
2B	J. Buchek	R	95	203	255	11	54	4.9	.977
	B. Johnson	R	39	72	82	2	21	4.0	.987
	C. Hiller (14G), B. Heise (12G), P. Linz (11G),								
	K. Boswell (6G), B. Shirley (3G), S. Alomar (2G),								
	K. Collins (2G)								
SS	B. Harrelson	R	149	254	467	32	88	5.1	.958
	B. Johnson (14G), S. Alomar (10G), J. Buchek (9G),								
	P. Linz (8G), B. Heise (3G)								
3B	E. Charles	R	89	85	201	17	16	3.4	.944
	K. Boyer	R	44	27	84	6	7	2.7	.949
	J. Buchek	R	17	17	29	0	3	2.7	1.000
	J. Moock (12G), T. Reynolds (5G), K. Boswell (4G),								
	S. Alomar (3G), B. Heise (2G), B. Johnson (1G),								
	P. Linz (1G), A. Otis (1G)								

POS	Player	T	G	PO	A	E	DP	TC/G	FA
OF	T. Davis	R	149	231	5	6	0	1.6	.975
	C. Jones	L	115	210	5	5	3	1.9	.977
	R. Swoboda	R	108	190	8	9	0	1.9	.957
	L. Stahl	L	43	90	4	3	0	2.3	.969
	T. Reynolds	R	72	65	3	2	1	1.0	.971
	A. Luplow	R	33	55	1	2	0	1.8	.966
	D. Bosch	R	39	55	2	0	0	1.5	1.000
	A. Otis	R	16	22	2	0	1	1.5	1.000
	J. Lewis (10G), P. Linz (1G)								
C	J. Grote	R	119	609	62	7	8	5.7	.990
	J. Sullivan	R	57	201	17	2	2	3.9	.991
	G. Goossen	R	23	101	7	3	2	4.8	.973
	H. Taylor (12G), T. Reynolds (1G)								

MONTHLY RECORD

	APR.	MAY	JUNE	JULY	AUG.	SEPT.	OCT.	FINAL
WINS	6	8	11	14	12	10	0	61
LOSSES	11	15	18	17	18	21	1	101
STANDING	9	10	10	10	10	10	10	10
GAMES BEHIND	7.5	12	18	22	30	39.5	40.5	40.5

MANAGER	W	L	PCT
Wes Westrum	57	94	.377
Salty Parker	4	7	.364

TEAM STATISTICS

	W	L	PCT	GB	R	OR	2B	3B	HR	BA	SA	SB	E	DP	FA	CG	BB	SO	ShO	SV	ERA
							Batting						**Fielding**			**Pitching**					
STL	101	60	.627		695	557	225	40	115	.263	.379	**102**	140	127	.977	44	431	956	17	**45**	3.05
SF	91	71	.562	10.5	652	**551**	201	39	140	.245	.372	22	134	149	.979	**64**	453	990	17	25	**2.92**
CHI	87	74	.540	14	**702**	624	211	49	128	.251	.378	63	**121**	143	**.980**	47	463	888	7	28	3.48
CIN	87	75	.537	14.5	604	563	251	54	109	.248	.372	92	**121**	124	.980	34	498	**1065**	**18**	39	3.05
PHI	82	80	.506	19.5	612	581	221	47	103	.242	.357	79	137	174	.978	46	403	967	17	23	3.10
PIT	81	81	.500	20.5	679	693	193	**62**	91	**.277**	**.380**	79	141	**186**	.978	35	561	820	5	35	3.74
ATL	77	85	.475	24.5	631	640	191	29	**158**	.240	.372	55	138	148	.978	35	449	862	5	32	3.47
LA	73	89	.451	28.5	519	595	203	38	82	.236	.332	56	160	144	.975	41	**393**	967	17	24	3.21
HOU	69	93	.426	32.5	626	742	**259**	46	93	.249	.364	88	159	120	.974	35	485	1060	8	21	4.03
NY	61	101	.377	40.5	498	672	178	23	83	.238	.325	58	157	147	.975	36	536	893	10	19	3.73
LEAGUE TOTAL					6218	6218	2133	427	1102	.249	.363	694	1408	1462	.978	417	4672	9468	121	291	3.37

TOTAL PITCHING

PITCHER	T	W	L	PCT	ERA	SV	G	GS	CG	IP	H	BB	SO	R	ER	ShO	H/9	BB/9	SO/9
Tom Seaver ★	R	16	13	.552	2.76	0	35	34	18	251	224	78	170	85	77	2	8.03	2.80	6.10
Jack Fisher	R	9	**18**	.333	4.70	0	39	30	7	220.1	251	64	117	**121**	**115**	1	10.25	2.61	4.78
Don Cardwell	R	5	9	.357	3.57	0	26	16	3	118.1	112	39	71	55	47	3	8.52	2.97	5.40
Bob Shaw	R	3	9	.250	4.29	0	23	13	3	98.2	105	28	49	54	47	1	9.58	2.55	4.47
Dick Selma	R	2	4	.333	2.77	2	38	4	0	81.1	71	36	52	29	25	0	7.86	3.98	5.75
Danny Frisella	R	1	6	.143	3.41	0	14	11	0	74	68	33	51	32	28	0	8.27	4.01	6.20
Ron Taylor	R	4	6	.400	2.34	8	50	0	0	73	60	23	46	21	19	0	7.40	2.84	5.67
Bob Hendley	L	3	3	.500	3.44	0	15	13	2	70.2	65	28	36	35	27	0	8.28	3.57	4.58
Bill Denehy	R	1	7	.125	4.70	0	15	8	0	53.2	51	29	35	38	28	0	8.55	4.86	5.87
Don Shaw	L	4	5	.444	2.98	3	40	0	0	51.1	40	23	44	19	17	0	7.01	4.03	7.71
Cal Koonce	R	3	3	.500	2.80	0	11	6	2	45	45	7	24	16	14	1	9.00	1.40	4.80
Hal Reniff	R	3	3	.500	3.35	4	29	0	0	43	42	23	21	20	16	0	8.79	4.81	4.40
Jack Lamabe	R	0	3	.000	3.98	1	16	2	0	31.2	24	8	23	15	14	0	6.82	2.27	6.54
Jack Hamilton	R	2	0	1.000	3.73	1	17	1	0	31.1	24	16	22	15	13	0	6.89	4.60	6.32
Bill Graham	R	1	2	.333	2.63	0	5	3	1	27.1	20	11	14	10	8	0	6.59	3.62	4.61
Dennis Bennett	L	1	1	.500	5.13	0	8	6	0	26.1	37	7	14	15	15	0	12.65	2.39	4.78
Jerry Koosman	L	0	2	.000	6.04	0	9	3	0	22.1	22	19	11	17	15	0	8.87	7.66	4.43
Chuck Estrada	R	1	2	.333	9.41	0	9	2	0	22	28	17	15	24	23	0	11.45	6.95	6.14
Tug McGraw	L	0	3	.000	7.79	0	4	4	0	17.1	13	13	18	16	15	0	6.75	6.75	9.35
Les Rohr	L	2	1	.667	2.12	0	3	3	0	17	13	9	15	7	4	0	6.88	4.76	7.94
Joe Grzenda	L	0	0	–	2.16	0	11	0	0	16.2	14	8	9	4	4	0	7.56	4.32	4.86
Bill Connors	R	0	0	–	6.23	0	6	1	0	13	8	5	13	9	9	0	5.54	3.46	9.00
Billy Wynne	R	0	0	–	3.12	0	6	1	0	8.2	12	2	4	4	3	0	12.46	2.08	4.15
Nick Willhite	L	0	1	.000	8.64	0	4	1	0	8.1	9	5	9	8	8	0	9.72	5.40	9.72
Jerry Hinsley	R	0	0	–	3.60	0	2	0	0	5	6	4	3	2	2	0	10.80	7.20	5.40
Ralph Terry	R	0	0	–	0.00	0	2	0	0	3.1	1	0	5	0	0	0	2.70	0.00	13.50
Al Schmelz	R	0	0	–	3.00	0	2	0	0	3	4	1	2	1	1	0	12.00	3.00	6.00
TEAM TOTAL		61	101	.377	3.73	19	439	162	36	1433.2	1369	536	893	672	594	8	8.59	3.36	5.51

STARTING PITCHING / RELIEF PITCHING

PITCHER	W	L	PCT	ERA	GS	CG	IP	H	BB	SO	W	L	PCT	ERA	SV	G	IP	H	BB	SO
T. Seaver ★	16	12	.571	2.74	34	18	249.2	220	77	170	0	1	.000	6.75	0	1	1.1	4	1	0
J. Fisher	8	17	.320	4.81	30	7	205.2	238	58	106	1	1	.500	3.07	0	9	14.2	13	6	11
D. Cardwell	4	9	.307	3.82	16	3	96.2	94	30	62	1	0	1.000	2.49	0	10	21.2	18	9	9
B. Shaw	2	8	.200	4.48	13	3	76.1	80	25	33	1	1	.500	3.63	0	10	22.1	25	3	16
D. Selma	0	1	.000	5.82	4	0	17	22	11	10	2	3	.400	1.96	2	34	64.1	49	25	42
D. Frisella	1	6	.142	3.82	11	0	66	64	27	44	0	0	–	0.00	0	3	8	4	6	7
B. Hendley	3	3	.500	3.54	13	2	68.2	64	27	34	0	0	–	0.00	0	2	2	1	1	2
B. Denehy	1	7	.125	5.82	8	0	38.2	42	25	29	0	0	–	1.80	0	7	15	9	4	6
C. Koonce	3	3	.500	2.97	6	2	39.1	42	6	19	0	0	–	1.59	0	5	5.2	3	1	5
J. Lamabe	0	2	.000	5.40	2	0	8.1	7	1	5	0	1	.000	3.47	1	14	23.1	17	7	18
J. Hamilton	0	0	–	12.00	1	0	3	4	2	2	2	0	1.000	2.86	1	16	28.1	20	14	20
B. Graham	1	2	.333	1.96	3	1	23	16	9	14	0	0	–	6.23	0	2	4.1	4	2	0
D. Bennett	1	1	.500	5.18	6	0	24.1	35	5	12	0	0	–	4.50	0	2	2	2	2	2
J. Koosman	0	2	.000	8.18	3	0	11	13	11	7	0	0	–	3.97	0	6	11.1	9	8	4
C. Estrada	0	2	.000	12.79	2	0	6.1	6	7	4	1	0	1.000	8.04	0	7	15.2	22	10	11
B. Connors	0	0	–	9.00	1	0	4	4	2	3	0	0	–	5.00	0	5	9	4	3	10
B. Wynne	0	0	–	20.25	1	0	1.1	6	0	0	0	0	–	1.80	0	5	7.1	6	2	4
N. Willhite	0	1	.000	22.50	1	0	2	5	1	2	0	0	–	4.26	0	3	6.1	4	4	7
TEAM TOTAL	42	80	.344	5.48	162	36	975.2	988	346	589	19	21	.475	2.89	19	277	458	381	190	304

POS	Player	B	G	AB	H	2B	3B	HR	HR %	R	RBI	BB	SO	SB	Pinch Hit AB	Pinch Hit H	BA	SA
REGULARS
1B	Ed Kranepool	L	127	373	86	13	1	3	0.8	29	20	19	39	0	16	3	.231	.295
2B	Phil Linz	R	78	258	54	7	0	0	0.0	19	17	10	41	1	9	1	.209	.236
SS	Bud Harrelson	B	111	402	88	7	3	0	0.0	38	14	29	68	4	6	0	.219	.251
3B	Ed Charles	R	117	369	102	11	1	15	4.1	41	53	28	57	5	15	6	.276	.434
RF	Ron Swoboda	R	132	450	109	14	6	11	2.4	46	59	52	113	8	9	4	.242	.373
CF	Tommie Agee	R	132	368	80	12	3	5	1.4	30	17	15	103	13	3	1	.217	.307
LF	Cleon Jones	R	147	509	151	29	4	14	2.8	63	55	31	98	23	10	1	.297	.452
C	Jerry Grote ★	R	124	404	114	18	0	3	0.7	29	31	44	81	1	8	2	.282	.349
SUBSTITUTES
2B	Ken Boswell	L	75	284	74	7	2	4	1.4	37	11	16	27	7	6	1	.261	.342
S2	Al Weis	B	90	274	47	6	0	1	0.4	15	14	21	63	3	3	0	.172	.204
UT	Jerry Buchek	R	73	192	35	4	0	1	0.5	8	11	10	53	1	18	3	.182	.219
3B	Kevin Collins	L	58	154	31	5	2	1	0.6	12	13	7	37	0	14	0	.201	.279
1B	Greg Goossen	R	38	106	22	7	0	0	0.0	4	6	10	21	0	6	0	.208	.274
SS	Bob Heise	R	6	23	5	0	0	0	0.0	3	1	1	1	0	0	0	.217	.217
1B	Mike Jorgensen	L	8	14	2	1	0	0	0.0	0	0	0	4	0	4	0	.143	.214
OF	Art Shamsky	L	116	345	82	14	4	12	3.5	30	48	21	58	1	23	1	.238	.406
OF	Larry Stahl	L	53	183	43	7	2	3	1.6	15	10	21	38	3	3	1	.235	.344
OF	Don Bosch	B	50	111	19	1	0	3	2.7	14	7	9	33	0	9	1	.171	.261
C1	J. C. Martin	L	78	244	55	9	2	3	1.2	20	31	21	31	0	8	1	.225	.316
C	Duffy Dyer	R	1	3	1	0	0	0	0.0	0	0	1	1	0	0	0	.333	.333
PITCHERS
P	Tom Seaver ★	R	38	95	15	2	0	0	0.0	5	3	3	44	0	0	0	.158	.179
P	Jerry Koosman ★	R	35	91	7	1	0	1	1.1	3	4	3	62	0	0	0	.077	.121
P	Don Cardwell	R	30	61	3	0	0	1	1.6	3	4	0	34	0	0	0	.049	.098
P	Dick Selma	R	39	58	12	2	0	0	0.0	4	1	0	20	1	0	0	.207	.241
P	Nolan Ryan	R	21	44	5	0	0	0	0.0	2	2	2	29	0	0	0	.114	.114
P	Al Jackson	L	27	28	7	1	0	0	0.0	2	2	2	9	0	0	0	.250	.286
P	Jim McAndrew	R	12	22	1	0	0	0	0.0	1	0	1	15	0	0	0	.045	.045
P	Cal Koonce	R	55	14	0	0	0	0	0.0	0	0	2	8	0	0	0	.000	.000
P	Danny Frisella	L	19	12	1	0	0	0	0.0	0	0	0	7	1	0	0	.083	.083
P	Ron Taylor	R	58	9	0	0	0	0	0.0	0	0	0	6	0	0	0	.000	.000
P	Bill Short	L	34	2	0	0	0	0	0.0	0	0	0	2	0	0	0	.000	.000
P	Bill Connors	R	9	1	1	0	0	0	0.0	0	0	1	0	0	0	0	1.000	1.000
P	Les Rohr	L	2	0	0	0	0	0	–	0	0	1	0	0	0	0		
P	Don Shaw	L	7	0	0	0	0	0	–	0	0	0	0	0	0	0		
	TEAM TOTAL			5503	1252	178	30	81	1.5	473	434	379	1203	72	170	26	.228	.315

INDIVIDUAL FIELDING

POS	Player	T	G	PO	A	E	DP	TC/G	FA
1B	E. Kranepool	L	113	921	75	6	76	8.9	.994
	G. Goossen	R	30	217	22	2	18	8.0	.992
	A. Shamsky	L	17	111	6	2	6	7.0	.983
	J. Martin (14G), L. Stahl (9G), M. Jorgensen (4G),								
	E. Charles (2G)								
2B	K. Boswell	R	69	154	203	13	37	5.4	.965
	P. Linz	R	71	136	162	10	36	4.3	.968
	A. Weis	R	29	42	62	2	15	3.7	.981
	J. Buchek (12G), K. Collins (6G), B. Heise (1G)								
SS	B. Harrelson	R	106	199	317	15	58	5.0	.972
	A. Weis	R	59	96	180	12	28	4.9	.958
	B. Heise (6G), K. Collins (1G)								
3B	E. Charles	R	106	69	200	13	19	2.7	.954
	J. Buchek	R	37	30	70	7	7	2.9	.935
	K. Collins	R	40	28	57	4	7	2.2	.955
	A. Weis (2G)								

POS	Player	T	G	PO	A	E	DP	TC/G	FA
OF	C. Jones	L	139	226	7	9	0	1.7	.963
	R. Swoboda	R	125	217	14	6	4	1.9	.975
	T. Agee	R	127	216	6	5	2	1.8	.978
	A. Shamsky	L	82	128	6	1	2	1.6	.993
	L. Stahl	L	47	110	5	2	1	2.5	.983
	D. Bosch	R	33	73	3	2	1	2.4	.974
	J. Buchek (9G), E. Kranepool (2G)								
C	J. Grote ★	R	115	754	60	5	8	7.1	.994
	J. Martin	R	53	334	24	2	4	6.8	.994
	G. Goossen (2G), D. Dyer (1G)								

MONTHLY RECORD

	APR.	MAY	JUNE	JULY	AUG.	SEPT.	OCT.	FINAL
WINS	7	13	16	13	14	10	0	73
LOSSES	9	15	14	20	18	13	0	89
STANDING	9	9	7	8	9	9	9	9
GAMES BEHIND	5	4.5	9	21.5	24	24	24	24

MANAGER	W	L	PCT
Gil Hodges	73	89	.451

TEAM STATISTICS

	W	L	PCT	GB	R	OR	Batting 2B	3B	HR	BA	SA	SB	Fielding E	DP	FA	Pitching CG	BB	SO	ShO	SV	ERA
STL	97	65	.599		583	472	227	48	73	.249	.346	110	140	135	.977	63	375	971	30	32	2.49
SF	88	74	.543	9	599	529	162	33	108	.239	.341	50	162	125	.974	77	344	942	20	16	2.71
CHI	84	78	.519	13	612	611	203	43	130	.242	.366	41	119	149	.981	46	392	894	12	32	3.41
CIN	83	79	.512	14	690	673	281	36	106	.273	.389	59	144	144	.977	24	573	963	16	38	3.56
ATL	81	81	.500	16	514	549	179	31	80	.252	.339	83	125	139	.980	44	362	871	16	29	2.92
PIT	80	82	.494	17	583	532	180	44	80	.252	.343	130	139	162	.978	42	485	897	19	30	2.74
LA	76	86	.469	21	470	509	202	36	67	.230	.319	57	144	144	.977	38	414	994	23	31	2.69
PHI	76	86	.469	21	543	615	178	30	100	.233	.333	58	127	163	.979	42	421	935	12	27	3.36
NY	73	89	.451	24	473	499	178	30	81	.228	.315	72	133	142	.979	45	430	1014	25	32	2.72
HOU	72	90	.444	25	510	588	205	28	66	.231	.317	44	156	129	.974	50	479	1021	12	23	3.26
LEAGUE TOTAL					5577	5577	1995	359	891	.243	.341	704	1389	1432	.978	471	4275	9502	185	290	2.98

TOTAL PITCHING

PITCHER	T	W	L	PCT	ERA	SV	G	GS	CG	IP	H	BB	SO	R	ER	ShO	H/9	BB/9	SO/9
Tom Seaver ★	R	16	12	.571	2.20	1	36	35	14	278	224	48	205	73	68	5	7.25	1.55	6.64
Jerry Koosman ★	L	19	12	.613	2.08	0	35	34	17	263.2	221	69	178	72	61	7	7.54	2.36	6.08
Don Cardwell	R	7	13	.350	2.95	1	29	25	5	180	156	50	82	69	59	1	7.80	2.50	4.10
Dick Selma	R	9	10	.474	2.75	0	33	23	4	170.1	148	54	117	63	52	3	7.82	2.85	6.18
Nolan Ryan	R	6	9	.400	3.09	0	21	18	3	134	93	75	133	50	46	0	6.25	5.04	8.93
Cal Koonce	R	6	4	.600	2.42	11	55	2	0	96.2	80	32	50	27	26	0	7.45	2.98	4.66
Al Jackson	L	3	7	.300	3.69	3	25	9	0	92.2	88	17	59	42	38	0	8.55	1.65	5.73
Jim McAndrew	R	4	7	.364	2.28	0	12	12	2	79	66	17	46	20	20	1	7.52	1.94	5.24
Ron Taylor	R	1	5	.167	2.70	13	58	0	0	76.2	64	18	49	24	23	0	7.51	2.11	5.75
Danny Frisella	R	2	4	.333	3.91	2	19	4	0	50.2	53	17	47	23	22	0	9.41	3.02	8.35
Bill Short	L	0	3	.000	4.85	1	34	0	0	29.2	24	14	24	17	16	0	7.28	4.25	7.28
Bill Connors	R	0	1	.000	9.00	0	9	0	0	14	21	7	8	14	14	0	13.50	4.50	5.14
Don Shaw	L	0	0	–	0.75	0	7	0	0	12	3	5	11	1	1	0	2.25	3.75	8.25
Les Rohr	L	0	2	.000	4.50	0	2	1	0	6	9	7	5	4	3	0	13.50	10.50	7.50
TEAM TOTAL		73	89	.451	2.72	32	375	163	45	1483.1	1250	430	1014	499	449	17	7.58	2.61	6.15

STARTING PITCHING / RELIEF PITCHING

PITCHER	W	L	PCT	ERA	GS	CG	IP	H	BB	SO	W	L	PCT	ERA	SV	G	IP	H	BB	SO
T. Seaver ★	16	12	.571	2.21	35	14	277	224	48	204	0	0	–	0.00	1	1	1	0	0	1
J. Koosman ★	19	12	.612	2.08	34	17	263.2	221	69	178	0	0	–	0.00	0	1		0	0	0
D. Cardwell	7	13	.350	3.02	25	5	166.2	145	49	76	0	0	–	2.03	1	4	13.1	11	1	6
D. Selma	9	10	.473	2.94	23	4	156.1	141	48	104	0	0	–	0.64	0	10	14	7	6	13
N. Ryan	6	9	.400	3.01	18	3	125.2	86	67	130	0	0	–	4.32	0	3	8.1	7	8	3
C. Koonce	1	0	1.000	3.12	2	0	8.2	9	0	5	5	4	.556	2.35	11	53	88	71	32	45
A. Jackson	2	6	.250	4.42	9	0	57	59	11	33	1	1	.500	2.52	3	16	35.2	29	6	26
D. Frisella	2	2	.500	5.24	4	0	22.1	24	4	18	0	2	.000	2.86	2	15	28.1	29	13	29
L. Rohr	0	1	.000	4.91	1	0	3.2	8	3	3	0	1	.000	3.86	0	1	2.1	1	4	2
TEAM TOTAL	66	72	.478	3.48	163	45	1160	983	316	797	7	17	.292	2.92	32	212	323.1	267	114	217

POS	Player	B	G	AB	H	2B	3B	HR	HR %	R	RBI	BB	SO	SB	Pinch Hit AB	Pinch Hit H	BA	SA
REGULARS																		
1B	Ed Kranepool	L	112	353	84	9	2	11	3.1	36	49	37	32	3	7	1	.238	.368
2B	Ken Boswell	L	102	362	101	14	7	3	0.8	48	32	36	47	7	10	1	.279	.381
SS	Bud Harrelson	B	123	395	98	11	6	0	0.0	42	24	54	54	1	0	0	.248	.306
3B	Wayne Garrett	L	124	400	87	11	3	1	0.3	38	39	40	75	4	14	1	.218	.268
RF	Ron Swoboda	R	109	327	77	10	2	9	2.8	38	52	43	90	1	9	2	.235	.361
CF	Tommie Agee	R	149	565	153	23	4	26	4.6	97	76	59	137	12	3	1	.271	.464
LF	Cleon Jones ★	R	137	483	164	25	4	12	2.5	92	75	64	60	16	4	2	.340	.482
C	Jerry Grote	R	113	365	92	12	3	6	1.6	38	40	32	59	2	4	1	.252	.351
SUBSTITUTES																		
S2	Al Weis	R	103	247	53	9	2	2	0.8	20	23	15	51	3	3	0	.215	.291
32	Bobby Pfeil	R	62	211	49	9	0	0	0.0	20	10	7	27	0	9	5	.232	.275
1B	Donn Clendenon	R	72	202	51	5	0	12	5.9	31	37	19	62	3	19	2	.252	.455
3B	Ed Charles	R	61	169	35	8	1	3	1.8	21	18	18	31	4	12	4	.207	.320
3B	Kevin Collins	L	16	40	6	3	0	1	2.5	1	2	3	10	0	3	0	.150	.300
SS	Bob Heise	R	4	10	3	1	0	0	0.0	1	0	3	2	0	1	1	.300	.400
OF	Art Shamsky	L	100	303	91	9	3	14	4.6	42	47	36	32	1	13	5	.300	.488
OF	Rod Gaspar	B	118	215	49	6	1	1	0.5	26	14	25	19	7	25	4	.228	.279
OF	Amos Otis	R	48	93	14	3	1	0	0.0	6	4	6	27	1	10	1	.151	.204
OF	Jim Gosger	L	10	15	2	2	0	0	0.0	0	1	1	6	0	4	0	.133	.267
C	J. C. Martin	L	66	177	37	5	1	4	2.3	12	21	12	32	0	18	3	.209	.316
C	Duffy Dyer	R	29	74	19	3	1	3	4.1	5	12	4	22	0	8	2	.257	.446
PITCHERS																		
P	Tom Seaver ★	R	39	91	11	3	0	0	0.0	7	6	7	34	1	0	0	.121	.154
P	Jerry Koosman ★	R	32	84	4	0	0	0	0.0	1	1	1	46	0	0	0	.048	.048
P	Gary Gentry	R	35	74	6	1	0	0	0.0	2	1	1	52	0	0	0	.081	.095
P	Don Cardwell	R	30	47	8	0	0	1	2.1	3	5	0	26	0	0	0	.170	.234
P	Jim McAndrew	R	27	37	5	1	0	0	0.0	3	2	0	26	0	0	0	.135	.162
P	Nolan Ryan	R	25	29	3	0	0	0	0.0	3	3	3	18	0	0	0	.103	.103
P	Tug McGraw	R	43	24	4	1	0	0	0.0	1	3	1	6	0	0	0	.167	.208
P	Cal Koonce	R	40	17	4	0	0	0	0.0	1	1	0	7	0	0	0	.235	.235
P	Jack DiLauro	B	23	12	0	0	0	0	0.0	0	0	0	9	0	0	0	.000	.000
P	Ron Taylor	R	59	4	1	0	0	0	0.0	0	0	0	2	0	0	0	.250	.250
P	Al Jackson	L	9	1	0	0	0	0	0.0	0	0	0	0	0	0	0	.000	.000
P	Danny Frisella	L	3	1	0	0	0	0	0.0	0	0	0	0	0	0	0	.000	.000
P	Les Rohr	L	1	0	0	0	0	0	—	0	0	0	0	0	0	0	—	—
P	Bob Johnson	L	2	0	0	0	0	0	—	0	0	0	0	0	0	0	—	—
P	Jessie Hudson	L	1	0	0	0	0	0	—	0	0	0	0	0	0	0	—	—
TEAM TOTAL				5427	1311	184	41	109	2.0	632	598	527	1089	66	176	36	.242	.351

INDIVIDUAL FIELDING

POS	Player	T	G	PO	A	E	DP	TC/G	FA
1B	E. Kranepool	L	106	809	64	6	76	8.3	.993
	D. Clendenon	R	58	420	29	7	47	7.9	.985
	C. Jones ★	L	15	99	7	0	3	7.1	1.000
	A. Shamsky (9G), J. Martin (2G)								
2B	K. Boswell	R	96	190	229	18	51	4.6	.959
	W. Garrett	R	47	102	97	3	27	4.3	.985
	A. Weis	R	43	73	90	5	23	3.9	.970
	B. Pfeil (11G)								
SS	B. Harrelson	R	119	243	347	19	70	5.1	.969
	A. Weis	R	52	65	128	8	27	3.9	.960
	W. Garrett (9G), B. Heise (3G)								
3B	W. Garrett	R	72	40	115	8	10	2.3	.951
	E. Charles	R	52	37	86	7	9	2.5	.946
	B. Pfeil	R	49	32	88	3	8	2.5	.976
	K. Collins (14G), A. Otis (3G), A. Weis (1G)								
OF	T. Agee	R	146	334	7	5	0	2.4	.986
	C. Jones ★	L	122	223	4	2	0	1.9	.991
	R. Swoboda	R	97	163	5	2	0	1.8	.988
	A. Shamsky	L	78	117	2	1	2	1.5	.992
	R. Gaspar	L	91	104	12	2	6	1.3	.983
	A. Otis	R	35	46	3	0	0	1.4	1.000
	J. Gosger (5G), E. Kranepool (2G), B. Pfeil (2G), D. Clendenon (1G)								
C	J. Grote	R	112	718	63	7	11	7.0	.991
	J. Martin	R	48	275	9	1	2	5.9	.996
	D. Dyer	R	19	105	10	1	0	6.1	.991

MONTHLY RECORD

	APR.	MAY	JUNE	JULY	AUG.	SEPT.	OCT.	FINAL
WINS	9	12	19	15	21	23	1	100
LOSSES	11	12	9	12	10	7	1	62
STANDING	3	3	2	2	2	1	1	1
GAMES BEHIND	5.5	9	8	7	5			

MANAGER	W	L	PCT
Gil Hodges	100	62	.617

TEAM STATISTICS

	W	L	PCT	GB	R	OR	Batting 2B	3B	HR	BA	SA	SB	Fielding E	DP	FA	CG	Pitching BB	SO	ShO	SV	ERA
EAST																					
NY	100	62	.617		632	541	184	41	109	.242	.351	66	122	146	.980	51	517	1012	28	35	2.99
CHI	92	70	.568	8	720	611	215	40	142	.253	.384	30	136	149	.978	58	475	1017	22	27	3.34
PIT	88	74	.543	12	725	652	220	52	119	.277	.398	74	155	169	.975	39	553	1124	9	33	3.61
STL	87	75	.537	13	595	540	228	44	90	.253	.359	87	138	144	.977	63	511	1004	12	26	2.94
PHI	63	99	.389	37	645	745	227	35	137	.241	.372	73	137	157	.977	47	570	921	14	21	4.14
MON	52	110	.321	48	582	791	202	33	125	.240	.359	52	184	179	.970	26	702	973	8	21	4.33
WEST																					
ATL	93	69	.574		691	631	195	22	141	.258	.380	59	115	114	.981	38	438	893	7	42	3.53
SF	90	72	.556	3	713	636	187	28	136	.242	.361	71	169	155	.974	71	461	906	15	17	3.25
CIN	89	73	.549	4	798	768	224	42	171	.277	.422	79	167	158	.973	23	611	818	11	44	4.11
LA	85	77	.525	8	645	561	185	52	97	.254	.359	80	126	130	.980	47	420	975	20	31	3.08
HOU	81	81	.500	12	676	668	208	40	104	.240	.352	101	153	136	.974	52	547	1221	11	34	3.60
SD	52	110	.321	41	468	746	180	42	99	.225	.329	45	156	140	.974	16	592	764	9	25	4.24
LEAGUE TOTAL					7890	7890	2455	471	1470	.250	.369	817	1758	1777	.977	531	6397	11628	166	356	3.59

TOTAL PITCHING

PITCHER	T	W	L	PCT	ERA	SV	G	GS	CG	IP	H	BB	SO	R	ER	ShO	H/9	BB/9	SO/9
Tom Seaver ★	R	25	7	.781	2.21	0	36	35	18	273.1	202	82	208	75	67	5	6.65	2.70	6.85
Jerry Koosman ★	L	17	9	.654	2.28	0	32	32	16	241	187	68	180	66	61	6	6.98	2.54	6.72
Gary Gentry	R	13	12	.520	3.43	0	35	35	6	233.2	192	81	154	94	89	3	7.40	3.12	5.93
Don Cardwell	R	8	10	.444	3.01	0	30	21	4	152.1	145	47	60	63	51	0	8.57	2.78	3.54
Jim McAndrew	R	6	7	.462	3.47	0	27	21	4	135	112	44	90	57	52	2	7.47	2.93	6.00
Tug McGraw	L	9	3	.750	2.24	12	42	4	1	100.1	89	47	92	31	25	0	7.98	4.22	8.25
Nolan Ryan	R	6	3	.667	3.53	1	25	10	2	89.1	60	53	92	38	35	0	6.04	5.34	9.27
Cal Koonce	R	6	3	.667	4.99	7	40	0	0	83	85	42	48	53	46	0	9.22	4.55	5.20
Ron Taylor	R	9	4	.692	2.72	13	59	0	0	76	61	24	42	23	23	0	7.22	2.84	4.97
Jack DiLauro	L	1	4	.200	2.40	1	23	4	0	63.2	50	18	27	19	17	0	7.07	2.54	3.82
Al Jackson	L	0	0	–	10.64	0	9	0	0	11	18	4	10	13	13	0	14.73	3.27	8.18
Danny Frisella	R	0	0	–	7.71	0	3	0	0	4.2	8	3	5	4	4	0	15.43	5.79	9.64
Jessie Hudson	L	0	0	–	4.50	0	1	0	0	2	2	2	3	1	1	0	9.00	9.00	13.50
Bob Johnson	R	0	0	–	0.00	1	2	0	0	1.2	1	1	1	0	0	0	5.40	5.40	5.40
Les Rohr	L	0	0	–	20.25	0	1	0	0	1.1	5	1	1	4	3	0	33.75	6.75	0.00
TEAM TOTAL		100	62	.617	2.99	35	365	162	51	1468.1	1217	517	1012	541	487	16	7.46	3.17	6.20

STARTING PITCHING   RELIEF PITCHING

PITCHER	W	L	PCT	ERA	GS	CG	IP	H	BB	SO	W	L	PCT	ERA	SV	G	IP	H	BB	SO
T. Seaver ★	25	7	.781	2.21	35	18	273	202	81	207	0	0	–	0.00	0	1	.1	0	1	1
D. Cardwell	7	9	.437	2.85	21	4	129.1	120	42	49	1	1	.500	3.91	0	9	23	25	5	11
J. McAndrew	6	7	.461	3.19	21	4	127	100	38	85	0	0	–	7.88	0	6	8	12	6	5
T. McGraw	1	1	.500	5.23	4	1	20.2	27	9	18	8	2	.800	1.47	12	38	79.2	62	38	74
N. Ryan	3	3	.500	3.65	10	2	56.2	41	28	51	3	0	1.000	3.31	1	15	32.2	19	25	41
J. DiLauro	0	3	.000	3.16	4	0	25.2	23	7	8	1	1	.500	1.89	1	19	38	27	11	19
TEAM TOTAL	72	51	.585	3.96	162	51	1107	892	354	752	28	11	.718	3.49	35	203	361.1	325	163	260

POS	Player	B	G	AB	H	2B	3B	HR	HR %	R	RBI	BB	SO	SB	Pinch Hit AB	Pinch Hit H	BA	SA
REGULARS
1B	Donn Clendenon	R	121	396	114	18	3	22	5.5	65	97	39	91	4	21	5	.288	.515
2B	Ken Boswell	L	105	351	89	13	2	5	1.4	32	44	41	32	5	7	2	.254	.345
SS	Bud Harrelson	B	157	564	137	18	8	1	0.2	72	42	95	74	23	2	0	.243	.309
3B	Joe Foy	R	99	322	76	12	0	6	1.9	39	37	68	58	22	2	0	.236	.329
RF	Ron Swoboda	R	115	245	57	8	2	9	3.7	29	40	40	72	2	19	5	.233	.392
CF	Tommie Agee	R	153	636	182	30	7	24	3.8	107	75	55	156	31	3	1	.286	.469
LF	Cleon Jones	R	134	506	140	25	8	10	1.9	71	63	57	87	12	5	0	.277	.417
C	Jerry Grote	R	126	415	106	14	1	2	0.5	38	34	36	39	2	1	0	.255	.308
SUBSTITUTES
1O	Art Shamsky	L	122	403	118	19	2	11	2.7	48	49	49	33	1	11	2	.293	.432
23	Wayne Garrett	L	114	366	93	17	4	12	3.3	74	45	81	60	5	5	0	.254	.421
S2	Al Weis	R	75	121	25	7	1	1	0.8	20	11	7	21	1	2	0	.207	.306
1O	Mike Jorgensen	L	76	87	17	3	1	3	3.4	15	4	10	23	2	14	2	.195	.356
1B	Ed Kranepool	L	43	47	8	0	0	0	0.0	2	3	5	2	0	31	4	.170	.170
S32	Tim Foli	R	5	11	4	0	0	0	0.0	1	0	0	2	0	1	1	.364	.364
2B	Teddy Martinez	R	4	16	1	0	0	0	0.0	0	0	0	3	0	0	0	.063	.063
OF	Dave Marshall	L	92	189	46	10	1	6	3.2	21	29	17	43	4	44	11	.243	.402
OF	Ken Singleton	B	69	198	52	8	0	5	2.5	22	26	30	48	1	18	4	.263	.379
OF	Rod Gaspar	B	11	14	0	0	0	0	0.0	4	0	1	4	1	1	0	.000	.000
OF	Leroy Stanton	R	4	4	1	0	1	0	0.0	0	0	0	0	0	3	0	.250	.750
C	Duffy Dyer	R	59	148	31	1	0	2	1.3	8	12	21	32	1	1	1	.209	.257
PITCHERS
P	Tom Seaver	R	42	95	17	1	1	1	1.1	9	10	10	31	0	1	0	.179	.242
P	Jerry Koosman	R	30	70	6	1	0	0	0.0	5	4	8	46	0	0	0	.086	.100
P	Gary Gentry	R	32	59	4	2	0	0	0.0	2	2	5	39	0	0	0	.068	.102
P	Jim McAndrew	R	32	54	8	3	0	0	0.0	6	2	5	17	0	0	0	.148	.204
P	Nolan Ryan	R	27	45	8	0	0	0	0.0	2	0	0	21	1	0	0	.178	.178
P	Ray Sadecki	L	28	39	8	0	0	0	0.0	2	3	2	10	0	0	0	.205	.205
P	Tug McGraw	R	57	13	4	1	0	0	0.0	1	5	0	2	0	0	0	.308	.385
P	Ron Herbel	R	12	0	0	0	0	0	0.0	0	0	0	0	0	0	0	.000	.000
P	Dan Frisella	R	30	13	4	0	0	0	0.0	0	1	1	4	0	0	0	.308	.308
P	Rich Folkers	L	16	6	2	0	0	0	0.0	1	0	0	0	0	0	0	.333	.333
P	Don Cardwell	R	16	5	0	0	0	0	0.0	0	1	0	3	0	0	0	.000	.000
P	Ron Taylor	R	57	4	0	0	0	0	0.0	0	0	1	4	0	0	0	.000	.000
P	Cal Koonce	R	13	1	0	0	0	0	0.0	0	0	0	1	0	0	0	.000	.000
P	Dean Chance	R	3	0	0	0	0	0	0.0	0	0	0	0	0	0	0	.000	.000
TEAM TOTAL				5443	1358	211	42	120	2.2	695	640	684	1062	118	193	38	.249	.370

INDIVIDUAL FIELDING

POS	Player	T	G	PO	A	E	TC	DP	AVG.	POS	Player	T	G	PO	A	E	TC	DP	AVG.
1B	Kranepool	L	8	47	3	0	50	5	1.000	OF	Swoboda	R	100	117	3	2	122	1	.984
	Shamsky	L	56	378	35	2	415	29	.995		Jones	L	130	243	10	5	258	3	.981
	Jorgensen	L	50	116	12	1	129	9	.992		Marshall	R	43	71	2	2	75	0	.973
	Clendenon	R	100	722	62	7	791	72	.991		Singleton	R	51	90	1	3	94	0	.968
2B	Martinez	R	4	8	7	0	15	3	1.000		Agee	R	150	374	4	13	391	3	.967
	Boswell	R	101	204	244	2	450	49	.996		Jorgensen	L	10	29	0	2	31	0	.935
	Garrett	R	45	94	92	2	188	28	.989	C	Grote	R	125	855	46	8	909	12	.991
	Weis	R	44	60	59	6	125	10	.952		Dyer	R	57	294	20	3	317	6	.991
3B	Foli	R	2	3	3	0	6	1	1.000	P	McAndrew	R	32	13	17	0	30	1	1.000
	Garrett	R	70	57	113	10	180	6	.944		Koosman	L	30	7	20	0	27	1	1.000
	Foy	R	97	90	179	18	287	20	.937		Taylor	R	57	5	12	0	17	0	1.000
											Frisella	R	30	3	8	0	11	1	1.000
SS	Foli	R	2	1	7	0	8	0	1.000		Folkers	L	16	0	10	0	10	2	1.000
	Martinez	R	1	1	4	0	5	1	1.000		Koonce	R	13	0	5	0	5	0	1.000
	Garrett	R	1	1	0	0	1	0	1.000		Chance	R	3	0	1	0	1	0	1.000
	Harrelson	R	156	305	401	21	727	84	.971		Gentry	R	32	15	17	1	33	1	.970
	Weis	R	15	15	22	2	39	3	.949		Seaver	R	37	19	46	3	68	3	.956
											Herbel*	R	76	8	17	2	27	0	.926
OF	Gaspar	L	8	13	0	0	13	0	1.000		McGraw	L	57	9	17	3	29	0	.897
	Stanton	R	1	1	0	0	1	0	1.000		Ryan	R	27	11	10	4	25	2	.840
	Shamsky	L	58	104	2	0	106	1	1.000		Sadecki	L	28	3	13	4	20	0	.800

* San Diego 64 games; Mets 12 games
PASSED BALLS—Grote (6).

MONTHLY RECORD

	APR.	MAY	JUNE	JULY	AUG.	SEPT.	OCT.	FINAL
WINS	10	15	15	15	13	15	0	83
LOSSES	9	14	10	13	18	14	1	79
STANDING	4	2	1	1			5	6
GAMES BEHIND	3½	2			1½		5	6

MANAGER	W	L	PCT.
Gil Hodges	83	79	.512

TEAM STATISTICS

	W	L	PCT.	GB	R	OR	2B	3B	HR	BA	SA	SB	E	DP	FA	CG	BB	SO	ShO	SV	ERA
EAST																					
PIT	89	73	.549		729	664	235	70	130	.270	.406	66	137	195	.979	36	625	990	13	43	3.70
CHI	84	78	.519	5	806	679	228	44	179	.259	.415	39	137	146	.978	59	475	1000	9	25	3.76
NY	83	79	.512	6	695	630	211	42	120	.249	.370	118	124	136	.979	47	575	1064	10	32	3.45
STL	76	86	.469	13	744	747	218	51	113	.263	.379	117	150	159	.977	51	632	960	11	20	4.05
PHI	73	88	.453	15½	594	730	224	58	101	.238	.356	72	114	134	.981	24	538	1047	8	36	4.17
MON	73	89	.451	16	687	807	211	35	136	.237	.365	65	141	193	.977	29	716	914	10	32	4.50
WEST																					
CIN	102	60	.630		775	681	253	45	191	.270	.436	115	151	173	.976	32	592	843	15	60	3.69
LA	87	74	.540	14½	749	684	233	67	87	.270	.382	138	135	135	.978	37	496	880	17	42	3.82
SF	86	76	.531	16	831	826	257	35	165	.262	.409	83	170	153	.973	50	604	931	7	30	4.23
HOU	79	83	.488	23	744	763	250	47	129	.259	.391	114	140	144	.977	45	577	942	6	35	4.33
ATL	76	86	.469	26	736	772	215	24	160	.270	.404	58	141	118	.975	24	478	960	9	24	4.36
SD	63	99	.389	39	681	788	208	36	172	.246	.391	60	158	159	.975	24	611	886	9	32	

TOTAL PITCHING

PITCHER	T	W	L	PCT.	ERA	SV	G	GS	CG	IP	H	BB	SO	R	ER	ShO	H/9	BB/9	SO/9
Tom Seaver	R	18	12	.600	2.81	0	37	36	19	290.2	230	83	283	103	91	2	7.11	2.52	8.73
Jerry Koosman	L	12	7	.632	3.14	0	30	29	5	212	189	71	118	87	74	1	8.01	2.97	5.04
Gary Gentry	R	9	9	.500	3.69	1	32	29	5	188.1	155	86	134	88	77	2	7.38	4.14	6.39
Jim McAndrew	R	10	14	.417	3.57	2	32	27	9	184.1	166	38	111	77	73	3	8.10	1.88	5.40
Ray Sadecki	L	8	4	.667	3.88	0	28	19	4	138.2	134	52	89	67	60	2	8.64	3.33	5.76
Nolan Ryan	R	7	11	.389	3.41	1	27	19	5	131.2	86	97	125	59	50	0	5.85	6.62	8.55
Tug McGraw	L	4	6	.400	3.26	10	57	0	0	90.2	77	49	81	40	33	0	7.65	4.86	8.01
Ron Taylor	R	5	4	.556	3.95	13	57	0	0	66.1	65	16	28	31	29	0	8.91	2.16	3.78
Dan Frisella	R	8	3	.727	3.00	1	30	1	0	65.2	49	34	54	23	22	0	6.66	4.59	7.38
Rich Folkers	L	0	2	.000	6.52	0	16	1	0	29.1	36	25	15	21	21	0	11.16	7.74	4.68
Don Cardwell	R	0	2	.000	6.48	0	16	1	0	25	31	6	8	19	18	0	11.16	2.16	3.60
Cal Koonce	R	0	2	.000	3.27	0	13	0	0	22	25	14	10	9	8	0	10.26	5.76	4.09
Ron Herbel	R	2	2	.500	1.38	1	12	0	0	13	14	2	8	3	2	0	9.72	1.35	5.54
Dean Chance	R	0	1	.000	13.50	1	3	0	0	2	3	2	0	3	3	0	13.50	9.00	0.00
TEAM TOTAL		83	79	.512	3.45	32	162	162	47	1459.2	1260	575	1064	630	559	10	7.74	3.51	6.57

POS	Player	B	G	AB	H	2B	3B	HR	HR %	R	RBI	BB	SO	SB	Pinch Hit AB	Pinch Hit H	BA	SA
REGULARS																		
1B	Ed Kranepool	L	122	421	118	20	4	14	3.3	61	58	38	33	0	8	2	.280	.447
2B	Ken Boswell	L	116	392	107	20	1	5	1.2	46	40	36	31	5	7	0	.273	.367
SS	Bud Harrelson	B	142	547	138	16	6	0	0.0	55	32	53	59	28	0	0	.252	.303
3B	Bob Aspromonte	R	104	342	77	9	1	5	1.5	21	33	29	25	0	7	1	.225	.301
RF	Ken Singleton	B	115	298	73	5	0	13	4.4	34	46	61	64	0	23	6	.245	.393
CF	Tommie Agee	R	113	425	121	19	0	14	3.3	58	50	50	84	28	6	3	.285	.428
LF	Cleon Jones	R	136	505	161	24	6	14	2.8	63	69	53	87	6	5	1	.319	.473
C	Jerry Grote	R	125	403	109	25	0	2	0.5	35	35	40	47	1	4	0	.270	.347
SUBSTITUTES																		
23S	Tim Foli	R	97	288	65	12	2	0	0.0	32	24	18	50	5	2	0	.226	.281
1B	Donn Clendenon	R	88	263	65	10	0	11	4.2	29	37	21	78	1	27	2	.247	.411
32	Wayne Garrett	L	56	202	43	2	0	1	0.5	20	11	28	31	1	2	0	.213	.238
S2	Teddy Martinez	R	38	125	36	5	2	1	0.8	16	10	4	22	6	1	0	.288	.384
23	Al Weis	R	11	11	0	0	0	0	0.0	3	1	2	4	0	4	0	.000	.000
OF	Dave Marshall	L	100	214	51	9	1	3	1.4	28	21	26	54	3	36	8	.238	.332
OF	Don Hahn	R	98	178	42	5	1	1	0.5	16	11	21	32	2	8	2	.236	.292
O1	Art Shamsky	L	68	135	25	6	2	5	2.9	13	18	21	18	1	24	3	.185	.370
O1	Mike Jorgensen	L	45	118	26	1	1	5	4.3	16	11	11	24	1	13	2	.220	.373
OF	Leroy Stanton	R	5	21	4	1	0	0	0.0	2	2	2	4	0	6	0	.190	.238
OF	John Milner	L	9	18	3	1	0	0	0.0	1	1	0	3	0	6	0	.167	.222
C	Duffy Dyer	R	59	169	39	7	1	2	1.2	13	18	14	45	1	9	4	.231	.320
C	Francisco Estrada	R	1	2	1	0	0	0	0.0	0	0	0	0	0	0	0	.500	.500
PITCHERS																		
P	Tom Seaver	R	39	92	18	3	0	1	1.1	8	7	6	31	0	0	0	.196	.261
P	Gary Gentry	R	32	68	5	0	0	0	0.0	2	3	0	36	0	0	0	.074	.074
P	Jerry Koosman	R	26	50	8	0	0	0	0.0	3	0	3	25	0	0	0	.160	.160
P	Ray Sadecki	L	34	50	10	0	0	0	0.0	2	2	2	12	0	0	0	.200	.200
P	Nolan Ryan	R	30	47	6	0	1	0	0.0	4	1	3	21	0	0	0	.128	.170
P	Jim McAndrew	R	24	23	1	1	0	0	0.0	0	1	1	11	0	0	0	.043	.087
P	Charlie Williams	R	31	23	2	0	0	0	0.0	1	1	2	11	0	0	0	.087	.087
P	Tug McGraw	R	51	18	4	2	0	1	5.5	3	2	0	5	0	0	0	.222	.500
P	Dan Frisella	R	53	13	3	0	0	0	0.0	1	1	1	2	0	0	0	.231	.231
P	Jon Matlack	L	7	11	3	0	0	0	0.0	1	0	1	6	0	0	0	.273	.273
P	Ron Taylor	R	45	4	1	0	0	0	0.0	1	0	0	3	0	0	0	.250	.250
P	Buzz Capra	R	3	1	0	0	0	0	0.0	0	0	0	0	0	0	0	.000	.000
P	Don Rose	R	1	0	0	0	0	0	0.0	0	0	0	0	0	0	0	.000	.000
TEAM TOTAL				5477	1365	203	29	98	1.8	588	546	547	958	89	192	34	.249	.351

INDIVIDUAL FIELDING

POS	Player	T	G	PO	A	E	TC	DP	AVG.	POS	Player	T	G	PO	A	E	TC	DP	AVG.
1B	Jorgensen	L	1	6	2	0	8	1	1.000	OF	Shamsky	L	38	57	6	1	64	1	.984
	Shamsky	L	1	2	0	0	2	1	1.000		Jones	L	132	248	4	5	257	1	.981
	Kranepool	L	108	786	61	2	849	67	.998		Agee	R	107	265	7	6	278	0	.978
	Clendenon	R	72	505	37	8	550	49	.985		Singleton	R	96	143	5	4	152	0	.974
2B	Garrett	R	9	18	11	0	29	4	1.000		Hahn	R	80	140	2	4	146	1	.973
	Weis	R	5	4	3	0	7	1	1.000		Jorgensen	L	31	58	0	3	61	0	.951
	Martinez	R	13	17	25	1	43	3	.977		Martinez	R	1	0	0	0	0	0	.000
	Boswell	R	109	191	234	12	437	56	.973	C	Estrada	R	1	1	0	0	1	0	1.000
	Foli	R	58	115	125	9	249	33	.964		Dyer	R	53	336	21	3	360	3	.992
3B	Weis	R	2	1	3	0	4	1	1.000		Grote	R	122	892	41	9	942	4	.990
	Martinez	R	3	2	1	0	3	0	1.000	P	Gentry	R	32	10	22	0	32	3	1.000
	Garrett	R	53	30	89	4	123	7	.967		Frisella	R	53	7	13	0	20	1	1.000
	Aspromonte	R	97	76	145	8	229	10	.965		Taylor	R	45	1	11	0	12	0	1.000
	Foli	R	36	17	54	3	74	5	.959		Matlack	L	7	1	2	0	3	0	1.000
SS	Foli	R	12	12	20	0	32	5	1.000		Capra	R	3	0	1	0	1	0	1.000
	Harrelson	R	140	257	441	16	714	86	.978		Seaver	R	36	17	38	1	56	3	.982
	Martinez	R	23	26	54	2	82	14	.976		Koosman	L	26	6	23	1	30	2	.967
OF	Kranepool	L	11	9	0	0	9	0	1.000		Sadecki	L	34	5	17	1	23	1	.957
	Stanton	R	5	9	0	0	9	0	1.000		McGraw	L	51	2	12	1	15	2	.933
	Milner	L	3	8	1	0	9	0	1.000		McAndrew	R	24	10	17	4	31	1	.871
	Foli	R	1	6	0	0	6	0	1.000		Ryan	R	30	5	15	3	23	2	.870
	Marshall	L	64	92	2	1	95	0	.989		Williams	R	31	6	7	2	15	1	.867
											Rose	R	1	0	0	0	0	0	.000

PASSED BALLS—Grote (10), Dyer (2), Estrada (1).

MONTHLY RECORD

	APR.	MAY	JUNE	JULY	AUG.	SEPT.	OCT.	FINAL
WINS	12	15	18	9	12	17	—	83
LOSSES	7	11	11	20	17	13	—	79
STANDING	1	3	2	4	4	3	—	3T
GAMES BEHIND		3	2	11½	12½	14	—	14

MANAGER	W	L	PCT.
Gil Hodges	83	79	.512

TEAM STATISTICS

	W	L	PCT.	GB	R	OR	2B	3B	HR	BA	SA	SB	E	DP	FA	CG	BB	SO	ShO	SV	ERA
EAST																					3.31
PIT	97	65	.599		788	599	223	61	154	.274	.416	65	133	164	.979	43	470	813	15	48	3.85
STL	90	72	.556	7	739	699	225	54	95	.275	.385	124	142	155	.978	56	576	911	14	22	3.61
CHI	83	79	.512	14	637	648	202	34	128	.258	.378	44	126	150	.980	75	411	900	17	13	2.99
NY	83	79	.512	14	588	550	203	29	98	.249	.351	89	114	135	.981	42	529	1157	13	22	4.12
MON	71	90	.441	25½	622	729	197	29	88	.246	.343	51	150	164	.976	49	658	829	8	25	3.71
PHI	67	95	.414	30	558	688	209	35	123	.233	.350	63	122	158	.981	31	525	838	10	25	
WEST																					3.32
SF	90	72	.556		706	644	224	36	140	.247	.378	101	179	153	.972	45	471	831	14	30	3.23
LA	89	73	.549	1	663	587	213	38	95	.266	.370	76	131	159	.979	48	399	853	18	33	3.75
ATL	82	80	.506	8	643	699	192	30	153	.257	.385	57	146	180	.977	40	485	823	11	31	3.35
CIN	79	83	.488	11	586	581	203	28	138	.241	.366	59	103	174	.984	27	501	750	11	38	3.13
HOU	79	83	.488	11	585	567	230	52	71	.240	.340	101	106	152	.983	43	475	914	10	25	3.22
SD	61	100	.379	28½	486	610	184	31	96	.233	.332	70	161	144	.974	47	559	923	10	17	

TOTAL PITCHING

PITCHER	T	W	L	PCT.	ERA	SV	G	GS	CG	IP	H	BB	SO	R	ER	ShO	H/9	BB/9	SO/9
Tom Seaver	R	20	10	.667	1.76	0	36	35	21	286.1	210	61	289	61	56	4	6.61	1.89	9.09
Gary Gentry	R	12	11	.522	3.24	0	32	31	8	203.1	167	82	155	84	73	3	7.38	3.64	6.84
Jerry Koosman	L	6	11	.353	3.04	0	26	24	4	165.2	160	51	96	66	56	0	7.56	2.79	5.22
Ray Sadecki	L	7	7	.500	2.93	0	34	20	5	163.1	139	44	120	56	53	2	7.65	2.43	6.66
Nolan Ryan	R	10	14	.417	3.97	0	30	26	3	152	125	116	137	78	67	0	7.38	6.84	8.10
Tug McGraw	L	11	4	.733	1.70	8	51	1	0	111	73	41	109	22	21	0	5.94	3.33	8.82
Dan Frisella	R	8	5	.615	1.98	12	53	0	0	90.2	76	30	93	28	20	0	7.47	2.97	9.18
Jim McAndrew	R	2	5	.286	4.40	0	24	10	0	90.1	78	32	42	50	44	0	7.80	3.20	4.20
Charlie Williams	R	5	6	.455	4.80	0	31	9	1	90.1	92	41	53	53	48	0	9.20	4.10	5.30
Ron Taylor	R	2	2	.500	3.65	2	45	0	0	69	71	11	32	28	28	0	9.27	1.44	4.14
Jon Matlack	L	0	3	.000	4.14	0	7	6	0	37	31	15	24	18	17	0	7.56	3.78	5.76
Buzz Capra	R	0	1	.000	9.00	0	3	0	0	5.1	3	5	6	6	5	0	5.31	8.82	10.62
Don Rose	R	0	0	.000	0.00	0	1	0	0	2	2	0	1	0	0	0	9.00	0.00	4.50
TEAM TOTAL		83	79	.512	2.99	22	162	162	42	1466.1	1227	529	1157	550	487	13	7.56	3.24	7.11

POS	Player	B	G	AB	H	2B	3B	HR	HR %	R	RBI	BB	SO	SB	Pinch Hit AB	Pinch Hit H	BA	SA
REGULARS																		
1B	Ed Kranepool	L	122	327	88	15	1	8	2.5	28	34	34	35	1	15	4	.269	.394
2B	Ken Boswell	L	100	355	75	9	1	9	2.5	35	33	32	35	2	7	1	.211	.318
SS	Bud Harrelson	B	115	418	90	10	4	1	0.2	54	24	58	57	12	0	0	.215	.266
3B	Jim Fregosi	R	101	340	79	15	4	5	1.5	31	32	38	71	0	1	0	.232	.344
RF	Rusty Staub	L	66	239	70	11	0	9	3.8	31	38	31	13	0	1	0	.293	.452
CF	Tommie Agee	R	114	422	96	23	0	13	3.1	52	47	53	92	8	4	0	.227	.374
LF	Cleon Jones	R	106	375	92	15	1	5	1.4	39	52	30	83	1	3	0	.245	.331
C	Duffy Dyer	R	94	325	75	17	3	8	2.5	33	36	28	71	0	3	2	.231	.375
SUBSTITUTES																		
2S3O	Teddy Martinez	R	103	330	74	5	5	1	0.3	22	19	12	49	7	4	0	.224	.279
32S	Wayne Garrett	L	111	298	69	13	3	2	0.7	41	29	70	58	3	8	0	.232	.315
1B	Jim Beauchamp	R	58	120	29	1	0	5	4.2	10	19	7	33	0	21	6	.242	.375
2B	Lute Barnes	R	24	72	17	2	2	0	0.0	5	6	6	4	0	3	0	.236	.319
1C	Bill Sudakis	B	18	49	7	0	0	1	2.0	3	7	6	14	0	6	1	.143	.204
OF	John Milner	L	117	362	86	12	2	17	4.7	52	38	51	74	2	12	3	.238	.423
O1	Willie Mays	R	69	195	52	9	1	8	4.1	27	19	43	43	1	8	2	.267	.446
OF	Dave Marshall	L	72	156	39	5	0	4	2.6	21	11	22	28	3	29	3	.250	.359
OF	Dave Schneck	L	37	123	23	3	2	3	2.4	7	10	10	26	0	4	0	.187	.317
OF	Don Hahn	R	17	37	6	0	0	0	0.0	0	1	4	12	0	6	0	.162	.162
C	Jerry Grote	R	64	205	43	5	1	3	1.5	15	21	26	27	1	2	0	.210	.288
C	Joe Nolan	L	4	10	0	0	0	0	0.0	0	0	1	3	0	1	0	.000	.000
PITCHERS																		
P	Tom Seaver	R	36	89	13	3	1	3	3.4	5	4	5	41	0	0	0	.146	.303
P	Jon Matlack	L	34	78	10	1	0	0	0.0	6	2	10	44	0	0	0	.128	.141
P	Gary Gentry	R	39	48	5	1	0	0	0.0	2	3	4	28	0	0	0	.104	.125
P	Jerry Koosman	R	34	47	4	0	0	0	0.0	1	1	0	18	0	0	0	.085	.085
P	Jim McAndrew	R	28	43	2	0	0	0	0.0	2	1	3	14	0	0	0	.047	.047
P	Tug McGraw	L	54	20	2	0	0	0	0.0	1	0	2	4	0	0	0	.100	.100
P	Ray Sadecki	L	34	13	2	0	0	0	0.0	1	1	0	5	0	0	0	.154	.154
P	Buzz Capra	R	14	12	3	0	0	0	0.0	1	1	3	3	0	0	0	.250	.250
P	Dan Frisella	R	39	7	2	0	0	0	0.0	0	1	0	0	0	0	0	.286	.286
P	Brent Strom	R	11	6	0	0	0	0	0.0	0	0	0	0	0	0	0	.000	.000
P	Hank Webb	R	6	5	0	0	0	0	0.0	0	0	0	0	0	0	0	.000	.000
P	Chuck Taylor	R	20	3	0	0	0	0	0.0	1	0	0	0	0	0	0	.000	.000
P	Bob Rauch	R	19	3	0	0	0	0	0.0	0	0	0	1	0	0	0	.000	.000
P	Tommy Moore	R	3	3	1	0	0	0	0.0	1	0	0	0	0	0	0	.333	.333
TEAM TOTAL				5135	1154	175	31	105	2.0	528	490	589	990	41	143	22	.225	.332

INDIVIDUAL FIELDING

POS	Player	T	G	PO	A	E	TC	DP	AVG.	POS	Player	T	G	PO	A	E	TC	DP	AVG.
1B	Milner	L	10	73	6	0	79	9	1.000	OF	Hahn	R	10	8	0	0	8	0	1.000
	Fregosi	R	3	7	1	0	8	0	1.000		Grote	R	1	1	0	0	1	0	1.000
	Kranepool	L	108	705	48	3	756	65	.996		Jones	L	84	136	8	2	146	1	.986
	Mays	R	11	75	2	1	78	3	.987		Schneck	L	33	63	1	1	65	0	.985
	Beauchamp	R	35	180	9	4	193	16	.979		Staub	R	65	108	4	2	114	2	.982
	Jones	L	20	174	12	4	190	9	.979		*Mays	R	63	138	3	3	144	1	.979
	Sudakis	R	7	51	7	2	60	3	.967		Marshall	R	42	70	0	2	72	0	.972
											Martinez	R	15	32	1	1	34	0	.971
2B	Martinez	R	47	81	77	1	159	9	.994		Milner	L	91	160	7	6	173	0	.965
	Boswell	R	94	208	183	4	395	53	.990		Agee	R	109	273	6	11	290	1	.962
	Barnes	R	14	35	35	3	73	11	.959		Beauchamp	R	5	8	0	1	9	0	.889
	Garrett	R	22	48	38	5	91	6	.945		Dyer	R	1	0	0	1	1	0	.000
											Kranepool	L	1	0	0	0	0	0	.000
3B	Martinez	R	2	0	6	0	6	0	1.000	P	Gentry	R	32	15	27	0	42	1	1.000
	Grote	R	3	1	1	0	2	0	1.000		McGraw	L	54	6	13	0	19	0	1.000
	Garrett	R	82	66	150	9	225	13	.960		Capra	R	14	5	10	0	15	2	1.000
	Fregosi	R	85	71	144	15	230	9	.935		Taylor	R	20	4	9	0	13	2	1.000
											Rauch	R	19	1	5	0	6	0	1.000
SS	Fregosi	R	6	13	17	0	30	6	1.000		Strom	L	11	0	2	0	2	0	1.000
	Barnes	R	6	5	15	0	20	2	1.000		Webb	R	6	3	4	0	7	0	1.000
	Martinez	R	42	62	110	3	175	21	.983		Moore	R	3	1	2	0	3	0	1.000
	Harrelson	R	115	191	334	16	541	51	.970		Matlack	L	34	8	33	1	42	1	.976
											McAndrew	R	28	16	16	1	33	0	.970
C	Sudakis	R	5	37	1	0	38	0	1.000		Koosman	L	34	4	23	1	28	1	.964
	Grote	R	59	405	42	1	448	5	.998		Frisella	R	39	5	15	1	21	0	.952
	Dyer	R	91	690	61	5	756	12	.993		Seaver	R	35	17	40	3	60	3	.950
	Nolan	R	3	12	3	1	16	0	.938		Sadecki	L	34	1	8	2	11	0	.818

* San Francisco 14 games, Mets 49 games.

PASSED BALLS—Dyer (3), Grote (2), Nolan (2).

MONTHLY RECORD

	APR.	MAY	JUNE	JULY	AUG.	SEPT.	OCT.	FINAL
WINS	8	21	12	11	11	15	5	83
LOSSES	4	7	15	15	17	14	1	73
STANDING	2	1	2	2	3	3	3	3
GAMES BEHIND	½		0	7	13	16	13½	13½

MANAGER	W	L	PCT.
Yogi Berra	83	73	.532

TEAM STATISTICS

	W	L	PCT.	GB	R	OR	2B	3B	HR	BA	SA	SB	E	DP	FA	CG	BB	SO	ShO	SV	ERA
EAST																					
PIT	96	59	.619		691	512	251	47	110	.274	.397	49	136	171	.978	39	433	838	15	48	2.81
CHI	85	70	.548	11	685	567	206	40	133	.257	.387	69	132	148	.979	54	486	824	19	32	3.22
NY	83	73	.532	13½	528	578	175	31	105	.225	.332	41	116	122	.980	32	486	1059	12	41	3.26
STL	75	81	.481	21½	568	600	214	42	70	.260	.355	104	141	146	.977	64	531	912	13	13	3.42
MON	70	86	.449	26½	513	609	156	22	91	.234	.325	68	134	141	.978	39	579	888	11	23	3.59
PHI	59	97	.378	37½	503	635	200	36	98	.236	.344	42	116	142	.981	43	536	927	13	15	3.66
WEST																					
CIN	95	59	.617		707	557	214	44	124	.251	.380	140	110	143	.982	25	435	806	15	60	3.21
HOU	84	69	.549	10½	708	636	233	38	134	.258	.393	111	116	151	.980	38	498	971	14	31	3.77
LA	85	70	.548	10½	584	527	178	39	98	.256	.360	82	162	145	.974	50	429	856	23	29	2.78
ATL	70	84	.455	25	628	730	186	17	144	.258	.382	47	156	130	.974	40	512	732	4	27	4.27
SF	69	86	.445	26½	662	649	211	36	150	.244	.384	123	156	121	.974	44	507	771	8	23	3.69
SD	58	95	.379	36½	488	665	168	38	102	.227	.332	78	144	146	.976	39	618	960	17	19	3.78

TOTAL PITCHING

PITCHER	T	W	L	PCT.	ERA	SV	G	GS	CG	IP	H	BB	SO	R	ER	ShO	H/9	BB/9	SO/9
Tom Seaver	R	21	12	.636	2.92	0	35	35	13	262	215	77	249	92	85	3	7.38	2.61	8.55
Jon Matlack	L	15	10	.600	2.32	0	34	32	8	244	215	71	169	79	63	4	7.92	2.61	6.21
Gary Gentry	R	7	10	.412	4.01	0	32	26	3	164	153	75	120	82	73	0	8.37	4.14	6.57
Jerry Koosman	L	11	12	.478	4.14	1	34	24	4	163	155	52	147	81	75	1	8.55	2.88	8.10
Jim McAndrew	R	11	8	.579	2.80	1	28	23	4	160.2	133	38	81	54	50	0	7.47	2.16	4.41
Tug McGraw	L	8	6	.571	1.70	27	54	0	0	106	71	40	92	26	20	0	6.03	3.42	7.83
Ray Sadecki	L	2	1	.667	3.09	0	34	2	0	75.2	73	31	38	33	26	0	8.64	3.69	4.50
Dan Frisella	R	5	8	.385	3.36	9	39	0	0	67.1	63	20	46	31	25	0	8.46	4.59	6.21
Buzz Capra	R	3	2	.600	4.58	0	14	6	0	53	50	27	45	27	27	0	8.46	2.70	7.65
Chuck Taylor	R	0	0	.000	5.52	2	20	0	0	31	44	9	9	19	19	0	12.78	2.61	2.61
Brent Strom	L	0	3	.000	6.90	0	11	5	0	30.1	34	15	20	25	23	0	10.17	4.50	6.00
Bob Rauch	R	0	1	.000	5.00	1	19	0	0	27	27	21	23	16	15	0	9.00	6.93	6.75
Hank Webb	R	0	0	.000	4.50	0	6	2	0	18.1	18	9	15	9	9	0	8.91	4.41	7.47
Tommy Moore	R	0	0	.000	3.00	0	3	1	0	12.1	12	1	5	4	4	0	8.91	0.75	3.69
TEAM TOTAL		83	73	.532	3.26	41	156	156	32	1414.2	1263	486	1059	578	513	12	8.01	3.06	6.75

POS	Player	B	G	AB	H	2B	3B	HR	HR %	R	RBI	BB	SO	SB	Pinch Hit AB	Pinch Hit H	BA	SA
REGULARS																		
1B	John Milner	L	129	451	108	12	3	23	5.1	69	72	62	84	1	4	0	.239	.432
2B	Felix Millan	R	153	638	185	23	4	3	0.5	82	37	35	22	2	0	0	.290	.353
SS	Bud Harrelson	B	106	356	92	12	3	0	0.0	28	20	48	49	5	0	0	.258	.309
3B	Wayne Garrett	L	140	504	129	20	3	16	3.2	76	58	72	74	6	4	4	.256	.403
RF	Rusty Staub	L	152	585	163	36	1	15	2.5	77	76	74	52	1	0	0	.279	.421
CF	Don Hahn	R	93	262	60	10	1	2	0.8	22	21	22	43	2	9	2	.229	.290
LF	Cleon Jones	R	92	339	88	13	0	11	3.2	48	48	28	51	1	4	3	.260	.395
C	Jerry Grote	R	84	285	73	10	2	1	0.4	17	32	13	23	0	1	0	.256	.316
SUBSTITUTES																		
1O	Ed Kranepool	L	100	284	68	12	2	1	0.4	28	35	30	28	1	16	2	.239	.306
UT	Teddy Martinez	R	92	263	67	11	0	1	0.4	34	14	13	38	3	1	0	.255	.308
3S	Jim Fregosi	R	45	124	29	4	1	0	0.0	7	11	20	25	1	5	0	.234	.282
32	Ken Boswell	L	76	110	25	2	1	2	1.8	12	14	12	11	0	51	12	.227	.318
1B	Jim Beauchamp	R	50	61	17	1	1	0	0.0	5	14	7	11	1	34	9	.279	.328
SS	Brian Ostrosser	L	4	5	0	0	0	0	0.0	0	0	0	2	0	1	1	.000	.000
O1	Willie Mays	R	66	209	44	10	0	6	2.9	24	25	27	47	1	7	2	.211	.344
OF	Jim Gosger	L	38	92	22	2	0	0	0.0	9	10	9	16	0	4	0	.239	.261
OF	Dave Schneck	L	13	36	7	0	1	0	0.0	2	0	1	4	0	1	0	.194	.250
O1	George Theodore	R	45	116	30	4	0	1	0.9	14	15	10	13	1	11	2	.259	.319
OF	Rich Chiles	L	8	25	3	2	0	0	0.0	2	1	0	2	0	0	0	.120	.200
C	Duffy Dyer	R	70	189	35	6	1	1	0.5	9	9	13	40	0	10	2	.185	.243
C	Ron Hodges	L	45	127	33	2	0	1	0.8	5	18	11	19	0	5	2	.260	.299
C	Jerry May	R	4	8	2	0	0	0	0.0	0	0	1	1	0	0	0	.250	.250
PH	Luther Barnes	R	3	2	1	0	0	0	0.0	0	1	0	1	0	0	0	.500	.500
PH	Greg Harts	L	3	2	1	0	0	0	0.0	0	0	0	0	0	2	1	.500	.500
PITCHERS																		
P	Tom Seaver	R	39	93	15	2	1	1	1.1	9	5	7	34	1	0	0	.161	.237
P	Jerry Koosman	R	35	78	8	1	0	0	0.0	3	3	2	37	0	0	0	.103	.115
P	Jon Matlack	L	35	65	9	0	0	0	0.0	5	2	13	38	0	0	0	.138	.138
P	George Stone	L	28	48	13	0	0	0	0.0	4	5	0	8	0	0	0	.271	.271
P	Ray Sadecki	L	31	31	7	2	0	0	0.0	3	1	0	5	0	0	0	.226	.290
P	Tug McGraw	R	60	24	4	0	0	0	0.0	0	2	2	9	0	0	0	.167	.167
P	Harry Parker	R	38	23	4	0	0	0	0.0	0	2	0	8	0	0	0	.174	.174
P	Jim McAndrew	R	24	15	2	1	0	0	0.0	0	2	6	7	0	0	0	.133	.200
P	Phil Hennigan	R	30	3	1	0	0	0	0.0	3	0	1	0	0	0	0	.333	.333
P	Buzz Capra	R	24	2	0	0	0	0	0.0	1	0	2	0	0	0	0	.000	.000
P	Craig Swan	R	3	2	0	0	0	0	0.0	0	0	0	0	0	0	0	.000	.000
P	George Strohmayer	R	7	0	0	0	0	0	0.0	0	0	0	0	0	0	0	.000	.000
P	Tommy Moore	R	4	0	0	0	0	0	0.0	1	0	0	0	0	0	0	.000	.000
P	Hank Webb	R	2	0	0	0	0	0	0.0	0	0	0	0	0	0	0	.000	.000
P	Bob Apodaca	R	1	0	0	0	0	0	0.0	0	0	0	0	0	0	0	.000	.000
P	Bob Miller	R	1	0	0	0	0	0	0.0	0	0	0	0	0	0	0	.000	.000
TEAM TOTAL			161	5457	1345	198	24	85	1.6	608	553	540	805	27	171	42	.246	.338

INDIVIDUAL FIELDING

POS	Player	T	G	PO	A	E	TC	DP	AVG.
1B	Theodore	R	4	20	2	0	22	3	1.000
	Fregosi	R	3	12	3	0	15	1	1.000
	Kranepool	L	51	395	27	1	423	39	.998
	Milner	L	95	771	47	9	827	66	.989
	Mays	R	17	143	4	3	150	9	.980
	Beauchamp	R	11	59	3	2	64	7	.969
2B	Martinez	R	5	5	4	0	9	1	1.000
	Millan	R	153	410	411	9	830	99	.989
	Garrett	R	6	14	18	1	33	6	.970
	Boswell	R	3	8	4	1	13	0	.923
3B	Martinez	R	14	12	23	0	35	2	1.000
	Boswell	R	17	7	29	1	37	3	.973
	Garrett	R	130	80	280	22	382	36	.942
	Fregosi	R	17	15	29	3	47	2	.936
SS	Ostrosser	R	4	1	4	0	5	0	1.000
	Harrelson	R	103	153	315	10	478	49	.979
	Martinez	R	44	66	110	11	187	12	.941
	Fregosi	R	17	20	38	6	64	10	.906
	Garrett	R	9	8	15	3	26	4	.885
OF	Gosger	L	35	45	0	0	45	0	1.000
	Schneck	L	12	28	0	0	28	0	1.000
	Chiles	L	8	22	1	0	23	1	1.000
	Mays	R	45	103	2	1	106	0	.991
	Hahn	R	87	176	2	2	180	0	.989
	Theodore	R	33	60	3	1	64	1	.984

POS	Player	T	G	PO	A	E	TC	DP	AVG.
OF	Kranepool	L	32	53	1	1	55	0	.982
	Staub	R	152	297	17	7	321	5	.978
	Martinez	R	21	36	2	1	39	0	.974
	Jones	L	92	168	6	6	180	0	.967
	Milner	L	29	33	4	2	39	0	.949
	Fregosi	R	1	0	0	0	0	0	.000
C	May	R	4	14	0	0	14	0	1.000
	Grote	R	81	545	34	3	582	0	.995
	Dyer	R	60	308	26	2	336	7	.994
	Hodges	R	40	241	13	2	256	6	.992
P	Stone	L	27	6	27	0	33	2	1.000
	Parker	R	38	4	14	0	18	0	1.000
	Strohmayer	R	7	1	2	0	3	0	1.000
	Capra	R	24	1	7	0	8	0	1.000
	Matlack	L	34	4	40	1	45	3	.978
	McGraw	L	60	8	19	1	28	1	.964
	Koosman	L	35	5	41	2	48	1	.958
	Seaver	R	36	26	35	5	66	1	.924
	Sadecki	L	31	1	7	1	9	0	.889
	Hennigan	R	30	4	4	1	9	0	.889
	McAndrew	R	23	3	9	2	14	0	.857
	Moore	R	3	1	0	1	2	0	.500
	Swan	R	3	0	1	1	2	0	.500
	Webb	R	2	0	0	0	0	0	.000
	Miller	R	1	0	0	0	0	0	.000
	Apodaca	R	1	0	0	0	0	0	.000

PASSED BALLS—Dyer (4), Grote (3).

MONTHLY RECORD									MANAGER		W	L	PCT.
	APR.	MAY	JUNE	JULY	AUG.	SEPT.	OCT.	FINAL	Yogi Berra		82	79	.509
WINS	12	9	11	12	18	19	1	82					
LOSSES	8	14	17	18	14	8	0	79					
STANDING	1	3	6	6	5	1	1	1					
GAMES BEHIND		5	10½	10½	5½								

TEAM STATISTICS

	W	L	PCT.	GB	R	OR	2B	3B	HR	BA	SA	SB	E	DP	FA	CG	BB	SO	ShO	SV	ERA
EAST																					
NY	82	79	.509		608	588	198	24	85	.246	.338	27	126	140	.980	47	490	1027	15	40	3.26
STL	81	81	.500	1½	643	603	240	35	75	.259	.357	100	159	149	.975	42	486	867	14	36	3.25
PIT	80	82	.494	2½	704	693	257	44	154	.261	.405	23	151	156	.976	26	564	839	11	44	3.73
MON	79	83	.488	3½	668	702	190	23	125	.251	.364	77	163	156	.974	26	681	866	6	38	3.71
CHI	77	84	.478	5	614	655	201	21	117	.247	.357	65	157	155	.975	27	438	885	13	40	3.66
PHI	71	91	.438	11½	642	717	218	29	134	.249	.371	51	134	179	.979	49	632	919	11	22	3.99
WEST																					
CIN	99	63	.611		741	621	232	34	137	.254	.383	148	115	162	.982	39	518	801	17	43	3.40
LA	95	66	.590	3½	675	565	219	29	110	.263	.371	109	125	166	.981	45	461	961	15	38	3.00
SF	88	74	.543	11	739	702	212	52	161	.262	.407	112	163	138	.974	33	485	787	8	44	3.79
HOU	82	80	.506	17	681	672	216	35	134	.251	.376	92	116	140	.981	45	575	907	14	26	3.75
ATL	76	85	.472	22½	799	774	219	34	206	.266	.427	84	166	142	.974	34	575	803	9	35	4.25
SD	60	102	.370	39	548	770	198	26	112	.244	.351	88	170	152	.973	34	548	845	10	23	4.16

TOTAL PITCHING

PITCHER	T	W	L	PCT.	ERA	SV	G	GS	CG	IP	H	BB	SO	R	ER	ShO	H/9	BB/9	SO/9
Tom Seaver	R	19	10	.655	2.08	0	36	36	18	290	219	64	251	74	67	3	6.79	1.98	7.79
Jerry Koosman	L	14	15	.483	2.84	0	35	35	12	263	234	76	156	93	83	3	8.01	2.61	5.31
Jon Matlack	L	14	16	.467	3.20	0	34	34	14	242	210	99	205	93	86	3	7.83	3.69	7.65
George Stone	L	12	3	.800	2.80	1	27	20	2	148	157	31	77	53	46	0	9.54	1.89	4.68
Tug McGraw	L	5	6	.455	3.86	25	60	2	0	118.2	106	55	81	53	51	0	8.01	4.14	6.12
Ray Sadecki	L	5	4	.556	3.38	1	31	11	1	116.2	109	41	87	47	44	0	8.37	3.15	6.66
Harry Parker	R	8	4	.667	3.34	5	38	9	0	96.2	79	36	63	40	36	0	7.29	3.33	5.85
Jim McAndrew	R	3	8	.273	5.40	1	23	12	0	80.1	109	31	38	60	48	0	12.24	3.15	4.23
Phil Hennigan	R	0	4	.000	6.28	3	30	0	0	43.1	50	16	22	30	30	0	10.44	3.33	4.59
Buzz Capra	R	2	7	.222	3.86	4	24	0	0	42	35	28	35	18	18	0	7.47	5.13	7.47
Geo. Strohmayer	R	0	0	.000	8.10	0	7	0	0	10	13	4	5	10	9	0	11.70	3.60	4.50
Craig Swan	R	0	1	.000	9.00	0	3	1	0	8.1	16	2	4	9	8	0	17.33	2.16	4.32
Tommy Moore	R	0	1	.000	12.00	0	3	1	0	3.1	6	3	1	5	4	0	16.38	8.19	2.88
Hank Webb	R	0	0	.000	9.00	0	2	0	0	1.2	2	2	1	2	2	0	15.03	15.03	7.47
Bob Miller	R	0	0	.000	0.00	0	1	0	0	1	0	0	1	0	0	0	0.00	0.00	0.00
Bob Apodaca	R	0	0	.000	0.00	0	1	0	0	0	0	2	0	1	1	0	0.00	—	0.00
TEAM TOTAL		82	79	.509	3.26	40	161	161	47	1465	1345	490	1027	588	531	15	8.28	2.97	6.31

ODDS AND ENDS

METS WON–LOST SUMMARY

WON–LOST–BY CLUB

TOTAL

	1962 W–L	1963 W–L	1964 W–L	1965 W–L	1966 W–L	1967 W–L	1968 W–L	1969 W–L	Total W–L	Pct.
Chicago	9–9	7–11	7–11	7–11	10–8	5–13	10–8	10–8	65–79	.451
Cincinnati	5–13	8–10	7–11	7–11	7–10	6–12	8–10	6–6	54–83	.394
Houston	3–13	5–13	9–9	4–14	11–7	7–11	8–10	2–10	49–87	.360
Los Angeles	2–16	2–16	3–15	6–12	6–12	6–12	11–7	8–4	44–94	.319
Mil-Atl	6–12	6–12	4–14	5–13	4–14	10–8	6–12	8–4	49–89	.355
Montreal	–	–	–	–	–	–	–	13–5	13–5	.722
Philadelphia	4–14	8–10	3–15	7–11	7–11	4–14	8–10	12–6	53–92	.366
Pittsburgh	2–16	4–14	6–12	4–14	5–13	11–7	9–9	10–8	51–93	.354
St. Louis	5–13	5–13	7–11	5–13	7–11	7–11	6–12	12–6	54–90	.375
San Diego	–	–	–	–	–	–	–	11–1	11–1	.917
San Francisco	4–14	6–12	7–11	5–13	9–9	5–13	7–11	8–4	51–87	.370
Total	40–120	51–111	53–109	50–112	66–95	61–101	73–89	100–62	494–799	
Pct.	.250	.315	.327	.309	.410	.377	.451	.617	.382	

	1970 W–L	1971 W–L	1972 W–L	1973 W–L	Total W–L	Pct.
Chicago	11–7	7–11	8–10	7–10	98–117	.456
Cincinnati	4–8	4–8	4–8	4–8	70–115	.378
Houston	6–6	7–5	6–6	6–6	74–110	.402
Los Angeles	5–7	7–5	5–7	5–7	66–120	.355
Mil.-Atl.	6–6	5–7	5–7	6–6	71–115	.382
Montreal	8–10	9–9	12–6	9–9	51–39	.567
Philadelphia	13–5	13–5	13–5	9–9	101–115	.468
Pittsburgh	6–12	10–8	8–6	13–5	88–124	.415
St. Louis	12–6	10–8	7–9	10–8	93–121	.434
San Diego	6–6	7–5	7–5	8–4	39–21	.650
San Francisco	6–6	4–8	8–4	5–7	74–112	.398
Total	83–79	83–79	83–73	82–79	825–1109	
Pct.	.512	.512	.532	.509	.426	

WINNING STREAKS
(7 or more games)

No. of Games	Year	Starting Date	Ending Date
11	1969	May 28	June 10
11	1972	May 12	May 21
10	1969	Sept. 6	Sept. 13
9	1969	Sept. 21	Oct. 1
7	1966	July 17	July 22
7	1969	July 2	July 9
7	1970	July 3	July 9
7	1972	Apr. 21	Apr. 28
7	1973	Sept. 18	Sept. 25

LOSING STREAKS
(10 or more games)

No. of Games	Year	Starting Date	Ending Date
17	1962	May 21	June 6
15	1963	June 28	July 14
13	1962	Aug. 9	Aug. 21
11	1962	July 15	July 26
11	1900	July 18	July 28
11	1965	Aug. 1	Aug. 13
10	1965	June 5	June 13
10	1965	July 7	July 20

BATTING HIGHLIGHTS

FIVE HITS IN ONE GAME

Dick Smith vs. Chicago, May 26, 1964
Jim Hickman vs. Milwaukee, Sept. 30, 1964
Phil Linz vs. Philadelphia, July 6, 1968
Joe Foy vs. San Francisco, July 19, 1970
Tommie Agee vs. Pittsburgh, Aug. 8, 1970
John Milner vs. St. Louis, Sept. 8, 1972
Rusty Staub vs. Los Angeles, May 24, 1973

THREE HOME RUNS IN ONE GAME

Jim Hickman vs. St. Louis, Sept. 3, 1965

GRAND SLAM HOME RUNS

Date	Player	Opponent	Pitcher
July 6, 1962	Rod Kanehl	St. Louis	Bobby Shantz
Aug. 1, 1962	Frank Thomas	Philadelphia	Jack Hamilton
April 21, 1963 (1st)	Jim Hickman	Milwaukee	Claude Raymond
June 26, 1963	Tim Harkness	Chicago	Jim Brewer
July 15, 1963 (1st)	Carl Willey	Houston	Ken Johnson
Aug. 9, 1963	Jim Hickman	Chicago	Lindy McDaniel
June 26, 1964	Joe Christopher	At Milwaukee	Bob Sadowski
Aug. 19, 1964	Jim Hickman	Pittsburgh	Vern Law
July 3, 1966 (1st)	Ed Bressoud	Pittsburgh	Bob Veale
Aug. 17, 1966	Hawk Taylor	Pittsburgh	Bob Veale
May 20, 1967	Jack Hamilton	St. Louis	Al Jackson
July 19, 1967 (2nd)	Tommy Davis	Houston	Dave Giusti
Aug. 30, 1968	Art Shamsky	St. Louis	Nelson Briles
May 14, 1969	Cleon Jones	Atlanta	George Stone
Sept. 13, 1969	Ron Swoboda	At Pittsburgh	Chuck Hartenstein
April 28, 1970	Dave Marshall	San Francisco	Gaylord Perry
July 9, 1970	Ron Swoboda	Montreal	Rich Nye
April 24, 1971	Tommie Agee	Chicago	Milt Pappas
May 11, 1971	Dave Marshall	Houston	George Culver
Aug. 7, 1971	Ken Boswell	Atlanta	Mike McQueen
April 28, 1972	Tommie Agee	Los Angeles	Jim Brewer
May 14, 1972	Rusty Staub	San Francisco	Sam McDowell
May 3, 1973	Rusty Staub	Cincinnati	
July 28, 1973	John Milner	Montreal	
Aug. 15, 1973	Jerry Grote	San Diego	
Aug. 18, 1973	John Milner	Cincinnati	
Aug. 27, 1973	Rusty Staub	San Diego	

METS HOME RUNS—BY CLUB

	1962 H-A	1963 H-A	1964 H-A	1965 H-A	1966 H-A	1967 H-A	1968 H-A	1969 H-A	1970 H-A	1971 H-A	1972 H-A	1973 H-A	Total H-A
Atlanta	–	–	–	–	5-6	6-6	5-5	4-2	8-5	2-9	5-13	1-6	36-52
Chicago	6-4	9-7	7-6	6-7	5-8	2-12	4-7	8-9	5-7	5-11	6-7	1-7	64-92
Cincinnati	18-8	6-5	3-6	14-6	6-4	5-6	4-8	7-4	5-4	1-0	2-7	3-4	74-62
Houston	8-1	5-1	6-1	6-1	6-2	8-1	5-1	5-2	3-4	4-1	5-5	0-3	61-23
Los Angeles	10-5	5-3	6-2	5-4	3-2	2-1	9-2	4-7	3-3	5-0	2-1	2-1	56-31
Milwaukee	8-10	8-4	12-5	7-4	–	–	–	–	–	–	–	–	35-23
Montreal	–	–	–	–	–	–	–	7-6	7-16	6-3	6-4	4-6	30-35
Philadelphia	17-3	9-5	8-9	2-10	5-5	1-1	3-1	5-3	8-4	8-10	7-6	6-7	79-64
Pittsburgh	7-1	4-1	5-1	1-5	6-1	7-3	6-2	3-5	3-2	5-8	3-2	9-2	59-33
St. Louis	16-7	5-3	6-10	4-14	8-6	7-6	4-3	5-6	4-2	4-3	4-6	4-3	71-69
San Diego	–	–	–	–	–	–	–	3-2	6-1	3-2	2-6	6-3	20-14
San Francisco	3-7	10-6	5-5	5-6	7-13	6-3	9-3	6-6	11-9	5-3	3-3	3-4	73-68
Total	93-46	61-35	58-45	50-57	51-47	44-39	49-32	57-52	63-57	48-50	45-60	39-46	658-566

PINCH-HIT HOME RUNS

1962 (9): Ed Bouchee (2), Choo Choo Coleman (2), Jim Hickman, Felix Mantilla, Marv Throneberry (2).
1963 (2): Joe Hicks, Frank Thomas
1964 (2): Larry Elliot, Frank Thomas
1965 (5): Jim Hickman, Johnny Lewis, Charley Smith, Ron Swoboda (2)
1966 (9): Jim Hickman, Chuck Hiller (2), Ed Kranepool, Billy Murphy, Johnny Stephenson,
   Ron Swoboda (2), Hawk Taylor
1967 (1): Jerry Buchek
1968 (4): Ed Charles (3), Art Shamsky
1969 (1): Duffy Dyer
1970 (4): Dave Marshall 2, Donn Clendenon, Ron Swoboda
1971 (1): Dave Marshall
1972 (0)
1973 (2): Ken Boswell 2

HITTING STREAKS
(14 or More Games)

Player	Games	Year	Dates
Cleon Jones	23	1970	Aug. 25–Sept. 15
Tommie Agee	20	1970	April 16–May 9
Tommie Agee	19	1970	June 22–July 8
Frank Thomas	18	1962	Aug. 12–Aug. 30
Felix Millan	18	1973	July 13–Aug. 1
Rusty Staub	15	1973	Sept. 15–Oct. 1
Felix Mantilla	14	1962	April 21–May 12
Jessie Gonder	14	1963	July 19–Aug. 4

METS TRIPLE PLAYS

Date	Opponent	Players Involved
May 30, 1962 (2nd)	Los Angeles	Chacon (SS)—Neal (2B)—Hodges (1B)
May 31, 1964 (2nd)	San Francisco	McMillan (SS)—Kranepool (1B)
April 15, 1965	At Houston	Lewis (RF)—Cannizzaro (C)—McMillan (SS)
Sept. 28, 1966 (1st)	Chicago	Bressoud (3B)—Hiller (2B)—Hickman (1B)

TRIPLE PLAYS HIT INTO BY METS

Date	Opponent	Batter
Sept. 30, 1962	At Chicago	Joe Pignatano
Aug. 15, 1964	Philadelphia	Bobby Klaus
May 2, 1967	San Francisco	Ken Boyer
Aug. 15, 1967 (2nd)	At Philadelphia	Phil Linz

LOW-HIT GAMES BY METS
(Two Hits or Less)

Date	Pitcher	Opponent	Mets W–L	Score
	One-Hitters			
June 22, 1962(1)	Jackson (Amalfitano, single in first)	Hou	W	2-0
May 4, 1966	Hamilton (Sadecki, bunt single in third)	At StL	W	9-0
July 9, 1969	Seaver (Qualls, one-out single in ninth)	Chi	W	4-0
April 18, 1970	Ryan (Doyle, single in first)	Phi	W	7-0
May 13, 1970	Gentry (Banks, single in eighth)	At Chi	W	4-0
May 15, 1970	Seaver (Compton, single in third)	At Phi	W	4-0
April 18, 1971(1)	Gentry (Clemente, triple in sixth)	Pit	W	5-2
Sept. 26, 1971	Seaver (Davalillo, single in seventh)	Pit	W	3-1
July 4, 1972(1)	Seaver (Lee, one-out single in ninth)	SD	W	2-0
July 10, 1973	Matlack (Helms, double in sixth)	Hou	W	1-0

LOW-HIT GAMES BY METS
(Two Hits or Less)

Two-Hitters

June 20, 1962(2)	Hunter	Mil	L	2-3(6)
May 30, 1963(2)	Hook	Chi	W	2-1
June 23, 1963(1)	Willey	Phi	W	5-0
May 2, 1964	Jackson	At Cin	W	3-0
May 17, 1964(2)	Fisher and Wakefield	At SF	L	0-1
May 28, 1964	Cisco and Bearnarth	At Chi	L	0-2
July 31, 1964(1)	Lary	Hou	W	3-0
July 21, 1965	Jackson	At Pit	W	1-0
May 8, 1966(1)	Hamilton and Bearnarth	Chi	L	1-3
June 28, 1966	Friend and Hamilton	Phi	L	0-1
Aug. 21, 1966(2)	McGraw	At Phi	W	5-1
June 21, 1967	Fisher	At Phi	W	2-0
May 10, 1968	Koosman and Koonce	At Chi	W	5-1
Aug. 29, 1968	Koonce and Taylor	Cin	W	2-0
Sept. 11, 1968	McAndrew, Short and Koonce	At Chi	W	1-0
Sept. 17, 1968	McAndrew	Chi	W	3-2
June 17, 1969(1)	Gentry	At Phi	W	1-0
June 24, 1969(2)	McAndrew and Taylor	Phi	W	5-0
Aug. 20, 1969	McAndrew	SF	W	6-0
Aug. 27, 1969	Koosman	At SD	W	4-1
April 22, 1970	Seaver	SD	W	2-1
April 25, 1970	Ryan	LA	L	0-1
May 24, 1970	Ryan	Chi	W	3-1
June 24, 1970(2)	Ryan and McGraw	At Chi	W	6-1
Sept. 20, 1970(1)	Koosman	Pit	W	4-1
June 18, 1971	Gentry	Phi	W	2-0
Sept. 6, 1971	Seaver	At Mon	W	7-0
May 2, 1972	Gentry	At SF	W	4-2
Sept. 29, 1972	Seaver	At Pit	W	1-0
May 12, 1973	Seaver	At Pit	W	6-0
Aug. 8, 1973	Matlack	At LA	W	1-0
Aug. 15, 1973	Seaver	At SD	W	7-0

LOW-HIT GAMES VS METS
(One Hit or Less)

Date	Pitcher	Team	Team W—L	Score

No-Hitters

June 30, 1962	Koufax	At LA	W	5-0
*June 21, 1964(1)	Bunning	Phi	W	6-0
†June 14, 1965	Maloney	At Cin	L	0-1(11)
Sept. 20, 1969	Moose	Pit	W	4-0
Oct. 2, 1972	Stoneman	Mon	W	7-0

*Perfect Game.
†Pitched 10 innings of no-hit ball. Mets got two hits in 11th and won the game.

One-Hitters

Sept. 25, 1964(1)	Maloney (Christopher, single in second)	Cin	W	3-0
May 20, 1965	Blasingame (Swoboda, single in seventh)	At Mil	W	7-1
June 20, 1965(1)	Koufax (Hickman, homer in fifth)	At LA	W	2-1
Sept. 10, 1965	Blasingame, O'Dell and Niekro (Hickman, homer in fourth)	Mil	W	3-1
Sept. 11, 1965	Cloninger (Jones, single in fifth)	Mil	W	9-0
July 1, 1966	Fryman (Hunt, single in first)	Pit	W	12-0
April 29, 1967	Arrigo (Grote, single in second)	At Cin	W	7-0
June 20, 1967	L. Jackson (Davis, double in second)	At Phi	W	4-0
July 28, 1968	Maloney and Carroll (Jones, double in first)	Cin	W	5-3
Aug. 4, 1968(2)	Kekich (Swoboda, single in seventh)	At LA	W	2-0
June 19, 1972	Dierker (Dyer, single In third)	Hou	W	3-0

ATTENDANCE

1962

	Home	Dates	Avg.	Road	Dates	Avg.
Los Angeles	243,054	8	30,382	208,552	9	23,172
San Francisco	229,972	7	32,853	131,135	7	18,734
St. Louis	91,496	8	11,437	93,797	7	13,400
Milwaukee	73,775	7	10,539	66,450	8	8,306
Cincinnati	69,566	7	9,938	89,488	8	11,186
Philadelphia	66,107	7	9,444	78,398	7	11,200
Pittsburgh	61,677	6	10,280	97,703	8	12,213
Chicago	60,632	8	7,579	39,053	7	5,579
Houston	26,251	5	5,250	72,204	9	8,023
Total	922,530	63	14,643	876,780	70	12,525

1963

	Home	Dates	Avg.	Road	Dates	Avg.
San Francisco	229,884	8	28,736	116,254	9	12,917
Los Angeles	220,247	8	27,531	206,197	8	25,775
St. Louis	119,526	8	14,941	70,026	8	8,753
Chicago	110,995	7	15,856	90,925	8	11,366
Pittsburgh	103,326	8	12,916	91,419	9	10,158
Milwaukee	99,250	8	12,406	65,271	8	8,159
Cincinnati	83,621	7	11,946	67,058	8	8,382
Philadelphia	69,759	8	8,720	68,417	7	9,774
Houston	43,500	7	6,214	53,526	9	5,947
Total	1,080,108	69	15,654	829,093	74	11,204

1964

	Home	Dates	Avg.	Road	Dates	Avg.
San Francisco	357,475	8	44,684	91,794	8	11,474
Los Angeles	326,231	8	40,779	204,281	9	22,698
Pittsburgh	209,882	9	23,320	65,550	8	8,194
Philadelphia	189,956	6	31,659	105,566	8	13,196
St. Louis	161,216	8	20,152	113,890	8	14,236
Milwaukee	133,810	8	16,726	63,971	8	7,996
Cincinnati	128,505	6	21,418	59,673	8	7,459
Chicago	125,746	7	17,964	63,500	9	7,056
Houston	99,776	6	16,629	46,727	8	5,841
Total	1,732,597	66	26,251	814,952	74	11,013

1965

	Home	Dates	Avg.	Road	Dates	Avg.
Los Angeles	337,910	8	42,239	227,123	8	28,390
San Francisco	336,278	8	42,035	115,777	8	14,472
St. Louis	178,344	8	22,293	132,612	8	16,577
Philadelphia	175,076	7	25,011	79,470	7	11,353
Cincinnati	168,991	8	21,124	64,646	8	8,081
Milwaukee	165,745	7	23,678	52,267	7	7,467
Pittsburgh	159,946	8	19,993	71,885	8	8,986
Chicago	136,574	7	19,511	75,248	7	10,750
Houston	109,525	7	15,646	256,403	9	28,489
Total	1,768,389	68	26,006	1,075,431	70	15,363

1966

	Home	Dates	Avg.	Road	Dates	Avg.
San Francisco	399,166	9	44,352	140,266	8	17,533
Los Angeles	358,518	8	44,815	235,773	8	29,472
Atlanta	211,705	9	23,523	160,897	8	20,112
Cincinnati	183,566	7	26,224	40,118	6	6,686
Philadelphia	175,566	8	21,946	108,891	7	15,556
Pittsburgh	174,554	8	21,819	150,233	8	18,779
Chicago	166,979	7	23,854	61,054	8	7,632
St. Louis	144,817	7	20,688	157,927	8	19,741
Houston	117,822	6	19,637	122,366	8	15,296
Total	1,932,693	69	28,010	1,177,525	69	17,066

1967

	Home	Dates	Avg.	Road	Dates	Avg.
San Francisco	246,942	8	30,868	78,911	7	11,273
Atlanta	216,751	8	27,094	105,593	9	11,733
St. Louis	207,210	8	25,901	156,301	7	22,329
Los Angeles	205,542	9	22,838	145,801	9	16,200
Pittsburgh	186,053	8	23,257	62,964	7	8,995
Philadelphia	141,662	7	20,237	85,788	8	10,724
Houston	134,987	7	19,284	131,227	8	16,403
Cincinnati	115,816	7	16,545	79,301	7	11,329
Chicago	110,529	5	23,854	90,159	8	11,270
Total	1,565,492	67	23,366	936,045	70	13,372

1968

	Home	Dates	Avg.	Road	Dates	Avg.
San Francisco	309,738	8	38,717	97,406	6	16,234
Los Angeles	280,141	8	35,018	126,584	8	15,823
St. Louis	260,717	8	32,590	192,903	8	24,113
Cincinnati	187,101	8	23,388	76,812	9	8,535
Pittsburgh	159,014	8	19,877	54,618	7	7,803
Atlanta	157,176	7	22,454	95,621	9	10,625
Philadelphia	152,266	8	19,033	43,867	7	6,267
Chicago	144,826	7	20,689	59,061	8	7,383
Houston	130,678	7	18,668	136,694	9	15,188
Total	1,781,657	69	25,821	883,566	71	12,445

1969

	Home	Dates	Avg.	Road	Dates	Avg.
St. Louis	307,907	9	34,212	116,240	7	16,606
Chicago	290,958	8	36,370	211,407	8	26,426
Pittsburgh	272,063	7	38,866	86,013	7	12,288
San Francisco	265,921	6	44,320	70,579	5	14,116
Los Angeles	219,012	6	36,502	155,235	6	25,873
Philadelphia	182,167	7	26,024	63,153	8	7,894
Cincinnati	170,587	6	28,431	82,403	5	16,481
Montreal	168,439	7	24,063	131,400	8	16,425
Atlanta	148,994	6	24,832	116,499	5	23,300
San Diego	79,283	4	19,821	38,154	5	7,361
Houston	70,042	4	17,511	126,123	6	21,021
Total	2,175,373	70	31,077	1,197,206	70	17,103

1970

	Home	Dates	Avg.	Road	Dates	Avg.
Atlanta	274,837	6	45,806	115,594	5	23,119
Chicago	336,536	9	37,393	193,042	7	27,577
Cincinnati	217,697	5	43,539	171,650	6	28,608
Houston	212,405	5	42,481	103,898	6	17,316
Los Angeles	209,149	6	34,858	183,451	6	30,575
Montreal	233,302	8	29,164	172,703	9	19,189
Philadelphia	205,424	7	29,346	77,403	8	9,676
Pittsburgh	304,069	8	38,008	324,716	9	36,079
St. Louis	311,129	9	34,569	195,143	9	21,683
San Diego	127,885	5	25,577	73,652	5	14,730
San Francisco	265,046	6	44,174	57,659	5	11,532
Total	2,697,479	74	36,452	1,668,911	75	22,252

1971

	Home	Dates	Avg.	Road	Dates	Avg.
Atlanta	226,337	6	37,723	106,412	6	17,735
Chicago	200,265	8	25,033	182,026	9	20,225
Cincinnati	151,752	5	30,350	103,565	5	20,713
Houston	147,586	6	24,597	126,932	6	21,155
Los Angeles	183,375	5	36,675	185,718	6	30,953
Montreal	148,719	7	21,246	154,333	8	19,292
Philadelphia	251,644	8	31,455	155,795	8	19,474
Pittsburgh	266,500	8	33,313	221,414	9	24,602
St. Louis	255,739	9	28,415	148,178	9	16,464
San Diego	147,332	6	24,555	40,654	5	8,131
San Francisco	287,431	6	47,905	100,155	6	16,693
Total	2,266,680	74	30,631	1,525,182	77	19,808

1972

	Home	Dates	Avg.	Road	Dates	Avg.
Atlanta	236,048	6	39,341	86,846	6	14,474
Chicago	209,971	7	29,996	175,167	9	19,463
Cincinnati	234,710	6	39,118	178,090	6	29,682
Houston	219,262	6	36,544	124,914	6	20,819
Los Angeles	189,464	6	31,577	181,801	6	30,300
Montreal	181,531	9	20,170	126,943	7	18,135
Philadelphia	188,904	8	23,613	176,976	8	22,122
Pittsburgh	183,403	8	22,925	156,262	5	31,252
St. Louis	146,765	5	29,353	156,165	9	17,352
San Diego	123,030	5	24,606	62,026	6	10,337
San Francisco	221,097	6	36,849	77,625	6	12,937
Total	2,134,185	72	29,641	1,502,815	74	20,308

1973

	Home	Dates	Avg.	Road	Dates	Avg.
Atlanta	127,445	6	21,241	55,828	6	9,304
Chicago	169,081	7	24,154	129,164	6	21,527
Cincinnati	154,476	6	25,746	139,169	5	27,834
Houston	111,986	6	18,664	118,080	6	19,680
Los Angeles	209,468	6	34,911	189,903	6	31,651
Montreal	222,720	7	31,817	130,891	8	16,361
Philadelphia	144,109	7	20,587	128,652	9	14,295
Pittsburgh	235,603	8	29,450	148,817	9	16,535
St. Louis	214,995	8	26,874	178,085	8	22,261
San Diego	134,644	6	22,441	36,375	6	6,063
San Francisco	187,863	6	31,311	68,630	6	11,438
Total	1,912,390	73	26,197	1,322,594	75	17,635

SUMMARY (1962–1973)

	Home	Dates	Avg.	Road	Dates	Avg.
*Atlanta	1,599,273	54	29,616	843,290	54	15,616
Chicago	2,063,092	87	24,863	1,369,806	94	14,572
Cincinnati	1,866,388	78	23,928	1,151,973	81	14,222
Houston	1,423,820	72	19,775	1,419,094	90	15,768
Los Angeles	2,982,111	86	34,676	2,250,419	89	25,285
*Milwaukee	472,580	30	15,753	247,959	31	7,999
Montreal	941,459	38	24,775	716,270	40	17,907
Philadelphia	1,942,640	88	22,075	1,172,376	92	12,743
Pittsburgh	2,316,090	94	24,639	1,531,594	94	16,294
St. Louis	2,399,861	95	25,262	1,711,267	96	17,826
San Diego	612,174	26	23,545	250,861	27	9,291
San Francisco	3,336,813	86	38,800	1,146,191	81	14,151
Total	21,969,573	834	26,342	13,810,100	869	15,892

*Braves in Milwaukee 1962-1965, in Atlanta thereafter.

Year-by-Year

Year	Home	Avg.	Road	Avg.
*1962	922,530	14,643	876,780	12,525
*1963	1,080,108	15,654	829,093	11,204
1964	1,732,597	26,251	814,952	11,013
1965	1,768,389	26,006	1,075,431	15,363
1966	1,932,693	28,010	1,177,525	17,066
1967	1,565,492	23,366	936,045	13,372
1968	1,781,657	25,821	883,566	12,445
1969	2,175,373	31,077	1,197,206	17,103
1970	2,697,479	36,452	1,668,911	22,252
1971	2,266,680	30,631	1,525,182	19,808
1972	2,134,185	29,641	1,502,815	20,308
1973	1,912,390	26,197	1,322,594	17,635
Total	21,969,573	26,342	13,810,100	15,892

*Home games at Polo Grounds in 1962, 1963; Shea Stadium thereafter.

WHERE THEY PLAYED

1B (35)	2B (30)	3B (46)
Bouchee 1962	Ashburn 1962	Chacon 1962
Herrscher 1962	Chacon 1962	Cook 1962-63
G. Hodges 1962-63	Drake 1962	Drake 1962
Kanehl 1962-64	Kanehl 1962-64	Herrscher 1962
Kranepool 1962-73	Mantilla 1962	Kanehl 1962-64
J. Marshall 1962	Neal 1962	Mantilla 1962
Thomas 1962-64	Burright 1963-64	Neal 1962-63
Throneberry 1962-63	Fernandez 1963	Thomas 1962-64
Carmel 1963	Hunt 1963-66	Zimmer 1962
Cook 1963	Schreiber 1963	Burright 1963
Harkness 1963-64	Klaus 1964-65	Fernandez 1963
D. Smith 1963-64	Samuel 1964	P. Green 1963
Hickman 1965-66	Cowan 1965	Hickman 1963-65
Kolb 1965	Hiller 1965-67	Hunt 1963-66
H. Taylor 1965	C. Smith 1965	Moran 1963-64
Boyer 1966-67	Bressoud 1966	Schreiber 1963
Bressoud 1966	Alomar 1967	W. Graham 1964
Stuart 1966	Boswell 1967-73	Klaus 1964-65
Davis 1967	Buchek 1967-68	Samuel 1964
B. Johnson 1967	Collins 1967-68	C. Smith 1964-65
Swoboda 1967	Heise 1967-68	Stephenson 1964
Charles 1968	B. Johnson 1967	Collins 1965, 68-69
Goossen 1968	Linz 1967-68	Hiller 1965-66
Jorgensen 1968, 70-71	Shirley 1967	Kolb 1965
Martin 1968-69	Weis 1968-71	Napoleon 1965
Shamsky 1968-71	Garrett 1969-73	Boyer 1966-67
Stahl 1968	Pfeil 1969	Bressoud 1966
Clendenon 1969-71	Martinez 1970-73	Grote 1966, 72-73
C. Jones 1969, 72-73	Foli 1971	Alomar 1967
Milner 1972-73	Barnes 1972	Boswell 1967
Fregosi 1972		Buchek 1967-68
Mays 1972-73		Charles 1967-69
Beauchamp 1972-73		Heise 1967
Sudakis 1972		B. Johnson 1967
Theodore 1973		Linz 1967
		Moock 1967
		Otis 1967, 69
		Reynolds 1967
		Weis 1968-71
		Garrett 1969-73
		Pfeil 1969
		Foy 1970
		Foli 1970-71
		Aspromonte 1971
		Martinez 1971-73
		Fregosi 1972-73

SS
(30)

Chacon 1962
Herrscher 1962
Kanehl 1962
Mantilla 1962
Neal 1962-63
Burright 1963
Fernandez 1963
Moran 1963-64
Schreiber 1963
Klaus 1964-65
McMillan 1964-66
Samuel 1964
C. Smith 1964-65
Collins 1965, 68
Cowan 1965
Harrelson 1965-73
Bressoud 1966
Hunt 1966
Alomar 1967
Buchek 1967
Heise 1967-69
B. Johnson 1967
Linz 1967
Weis 1968-71
Garrett 1969-70, 73
Foli 1970-71
Martinez 1970-73
Barnes 1972
Fregosi 1972
Ostrosser, 1973

OF
(65)

Ashburn 1962
Bell 1962
Cannizzaro 1962
Christopher 1962-65
Cook 1962-63
DeMerit 1962
Herrscher 1962
Hickman 1962-66
Kanehl 1962-64
J. Marshall 1962
B. G. Smith 1962
Thomas 1962-64
Woodling 1962
Carmel 1963
Coleman 1963
Hicks 1963
C. Jones 1963, 65-73
Kranepool 1963-64, 66, 68-69, 71-73
Piersall 1963
D. Smith 1963-64
Snider 1963
Altman 1964
Elliot 1964, 66
C. Smith 1964
Stephenson 1964-66
H. Taylor 1964
Cowan 1965
Hiller 1965-66
Kolb 1965
Lewis 1965-67
Napoleon 1965-66
Swoboda 1965-70
Fitzmaurice 1966
Luplow 1966-67
Murphy 1966
Bosch 1967-68
Davis 1967
Linz 1967
Otis 1967, 69
Reynolds 1967
Stahl 1967, 68
Agee 1968-72
Buchek 1968
Shamsky 1968-71
Clendenon 1969-71
Gaspar 1969-70
Gosger 1969

Pfeil 1969
Stanton 1970-71
D. Marshall 1970-72
Singleton 1970-71
Jorgensen 1970-71
Milner 1971-73
Foli 1971
Hahn 1971-73
Martinez 1971-73
Grote 1972
Schneck 1972-73
Staub 1972-73
Mays 1972-73
Beauchamp 1972-73
Dyer 1972
Chiles 1973
Theodore 1973
Fregosi 1973

C
(24)

Cannizzaro 1962-65
Chiti 1962
Coleman 1962, 63, 66
Ginsberg 1962
Landrith 1962
Pignatano 1962
S. Taylor 1962-63
Gonder 1963-65
Sherry 1963
Berra 1965
Goossen 1965-68
Schaffer 1965
Stephenson 1965-66
Grote 1966-73
Reynolds 1967
Sullivan 1967
H. Taylor 1964-67
Dyer 1968-73
Martin 1968-69
Estrada 1971
Sudakis 1972
Nolan 1972
R. Hodges 1973
May 1973

WORLD SERIES
AND
NATIONAL LEAGUE
CHAMPIONSHIP SERIES

Game 1—New York (East) defeats Atlanta (West) 9-5

New York	AB	R	H	PO	A	E
Agee, cf	5	0	0	2	0	0
Garrett, 3b	4	1	2	1	2	0
Jones, lf	5	1	1	5	0	0
Shamsky, rf	4	1	3	2	0	0
a-Weis, 2b	0	0	0	1	1	0
Boswell, 2b	3	2	0	0	1	1
Gaspar, rf	0	0	0	0	0	0
Kranepool, 1b	4	2	1	7	2	0
Grote, c	3	1	1	5	1	0
Harrelson, ss	3	1	1	2	1	0
Seaver, p	3	0	0	1	1	0
b-Martin	1	0	1	0	0	0
Taylor, p	0	0	0	1	0	0
Totals	35	9	10	27	9	1

New York	020 200 050	—9
Atlanta	012 010 100	—5

New York	IP	H	R	ER	BB	SO
Seaver	7	8	5	5	3	3
Taylor SV	2	2	0	0	0	1

Atlanta	IP	H	R	ER	BB	SO
Niekro	8	9	9	4	4	4
Upshaw	1	1	0	0	0	1

Atlanta	AB	R	H	PO	A	E
Millan, 2b	5	1	2	3	2	0
Gonzalez, cf	5	2	2	0	1	1
H. Aaron, rf	5	1	2	1	0	0
Carty, lf	3	1	1	0	0	0
Lum, lf	1	0	1	0	0	0
Cepeda, 1b	4	0	1	14	0	1
Boyer, 3b	1	0	0	2	5	0
Didier, c	4	0	0	5	0	0
Garrido, ss	4	0	1	2	7	0
Niekro, p	3	0	0	0	3	0
c-Aspromonte	1	0	0	0	0	0
Upshaw, p	0	0	0	1	0	0
Totals	36	5	10	27	19	2

Bases on balls—Off Seaver 3 (Boyer 2, Carty), off Niekro 4 (Boswell, Garrett, Grote, Harrelson). Strikeouts—By Seaver 3 (Niekro, Didier, Garrido), by Taylor 1 (Gonzalez), by Niekro 4 (Agee 2, Harrelson, Kranepool), by Upshaw 1 (Agee). Hit batsman—By Seaver 1 (Cepeda).

a-Ran for Shamsky in eighth. b-Singled for Seaver in eighth. c-Grounded out for Niekro in eighth. Runs batted in—Harrelson 2, Martin 2, Grote, Jones, H. Aaron 2, Gonzalez 2, Boyer. Two-base hits—Garrett, H. Aaron, Carty, Gonzalez, Lum, Millan. Three-base hit—Harrelson. Home runs—H. Aaron, Gonzalez. Stolen bases—Jones, Cepeda. Sacrifice fly—Boyer. Grounded into double plays—Jones 2. Double plays—Garrido, Millan, and Cepeda; Upshaw, Garrido, and Cepeda. Passed balls—Didier, Grote. Left on bases—New York 3, Atlanta 9. Umpires—Barlick, Donatelli, Sudol, Vargo, Pelekoudas, Steiner. Time—2:37. Attendance—50,122.

Game 2—New York (East) defeats Atlanta (West) 11-6

New York	AB	R	H	PO	A	E
Agee, cf	4	3	2	3	0	0
Garrett, 3b	5	1	2	0	1	0
Jones, lf	5	2	3	3	0	0
Shamsky, rf	5	1	3	0	0	0
c-Gaspar, rf	0	0	0	2	0	0
Boswell, 2b	5	1	1	2	1	0
McGraw, p	0	0	0	0	0	0
Kranepool, 1b	4	0	1	6	0	0
Grote, c	5	1	0	9	0	0
Harrelson, ss	5	1	1	2	2	1
Koosman, p	2	1	0	0	1	0
Taylor, p	0	0	0	0	0	0
b-Martin	1	0	0	0	0	0
Weis, 2b	1	0	0	0	2	0
Totals	42	11	13	27	7	1

New York	132 210 200	—11
Atlanta	000 150 000	—6

New York	IP	H	R	ER	BB	SO
Koosman	4.2	7	6	6	4	5
Taylor	1.1	1	0	0	0	2
McGraw SV	3	1	0	0	1	1

Atlanta	IP	H	R	ER	BB	SO
Reed	1.2	5	4	4	3	3
Doyle	1	2	2	0	1	3
Pappas	2.1	4	3	3	0	4
Britton	.1	0	0	0	1	0
Upshaw	2.2	2	2	2	1	1
Neibauer	1	0	0	0	0	1

Atlanta	AB	R	H	PO	A	E
Millan, 2b	2	1	2	0	5	0
Gonzalez, cf	4	1	1	2	0	0
H. Aaron, rf	5	1	1	3	0	1
Carty, lf	4	2	1	1	0	0
Cepeda, 1b	4	1	2	8	0	1
Boyer, 3b	4	1	1	1	2	1
Didier, c	4	0	0	12	1	0
Garrido, ss	4	0	1	0	0	0
Reed, p	0	0	0	0	1	0
Doyle, p	0	0	0	0	0	0
Pappas, p	1	0	0	0	0	0
a-T. Aaron	1	0	0	0	0	0
Britton, p	0	0	0	0	0	0
Upshaw, p	1	0	0	0	0	0
d-Aspromonte	1	0	0	0	0	0
Neibauer, p	0	0	0	0	0	0
Totals	35	6	9	27	9	3

Bases on balls—Off Koosman 4 (Millan 2, Carty, Gonzalez), off McGraw 1 (Millan), off Reed 3 (Garrett, Jones, Koosman), off Doyle 1 (Agee), off Britton 1 (Kranepool), off Upshaw 1 (Carty). Strikeouts—By Koosman 5 (Boyer, Cepeda, Didier, Gonzalez, Pappas), by Taylor 2 (Gonzalez, Upshaw), by McGraw 1 (H. Aaron), by Reed 3 (Boswell, Grote, Shamsky), by Doyle 3 (Boswell, Koosman, Kranepool), by Pappas 4 (Agee, Jones, Koosman, Shamsky), by Upshaw 1 (Harrelson), by Neibauer 1 (Garrett).

a-Grounded out for Pappas in fifth. b-Flied out for Taylor in seventh. c-Ran for Shamsky in seventh. d-Fouled out for Upshaw in eighth. Runs batted in—Jones 3, Agee 2, Boswell 2, Garrett, Harrelson, Kranepool, Shamsky, H. Aaron 3, Boyer 2, Cepeda. Two base hits—Garrett, Harrelson, Jones, Carty, Cepeda. Home runs—Agee, Boswell, Jones, H. Aaron. Stolen bases—Agee 2, Garrett, Jones. Caught Stealing—Kranepool. Grounded into double plays—H. Aaron, Carty. Double plays—Harrelson, Boswell, and Kranepool; Weis, Harrelson, and Kranepool; Didier and Boyer. Left on bases—New York 10, Atlanta 7. Umpires—Donatelli, Sudol, Vargo, Pelekoudas, Steiner, Barlick. Time—3:10. Attendance—50,270.

Game 3—New York (East) defeats Atlanta (West) 7-4

Atlanta	AB	R	H	PO	A	E
Millan, 2b	5	0	0	2	1	1
Gonzalez, cf	5	1	2	1	0	0
H. Aaron, rf	4	1	2	1	1	0
Carty, lf	3	1	1	1	0	0
Cepeda, 1b	3	1	2	7	1	0
Boyer, 3b	4	0	0	1	1	0
Didier, c	3	0	0	7	0	0
b-Lum	1	0	1	0	0	0
Jackson, ss	0	0	0	0	0	0
Garrido, ss	2	0	0	2	1	0
c-Alou	1	0	0	0	0	0
Tillman, c	0	0	0	2	0	0
Jarvis, p	2	0	0	1	2	0
Stone, p	1	0	0	1	1	0
Upshaw, p	0	0	0	0	0	0
d-Aspromonte	1	0	0	0	0	0
Totals	35	4	8	24	8	1

Atlanta	200 020 000	—4
New York	001 231 00X	—7

Atlanta	IP	H	R	ER	BB	SO
Jarvis	4.1	10	6	6	0	6
Stone	1	2	1	1	0	0
Upshaw	2.2	2	0	0	0	2

New York	IP	H	R	ER	BB	SO
Gentry	2*	5	2	2	1	1
Ryan	7	3	2	2	2	7

*pitched to two batters in third.

New York	AB	R	H	PO	A	E
Agee, cf	5	1	3	4	0	0
Garrett, 3b	4	1	1	0	3	0
Jones, lf	4	1	2	3	0	0
Shamsky, rf	4	1	1	1	0	0
a-Gaspar, rf	0	0	0	0	0	0
Boswell, 2b	4	1	3	1	0	0
Weis, 2b	0	0	0	0	0	0
Kranepool, 1b	4	0	1	7	1	0
Grote, c	4	1	1	8	0	0
Harrelson, ss	3	0	0	2	3	0
Gentry, p	0	0	0	0	0	0
Ryan, p	4	1	2	1	0	0
Totals	36	7	14	27	7	0

Bases on balls—Off Gentry 1 (Garrido), off Ryan 2 (Carty, Cepeda). Strikeouts—By Jarvis 6 (Grote 2, Garrett, Gentry, Jones, Shamsky), by Upshaw 2 (Agee, Grote), by Gentry 1 (Jarvis), by Ryan 7 (Boyer, Carty, Cepeda, Gonzalez, Jarvis, Stone).

a-Ran for Shamsky in seventh. b-Singled for Didier in eighth. c-Lined out for Garrido in eighth. d-Flied out for Upshaw in ninth. Runs batted in—H. Aaron 2, Cepeda 2, Boswell 3, Agee 2, Garrett 2. Two-base hits—H. Aaron, Cepeda, Agee, Grote, Jones, Kranepool. Home runs—H. Aaron, Cepeda, Agee, Boswell, Garrett. Sacrifice—Harrelson. Double play—Jarvis and Garrido. Left on bases—Atlanta 7, New York 6. Umpires—Sudol, Vargo, Pelekoudas, Steiner, Barlick, Donatelli. Time—2:24. Attendance—53,195.

R	H	E	PITCHERS (inn. pit.)	HOME RUNS (men on)	HIGHLIGHTS

New York (East) defeats Atlanta (West) 3 games to 0

GAME 1 - OCTOBER 4

		R	H	E	PITCHERS	HOME RUNS	HIGHLIGHTS
NY	E	9	10	1	Seaver (7), Taylor (2) **SV**		Aaron's home run off Seaver gives Atlanta a 5-4 lead in the seventh. But in the eighth, the Mets score five runs off Niekro as Garrett doubles past Boyer, Jones loops a single to left, Shamsky singles, Jones steals third when caught off second, Cepeda makes a wild throw home on Kranepool's grounder and Martin pinch hits a two-run single after an intentional pass to Harrelson. The fifth run scores as Gonzalez lets Martin's hit bounce past in center.
ATL	W	5	10	2	**Niekro** (8), Upshaw (1)	Gonzalez, H. Aaron	

GAME 2 - OCTOBER 5

		R	H	E	PITCHERS	HOME RUNS	HIGHLIGHTS
NY	E	11	13	1	Koosman (4.2), **Taylor** (1.1), McGraw (3) **SV**	Agee (1 on), Boswell (1 on), Jones (1 on), H. Aaron (2 on)	The Mets pile up an 8-0 lead in four innings, scoring on a double steal and an infield hit in the first, on Agee's homer and a scoring single by Shamsky in the second, on two unearned runs in the third and Boswell's homer in the fourth. Koosman is knocked out in the fifth by Aaron's homer, a walk, Cepeda's double and Boyer's two-run single, all with two out. But with the score 9-6, Taylor and McGraw stifle the Braves while Jones' homer gives New York an extra safety margin in the seventh.
ATL	W	6	9	3	Reed (1.2), Doyle (1), Pappas (2.1), Britton (0.1), Upshaw (2.2), Neibauer (1)		

GAME 3 - OCTOBER 6

		R	H	E	PITCHERS	HOME RUNS	HIGHLIGHTS
ATL	W	4	8	1	**Jarvis** (4.1), Stone (1), Upshaw (2.2)	H. Aaron (1 on), Cepeda (1 on)	After Aaron's homer in the first, Ryan relieves Gentry with two on, none out in the third and a one-ball, two-strike count on Carty. He strikes out Carty, and gets out of the inning. Agee's homer in the third and Boswell's homer in the fourth put the Mets ahead, 3-2, but Cepeda's homer in the fifth makes the score 4-3. But in the Met fifth, Garrett greets reliever Stone with a homer and Jones follows with a double. Boswell's single off Upshaw makes it 6-4 and Ryan keeps command.
NY	E	7	14	0	Gentry (2), **Ryan** (7)	Agee, Boswell (1 on), Garrett (1 on)	

Team Totals

		W	AB	H	2B	3B	HR	R	RBI	BA	BB	SO	ERA
NY	E	3	113	37	8	1	6	27	24	.327	10	25	5.00
ATL	W	0	106	27	9	0	5	15	15	.255	11	20	6.92

Individual Batting

NEW YORK (EAST)

	AB	H	2B	3B	HR	R	RBI	BA
T. Agee, of	14	5	1	0	2	4	4	.357
C. Jones, of	14	6	2	0	1	4	4	.429
W. Garrett, 3b	13	5	2	0	1	3	3	.385
A. Shamsky, of	13	7	0	0	0	3	1	.538
K. Boswell, 2b	12	4	0	0	2	4	5	.333
E. Kranepool, 1b	12	3	1	0	0	2	1	.250
J. Grote, c	12	2	1	0	0	3	1	.167
B. Harrelson, ss	11	2	1	1	0	2	3	.182
N. Ryan, p	4	2	0	0	0	1	0	.500
T. Seaver, p	3	0	0	0	0	1	0	.000
J. Koosman, p	2	0	0	0	0	1	0	.000
J. Martin	2	1	0	0	0	0	2	.500
A. Weis, 2b	1	0	0	0	0	0	0	.000
R. Gaspar, of	0	0	0	0	0	0	0	—

Errors: K. Boswell, B. Harrelson
Stolen bases: C. Jones (2), T. Agee (2), W. Garrett

ATLANTA (WEST)

	AB	H	2B	3B	HR	R	RBI	BA
T. Gonzalez, of	14	5	1	0	1	4	2	.357
H. Aaron, of	14	5	2	0	3	3	7	.357
F. Millan, 2b	12	4	1	0	0	2	0	.333
O. Cepeda, 1b	11	5	2	0	1	2	3	.455
B. Didier, c	11	0	0	0	0	0	0	.000
R. Carty, of	10	3	2	0	0	4	0	.300
G. Garrido, ss	10	2	0	0	0	0	0	.200
C. Boyer, 3b	9	1	0	0	0	0	3	.111
B. Aspromonte	3	0	0	0	0	0	0	.000
P. Niekro, p	3	0	0	0	0	0	0	.000
M. Lum, of	2	2	1	0	0	0	0	1.000
P. Jarvis, p	2	0	0	0	0	0	0	.000
G. Stone, p	1	0	0	0	0	0	0	.000
C. Upshaw, p	1	0	0	0	0	0	0	.000
T. Aaron	1	0	0	0	0	0	0	.000
M. Pappas, p	1	0	0	0	0	0	0	.000
F. Alou	1	0	0	0	0	0	0	.000
B. Tillman, c	0	0	0	0	0	0	0	—
S. Jackson, ss	0	0	0	0	0	0	0	—

Errors: O. Cepeda (2), T. Gonzalez, F. Millan, H. Aaron, C. Boyer
Stolen bases: O. Cepeda

Individual Pitching

NEW YORK (EAST)

	W	L	ERA	IP	H	BB	SO	SV
T. Seaver	1	0	6.43	7	8	3	2	0
N. Ryan	1	0	2.57	7	3	2	7	0
J. Koosman	0	0	11.57	4.2	7	4	5	0
R. Taylor	1	0	0.00	3.1	3	0	4	1
T. McGraw	0	0	0.00	3	1	1	1	1
G. Gentry	0	0	9.00	2	5	1	1	0

ATLANTA (WEST)

	W	L	ERA	IP	H	BB	SO	SV
P. Niekro	0	1	4.50	8	9	4	4	0
C. Upshaw	0	0	2.84	6.1	5	1	4	0
P. Jarvis	0	1	12.46	4.1	10	0	6	0
M. Pappas	0	0	11.57	2.1	4	4	4	0
R. Reed	0	1	21.60	1.2	5	3	3	0
G. Neibauer	0	0	0.00	1	0	1	0	0
P. Doyle	0	0	0.00	1	2	1	3	0
G. Stone	0	0	9.00	1	2	0	0	0
J. Britton	0	0	0.00	0.1	0	1	0	0

Game 1—Baltimore (A.L.) defeats New York (N.L.) 4-1

New York (N.L.)	AB	R	H	PO	A	E
Agee, cf	4	0	0	4	0	0
Harrelson, ss	3	0	1	0	1	0
Jones, lf	4	0	1	1	0	0
Clendenon, 1b	4	1	2	9	1	0
Swoboda, rf	3	0	1	0	0	0
Charles, 3b	4	0	0	1	4	0
Grote, c	4	0	1	6	0	0
Weis, 2b	1	0	0	3	1	1
Seaver, p	1	0	0	0	0	0
a-Dyer	1	0	0	0	0	0
Cardwell, p	0	0	0	0	0	0
b-Gaspar	1	0	0	0	0	0
Taylor, p	0	0	0	0	1	0
c-Shamsky	1	0	0	0	0	0
Totals	31	1	6	24	8	1

Baltimore (A.L.)	AB	R	H	PO	A	E
Buford, lf	4	1	2	2	0	0
Blair, cf	3	0	0	2	0	0
F. Robinson, rf	4	0	0	2	0	0
Powell, 1b	4	0	1	11	0	0
B. Robinson, 3b	4	0	0	0	6	0
Hendricks, c	3	1	1	8	0	0
Johnson, 2b	2	1	0	1	3	0
Belanger, ss	3	1	1	1	3	0
Cuellar, p	3	0	1	0	0	0
Totals	30	4	6	27	12	0

New York (N.L.)	000 000 100	—1
Baltimore (A.L.)	100 300 00X	—4

New York (N.L.)	IP	H	R	ER	BB	SO
Seaver	5	6	4	4	1	3
Cardwell	1	0	0	0	0	0
Taylor	2	0	0	0	1	3

Baltimore (A.L.)	IP	H	R	ER	BB	SO
Cuellar	9	6	1	1	4	8

Bases on balls—Off Seaver 1 (Johnson), off Taylor 1 (Blair), off Cuellar 4 (Weis 2, Harrelson, Swoboda). **Strikeouts**—By Seaver 3 (Blair, Cuellar, F. Robinson), by Taylor 3 (Cuellar, B. Robinson, F. Robinson), by Cuellar 8 (Agee 2, Clendenon 2, Charles, Grote, Seaver, Swoboda).

a-Grounded out for Seaver in sixth. b-Grounded out for Cardwell in seventh. c-Grounded out for Taylor in ninth. **Runs batted in**—Weis, Buford 2, Belanger, Cuellar. **Two-base hits**—Clendenon, Buford. **Home run**—Buford. **Sacrifice fly**—Weis. **Caught stealing**—Blair. **Grounded into double play**—Agee. **Double play**—Belanger, Johnson, and Powell. **Left on bases**—New York 8, Baltimore 4. **Umpires**—Soar (A.L.), Secory (N.L.), Napp (A.L.), Crawford (N.L.), DiMuro (A.L.), Weyer (N.L.). **Time**—2:13. **Attendance**—50,429.

Game 2—New York (N.L.) defeats Baltimore (A.L.) 2-1

New York (N.L.)	AB	R	H	PO	A	E
Agee, cf	4	0	0	3	0	0
Harrelson, ss	3	0	0	3	3	0
Jones, lf	4	0	0	2	0	0
Clendenon, 1b	3	1	1	7	0	0
Swoboda, rf	4	0	0	5	0	0
Charles, 3b	4	1	2	0	3	0
Grote, c	4	0	1	4	0	0
Weis, 2b	3	0	2	3	1	0
Koosman, p	4	0	0	0	1	0
Taylor, p	0	0	0	0	0	0
Totals	33	2	6	27	8	0

Baltimore (A.L.)	AB	R	H	PO	A	E
Buford, lf	4	0	0	1	0	0
Blair, cf	4	1	1	2	0	0
F. Robinson, rf	3	0	0	2	0	0
a-Rettenmund	0	0	0	0	0	0
Powell, 1b	3	0	0	10	1	0
B. Robinson, 3b	4	0	1	0	2	0
Johnson, 2b	2	0	0	1	3	0
Etchebarren, c	3	0	0	8	0	0
Belanger, ss	3	0	0	2	4	0
McNally, p	3	0	0	1	1	0
Totals	29	1	2	27	11	0

New York (N.L.)	000 100 001	—2
Baltimore (A.L.)	000 000 100	—1

New York (N.L.)	IP	H	R	ER	BB	SO
Koosman	8.2	2	1	1	3	4
Taylor SV	.1	0	0	0	0	0

Baltimore (A.L.)	IP	H	R	ER	BB	SO
McNally	9	6	2	2	3	7

Bases on balls—Off Koosman 3 (Johnson, Powell, F. Robinson), off McNally 3 (Clendenon, Harrelson, Weis). **Strikeouts**—By Koosman 4 (Belanger, Buford, McNally, Powell), by McNally 7 (Agee 2, Koosman 2, Clendenon, Swoboda, Weis). **Wild pitch**—McNally.

a-Ran for F. Robinson in ninth. **Runs batted in**—Clendenon, Weis, B. Robinson. **Two-base hit**—Charles. **Home run**—Clendenon. **Stolen base**—Blair. **Left on bases**—New York 7, Baltimore 4. **Umpires**—Secory (N.L.), Crawford (N.L.), DiMuro (A.L.), Weyer (N.L.), Soar (A.L.). **Time**—2:20. **Attendance**—50,850.

Game 3—New York (N.L.) defeats Baltimore (A.L.) 5-0

Baltimore (A.L.)	AB	R	H	PO	A	E	New York (N.L.)	AB	R	H	PO	A	E
Buford, lf	3	0	0	2	0	0	Agee, cf	3	1	1	6	0	0
Blair, cf	5	0	0	0	0	0	Garrett, 3b	1	0	0	1	0	0
F. Robinson, rf	2	0	1	7	0	0	Jones, lf	4	0	0	0	0	0
Powell, 1b	4	0	2	5	1	0	Shamsky, rf	4	0	0	1	0	0
B. Robinson, 3b	4	0	0	0	1	0	Boswell, 2b	3	1	1	0	1	0
Hendricks, c	4	0	0	6	0	0	Weis, 2b	0	0	0	0	0	0
Johnson, 2b	4	0	0	1	3	0	Gaspar, rf	1	0	0	2	0	0
Belanger, ss	2	0	0	2	0	0	Kranepool, 1b	4	1	1	7	0	0
Palmer, p	2	0	0	1	0	1	Grote, c	3	1	1	7	0	0
a-May	0	0	0	0	0	0	Harrelson, ss	3	1	1	3	5	0
Leonhard, p	0	0	0	0	1	0	Gentry, p	3	0	1	0	0	0
b-Dalrymple	1	0	1	0	0	0	Ryan, p	0	0	0	0	0	0
c-Salmon	0	0	0	0	0	0	Totals	29	5	6	27	6	0
Totals	31	0	4	24	6	1							

Baltimore (A.L.)	000 000 000 —0
New York (N.L.)	120 001 01X —5

Baltimore (A.L.)	IP	H	R	ER	BB	SO	New York (N.L.)	IP	H	R	ER	BB	SO
Palmer	6	5	4	4	4	5	Gentry	6.2	3	0	0	5	4
Leonhard	2	1	1	1	1	1	Ryan SV	2.1	1	0	0	2	3

Bases on balls—Off Palmer 4 (Garrett 2, Grote, Harrelson), off Leonhard 1 (Agee), off Gentry 5 (F. Robinson 2, Belanger, Buford, May), off Ryan 2 (Belanger, Buford). **Strikeouts**—By Palmer 5 (Gentry 2, Garrett, Harrelson, Jones), by Leonhard 1 (Harrelson), by Gentry 4 (Buford 2, Blair, B. Robinson), by Ryan 3 (Blair, Powell, B. Robinson).

a-Walked for Palmer in seventh. b-Singled for Leon-
hard in ninth. c-Ran for Dalrymple in ninth. **Runs batted in**—Gentry 2, Agee, Grote, Kranepool. **Two-base hits**—Gentry, Grote. **Home runs**—Agee, Kranepool. **Sacrifice hit**—Garrett. **Left on bases**—Baltimore 11, New York 6. **Umpires**—Napp (A.L.), Crawford (N.L.), DiMuro (A.L.), Weyer (N.L.), Soar (A.L.), Secory (N.L.). **Time**—2:23. **Attendance**—56,335.

Game 4—New York (N.L.) defeats Baltimore (A.L.) 2-1

Baltimore (A.L.)	AB	R	H	PO	A	E	New York (N.L.)	AB	R	H	PO	A	E
Buford, lf	5	0	0	2	0	0	Agee, cf	4	0	1	2	0	0
Blair, cf	4	0	1	0	0	0	Harrelson, ss	4	0	1	5	2	0
F. Robinson, rf	4	1	1	0	0	0	Jones, lf	4	1	1	1	0	0
Powell, 1b	4	0	1	14	0	0	Clendenon, 1b	4	1	1	6	3	0
B. Robinson, 3b	3	0	0	0	3	0	Swoboda, rf	4	0	3	4	0	0
Hendricks, c	3	0	0	7	1	0	Charles, 3b	3	0	0	2	1	0
Johnson, 2b	4	0	0	4	6	0	b-Shamsky	1	0	0	0	0	0
Belanger, ss	4	0	1	0	6	0	Garrett, 3b	0	0	0	0	0	1
Cuellar, p	2	0	1	0	1	0	Grote, c	4	0	1	7	2	0
a-May	1	0	0	0	0	0	d-Gaspar	0	1	0	0	0	0
Watt, p	0	0	0	0	0	0	Weis, 2b	3	0	2	1	1	0
c-Dalrymple	1	0	1	0	0	0	Seaver, p	3	0	0	2	1	0
Hall, p	0	0	0	0	0	0	e-Martin	0	0	0	0	0	0
Richert, p	0	0	0	0	0	1	Totals	34	2	10	30	10	1
Totals	35	1	6	27	17	1							

Baltimore (A.L.)	000 000 001 0 —1
New York (N.L.)	010 000 000 1 —2

Baltimore (A.L.)	IP	H	R	ER	BB	SO	New York (N.L.)	IP	H	R	ER	BB	SO
Cuellar	7	7	1	1	0	5	Seaver	10	6	1	1	2	6
Watt	2	2	0	0	0	2							
Hall	0*	1	1	0	1	0							
Richert	0+	0	0	0	0	0							

*Pitched to two batters in tenth. +Pitched to one batter in tenth. None out when winning run scored.

Bases on balls—Off Hall 1 (Weis), off Seaver 2 (Blair, Hendricks). **Strikeouts**—By Cuellar 5 (Grote 2, Charles, Clendenon, Seaver), by Watt 2 (Agee, Clendenon), by Seaver 6 (Blair, Buford, Cuellar, Johnson, May, Powell).

a-Struck out for Cuellar in eighth. b-Grounded out for Charles in ninth. c-Singled for Watt in tenth. d-Ran for Grote in tenth. e-Sacrificed and safe on error for Seaver in tenth. **Runs batted in**—B. Robinson, Clendenon. **Two-base**
hit—Grote. **Home run**—Clendenon. **Sacrifice**—Martin. **Sacrifice fly**—B. Robinson. **Caught stealing**—Johnson, Swoboda. **Grounded into double plays**—Jones, Seaver. **Double plays**—Belanger, Johnson, and Powell 2; Hendricks and Johnson. **Left on bases**—Baltimore 7, New York 7. **Umpires**—Crawford (N.L.), DiMuro (A.L.), Weyer (N.L.), Soar (A.L.), Secory (N.L.), Napp (A.L.). **Time**—2:33. **Attendance**—57,367.

Game 5—New York (N.L.) defeats Baltimore (A.L.) 5-3

Baltimore (A.L.)	AB	R	H	PO	A	E
Buford, lf	4	0	0	1	0	0
Blair, cf	4	0	0	3	0	0
F. Robinson, rf	3	1	1	2	0	0
Powell, 1b	4	0	1	6	0	1
b-Salmon	0	0	0	0	0	0
B. Robinson, 3b	4	0	0	1	4	0
Johnson, 2b	4	0	1	1	0	0
Etchebarren, c	3	0	0	8	0	0
Belanger, ss	3	1	1	2	1	0
McNally, p	2	1	1	0	0	0
a-Motton	1	0	0	0	0	0
Watt, p	0	0	0	0	0	1
Totals	32	3	5	24	5	2

New York (N.L.)	AB	R	H	PO	A	E
Agee, cf	3	0	1	4	0	0
Harrelson, ss	4	0	0	1	6	0
Jones, lf	3	2	1	3	0	0
Clendenon, 1b	3	1	1	8	0	0
Swoboda, rf	4	1	2	5	0	0
Charles, 3b	4	0	0	0	1	0
Grote, c	4	0	0	5	0	0
Weis, 2b	4	1	1	1	2	0
Koosman, p	3	0	1	0	1	0
Totals	32	5	7	27	10	0

Baltimore (A.L.)	003 000 000	—3
New York (N.L.)	000 002 12X	—5

Baltimore (A.L.)	IP	H	R	ER	BB	SO
McNally	7	5	3	3	2	6
Watt	1	2	2	1	0	1

New York (N.L.)	IP	H	R	ER	BB	SO
Koosman	9	5	3	3	1	5

Bases on balls—Off McNally 2 (Agee, Clendenon), off Koosman 1 (F. Robinson). **Strikeouts**—By McNally 6 (Harrelson 2, Koosman 2, Clendenon, Swoboda), by Watt 1 (Weis), by Koosman 5 (Blair, Etchebarren, McNally, Powell, F. Robinson). **Hit batsman**—By McNally 1 (Jones).

a-Grounded out for McNally in eighth. b-Ran for Powell in ninth. **Runs batted in**—McNally 2, F. Robinson, Clendenon 2, Weis, Swoboda. **Two-base hits**—Jones, Koosman, Swoboda. **Home runs**—McNally, F. Robinson, Clendenon, Weis. **Stolen base**—Agee. **Left on bases**—Baltimore 3, New York 6. **Umpires**—DiMuro (A.L.), Weyer (N.L.), Soar (A.L.), Secory (N.L.), Napp (A.L.), Crawford (N.L.). **Time**—2:14. **Attendance**—57,397.

R H E	PITCHERS (inn. pit.)	HOME RUNS (men on)	HIGHLIGHTS

New York (N.L.) defeats Baltimore (A.L.) 4 games to 1

GAME 1 - OCTOBER 11

NY N | 1 6 1 | **Seaver** (5), Cardwell (1), Taylor (2) | Buford | Buford greets Seaver with a home run on second pitch. With two out in fourth, Hendricks singles, Johnson walks, Belanger singles for a run, Cuellar singles for another and Buford doubles in a third.
BAL A | 4 6 0 | **Cuellar** (9) |

GAME 2 - OCTOBER 12

NY N | 2 6 0 | **Koosman** (8.2), Taylor (0.1) **SV** | Clendenon | Clendenon's homer in fourth is matched in the seventh by the first two Oriole hits: a single by Blair, who steals second, and Brooks Robinson's single with two out. Successive singles by Charles, Grote and Weis with two out make it 2-1 in ninth, and Taylor gets last out after Koosman walks two with two out in bottom half.
BAL A | 1 2 0 | **McNally** (9) |

GAME 3 - OCTOBER 14

BAL A | 0 4 1 | Palmer (6), Leonard (2) | Agee, Kranepool | Agee homers in first and Gentry drives in two with two-out double in second. But when Gentry walks three men with two out in seventh, Agee saves three runs with sliding catch in right center as Ryan relieves. Agee saved two runs in fourth with one-hand running catch at left field wall.
NY N | 5 6 0 | **Gentry** (6.2), Ryan (2.1) **SV** |

GAME 4 - OCTOBER 15

BAL A | 1 6 1 | Cuellar (7), Watt (2), **Hall** (0), Richert (0) | | Seaver takes 1-0 lead into ninth, thanks to Clendenon's homer in second. But Frank Robinson and Powell single with one out, and Swoboda's diving catch robs Brooks Robinson of a triple but tying run scores. Buford misplays Grote's fly into a double leading off the 10th, and Richert's wild throw to first on Martin's pinch bunt lets winning run score.
NY N | 2 10 1 | **Seaver** (10) | Clendenon |

GAME 5 - OCTOBER 16

BAL A | 3 5 2 | McNally (7), **Watt** (1) | McNally (1 on), F. Robinson, Clendenon (1 on), Weis | Third-inning homers by McNally and Frank Robinson give Baltimore 3-0 lead. But Clendenon's homer in sixth, after a pitch nicks Jones' shoe, and Weis' homer in seventh tie it. Doubles by Jones and Swoboda off Watt score winning run in eighth.
NY N | 5 7 0 | **Koosman** (9) |

Team Totals

	W	AB	H	2B	3B	HR	R	RBI	BA	BB	SO	ERA
NY N	4	159	35	8	0	6	15	13	.220	15	35	1.80
BAL A	1	157	23	1	0	3	9	9	.146	15	28	2.72

Individual Batting

NEW YORK (N.L.)

	AB	H	2B	3B	HR	R	RBI	BA
J. Grote, c	19	4	2	0	0	1	1	.211
C. Jones, of	19	3	1	0	0	2	0	.158
T. Agee, of	18	3	0	0	1	1	1	.167
B. Harrelson, ss	17	3	0	0	0	1	0	.176
R. Swoboda, of	15	6	1	0	0	1	1	.400
E. Charles, 3b	15	2	1	0	0	1	0	.133
D. Clendenon, 1b	14	5	1	0	3	4	4	.357
A. Weis, 2b	11	5	0	0	1	1	3	.455
J. Koosman, p	7	1	1	0	0	0	0	.143
A. Shamsky, of	6	0	0	0	0	0	0	.000
T. Seaver, p	4	0	0	0	0	0	0	.000
E. Kranepool, 1b	4	1	0	0	1	1	1	.250
K. Boswell, 2b	3	1	0	0	0	1	0	.333
G. Gentry, p	3	1	1	0	0	0	2	.333
R. Gaspar, of	2	0	0	0	0	1	0	.000
D. Dyer	1	0	0	0	0	0	0	.000
W. Garrett, 3b	1	0	0	0	0	0	0	.000
J. Martin	0	0	0	0	0	0	0	—

Errors: W. Garrett, A. Weis
Stolen bases: T. Agee

BALTIMORE (A.L.)

	AB	H	2B	3B	HR	R	RBI	BA
D. Buford, of	20	2	1	0	1	1	2	.100
P. Blair, of	20	2	0	0	0	1	0	.100
B. Robinson, 3b	19	1	0	0	0	0	2	.053
B. Powell, 1b	19	5	0	0	0	0	0	.263
D. Johnson, 2b	16	1	0	0	0	1	0	.063
F. Robinson, of	16	3	0	0	1	2	1	.188
M. Belanger, ss	15	3	0	0	0	2	1	.200
E. Hendricks, c	10	1	0	0	0	1	0	.100
Etchebarren, c	6	0	0	0	0	0	0	.000
M. Cuellar, p	5	2	0	0	0	0	1	.400
D. McNally, p	5	1	0	0	1	1	2	.200
J. Palmer, p	2	0	0	0	0	0	0	.000
C. Dalrymple	2	2	0	0	0	0	0	1.000
C. Motton	1	0	0	0	0	0	0	.000
D. May	1	0	0	0	0	0	0	.000
M. Rettenmund	0	0	0	0	0	0	0	—
C. Salmon	0	0	0	0	0	0	0	—

Errors: P. Richert, E. Watt, J. Palmer, B. Powell
Stolen bases: P. Blair

Individual Pitching

NEW YORK (N.L.)

	W	L	ERA	IP	H	BB	SO	SV
J. Koosman	2	0	2.04	17.2	7	4	9	0
T. Seaver	1	1	3.00	15	12	3	9	0
G. Gentry	1	0	0.00	6.2	3	5	4	0
R. Taylor	0	0	0.00	2.1	0	1	3	1
N. Ryan	0	0	0.00	2.1	1	2	3	1
D. Cardwell	0	0	0.00	1	0	0	0	0

BALTIMORE (A.L.)

	W	L	ERA	IP	H	BB	SO	SV
D. McNally	0	1	2.81	16	11	5	13	0
M. Cuellar	1	0	1.13	16	13	4	13	0
J. Palmer	0	1	6.00	6	5	4	5	0
E. Watt	0	1	3.00	3	4	0	3	0
D. Leonhard	0	0	4.50	2	1	1	1	0
D. Hall	0	1	—	0.0	1	1	0	0
P. Richert	0	0	—	0.0	0	0	0	0

		R	H	E	PITCHERS (inn. pit.)	HOME RUNS (men on)	HIGHLIGHTS

New York (East) defeats Cincinnati (West) 3 games to 2

GAME 1 - OCTOBER 6

		R	H	E	PITCHERS (inn. pit.)	HOME RUNS (men on)	HIGHLIGHTS
NY	E	1	3	0	Seaver (9)	Rose, Bench	Tom Seaver set a league playoff record striking out 13 Reds, but after pitching seven superb scoreless innings, he served a game-tying home run to Pete Rose in the eighth and another to Johnny Bench in the ninth as the Reds came from behind to win 2–1. Seaver drove in the only New York run, doubling home Bud Harrelson in the second. Pedro Borbon, in relief of Jack Billingham, was the winner.
CIN	W	2	6	0	Billingham (8), Hall (0), Borbon (1)		

GAME 2 - OCTOBER 7

		R	H	E	PITCHERS (inn. pit.)	HOME RUNS (men on)	HIGHLIGHTS
NY	E	5	7	0	Matlack (0)	Staub	Jon Matlack pitched a two-hitter and struck out nine pitching the Mets to a 5–0 triumph that evened the Series. The Mets, nursing a 1–0 lead going into the ninth, on a homer by Rusty Staub, teed off on relievers Tom Hall and Pedro Borbon for four runs to put the game out of reach.
CIN	W	0	2	0	Gullett (5), Carroll (3), Hall (0.1), Borbon (0.2)		

GAME 3 - OCTOBER 8

		R	H	E	PITCHERS (inn. pit.)	HOME RUNS (men on)	HIGHLIGHTS
CIN	W	2	8	1	Grimsley (1.2), Hall (0.1), Tomlin (1.2), Nelson (2.1), Borbon (2)	Menke	Rusty Staub homered in his first two times at bat, his second homer coming in the second inning to highlight a five-run outburst that helped Jerry Koosman and the Mets to an easy 9–2 triumph. A tussle between Pete Rose of the Reds and Bud Harrelson of the Mets precipitated a bottle-throwing, garbage-throwing shower upon Rose in leftfield. Reds' manager Sparky Anderson pulled the Reds from the field and Mets players had to plead with the fans to cease and desist. Play was interrupted for 15 minutes before order was finally restored.
NY	E	9	11	1	Koosman (9)	Staub, Staub (2 on)	

GAME 4 - OCTOBER 9

		R	H	E	PITCHERS (inn. pit.)	HOME RUNS (men on)	HIGHLIGHTS
CIN	W	2	8	0	Norman (5), Gullett (4), Carroll (2), Borbon (1), SV	Perez, Rose	Pete Rose got his revenge, hitting a home run off Harry Parker in the 12th inning to give the Reds a 2–1 victory and even the Series at two games apiece. George Stone of the Mets carried a 1–0 lead until the seventh when Tony Perez homered to tie the score. Rose got three of the Reds eight hits while Harrelson went hitless. Rusty Staub jammed his right shoulder crashing into the fence to make a spectacular catch with two on base in the 11th inning.
NY	E	1	3	2	Stone (6.2), McGraw (4.1), Parker (1)		

GAME 5 - OCTOBER 10

		R	H	E	PITCHERS (inn. pit.)	HOME RUNS (men on)	HIGHLIGHTS
CIN	W	2	7	1	Billingham (4), Gullett (0), Carroll (2), Grimsley (2)		Tom Seaver, a victim of non-support most of the regular season, was backed by a 13-hit attack and easily outpitched Cincinnati ace Jack Billingham to give the Mets a 7–2 victory and the National League championship. The Mets sent eight men to the plate in the fifth and scored half of them to break a 1–1 tie. Cleon Jones led the attack with a double and two singles, driving in two runs. The fans went on a rampage at the game's end and the players had to run for their lives to escape possible bodily injury.
NY	E	7	13	1	Seaver (8.1), McGraw (0.2), SV		

Team Totals

	W	AB	H	2B	3B	HR	R	RBI	BA	BB	SO	ERA
NY E	3	168	37	5	0	3	23	22	.220	19	28	1.33
CIN W	2	166	31	4	0	4	8	8	.187	13	42	4.45

Individual Batting

NEW YORK (EAST)

	AB	H	2B	3B	HR	R	RBI	BA
W. Garrett, 3b	23	2	1	0	0	1	1	.087
C. Jones, of	20	6	2	0	0	3	3	.300
J. Grote, c	19	4	0	0	0	2	2	.211
F. Millan, 2b	19	6	0	0	0	5	2	.316
B. Harrelson, ss	18	3	0	0	0	1	2	.167
D. Hahn, of	17	4	0	0	0	2	1	.235
J. Milner, 1b	17	3	0	0	0	2	1	.176
R. Staub, of	15	3	0	0	3	4	5	.200
T. Seaver, p	6	2	2	0	0	1	1	.333
J. Koosman, p	4	2	0	0	0	1	1	.500
W. Mays, of	3	1	0	0	0	1	1	.333
E. Kranepool,1b	2	1	0	0	0	0	2	.500
J. Matlack, p	2	0	0	0	0	0	0	.000
T. McGraw, p	1	0	0	0	0	0	0	.000
G. Stone, p	1	0	0	0	0	0	0	.000
K. Boswell	1	0	0	0	0	0	0	.000
H. Parker, p	0	0	0	0	0	0	0	.000

Errors: W. Garrett, T. McGraw, J. Grote, C. Jones
Stolen bases: None

CINCINNATI (WEST)

	AB	H	2B	3B	HR	R	RBI	BA
T. Perez, 1b	22	2	0	0	1	1	2	.091
P. Rose, of	21	8	1	0	2	3	2	.381
J. Morgan, 2b	20	2	1	0	0	1	1	.100
J. Bench, c	19	5	1	0	1	1	1	.263
C. Geronimo, of	15	1	0	0	0	0	0	.067
D. Driessen, 3b	12	2	1	0	0	0	1	.167
A. Kosco, rf	10	3	0	0	0	0	0	.300
D. Menke, 3s	9	2	0	0	1	1	1	.222
D. Chaney, ss	9	0	0	0	0	0	0	.000
K. Griffey, o	7	1	1	0	0	0	0	.143
E. Armbrister, of	6	1	0	0	0	0	0	.167
L. Stahl	4	2	0	0	0	1	0	.500
J. Billingham, p	3	0	0	0	0	0	0	.000
P. Gagliano	3	0	0	0	0	0	0	.000
H. King	2	1	0	0	0	0	0	.500
E. Crosby	2	1	0	0	0	0	0	.500
R. Nelson, p	1	0	0	0	0	0	0	.000
D. Gullett, p	1	0	0	0	0	0	0	.000
F. Norman, p	1	0	0	0	0	0	0	.000
R. Grimsley, p	0	0	0	0	0	0	0	.000
T. Hall, p	0	0	0	0	0	0	0	.000
D. Tomlin, p	0	0	0	0	0	0	0	.000
P. Borbon, p	0	0	0	0	0	0	0	.000
C. Carroll, p	0	0	0	0	0	0	0	.000

Errors: A. Kosko, D. Driessen
Stolen bases: None

Individual Pitching

NEW YORK (EAST)

	W	L	ERA	IP	H	BB	SO	SV
T. Seaver	1	1	1.62	16.2	13	5	17	0
J. Koosman	1	0	2.00	9	8	0	9	0
J. Matlack	1	0	0.00	9	2	3	9	0
G. Stone	0	0	1.35	6.2	3	2	4	0
T. McGraw	0	0	0.00	5	4	3	3	1
H. Parker	0	1	9.00	1	1	0	0	0

CINCINNATI (WEST)

	W	L	ERA	IP	H	BB	SO	SV
J. Billingham	0	1	4.50	12	9	4	9	0
D. Gullett	0	1	2.00	9	4	3	6	0
C. Carroll	1	0	1.29	7	5	1	2	0
F. Norman	0	0	1.80	5	1	3	3	0
P. Borbon	1	0	0.00	4.2	3	0	3	1
R. Grimsley	0	1	13.63	3.2	7	2	3	0
R. Nelson	0	0	0.00	2.1	0	1	0	0
D. Tomlin	0	0	16.20	1.2	5	1	1	0
T. Hall	0	0	67.00	0.2	3	4	1	0

GAME NO. 1
GAME OF SATURDAY, OCTOBER 6

New York	ab	r	h	rbi	Cincinnati	ab	r	h	rbi
Garrett, 3b	4	0	1	0	Rose, lf	4	1	1	1
Millan, 2b	3	0	0	0	Morgan, 2b	4	0	0	0
Staub, rf	2	0	0	0	Driessen, 3b	4	0	1	0
Milner, 1b	3	0	1	0	Perez, 1b	4	0	0	0
Jones, lf	4	0	0	0	Bench, c	4	1	3	1
Grote, c	4	0	0	0	Griffey, rf	2	0	0	0
Hahn, cf	3	0	0	0	Geronimo, cf	3	0	1	0
Harrelson, ss	2	1	0	0	Chaney, ss	2	0	0	0
Seaver, p	3	0	1	1	Stahl, ph	1	0	0	0
					Crosby, ss	0	0	0	0
					Billingham, p	1	0	0	0
					King, ph	1	0	0	0
					Hall, p	0	0	0	0
					Borbon, p	0	0	0	0
Totals	28	1	3	1	**Totals**	30	2	6	2

```
New York      0 1 0   0 0 0   0 0 0—1
Cincinnati    0 0 0   0 0 0   0 1 1—2
```
One out when winning run scored.

	IP	H	R	ER	BB	SO
Seaver (Loser)	8⅓	6	2	2	0	13

Cincinnati	IP	H	R	ER	BB	SO
Billingham	8	3	1	1	3	6
Hall	0*	0	0	0	1	0
Borbon (Winner)	1	0	0	0	0	0

*Pitched to one batter in ninth.

E—None. DP—Cincinnati 1. LOB—New York 5, Cincinnati 5. 2B—Seaver, Bench, Driessen. HR—Rose, Bench. SH—Millan, Billingham. HBP—By Seaver (Griffey). U—Sudol, Vargo, Pelekoudas, Engel, Froemming and Dale. T—2:00. A—53,431.

GAME NO. 2
GAME OF SUNDAY, OCTOBER 7

New York	ab	r	h	rbi	Cincinnati	ab	r	h	rbi
Garrett, 3b	5	0	0	0	Rose, lf	4	0	0	0
Millan, 2b	4	1	1	0	Morgan, 2b	4	0	0	0
Staub, rf	3	2	1	1	Perez, 1b	4	0	0	0
Jones, lf	3	1	1	1	Bench, c	4	0	0	0
Milner, 1b	3	1	0	0	Kosco, rf	2	0	2	0
Grote, c	4	0	1	2	Driessen, 3b	3	0	0	0
Hahn, cf	3	0	2	0	Geronimo, cf	3	0	0	0
Harrelson, ss	4	0	1	1	Chaney, ss	0	0	0	0
Matlack, p	2	0	0	0	Armbris'r, ph	1	0	0	0
					Hall, p	0	0	0	0
					Borbon, p	0	0	0	0
					Gullett, p	0	0	0	0
					Gagliano, ph	1	0	0	0
					Carroll, p	0	0	0	0
					Menke, ph-ss	1	0	0	0
Totals	31	5	7	5	**Totals**	27	0	2	0

```
New York      0 0 0   1 0 0   0 0 4—5
Cincinnati    0 0 0   0 0 0   0 0 0—0
```

New York	IP	H	R	ER	BB	SO
Matlack (Winner)	9	2	0	0	3	9

Cincinnati	IP	H	R	ER	BB	SO
Gullett (Loser)	5	2	1	1	2	3
Carroll	3	0	0	0	1	2
Hall	⅓	2	4	4	2	0
Borbon	⅔	3	0	0	0	1

E—None. DP—Cincinnati 1. LOB—New York 5, Cincinnati 4. HR—Staub. SH—Gullett, Matlack. U—Vargo, Pelekoudas, Engel, Froemming, Dale and Sudol. T—2:19. A—54,041.

GAME NO. 3
GAME OF MONDAY, OCTOBER 8

Cincinnati	ab	r	h	rbi	New York	ab	r	h	rbi
Rose, lf	4	0	2	0	Garrett, 3b	4	0	0	1
Morgan, 2b	4	0	1	1	Millan, 2b	3	2	1	1
Perez, 1b	4	0	0	0	Staub, rf	5	2	2	4
Bench, c	4	0	1	0	Jones, lf	3	1	2	0
Kosco, rf	4	0	1	0	Milner, 1b	4	0	1	1
Armbris'r, cf	4	0	1	0	Grote, c	3	2	1	0
Menke, 3b	4	1	1	1	Hahn, cf	4	1	2	0
Chaney, ss	3	0	0	0	Harrelson, ss	4	0	0	0
Gagliano, ph	1	0	0	0	Koosman, p	4	1	2	1
Grimsley, p	0	0	0	0					
Hall, p	0	0	0	0					
Stahl, ph	1	1	1	0					
Tomlin, p	1	0	0	0					
Nelson, p	1	0	0	0					
King, ph	1	0	1	0					
Borbon, p	0	0	0	0					
Totals	35	2	8	2	**Totals**	34	9	11	8

```
Cincinnati    0 2 0   0 0 0   0 0 0—2
New York      1 5 1   2 0 0   0 x—9
```

Cincinnati	IP	H	R	ER	BB	SO
Grimsley (Loser)	1⅔	5	5	5	1	2
Hall	⅓	1	1	1	1	1
Tomlin	1⅔	5	3	3	1	1
Nelson	2⅓	0	0	0	1	0
Borbon	2	0	0	0	0	2

New York	IP	H	R	ER	BB	SO
Koosman (Winner)	9	8	2	2	0	9

E—Kosco, Garrett. DP—New York 1. LOB—Cincinnati 6, New York 6. 2B—Jones, Bench. HR—Staub 2, Menke. SF—Garrett. U—Pelekoudas, Engel, Froemming, Dale, Sudol and Vargo. T—2:48. A—53,967.

GAME NO. 4
GAME OF TUESDAY, OCTOBER 9

Cincinnati	ab	r	h	rbi	New York	ab	r	h	rbi
Rose, lf	5	1	3	1	Garrett, 3b	5	0	0	0
Morgan, 2b	4	0	0	0	Millan, 2b	5	0	2	1
Perez, 1b	6	1	1	1	Staub, rf	5	0	0	0
Bench, c	4	0	1	0	Jones, lf	5	0	0	0
Kosco, rf	4	0	1	0	Milner, 1b	4	0	0	0
Menke, 3b-ss	4	0	1	0	Grote, c	4	0	1	0
Geronimo, cf	5	0	0	0	Hahn, cf	3	1	0	0
Chaney, ss	2	0	0	0	Harrelson, ss	4	0	0	0
Armbris'r, ph	1	0	0	0	Stone, p	1	0	0	0
Crosby, ss	1	0	1	0	McGraw, p	1	0	0	0
Dr'sen, pr-3b	1	0	0	0	Boswell, ph	1	0	0	0
Norman, p	0	0	0	0	Parker, p	0	0	0	0
Stahl, ph	1	0	0	0					
Gullett, p	1	0	0	0					
Gagliano, ph	1	0	0	0					
Carroll, p	0	0	0	0					
Griffey, ph	1	0	0	0					
Borbon, p	0	0	0	0					
Totals	42	2	8	2	**Totals**	38	1	3	1

```
Cincinnati    0 0 0   0 0 0   1 0 0   0 1—2
New York      0 0 1   0 0 0   0 0 0   0 0—1
```

Cincinnati	IP	H	R	ER	BB	SO
Norman	5	1	1	1	3	3
Gullett	4	2	0	0	0	3
Carroll (Winner)	2	0	0	0	0	0
Borbon (Save)	1	0	0	0	0	0

New York	IP	H	R	ER	BB	SO
Stone	6⅔	3	1	1	2	4
McGraw	4⅓	4	0	0	3	3
Parker (Loser)	1	1	1	1	0	0

E—McGraw, Grote. DP—Cincinnati 1, New York 2. LOB—Cincinnati 10, New York 4. HR—Perez, Rose. SH—Morgan. WP—McGraw. U—Engel, Froemming, Dale, Sudol, Vargo and Pelekoudas. T—3:07. A—50,786.

GAME NO. 5
GAME OF WEDNESDAY, OCTOBER 10

Cincinnati	ab	r	h	rbi	New York	ab	r	h	rbi
Rose, lf	4	1	2	0	Garrett, 3b	5	1	1	0
Morgan, 2b	4	1	1	.0	Millan, 2b	4	2	2	0
Driessen, 3b	4	0	1	1	Jones, rf-lf	5	1	3	2
Perez, 1b	4	0	1	1	Milner, 1b	3	1	1	0
Bench, c	3	0	0	0	Kranepool, lf	2	0	1	2
Griffey, rf	4	0	1	0	Mays, ph-cf	3	1	1	1
Geronimo, cf	4	0	0	0	Grote, c	4	0	1	0
Chaney, ss	2	0	0	0	Hahn, cf-rf	4	0	0	1
Stahl, ph	1	0	1	0	Harrelson, ss	4	0	2	1
Billingham, p	2	0	0	0	Seaver, p	3	1	1	0
Gullett, p	0	0	0	0	McGraw, p	0	0	0	0
Carroll, p	0	0	0	0					
Crosby, ph	1	0	0	0					
Grimsley, p	0	0	0	0					
King, ph	0	0	0	0					
Totals	**33**	**2**	**7**	**2**	**Totals**	**37**	**7**	**13**	**7**

```
Cincinnati    0 0 1   0 1 0   0 0 0—2
New York      2 0 0   0 4 1   0 0 x—7
```

Cincinnati	IP	H	R	ER	BB	SO
Billingham (Loser)	4*	6	5	5	1	3
Gullett	0†	0	1	1	1	0
Carroll	2	5	1	1	0	0
Grimsley	2	2	0	0	1	1
New York	IP	H	R	ER	BB	SO
Seaver (Winner)	8⅓	7	2	1	5	4
McGraw (Save)	⅔	0	0	0	0	0

*Pitched to three batters in fifth.
†Pitched to one batter in fifth.

E—Jones, Driessen. LOB—Cincinnati 10, New York 10. 2B—Morgan, Griffey, Rose, Garrett, Jones, Seaver. SH—Millan. SF—Driessen. WP—Seaver. U—Froemming, Dale, Sudol, Vargo, Pelekoudas and Engel. T—2:40. A—50,323.

World Series 1973

		R	H	E	PITCHERS (inn. pit.)	HOME RUNS (men on)	HIGHLIGHTS

Oakland (A.L.) defeats New York (N.L.) 4 games to 3

GAME 1 - OCTOBER 13

		R	H	E	PITCHERS (inn. pit.)	HOME RUNS	HIGHLIGHTS
NY	N	1	7	2	Matlack (6), McGraw (2)		A's score two unearned runs in third inning, with help of errors by Millan and Mays, plus double by Holtzman and RBI single by Rudi, and hang on behind tight pitching.
OAK	A	2	4	0	Holtzman (5), Fingers (3.1), Knowles (0.2), SV		

GAME 2 - OCTOBER 14

		R	H	E	PITCHERS (inn. pit.)	HOME RUNS	HIGHLIGHTS
NY	N	10	15	1	Koosman (2.1), Sadecki (1.2), Parker (1), McGraw (6), Stone (1), SV	Jones, Garrett	In longest (4:13) and one of loosest Series' games in history, Mets finally prevail by virtue of two costly errors by Andrews in 12th inning, when New York pushes across four runs. Teams tie record with total of 11 pitchers.
OAK	A	7	13	5	Blue (5.1), Pina (0), Knowles (3.2), Odom (2), Fingers (2.2), Lindblad (0.1)		

GAME 3 - OCTOBER 16

		R	H	E	PITCHERS (inn. pit.)	HOME RUNS	HIGHLIGHTS
OAK	A	3	10	1	Hunter (6), Knowles (2), Lindblad (2), Fingers (1), SV		Campaneris gets decisive hit, rapping single following walk and passed ball on third strike in 11th. Seaver fans 12 in eight innings.
NY	N	2	10	2	Seaver (8), Sadecki (0), McGraw (2), Parker (1)	Garrett	

GAME 4 - OCTOBER 17

		R	H	E	PITCHERS (inn. pit.)	HOME RUNS	HIGHLIGHTS
OAK	A	1	5	1	Holtzman (0.1), Odom (2.2), Knowles (1), Pina (0), Lindblad (1)	Staub (2 on)	Staub has perfect game with three singles and three-run homer, and picks up five RBI, while Matlack throttles A's on three hits in eight innings.
NY	N	6	13	1	Matlack (8), Sadecki (1), SV		

GAME 5 - OCTOBER 18

		R	H	E	PITCHERS (inn. pit.)	HOME RUNS	HIGHLIGHTS
OAK	A	0	3	1	Blue (5.2), Knowles (0.1), Fingers (2)		Jones doubles in run in second and Hahn triples home run in sixth, while Koosman and McGraw blank A's on two singles and a double.
NY	N	2	7	1	Koosman (6.1), McGraw (2.2), SV		

GAME 6 - OCTOBER 20

		R	H	E	PITCHERS (inn. pit.)	HOME RUNS	HIGHLIGHTS
NY	N	1	6	2	Seaver (7), McGraw (1)		Jackson rips two RBI doubles then singles and scores A's other run.
OAK	A	3	7	0	Hunter (7.1), Knowles (0.1), Fingers (1.1)		

GAME 7 - OCTOBER 21

		R	H	E	PITCHERS (inn. pit.)	HOME RUNS	HIGHLIGHTS
NY	N	2	8	1	Matlack (2.2), Parker (1.1), Sadecki (2), Stone (2)	Campaneris (1 on), Jackson (1 on)	Campaneris and Jackson bash two-run homers in third inning—A's first two homers of Series—and Oakland captures second World Series title in row. After game, winning manager Dick Williams quits.
OAK	A	5	9	1	Holtzman (5.1), Fingers (3.1), Knowles (0.1), SV		

Team Totals

	W	AB	H	2B	3B	HR	R	RBI	BA	BB	SO	ERA
OAK A	4	241	51	12	3	2	21	20	.212	28	62	2.32
NY N	3	261	66	7	2	4	24	16	.253	26	36	2.22

Individual Batting

OAKLAND (A.L.)

	AB	H	2B	3B	HR	R	RBI	BA
Campaneris, ss	31	9	0	1	1	6	3	.290
Rudi, lf	27	9	2	0	0	3	4	.333
Bando, 3b	26	6	1	1	0	5	1	.231
Jackson, rf	29	9	3	1	1	3	6	.310
Tenace, 1b	19	3	1	0	0	0	3	.158
Alou, rf	19	3	1	0	0	0	3	.158
Davalillo, cf	11	1	0	0	0	0	0	.091
Fosse, c	19	3	1	0	0	0	0	.158
Green, 2b	16	1	0	0	0	0	0	.603
Holtzman, p	3	2	2	0	0	2	0	.667
Mangual, cf	6	0	0	0	0	0	0	.000
Fingers, p	3	1	0	0	0	0	0	.333
Knowles, p	0	0	0	0	0	0	0	.000
Kubiak, 2b	3	0	0	0	0	1	0	.000
Andrews, 2b	3	0	0	0	0	0	0	.000
Blue, p	4	0	0	0	0	0	0	.000
Pina, p	0	0	0	0	0	0	0	.000
Conigliari, ph	3	0	0	0	0	0	0	.000
Odom, p	1	0	0	0	0	0	0	.000
Johnson, 1b	10	3	1	0	0	0	0	.300
Lewis, pr	0	0	0	0	0	1	0	.000
Lindblad, p	1	0	0	0	0	0	0	.000
Bourque, 1b	2	1	0	0	0	0	0	.500
Hunter, p	5	0	0	0	0	0	0	.000

NEW YORK (N.L.)

	AB	H	2B	3B	HR	R	RBI	BA
Garrett, 3b	30	5	0	0	2	4	2	.167
Millan, 2b	32	6	1	1	0	3	1	.187
Mays, cf	7	2	0	0	0	1	1	.286
Jones, lf	28	8	2	0	1	5	1	.286
Milner, 1b	27	8	0	0	0	2	2	.296
Grote, c	30	8	0	0	0	2	0	.267
Hahn, cf	29	7	1	1	0	2	2	.241
Kranepool, ph	3	0	0	0	0	0	0	.000
Harrelson, ss	24	6	1	0	0	2	1	.250
Hodges, ph	0	0	0	0	0	0	0	.000
Martinez, pr	0	0	0	0	0	0	0	.000
Matlack, p	4	1	0	0	0	0	0	.250
Boswell, ph	3	3	0	0	1	0	0	1.000
McGraw, p	3	1	0	0	0	1	0	.333
Staub, rf	26	11	2	0	1	1	6	.423
Beauchamp, ph	4	0	0	0	0	0	0	.000
Koosman, p	4	0	0	0	0	0	0	.000
Sadecki, p	0	0	0	0	0	0	0	.000
Theodore, lf	2	0	0	0	0	0	0	.000
Parker, p	0	0	0	0	0	0	0	.000
Stone, p	0	0	0	0	0	0	0	.000
Seaver, p	5	0	0	0	0	0	0	.000

Individual Pitching

OAKLAND (A.L.)

	W	L	ERA	IP	H	BB	SO	SV
Holtzman	2	1	4.22	10.2	13	5	6	0
Fingers	0	1	0.66	13.2	13	4	8	0
Knowles	0	0	0.00	6.1	4	5	5	0
Blue	0	1	4.91	11	10	3	8	0
Pina	0	0	0.00	3	6	2	0	0
Odom	0	0	3.86	4.2	5	2	2	0
Lindblad	1	0	0.00	3.1	4	1	1	0
Hunter	1	0	2.03	13.1	11	4	6	0

NEW YORK (N.L.)

	W	L	ERA	IP	H	BB	SO	SV
Matlack	1	2	2.16	16.2	10	5	11	0
McGraw	1	0	2.63	13.2	8	9	14	0
Koosman	1	0	3.12	8.2	9	7	8	0
Sadecki	0	0	1.93	4.2	5	1	6	0
Parker	0	1	0.00	3.1	2	2	2	0
Stone	0	0	4.00	3	4	1	3	0
Seaver	0	1	2.40	15	13	3	18	0

GAME NO. 1 AT OAKLAND
SATURDAY, OCTOBER 13

New York	AB	R	H	PO	A	E
Garrett, 3b	5	0	0	0	0	0
Millan, 2b	4	0	1	1	2	1
Mays, cf	4	0	1	0	0	1
Jones, lf	4	1	2	3	0	0
Milner, 1b	4	0	2	11	0	0
Grote, c	4	0	0	5	2	0
Hahn, rf	2	0	0	0	0	0
cKranepool	1	0	0	0	0	0
Harrelson, ss	2	0	0	4	6	0
dHodges	0	0	0	0	0	0
eMartinez	0	0	0	0	0	0
Matlack, p	0	0	0	0	0	0
bBoswell	1	0	1	0	0	0
McGraw, p	0	0	0	0	0	0
fStaub	0	0	0	0	0	0
gBeauchamp	1	0	0	0	0	0
Totals	32	1	7	24	10	2

Oakland	AB	R	H	PO	A	E
Campaneris, ss	4	1	1	3	1	0
Rudi, lf	3	0	1	0	0	0
Bando, 3b	3	0	1	1	3	0
Jackson, cf-rf	3	0	0	4	0	0
Tenace, 1b	3	0	0	11	0	0
Alou, rf	3	0	0	1	0	0
Davalillo, cf	0	0	0	0	0	0
Fosse, c	3	0	0	4	1	0
Green, 2b	2	0	0	2	3	0
Holtzman, p	1	1	1	1	3	0
aMangual	1	0	0	0	0	0
Fingers, p	1	0	0	0	0	0
Knowles, p	0	0	0	0	0	0
Totals	27	2	4	27	11	0

New York	IP	H	R	ER	BB	SO
Matlack (L)	6	3	2	0	2	3
McGraw	2	1	0	0	1	1

Oakland	IP	H	R	ER	BB	SO
Holtzman (W)	5	4	1	1	3	2
Fingers	3⅓	3	0	0	1	3
Knowles (S)	⅔	0	0	0	0	0

New York					
New York	000	100	000—1
Oakland	002	000	00x—2

Bases on balls—Off Matlack 2 (Green, Jackson), off McGraw 1 (Bando), off Holtzman 3 (Harrelson, Hahn, Matlack), off Fingers 1 (Hodges).

Strikeouts—By Matlack 3 (Tenace, Green, Campaneris), by McGraw 1 (Fingers), by Holtzman 2 (Hahn, Harrelson), by Fingers 3 (Hahn, Harrelson, Mays).

aLined out for Holtzman in fifth. bSingled for Matlack in seventh. cLined out for Hahn in ninth. dWalked for Harrelson in ninth. eRan for Hodges in ninth. fAnnounced to bat for McGraw in ninth. gPopped out for Staub in ninth. Runs batted in—Rudi, Milner. Two-base hits—Holtzman, Jones. Three-base hit—Millan. Stolen base—Campaneris. Caught stealing—Green. Sacrifice hits—Matlack, Rudi. Double plays—Holtzman and Tenace; Green, Campaneris and Tenace. Passed ball—Fosse. Left on bases—New York 9, Oakland 5. Umpires—Springstead (AL) plate, Donatelli (NL) first base, Neudecker (AL) second base, Pryor (NL) third base, Goetz (AL) left field, Wendelstedt (NL) right field. Time—2:26. Attendance—46,021.

GAME NO. 2 AT OAKLAND
SUNDAY, OCTOBER 14

New York	AB	R	H	PO	A	E
Garrett, 3b	6	1	1	1	5	0
Millan, 2b	6	0	0	4	5	0
Staub, rf	5	0	1	0	0	0
gMays, cf	2	1	1	1	0	0
Jones, lf	5	3	3	0	0	0
Milner, 1b	6	1	2	15	0	0
Grote, c	6	1	2	15	2	0
Hahn, cf-rf	7	1	1	0	0	0
Harrelson, ss	6	1	3	0	4	0
Koosman, p	1	0	0	0	0	1
Sadecki, p	0	0	0	0	1	0
aTheodore	1	0	0	0	0	0
Parker, p	0	0	0	0	0	0
bKranepool	0	0	0	0	0	0
cBeauchamp	1	0	0	0	0	0
McGraw, p	2	1	1	0	2	0
Stone, p	0	0	0	0	0	0
Totals	54	10	15	36	19	1

Oakland	AB	R	H	PO	A	E
Campaneris, ss	6	2	1	0	6	0
Rudi, lf	5	1	2	3	1	1
Bando, 3b	5	2	1	1	4	0
Jackson, cf	6	1	4	3	0	0
Tenace, 1b	3	0	1	14	0	1
Alou, rf	6	0	3	2	0	0
Fosse, c	5	0	0	11	0	0
Green, 2b	2	0	0	2	1	0
dMangual	1	0	0	0	0	0
Kubiak, 2b	0	0	0	0	0	0
fAndrews, 2b	2	0	0	0	0	2
Blue, p	2	0	0	0	0	0
Pina, p	0	0	0	0	0	0
Knowles, p	0	0	0	0	0	1
eConigliaro	1	0	0	0	0	0
Odom, p	0	0	0	0	0	0
hJohnson	1	0	1	0	0	0
iLewis	0	1	0	0	0	0
Fingers, p	1	0	0	0	1	0
Lindblad, p	0	0	0	0	0	0
jDavalillo	1	0	0	0	0	0
Totals	47	7	13	36	13	5

New York	011	004	000	004—10	
Oakland	210	000	102	001— 7	

New York	IP	H	R	ER	BB	SO
Koosman	2⅓	6	3	3	3	4
Sadecki	1⅔	0	0	0	0	3
Parker	1	1	0	0	0	0
McGraw (W)	6†	5	4	4	3	8
Stone (S)	1	1	0	0	1	0

Oakland	IP	H	R	ER	BB	SO
Blue	5⅓	4	4	4	2	4
Pina	0*	2	2	0	0	0
Knowles	1⅔	1	0	0	2	0
Odom	2	2	0	0	0	2
Fingers (L)	2⅔	6	4	1	0	2
Lindblad	⅓	0	0	0	0	0

*Pitched to three batters in sixth.
†Pitched to two batters in twelfth.

Bases on balls—Off Koosman 3 (Tenace 2, Fosse), off McGraw 3 (Rudi, Bando, Tenace), off Stone 1 (Andrews), off Blue 2 (Garrett, Jones), off Knowles 2 (Millan, Milner).

Strikeouts—By Koosman 4 (Jackson, Green, Blue, Bando), by Sadecki 3 (Green, Blue, Campaneris), by McGraw 8 (Mangual, Bando 2, Tenace, Campaneris, Fosse, Andrews, Rudi), by Blue 4 (Garrett, Millan, Harrelson, Staub), by Knowles 2 (Garrett, Hahn), by Odom 2 (McGraw, Garrett), by Fingers 2 (Milner, Garrett).

aGrounded out for Sadecki in fifth. b Announced to bat for Parker in sixth. cSafe on error for Kranepool in sixth. dStruck out for Green in sixth. eGrounded out for Knowles in seventh. fGrounded out for Kubiak in eighth. gRan for Staub in ninth. hDoubled for Odom in ninth. iRan for Johnson in ninth. jPopped out for Lindblad in twelfth. Runs batted in—Bando, Alou 2, Rudi, Jackson 2, Tenace, Jones, Garrett, Hahn, Harrelson, Mays. Two-base hits—Rudi, Alou, Jackson, Johnson, Harrelson. Three-base hits—Bando, Campaneris, Jackson. Home runs—Jones, Garrett. Stolen base—Campaneris. Caught stealing—Rudi, Tenace. Sacrifice hit —McGraw. Double plays—Garrett, Millan and Milner; Rudi and Fosse. Hit by pitcher—By Pina (Grote), by McGraw (Campaneris), by Fingers (Jones). Left on bases—New York 15, Oakland 12. Umpires—Donatelli (NL) plate, Neudecker (AL) first base, Pryor (NL) second base, Goetz (AL) third base, Wendelstedt (NL) left field, Springstead (AL) right field. Time—4:13. Attendance—49,151.

GAME NO. 3 AT N.Y.
TUESDAY, OCTOBER 16

Oakland	AB	R	H	PO	A	E
Campaneris, ss	6	1	3	2	7	0
Rudi, lf	5	0	2	7	0	0
Bando, 3b	4	1	2	0	1	0
Jackson, rf	5	0	0	2	0	0
Tenace, 1b-c	3	0	1	4	0	0
Davalillo, cf-1b	5	0	1	7	0	0
Fosse, c	2	0	0	5	0	0
aBourque, 1b	2	0	1	2	0	0
eLewis	0	0	0	0	0	0
Lindblad, p	1	0	0	0	0	0
Fingers, p	0	0	0	0	0	0
Green, 2b	2	0	0	1	0	0
bAlou	1	0	0	0	0	0
Kubiak, 2b	1	1	0	2	2	0
Hunter, p	2	0	0	0	2	1
cJohnson	1	0	0	0	0	0
Knowles, p	0	0	0	0	0	0
fMangual, cf	2	0	0	1	0	0
Totals	42	3	10	33	12	1

New York	AB	R	H	PO	A	E
Garrett, 3b	4	1	2	1	2	0
Millan, 2b	5	1	2	3	2	2
Staub, rf	6	0	2	2	0	0
Jones, lf	5	0	0	2	1	0
Milner, 1b	3	0	1	5	1	0
Grote, c	5	0	0	15	0	0
Hahn, cf	5	0	1	4	1	0
Harrelson, ss	5	0	2	1	3	0
Seaver, p	3	0	0	0	0	0
dBeauchamp	1	0	0	0	0	0
Sadecki, p	0	0	0	0	0	0
McGraw, p	0	0	0	0	1	0
gMays	1	0	0	0	0	0
Parker, p	0	0	0	0	0	0
Totals	43	2	10	33	11	2

Oakland	000	001	010	01—3	
New York	200	000	000	00—2	

GAME NO. 3 AT N.Y.
TUESDAY, OCTOBER 16

Oakland	IP	H	R	ER	BB	SO
Hunter	6	7	2	2	3	5
Knowles	2	0	0	0	1	0
Lindblad (W)	2†	3	0	0	1	0
Fingers (S)	1	0	0	0	0	0

New York	IP	H	R	ER	BB	SO
Seaver	8	7	2	2	1	12
Sadecki	0*	1	0	0	0	0
McGraw	2	1	0	0	1	1
Parker (L)	1	1	1	0	1	1

*Pitched to two batters in ninth.
†Pitched to one batter in eleventh.

Bases on balls—Off Hunter 3 (Garrett 2, Milner), off Knowles 1 (Milner), off Lindblad 1 (Jones), off Seaver 1 (Tenace), off McGraw 1 (Tenace), off Parker 1 (Kubiak).

Strikeouts—By Hunter 5 (Jones, Grote, Seaver 2, Garrett), by Seaver 12 (Bando, Jackson 3, Tenace 2, Davalillo, Fosse, Green, Hunter, Cam-

paneris, Johnson), by McGraw 1 (Mangual), by Parker 1 (Mangual).

aFlied out for Fosse in seventh. bGrounded out for Green in seventh. cStruck out for Hunter in seventh. dFlied out for Seaver in eighth. eRan for Bourque in ninth. fStruck out for Knowles in ninth. gGrounded into force out for McGraw in tenth. Runs batted in—Garrett, Tenace, Rudi, Campaneris. Two-base hits—Rudi, Hahn, Bando, Tenace, Staub. Home run—Garrett. Stolen base—Campaneris. Sacrifice hits—Bando, Millan. Wild pitch—Hunter. Passed ball—Grote. Left on bases—Oakland 10, New York 14. Umpires—Neudecker (AL) plate, Pryor (NL) first base, Goetz (AL) second base, Wendelstedt (NL) third base, Donatelli (NL) right field. Time—3:15. Attendance—54,817.

GAME NO. 4 AT N.Y.
WEDNESDAY, OCTOBER 17

Oakland	AB	R	H	PO	A	E
Campaneris, ss	4	0	0	1	2	0
Rudi, lf	4	0	1	1	1	0
Bando, 3b	3	1	0	3	4	0
Jackson, cf	4	0	1	0	0	0
Tenace, 1b	3	0	1	12	0	0
Alou, rf	4	0	0	1	0	0
Fosse, c	4	0	1	4	2	0
Green, 2b	1	0	0	1	3	1
aMangual	1	0	0	0	0	0
Kubiak, 2b	1	0	0	1	3	0
dJohnson	1	0	1	0	0	0
Holtzman, p	0	0	0	0	0	0
Odom, p	1	0	0	0	1	0
Knowles, p	0	0	0	0	1	0
bConigliaro	1	0	0	0	0	0
Pina, p	0	0	0	0	0	0
cAndrews	1	0	0	0	0	0
Lindblad, p	0	0	0	0	0	0
eDavalillo	0	0	0	0	0	0
Totals	33	1	5	24	17	1

New York	AB	R	H	PO	A	E
Garrett, 3b	4	2	1	0	4	1
Millan, 2b	5	1	1	4	1	0
Staub, rf	4	1	4	1	0	0
Jones, lf	3	0	1	2	0	0
Theodore, lf	1	0	0	1	0	0
Milner, 1b	3	0	0	9	0	0
Grote, c	4	0	3	7	0	0
Hahn, cf	4	1	1	2	0	0
Harrelson, ss	2	1	1	1	3	0
Matlack, p	3	0	1	0	1	0
Sadecki, p	0	0	0	0	0	0
Totals	33	6	13	27	9	1

Oakland	0 0 0	1 0 0	0 0 0—1
New York	3 0 0	3 0 0	0 0 x—6

Oakland	IP	H	R	ER	BB	SO
Holtzman (L)	⅓	4	3	3	1	0
Odom	2⅔*	3	2	2	2	0
Knowles	1	1	1	0	1	1
Pina	3	4	0	0	2	0
Lindblad	1	1	0	0	0	1

New York	IP	H	R	ER	BB	SO
Matlack (W)	8	3	1	0	2	5
Sadecki (S)	1	2	0	0	1	2

*Pitched to two batters in fourth.

Bases on balls—Off Holtzman 1 (Milner), off Odom 2 (Matlack, Staub), off Knowles 1 (Jones), off Pina 2 (Harrelson 2), off Matlack 2 (Bando, Tenace), off Sadecki 1 (Davalillo).

Strikeouts—By Knowles 1 (Matlack), by Lindblad 1 (Garrett), by Matlack 5 (Jackson, Tenace, Green, Odom, Rudi), by Sadecki 2 (Fosse, Campaneris).

aPopped out for Green in fifth. bFlied out for Knowles in fifth. cGrounded out for Pina in eighth. dSingled for Kubiak in ninth. eWalked for Lindblad in ninth. Runs batted in—Staub 5, Tenace. Home run—Staub. Double plays—Bando, Green and Tenace; Green, Campaneris and Tenace; Knowles, Fosse and Tenace; Kubiak and Tenace. Wild pitch—Odom. Hit by pitcher—by Knowles (Garrett), by Matlack (Campaneris). Left on bases—Oakland 9, New York 10. Umpires—Pryor (NL) plate, Goetz (AL) first base, Wendelstedt (NL) second base, Springstead (AL) third base, Donatelli (NL) left field, Neudecker (AL) right field. Time—2:41. Attendance—54,817.

GAME NO. 5 AT N.Y.
THURSDAY, OCTOBER 18

Oakland	AB	R	H	PO	A	E
Campaneris, ss	3	0	1	0	4	1
Rudi, lf	4	0	0	3	0	0
Bando, 3b	3	0	1	1	1	0
Jackson, cf	3	0	0	1	0	0
Tenace, 1b	1	0	0	7	2	0
dOdom	0	0	0	0	0	0
Bourque, 1b	0	0	0	1	1	0
Alou, rf	4	0	0	0	0	0
Fosse, c	4	0	1	6	0	0
Green, 2b	2	0	0	1	0	0
aJohnson	0	0	0	0	0	0
bLewis	0	0	0	0	0	0
Kubiak, 2b	1	0	0	2	2	0
Blue, p	2	0	0	2	1	0
Knowles, p	0	0	0	0	0	0
cMangual	1	0	0	0	0	0
Fingers, p	0	0	0	0	0	0
eConigliaro	1	0	0	0	0	0
Totals	29	0	3	24	11	1

New York	AB	R	H	PO	A	E
Garrett, 3b	3	0	0	1	2	1
Millan, 2b	4	0	0	2	1	0
Staub, rf	3	0	1	0	0	0
Jones, lf	4	1	2	2	0	0
Milner, 1b	4	0	2	7	0	0
Grote, c	3	1	1	10	0	0
Hahn, cf	4	0	1	2	0	0
Harrelson, ss	2	0	0	3	4	0
Koosman, p	3	0	0	0	1	0
McGraw, p	1	0	0	0	0	0
Totals	31	2	7	27	8	1

```
Oakland      000  000  000—0
New York     010  001  00x—2
```

Oakland	IP	H	R	ER	BB	SO
Blue (L)	5⅔	6	2	2	1	4
Knowles	⅓	0	0	0	1	1
Fingers	2	1	0	0	2	1

New York	IP	H	R	ER	BB	SO
Koosman (W)	6⅓	3	0	0	4	4
McGraw (S)	2⅔	0	0	0	3	3

Bases on balls—Off Blue 1 (Garrett), off Knowles 1 (Harrelson), off Fingers 2 (Staub, Harrelson), off Koosman 4 (Bando, Tenace 2, Campaneris, off McGraw 3 (Johnson, Jackson, Tenace).

Strikeouts—By Blue 4 (Garrett 2, Koosman 2), by Knowles 1 (Koosman), by Fingers 1 (Hahn), by Koosman 4 (Jackson, Tenace, Blue 2), by McGraw 3 (Campaneris, Kubiak, Conigliaro).

aWalked for Green in seventh. bRan for Johnson in seventh. cPopped out for Knowles in seventh. dRan for Tenace in eighth. eStruck out for Fingers in ninth. Runs batted in—Milner, Hahn. Two-base hits—Jones, Fosse. Three-base hit—Hahn. Sacrifice hit—Grote. Double play—Millan, Harrelson and Milner. Wild pitch—Blue. Left on bases—Oakland 9, New York 10. Umpires—Goetz (AL) plate, Wendelstedt (NL) first base, Springstead (AL) second base, Donatelli (NL) third base, Neudecker (AL) left field, Pryor (NL) right field. Time—2:30. Attendance—54,817.

GAME NO. 6 AT OAKLAND
SATURDAY, OCTOBER 20

New York	AB	R	H	PO	A	E
Garrett, 3b	3	0	1	0	2	1
Millan, 2b	4	0	1	2	1	0
Staub, rf	4	0	1	0	0	0
Jones, lf	4	0	0	1	0	0
Milner, 1b	4	0	1	10	0	0
Grote, c	4	0	1	7	1	0
Hahn, cf	3	0	0	4	0	1
cKranepool	1	0	0	0	0	0
Harrelson, ss	3	0	0	2	0	0
Seaver, p	2	0	0	0	2	0
aBoswell	1	1	1	0	0	0
McGraw, p	0	0	0	0	0	0
Totals	33	1	6	24	8	2

Oakland	AB	R	H	PO	A	E
Campaneris, ss	4	0	0	2	4	0
Rudi, lf	3	1	1	3	0	0
Bando, 3b	4	1	1	0	0	0
Jackson, rf-cf	4	1	3	2	0	0
Tenace, c-1b	3	0	0	3	0	0
Davalillo, cf	2	0	0	6	0	0
bAlou, rf	0	0	0	1	0	0
Johnson, 1b	4	0	1	5	1	0
Fosse, c	0	0	0	0	0	0
Green, 2b	3	0	1	4	2	0
Hunter, p	3	0	0	1	0	0
Knowles, p	0	0	0	0	0	0
Fingers, p	0	0	0	0	0	0
Totals	30	3	7	27	7	0

```
New York     000  000  010—1
Oakland      101  000  01x—3
```

New York	IP	H	R	ER	BB	SO
Seaver (L)	7	6	2	2	2	6
McGraw	1	1	1	0	1	1

Oakland	IP	H	R	ER	BB	SO
Hunter (W)	7⅓	4	1	1	1	1
Knowles	⅓	2	0	0	0	1
Fingers (S)	1⅓	0	0	0	0	0

Bases on balls—Off Seaver 2 (Davalillo, Rudi), off McGraw 1 (Tenace), off Hunter 1 (Garrett).

Strikeouts—By Seaver 6 (Bando, Tenace, Hunter 2, Rudi, Campaneris), by McGraw 1 (Johnson), by Hunter 1 (Hahn), by Knowles 1 (Staub).

aSingled for Seaver in eighth. bHit sacrifice fly for Davalillo in eighth. cPopped out for Hahn in ninth. Runs batted in—Jackson 2, Alou, Millan. Two-base hits—Jackson 2. Sacrifice fly—Alou. Double play—Grote and Millan. Caught stealing—Tenace. Wild pitch—Seaver. Left on bases—New York 6, Oakland 7. Umpires—Wendelstedt (NL) plate, Springstead (AL), first base, Donatelli (NL) second base, Neudecker (AL) third base, Pryor (NL) left field, Goetz (AL) right field. Time—2:07. Attendance—49,333.

GAME NO. 7 AT OAKLAND
SUNDAY, OCTOBER 21

New York	AB	R	H	PO	A	E
Garrett, 3b	5	0	0	1	4	0
Millan, 2b	4	1	1	0	1	0
Staub, rf	4	0	2	2	0	0
Jones, lf	3	0	0	1	0	1
Milner, 1b	3	1	0	9	0	0
Grote, c	4	0	1	8	0	0
Hahn, cf	4	0	3	1	0	0
Harrelson, ss	4	0	0	2	2	0
Matlack, p	1	0	0	0	0	0
Parker, p	0	0	0	0	0	0
bBeauchamp	1	0	0	0	0	0
Sadecki, p	0	0	0	0	0	0
cBoswell	1	0	1	0	0	0
Stone, p	0	0	0	0	0	0
dKranepool	1	0	0	0	0	0
eMartinez	0	0	0	0	0	0
Totals	35	2	8	24	7	1

Oakland	AB	R	H	PO	A	E
Campaneris, ss	4	2	3	2	4	0
Rudi, lf	3	1	2	3	0	0
Bando, 3b	4	0	0	0	1	0
Jackson, cf-rf	4	1	1	5	0	0
Tenace, c-1b	3	0	0	7	0	1
Alou, rf	1	0	0	0	0	0
aDavalillo, cf	3	0	0	2	0	0
Johnson, 1b	3	0	0	3	0	0
Fosse, c	1	0	1	2	0	0
Green, 2b	4	0	0	3	2	0
Holtzman, p	2	1	1	0	0	0
Fingers, p	1	0	1	0	1	0
Knowles, p	0	0	0	0	0	0
Totals	33	5	9	27	8	1

New York	000	001	001—2
Oakland	004	010	00x—5

New York	IP	H	R	ER	BB	SO
Matlack (L)	2⅔	4	4	4	1	3
Parker	1⅓	0	0	0	1	1
Sadecki	2	2	1	1	0	1
Stone	2	3	0	0	0	3

Oakland	IP	H	R	ER	BB	SO
Holtzman (W)	5⅓	5	1	1	1	4
Fingers	3⅓	3	1	0	1	2
Knowles (S)	⅓	0	0	0	0	0

Bases on balls—Off Matlack 1 (Rudi), off Parker 1 (Tenace), off Holtzman 1 (Jones), off Fingers 1 (Milner).

Strikeouts—By Matlack 3 Bando, Tenace, Green), by Parker 1 (Johnson), by Sadecki 1 (Johnson), by Stone 3 (Rudi, Bando, Jackson), by Holtzman 4 (Garrett 2, Hahn, Beauchamp), by Fingers 2 (Garrett, Jones).

aFlied out for Alou in third. bStruck out for Parker in fifth. cSingled for Sadecki in seventh. dSafe on error for Stone in ninth. eRan for Kranepool in ninth. Runs batted in—Campaneris 2, Jackson 2, Rudi, Staub. Two-base hits—Holtzman, Millan, Staub. Home runs—Campaneris, Jackson. Double play—Bando, Campaneris and Green. Left on bases—New York 8, Oakland 6. Umpires—Springstead (AL) plate, Donatelli (NL) first base, Neudecker (AL) second base, Pryor (NL) third base, Goetz (AL) left field, Wendelstedt (NL) right field. Time—2:37. Attendance—49,333.

NEW YORK METS' BATTING AND FIELDING AVERAGES

Player—Position	G	AB	R	H	2B	3B	HR	RBI	BB	SO	BA	PO	A	E	FA
Boswell, ph	3	3	1	3	0	0	0	0	0	0	1.000	0	0	0	.000
Staub, ph-rf	7	26	1	11	2	0	1	6	2	2	.423	5	0	0	1.000
McGraw, p	5	3	1	1	0	0	0	0	0	1	.333	0	3	0	1.000
Milner, 1b	7	27	2	8	0	0	0	2	5	1	.296	66	1	0	1.000
Jones, lf	7	28	5	8	2	0	1	1	4	2	.286	11	1	1	.923
Mays, cf-pr-ph	3	7	1	2	0	0	0	1	0	1	.286	1	0	1	.500
Grote, c	7	30	2	8	0	0	0	0	0	1	.267	67	5	0	1.000
Harrelson, ss	7	24	2	6	1	0	0	1	5	3	.250	11	24	0	1.000
Matlack, p	3	4	0	1	0	0	0	0	2	1	.250	0	1	0	1.000
Hahn, rf-cf	7	29	2	7	1	1	0	2	1	6	.241	13	1	1	.933
Millan, 2b	7	32	3	6	1	1	0	1	1	1	.188	16	13	3	.906
Garrett, 3b	7	30	4	5	0	0	2	2	5	11	.167	4	19	3	.885
Martinez, pr	2	0	0	0	0	0	0	0	0	0	.000	0	0	0	.000
Hodges, ph	1	0	0	0	0	0	0	0	1	0	.000	0	0	0	.000
Stone, p	2	0	0	0	0	0	0	0	0	0	.000	0	0	0	.000
Parker, p	3	0	0	0	0	0	0	0	0	0	.000	0	0	0	.000
Sadecki, p	4	0	0	0	0	0	0	0	0	0	.000	0	1	0	1.000
Theodore, ph-lf	2	2	0	0	0	0	0	0	0	0	.000	1	0	0	1.000
Kranepool, ph	4	3	0	0	0	0	0	0	0	0	.000	0	0	0	.000
Beauchamp, ph	4	4	0	0	0	0	0	0	0	1	.000	0	0	0	.000
Koosman, p	2	4	0	0	0	0	0	0	0	3	.000	0	1	1	.500
Seaver, p	2	5	0	0	0	0	0	0	0	2	.000	0	2	0	1.000
Totals	7	261	24	66	7	2	4	16	26	36	.253	195	72	10	.964

OAKLAND ATHLETICS' BATTING AND FIELDING AVERAGES

Player—Position	G	AB	R	H	2B	3B	HR	RBI	BB	SO	BA	PO	A	E	FA
Holtzman, p	3	3	2	2	2	0	0	0	0	0	.667	1	3	0	1.000
Bourque, ph-1b	2	2	0	1	0	0	0	0	0	0	.500	3	1	0	1.000
Rudi, lf	7	27	3	9	2	0	0	4	3	4	.333	20	2	0	1.000
Fingers, p	6	3	0	1	0	0	0	0	0	1	.333	0	2	0	1.000
Jackson, cf-rf	7	29	3	9	3	1	1	6	2	7	.310	17	0	0	1.000
Johnson, ph-1b	6	10	0	3	1	0	0	0	1	4	.300	8	1	0	1.000
Campaneris, ss	7	31	6	9	0	1	1	3	1	7	.290	10	28	1	.974
Bando, 3b	7	26	5	6	1	1	0	1	4	7	.231	6	14	1	.952
Alou, rf-ph	7	19	0	3	1	0	0	3	0	0	.158	5	0	0	1.000
Fosse, c	7	19	0	3	1	0	0	0	1	4	.158	32	3	0	1.000
Tenace, 1b-c	7	19	0	3	1	0	0	3	11	7	.158	57	2	2	.967
Davalillo, cf-ph-1b	6	11	0	1	0	0	0	0	2	1	.091	15	0	0	1.000
Green, 2b	7	16	0	1	0	0	0	0	1	6	.063	14	11	1	.962
Knowles, p	7	0	0	0	0	0	0	0	0	0	.000	0	1	1	.500
Lewis, pr	3	0	1	0	0	0	0	0	0	0	.000	0	0	0	.000
Pina, p	2	0	0	0	0	0	0	0	0	0	.000	0	0	0	.000
Lindblad, p	3	0	0	0	0	0	0	0	0	0	.000	0	0	0	.000
Odom, p-pr	3	1	0	0	0	0	0	0	0	1	.000	0	1	0	1.000
Conigliaro, ph	3	3	0	0	0	0	0	0	0	1	.000	0	0	0	.000
Andrews, ph-2b	2	3	0	0	0	0	0	0	1	1	.000	1	0	2	.333
Kubiak, 2b	4	3	1	0	0	0	0	0	1	1	.000	5	7	0	1.000
Blue, p	2	4	0	0	0	0	0	0	0	4	.000	2	1	0	1.000
Hunter, p	2	5	0	0	0	0	0	0	0	3	.000	1	2	1	.750
Mangual, ph-cf	5	6	0	0	0	0	0	0	0	3	.000	1	0	0	1.000
Totals	7	241	21	51	12	3	2	20	28	62	.212	198	79	9	.969

OAKLAND ATHLETICS' PITCHING RECORDS

Pitcher	G	GS	CG	IP	H	R	ER	BB	SO	HB	WP	W	L	Pct	ERA
Knowles	7	0	0	6⅓	4	1	0	5	5	1	0	0	0	.000	0.00
Lindblad	3	0	0	3⅓	4	0	0	1	1	0	0	1	0	1.000	0.00
Pina	2	0	0	3	6	2	0	2	0	1	0	0	0	.000	0.00
Fingers	6	0	0	13⅔	13	5	1	4	8	1	0	0	1	.000	0.66
Hunter	2	2	0	13⅓	11	3	3	4	6	0	1	1	0	1.000	2.03
Odom	2	0	0	4⅔	5	2	2	2	2	0	1	0	0	.000	3.86
Holtzman	3	3	0	10⅔	13	5	5	5	6	0	0	2	1	.667	4.22
Blue	2	2	0	11	10	6	6	3	8	0	1	0	1	.000	4.91
Totals	7	7	0	66	66	24	17	26	36	3	3	4	3	.571	2.32

Saves—Fingers 2, Knowles 2.

NEW YORK METS' PITCHING RECORDS

Pitcher	G	GS	CG	IP	H	R	ER	BB	SO	HB	WP	W	L	Pct	ERA
Parker	3	0	0	3⅓	2	1	0	2	2	0	0	0	1	.000	0.00
Stone	2	0	0	3	4	0	0	1	3	0	0	0	0	.000	0.00
Sadecki	4	0	0	4⅔	5	1	1	1	6	0	0	0	0	.000	1.93
Matlack	3	3	0	16⅔	10	7	4	5	11	1	0	1	2	.333	2.16
Seaver	2	2	0	15	13	4	4	3	18	0	1	0	1	.000	2.40
McGraw	5	0	0	13⅔	8	5	4	9	14	1	0	1	0	1.000	2.63
Koosman	2	2	0	8⅔	9	3	3	7	8	0	0	1	0	1.000	3.12
Totals	7	7	0	65	51	21	16	28	62	2	1	3	4	.429	2.22

Saves—Stone, Sadecki, McGraw.
Combination Shutout—Koosman and McGraw.

COMPOSITE SCORE BY INNINGS

Oakland	3	1	7	1	1	1	1	2	2	0	1	1—21
New York	5	2	1	4	0	6	0	1	1	0	0	4—24

Sacrifice hits—Bando, Grote, Matlack, McGraw, Millan, Rudi.

Sacrifice fly—Alou.

Stolen bases—Campaneris 3.

Caught stealing—Tenace 2, Green, Rudi.

Double plays—Green, Campaneris and Tenace 2; Holtzman and Tenace; Rudi and Fosse; Bando, Green and Tenace; Knowles, Fosse and Tenace; Kubiak and Tenace; Bando, Campaneris and Green; Garrett, Millan and Milner; Millan, Harrelson and Milner; Grote and Millan.

Passed balls—Fosse, Grote.

Hit by pitcher—By Pina 1 (Grote), by Fingers 1 (Jones), by Knowles 1 (Garrett), by Matlack 1 (Campaneris), by McGraw 1 (Campaneris).

		G	W	L	PCT	Standing				G	W	L	PCT	Standing	

Casey Stengel

STENGEL, CHARLES DILLON (The Old Professor)
B. July 30, 1890, Kansas City, Mo.
Hall of Fame 1966.

		G	W	L	PCT	Standing
1934	BKN N	153	71	81	.467	6
1935		154	70	83	.458	5
1936		156	67	87	.435	7
1938	BOS N	153	77	75	.507	5
1939		152	63	88	.417	7
1940		152	65	87	.428	7
1941		156	62	92	.403	7
1942		150	59	89	.399	7
1943		153	68	85	.444	6
1949	NY A	155	97	57	.630	1
1950		155	98	56	.636	1
1951		154	98	56	.636	1
1952		154	95	59	.617	1
1953		151	99	52	.656	1
1954		155	103	51	.669	2
1955		154	96	58	.623	1
1956		154	97	57	.630	1
1957		154	98	56	.636	1
1958		155	92	62	.597	1
1959		155	79	75	.513	3
1960		155	97	57	.630	1
1962	NY N	161	40	120	.250	10
1963		162	51	111	.315	10
1964		163	53	109	.327	10
1965		96	31	64	.326	10	10
25 yrs.		3812	1926	1867	.508	
4 yrs.		582	175	404	.302	

WORLD SERIES RECORD

		G	W	L	PCT	
1949	NY A	5	4	1	.800	
1950		4	4	0	1.000	
1951		6	4	2	.667	
1952		7	4	3	.571	
1953		6	4	2	.667	
1955		7	3	4	.429	
1956		7	4	3	.571	
1957		7	3	4	.429	
1958		7	4	3	.571	
1960		7	3	4	.429	
10 yrs.		63	37	26	.587	

Wes Westrum

WESTRUM, WESLEY NOREEN
B. Nov. 28, 1922, Clearbrook, Minn.

		G	W	L	PCT	Standing	
1965	NY N	68	19	48	.284	10	10
1966		161	66	95	.410	9	
1967		151	57	94	.377	10	10
3 yrs.		380	142	237	.375		

Salty Parker

PARKER, FRANCIS JAMES
B. July 8, 1913, East St. Louis, Ill.

		G	W	L	PCT	Standing	
1967	NY N	11	4	7	.364	10	10

Gil Hodges

HODGES, GILBERT RAYMOND
B. Apr. 4, 1924, Princeton, Ind.

		G	W	L	PCT	Standing	
1963	WAS A	122	42	80	.344	10	10
1964		162	62	100	.383	9	
1965		162	70	92	.432	8	
1966		159	71	88	.447	8	
1967		161	76	85	.472	6	
1968	NY N	163	73	89	.451	9	
1969		162	100	62	.617	1	
7 yrs.		1091	494	596	.453		
2 yrs.		325	173	151	.534		

LEAGUE CHAMPIONSHIP SERIES RECORD

		G	W	L	PCT	
1969	NY N	3	3	0	1.000	

WORLD SERIES RECORD

		G	W	L	PCT	
1969	NY N	5	4	1	.800	

Yogi Berra

BERRA, LAWRENCE PETER
B. May 12, 1925, St. Louis, Mo.

		G	W	L	PCT	Standing	
1964	NY A	162	99	63	.611	1	
1972	NY N	156	83	73	.532	3	
1973	NY N	161	82	79	.509	1	
3 yrs.		479	264	215	.553		
2 yrs.		317	165	152	.522		

LEAGUE CHAMPIONSHIP SERIES RECORD

		G	W	L	PCT	
1973	NY N	5	3	2	.600	

WORLD SERIES RECORD

		G	W	L	PCT	
1964	NY A	7	3	4	.429	
1973	NY N	7	3	4	.429	
2 yrs.		14	6	8	.429	

PLAYER AND MANAGER ROSTER

(Participated in at least one game)

AGEE, Tommie 1968-72
ALOMAR, Sandy 1967
ALTMAN, George 1964
ANDERSON, Craig 1962-64
APODACA, Bob 1973-
ARRIGO, Gerry 1966
ASHBURN, Richie 1962
ASPROMONTE, Bob 1971

BARNES, Lute 1972
BAUTA, Ed 1963-64
BEAUCHAMP, Jim 1972
BEARNARTH, Larry 1963-66
BELL, Gus 1962
BENNETT, Dennis 1967
BERRA, Yogi 1965
BETHKE, Jim 1965
BOSCH, Don 1967-68
BOSWELL, Ken 1967-
BOUCHEE, Ed 1962
BOYER, Ken 1966-67
BRESSOUD, Ed 1966
BUCHEK, Jerry 1967-68
BURRIGHT, Larry 1963-64

CANNIZZARO, Chris 1962-65
CAPRA, Buss 1971-
CARDWELL, Don 1967-70
CARMEL, Duke 1963
CHACON, Elio 1962
CHANCE, Dean 1970
CHARLES, Ed 1967-69
CHILES, Rich 1973-
CHITI, Harry 1962
CHRISTOPHER, Joe 1962-65
CISCO, Galen 1962-65
CLENDENON, Donn 1969-71
COLEMAN, Clarence 1962-63, 65
COLLINS, Kevin 1965, 67-69
CONNORS, Bill 1967-68
COOK, Cliff 1962-63
COWAN, Billy 1965
CRAIG, Roger 1962-63

DAVIAULT, Ray 1962
DAVIS, Tommy 1967
DeMERIT, John 1962
DENEHY, Bill 1967
DiLAURO, Jack 1969
DILLON, Steve 1963-64
DRAKE, Sammy 1962
DYER. Don 1968-

EILERS, Dave 1965-66
ELLIOT, Larry 1964, 66
ESTRADA, Chuck 1967
ESTRADA, Francisco 1971

FERNANDEZ, Chico 1963
FISHER, Jack 1964-67
FITZMAURICE, Shaun 1966
FOLI, Tim 1970-71
FOLKERS, Rich 1970
FOSS, Larry 1962
FOY, Joe 1970
FREGOSI, Jim 1972
FRIEND, Bob 1966
FRISELLA, Danny 1967-72

GARDNER, Rob 1965-66
GARRETT, Wayne 1969-
GASPAR, Rod 1969-70
GENTRY, Gary 1969-72
GINSBERG, Joe 1962
GONDER, Jesse 1963-65
GOOSSEN, Greg 1965-68
GOSGER, Jim 1969
GRAHAM, Bill 1967
GRAHAM, Wayne 1964
GRZENDA, Joe 1967
GREEN, Dallas 1966
GREEN, Pumpsie 1963
GROTE, Jerry 1966-

HAHN, Don 1971-
HAMILTON, Jack 1966-67
HARKNESS, Tim 1963-64
HARRELSON, Bud 1965-
HARTS, Greg 1973-
HEISE, Bob 1967-69
HENDLEY, Bob 1967
HENNIGAN, Phil 1973-
HEPLER, Bill 1966
HERBEL, Ron 1970
HERRSCHER, Rick 1962
HICKMAN, Jim 1962-66
HICKS, Joe 1963
HILLER, Chuck 1965-67
HILLMAN, Dave 1962
HINSLEY, Jerry 1964, 67
HODGES, Gil 1962-63
HODGES, Ron 1973-
HOOK, Jay 1962-64
HUDSON, Jesse 1969
HUNT, Ron 1963-66
HUNTER, Willard 1962, 64

JACKSON, Al 1962-65, 68-69
JOHNSON, Bob D. 1969
JOHNSON, Bob W. 1967
JONES, Cleon 1963, 65-
JONES, Sherman 1962
JORGENSEN, Mike 1968, 70-71

KANEHL, Rod 1962-64
KLAUS, Bobby 1964-65
KLIMCHOCK, Lou 1966
KOLB, Gary 1965
KOONCE, Cal 1967-70
KOOSMAN, Jerry 1967-
KRANEPOOL, Ed 1962-
KROLL, Gary 1964-65

LABINE, Clem 1962
LAMABE, Jack 1967
LANDRITH, Hobie 1962
LARY, Frank 1964-65
LEWIS, Johnny 1965-67
LINZ, Phil 1967-68
LOCKE, Ron 1964
LUPLOW, Al 1966-67

MacKENZIE, Ken 1962-63
McANDREW, Jim 1968-
McGRAW, Frank 1965-67, 69-
McMILLAN, Roy 1964-66
MANTILLA, Felix 1962

MARSHALL, Dave 1970-72
MARSHALL, Jim 1962
MARTIN, J. C. 1968-69
MARTINEZ, Teddy 1970-
MATLACK, Jon 1971-
MAY, Jerry 1973
MAYS, Willie 1972
MILLAN, Felix 1973-
MILLER, Bob G. 1962
MILLER, Bob L. 1962
MILLER, Larry 1965-66
MILNER, John 1971-
MIZELL, Wilmer 1962
MOFORD, Herb 1962
MOOCK, Joe 1967
MOORE, Tommy 1972
MOORHEAD, Bob 1962, 65
MORAN, Al 1963-64
MURPHY, Bill 1966
MUSGRAVES, Dennis 1965

NAPOLEON, Dan 1965-66
NEAL, Charlie 1962-63
NOLAN, Joe 1972

OSTROSSER, Brian 1973-
OTIS, Amos 1967, 69

PARKER, Harry 1973-
PARSONS, Tom 1964-65
PFEIL, Bob 1969
PIERSALL, Jim 1963
PIGNATANO, Joe 1962
POWELL, Grover 1963

RAUCH, Bob 1972
RENIFF, Hal 1967
REYNOLDS, Tom 1967
RIBANT, Dennis 1964-66
RICHARDSON, Gordon 1965-66
ROHR, Les 1967-69
ROSE, Don 1971
ROWE, Don 1963
RUSTECK, Dick 1966
RYAN, Nolan 1966, 68-71

SADECKI, Ray 1970-
SAMUEL, Amado 1964
SCHAFFER, Jim 1965
SCHMELZ, Al 1967
SCHNECK, Dave 1972
SCHREIBER, Ted 1963
SEAVER, Tom 1967-
SELMA, Dick 1965-68
SHAMSKY, Art 1968-71
SHAW, Bob 1966-67
SHAW, Don 1967-68
SHERRY, Norm 1963
SHIRLEY, Bart 1967
SHORT, Bill 1968
SINGLETON, Ken 1970-71
SMITH, Bobby Gene 1962
SMITH, Charley 1964-65
SMITH, Dick 1963-64
SNIDER, Duke 1963
SPAHN, Warren 1965
STAHL, Larry 1967-68
STALLARD, Tracy 1963-64
STANTON, Leroy 1970-71

383

STAUB, Rusty 1972-
STEPHENSON, John 1965-66
STROM, Brent 1972
STONE, George 1973-
STROHMAYER, John 1973-
STUART, Dick 1966
STURDIVANT, Tom 1964
SUDAKIS, Bill 1972
SULLIVAN, John 1967
SUTHERLAND, Darrell 1964-66
SWAN, Craig 1973-
SWOBODA, Ron 1965-70

TAYLOR, Bob 1964-67
TAYLOR, Chuck 1972
TAYLOR, Ron 1967-71
TAYLOR, Sammy 1962-63
TERRY, Ralph 1966-67
THEODORE, George 1973-
THOMAS, Frank 1962-64
THRONEBERRY, Marv 1962-63

WAKEFIELD, Bill 1964
WEBB, Hank 1972
WEIS, Al 1968-71
WILLEY, Carl 1963-65
WILLHITE, Nick 1967
WILLIAMS, Charlie 1971
WOODLING, Gene 1962
WYNNE, Billy 1967

ZIMMER, Don 1962

MANAGERS
BERRA, Yogi 1972-
HODGES, Gil 1968-71
*PARKER, Salty 1967
STENGEL, Casey 1962-65
WESTRUM, Wes 1965-67
*Interim manager from Sept. 21
to end of season.

COACHES
BERRA, Yogi 1965-71
HADDIX, Harvey 1966-67
HARDER, Mel 1964
HEFFNER, Don 1964-65
HEMUS, Solly 1962-63
HERZOG, Whitey 1966
HORNSBY, Rogers 1962
KRESS, Red 1962
LAVAGETTO, Cookie 1962-63
McCULLOUGH, Clyde 1963
McMILLAN, Roy 1973
MURPHY, John 1967
PARKER, Salty 1967
PIGNATANO, Joe 1968-
ROBINSON, Sheriff 1964-67, 72
RUFFING, Red 1962
SPAHN, Warren 1965
WALKER, Al 1968-
WESTRUM, Wes 1964-65
WHITE, Ernie 1963
YOST, Ed 1968-